The Best
Midwestern Colleges

The Princeton Review

The Best Midwestern Colleges

150 Great Schools to Consider

By Robert Franek,
Tom Meltzer, Roy Opochinski,
Tara Bray, Christopher Maier, Carson Brown,
Julie Doherty, K. Nadine Kavanaugh,
Catherine Monaco, and Dinaw Mengestu

Random House, Inc.

New York

www.PrincetonReview.com

Princeton Review Publishing, L. L. C.
2315 Broadway
New York, NY 10024
E-mail: bookeditor@review.com

ISBN 0-375-76335-X

Editorial Director: Robert Franek
Editors: Robert Franek, Erik Olson, and Erica Magrey
Designer: Scott Harris
Production Editor: Julieanna Lambert
Production Coordinator: Scott Harris

Manufactured in the United States of America.

9 8 7 6 5 4 3 2 1

FOREWORD

Every year, about three million high school graduates go to college. To make sure they end up at the *right* school, they spend several billion dollars on the admissions process. This money pays for countless admissions officers and counselors, a bunch of standardized tests (and preparation for them), and many books similar to—but not as good as—this one.

It's so expensive because most admissions professionals have a thing about being in control. As a group, colleges resist almost every attempt to standardize or otherwise simplify the process. Admissions officers want you to believe that every admissions decision that they render occurs within systems of weights, measures, and deliberations that are far too complex for you to comprehend. They shudder at the notion of having to respond to students and their parents in down-to-earth language that might reveal the arbitrary nature of a huge percentage of the admissions and denials that they issue during each cycle. That would be admitting that good luck and circumstance play a major part in many successful applications. So, in flight from public accountability, they make the process a lot more mysterious than it needs to be.

Even the most straightforward colleges hide the information you would want to know about the way they'll evaluate your application: What grades and SATs are they looking for? Do their reported SAT averages include minority students, athletes, and legacies (kids whose parents went to their school)? Exactly how much do extracurricular activities count? What percentage of the aid that they give out is in loans and what percentage is in grants?

We couldn't get answers to these questions from many colleges. In fact, we couldn't get answers to *any* questions from some schools. Others who supplied this information to us for earlier editions of this guide have since decided that they never should have in the first place. After all, knowledge is power.

Colleges seem to have the time and money to create beautiful brochures that generally show that all college classes are held under a tree on a beautiful day. Why not just tell you what sort of students they're looking for, and what factors they'll use to consider your application?

Until the schools demystify the admissions process, this book is your best bet. It's not a phone book containing every fact about every college in the country. And it's not a memoir written by a few graduates describing their favorite dining halls or professors. We've given you the facts you'll need to apply to the few hundred best schools in the country. And enough information about them—which we gathered from hundreds of counselors and admissions officers and more than 100,000 college students—to help you make a smart decision about which school to attend.

One note: We don't talk a lot about majors. This is because most high school students really don't know what they want to major in—and the ones who do almost always change their minds by the beginning of junior year. Choosing a school because of the reputation of a single department is often a terrible idea.

If you're interested in learning about majors and the colleges that offer them, pick up our *Guide to College Majors* or visit our website, www.princetonreview.com, where we explain majors and list the colleges that offer them.

As complicated and difficult as the admissions process is, we think you'll love college itself—especially at the schools listed in this book.

Good luck in your search.

John Katzman

June 2003

ACKNOWLEDGMENTS

I am blessed year after year with a talented group of colleagues working together to produce our guidebooks. This book, part of our "building out" of the concept of our flagship college guide, *The Best 351 Colleges,* yields, like its predecessor, what prospective college students really want: the most honest, accessible, and pertinent information on the colleges they are considering attending for the next four years of their lives. Collectively including profiles of more than 600 colleges and universities, our *Best Regional Colleges* series was an unprecedented undertaking, requiring well-coordinated student-survey, editorial, and production efforts, and my sincere thanks go to the many who contributed to this tremendous project. I am proud to note here that we have again successfully provided an uncompromising look into the true nature of each profiled college or university, based on the opinions of each college's current students. I know our readers will benefit from our cumulative efforts.

A special thank you goes to our authors, Tom Meltzer, Tara Bray, Roy Opochinski, Christopher Maier, Carson Brown, Julie Doherty, Nadine Kavanaugh, Catherine Monaco, and Dinaw Mengestu for their dedication in sifting through thousands of surveys to produce the essence of each school in three paragraphs! Very special thanks go to two stellar producers from our editorial staff: Erik Olson and Erica Magrey. Erik, our Senior Editor, is an essential resource to our department and a clear driver of this series. I can always trust Erik to provide clear direction in both the voice and sensibilities of The Princeton Review; he has proven himself again here. Erica, in her freshman performance, took this trial by fire with grace and moxie. On a daily basis, Erica brought quiet competence to the student survey process, adhering meticulously to our standards and goals for each book's narrative profiles.

Sincere thanks go to Jillian Taylor, our Student Survey Manager. Jillian provided clear messaging on our survey methodology and editorial procedure, remaining even-handed and approachable throughout the process. A special note goes to Amy Kinney, a veteran student surveyor, for her unwavering dedication to relaying our books' mission to the schools included in these pages. She provided sincere representation of the mission of The Princeton Review. Michael Palumbo also deserves praise for his indispensable contributions in the last days of production.

My continued thanks go to our data collection staff—David Soto, Ben Zelavansky, and Yojaira Cordero—for their successful efforts in collecting and accurately representing the statistical data that appear with each college profile. In turn, my gratitude goes to Chris Wujciak for his competence in all of our book pours.

The enormity of this project and its deadline constraints could not have been realized without the calm presence of our production team, Julieanna Lambert and Scott Harris. Their ability to remain focused throughout the production of this project inspires and impresses me. They deserve great thanks for their flexible schedules and uncompromising efficiency.

Special thanks go to Jeanne Krier, our Random House publicist, for the work she has done on this new series and the overall work she has done on our flagship book, *The Best 351 Colleges*, since its first edition. Jeanne continues to be my trusted colleague, media advisor and friend. I would also like to make special mention of Tom Russell, our publisher, for his continuous investment in our new book ideas.

Lastly, I thank John Katzman and Mark Chernis for their steadfast confidence in both this series and our publishing department, and for always being the champions of student opinion. It is pleasure to work with you both.

Again, to all who contributed so much to these publications, thank you for your efforts; they do not go unnoticed.

Robert Franek

Editorial Director

Lead Author—The Best Regional Colleges

CONTENTS

PART 1

INTRODUCTION

A P _ LIC _ T _ O_.

What's *that*?!?!

It's APPLICATION with P-A-I-N removed from the process.

We removed the paper, too.

With PrincetonReview.com's Online College Applications there are no endless piles to shuffle. No leaky pens, no hand cramps, no trying to figure out how many stamps to stick on that envelope.

The process is so painless, online applications practically submit themselves for you. Watch . . .

Type in your main contact information just once in our application profile and every subsequent application you file from our database—picking from hundreds of top schools—is automatically filled in with your information.

Not only are online applications:

- Faster to fill out

- Completely safe and secure

- Instantly trackable (check your application status online!)

- And . . . impossible to lose in the mail (they reach schools instantly)

But also: On PrincetonReview.com, there's no extra fee to submit your application online—our technology is totally FREE for you to use. In fact, some colleges even *waive* the application fee if you apply online.

Still have questions?

- Can I start an application now and finish it later?

- Are there easy-to-use instructions or someone I can call if I have a question? If I get stuck are there application instructions?

- Do schools *really* want to receive applications online?

Yes, yes, and yes!

It's easy to see the advantages of online applications. Almost as easy as actually applying.

Just log on and apply. It's that easy.

PrincetonReview.com—Applications without the pain.

HOW WE PRODUCE THIS BOOK

Welcome to the first edition of *The Best Midwestern Colleges*, one-fifth of our *Best* regional guidebook series. Our decision to produce this series was fueled by a desire to raise awareness of academically excellent but lesser-known regional colleges for those looking to study within a specific geographic area. Many of the schools within these pages are nationally competitive institutions of higher learning; we therefore also include their profiles in the 2004 edition of our best-selling *The Best 351 Colleges*. In fact, for these regional guides, we employ the same methodology for collecting student surveys and distilling them into college profiles as we do for *The Best 351 Colleges*. An important difference between this series and *The Best 351 Colleges*, however, is that we do not include any ranking lists. The profiles in these regional guides also appear in a slightly different format than those in *The Best 351 Colleges*.

But why are some of the outstanding schools in this book *not* included in *Best 351*? For one or both of two possible reasons. First, it may be because—at this time—they have a regional, rather than a national, focus. That is, they draw their students primarily from the state in which they are located, or from bordering states. A second possible reason is that—again, at this time—they have not met the rather rigorous standards for inclusion in *The Best 351 Colleges*. Is that meant as a snub to the schools that didn't make it into *Best 351*? Absolutely not. There are more than 3,000 institutions of higher learning in the United States, and *The Best 351 Colleges* profiles the top 10 percent, academically, of those schools. These regional guides, on the other hand, offer student opinion–driven information on all of those top colleges as well as the colleges just outside of that highest 10 percent.

For each school, we provide both in-depth statistical data (on admissions, financial aid, student body demographics, and academics) and narrative descriptions of academic and social life based on the opinions of the very students who attend them. Although we have expanded the scope of schools profiled from *Best 351*, we have also narrowed our focus to aid students for whom location is a key consideration.

We avoided using any sort of mathematical calculations or formulas to determine which colleges and universities to include in the regional guides. For each region, we aim to provide an inclusive cross-section of colleges: large and small, public and private, all-male and all-female, historically black colleges and universities, science and technology–focused institutions, nontraditional colleges, highly selective and virtually open-door admissions, great buys and the wildly expensive. Like the other schools in these guides, all are institutions well worth considering. Though not every college included will appeal to every student, this guide represents the top 150 colleges in the Midwestern states. We've surveyed students at 604 colleges across the nation and sorted their profiles into five regional guides. The following books complete the series:

The Best Mid-Atlantic Colleges

The Best Northeastern Colleges

The Best Southeastern Colleges

The Best Western Colleges

Each college we surveyed this year had to meet two criteria: first, they had to meet our standards for academic excellence within their region, and second, we had to be able to survey their students anonymously, either through our online survey (http://survey.review.com) or through our paper survey, which we distribute and collect during an on-campus visit.

Surveying thousands of students on hundreds of campuses is a mammoth undertaking, but the launch of our online student survey, available 24/7, has made it possible for students to complete a survey anytime and anywhere an Internet-enabled computer can be found. We've surveyed anywhere from all twenty-odd men at Deep Springs College in the California desert to thousands of collegians at places like Clemson University and Utah State University.

So how do we do it? All colleges and universities we plan to visit are notified through established campus contacts that we wish to arrange a survey; we depend on these contacts for assistance in identifying common, high-traffic areas on campus in which to distribute our paper survey and to help us make any necessary arrangements as required by campus policies. When possible, and when the college is willing, our contacts will arrange for an e-mail to be sent to the entire student body encouraging them to fill out our online survey. (In recent years, many schools have chosen to send an e-mail to the entire student body, which in some cases yielded astonishing results.) At colleges in the New York metropolitan area (we call it home), we most often send our own team to conduct the typically half-day surveys; at colleges that are further afield, we typically either send Princeton Review people from our field offices or hire current students at the college to conduct the surveys. Some of the colleges also included in *The Best 351 Colleges* series were surveyed this past year, but not *all*; each is surveyed *at least* once every three years. The reality is that, unless there's been some grand upheaval at a campus, we've found that there's little change in student opinion from one year to the next. Colleges that wish to be resurveyed prior to their turn in the regular survey cycle are accommodated with an earlier visit if at all possible.

The survey itself is extensive, divided into four fundamental sections—"About Yourself," "Your School's Academics/Administration," "Students," and "Life at Your School"—that collectively include more than 70 questions. We ask about everything imaginable, from

"How many out-of-class hours do you spend studying each day?" to "How widely used is beer?" Most questions are multiple-response in nature, but several offer students the opportunity to expand on their answers with narrative responses. These narrative responses are the source of the student quotes that appear throughout each college profile in *The Best Midwestern Colleges*.

Once the surveys have been completed and the responses stored in our database, each college is given a grade point average (GPA) for its students' answers to each multiple-response question. It is these GPAs that enable us to compare student opinions from college to college, and to gauge which aspects of the complete experience at each college rate highest and lowest according to the institution's own students. (They are also the basis for three of the ratings—Quality of Life, Financial Aid, and Academic—that appear at the top of each college profile.) Once we have this information in hand, we write the individual college profiles. Student quotes within the profiles are not chosen for their extreme nature, humor, or singular perspective—in all cases the intention is that they represent closely the sentiments expressed by the majority of survey respondents from the college or that they illustrate one side or another of a mixed bag of student opinion (in which case the counterpoint will also appear within the text). And of course, if a student's quote accomplishes this *and* is noteworthy for it's wittiness, it'll definitely make it into the guide.

The profiles in general seek to accomplish that which a college admissions viewbook by its very nature can never really hope to achieve—to provide a (relatively) uncensored view of life at a particular college, and acknowledge that even the best colleges have their shortcomings. Though some college administrators find this book hard to accept, most have come to recognize that college officials no longer enjoy the luxury of controlling every word that students hear or read about their institutions and that the age of consumerism in the college search process is here to stay.

Our survey is qualitative and anecdotal. While this approach sometimes means we blow a result—such as when we surveyed at Stephens College during the week the administration was debating the abolition of women's studies as a major at that small women's college and *(surprise!)* the survey results indicated an unhappy student body—most of our results are confirmed by feedback we get from alums, current students, counselors, and prospective students who visit the campuses. In order to help guard against the likelihood that we produce an entry that's way off the mark, we send administrators at each school a copy of the entry we intend to publish prior to its actual publication date, with ample opportunity to respond with corrections, comments, and/or outright objections. In every case in which we receive a reply, we take careful steps to ensure that we review their suggestions and make appropriate changes when warranted.

Far more important than what college administrators think is what *you* think. Take our information on colleges as you should take information from all sources—as input that reflects the values and opinions of others, which may be helpful to you as you *form your own opinions*. This guide is not an end point from which you should cull your list of possible colleges but rather a starting point, a tool that can help you to probe the surface and get a sense of the college experience. You must do your own investigation, refer to other sources, visit the campuses, and develop your own list of best colleges. Only then will this book be the useful tool that it is intended to be.

How This Book Is Organized

Each of the colleges and universities listed in this book has its own two-page spread. To make it easier to find information about the schools of your choice, we've used the same format for every school. Look at the sample pages below:

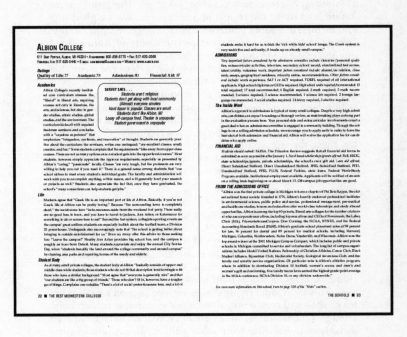

Each spread has several components. First, at the very top of the spread you will see the school's address, telephone and fax numbers for the admissions office, the telephone number for the financial aid office, and the school's website and/or e-mail address. Next, you will find the school's ratings in four categories: Quality of Life, Academics, Admissions, and Financial Aid, which are described further below. Then you will see our "Survey Says . . ." bubble and the first three sections—"Academics," "Life," and "Student Body"—which are drawn primarily from student survey responses for that particular college. Then comes the "Admissions" section with information on how the admissions office weighs the different components of your application; followed by the "Inside Word" on admissions, academics, life, or demographics at that school; "Financial Aid" application pointers; and an institution-authored message under the title "From the Admissions Office." Finally, at the end of the profile is the page number on which the school's statistical data appears. Here's an explanation of each part:

1. Contact Information

Includes school address, admissions phone and fax numbers, financial aid phone number, admissions e-mail address, and school website.

2. Quality of Life Rating

How happy students are with their lives outside the classroom. This rating is given on a scale of 60 to 99. The ratings were determined using the results of our surveys. We weighed several factors, including students' overall happiness; the beauty, safety, and location of the campus; comfort of dorms; food quality; and ease in dealing with the administration. Note that even if a school's rating is in the low 60s, it does not mean that the quality of life is horrible—there are no "failing" schools. A low ranking just means that the school placed low compared with others in our *Best* regional series. This individual rating places each college on a continuum for purposes of comparing all colleges within this edition of the series only. Though similar, these ratings are not intended to be compared directly to those within any subsequent edition, as our ratings computations are refined and change somewhat annually.

3. Academic Rating

On a scale of 60 to 99, how hard students work at the school and how much they get back for their efforts. The ratings are based on results of our surveys of students and administrators. Factors weighed included how many hours students study and the quality of students the school attracts; we also considered students' assessments of their professors' abilities and helpfulness. This individual rating places each college on a continuum for purposes of comparing all colleges within this edition only. Though similar, these ratings are not intended to be compared directly to those within any other edition, as our ratings computations are refined and change somewhat annually.

4. Admissions Rating

How competitive admission is at the school, on a scale of 60 to 99. This rating is determined by several factors, including the class rank of entering freshmen, their test scores, and the percentage of applicants accepted. By incorporating all these factors, our competitiveness rating adjusts for "self-selecting" applicant pools. University of Chicago, for example, has a very high competitiveness rating, even though it admits a surprisingly large proportion of its applicants. Chicago's applicant pool is self-selecting; that is, nearly all the school's applicants are exceptional students. This individual rating places each college on a continuum for purposes of comparing all colleges within this edition only. Though similar, these ratings are not intended to be compared directly to those within any other edition, as our ratings computations are refined and change somewhat annually.

5. Financial Aid Rating

Based on school-reported data on financial aid awards to students and students' satisfaction as collected on our survey with the financial aid they receive. Again, this is on a scale of 60 to 99. This individual rating places each college on a continuum for purposes of comparing all colleges within this edition only. Though similar, these ratings are not intended to be compared directly to those within any other edition, as our ratings computations are refined and change somewhat annually.

6. Survey Says . . .

Our "Survey Says" list, located under the ratings on each school's two-page spread, is based entirely on the results of our student surveys. In other words, the items on this list are based on the opinions of the students we surveyed at those schools (*not* on any numerical analysis of library size, endowment, etc.). Items listed are those that are unusually popular or unpopular on that campus. Some of the terms that appear on the list are not entirely self-explanatory; these terms are defined below.

Diverse students interact: We asked whether students from different class and ethnic backgrounds interacted frequently and easily. When students' collective response is "yes," the heading "Diverse students interact" appears on the list. When student response indicates there are not many interactions between students from different class and ethnic backgrounds, the heading "Students are cliquish" appears on the list.

Cheating: We asked students how prevalent cheating is at their school. If students reported cheating to be rare, "No one cheats" shows up on the list.

Students are happy: This category reflects student responses to the question "Overall, how happy are you with your school?"

TAs teach upper-level classes: At some large universities, you'll continue to be taught by teaching assistants even in your upper-level courses. It is safe to assume that when "Lots of TAs teach upper-level courses" appears on the list, TAs also teach a disproportionate number of intro courses as well.

Students are very religious or **Students aren't religious:**
We asked students how religious they are. Their responses
are reflected in this category.

Diverse student body: We asked students whether their
student body is made up of a variety of ethnic groups. This
category reflects their answers, and shows up as "Diversity
lacking on campus" or "Ethnic diversity on campus."

Town-gown relations: We asked students whether they got
along with local residents; their answers are reflected by
this category.

7. Academics, Life, and Student Body

The first three sections summarize the results of the surveys we
distributed to students at the school. The "Academics" section
reports how hard students work and how satisfied they are
with the education they are getting. It also often tells you
which academic departments our respondents rated favorably.
Student opinion regarding administrative departments often
works its way into this section, as well. The "Life" section describes life outside the classroom and addresses questions
ranging from "How nice is the campus?" and "How comfortable are the dorms?" to "How popular are fraternities and sororities?" The "Student Body" section tells you about what
type of student the school usually attracts and how the students view the level of interaction between various groups,
including those of different ethnic origins. All quotes in these
three sections are from students' essay responses to our surveys. We choose quotes based on the accuracy with which they
reflect our overall survey results for that school.

8. Admissions

This section tells you what aspects of your application are most
important to the school's admissions officers. It also lists the
high school curricular prerequisites for applicants, which standardized tests (if any) are required, and special information
about the school's admissions process (e.g., Do minority students and legacies, for example, receive special consideration?
Are there any unusual application requirements for applicants
to special programs?).

9. The Inside Word

This section contains our own insights into each school's admissions process, student-body demographics, life on campus,
or unique academic attributes.

10. Financial Aid

This section summarizes the financial aid process at the school—what forms you need and what types of aid and loans are available. (More information about need-based aid is listed under "Financial Facts" in the school's statistical profile at the back of the book.) While this section includes specific deadline dates as reported by the colleges, we strongly encourage students seeking financial aid to file all forms—federal, state, and institutional—as soon as they become available. In the world of financial aid, the early birds almost always get the best worms (provided, of course, that they're eligible for a meal!).

11. From the Admissions Office

This section contains text supplied by the colleges in response to our invitation that they use this space to "speak directly to the readers of our guide."

12. For More Information

We refer you to the page number in our school statistics section where you can find detailed statistical information for the particular school you're reading about.

SCHOOL STATISTICS

This section, located in the back of the book, contains various statistics culled from our student surveys and from questionnaires school administrators fill out. Keep in mind that not every category will appear for every school, since in some cases the information is not reported or not applicable. Please note that ratings for Quality of Life, Academics, Admissions, and Financial Aid are explained on pages 10-11.

If a school has completed each and every data field, the headings will appear in the following order:

Type of school: Whether the school is public or private.

Affiliation: Any religious order with which the school is affiliated.

Environment: Whether the campus is located in an urban, suburban, or rural setting.

Total undergrad enrollment: The total number of undergraduates who attend the school.

% male/female through **# countries represented:** The demographic breakdown of the full-time undergraduate student body, a listing of what percentage of the student body lives on campus, the percentage belonging to Greek organizations, and finally, the number of countries represented by the student body.

Calendar: The school's schedule of academic terms. A "semester" schedule has two long terms, usually starting in September and January. A "trimester" schedule has three terms, one usually beginning before Christmas and two after. A "quarterly" schedule has four terms, which go by very quickly: the entire term, including exams, usually lasts only nine or ten weeks. A "4-1-4" schedule is like a semester schedule, but with a month-long term in between the fall and spring semesters. (Similarly, a "4-4-1" has a short term following two longer semesters.) When a school's academic calendar doesn't match any of these traditional schedules we note that by saying "other." For schools that have "other" as their calendar, it is best to call the admissions office for details.

Student/faculty ratio: The ratio of full-time undergraduate instructional faculty members to all undergraduates.

Profs interesting rating: Based on the answers given iby students to the survey question, "In general, how good are your instructors as teachers?"

Profs accessible rating: Based on the answers given by students to the survey question, "In general, how accessible are your instructors outside the classroom?"

% profs teaching UG courses: Largely self-explanatory; this category shows the percentage of professors who teach undergraduates and doesn't include any faculty whose focus is solely on research.

% classes taught by TAs: Many universities that offer graduate programs use graduate students as teaching assistants (TAs). They teach undergraduate courses, primarily at the introductory level. This category reports on the percentage of classes that are taught by TAs instead of regular faculty.

Avg lab size; Avg reg class size: College-reported figures on class size averages for regular courses and for labs/discussion sections.

Most Popular Majors: The three most popular majors at the school.

% of applicants accepted: The percentage of applicants to which the school offered admission.

% of acceptees attending: The percentage of those who were accepted who eventually enrolled.

 # accepting a place on wait list: The number of students who decided to take a place on the wait list when offered this option.

% admitted from wait list: The percentage of applicants who opted to take a place on the wait list and were subsequently offered admission. These figures will vary tremendously from college to college and should be a consideration when deciding whether to accept a place on a college's wait list.

# of early decision applicants: The number of students who applied under the college's early decision or early action plan.

% accepted early decision: The percentage of early decision or early action applicants who were admitted under this plan. By the nature of these plans, the vast majority who are admitted wind up enrolling. (See the early decision/action description on the next page for more detail.)

Range/Average SAT Verbal, Range/Average SAT Math, Range/Average ACT Composite: The average and the middle 50 percent range of test scores for entering freshmen. Don't be discouraged from applying to the school of your choice even if your combined SAT scores are 80 or even 120 points below the average, because you may still have a chance of getting in. Remember that many schools emphasize other aspects of your application (e.g., your grades, how good a match you make with the school) more heavily than test scores.

Minimum TOEFL: The minimum test score necessary for entering freshmen who are required to take the TOEFL (Test of English as a Foreign Language). Most schools will require all international students or non-native English speakers to take the TOEFL in order to be considered for admission.

Average HS GPA: We report this on a scale of 0.0 to 4.0 (occasionally colleges report averages on a 100 scale, in which case we report those figures). This is one of the key factors in college admissions. Be sure to keep your GPA as high as possible straight through until graduation from high school.

% graduated top 10%, top 25%, top 50% of class: Of those students for whom class rank was reported, the percentage of entering freshmen who ranked in the top tenth, quarter, and half of their high school classes.

Early decision/action deadlines: The deadline for submission of application materials under the early decision or early action plan. Early decision is generally for students for whom the school is a first choice. The applicant commits to attending the school if admitted; in return, the school renders an early decision, usually in December or January. If accepted, the applicant doesn't have to spend the time and money applying to other schools. In most cases, students may apply for early decision to only one school. Early action is similar to early decision, but less binding; applicants need not commit to attending the school and in some cases may apply early action to more than one school. The school, in turn, may not render a decision, choosing to defer the applicant to the regular admissions pool. Each school's guidelines are a little different, and the policies of a few of the most selective colleges in the country have changed quite dramatically recently. Some colleges offer more than one early decision cycle, so it's a good idea to call and get full details if you plan to pursue one of these options.

Early decision, early action, priority, and regular admission deadlines: The dates by which all materials must be postmarked (we'd suggest "received in the office") in order to be considered for admission under each particular admissions option/cycle for admission for the fall term.

Early decision, early action, priority, and regular admission notification: The dates by which you can expect a decision on your application under each admissions option/cycle.

Nonfall registration: Some schools will allow applicants or transfers to matriculate at times other than the fall term—the traditional beginning of the academic calendar year. Other schools will only allow you to register for classes if you can begin in the fall term. A simple "yes" or "no" in this category indicates the school's policy on nonfall registration.

Tuition, In-state tuition: The tuition at the school, or for public colleges, for a resident of the school's state. In-state tuition is usually much lower than out-of-state tuition for state-supported public schools.

Out-of-state tuition: For public colleges, the tuition for a nonresident of the school's state. This entry appears only for public colleges, since tuition at private colleges is generally the same regardless of state of residence.

Room and board: Estimated room and board costs.

Books and supplies: Estimated annual cost of necessary textbooks and/or supplies.

% frosh receiving aid: According to the school's financial aid department, the percentage of all freshmen who received need-based aid.

% undergrads receiving aid: According to the school's financial aid department, the percentage of all undergrads who receive need-based financial aid.

Avg frosh grant: The average grant or scholarship amount awarded to freshmen.

Avg frosh loan: The average amount of loans disbursed to freshmen.

If you have any questions, comments, or suggestions, please contact us at Editorial Department, Admissions Services, 2315 Broadway, New York, NY 10024, or e-mail us at bookeditor@review.com. We appreciate your input and want to make our books as useful to you as they can be.

GLOSSARY

ACT: Like the SAT I but less tricky. Many schools accept either SAT or ACT scores; if you consistently get blown away by the SAT, you might want to consider taking the ACT instead.

College-prep curriculum: 16 to 18 academic credits (each credit equals a full year of a high school course), usually including 4 years of English, 3 to 4 years of social studies, and at least 2 years each of science, mathematics, and foreign language.

Core curriculum: Students at schools with core curricula must take a number of required courses, usually in such subjects as world history and/or western civilization, writing skills, and fundamental math and science.

CSS/Financial Aid PROFILE: The College Scholarship Service PROFILE, an optional financial aid form required by some colleges in addition to the FAFSA.

Distribution requirements: Students at schools with distribution requirements must take a number of courses in various subject areas, such as foreign language, humanities, natural science, and social science. Distribution requirements do not specify which courses you must take, only which types of courses.

FAFSA: The Free Application for Federal Student Aid. Schools are required by law to accept the FAFSA; some require that applicants complete at least one other form (usually a CSS/Financial Aid PROFILE or the college's own form) to be considered for financial aid.

4-1-4: A type of academic schedule. It's like a semester schedule, but with a short semester (usually one month long) between the two semesters. Most schools offer internship programs or nontraditional studies during the short semester. A 4-4-1 schedule is similar to this one, except the short semester comes after the second long semester, usually in the late spring or early summer.

GDI: "Goddamned independent," a term frequently used by students in fraternities and sororities to describe those not in fraternities and sororities.

Greek system, Greeks: Fraternities and sororities and their members.

Humanities: These include such disciplines as art history, drama, English, foreign languages, music, philosophy, and religion.

Merit-based grant: A scholarship (not necessarily full) given to students because of some special talent or attribute. Artists, athletes, community leaders, and geniuses are typical recipients.

Natural sciences: These include such disciplines as astronomy, biology, chemistry, genetics, geology, mathematics, physics, and zoology.

Need-based grant: A scholarship (not necessarily full) given to students because they would otherwise be unable to afford college. Student need is determined on the basis of the FAFSA. Some schools also require the CSS PROFILE and/or institutional applications.

Priority deadline: Some schools will list a deadline for admission and/or financial aid as a "priority deadline," meaning that while they will accept applications after that date, all applications received prior to the deadline are assured of getting the most thorough, and in some instances potentially more generous, appraisal possible.

RA: Residence assistant (or residential advisor). Someone, usually an upperclassman or graduate student, who supervises a floor or section of a dorm, usually in return for free room and board. RAs are responsible for enforcing the drinking and noise rules.

SAT I: A college entrance exam required by many schools.

SAT II: Subject Tests: Subject-specific exams administered by the Educational Testing Service (the SAT people). These tests are required by some, but not all, admissions offices. English Writing and Math Level I or IIC are the tests most frequently required.

Social sciences: These include such disciplines as anthropology, economics, geography, history, international studies, political science, psychology, and sociology.

TA: Teaching assistant. Most often a graduate student, a TA will often teach discussion sections of large lectures. At some schools, TAs and graduate students teach a large number of introductory-level and even some upper-level courses. At smaller schools, professors generally do all the teaching.

Work-study: A government-funded financial aid program that provides assistance to financial aid recipients in return for work in the school's library, labs, etc.

PART 2

THE SCHOOLS

ALBION COLLEGE

611 EAST PORTER, ALBION, MI 49224 • ADMISSIONS: 800-858-6770 • FAX: 517-629-0569
FINANCIAL AID: 517-629-0440 • E-MAIL: ADMISSIONS@ALBION.EDU • WEBSITE: WWW.ALBION.EDU

Ratings
Quality of Life: 77   **Academic:** 78   **Admissions:** 80   **Financial Aid:** 87

Academics

Albion College's recently instituted core curriculum stresses the "liberal" in liberal arts, requiring courses not only in literature, the arts, and sciences, but also in gender studies, ethnic studies, global studies, and the environment. The curriculum kicks off with required freshman seminars and concludes with a "capstone experience" that

> **SURVEY SAYS . . .**
> *Students aren't religious*
> *Students don't get along with local community*
> *(Almost) everyone smokes*
> *Hard liquor is popular, Classes are small*
> *Students don't like Albion, MI*
> *Lousy off-campus food, Theater is unpopular*
> *Student government is unpopular*

emphasizes "integration, synthesis, and innovation" of thought. Students are generally positive about the curriculum: the seminars, writes one undergrad, "are excellent classes, small, creative, and fun." Some students complain that the requirements "take away from upper-class courses. There are not as many options once a student gets into the upper-level courses." Most students, however, simply appreciate the rigorous requirements, especially as presented by Albion's "caring," "passionate" faculty. Classes "are very tough, but the professors are very willing to help you out if you need it." There is a general sense among students that "our school strives to meet every student's individual goals. The faculty and administration will work with you to accomplish anything, within reason, and will generally fund your research or projects as well." Students also appreciate the fact that, once they have graduated, the school's "many connections can help students get jobs."

Life

Students agree that "Greek life is an important part of life at Albion. Basically, if you're not Greek, life at Albion can be pretty boring." Because "the surrounding town is completely dead," the social scene here "lacks resources aside from the weekend frat party. There really are no good bars in town, and you have to travel to Jackson, Ann Arbor, or Kalamazoo for something to do or somewhere to eat!" Beyond the frat system, collegiate sporting events are the campus' great unifiers: students are especially bullish about the football team, a Division III powerhouse. Undergrads also encouragingly note that "the school is getting better about bringing in outside entertainment for us." Even so, many offer this advice to those seeking fun: "Leave the campus!" Nearby Ann Arbor provides big school fun, and the campus is roughly an hour from Detroit. Many students appreciate and enjoy the annual City Service Day, when "students beautify the land around the college community and around campus" by cleaning area parks and repairing homes of the needy and elderly.

Student Body

As at many small private colleges, the student body at Albion "basically consists of upper- and middle-class white students; those students who do not fit that description tend to mingle with those who have a similar background." Most agree that "everyone is generally nice" and that "our students are like a big group of friends." Those who don't fit in, however, have a tougher go of things. Complains one outsider, "There's a lot of social pretentiousness here, and a lot of students make it hard for us to kick the 'rich white kids' school' image. The Greek system is very restrictive and anti-unity; it breaks up an already small campus."

ADMISSIONS

Very important factors considered by the admissions committee include: character/personal qualities, extracurricular activities, interview, secondary school record, standardized test scores, talent/ability, volunteer work. *Important factors considered include:* alumni/ae relation, class rank, essays, geographical residence, minority status, recommendations. *Other factors considered include:* work experience. SAT I or ACT required. TOEFL required of all international applicants. High school diploma or GED is required. *High school units required/recommended:* 15 total required; 17 total recommended; 4 English required, 2 math required, 3 math recommended, 2 science required, 3 science recommended, 1 science lab required, 2 foreign language recommended, 3 social studies required, 1 history required, 3 elective required.

The Inside Word

Albion's approach to admissions is typical of many small colleges. Despite a very high admit rate, candidates can expect to undergo a thorough review, as matchmaking plays a strong part in the evaluation process here. Your personal side and extracurricular involvements count a great deal when an admissions committee is engaged in community building. Though the college is on a rolling admission schedule, we encourage you to apply early in order to have the best shot at both admission and financial aid. Albion will waive the application fee for candidates who apply online.

FINANCIAL AID

Students should submit: FAFSA. The Princeton Review suggests that all financial aid forms be submitted as soon as possible after January 1. *Need-based scholarships/grants offered:* Pell, SEOG, state scholarships/grants, private scholarships, the school's own gift aid. *Loan aid offered:* Direct Subsidized Stafford, Direct Unsubsidized Stafford, FFEL Subsidized Stafford, FFEL Unsubsidized Stafford, FFEL PLUS, Federal Perkins, state loans. Federal Work-Study Program available. Institutional employment available. Applicants will be notified of awards on a rolling basis beginning on or about March 15. Off-campus job opportunities are good.

FROM THE ADMISSIONS OFFICE

"Albion was the first private college in Michigan to have a chapter of Phi Beta Kappa, the oldest national honor society, founded in 1776. Albion's heavily endowed professional institutes in environmental science, public policy and service, professional management, pre-medical and healthcare studies, honors and education offer world-class internships and study abroad opportunities. Albion is among the top 85 private, liberal arts colleges for the number of alumni who are corporate executives, including top executives and CEOs of Newsweek, the Lahey Clinic (MA), PricewaterhouseCoopers, Dow Corning, the NCAA, NYNEX, and the Federal Accounting Standards Board (FASB). Albion's graduate school placement rates at 98 percent for law, 96 percent for dental and 89 percent for medical schools, including Harvard, Michigan, Columbia, Northwestern, Notre Dame, Vanderbilt, and Wisconsin. Albion was the top award winner at the 2001 Michigan Campus Compact, which includes public and private schools in Michigan committed to service and volunteerism. The long list of campus organizations includes Model United Nations, Fellowship of Christian Athletes, Canoe Club, Black Student Alliance, Equestrian Club, Medievalist Society, Ecological Awareness Club, and fraternity and sorority service organizations. Of particular note is Albion's athletics program, where in addition to dominating Division III football, women's soccer, and men's and women's golf and swimming, five varsity teams have earned the highest grade-point average in the MIAA conference, NCAA Division III, or any division nationwide."

For even more information on this school, turn to page 324 of the "Stats" section.

Alma College

614 West Superior Street, Alma, MI 48801-1599 • Admissions: 989-463-7139 • Fax: 989-463-7057
E-mail: admissions@alma.edu • Website: www.alma.edu

Ratings

Quality of Life: 72   **Academic:** 80   **Admissions:** 76   **Financial Aid:** 75

Academics

Students come to Alma, a small liberal arts college in the middle of Michigan's Lower Peninsula, expecting to have their limits pushed. Few are disappointed. As one student told us, "Alma has excellent academic programs. Students receive a quality educa-

> **SURVEY SAYS . . .**
> *Classes are small, Registration is a breeze*
> *Students are religious*
> *Student publications are ignored*
> *(Almost) everyone plays intramural sports*
> *Lots of beer drinking, Lousy food on campus*

tion here. Be ready to devote a lot of time to your studies." Noted another, "My overall academic experience has been excellent so far. The classes are tough, and it's really trying at times, but as long as you remember how accessible [the] faculty is, it's much easier to get through!" Alma undergraduates "have high academic standards. I've received many sympathetic looks after telling them I got a B on my exam," reports one student. "It's a B! I didn't fail or anything." Students navigate the difficult curriculum under the guidance of "faculty who are willing to help you. [If] you go to a professor's office hours once, it's hard to stop going." Administrators likewise "are awesome! Everyone is very accessible and our president frequently has students . . . for dinner." Student complaints here are few, although one undergrad did warn that "due to the lack of teamwork among the different divisions of the college, it's hard to get things like interdisciplinary study done sometimes. I expect for large universities to have this problem but not a small liberal arts college."

Life

As one student put it: "Life at Alma is pretty laid back. Some people might think that it's hard because it is a private Christian school, but it's not that horrible at all! For fun, we hang out with our friends, whether it's at a fraternity house (not even partying...) or just in our rooms. The more-Christian students do things differently from the less-Christian students, and everyone still seems to get along fairly well." Alma undergrads "are very involved in the Greek social life. One out of three [sic] is Greek at Alma. So if you're not fraternity or sorority type, you probably won't fit in very well, or at least [you] will have a dull social life." Many non-Greeks simply leave campus come Friday afternoon: reports one student, "It's a typical suitcase campus . . . . The ones that stay either can't go home and mope about it, or "they party. Off campus "there are a few bars/clubs in town that cater to the college crowd. They actually cut their hours almost in half in the summer when there are no students around. They make most of their money off of us, so they have a lot of deals for those 21 and over." Some feel that "Alma's sports could improve, but considering our academics are our main priority, this isn't such a big deal."

Student Body

Alma undergrads brag, "The students are the greatest strength of Alma. While it doesn't seem like a very diverse campus, and we joke about all being 'white, middle-class kids' because we don't have a large minority community, it is very diverse. We have all kinds of people on our campus that make it very interesting." An African American student disagrees, however, telling us that "diversity at this school is lacking. . . . Most minority students who come here end up transferring because they feel alone and lost. . . . We end up having to support each other, and most of the time that is not enough." Though Alma undergrads can be cliquish, "there's a lot of unity within groups here on campus. Wherever you go [to school], people are going to find those whom they mesh with, and those people become their circle of friends. The difference with Alma is that people regularly are a part of multiple circles, and their friends are fine with that."

ADMISSIONS

Very important factors considered by the admissions committee include: secondary school record and standardized test scores. *Important factors considered include:* class rank and essays. *Other factors considered include:* alumni/ae relation, character/personal qualities, extracurricular activities, interview, recommendations, talent/ability, and volunteer work. SAT I or ACT required. TOEFL required of all international applicants. High school diploma is required and GED is accepted. *High school units required/recommended:* 16 total are required; 4 English required, 3 math required, 3 science required, 2 foreign language recommended, 3 social studies required.

The Inside Word

Alma College admits students on a rolling basis, meaning that applicants for regular admission can apply and receive a decision early in the calendar year. Those for whom Alma is a first choice should consider applying Early Action; the deadline is early November, and students receive a decision by mid-November. Early Action admits are eligible for scholarships not typically available to regular admission candidates.

FINANCIAL AID

Students should submit: FAFSA. No deadline for regular filing. The Princeton Review suggests that all financial aid forms be submitted as soon as possible after January 1. *Need-based scholarships/grants offered:* Pell, SEOG, state scholarships/grants, private scholarships, and the school's own gift aid. *Loan aid offered:* Direct Subsidized Stafford, Direct Unsubsidized Stafford, Direct PLUS, Federal Perkins, and college/university loans from institutional funds. Federal Work-Study Program available. Institutional employment available. Applicants will be notified of awards on a rolling basis beginning on or about March 1. Off-campus job opportunities are fair.

FROM THE ADMISSIONS OFFICE

"Alma College, a Phi Beta Kappa institution, is a private, liberal arts and sciences college in central Michigan. Located one hour north of Michigan's capital, Lansing, and about two and a half hours north of Detroit, the residential campus is just a five-minute walk from downtown shops or local churches and a short drive from national fast-food chains and pizza shops. More than 1,300 students come to Alma's friendly campus from 19 states and several foreign countries. Founded in 1886 and affiliated with the Presbyterian Church (U.S.A.), Alma is committed to a quality undergraduate education. Academic excellence and a deep regard for students as individuals are fundamental to its educational residential programs. The College offers nearly 40 programs of study. Its small size enables many opportunities for one-on-one collaboration with faculty.

"High school students should have approximately a B average and an ACT composite score of 22 or a combined SAT score of 1030. A total of 16 high school units are required, including 4 of English, 3 of mathematics, 3 of social studies, and 3 of science; 2 units of foreign language are strongly recommended. An interview and campus visit are encouraged and Advanced Placement is accepted.

"International study options include formal programs in Australia, Austria, Ecuador, France, Germany, Italy, London, Mexico, New Zealand, Scotland, and Spain. Intercollegiate athletics are played at the NCAA Division III level, and Alma fields a total of 18 sports teams for men and women."

For even more information on this school, turn to page 324 of the "Stats" section.

ANDERSON UNIVERSITY

1100 EAST FIFTH STREET, ANDERSON, IN 46012 • ADMISSIONS: 765-641-4080 • FAX: 765-641-4091
E-MAIL: INFO@ANDERSON.EDU • WEBSITE: WWW.ANDERSON.EDU

Ratings
Quality of Life: 77   **Academic:** 78   **Admissions:** 76   **Financial Aid:** 78

Academics

Music and a nurturing Christian environment are the standout features of Anderson University, a small liberal arts school affiliated with the Church of God. "We have a great music program that has

> **SURVEY SAYS . . .**
> *Profs teach upper levels*
> *Diversity lacking on campus*
> *Instructors are good teachers, Students are happy*

produced wonderful musicians. I love to go to their concerts and the activities they put on," enthuses one undergrad. Notes another student, "The school of business, the music program, and the nursing program are all excellent." Anderson's small-school atmosphere facilitates lots of one-on-one learning opportunities; explains one student, "The class sizes are always small; I've never had a class with more than 30 students. The professors are extremely in tune with the students' needs." Students also happily report that "for the most part, administrators, professors, and staff are very friendly and available to the students. The majority of the faculty and staff are Christians, and Christian values are reflected in their teaching." A few here warn about the drawbacks of Anderson's size; writes one, "The only frustrating experience I have had was in registering for classes. That's the difficulty of being at a small school: classes get full fast and are a pain to schedule around each other. Some are only offered every other year and have odd hours that make it difficult to fit in the other classes I want to take."

Life

Those who enjoy life at Anderson University either embrace the school's religious ideals or take pleasure in skirting AU's many rules. Not everyone can adapt: "You either love AU or you hate it," explains one student. "I love it. Well, most of the time. For fun, they usually have stuff planned around campus." Stuff around campus includes "karaoke, horseback-riding trips, a square dance, and movies [projected onto] the side of a dorm. The social clubs put on a lot of fun shows like Encore (a talent show) and Cheap Thrills (a comedy). There are also lots of great musicians on our campus who put on concerts. Organizations like FCA, Campus Crusade for Christ, and other service groups meet regularly and have a strong attendance." Many here are athletically inclined; reports one such student, "In nice weather, it's hard to keep people indoors. Pick-up games of volleyball, Frisbee, soccer, basketball, kickball, and softball can be found all around campus." Students note that "there aren't any fraternities/sororities, but the equivalents are social clubs . . . . You aren't allowed to join them until sophomore year, and there are very strict regulations about rush. The social clubs are supposed to be service-based." Immediately beyond campus lies the town of Anderson, which "is kind of dull. Lots of cheap, tasty places to eat, though . . . . [And] it's about a half an hour to [Indianapolis]." On the upside, town-gown relations are good; writes one student, "People in the town really like AU students because they are typically very respectful and kind." Anderson is not for everyone though; warns one detractor, "Partying is not allowed by the administration, nor is dancing." Another notes that "there are only certain hours you can have a person of the opposite sex on your room."

Student Body

Many at Anderson agree that "the students here are great! Unlike many schools, the students who drink, smoke, and are sexually involved are in the minority. Students are friendly, outgoing, caring, encouraging, and desire to build each other up as brothers and sisters in Christ." "Most are Bible thumpers, (if that is an acceptable term)," is how another student put it. Undergrads appreciate the "small classes, group projects, small campus, and dorm life that help make this a closely connected community," the type of place where "everyone says 'hi' to everyone. . . . It doesn't matter if you know them or not!" Some, however, feel that "most are living in a dream world, a bubble. It's as if they think going to a Christian school means it should be like summer church camp every day."

ADMISSIONS

Very important factors considered by the admissions committee include: recommendations. *Important factors considered include:* character/personal qualities, class rank, extracurricular activities, interview, religious affiliation/commitment, standardized test scores, and volunteer work. *Other factors considered include:* alumni/ae relation, essays, minority status, secondary school record, talent/ability, and work experience. SAT I or ACT required; SAT I recommended. TOEFL required of all international applicants. High school diploma or GED is required. *High school units required/recommended:* 16 total required; 20 total recommended; 4 English required, 3 math required, 2 science required, 3 science recommended, 2 science lab required, 3 science lab recommended, 2 foreign language recommended, 2 social studies required, 3 social studies recommended, 2 history required, 5 elective recommended.

The Inside Word

Anderson University strongly recommends that candidates visit the campus, an excellent suggestion given that students here lead a less-than-typical college existence. The all-pervasive influence of religion is not for everyone, and visitors will soon sense whether AU is a good fit for them.

FINANCIAL AID

Students should submit: FAFSA. No deadline for regular filing. The Princeton Review suggests that all financial aid forms be submitted as soon as possible after January 1. *Need-based scholarships/grants offered:* Pell, SEOG, state scholarships/grants, private scholarships, and the school's own gift aid. *Loan aid offered:* FFEL Subsidized Stafford, FFEL Unsubsidized Stafford, FFEL PLUS, Federal Perkins, and college/university loans from institutional funds. Federal Work-Study Program available. Institutional employment available. Applicants will be notified of awards on a rolling basis beginning on or about February 15. Off-campus job opportunities are excellent.

FROM THE ADMISSIONS OFFICE

"Anderson University has been dedicated to Christian higher education in the liberal arts since 1917; this means scholarship and quality academics in the context of faith and service to church and society. Daily, the institution seeks to foster and nurture graduates who have a global perspective—who are competent, caring, creative, generous persons of character and potential. Campus programs are created to enable each member of the university to become stronger in body, mind, and spirit.

"Anderson University is a member of the Council for Christian Colleges and Universities and recognized for providing outstanding undergraduate and graduate academic quality within a faith community. Classes, taught by full-time faculty, are designed to be small and intimate, encouraging teacher/student interaction. University facilities provide approximately 2,500 students with state-of-the-art equipment, fully networked classrooms, and comfortable residences halls within a well-maintained 120-acre campus. For more information about Anderson University, visit www.anderson.edu."

For even more information on this school, turn to page 325 of the "Stats" section.

ASHLAND UNIVERSITY

401 College Avenue, Ashland, OH 44805 • Admissions: 419-289-5052 • Fax: 419-289-5999
E-mail: auadmsn@ashland.edu • Website: www.ashland.edu

Ratings

Quality of Life: 76   Academic: 73   Admissions: 68   Financial Aid: 74

Academics

"Accent on the individual" is the motto of Ashland University, a small college in Amish country, founded by the Brethren Church in 1878, where students benefit from a "close-knit atmosphere very conducive to learning." As there are typically no more than "6 to 20 peo-

> **SURVEY SAYS . . .**
> Students get along with local community
> Classes are small, Students are religious
> Profs teach upper levels, Theater is hot
> Student publications are popular
> Hard liquor is popular, School is well run

ple" per class and "a good majority of professors truly enjoy what they are doing and working with the students," an Ashland undergrad never feels like a face in the crowd. The support from the faculty facilitates the transition from high school, and the "wonderful," "understanding," and "very helpful" professors generally go "above and beyond the call of duty." Students are generally pleased with the academic caliber of their institution, doling out praise for the education and business departments, as well as the notable Ashbrook Scholars program in political science, in which a bunch of "bright, politically active students" works together in a small class setting. Though most say the school is well run, students are not unilaterally impressed with the administration. One student criticizes, "The school is very conservative and occasionally will not be open-minded about student issues." Though administrators hype an open-door policy, students complain, "When speaking to the administration, the door is the only thing open."

Life

When asked what the best part of campus life is, Ashland students give a surprising reply: "Definitely the food." Described as "amazing," "fresh," and "constantly changing," the fare at AU's dining hall has "won national awards." Feasting aside, students keep busy with campus clubs and organizations, of which the Division II athletics program and theatre are among the most popular. In addition, "many students participate in church activities." Since Ashland is a "dry campus," meaning "no alcohol allowed," "things are pretty tame," and there are "serious fines" to be paid for not following the rules. These rules are met with mixed reviews. One student gripes, "I just wish . . . that we weren't treated like children," while another supports the university's intentions: "The school tries to provide the safest, yet enjoyable, atmosphere." Although "there's not much to do in Amish county," Ashland's campus is an idyllic place to be stranded, as it is both "incredibly beautiful" and "extremely safe." Consequently, most remain on campus during the weekends to "watch movies, talk to friends, or go to a party," although "small dance clubs, bowling lanes, a movie theatre, and restaurants" draw students off campus. If you're on the fence about whether Ashland is a good fit for you, take one student's advice into account: "Anyone who is considering coming to Ashland should know that they are not coming here to party. Those who come to Ashland without understanding the goal/mission of the university often dislike the atmosphere."

Student Body

Students generally describe each other as "friendly and caring." "Most people know just about everyone" in this small community, though due to varying interests, there are a number of "major cliques that don't mix." Notes one theatre major, "I stay away from the jocks, and they stay away from the theatre majors. It's civil, but we aren't hugging and singing Kumbaya." Although the vibe is mostly amiable, "white, upper-middle-class Republicans" constitute a majority of Ashland's student body and faculty, making it "a difficult school to be a minority at." One undergrad reports that her classmates "seem to have the best intentions in life, but their narrow views will only get them so far." "Some of them are complete idiots," one student comments of his peers, "and some are bloody brilliant. It's the same with any group of people."

ADMISSIONS

Very important factors considered by the admissions committee include: secondary school record and standardized test scores. *Important factors considered include:* alumni/ae relation, character/personal qualities, class rank, essays, extracurricular activities, and interview. *Other factors considered include:* geographical residence, recommendations, religious affiliation/commitment, and work experience. SAT I or ACT required. TOEFL required of all international applicants. High school diploma or GED is required. *High school units required/recommended:* 3 English required, 4 English recommended, 2 math required, 3 math recommended, 2 science required, 3 science recommended, 2 foreign language recommended, 2 social studies required, 3 social studies recommended, 1 history required.

The Inside Word

Like most schools at which religion defines daily life, Ashland takes a strong interest in all indicators of a candidate's character. Applicants are encouraged to provide letters of recommendation from a counselor or principal; the school also suggests that applicants visit the school and interview with an admissions officer.

FINANCIAL AID

Students should submit: FAFSA and institution's own financial aid form. No deadline for regular filing. The Princeton Review suggests that all financial aid forms be submitted as soon as possible after January 1. *Need-based scholarships/grants offered:* Pell, SEOG, state scholarships/grants, private scholarships, and the school's own gift aid. *Loan aid offered:* Direct Subsidized Stafford, Direct Unsubsidized Stafford, Direct PLUS, Federal Perkins, Federal Nursing, and state loans. Federal Work-Study Program available. Applicants will be notified of awards on a rolling basis.

FROM THE ADMISSIONS OFFICE

"Ashland University will celebrate its 125th anniversary during the year 2003. Alumni and friends are invited to join Ashland University for this 'Year of Celebration' to honor its past, celebrate its accomplishments and milestones, and remember those whose dedication and hard work helped take this institution from a small, struggling college to the vibrant institution of higher education we see today. This 'Year of Celebration' comes at a time when Ashland University is stronger and better positioned to achieve its educational mission than at any point in its history. This yearlong observance will mark the return to campus of many alumni and friends.

"Some of the scheduled events for the 125th Anniversary include the following: a number of well-known speakers, including Barbara Bush as the Ashbrook Center 19th Annual Memorial Dinner speaker on April 4 and Bill Cosby presenting two shows as part of Homecoming Weekend on October 3; academic events such as author Terrence Deal speaking for an event sponsored by the Spectrum Series and the Colleges of Education and Business and Economics; a College of Arts and Sciences' Human Nature Symposium featuring four speakers; special events such as the Arctic Blast ice sculpting event, a Homecoming Parade to be 'the parade of all parades,' an Ohio Bicentennial Historical Marker dedication, and the burial of four time capsules."

For even more information on this school, turn to page 325 of the "Stats" section.

AUGSBURG COLLEGE

2211 RIVERSIDE AVENUE SOUTH, MINNEAPOLIS, MN 55454 • ADMISSIONS: 612-330-1001
FAX: 612-330-1590 • E-MAIL: ADMISSIONS@AUGSBURG.EDU • WEBSITE: WWW.AUGSBURG.EDU

Ratings
Quality of Life: 83   **Academic:** 70   **Admissions:** 64   **Financial Aid:** 79

Academics

Students at Augsburg College, "a small Lutheran" institution in the heart of Minneapolis, insist that "the faculty is one of Augsburg's greatest strengths." With an average class size of less than 20 students, undergrads here have plenty

> **SURVEY SAYS . . .**
> *Instructors are good teachers, Students are happy*
> *Classes are small, Students are religious*
> *Profs teach upper levels, No one cheats*
> *Class discussions encouraged*

of opportunity to get to know their professors; many discover that they're "knowledgeable, witty, engaging, creative, easy to talk to, and encouraging." A science student appreciates his profs, as they make "coming to Augsburg a pleasure, and they even make it worth getting up for your 8:00 class." "Not only do they provide the students with valuable information," reveals one student, "they also provide the knowledge for how to use the information with relation to life"; another adds that they "encourage students to reach out into the city and get first-hand experience" through internships. The administration is not so well received; generally described as "definitely lacking," with a "narrow-minded" staff, students hope that after the administration's "transitional period," communication with students will improve. Among the distinctions of the academic curriculum are majors in youth and family ministry, music therapy, and space physics, but if Augsburg doesn't offer a particular course, students have the option of taking classes at one of four other area colleges—St. Thomas, St. Catherine, Hamline, and Macalester. Students won't have to go far to find great facilities, though, as Augsburg has recently created "wonderful," "24-hour" computer labs and constructed a new library.

Life

Located about 10 blocks from the heart of downtown Minneapolis, Augsburg's campus offers perpetual access to urban pleasures like "theatrical events," "art," "museums," "historical places," "free parks," "bars," "night clubs," and "coffee shops." Fifteen minutes from the city, you'll find the world famous Mall of America, "the largest mall in the country," which "has everything from an amusement park, aquarium, nightclubs, and a wedding chapel to some awesome shopping." "People work their butts off" on campus, and aside from studying, students are involved with "countless clubs, organizations, and jobs." Clubs and support groups exist for a wide range of people and include "the CLASS program for students with physical and learning disabilities; the Step-up program for students [recovering from] alcohol/drug abuse issues; Pan-Asian, Pan-African, and American Indian student unions; and a huge international organization." The gym and the on-campus coffee shops are popular leisure-time destinations. Unlike many of America's other religiously affiliated schools, Augsburg is not a dry campus. "There is usually a party or 10 if you want to find one on a weekend," says a student, but partying doesn't occur to "the point where everywhere you go people are drunk." In fact, the wildest residents at Augsburg are probably the campus squirrels. A junior explains, "Our crazy squirrels . . . climb into people's open car windows."

Student Body

Augsburg College boasts "a lot of diversity"—at least as far as a 3,000-student, religious college is concerned. While 70 percent of the student body is white and more than 50 percent comes from a Lutheran background, the campus is composed of people from 40 states, 40 countries, and a mix of races, ethnicities, religions, and sexual orientations. "The friends I have made are more different and diversified than the colors in a crayon box," claims one student. Another asserts, "We are encouraged to embrace differences." Despite the religious lean of the school, "they don't force religion upon anyone." A "liberal," "friendly environment," Augsburg is home to students who "are interested in many different things, ranging from wrestling to campus ministry, and the History Club to Queer and Straight Unity (QSU)," while there's also a notable pocket of disinterested students who've been struck by the so-called "Auggie Apathy." To sum it up, one student writes: "Whatever type of person you are looking for, you will find it here."

ADMISSIONS

Very important factors considered by the admissions committee include: class rank, essays, secondary school record, and standardized test scores. *Important factors considered include:* character/personal qualities, extracurricular activities, and recommendations. *Other factors considered include:* alumni/ae relation, interview, talent/ability, volunteer work, and work experience. TOEFL required of all international applicants. High school diploma or GED is required. *High school units required/recommended:* 15 total required; 6 total recommended; 4 English required, 3 math required, 3 science required, 2 foreign language required, 3 social studies required, 4 social studies recommended, 2 history recommended.

The Inside Word

Augsburg knows how to turn a sow's ear into a silk purse: when the school learned that one of its donors had sent racist letters to intermarried couples, it rededicated the person's $500,000 donation to create new minority scholarships. Apparently, the school's dedication to diversity is paying off.

FINANCIAL AID

Students should submit: FAFSA and institution's own financial aid form. Regular filing deadline is August 1. The Princeton Review suggests that all financial aid forms be submitted as soon as possible after January 1. *Need-based scholarships/grants offered:* Pell, SEOG, state scholarships/grants, private scholarships, and the school's own gift aid. *Loan aid offered:* FFEL Subsidized Stafford, FFEL Unsubsidized Stafford, FFEL PLUS, Federal Perkins, Federal Nursing, and state loans. Federal Work-Study Program available. Institutional employment available. Applicants will be notified of awards on a rolling basis beginning on or about March 1. Off-campus job opportunities are good.

FROM THE ADMISSIONS OFFICE

"Minneapolis is a great place to go to college (an Internet research company recently rated it number two of big-city 'best college towns') and at Augsburg College students find many ways to take advantage of the opportunities at their doorstep—from internships and job prospects to cultural events, sports, and shopping. Augsburg offers a broad liberal arts education 60 and is recognized nationally for its emphasis on experiential learning—the 'hands-on' experience that employers seek in today's technological workplace. During their four years, students explore their interests and talents as they search for meaning in their lives and careers. Built into the curriculum are opportunities for study abroad, research, internships, and service-learning. On Augsburg's small campus, students get to know their professors beyond the classroom—working together on research questions, developing poster presentations, or playing in the same music ensemble. A college of the Evangelical Lutheran Church in America (ELCA), Augsburg welcomes students from all cultural, social, and religious backgrounds. The College also offers an undergraduate weekend program for working adults and five graduate programs. Augsburg is a leader in supporting students with learning and physical disabilities, and its Center for Global Education provides study and travel programs for universities around the country."

For even more information on this school, turn to page 326 of the "Stats" section.

AUGUSTANA COLLEGE (IL)

639 38TH STREET, ROCK ISLAND, IL 61201-2296 • ADMISSIONS: 309-794-7341 • FAX: 309-794-7422
E-MAIL: ADMISSIONS@AUGUSTANA.EDU • WEBSITE: WWW.AUGUSTANA.EDU

Ratings
Quality of Life: 72   Academic: 84   Admissions: 79   Financial Aid: 69

Academics

Students looking for a true small-college experience will do well at Augustana College. Augie undergrads praise not just the quality but the openness and availability of their professors. Writes one, "Because the school is small, students really do receive that 'quality time' from their teachers." Augustana instructors go the extra mile to show students they

> **SURVEY SAYS . . .**
> *Intercollegiate sports are popular*
> *Diversity lacking on campus*
> *Classes are small*
> *School is well run*
> *Students are religious*
> *Lots of beer drinking*
> *Students get along with local community*
> *(Almost) everyone plays intramural sports*

care, from giving out their home phone numbers in class to inviting students to dinner. Recounts one freshman, "My philosophy professor last term connected with students by inviting them over to a Halloween celebration. Many of my professors have opened up their homes for get-togethers." Agrees another, "The professors are very accessible, and I have gotten to know many of them well. They are very concerned with the well-being of their students." Many students choose Augustana for the number of different majors it offers, despite its small size. Others complain that academic diversity and course offerings need to be expanded. One student claims that the old-fashioned administration has all but shut down the Asian Studies department, while another complains that the general education requirements are in need of "a more global perspective."

Life

Augustana churns out happy students. Most say they love college life and report that on-campus activities and clubs flourish, catering to varied interests, from fraternities to choir. In the words of a female junior: "Augustana offers a great variety of activities for their students—on-campus movies, intramural sports, and just fun opportunities for students to socialize!" Though Augustana is technically a dry campus, parties and mixers are a big part of collegiate social life. As the surrounding city is not much more than a sleepy town, students rely heavily on campus-based activities, which can feel limiting to students looking for stimulation outside the college bubble. One freshman moans, "There isn't always something interesting to do on campus. People watch movies and drink." Another junior further explains, "I feel detached from the 'outside world.'"

Student Body

Augustana students love their school and they love each other. Raves one freshman, "Everyone is awesome." Enthuses another sophomore, "Right from the beginning everyone was friendly. Upperclassmen talked to me and gave me advice." Indeed, the small campus encourages a community feeling. "At our school, wherever you go you recognize a friendly face." Concurs another, "You can't walk anywhere without saying 'hi' at least five times." This camaraderie, however, may stem from the fact that a vast majority of Augie students come from the same economic and geographic backgrounds. One senior explains, "It seems like 98 percent of this campus is upper-middle-class white Chicago suburbanites." Another agrees that "the campus here is pretty much overrun by rich, preppy, white kids from the suburbs of Chicago," and further warns, "if you're looking for diversity and activism in your fellow students, don't come here!"

ADMISSIONS

Very important factors considered by the admissions committee include: class rank, secondary school record, and standardized test scores. *Important factors considered include:* character/personal qualities, essays, extracurricular activities, interview, and talent/ability. *Other factors considered include:* alumni/ae relation, minority status, recommendations, volunteer work, and work experience. SAT I or ACT required. TOEFL required of all international applicants. High school diploma or GED is required. *High school units required/recommended:* 16 total recommended; 4 English recommended, 3 math recommended, 2 science recommended, 1 foreign language recommended, 1 social studies recommended, 1 history recommended, 4 elective recommended.

The Inside Word

Previous academic performance weighs very heavily in admissions decisions at Augustana, as the school attracts an accomplished applicant pool. For marginal candidates, a visit to campus is a great way to make a solid impression and let admissions officers here know that you're serious about attending.

FINANCIAL AID

Students should submit: FAFSA and institution's own financial aid form. The Princeton Review suggests that all financial aid forms be submitted as soon as possible after January 1. *Need-based scholarships/grants offered:* Pell, SEOG, state scholarships/grants, private scholarships, and the school's own gift aid. *Loan aid offered:* FFEL Subsidized Stafford, FFEL Unsubsidized Stafford, FFEL PLUS, and Federal Perkins. Federal Work-Study Program available. Institutional employment available. Applicants will be notified of awards on a rolling basis beginning on or about February 15. Off-campus job opportunities are good.

FROM THE ADMISSIONS OFFICE

"Augustana College seeks to develop in students the characteristics of liberally educated persons: clarity of thought and expression, curiosity, fair-mindedness, appreciation for the arts, intellectual honesty, and a considered set of personal values and commitments in a culturally diverse world. Students combine a unique, newly developed general education curriculum with in-depth study in their major field(s). The program is designed to enhance student abilities to think critically and creatively, read and listen carefully, write and speak effectively, and use information efficiently and responsibly. Guided by a highly qualified, enthusiastic faculty, students are both inspired and compelled toward excellence in an atmosphere of mentoring and informal camaraderie. Augustana's three-term calendar provides plenty of time to pursue interests outside of the classroom, without sacrificing academics. Here students find a vibrant, active, residential community with the majority of our students (including first-year), becoming members of two or more clubs and organizations. With more than 100 social, religious, political, performing, and recreational opportunities to choose from, belonging at Augustana is easy. So, if you seek a complete college experience that will prepare you to lead, live well, and compete, then Augustana might be just the place for you."

For even more information on this school, turn to page 327 of the "Stats" section.

Augustana College (SD)

2001 South Summit Avenue, Sioux Falls, SD 57197 • Admissions: 605-274-5516 • Fax: 605-274-5518
E-mail: info@inst.augie.edu • Website: www.augie.edu

Ratings

Quality of Life: 71   Academic: 79   Admissions: 71   Financial Aid: 72

Academics

What separates Augustana College from the pack? "I would have to say it's the caring atmosphere," observes a typical undergrad. "When my parents came out to see the school, their first words were [about] how nice the people were." Agrees another, "The whole school is a community. The professors, staff, and students all

> **SURVEY SAYS . . .**
> *Classes are small*
> *Students love Sioux Falls*
> *Students are religious*
> *Very little beer drinking*
> *Students don't get along with local community*
> *Student publications are ignored*
> *No one cheats*

are friendly with each other, and the campus is pretty close-knit." Augie's faculty and small student body facilitate this strong sense of belonging; as one student told us, "I love Augustana because the faculty and administrators know you by name and their doors are almost always open to their students. Also, I feel that I'm getting an excellent liberal arts education because as a science major, not only am I challenged in my major, but my liberal arts classes force me to question preconceived beliefs that I hold and open my mind to other perspectives." Professors "have an interest in the students and will do what they can to help [them]." Enthuses yet another undergrad, "They are not only my professors, but my friends. . . . They care about what I bring to the class/school, my personal life, and everything. They are my 'family' away from home!" Others point out that "the study abroad program is excellent" and "the school's reputation helps when you are looking for a job in the community." As at many small liberal arts schools these days, "Financial difficulties currently beset us. The administration needs to rethink its plan of action [for] eliminating certain departments and positions and how to handle these cuts."

Life

Because Augustana's hometown of Sioux Falls "is relatively small and not real exciting," "students at Augustana stay pretty near campus. It's a real campus community. Friends hang out together in the dorms and there are many on-campus activities: movies, athletic activities, guest lecturers, etc." Students praise the "great aesthetic qualities of the campus and city," adding, "It's a pretty safe campus, so safe that campus safety officers spend their time eating donuts and playing Solitaire." Life here is relatively quiet; as one student put it, "During the week, when studying isn't an issue, a movie, pizza, and beer will usually suffice for fun." On weekends, students enjoy "bowling, watching movies (videos and widescreen), hiking, backpacking, cross-country skiing, and camping." Augie intramurals are "huge, and house parties are very big." In short, "Augie has something for everyone. There are parties for people who like that, both with and without alcohol. There are a lot of speakers, like Queen Noor of Jordan and James Earl Jones, that come to campus. Augie intercollegiate sports are well attended." Augustana is a Lutheran school, and as such sets some tougher-than-usual rules for student behavior. Alcohol, for example, is banned on campus and at all school-sponsored events. Visitation policies in the dorms (co-ed residence halls with single-sex floors) are also strict, leading one student to grouse about "a few strange regulations that could be changed to make campus life more fair."

Student Body

Augustana students want you to know that "contrary to world belief, we are not all 'country folk' in the Midwest!" In fact, "we embody all of the characteristics and cliques of our generation. Everyone (with the exception of a few) is good-hearted and friendly! We will also be nosy and follow the basic 'soap operas' going on in the dorms, but [we] care about people at the same time. We are a fun bunch of kids from the Midwest!" Male students note gleefully, "The girl-to-guy ratio is around 3 to 1, so ya can imagine what I love to do. I wasn't really into girls in high school, but I've got dozens of female friends here at Augie already." Don't expect wild times, though, as "most people here are very religious." Improvements? Augies would like to see their monochromatic hue suffused with a little more color: "The majority of people here are white. There are very few minorities. Some diversity would be nice."

ADMISSIONS

Very important factors considered by the admissions committee include: secondary school record. *Important factors considered include:* alumni/ae relation, class rank, standardized test scores, and volunteer work. *Other factors considered include:* character/personal qualities, extracurricular activities, geographical residence, interview, minority status, recommendations, religious affiliation/commitment, state residency, talent/ability, and work experience. SAT I or ACT required. TOEFL required of all international applicants. High school diploma is required and GED is accepted. *High school units required/recommended:* 16 total are recommended; 4 English recommended, 3 math recommended, 3 science recommended, 2 foreign language recommended, 2 social studies recommended, 2 history recommended.

The Inside Word

Borderline candidates to Augustana (those that don't meet or exceed reported admissions averages) should stress personal traits that will contribute to the campus community. A dedication to public service will be seen as a plus here; so too will musical talent, as the school has a large and well-regarded music program.

FINANCIAL AID

Students should submit: FAFSA. The Princeton Review suggests that all financial aid forms be submitted as soon as possible after January 1. *Need-based scholarships/grants offered:* Pell, SEOG, private scholarships, and the school's own gift aid. *Loan aid offered:* FFEL Subsidized Stafford, FFEL Unsubsidized Stafford, FFEL PLUS, Federal Perkins, Federal Nursing, and college/university loans from institutional funds. Federal Work-Study Program available. Institutional employment available. Applicants will be notified of awards on or about . Off-campus job opportunities are excellent.

For even more information on this school, turn to page 327 of the "Stats" section.

BAKER UNIVERSITY

EIGHTH AND GROVE, BALDWIN CITY, KS 66006 • ADMISSIONS: 785-594-8307 • FAX: 785-594-8372
E-MAIL: ADMISSION@BAKERU.EDU • WEBSITE: WWW.BAKERU.EDU

Ratings

Quality of Life: 70 **Academic:** 78 **Admissions:** 74 **Financial Aid:** 69

Academics

Let's get one thing straight about Baker undergraduate students: if there's one thing they love about their school it's the "caring faculty" who "bend over backwards" to help a student in need. Profs here enjoy nearly universal praise from students for their accessibility and vigor. It's common for professors to hand out their home phone num-

> **SURVEY SAYS . . .**
> *Students get along with local community*
> *Intercollegiate sports are popular*
> *Lots of beer drinking*
> *Student publications are popular*
> *School is well run, Hard liquor is popular*
> *Popular college radio*
> *(Almost) everyone plays intramural sports*

bers so students can contact them with questions at any hour. Professors "know who you are and they know about you—they care!" They're not just attentive and available, though; they're "extremely dynamic and excellent" at what they teach. "The science teachers are off the wall and can't help but keep your attention. The physics chair was lead guitar in a band and worked for NASA." Students do complain, however, that the science labs are a little behind the times. Most students feel that the administration is on their side as well: "Both professors and administration want you to be there, and if you are having trouble adjusting or with school work, there are lots of places to go for help." Students report that administrators are just as personable as the faculty, especially the higher-ups. Writes one student, "You can walk past the dean of students and have him greet you by name." Marvels another: "On my first day of classes I was standing in the lunch line waiting for my chicken strips when a guy in a suit tapped me on the shoulder and said, 'Lydia, it's so good to have you here!' I had to ask the lunch lady who he was . . . . Turns out it was the president of the university, who somehow already knew my name. This is typical at Baker." Some students worry that the administration is too focused on increasing enrollment ("We don't have the facilities or the staff") and should concern itself more with increasing the standard of living for the students already enrolled. Still, the small school atmosphere provides plenty of opportunities "for one-on-one contact with professors, seminars, conferences, trips, research, community service, Greek life, and [the] administration."

Life

Baker's hometown of Baldwin City is fairly small, so when students want off-campus fun, they head to Lawrence (about a 15-minute drive) or Kansas City (30 minutes) for bars, clubs, shopping, or just a change of scene. On campus, though, students do a good job of making their own amusement: "We watch a lot of movies, play some great games, and make prank phone calls." For outdoor fun, students enjoy visiting the Baker Wetlands, Boyd Woods, and the Prairie Reserve. Old trees and buildings beautify the campus, and a student admires the "brick roads" that make the campus look like "an old movie." Complaints about Baker include a dearth of parking space and the ubiquitous desire for better cafeteria food. (More chicken strips? See above.) Vegetarian students grouse that they "cannot live by cheese and pasta alone." Greek life is huge; almost every student is a member of a fraternity or sorority, and the brother- and sisterhoods do their best to keep the campus hopping with parties. Still, "this school is pretty tough, so in between the parties, you kind of have to study. . . ."

Student Body

The general consensus: "Everyone is really nice and wants you to be happy with Baker." A freshman opines, "Overall, the students mesh and work together, and are understanding of each other's differences." The small campus comes in handy here, too, as students "get to know almost everyone." On the down side, undergrads note that "there is little diversity in terms of race, sexual orientation, nationality, religion, etc." Admits one student, "The majority are rather sheltered rich kids, but for the most part they are all really cool." Raising a toast to his future alma mater, one student muses, "The Cheers theme song pretty much sums it up," adding, "At Baker everybody knows your name."

ADMISSIONS

Very important factors considered by the admissions committee include: class rank, secondary school record, and standardized test scores. *Important factors considered include:* recommendations. *Other factors considered include:* character/personal qualities and essays. SAT I or ACT required. TOEFL required of all international applicants. High school diploma or GED is required. *High school units required/recommended:* 16 total recommended; 4 English recommended, 3 math recommended, 3 science recommended, 2 foreign language recommended, 2 social studies recommended, 2 history recommended.

The Inside Word

Baker University does not set inordinately high admissions standards; the school's website reports that "in most cases, freshman applicants with an ACT composite score of 21 or a 3.0 high school GPA will be admitted." Those not meeting these requirements are not automatically disqualified, but rather are "evaluated on an individual basis."

FINANCIAL AID

Students should submit: FAFSA and institution's own financial aid form. Priority deadline is March 1. The Princeton Review suggests that all financial aid forms be submitted as soon as possible after January 1. *Need-based scholarships/grants offered:* Pell, SEOG, state scholarships/grants, private scholarships, and the school's own gift aid. Non-need-based scholarships are offered as well. *Loan aid offered:* FFEL Subsidized Stafford, FFEL Unsubsidized Stafford, FFEL PLUS, Federal Perkins, and college/university loans from institutional funds. Federal Work-Study Program available. Institutional employment available. Applicants will be notified of awards on a rolling basis beginning on or about February 15. Off-campus job opportunities are good.

FROM THE ADMISSIONS OFFICE

"Baker offers a prestigious private education at a price comparable to those of public universities. Nine out of ten Baker students receive financial aid and most packages cover the majority of tuition costs. If your aid doesn't cover the total cost of attending Baker, the University allows students to pay in installments. The payment options can range from 8 to 12 months and there are no interest charges.

"Any time you walk across Baker's campus you're likely to see a construction project underway. A recent project, the re-creation of Baker's library, was completed in December 2002. The $6 million project changed the scope and appearance of Collins Library, while emphasizing technology and small-group learning. The more than 14,000-square-foot expansion includes high technology and distance learning classrooms and a state-of-the-art learning resource area with an adjacent coffee bar. Just as the library project was nearing completion, the University began an $8 million campaign to revitalize its outdoor athletic facilities. Several parts of the project, including a new press box, new stadium seats, new field turf, a new scoreboard, and new locker facilities were completed in time for the 2002 football season."

For even more information on this school, turn to page 328 of the "Stats" section.

BALDWIN-WALLACE COLLEGE

275 EASTLAND ROAD, BEREA, OH 44017 • ADMISSIONS: 440-826-2222 • FAX: 440-826-3830
E-MAIL: ADMIT@BW.EDU • WEBSITE: WWW.BW.EDU

Ratings

Quality of Life: 74   **Academic:** 72   **Admissions:** 67   **Financial Aid:** 82

Academics

With a leading music conservatory and musical theatre program, Baldwin-Wallace College may "not be the place for you . . . if you aren't into music and acting." For the most part, however, the 4,000 or so students attending B-W seem quite happy with the education they're receiving (even those not majoring in theatre or music,

SURVEY SAYS . . .
Theater is unpopular
Classes are small
Students are religious
Instructors are good teachers
Class discussions encouraged
Very little hard liquor
Student publications are ignored

which is most of them). One B-W student highlighted "the small class size and engaging discussion format" as the most pleasing aspects of her academic experience. In such a setting, "the professors can give their students more personalized attention." Students are split when it comes to rating professorial quality. While many find that "the full-time faculty are excellent, very knowledgeable and understanding" as well as "extremely hands on," others opine that they're "nothing to brag home about" and feel that "classes could be more challenging." Students acknowledge the growing pains concomitant with the ascension of a new president, but overall, most feel as though the people in charge have their "best interests at heart even though at times it feels like they [administrators] are our worst enemies." But with its "friendly faculty and staff" who are "more than willing to help out," most B-W students are pleased that they study at a college where they "work you hard, but give you the resources to succeed."

Life

Hometown Berea is only 20 minutes from the heart of Cleveland. With The Rock & Roll Hall of Fame, "the great nightlife in the Flats area," and Broadway shows at Playhouse Square, students quickly learn that "Cleveland is a great city and there is always something exciting to go and see or do downtown." Which is a good thing since many find the actual campus to be "drab and boring." One musical theatre major wishes that B-W "could become a more vibrant place—granted it's small, but it doesn't have to be downright dead." One problem might be that "B-W is what we like to call a 'suitcase' school, meaning that nearly half of the students go home or elsewhere during the weekends." While many find that "Greek life . . . provides much entertainment," there are those that see the fraternity/sorority scene as "kind of lame. There are no houses and all they do is sit around in a tiny little dorm room that smells and drink really, really cheap beer." For those not ready to imbibe massive doses of Natty Light, one student recommends hitting "one of the local bars: Panini's, Mad Jacks, or the Berea Café around midnight or later . . . [where] there is dancing and drinking galore." But if you plan to drink galore, beware: "The alcohol policy is way too strict. For your first offense you have to pay $100, go through all this counseling, and are labeled an alcoholic." And then there are the "opposite sex visitor hours" complaints. That's a whole other can of worms, though.

Student Body

"The thing I love most about B-W is the fact that I can walk down the street and nearly every face I pass is a familiar one." There are a lot of lines dividing this student body, like the one "between the liberal arts students and the conservatory students." Others comment obliquely on "a lack of communication between Greek and non-Greek students." And there is interdepartmental tension, too. If you are a musical theatre major, be prepared for "a lot of back-biting. . . . [Students] are vicious and horrible to one another." While one student finds B-W "quite open and accepting for a midwestern school," another notes, "Kids at this school are very jaded and sheltered and are not used to other races or ethnicities." One student pithily labels classmates "really strong unique individuals," while another delves a bit deeper to describe the true soul of the B-W undergrad: "Overall the average student is an indestructible being, able to consume massive quantities of wings and beer, and in so doing, able to beat up small buildings in a single bout."

ADMISSIONS

Very important factors considered by the admissions committee include: class rank and secondary school record. *Important factors considered include:* essays, extracurricular activities, recommendations, and standardized test scores. *Other factors considered include:* alumni/ae relation, character/personal qualities, geographical residence, interview, minority status, religious affiliation/commitment, state residency, talent/ability, volunteer work, and work experience. SAT I or ACT required. TOEFL required of all international applicants. High school diploma or GED is required. *High school units required/recommended:* 15 total required; 19 total recommended; 4 English required, 3 math required, 4 math recommended, 3 science required, 4 science recommended, 2 science lab required, 2 foreign language required, 2 social studies required, 2 social studies recommended, 1 history required, 2 elective recommended.

The Inside Word

Admission is most competitive at Baldwin-Wallace's popular Conservatory of Music. All conservatory applicants must audition; instrumentalists may submit an audition videotape. For all other divisions, admission criteria are less stringent. With approximately four-fifths of all applicants gaining admission here, the average college-bound high school senior is nearly assured admittance to Baldwin-Wallace.

FINANCIAL AID

Students should submit: FAFSA. Regular filing deadline is September 1. The Princeton Review suggests that all financial aid forms be submitted as soon as possible after January 1. *Need-based scholarships/grants offered:* Pell, SEOG, state scholarships/grants, private scholarships, and the school's own gift aid. *Loan aid offered:* FFEL Subsidized Stafford, FFEL Unsubsidized Stafford, FFEL PLUS, Federal Perkins, and college/university loans from institutional funds. Federal Work-Study Program available. Institutional employment available. Applicants will be notified of awards on a rolling basis beginning on or about February 14. Off-campus job opportunities are good.

For even more information on this school, turn to page 328 of the "Stats" section.

BALL STATE UNIVERSITY

OFFICE OF ADMISSIONS, 2000 UNIVERSITY AVENUE, MUNCIE, IN 47306 • ADMISSIONS: 765-285-8300
FAX: 765-285-1632 • E-MAIL: ASKUS@BSU.EDU • WEBSITE: WWW.BSU.EDU

Ratings
Quality of Life: 71   **Academic:** 66   **Admissions:** 63   **Financial Aid:** 77

Academics

Pick up the course catalog at Ball State University, and you realize that you're at a big state school. The offerings are expansive, culled from 155 undergraduate programs offered by 48 departments in 7 colleges. The colleges

> **SURVEY SAYS . . .**
> *Frats and sororities dominate social scene*
> *Classes are small*
> *No one cheats*
> *Lots of beer drinking*

that comprise Ball State—Applied Sciences and Technology; Architecture and Planning; Business; Communication, Information, and Media; Fine Arts; Science and Humanities; and the Teacher's College—offer courses ranging from "food preparation science" to "contemporary forms of persuasion." Despite the vast list of courses, students grumble that they'd "like to see more of the classes in our catalogs offered" on a regular basis rather than "once every two to five years." While BSU's programs receive mixed reviews, there's a general consensus that the education and the telecommunications programs are not only outstanding, but are also among "the best programs in the nation." The honors college also comes with high recommendations, as it "offers smaller, more discussion-based courses and a wider variety of core classes to choose from." The average class size is under 30, allowing for closer classroom bonds. Says one student of her professors, "If they can help you with anything they generally will, without hesitation." And students feel that the school's downfalls are diminishing due to recent changes. "We just got a new president, so the administrative theory has radically shifted," comments a student. "It appears that the new administration is student oriented, as it has really not been in the past."

Life

Students at BSU make no bones about the fact that "Ball State is a party school and will stay that way no matter what anyone tries to do." To many students' consternation, frat house kegs have recently run dry, but university hometown Muncie offers revelers some "sweet bars" and plenty of leeway for fun. "You can pretty much relax if you're drinking underage," a student says. "The cops here are pretty cool as long as you don't break anything, puke on them, or try to fight everyone." The revelry begins on "Tipsy Tuesday" and drifts through "Wobbly Wednesday" to "Thirsty Thursday," when the true partying gets underway. Of course, not every single one of the 16,000 students here is seeing life through a pint glass. "Muncie has every basic thing you'd expect to be available for college students," explains one student. "I often go to movies, go bowling, hang out at coffeehouses, and go out to eat on the weekends." Another adds, "There are also a great number of churches and religous groups to be found for students who prefer to remember most of their college years." The university is also home to student clubs, activities, and Division I athletic teams that provide options "for almost every taste." Students with cars and the will to travel can even venture to big cities Indianapolis, Chicago, Dayton, or Cincinnati for urban entertainment.

Student Body

Ball State is "a central Indiana school," and about 90 percent of its students are central Indiana people. One feels that the prevalence of "white farm kids" at BSU sometimes leads to a "sheltered" mentality: some students tend to be "apprehensive of minorities and other students from different backgrounds than themselves." While most students admit that, yes, they "could use a lot more diversity" on campus, they contend that BSU's student body is "welcoming when it comes to different lifestyles and different people." And the rural midwestern fabric of these students has weeded out some of the pretentiousness that you find at other universities. A mathematical economics major explains, "Many of us were raised in the same working-class atmosphere. The populace isn't made up of students who will look down on you if you aren't wearing the latest item from Banana Republic, J.Crew, or Abercrombie." Many students expressed the sentiment that "most students are very congenial people and easy to approach with questions and comments. During my first couple weeks of school I had many questions about places/activities on campus and the veteran students were more than happy to help me."

ADMISSIONS

Very important factors considered by the admissions committee include: secondary school record. *Important factors considered include:* standardized test scores and talent/ability. *Other factors considered include:* alumni/ae relation, essays, interview, minority status, and recommendations. SAT I or ACT required. TOEFL required of all international applicants. High school diploma or GED is required. *High school units required/recommended:* 4 English required, 3 math required, 4 math recommended, 3 science required, 4 science recommended, 3 science lab required, 3 foreign language recommended, 3 social studies required.

The Inside Word

With decent grades and test scores, you should have little trouble getting in to Ball State. Some programs are smaller than others and therefore more competitive. Check the school's website frequently for updates; the school posts notices (www.bsu.edu/admissions) that warn when space in a particular program is getting tight.

FINANCIAL AID

Students should submit: FAFSA. No deadline for regular filing. The Princeton Review suggests that all financial aid forms be submitted as soon as possible after January 1. *Need-based scholarships/grants offered:* Pell, SEOG, state scholarships/grants, private scholarships, and the school's own gift aid. *Loan aid offered:* Direct Subsidized Stafford, Direct Unsubsidized Stafford, Direct PLUS, and Federal Perkins. Federal Work-Study Program available. Institutional employment available. Applicants will be notified of awards on a rolling basis beginning on or about April 15. Off-campus job opportunities are good.

For even more information on this school, turn to page 329 of the "Stats" section.

BELOIT COLLEGE

700 COLLEGE STREET, BELOIT, WI 53511 • ADMISSIONS: 608-363-2500 • FAX: 608-363-2075
FINANCIAL AID: 608-363-2500 • E-MAIL: ADMISS@BELOIT.EDU • WEBSITE: WWW.BELOIT.EDU

Ratings
Quality of Life: 84   Academic: 87   Admissions: 80   Financial Aid: 95

Academics

"Beloit seriously is about inventing yourself," writes one student, echoing the unofficial motto of this small southern Wisconsin liberal arts school. "Come to this school if you have initiative and motivation to do creative things of your own design. If you build it . . . they will pay for it to be done. I love it here." Agrees another undergrad, "Beloit College is a bombardment of opportunities, and if you are lucky and smart, you will take the opportunities that are best for you as a person and academically." Students here especially love the school's "multidisciplinary approach, which allows you to view events from the perspectives of different disciplines." They also appreciate the little things, from the academic advising to the uncommon sense of community that students, faculty, and administrators share ("Last weekend, all sophomores and a number of professors and administrators were treated to a weekend away from campus at a resort," reports a typical student.) Students also approvingly declare, "Beloit College runs based on the desires of the student body. Money is allotted to groups by student funding boards so that there isn't any discrepancy between the interests of the students and college bureaucracy about distribution of funds." Profs here, by all accounts, "are amazing. They will all take the time to talk to anybody about anything. They all really care about making the students interested in the material. Seriously."

> **SURVEY SAYS . . .**
> *Campus easy to get around*
> *Lots of beer drinking*
> *Campus feels safe*
> *Campus is beautiful*
> *Dorms are like palaces*
> *Hard liquor is popular*
> *(Almost) everyone smokes*
> *Students are happy*

Life

Explains one student, "If you're okay with staying on campus all the time, Beloit's your school. If seeing the same places and the same people day after day after day bothers you, you might want to think over your decision to apply here." Given the situation, it's fortunate that "Beloit students are resourceful. Since there's not much to do in a dying town, we learn to entertain ourselves and each other. We love theme parties ('Come As Another Beloit Student,' 'Dress Like Your Celebrity Look-Alike'), and ultimate Frisbee has a cult-like participation and following." "Clubs and student organizations thrive on this campus," and "besides the many student clubs, there are establishments such as the Coughy-Haus (which serves alcohol, allows smoking, and features loud bands) and the Java Joint (quiet music, no smoking, no alcohol, good for studying or playing board games) that one can go to for fun." There's also "sporting events, theater choir and band performances, intramurals, talks, lectures, discussions, Greek-sponsored events, all-campus activities, and movies at cinema for additional entertainment. There's definitely always something going on at Beloit College." Students here appreciate the school alcohol policy, which is "to treat us like adults unless we give them a reason to do differently." Those with cars occasionally escape to "Rockford and Janesville, which are 20 minutes away. Also, Milwaukee, Madison, and Chicago are all within 90 minutes, so there's always chances for breaking out of the bubble."

Student Body

Undergraduates insist, "There really is no 'typical student' at Beloit. People here are free to be whomever they want to be and definitely exercise that freedom." Most would concede, however, that the majority is a little on the nerdy side: "Beloit College is like high school, only now the misfits are the popular cliques, and they exclude people that seem too normal," notes one student. Many here are "always overly involved. I don't know anyone on campus that isn't involved in more than one club, sport, philanthropy, or Greek organization." The few conservative students warn, "A Beloit student will open his arms and celebrate just about any kind of person so long as that person is a liberal passionate activist who says he is open-minded. Oh yeah, and dreadlocks help." Beloit is also home to "a large, vocal international population [that] provides a worldview not available at most schools."

ADMISSIONS

Very important factors considered by the admissions committee include: essays, recommendations, secondary school record. *Important factors considered include:* class rank, interview, standardized test scores. *Other factors considered include:* alumni/ae relation, character/personal qualities, extracurricular activities, talent/ability, volunteer work, work experience. SAT I or ACT required. TOEFL required of all international applicants. High school diploma or GED is required. *High school units required/recommended:* 4 English recommended, 4 math recommended, 3 science recommended, 2 foreign language recommended, 4 social studies recommended, 4 history recommended.

The Inside Word

Beloit expects to find evidence of sensitivity and thoughtfulness in successful candidates. There is tough competition for students among colleges in the Midwest, which gives those Beloit applicants who don't show consistent strength a bit of a break.

FINANCIAL AID

Students should submit: FAFSA, institution's own financial aid form, state aid form. CSS/Financial Aid PROFILE is accepted. No deadline for regular filing. The Princeton Review suggests that all financial aid forms be submitted as soon as possible after January 1. *Need-based scholarships/grants offered:* Pell, SEOG, state scholarships/grants, private scholarships, the school's own gift aid. *Loan aid offered:* FFEL Subsidized Stafford, FFEL Unsubsidized Stafford, FFEL PLUS, Federal Perkins, college/university loans from institutional funds. Federal Work-Study Program available. Institutional employment available. Applicants will be notified of awards on a rolling basis beginning on or about April 1. Off-campus job opportunities are fair.

FROM THE ADMISSIONS OFFICE

"While Beloit students clearly understand the connection between college and career, they are more apt to value learning for its own sake than for the competitive advantage that it will afford them in the workplace. As a result, Beloit students adhere strongly to the concept than an educational institution, in order to be true to its own nature, must imply and provide a context in which a free exchange of ideas can take place. This precept is embodied in the mentoring relationship that takes place between professor and student and the dynamic, participatory nature of the classroom experience."

For even more information on this school, turn to page 330 of the "Stats" section.

BETHEL COLLEGE (KS)

300 EAST 27TH STREET, NORTH NEWTON, KS 67117-0531 • ADMISSIONS: 316-284-5230 • FAX: 316-284-5870
E-MAIL: ADMISSIONS@BETHELKS.EDU • WEBSITE: WWW.BETHELKS.EDU

Ratings

Quality of Life: 73   Academic: 73   Admissions: 69   Financial Aid: 78

Academics

Bethel College of Kansas, a small Mennonite liberal arts school south of Wichita, attracts an exceptional student body, boasting one of the highest per capita rates of National Merit finalists in the state. Accounting, pre-law, and pre-medical studies are tops with the hard workers who submit to Bethel's rigors. Writes one

> **SURVEY SAYS . . .**
> *Classes are small*
> *Theater is unpopular*
> *Students are religious*
> *Very little hard liquor*
> *No one plays intramural sports*
> *Very little beer drinking*
> *No one watches intercollegiate sports*

student, "Finals week we all look like zombies. . . . I hear many people complain about the school and claim they are going to leave. However, when they show up on campus the next fall, a common answer is simply that there is just something about the college that 'gets you' and makes it hard to leave." What 'gets them' may be the quality of instruction: as one student put it, "The greatest strengths of the school lie in the professors. They are personable and positive, and they give up a lot to ensure that the academic reputation of the school survives." Classes, many of which "use graduate-level texts" are "held in seminar-like format, and conversation is encouraged," fostering "a good student attitude. . . . The classes may be more demanding than a state college, but it is worth the pain." Students are also drawn in by the school's placement programs and claim that Bethel "can hook you up with some of the best internships." Mix that in with the "common aura of meta-analysis going on all over the campus" and you'll find a student body balanced between theory and practice. Students also comment on the frequency with which they see the President on campus, "on average . . . about three times a week just in passing."

Life

Because of the intense academic environment at Bethel College, students aren't always awash in the pleasures of extracurricular life. "Getting away occasionally is advised, as much of the time here is spent closeted with a book," notes one undergrad. Compounding the quietude is a dearth of activity on campus; "Bethel College could use more student weekend functions," complains a typical student. Adds another, "Weekends usually are boring if you don't find or make an excuse to get away to Wichita, about 30 miles south." Students make their own fun; some are fanatical about Ultimate Frisbee ("Ultimate Frisbee has a faithful following; people get together and play everyday," says one student), while others "may go drunken bowling or mini-golfing. Otherwise we usually drink on campus. . . . It is nice, because there is absolutely no pressure to do any of this. It is just a lot of fun." Another notes "Athletics are very well organized and add a nice dimension to life. I played volleyball and found it optimal, as all the schools in our conference were also in our state, minimizing travel." When they can lift their eyes from the books, students often notice that "the campus itself is beautifully taken care of, having many trees and an open area in the center of all the buildings. The grounds and air are both very clean, and there is nearly no sound pollution."

Student Body

Bethel undergrads report that "There is a diverse array of students who attend the school," but "because enrollment is typically under 500, it is very easy to see the division of people. For the most part, people are extremely friendly, at first especially, but it is difficult to break into pre-formed cliques." One student notes the diversity on campus: "There are a lot of different kinds of people. There are people who get into Earth Day and people who love to watch and play sports. The nice thing is all kinds of people don't let their differences get in the way of their attitude and personality. Everyone is treated with respect." Students are also quick to add that "there are many positive aspects to the tiny campus. Everyone knows everyone else, and trust is easily come by. Doors are left unlocked, and cases of theft or vandalism are rare and surprising."

ADMISSIONS

Very important factors considered by the admissions committee include: alumni/ae relation, character/personal qualities, interview, and secondary school record. *Important factors considered include:* class rank, extracurricular activities, recommendations, religious affiliation/commitment, standardized test scores, talent/ability, and volunteer work. *Other factors considered include:* essays, geographical residence, minority status, state residency, and work experience. SAT I or ACT required. TOEFL required of all international applicants. High school diploma is required and GED is accepted. *High school units required/recommended:* 16 total are recommended; 4 English recommended, 4 math recommended, 3 science recommended, 2 foreign language recommended, 3 social studies recommended.

The Inside Word

Bethel's admissions criteria are not strict; according to the school's website, "Automatic admission is generally given to students with a GPA of 2.5 and an ACT of 19 or SAT I of 890." The school reserves the right, however, to turn away those whom it feels would not fit well in this quiet community.

FINANCIAL AID

Students should submit: FAFSA. No deadline for regular filing. The Princeton Review suggests that all financial aid forms be submitted as soon as possible after January 1. *Need-based scholarships/grants offered:* Pell, SEOG, state scholarships/grants, private scholarships, and the school's own gift aid. *Loan aid offered:* FFEL Subsidized Stafford, FFEL Unsubsidized Stafford, FFEL PLUS, and Federal Perkins. Federal Work-Study Program available. Institutional employment available. Applicants will be notified of awards on a rolling basis beginning on or about March 15. Off-campus job opportunities are good.

For even more information on this school, turn to page 330 of the "Stats" section.

BETHEL COLLEGE (MN)

3900 BETHEL DRIVE, SAINT PAUL, MN 55112 • ADMISSIONS: 651-638-6242 • FAX: 651-635-1490
E-MAIL: BCOLL-ADMIT@BETHEL.EDU • WEBSITE: WWW.BETHEL.EDU

Ratings

Quality of Life: 75   Academic: 77   Admissions: 76   Financial Aid: 72

Academics

Bethel College offers its students a cozy liberal arts education with a Christian tilt. Because there are "such small class sizes," it's easy for students and professors "to develop relationships that go beyond simply the academics." Students describe their professors as "approachable" instructors who "genuinely care" and "choose to invest in the lives of students." In the classroom, profs "incorporate Christianity into their class." A student comments, "This was different for me and I have just fallen in love with it." "Challenging and fulfilling" is how a classmate describes the courses at Bethel. "Challenging enough," adds another student, "but not so overwhelming that I can't give my time to other things I enjoy." The majors that draw in the most students are education, business, and biology, though students recommend nursing, physics, and biblical and theological studies as well. Satisfied though they may be, students still chant the popular small-school complaint: "More variety of courses," please. They also warn of the occasional professors who are "not knowledgeable about what they are teaching and unapproachable outside of the classroom." But these are the anomalies. As a general rule, Bethel's educational mission is shaped by accessibility and personal relationships. To this effect, a student says, "We work hard building up each other . . . 1st Thes. 5:11." A wisenheimer chides, "Gotta love them Baptists!"

> ### SURVEY SAYS . . .
> *Theater is hot*
> *Students love Saint Paul*
> *Students are religious*
> *Diversity lacking on campus*
> *High cost of living*
> *School is well run*
> *Popular college radio*
> *Student publications are popular*

Life

A Bethel student's college years are shaped by a "lifestyle statement" that everyone—students and faculty—signs "before coming" to school. A student describes some of the rules outlined in the statement: "Dancing is prohibited . . . Drinking, smoking, sex (except in marriage), and drugs are also prohibited." These rules, students say, create an atmosphere of "good, clean fun" within a community that's visibly "committed to Christian values." A female undergrad describes an incident in her first year when she returned to her dorm room and was told that her roommate was behind closed doors with her boyfriend. "'Oh no!' I thought to myself. 'What's going on in there?' I went in—and they were praying together. It was awesome." Of course, there are less devout students "who prefer to drink and use drugs" and take advantage of Bethel's "underground party scene," but they are in a small minority. Most students are "involved in the student body . . . whether through ministry, music, theatre, sports, Bible studies, student life" or student activities, which include "weekend events, midnight movies, late-night roller-skating, BBQs, banquets," "bonfires, trips to the Mall of America," or "sporting events." Bethel is situated on the banks of Lake Valentine in "the northern side of St. Paul," about "15 minutes from downtown." In the Twin Cities metro area, students find high culture, like "concerts, plays, and the Walker and MIA art museums," and the staple delights of any college student's life—namely, bowling alleys, diners, coffee shops, and movie theatres. "If you're bored," says one student, "it's your own fault."

Student Body

As a student explains, the "common ground" that ties all Bethel students together is "that we have a relationship with Jesus Christ." Another chimes in: "The majority of students who attend Bethel have chosen to come here because they are looking for a Christian environment, to grow in their faith while receiving a quality education." Aside from their intense faith, many students here share "wealthy" or "middle-class, suburban white backgrounds." About 70 percent of the students hail from Minnesota, an area rife with Scandinavian ancestry— thus, the "blonde hair, blue eyes" that you see all over campus. Generally, the only tension that touches the Bethel crowd results from "hypocrisy," as one student puts it, adding that sometimes "people say one thing on Sundays and do another thing Saturday night. That makes me sad that people say that they are serving God, but they aren't even trying. I think it makes God sad also." The pervasive "ultraconservative" disposition of the students sometimes makes them seem "closed-minded and judgmental," but overall students find their classmates to be "accepting, encouraging, and inspiring."

ADMISSIONS

Very important factors considered by the admissions committee include: class rank, recommendations, religious affiliation/commitment, secondary school record, and standardized test scores. *Important factors considered include:* character/personal qualities, essays, and interview. *Other factors considered include:* alumni/ae relation, extracurricular activities, minority status, and volunteer work. SAT I or ACT required. TOEFL required of all international applicants. High school diploma or GED is required. *High school units required/recommended:* 4 English recommended, 3 math recommended, 3 science recommended, 2 foreign language recommended, 4 social studies recommended, 3 history recommended.

The Inside Word

According to its website, Bethel admits freshman candidates who rank in the top half of their high school class and earn a 21 composite ACT score or a combined SAT I score of 920. Applicants must also demonstrate a commitment to Bethel's "Christian lifestyle standards," which can be reviewed on the school's website.

FINANCIAL AID

Students should submit: FAFSA, institution's own financial aid form, and state aid form. No deadline for regular filing. The Princeton Review suggests that all financial aid forms be submitted as soon as possible after January 1. *Need-based scholarships/grants offered:* Pell, SEOG, state scholarships/grants, private scholarships, and the school's own gift aid. *Loan aid offered:* FFEL Subsidized Stafford, FFEL Unsubsidized Stafford, FFEL PLUS, Federal Perkins, state loans, and private alternative bank loans. Federal Work-Study Program available. Institutional employment available. Applicants will be notified of awards on a rolling basis beginning on or about March 1. Off-campus job opportunities are excellent.

For even more information on this school, turn to page 331 of the "Stats" section.

BRADLEY UNIVERSITY

1501 WEST BRADLEY AVENUE, PEORIA, IL 61625 • ADMISSIONS: 309-677-1000 • FAX: 309-677-2797
FINANCIAL AID: 309-677-3089 • E-MAIL: ADMISSIONS@BRADLEY.EDU • WEBSITE: WWW.BRADLEY.EDU

Ratings
Quality of Life: 77   **Academic:** 69   **Admissions:** 77   **Financial Aid:** 84

Academics

Career-oriented undergraduates seeking the intimacy of a small college and the resources of a research institution might want to consider Bradley University. With just under 5,000 undergrads and nearly 1,000 grad students, Bradley is small enough to allow personal interaction between students and professors and big enough to offer more than 90 academic and pre-professional majors in five undergraduate col-

> **SURVEY SAYS . . .**
> *Frats and sororities dominate social scene*
> *(Almost) everyone smokes*
> *Popular college radio*
> *Hard liquor is popular*
> *Lots of beer drinking*
> *Athletic facilities need improving*
> *Library needs improving*
> *Students don't like Peoria, IL*
> *Lousy food on campus*

leges. Many who attend agree that "Bradley is the perfect size. The smaller school atmosphere has allowed me to get more involved in campus." Indicative of the level of intimacy here is the fact that "many professors include their home number on the syllabus so we can contact them. One even said we could call until 1 a.m. because they're on a college schedule, but after that to wait until the next day." The business, chemistry, and engineering departments all receive high marks here, and liberal arts faculty members have their advocates as well. Professors generally "are good. With small schools, the classes are small and close-knit, but class variety is limited. The trade-off is good, though." The administration gets mixed reviews; explains one student, "Academically, Bradley is run very well. But in the area of nonacademics, the administration needs to be more open." Writes another, "Administrators seem willing to hear students' questions but not necessarily as willing to do anything about them." Other student complaints center on the library ("out of date") and technology services. All in all, though, the students tell us that they're happy with the "memorable" and "excellent" academic experience that Bradley offers. "I love Bradley University," beams one sophomore. "I have never regretted my decision [to attend] at all."

Life

Students describe a "laid-back," midwestern vibe permeating the "self-contained" and "pretty campus" at Bradley University. For some, especially those outside the Greek system, it's a little too laid back. Explains one student, "Bradley is a good school if you don't care about a social life." Those within Greek society, however, find plenty to fill their extracurricular hours. "Social life is somewhat Greek-oriented," concedes one frat member. Adds another student, "If you don't like Greek parties you are kind of screwed." For the alternatively inclined, "art parties are pretty hip, or you could go to local rock shows. Local bars are also popular." For all others, the school provides a few activities "specifically designed to get everyone on campus involved," but for the most part, students find few distractions enticing them from their studies. The gym facilities, a potential source of diversion, "need serious improvement." To make matters worse, most students agree that Peoria "is boring." On the positive side, it is "easy, quick, and convenient to get to and from class" at Bradley, especially considering the size of the undergraduate population. Also, brand new dorms are soon to be available for upperclassmen; in just a few years you'll be living in really swank digs.

Student Body

"Most people are either athletes or Greeks" at Bradley, where the "atmosphere is on the conservative side, not so open to activism." However, "people are friendly for the most part," writes one student, and others further characterize their classmates as "outgoing," "courteous," "wealthy, educated," and "slightly motivated." Because the student body is small, "everyone knows everyone else [by the beginning of senior year], which can be a good thing or a bad thing." Some students say self-imposed racial and ethnic segregation is "obvious," but others feel that tolerance and unity are hallmarks here. "Bradley is like a family," coos a junior. "People from all different backgrounds are constantly interacting."

ADMISSIONS

Very important factors considered by the admissions committee include: secondary school record. *Important factors considered include:* class rank, standardized test scores. *Other factors considered include:* alumni/ae relation, character/personal qualities, essays, extracurricular activities, interview, personal experience and cultural background, recommendations, talent/ability, volunteer work, work experience. SAT I or ACT required. TOEFL required of all international applicants. High school diploma or GED is required. *High school units required/recommended:* 16 total required; 4 English required, 5 English recommended, 3 math required, 4 math recommended, 2 science required, 3 science recommended, 2 science lab required, 3 science lab recommended, 2 foreign language recommended, 2 social studies required, 3 social studies recommended, 2 history recommended.

The Inside Word

Though students come here from far and wide, Bradley is best known within the Midwest and its reach is primarily regional. As a result, the admission process at Bradley is not super competitive; combined with solid academic quality and a broad range of offerings, this makes Bradley a worthwhile choice for those seeking to attend a strong school without running a grueling admissions gauntlet.

FINANCIAL AID

Students should submit: FAFSA. The Princeton Review suggests that all financial aid forms be submitted as soon as possible after January 1. *Need-based scholarships/grants offered:* Pell, SEOG, state scholarships/grants, private scholarships, the school's own gift aid. *Loan aid offered:* Direct Subsidized Stafford, Direct Unsubsidized Stafford, Direct PLUS, Federal Perkins, Federal Nursing, college/university loans from institutional funds. Federal Work-Study Program available. Institutional employment available. Applicants will be notified of awards on a rolling basis. Off-campus job opportunities are good.

FROM THE ADMISSIONS OFFICE

"Does the size of a college make a difference? Bradley's 5,000 undergraduates and 1,000 graduates think so. They like the opportunities, choices, and technologies of a larger university and the quality, personal attention, and challenge of a small, private college. Bradley's size makes so many things possible—recognition instead of anonymity, accessibility instead of bureaucracy, and academic choices instead of limits. Bradley students choose from more than 90 programs of study in the Foster College of Business Administration, Slane College of Communications and Fine Arts, College of Education and Health Sciences, College of Engineering and Technology, and Liberal Arts and Sciences. Clearly, size does make a difference."

For even more information on this school, turn to page 331 of the "Stats" section.

BUENA VISTA UNIVERSITY

610 WEST FOURTH STREET, STORM LAKE, IA 50588-1798 • ADMISSIONS: 712-749-2235
FAX: 712-749-1459 • E-MAIL: ADMISSIONS@BVU.EDU • WEBSITE: WWW.BVU.EDU

Ratings
Quality of Life: 75   Academic: 80   Admissions: 77   Financial Aid: 89

Academics

Buena Vista University bills itself as the nation's first truly "wireless community." What that means is that every student, upon commencement of his or her freshman year, is issued a notebook computer and granted wireless Internet access. That's right: check your e-mail from anywhere at anytime! While the university is

> **SURVEY SAYS . . .**
> *No one plays intramural sports*
> *Diversity lacking on campus*
> *Classes are small*
> *Students are religious*
> *Very little beer drinking*
> *(Almost) no one listens to college radio*

remaining at the forefront of the technological revolution, students here complain that there's not much of an academic revolution going on. "I haven't really learned anything new," admits one student who would like to confront more challenges in the classroom. Another agrees, "The classes aren't tough at all." Most concur, however, that the professors are available to students looking to go the extra mile. "The professors are really good about being there when you need them," enthuses an undergrad. "You can call them at home if you have a problem and they are really friendly." And when the student is willing, the professors "take time to get to know you as an individual." The key at Buena Vista is to show up with drive—and then keep one's self in gear. "You get outta college life what you put into college life," advises one self-motivated undergraduate.

Life

"Nearly 50 percent of the campus goes home on the weekends, and when you consider how small we are," that doesn't leave many students hanging around for weekend events. But, students tell us, the people who leave on weekends are the ones who are missing out. "For those who do stay, pretty much it's party central." There are definitely students who prefer to invest their time in one—or two, or three, or a dozen—of the campus' 50 or so organizations and the host of activities they foster. One of the biggest days on campus is the annual Buenafication Day, when "bands come here and play" and other student activities create a festive mood. All sorts of sports can be seen when the weather permits, and there's "sledding and such in the winter." Other students say they are content to simply walk (or jog, or Rollerblade) along the 3,200-acre Storm Lake, one of the campus' closest neighbors. And when all else fails, the promising young minds at Buena Vista are content to simply "go to movies or hang out in each other's rooms."

Student Body

When the students at Buena Vista describe themselves as "midwestern kids," they aren't kidding. About 85 percent of the populace hails from within the state, and most others come from Iowa's next-door neighbors. Because the Midwest is rife with open spaces and farmlands, it shouldn't be surprising that "many of the students" at BVU "come from rural areas." This has its pros and cons. On the con side, many incomers "have not been exposed or know how to react to students of different ethnic backgrounds or sexual orientations." On the flipside, the inherent midwestern congeniality spawns a great deal of "really friendly" and "laid back" students. unfortunately, it's sometimes hard to appreciate the friendliness of the student body; because of their regional origins, many students head back home on the weekends rather than sticking around to have a hand in Buena Vista's social life.

ADMISSIONS

Very important factors considered by the admissions committee include: standardized test scores. *Important factors considered include:* class rank and secondary school record. *Other factors considered include:* alumni/ae relation, character/personal qualities, essays, extracurricular activities, geographical residence, interview, minority status, recommendations, religious affiliation/commitment, state residency, talent/ability, volunteer work, and work experience. SAT I or ACT required. TOEFL required of all international applicants. High school diploma or GED is required. *High school units required/recommended:* 4 English required, 4 math recommended, 2 science required, 4 science recommended, 2 foreign language recommended, 2 social studies required, 2 history recommended.

The Inside Word

In its efforts to attract top students, Buena Vista offers a number of generous scholarships to candidates with excellent academic records. These include four "multicultural" full scholarships per year, each earmarked for a student of color.

FINANCIAL AID

Students should submit: FAFSA and institution's own financial aid form. The Princeton Review suggests that all financial aid forms be submitted as soon as possible after January 1. *Need-based scholarships/grants offered:* Pell, SEOG, state scholarships/grants, private scholarships, and the school's own gift aid. *Loan aid offered:* Direct Subsidized Stafford, Direct Unsubsidized Stafford, Direct PLUS, FFEL Subsidized Stafford, FFEL Unsubsidized Stafford, FFEL PLUS, Federal Perkins, and college/university loans from institutional funds. Federal Work-Study Program available. Institutional employment available. Applicants will be notified of awards on or about February 20. Off-campus job opportunities are excellent.

FROM THE ADMISSIONS OFFICE

"So why do students chose BVU? Because they love this place! Our lakeside campus is not only beautiful, but has all the best facilities—including a brand new triple-court recreation center with an indoor 200-meter track, plus a $26 million science center currently under construction. Then you have our faculty members, who not only care about their students, but also what they teach; in fact, the faculty just made better-than-ever changes to BVU's degree plans. Add in all the opportunities to participate in our 21 varsity sports or to get involved in campus organizations that let students do everything from be a deejay on the radio to decide what food the cafeteria serves. Plus there's our interim session, which lets students travel internationally or within the U.S., or work at an internship with companies all over the nation. And don't forget how we make college affordable for our students, with 98 percent of them receiving financial assistance. But perhaps best of all, we really do give all our students their own laptop computer! Thanks to our wireless network that stretches over the entire campus, students can stay logged on to the Internet (yes, for free!) no matter where they are—in classrooms, in their residence halls, or out by the lake. In all these ways and more, Buena Vista University's bold vision of what an education should be is providing bright futures for our students."

For even more information on this school, turn to page 332 of the "Stats" section.

BUTLER UNIVERSITY

4600 SUNSET AVENUE, INDIANAPOLIS, IN 46208 • ADMISSIONS: 317-940-8100 • FAX: 317-940-8150
E-MAIL: ADMISSION@BUTLER.EDU • WEBSITE: WWW.BUTLER.EDU

Ratings
Quality of Life: 83   **Academic:** 73   **Admissions:** 68   **Financial Aid:** 76

Academics

With a little more than 3,000 students, Butler University provides an intimate learning environment that allows professors to cater "to the needs of their students," "where professors actually know my name and they are concerned if they think I am not understand-

> **SURVEY SAYS . . .**
> *Instructors are good teachers*
> *Classes are small, Profs teach upper levels*
> *Lousy food on campus, Students are happy*
> *Student publications are popular, School is well run*
> *(Almost) everyone plays intramural sports*

ing the material." At Butler, "classes are often taught by people in the actual profession," and through the real-world experience of Butler's instructors, students are able to relate their studies to the working world that awaits them. While you'll certainly find some "excellent professors" at Butler, you'll also come across some who have an uncanny knack for making "lectures about very interesting subjects incredibly boring." "At least we don't have teaching assistants," shrugs a student. The most popular majors at Butler are pharmacy, marketing, journalism, and biological sciences. And numerous smaller programs, such as ballet and education, are held in high repute. When students discover the right major or the right professors for them, they report an "outstanding" academic ride at Butler. One satisfied student shares, "I constantly find myself motivated to find my own opinion and seek out new answers."

Life

If you thought Greek life was big in the Mediterranean, just wait until you get to Butler. "Everything revolves around the Greek system," admits a student, despite the fact that only 25 percent of Butler undergrads go Greek. With eight sororities and eight fraternities, Butler's social life (especially for those under 21) consists largely of "frat parties." But "if you don't get involved in a frat or sorority . . . you won't be left out," assures an appeasing student. "There are campus events for everyone." Aside from more than 100 campus organizations, students have access to "guest speakers," "sporting events," on-campus "entertainment," and "free movies" that "are offered each weekend." "The student government provides numerous activities throughout the year, such as skydiving, theatre, concert trips, and Pacers games." The university also hosts springtime community-building competitions, such as "all-campus cookouts on the lawn" or "all-night sports competitions between housing units." There's also the "Spring Sports Spectacular" (athletics), "Geneva Stunts" (acting), and "Spring Sing" (um, singing). And let's not forget that Butler has all the thrills of Indianapolis. "There are a lot of bars and dance clubs" in the city, especially in "the popular Broad Ripple area." Indianapolis also offers "good shopping, good food, and good places to go for entertainment," such as "theatre productions, comedy clubs, and museums." And, of course, the hometown pro sports teams provide another host of options. But come to the BU campus during college basketball's March Madness and you'll see that the most important sports team in town—at least in the minds of Butler students—is the Butler Bulldogs. Or simply, "the Dawgs," as a student fan informs us.

Student Body

"Whether you know them or not," the students at Butler "are friendly. That's just the way campus is. Everyone is very welcoming." This sense of friendliness is what leads many students to choose Butler. But there are some students who contend that Butler's young scholars aren't always as nice as they initially seem. "I think that many of them are spoiled and don't necessarily care for others," says a pharmacy student. Because Butler is a private university with a sizable tuition, it tends to attract "rich kids" who look "like they just stepped out of an Abercrombie and Fitch catalogue. Talk about some good-lookin', well-dressed kids!" jokes a student. Greek life is a defining factor in these students' lives: you're either Greek, or you're not, and everyone knows it. While Butler is by no means a portrait of diversity—"mostly Caucasian females," describes one student—it has a healthy mix of students from the city and students "from small rural communities." Overall, the tenor of the campus populace is "conservative," perhaps in part because of the "many so-called 'religious' students" who attend Butler. But if you're a liberal pagan, don't worry: "There are all types of people here."

ADMISSIONS

Very important factors considered by the admissions committee include: class rank, essays, recommendations, secondary school record, and standardized test scores. *Important factors considered include:* extracurricular activities. *Other factors considered include:* alumni/ae relation, character/personal qualities, interview, minority status, talent/ability, volunteer work, and work experience. SAT I or ACT required. TOEFL required of all international applicants. High school diploma or GED is required. *High school units required/recommended:* 17 total required; 4 English required, 3 math required, 3 science required, 2 foreign language required, 2 history required, 2 elective required.

The Inside Word

Butler offers two nonbinding early application programs, meaning that students can gain early acceptance without committing to attend. Those who apply early are eligible for special scholarships, unique housing opportunities, and consideration for the honors program.

FINANCIAL AID

Students should submit: FAFSA and institution's own financial aid form, both due March 1. Regular filing deadline is October 1. The Princeton Review suggests that all financial aid forms be submitted as soon as possible after January 1. *Need-based scholarships/grants offered:* Pell, SEOG, state scholarships/grants, and the school's own gift aid. *Loan aid offered:* Direct Subsidized Stafford, Direct Unsubsidized Stafford, Direct PLUS, and Federal Perkins. Federal Work-Study Program available. Institutional employment available. Applicants will be notified of awards on a rolling basis beginning on or about March 15. Off-campus job opportunities are excellent.

FROM THE ADMISSIONS OFFICE

"Butler students commonly identify the University's strengths as academic excellence, personal attention from faculty, a wide range of academic programs, quality facilities, and proven preparation for graduate school and career. Butler students represent almost every state in the nation and more than 40 countries, reflecting a diversity of cultures, interests, aspirations, personalities, and experience. Students can take advantage of more than 100 student organizations, including student government; intramural sports; NCAA Division I varsity athletics; social, religious, and volunteer organizations; service clubs; honorary societies; and performance groups. A core curriculum affords students the opportunity to gain knowledge in the humanities, the arts, social sciences, natural sciences, and mathematics. Baccalaureate degrees are offered through Butler's five colleges. For students who are undecided about their major field of study, there is an Exploratory Studies Program, where students develop a personalized academic plan to help choose the major that best suits their interests and abilities. Butler also offers an individualized major that allows students to create their own major such as women's studies."

For even more information on this school, turn to page 333 of the "Stats" section.

CALVIN COLLEGE

3201 Burton Street, SE, Grand Rapids, MI 49546 • Admissions: 616-526-6106 • Fax: 616-526-6777
Financial Aid: 616-526-6134 • E-mail: admissions@calvin.edu • Website: www.calvin.edu

Ratings
Quality of Life: 93   Academic: 82   Admissions: 78   Financial Aid: 90

Academics

Christian values are certainly front-and-center at Calvin College, a midsize midwestern school affiliated with the Christian Reformed Church. Rigid dogma, however, is not on the agenda; writes one student, "Calvin gives students the opportunities to explore their faith at an academic and spiritual level. Students can take advantage of religion classes, Bible studies, and fun worship groups, or they can choose to ignore all of that." Agrees another, "Calvin gets people to think for themselves and not just regurgitate the political and religious ideals of their parents." Students praise requirements that "encourage you to delve into subjects you wouldn't have necessarily considered if you didn't have to take them for the fulfillment of the core curriculum." Of course, an excellent program can go only so far without an excellent faculty; fortunately, "Calvin College's professors are dedicated to serving the student body in any way possible." Notes one student, "Professors often have students to their house for dinner, eat in the cafeteria with students, keep their doors open, follow office hours, and accept home phone calls." Similarly, administrators are "always eager to help solve problems and give suggestions as to how to improve" the school, "know students by name," and "often attend student functions, like chapel and sports events. They aren't holed up in their offices; they are a part of the community."

> **SURVEY SAYS . . .**
> *Very small frat/sorority scene*
> *Students are very religious*
> *Very little hard liquor, Very little beer drinking*
> *(Almost) no one smokes*
> *Lots of conservatives on campus*
> *Classes are small*
> *Diversity lacking on campus*
> *Musical organizations are hot*
> *Very little drug use*

Life

Calvin undergrads appreciate the efforts their school makes to provide "plenty of things to do outside of the classroom. There is always a show of some sort, whether it is improv or a band." Adds one student, "Calvin offers great entertainment. The Student Activities Board brings in great concerts like Bela Fleck, Ben Harper, and Emmylou Harris. The Film Arts committee shows artsy movies every weekend, and the dorms all plan activities on the weekend, from floor dates for sundaes to massive broom ball tournaments." Students are especially grateful for on-campus diversions during the tundra-like winters, during which there is "way too much snow and the sun doesn't shine." (But hey, "that provides a great study environment.") Students enjoy a surprising amount of freedom on campus: explains one undergrad, "Our values are good, but we are a lot less strict than many Christian schools. Chapels are not mandatory, smoking is permitted, alcohol and most other policies are under 'responsible freedom' guidelines. The school trusts students to make their own decisions and expects that students want to learn." Despite its nickname of "Bland Rapids," hometown Grand Rapids earns the praise of many undergrads. Offers one, "Grand Rapids has one area of town, Eastown, which has lots of fun coffee shops and artsy shops, and is much more diverse than the rest of GR. A lot of Calvin students live there." The campus "is very beautiful, especially in the fall—great time to visit!"

Student Body

A number of Calvin respondents this year noted a broadening of the school's traditionally narrow demographic. Wrote one, "Historically, Calvin has been a conservative, Christian, suburban, white school with few people from other religious denominations . . . [but] in the past few years, Calvin has taken great strides to promote a more diverse campus, and it shows. I think the students here are genuinely benefiting from the progress Calvin has made." Things haven't changed that much, though; you can still "learn Dutch without taking a class" here. As one would expect, students are religious, "but not freaky about religion. Calvin students are very intelligent, so they enjoy talking theology and philosophy, and such. Because of this, they are generally accepting of a lot of viewpoints."

ADMISSIONS

Very important factors considered by the admissions committee include: religious affiliation/commitment, secondary school record, standardized test scores. *Important factors considered include:* character/personal qualities, essays, extracurricular activities, recommendations. *Other factors considered include:* class rank, volunteer work, work experience. SAT I or ACT required; ACT preferred. TOEFL required of all international applicants. High school diploma or GED is required. *High school units required/recommended:* 12 total required; 17 total recommended; 3 English required, 4 English recommended, 3 math required, 2 science required, 1 science lab recommended, 2 foreign language recommended, 2 social studies required, 3 social studies recommended, 3 elective required.

The Inside Word

Calvin's applicant pool is highly self-selected and small. Nearly all candidates get in, and over half choose to enroll. The freshman academic profile is fairly solid, but making a good match with the college philosophically is much more important for gaining admission than anything else.

FINANCIAL AID

Students should submit: FAFSA, institution's own financial aid form. No deadline for regular filing. The Princeton Review suggests that all financial aid forms be submitted as soon as possible after January 1. *Need-based scholarships/grants offered:* Pell, SEOG, state scholarships/grants, private scholarships, the school's own gift aid. *Loan aid offered:* Direct Subsidized Stafford, Direct Unsubsidized Stafford, Direct PLUS, Federal Perkins, state loans, college/university loans from institutional funds, private alternative loans. Federal Work-Study Program available. Institutional employment available. Applicants will be notified of awards on a rolling basis beginning on or about March 15. Off-campus job opportunities are excellent.

FROM THE ADMISSIONS OFFICE

"Calvin's well-respected faculty, innovative core curriculum, and inquiring student body come together in an environment that links intellectual freedom with a heart for service. Calvin's 400-acre campus is home to more than 4,300 students and 300 professors who chose Calvin because of its national reputation for academic excellence and faith-shaped thinking. Calvin encourages students to explore all things and offers nearly 100 academic options to choose from. Quality teaching and accessibility to students are considered top priorities by faculty members. More than 80 percent of Calvin professors hold the highest degree in their field, the student/faculty ratio is 13:1, and the average class size is 23. The College's 4-1-4 calendar offers opportunities for off-campus and international study, while service-learning projects draw Calvin students into the local community. Internships allow students to try their individual gifts in the workplace while gaining professional experience. In a recent survey, 96 percent of Calvin graduates reported that they had either secured a job or begun graduate school within six months of graduation. Calvin is among the top 3 percent of four-year private colleges in the number of graduates who go on to earn a PhD."

For even more information on this school, turn to page 333 of the "Stats" section.

CARLETON COLLEGE

100 SOUTH COLLEGE STREET, NORTHFIELD, MN 55057 • ADMISSIONS: 507-646-4190 • FAX: 507-646-4526
FINANCIAL AID: 507-646-4190 • E-MAIL: ADMISSIONS@ACS.CARLETON.EDU • WEBSITE: WWW.CARLETON.EDU

Ratings
Quality of Life: 89　　　Academic: 98　　　Admissions: 97　　　Financial Aid: 83

Academics

At this "blazingly liberal" college the classes are small, and the class discussions "well-modulated" and "enlightening." "WOW," says a student about the professors, who provide a "wonderful support system here for dealing with academic issues." Students have every right to be proud; Carleton is a nationally preeminent liberal arts college. It divides the academ-

> **SURVEY SAYS . . .**
> *(Almost) everyone plays intramural sports*
> *No one cheats*
> *Students aren't religious*
> *Lab facilities need improving*
> *Great computer facilities*
> *Theater is hot*
> *(Almost) no one smokes*
> *Musical organizations are hot*

ic year into trimesters, and students take only three classes per term, which "allows students to concentrate more fully on each subject." The workload's not light, though; students are "committed," and by the end of the term "the entire campus suffers from sleep deprivation." Students compete academically, "not with other students—but with themselves." And if one needs it, Carleton provides free tutoring in various academic subjects. Carleton has "first-rate everything," but in spirit the school "doesn't take itself too seriously." It is common for students to call professors by their first names, and professors often give out their home phone numbers. The administration is highly accessible, too, and even the president holds office hours every Tuesday. He also "read Winnie the Pooh stories to my floor last term, one Sunday evening—he does a great Eeyore." Students don't find much to complain about, though the library's resources are "limited," and the on-campus food "sucks."

Life

"Ultimate Frisbee and Carleton are practically synonymous," so much so that entering students are each given a Frisbee. But Frisbee's not all that Carleton students ("Carls" for short) find to do in Northfield, Minnesota. On weekdays there is little drinking and few parties, as "people study all the time, but it's just considered normal." Students "always complain about having work to do, but the truth is, we love it and become totally engaged in it." During moments of free time and on the weekends, Carls find all sorts of "weird" ways to have fun. Hints one students, "A word to the wise—if streaking embarrasses you, stay away. Carls aren't afraid to bare all." When there's snow (and there's plenty of it) students go "traying," which is "sledding using a tray from the dining hall." Hungry in the middle of the night? There's Dace Moses House, where students can go whenever the urge strikes to "make cookies—chocolate chip, to be exact. The rule is that you have to leave what you don't eat at the house." And in the spring (when all that snow melts) there's "Rottblatt. A 'softball' game with an inning for each year the college has been in existence (135 in 2001). Traditionally, a keg is at each base, and it is an excuse to get up early on Saturday and drink." While "there is a lot of boozing around," Carls don't feel pressured to drink. Complaints? You guessed it: the "ridiculous cold." Minnesota winters are brutal. And, while the school does provide shuttle service for trips to the nearby Twin Cities and the Mall of America, it's "not very frequent or very cheap."

Student Body

"People who go to Carleton know that they are smart and are willing to demonstrate it." The "quirky," "creative" students are "independent thinkers" and "share a respect for one another that seems unique to Carleton." Some students, however, can be arrogant about their high intelligence. Students dress "a little weird," with "bat ears" or "without shoes," but "no one can be placed by the way they look." The "traditional stereotypes don't apply at all to anyone. Everyone is much more deep and interesting than they first appear." And students are "so friendly, I feel like I'm in Mr. Roger's neighborhood." But while Carleton is "diverse in terms of personalities," the school is primarily Caucasian, and both students and administrators would like to see more racial and ethnic diversity. A gay student also warns that "it's really really really hard to hook up with another guy."

ADMISSIONS

Very important factors considered by the admissions committee include: secondary school record. *Important factors considered include:* character/personal qualities, class rank, essays, extracurricular activities, minority status, recommendations, standardized test scores, talent/ability, volunteer work, work experience. *Other factors considered include:* alumni/ae relation, geographical residence, interview, state residency. SAT I or ACT required; SAT II recommended. TOEFL required of all international applicants. High school diploma or GED is required. *High school units required/recommended:* 4 English recommended, 3 math recommended, 3 science recommended, 1 science lab recommended, 3 foreign language recommended.

The Inside Word

Admission to Carleton would be even more difficult if the college had more name recognition. Current applicants should be grateful for this, because standards are already rigorous. Only severe competition with the best liberal arts colleges in the country prevents an even lower admit rate.

FINANCIAL AID

Students should submit: FAFSA, CSS/Financial Aid PROFILE, noncustodial (divorced/separated) parent's statement, business/farm supplement. Regular filing deadline is February 15. The Princeton Review suggests that all financial aid forms be submitted as soon as possible after January 1. *Need-based scholarships/grants offered:* Pell, SEOG, state scholarships/grants, private scholarships, the school's own gift aid. *Loan aid offered:* FFEL Subsidized Stafford, FFEL Unsubsidized Stafford, FFEL PLUS, Federal Perkins, state loans, college/university loans from institutional funds, Minnesota SELF Loan program. Federal Work-Study Program available. Institutional employment available. Applicants will be notified of awards on or about April 15. Off-campus job opportunities are good.

FROM THE ADMISSIONS OFFICE

"In an annual college freshmen survey, Carleton students self-identify along the full conservative-to-liberal spectrum, with a majority identifying as moderate to liberal. Individualistic and energetic, Carls take academics seriously but not themselves. Participation in athletics, theater, or music and in activities from religious events to dining hall discussion over hearty fare marks the Carleton experience. More than two-thirds of students spend time studying abroad. Cool fact: More snow fell in the northeast than here in the past three years."

For even more information on this school, turn to page 334 of the "Stats" section.

CARTHAGE COLLEGE

2001 ALFORD PARK DRIVE, KENOSHA, WI 53140-1994 • ADMISSIONS: 262-551-6000 • FAX: 262-551-5762
E-MAIL: ADMISSIONS@CARTHAGE.EDU • WEBSITE: WWW.CARTHAGE.EDU

Ratings
Quality of Life: 84   Academic: 72   Admissions: 72   Financial Aid: 75

Academics

Carthage College is a small liberal arts school affiliated with the Evangelical Lutheran Church, situated on a "really comfortable and close-knit campus" on the shores of Lake Michigan. Characterized as "fun, caring, patient, and most of all, experienced in their fields," professors at Carthage "aren't untouchable figures that talk at you in class and are never available for discussion." On the contrary, students say "professors are very approachable" and "even go so far as to give you their personal home phone numbers as well as office in case you need to talk to them after hours." Students thrive in this supportive academic environment, where class sizes are "very small," "the teacher/student ratio is excellent," and the courses are tough but "aren't overly intimidating." There are those, however, who feel that the school needs to take academic programs more seriously. Many report that the school "worships athletic departments above all else," and consequently "football and other sports get all the money and attention" at the expense of academic programs and facilities. One student laments, "The faculty is overworked, underpaid, understaffed, and not given the credit they deserve." Another adds, "The few good professors we have are under-appreciated and get lost in the shuffle." Generally, students are quick to question the administration's priorities when it comes to spending. One student complains that the school is guilty of "wasting money building buildings that don't necessarily need to built," while another claims, "The administration will take your money whenever they can and spend it on landscaping."

> **SURVEY SAYS . . .**
> *Diversity lacking on campus*
> *Students are religious*
> *No one cheats*
> *Class discussions encouraged*
> *(Almost) everyone plays intramural sports*
> *Lots of beer drinking*

Life

Set in small town Kenosha but close to Chicago and Milwaukee, Carthage College offers plenty of campus entertainment. When it comes to extracurricular activities, "Greek organizations," "academic or performing arts groups," and "athletic teams" are extremely popular. During off-hours, students get together to "have movie marathons, play midnight games of tag, and go clubbing in Milwaukee or Chicago." Though technically a dry campus, the rules are lenient, and "a large number of people spend their weekends—and some their weekdays—drinking and having a good time." Not everyone, though, is thrilled about the campus programming and transportation services. The school is "somewhat secluded," and therefore, "if you don't have a car, you're pretty much bored out of your mind." Grumbles one student, "the school brings entertainers and plays movies on Saturday nights, so there are a few things going on for those stranded here, but not many."

Student Body

Carthage College attracts students with such "diversity in interests and personalities" that they run the gamut from "petty" and "immature" to "genuinely friendly," according to their classmates. One undergrad describes "two hemispheres" on campus: "There are the beer drinkers, and the organizational overachievers, and admittedly, these two groups are not mutually exclusive, not by any means." Unfortunately, many also characterize fellow students as "sometimes too closed-minded." One suggests that her classmates "need to open themselves up to diversity in sexual orientation—it's such a taboo around here, unfortunately." Confers another, "People are very intolerant at my school, especially toward Goths and homosexuals." Most, however, maintain that they "haven't seen any racial discrimination or prejudice," and for the most part, "everyone gets along very well." One student confesses, "I'm from a lower-class family and tend to dress gothic, and I've never had any problems with anyone."

ADMISSIONS

Very important factors considered by the admissions committee include: character/personal qualities, secondary school record, standardized test scores, and talent/ability. *Important factors considered include:* class rank and extracurricular activities. *Other factors considered include:* alumni/ae relation, geographical residence, interview, minority status, recommendations, state residency, volunteer work, and work experience. SAT I or ACT required, ACT preferred. TOEFL required of all international applicants. High school diploma or GED is required. *High school units required/recommended:* 16 total required; 16 total recommended; 4 English required, 3 math required, 3 science required, 2 foreign language recommended, 3 social studies required, 3 social studies recommended, 3 elective required.

The Inside Word

Carthage admitted 90 percent of its applicants last year, but that number is deceiving; the school's reputation and price tag scare off all but those who are reasonably sure they will get in and be able to foot the bill. You shouldn't let the cost of a Carthage education scare you off, though; over 90 percent of students here receive financial assistance.

FINANCIAL AID

Students should submit: FAFSA. The Princeton Review suggests that all financial aid forms be submitted as soon as possible after January 1. *Need-based scholarships/grants offered:* Pell, SEOG, state scholarships/grants, private scholarships, and the school's own gift aid. *Loan aid offered:* FFEL Subsidized Stafford, FFEL Unsubsidized Stafford, FFEL PLUS, Federal Perkins, state loans, and college/university loans from institutional funds. Federal Work-Study Program available. Institutional employment available. Off-campus job opportunities are good.

For even more information on this school, turn to page 334 of the "Stats" section.

Case Western Reserve University

103 Tomlinson Hall, 10900 Euclid Avenue, Cleveland, OH 44106-7055 • Admissions: 216-368-4450
Fax: 216-368-5111 • Financial Aid: 216-368-4530 • E-mail: admission@po.cwru.edu
Website: www.cwru.edu

Ratings
Quality of Life: 70   Academic: 80   Admissions: 86   Financial Aid: 82

Academics

Though CWRU was officially born out of the union of the engineering-intense Case Institute of Technology and the liberal arts-focused Western Reserve University, there's no mistaking that the academic scales are tipped in favor of the former; the extensive engineering offerings leave some "humanities people feeling left in the dust." Many students choose CWRU for its strong academic reputation, but prospectives

> **SURVEY SAYS . . .**
> *Ethnic diversity on campus*
> *Students love Cleveland, OH*
> *Great library*
> *Great computer facilities*
> *Class discussions are rare*
> *Intercollegiate sports are unpopular*
> *or nonexistent*
> *Registration is a pain*
> *Campus difficult to get around*
> *Unattractive campus*

are advised by current students to do their homework before signing up for classes in any given department, as shown in their remarkably even-handed appraisal of instructional quality. While one complains that "some professors . . . don't speak English, don't teach, waste class time rambling about their native countries, or take pride in failing all their students," another beams, "Many of the professors are not only staggeringly intelligent and excited about their area of study, but are [also] eager to share their enthusiasm for their research with students." Students are equally split on the administration; descriptions of deans range from "always accessible" to "not terribly bright."

Life

According to a female sophomore, "Case is fun if you make it fun, but it's not a top-ten party school. If you're looking for that, go somewhere else." Why? Academic demands dilute the bacchanalia that might otherwise go on in Cleveland. One student complains that life is "kinda boring" because there is "a lot to do but no time to do it." Those who make time for something besides studying, however, get involved in theater and music, hang out with friends, or go Greek. Writes one senior, "Greek life is fun. I am very involved with it and hang out with my sisters a lot." Beyond these activities, many feel "there is very little to do on campus" and turn to surrounding Cleveland for entertainment. "I don't understand how people are bored living in Cleveland. This city has so many possibilities . . . being bored on this campus is a choice," declares a senior. Another elucidates, "For fun, we spend time with friends, go to movies and plays, and go to Severance Hall to hear the world-class Cleveland Orchestra." Furthermore, the city provides a great opportunity for students who want to lend a hand in the greater community. Claims a sophomore, "I get involved in all the social and environmental justice activities I can. There's a small but growing group of very liberal activists on campus."

Student Body

CWRU's diverse student population shares one thing in common: they are serious about school. While this seriousness means excellent classmates to some, it means a campus full of losers to others. Some undergrads say their fellow students are "centered and want to learn," "studious," and "respectful and friendly," while others describe them as "antisocial, unfriendly, and very self-centered." Given the conflicting attitudes, the campus has something of a split personality. A female junior sums it up: "It seems there is a dichotomy in the social life. Either you're very social and go out a lot or you never leave your room." A sardonic sophomore agrees, "There seem to be two distinct social groups here: people who accept that they are total dorks and the rest who try to party their dorkiness away."

ADMISSIONS

Very important factors considered by the admissions committee include: extracurricular activities, secondary school record, talent/ability, volunteer work, work experience. *Important factors considered include:* alumni/ae relation, character/personal qualities, class rank, essays, interview, minority status, recommendations, standardized test scores. SAT I or ACT required; SAT II recommended. TOEFL required of all international applicants. High school diploma or GED is required. *High school units required/recommended:* 16 total required; 4 English required, 3 math required, 4 math recommended, 3 science required, 1 science lab required, 2 science lab recommended, 2 foreign language required, 3 foreign language recommended, 3 social studies required, 4 social studies recommended.

The Inside Word

Case Western faces tough competition, and they handle it very well. The university received a record number of applications last year, and as a result it's quite a bit tougher to get admitted. Even if you solidly meet the academic profile, don't be complacent—Case's freshman profile reflects well on the academic preparedness of its candidates, and due to their good fortune they've got an opportunity to be significantly more choosy about who gets an offer.

FINANCIAL AID

Students should submit: FAFSA, CSS/Financial Aid PROFILE, noncustodial (divorced/separated) parent's statement, business/farm supplement, parent and student income tax returns and W-2 forms. Regular filing deadline is April 15. The Princeton Review suggests that all financial aid forms be submitted as soon as possible after January 1. *Need-based scholarships/grants offered:* Pell, SEOG, state scholarships/grants, private scholarships, the school's own gift aid. *Loan aid offered:* Direct Subsidized Stafford, Direct Unsubsidized Stafford, FFEL PLUS, Federal Perkins, Federal Nursing, state loans, college/university loans from institutional funds. Federal Work-Study Program available. Institutional employment available. Applicants will be notified of awards on a rolling basis beginning on or about March 15. Off-campus job opportunities are good.

FROM THE ADMISSIONS OFFICE

"An important part of CWRU's philosophy is that education is best accomplished through experience. We've begun a new undergraduate program called SAGES that strives to blur the distinctions between learning and life. SAGES students engage with faculty, peers, and the larger Cleveland community through small seminars, research projects, internships, and community service. Their seminar professors serve as mentors, helping them design their educational plan. The opportunities CWRU students have to work with some of the top curators, scientists, musicians, educators, and professionals (to name a few) are truly exciting."

For even more information on this school, turn to page 335 of the "Stats" section.

CEDARVILLE UNIVERSITY

251 N. MAIN STREET, CEDARVILLE, OH 45314 • ADMISSIONS: 937-766-7700 • FAX: 937-766-7575
E-MAIL: ADMISSIONS@CEDARVILLE.EDU • WEBSITE: WWW.CEDARVILLE.EDU

Ratings

Quality of Life: 77   Academic: 78   Admissions: 73   Financial Aid: 74

Academics

Nestled in the cornfields of Ohio, Cedarville University offers a well-rounded, Christian education to its small undergraduate population. Students inform us that academics are "challenging but not impossible" and that professors "want to help you succeed in your studies" and "are always willing to meet with students and

> **SURVEY SAYS . . .**
> *Students get along with local community*
> *Classes are small*
> *Diversity lacking on campus*
> *Students are religious*
> *Instructors are good teachers*
> *Popular college radio*
> *School is well run, Theater is hot*

talk with them, whether it's about class material or not." Cedarville professors "emphasize educating the whole person, not just the intellect," and "are knowledgeable in their field of study, but also in life in general." But students believe that what really distinguishes Cedarville professors is that "they don't try to make us all the same"; instead, they "give us room to grow into professional adults who can think on our own." In addition, Christianity is a fundamental part of the school's curriculum: "Every class starts with prayer, and the Bible is integrated into every subject." As one devout student shares, "Christianity is not separate from our academic or social lives. Christ-like living permeates the classroom." Though most feel they are receiving a balanced education at Cedarville, some feel that the university could better serve the students by placing more emphasis on intellectual growth. One student explains, "The administration is not terribly concerned with academics. . . . It is apparent to the student body that their performance academically is less important than their campus involvement, service in ministry, and contribution to the school's separatist image."

Life

Cedarville University is located "in the middle of a cornfield, in a town with two stoplights, two pizza places, three restaurants, a coffee shop, and a car wash." But unlike many small-town collegians, Cedarville students don't complain of isolation or boredom. Comments one satisfied student, "I love the setting. We're out in the cornfields and yet within an hour of anything you could want to do." For recreation, students say they "have to get creative," but that popular activities include "going out to eat, catching a movie, crashing at a coffee shop, playing sports," trekking out to "a nearby town where there is an ice-cream place, mini-golf, and a driving range," and going to "concerts, roller-skating, bowling, films, and parties." In addition, "athletic events and evangelical community outreach are hugely popular." If you're hoping college life will feel like a remake of Animal House, Cedarville isn't for you; the majority of students say they "don't find fun in getting drunk and sleeping around" and "nothing too wild goes on" on campus. In fact, Cedarville is "very strict" in terms of personal presentation and behavior; some students are opposed to the "curfew of 12 on weekdays and 1 on weekends" and say the "dress code is the most annoying thing, but since everyone abides by it, it just becomes second nature." Cedarville also provides guidelines for media, music, dancing, and dating in order to protect and uphold Christian values.

Student Body

One Cedarville coed exclaims, "I love the girls in my dorm, and I wouldn't trade the experience for a dozen boxes of powdered sugar donuts!" Her sentiments are echoed throughout the Cedarville student body, who say their classmates are "very friendly," "always smiling and ready to lend a hand," and "genuine in their faith," though, occasionally cliquey as well. Common religious faith unites the campus population, and students are keen on the "family-like atmosphere that chapel creates." Since the majority of the student body is "conservative Christian," you may expect a friendly smile but not much diversity from Cedarville students. Notes one, "There isn't much room for left-wing politics or opinions that go against the grain." Another explains, "Sometimes it is hard for them to accept students from other backgrounds, but with the growing number of "non-Baptist" students, this problem is decreasing." Diversifying the student body is in fact a priority in the administration, and "the university has just started a minority recruitment program that should help diversify our campus."

ADMISSIONS

Very important factors considered by the admissions committee include: character/personal qualities, essays, religious affiliation/commitment, secondary school record, and standardized test scores. *Important factors considered include:* minority status and recommendations. *Other factors considered include:* alumni/ae relation, class rank, extracurricular activities, interview, talent/ability, and volunteer work. SAT I or ACT required, ACT preferred. TOEFL required of all international applicants. High school diploma or GED is required. *High school units required/recommended:* 15 total recommended; 4 English recommended, 3 math recommended, 3 science lab recommended, 2 foreign language recommended, 3 social studies recommended.

The Inside Word

Cedarville reviews applications on a rolling basis; those that arrive early in the year are likely to receive a more favorable review than those arriving later. Religious commitment is a must for admission; this much is clearly spelled out on the school's website.

FINANCIAL AID

Students should submit: FAFSA and institution's own financial aid form. No deadline for regular filing. The Princeton Review suggests that all financial aid forms be submitted as soon as possible after January 1. *Need-based scholarships/grants offered:* Pell, SEOG, state scholarships/grants, private scholarships, and the school's own gift aid. *Loan aid offered:* FFEL Subsidized Stafford, FFEL Unsubsidized Stafford, FFEL PLUS, Federal Perkins, Federal Nursing, state loans, and college/university loans from institutional funds. Federal Work-Study Program available. Institutional employment available. Applicants will be notified of awards on a rolling basis beginning on or about March 1. Off-campus job opportunities are excellent.

For even more information on this school, turn to page 336 of the "Stats" section.

CENTRAL COLLEGE

812 University Street, Pella, IA 50219-1999 • Admissions: 877-462-3687 • Fax: 641-628-5316
E-mail: admission@central.edu • Website: www.central.edu

Ratings

Quality of Life: 75   Academic: 78   Admissions: 73   Financial Aid: 79

Academics

Central College, which lays claim to a "good name inside the state" of Iowa, attracts professors who are "professional in their jobs and personable as mentors and resources," according to students. Outside of the classroom, under-

> **SURVEY SAYS . . .**
> *School is well run, Student publications are popular*
> *Students are religious, Diversity lacking on campus*
> *Profs teach upper levels*
> *(Almost) everyone plays intramural sports*

graduates receive support from a well-run academic center, "where you can get your papers checked and proofread and be tutored in any subject you need." Study abroad programs enjoy a high degree of popularity, with more than half of Central students venturing to foreign shores. The administration's "hands-on approach" wins approval with students, who say, "They want everyone to get involved." Even the financial aid office is "always willing to take time to make sense out of your package." Head honcho President Roe, who is also the football team's kicking coach, is generally considered a "rock star." Because "the school puts its budget back into the students," new facilities pop up regularly, including updated computer labs. There are a few complaints here and there among the student body; one such complaint alleges that Central "does not cater to the needs of commuter students," while others claim that it's "commuter-friendly." Another student suggests that Central "recognize how strong our school is in the arts. We have amazing theatre and music departments, but no one knows about them because we are plugged as a football/volleyball school."

Life

One Central student explains that campus life centers around one of three things: "church, sports, or beer." Christian organizations exert a strong presence, and "there are many religous activities on campus to partake in," writes one student. "Because Central is located in small-town Iowa, there isn't a lot of entertainment in the community. The school does a really good job at bringing comedians, magicians, singers/songwriters, etc., to campus. Being at a small school gives you the chance to hang out with friends and get to know each other well." Some students turn to the bottle and ignore the no-alcohol policy, which "is violated on a daily basis." One student sees this ban on alcohol and the strict visitation policy as "two unenforceable rules that Central should drop and come into the 21st century." Another disagrees: "One thing we don't participate in are activities that involve alcohol. My friends and I aren't interested in killing our brain cells." Hometown Pella offers movies and eateries; for relief from the small-town blues, students can travel a mere 45 minutes to Des Moines or a little over an hour to the excitement that awaits in Iowa City.

Student Body

Says one undergrad of Central's student body, "I feel that most people here are friendly and open and most everyone gets along." Though many people wish the population was "more representative of the world," another undergraduate explains, "There are enough farm kids and out-of-state kids to add economic diversity and some ethnic diversity, but in a state like Iowa, that latter goal is tough." While the school manages to attract "many foreign students," there are "few American minorities." In terms of sexual preference, "people in the GLBT community are afraid to be themselves because of harassment and safety issues." Certain respondents feel that "some students are not even willing to be educated about diversity issues," while others believe "most of the students recognize the differences people have and learn to live with those differences." In general, the community of "jocks, Bible beaters, and arts and theatre people" shares an "unwritten bond" that derives from attending the same school. A content student boasts, "I don't think you will find a more friendly campus."

ADMISSIONS

Important factors considered by the admissions committee include: class rank, recommendations, secondary school record, and standardized test scores. *Other factors considered include:* essays and recommendations. SAT I or ACT required, ACT preferred. TOEFL required of all international applicants. High school diploma or GED is required. *High school units required/recommended:* 15 total required; 4 English recommended, 3 math recommended, 2 science recommended, 2 foreign language recommended, 3 social studies recommended, 2 history recommended.

The Inside Word

Central is in the midst of a ten-year program to expand undergraduate size by about 20 percent; this means extra spaces are available in the next few incoming classes. Aid candidates who submit applications before December 1 receive a free financial aid estimate from the school. Those seeking scholarships must apply by January 20.

FINANCIAL AID

Students should submit: FAFSA. The Princeton Review suggests that all financial aid forms be submitted as soon as possible after January 1. *Need-based scholarships/grants offered:* Pell, SEOG, state scholarships/grants, private scholarships, and the school's own gift aid. *Loan aid offered:* Direct Subsidized Stafford, Direct Unsubsidized Stafford, Direct PLUS, Federal Perkins, and college/university loans from institutional funds. Federal Work-Study Program available. Institutional employment available. Applicants will be notified of awards on a rolling basis beginning on or about March 10. Off-campus job opportunities are excellent.

FROM THE ADMISSIONS OFFICE

"'Challenging yet supportive' describes Central College in Pella, Iowa. Students establish one-to-one relationships with their professors, while the curriculum engages students and prepares them for a career or graduate school. More than 97 percent of Central's May 2001 graduates either accepted professional employment or enrolled in a graduate school of their choice within one year after graduation. *U.S. News & World Report* calls Central College one of the top 10 best comprehensive colleges for a bachelor's degree in the Midwest and one of the top 10 comprehensive 'Great Schools at Great Prices' for bachelor's degrees in the Midwest. In addition, Central's international study abroad program is ranked number 10 in the nation under the magazine's 'Programs that Really Work.' Central has 10 study abroad sites, in Austria, China, England, France, Kenya, Mexico, the Netherlands, Spain, and Wales.

"In addition to enjoying the largest enrollment in a decade, Central is also seeing an increase in faculty, programs, and facilities across campus. Since 1999, three new buildings have been added, including the Weller Center for Business and International Studies, the Ron Schipper Fitness Center, and a new 72-bed residence hall. The Vermeer Science Center for the natural sciences, math, and computer science underwent a $20 million renovation in 2002. The music program was highlighted again this year on Iowa Public Television and the athletic program continues to produce Iowa Conference Champions. For more information about the exciting things happening at Central, check out our website at www.central.edu."

For even more information on this school, turn to page 336 of the "Stats" section.

CENTRAL MICHIGAN UNIVERSITY

105 WARRINER HALL, MOUNT PLEASANT, MI 48859 • ADMISSIONS: 989-774-3076 • FAX: 989-774-7267
E-MAIL: CMUADMIT@CMICH.EDU • WEBSITE: WWW.CMICH.EDU

Ratings

Quality of Life: 77   Academic: 72   Admissions: 67   Financial Aid: 75

Academics

Central Michigan University offers its nearly 20,000 undergrads more than 150 programs of study, with majors in business and education topping the popularity list. Students also point to the university's programs in music, theatre, broadcasting, education, and the health professions, describing them as major assets to the academic climate in Mount

SURVEY SAYS . . .
Student publications are popular
No one cheats
Classes are small
Frats and sororities dominate social scene
School is well run
Intercollegiate sports are popular
Lots of beer drinking
Students get along with local community

Pleasant. But with so many classes and instructors to choose from, students admit that there are both strong and weak spots here. On the weaker side, there are "many foreign teachers" who are "hard to understand" in the classroom. And some classes are "taught by grad students who are not experienced at what they are doing." But within the ranks of the full-time faculty, it's not hard to find professors who "are willing to do anything for their students. They give out home numbers and are willing to work with you at any time and [in] any way they can to help you achieve the highest grades possible." In general, the education offered by CMU is one that allows students to grow inside and outside of the classroom. "The classes are challenging but not overwhelming," explains a student, "and I have time to live a well-rounded college life, aside from hitting the books. It's probably not the most rigorous school academically, but I feel I'm receiving a good education." A freshman adds that the university's mission is "not only to have us graduate with a degree, but graduate with an education." Should anything ever go awry along their educational paths, students here feel comfortable approaching members of the staff and administration for assistance—even the president, who "has many forums for communication with students."

Life

Mount Pleasant, where you'll find Central Michigan University, gets mixed reviews from the student-set. A glass-is-half-full type opines, "In Mount Pleasant, there is a lot to do. There are two cinemas, three clubs, a casino, and coffeehouses and restaurants galore." Half-empty types, on the other hand, argue, "There is nothing to do in Mount Pleasant," and, "despite the name, Mount Pleasant is neither mountainous nor pleasant." Truth of the matter is that Mount Pleasant is by no means a cultural Mecca, but it provides a healthy handful of distractions for interested students. Probably the two most popular distractions are The Pub and The Wayside—the unofficial watering holes of CMU. Wherever they end up, CMU students "like to go out and party, and get drunk all the time." In fact, students here contend that CMU is a bigger "party school" than most people realize, and they want to get more recognition for it. "Party Central" is the university's unofficial, student-designated nickname. All of CMU's 16,000-plus undergrads can get involved in more than 200 organizations on campus, as well as take advantage of the "brand new Student Activity Center, which has gym facilities, a pool, an indoor track, bowling lanes, and a lot more." A third of CMU students live on campus in "some of the nicest dorms in the country." But one upperclassman recommends, "First-year students [should] try to avoid living in the Towers complex on campus, as they tend to be crazy and a high percentage of kids there drop out."

Student Body

To say the least, CMU students are not above criticizing themselves. They'll readily admit that theirs is a homogenous, self-segregating campus. Most students are white, "most are from Michigan," and most are "conservatives." The Greek/GDI divide bothers some, but that's a natural repercussion of any fraternity/sorority system. CMU's liberal admissions policy is a sore spot for the many motivated students who would like to see the university weed out those unprepared academically. But this tension aside, the CMU population is a rather "laid-back" group that shares a common pastime: "partying." Parties give students regular, bibulous opportunities to get together and socialize. And while students may criticize each other anonymously in certain student surveys, they "generally get along great with each other."

ADMISSIONS

Very important factors considered by the admissions committee include: secondary school record. *Important factors considered include:* extracurricular activities, recommendations, and standardized test scores. *Other factors considered include:* alumni/ae relation, class rank, essays, geographical residence, interview, state residency, talent/ability, volunteer work, and work experience. ACT required. TOEFL required of all international applicants. High school diploma or GED is required. *High school units required/recommended:* 19 total recommended; 4 English recommended, 4 math recommended, 3 science recommended, 2 foreign language recommended, 2 social studies recommended, 2 history recommended.

The Inside Word

CMU admits more than 9,000 freshman candidates every year, so nearly all its admissions decisions must be made by formula. The school looks at candidates' high school GPA and standardized test scores, and that's about it. If you're at least a C+/B- student who scored 20 or better on the ACT, you're in.

FINANCIAL AID

Students should submit: FAFSA. No deadline for regular filing. The Princeton Review suggests that all financial aid forms be submitted as soon as possible after January 1. *Need-based scholarships/grants offered:* Pell, SEOG, state scholarships/grants, private scholarships, and the school's own gift aid. *Loan aid offered:* Direct Subsidized Stafford, Direct Unsubsidized Stafford, Direct PLUS, Federal Perkins, state loans, and alternative loans. Federal Work-Study Program available. Institutional employment available. Applicants will be notified of awards on a rolling basis beginning on or about April 1. Off-campus job opportunities are good.

For even more information on this school, turn to page 337 of the "Stats" section.

CENTRAL MISSOURI STATE UNIVERSITY

OFFICE OF ADMISSIONS, ADMINISTRATION 104, WARRENSBURG, MO 64093 • ADMISSIONS: 660-543-4290
FAX: 660-543-8517 • E-MAIL: ADMIT@CMSUVMB.CMSU.EDU • WEBSITE: WWW.CMSU.EDU

Ratings

Quality of Life: 77   Academic: 73   Admissions: 71   Financial Aid: 71

Academics

Students come to Central Missouri State University for its wide offerings in pre-professional studies, ranging from the commonplace (education, business, nursing, criminal justice) to the singular (safety science, aerospace manufacturing, railway signal engineering). Of particular note is

> **SURVEY SAYS . . .**
> No one plays intramural sports
> Classes are small
> Frats and sororities dominate social scene
> Student publications are ignored
> Very little hard liquor
> Very little beer drinking, No one cheats

CMSU's aviation department, whose attractive and affordable program "is very well done for the pilots and flight team. Many great aviation students graduate each year and go on to get excellent jobs." CMSU undergraduates praise the school for "keeping classes pretty small; I was able to get into the working part of my major right away." They also report that the school demonstrates "the ability to welcome new students, both traditional and nontraditional" and boasts a "small beautiful campus that makes for ease of getting to class." The faculty receives mixed reviews; writes one typical undergrad, "I have had a mix of professors that are great teachers, good smartasses, or even just plain terrible teachers." Although some students say they "have yet to run into any problems" with the administration, poor marks are more commonly dished out; one complaint: "The administration claims that students are the top concern. My experience with this is that it is pure BS. We are only income to our administration." Many complain of the red tape typical of state institutions; reports one undergrad, "You might have to visit, not call mind you, three to six different people or departments, all giving you separate and distinct information, to get something accomplished."

Life

Students describe a fairly one-dimensional social scene at CMSU. Sums up one undergrad, "Here in Warrensburg there is nothing really to do, so many people turn to alcohol to have fun. That is about all that goes on: drinking, drinking, and more drinking." Because many students leave campus for the weekend after Thursday classes end ("the people who don't like to party go home"), "people go out every Wednesday and party hard" at the bars up and down Pine Street, most of which cater primarily to students. Hometown Warrensburg offers little besides bars, students say, and as one student informed us: "We have a movie theatre, but it sucks: the sound isn't great, the seating isn't comfortable. . . . Besides the bars and the movie theatre, all there is here is class and Chinese food." Many agree that "the school needs to support events that students could go to. Those of us who stick around need something to do on the weekend." Students are also disgruntled with campus housing and food services here; writes one, "I would strongly suggest students find housing other than on-campus. My room is missing tiles, the window fell off (really), my door lock did not work, my light bulbs blew out and it took three days to have them replaced (try studying in the dark)." Another warned that the dining hall services, "provided by none other than Marriott," aren't worth the price. "I have never been fed worse food in all my life."

Student Body

The majority of CMSU undergrads "seem to be white and from small towns," creating a community that is not for everyone; writes one dissatisfied undergrad, "I don't get along with most of my classmates. I'm an open-minded, cultured city girl, and it seems that most of the student body come from small towns where drinking, drugs, and sex are more important than studies and interaction with diverse groups." Students report that "the Greek thing is big here, so all those Greeks stick with their frat/sorority. The general rule is to stick with your own; most don't venture out of their comfort zone." Many love the culture, however, telling us, "The people at CMSU are very interesting. It is a 'small-town' atmosphere, and everyone gets along. I have had no problems with my roommates or people in my classes. Everyone is willing to help you out. They are also very friendly. People with smiles on their faces . . . that's what I like about CMSU."

ADMISSIONS

Very important factors considered by the admissions committee include: class rank, secondary school record, and standardized test scores. *Other factors considered include:* alumni/ae relation, character/personal qualities, extracurricular activities, recommendations, and talent/ability. SAT I or ACT required, ACT preferred. TOEFL required of all international applicants. High school diploma or GED is required. *High school units required/recommended:* 16 total required; 4 English required, 3 math required, 2 science required, 1 science lab required, 2 foreign language recommended, 3 social studies required, 3 elective required.

The Inside Word

CMSU uses an admissions index to determine whether students qualify for admission. Students in the 50th percentile of their graduating class need combined SAT scores of 980 or composite ACT scores of 21. You can calculate your admissions index at the school's website.

FINANCIAL AID

Students should submit: FAFSA. No deadline for regular filing. The Princeton Review suggests that all financial aid forms be submitted as soon as possible after January 1. *Need-based scholarships/grants offered:* Pell, SEOG, state scholarships/grants, private scholarships, and the school's own gift aid. *Loan aid offered:* Direct Subsidized Stafford, Direct Unsubsidized Stafford, Direct PLUS, Federal Perkins, and state loans. Federal Work-Study Program available. Institutional employment available. Applicants will be notified of awards on a rolling basis. Off-campus job opportunities are excellent.

For even more information on this school, turn to page 337 of the "Stats" section.

CLARKE COLLEGE

1550 CLARKE DRIVE, DUBUQUE, IA 52001-3198 • ADMISSIONS: 563-588-6300 • FAX: 563-588-6789
E-MAIL: ADMISSIONS@CLARKE.EDU • WEBSITE: WWW.CLARKE.EDU

Ratings
Quality of Life: 80   Academic: 75   Admissions: 72   Financial Aid: 82

Academics

Students at tiny Clarke College appreciate the little personal touches that their school provides. "Clarke has wonderful teachers and staff that [are] dedicated to helping you truly get the most of the full college experience," explains one student. "The counselors, advisors, and professors are purely there to help you succeed, and they [all] complete this with smiles." Adds another, "It really is a great school. . . . It's small, but that [provides] great opportunities for student/teacher interaction." Undergrads tell us that "Clarke has a good nursing program, as well as a good physical therapy program, so students appear to be more goal-oriented than some other universities are. People in those majors are submerged full force into their curriculum." Business and education are also popular majors at Clarke. All students must complete 51 hours of general education requirements, which include study in the humanities, sciences, mathematics, computer science, philosophy, religious studies, and multicultural studies. Undergrads report that the curriculum is difficult; writes one, "I am somewhat challenged in my classes, but I know that if I need help with anything, other resources such as tutors and the writing lab are there." Many appreciate the fact that "the administration is of the Catholic faith (a large part of the staff are nuns), but you won't see much Bible-beating here."

> **SURVEY SAYS . . .**
> *Classes are small*
> *Diversity lacking on campus*
> *Instructors are good teachers*
> *Profs teach upper levels*
> *No one plays intramural sports*
> *Theater is unpopular*
> *Very little hard liquor*
> *Student publications are ignored*

Life

Life on the Clarke campus is quiet: too quiet for some, just right for others. Writes one student, "The town where Clarke is located, Dubuque, has nothing to do, and the college is small so it offers very little to do on the weekends." Counters another, "At school, we often sit in our dorms and complain, 'There's nothing to do.' But we forget that's a good thing. Plans are made 30 seconds in advance. On a Friday night, I could be anywhere. You could see me at a local coffee shop, sitting in my dorm watching MTV, or downing beers in friends' dorms. Either way, I know I'll be having fun. Party schools get monotonous; they are only breeding grounds for alcoholics. Variety is the spice of life." Another student agrees, reporting that "a lot of people get drunk on weekends, but there are other things to do. Just hanging out playing games, going to dances or to parties or out to eat can be a lot of fun! I don't really drink that much, but there are plenty of other things to do. I run, I'm involved in a couple of clubs, I volunteer and work, and hang out with friends. There are also a lot of free activities offered for people to participate in, like golfing, bowling, canoeing, as well as kickboxing and yoga." Students appreciate the fact that "Clarke is a very secure campus. To get into the girl's dorm you need to have a chip that is accessed only for girls living in that building; the chip policy also is the same with the on-campus apartments and the coed building here on campus." They are less thrilled with the strict curfews in dorms; writes one, "Visitation hours in the lower-classmen dorms need to change. Men are supposed to be out of the girls' dorm at midnight on weekdays, 2 A.M. on weekends. The same goes for women in the men's dorm."

Student Body

Clarke students "are just like any other college students. Some drink, some don't, some are very religious, while others aren't even affiliated with a religion." The small, predominantly Catholic, predominantly female student population is "supportive, constructive, and happy." Students do, however, admit, "Clarke is a very 'clique-oriented' school. We all feel welcome with one another, and due to the size of Clarke you know basically everyone, but people tend to stay with whom they are comfortable with a little too much at times." Undergrads report that "even though the amount of diversity at this school is not high, there is a constant presence of different cultures. The multicultural student services team makes sure that all students are represented in the school community."

ADMISSIONS

Very important factors considered by the admissions committee include: secondary school record and standardized test scores. *Important factors considered include:* class rank. *Other factors considered include:* extracurricular activities, interview, minority status, talent/ability, and volunteer work. SAT I or ACT required. TOEFL required of all international applicants. High school diploma or GED is required. *High school units required/recommended:* 21 total required; 4 English required, 3 math required, 4 math recommended, 3 science required, 4 science recommended, 2 science lab required, 2 foreign language required, 3 social studies required, 4 elective required.

The Inside Word

Clarke is looking to grow: its 2002–2003 incoming class was 41 percent larger than its predecessor. That's a lot of extra spaces to fill, meaning that a few extra borderline candidates should be able to sneak in under the wire.

FINANCIAL AID

Students should submit: FAFSA. No deadline for regular filing. The Princeton Review suggests that all financial aid forms be submitted as soon as possible after January 1. *Need-based scholarships/grants offered:* Pell, SEOG, state scholarships/grants, private scholarships, and the school's own gift aid. *Loan aid offered:* FFEL Subsidized Stafford, FFEL Unsubsidized Stafford, FFEL PLUS, Federal Perkins, Federal Nursing, state loans, and college/university loans from institutional funds. Federal Work-Study Program available. Institutional employment available. Off-campus job opportunities are excellent.

For even more information on this school, turn to page 338 of the "Stats" section.

COE COLLEGE

1220 First Avenue NE, Cedar Rapids, IA 52402 • Admissions: 319-399-8500 • Fax: 319-399-8816
Financial Aid: 319-399-8540 • E-mail: admission@coe.edu • Website: www.coe.edu

Ratings

Quality of Life: 74   Academic: 80   Admissions: 83   Financial Aid: 80

Academics

In the minds of many of Coe students, the powers-that-be are divided into two distinct factions: the "excellent" faculty and the "approachable" administrators. Important to note: The administration and students do not always see eye to eye; however, students are quick to credit the administration with an ability to internalize feedback—no matter if

> **SURVEY SAYS . . .**
> *Classes are small*
> *Athletic facilities are great, Great library*
> *Registration is a breeze*
> *Everyone loves the Kohawks*
> *Musical organizations are hot*
> *Student publications are popular*
> *Diverse students interact*
> *(Almost) no one listens to college radio*

it's good or bad. One student notes, "If there's one thing I love about my school, it's how willing the faculty and administration are to work with you." And most students hold warm and venerable feelings for the college's president, who's "always smoking a cigar and waving at students." As for the "outstanding" professors, they "are very friendly" and "easily accessible outside of the classroom." As you're likely to find at many small colleges, at Coe you may discover that "access to specifics within" your field is "limited to what the two or three professors in your department specialize in. If you want a very specific field, think hard before coming to Coe." "All in all, you make the academic experience what you want it to be, mediocre, satisfying, or challenging." The choice is yours.

Life

"Life at Coe is fun!" exclaims one underclassman. While there are definitely a handful of students who "frickin' study for fun," you'll find that the most popular pastime at this "partying school" is to "drink, and drink heavily." However, there are "tons of activities to get involved in." "Greek life is rampant" and provides its fair share of social outlets. Whether in a frat or not, students here "like to get together in big groups and party til you can't party anymore." Students will tell you that "student clubs and organizations" run a close second to these wild parties when it comes to "what people do for fun." Coe offers "everything from social and academic fraternities and sororities to music and theater to outdoor activities clubs to sports and intramurals to volunteering." And let's not forget the "campuswide" events like "Block Party, Homecoming, Presidential Ball, Flunk Day"—"an official cutting-class and beer-drinking day"—and "Winter Games." Students believe that Cedar Rapids is an agreeable place, even if it does feel like "one of those mid-size midwestern towns that all seem much the same." "Iowa City, the home of the University of Iowa" is only "20 minutes south," and this offers a world of social opportunities to antsy Coe undergrads. And when students feel especially eager to escape "the Coe bubble," they know that it's only "four hours to Chicago, St. Louis, [and] the Twin Cities."

Student Body

Because "lots of juniors and seniors live on campus," students feel that the entire "community" exists within what they call "the Coe bubble." Inside this bubble, you'll find "a somewhat polar" group of students "made of up of segments, each with [its] own concerns and inter-ests." "We have every clique," explains one student. There are "the jocks, the ditzies [sic], the band geeks, the volunteer people, the incredibly cute smart men, the loud and proud GLBT community, the incredibly cute, incredibly smart women, the small-town farm kids, the city-slickers, the gangsta wannabes, the playas, the chicks that absolutely hate the world and every man in it, and the Greeks, the cheerleaders, the 'fresh meat' girls, the Weezer-lovin' dudes, and probably every other stereotypical group you can think of shaking a stick at." There are also "quite a few foreign students," though "the American minority students are few and far between." Whether you like them or not, you'll be sure to get to know your classmates at Coe. "It's a close-knit community and just about everybody knows everyone else in some way."

ADMISSIONS

Very important factors considered by the admissions committee include: secondary school record. *Important factors considered include:* class rank, essays, recommendations, standardized test scores. *Other factors considered include:* alumni/ae relation, character/personal qualities, extracurricular activities, interview, minority status, talent/ability, volunteer work. SAT I or ACT required. TOEFL required of all international applicants. High school diploma or GED is required. *High school units required/recommended:* 18 total recommended; 4 English recom-mended, 3 math recommended, 3 science recommended, 1 science lab recommended, 2 for-eign language recommended, 3 social studies recommended, 2 elective recommended.

The Inside Word

Coe's admissions process places a very high level of importance on your numbers. Candidates who don't have at least a 2.75 high school GPA and at least a 22 on the ACT may find tough going with the admissions committee. As is true of nearly all small liberal arts col-leges, Coe conducts a thorough application review that also considers your personal back-ground and involvements, but an emerging national reputation enables them to keep their focus upon academic achievement as the primary gatekeeper.

FINANCIAL AID

Students should submit: FAFSA. Regular filing deadline is April 30. The Princeton Review sug-gests that all financial aid forms be submitted as soon as possible after January 1. *Need-based scholarships/grants offered:* Pell, SEOG, state scholarships/grants, private scholarships, the school's own gift aid. *Loan aid offered:* Direct Subsidized Stafford, Direct Unsubsidized Stafford, Direct PLUS, Federal Perkins, college/university loans from institutional funds. Federal Work-Study Program available. Institutional employment available. Applicants will be notified of awards on a rolling basis beginning on or about March 1. Off-campus job oppor-tunities are excellent.

FROM THE ADMISSIONS OFFICE

"A Coe education begins to pay off right away. In fact, 98 percent of last year's graduating class was either working or in graduate school within six months of graduation. One reason our graduates do so well is the Coe Plan—a step-by-step sequence of activities designed to prepare our students for life after Coe. This required sequence stretches from the first-year seminar to community service, issue dinners, career planning seminars, and the required hands-on experience. The hands-on component may be satisfied through an internship, research, practicum, or study abroad. One student lived with a Costa Rican family while she studied the effects of selective logging on rain forest organisms. Others have interned at places like Warner Brothers in Los Angeles and the Chicago Board of Trade. Still others com-bine travel with an internship or student teaching for an unforgettable off-campus experience. Coe College is one of the few liberal arts institutions in the country to require hands-on learn-ing for graduation."

For even more information on this school, turn to page 339 of the "Stats" section.

COLLEGE OF SAINT BENEDICT/SAINT JOHN'S UNIVERSITY

PO Box 7155, COLLEGEVILLE, MN 56321-7155 • ADMISSIONS: 320-363-2196 • FAX: 320-363-3206
FINANCIAL AID: 320-363-3664 • E-MAIL: ADMISSIONS@CSBSJU.EDU • WEBSITE: WWW.CSBSJU.EDU

Ratings
Quality of Life: 79   Academic: 76   Admissions: 81   Financial Aid: 88

Academics

Ninety miles northwest of Minnesota's Twin Cities lay the twin campuses of the all-women's College of Saint Benedict and the all-men's Saint John's University. The two schools forged their partnership in 1964 in an effort to "take the best of what women's, men's, and co-ed colleges offer and combine them in a way you won't find at another pair of colleges in the nation." According to students, CSB/SJU more than meets the challenge it initially set for itself. Writes one, "Our school is more than a school. It's tradition, family, beauty, and presence all rolled into a tiny backwoods campus. You can't help but fall in love with the place, everything from the people to the profs." Agrees another, "Community is the greatest strength" of CSB/SJU. Students are particularly pleased at the way in which the curriculum here stresses critical thinking. Writes one, "Not only do you learn about skills for a major, you learn a better, open, and more knowledgeable way of thinking and applying it to real-life situations." Professors receive rave reviews, with undergrads gushing that "some of the profs are real gems. They're great teachers, some even friends, who would bend over backwards to make sure you learn what you have to know, and do their best to let you enjoy it." Adds another, "Several of my professors have become close friends of mine. They really get involved with the students on a personal level. CSB/SJU has great academics, and I feel it comes directly from the attitudes of the professors."

> **SURVEY SAYS . . .**
> *Great food on campus*
> *Athletic facilities are great*
> *Ethnic diversity lacking on campus*
> *(Almost) everyone plays intramural sports*
> *Students pack the stadium, Theater is unpopular*
> *Students are very religious*
> *Students get along with local community*
> *Low cost of living*

Life

The gorgeous natural setting of CSB/SJU sets the tone for many student pastimes. Writes one student, "Saint John's is nestled on 2,400 acres of woodland that's surrounded by five lakes. The outdoor activities available are virtually unrivaled by any other college." To facilitate students' passion for the outdoors, the school has "a place on campus called the Outdoor Leadership Center, which rents out equipment to students (e.g., camping equipment, cross-country skis, rollerblades, and snowshoes)." Students also participate in "a wide range of athletics and intramural activities." For entertainment, "the school brings many things onto campus for us to do, such as musical performers, movies, and dances. Since these are all free, there are many great, cheap ways to have fun." Writes one student, "There is truly something for everyone. For those who like to party, you can find one just about every night of the week. For those who like to sit back and relax all week, you can do that too—it's really nice to do by Lake Sagatagan at St. John's." The fact that the two campuses are about five miles apart seems to have little effect on social life; the two schools coordinate events through the Joint Events Council. And, "when there isn't anything going on here, Minneapolis is only an hour away. . . . When the serenity gets [to be] too much for you, the hustle and bustle of big city life is in reach. I have yet to be bored here."

Student Body

The student body of CSB/SJU "is basically a bunch of white suburban kids from Minnesota and a bunch of white farm kids from Minnesota mixed together, and a few international students mainly from the Bahamas and a few out-of-state students thrown in to spice things up a bit." Students are "friendly, motivated, and courteous. Most people get along and socialize with many people." Reports one student, "It's not uncommon to say 'hello' to people you don't even know." Another points out that "there are a number of students here that do come from wealthy backgrounds, so sometimes it's tough for myself and others from not-so-wealthy backgrounds to see so many nice cars and people wearing Abercrombie. The students are in no way separated by money or what they wear, though. Everyone gets along very well."

ADMISSIONS

Very important factors considered by the admissions committee include: class rank, essays, secondary school record, standardized test scores. *Important factors considered include:* alumni/ae relation, character/personal qualities, extracurricular activities, geographical residence, minority status, recommendations, religious affiliation/commitment, state residency, talent/ability, volunteer work, work experience. *Other factors considered include:* interview. SAT I or ACT required. TOEFL required of all international applicants. High school diploma or GED is required. *High school units required/recommended:* 17 total recommended; 4 English recommended, 3 math recommended, 2 science recommended, 2 science lab recommended, 2 foreign language recommended, 2 social studies recommended, 4 elective recommended.

The Inside Word

Though Saint John's University and the College of Saint Benedict have combined most of their efforts and operations on campus, admission remains distinct. Women must apply to the College of Saint Benedict and men to Saint John's. Since it is a joint admissions office, both are seeking exactly the same qualities in their students; in addition to solid academic records from high school, much attention is paid to the match a student makes with the schools. Candidates can expect their personal side to receive thorough evaluation within the admissions processes here.

FINANCIAL AID

Students should submit: FAFSA, institution's own financial aid form, federal tax forms and W-2s. The Princeton Review suggests that all financial aid forms be submitted as soon as possible after January 1. *Need-based scholarships/grants offered:* Pell, SEOG, state scholarships/grants, private scholarships, the school's own gift aid. *Loan aid offered:* FFEL Subsidized Stafford, FFEL Unsubsidized Stafford, FFEL PLUS, Federal Perkins, state loans, various private loans. Federal Work-Study Program available. Institutional employment available. Applicants will be notified of awards on a rolling basis beginning on or about March 15. Off-campus job opportunities are good.

FROM THE ADMISSIONS OFFICE

"CSB/SJU believes that a student's hard work in high school deserves recognition—that's why renewable scholarships such as the Regents'/Trustees' (worth $38,000 over four years); the President's (worth from $22,000 to $32,000 over four years); and the Dean's (worth from $12,000 to $20,000 over four years) are awarded competitively based on the student's past academic achievement, college entrance test scores, and demonstrated leadership and service. Diversity Leadership Scholarships (worth up to $20,000 over four years) are awarded to students who have promoted diversity in their leadership and service work. Performing and Fine Arts Scholarships (worth up to $8,000 over four years) are awarded to students who have participated in and excelled in art, music, or theater in high school. Approximately 90 percent of the students currently attending the colleges receive financial assistance; many receive both scholarship and need-based assistance."

For even more information on this school, turn to page 339 of the "Stats" section.

COLLEGE OF ST. CATHERINE

2004 RANDOLPH AVENUE, SAINT PAUL, MN 55105 • ADMISSIONS: 651-690-6505 • FAX: 651-690-8824
E-MAIL: ADMISSIONS@STKATE.EDU • WEBSITE: WWW.STKATE.EDU

Ratings
Quality of Life: 78   **Academic:** 78   **Admissions:** 70   **Financial Aid:** 80

Academics

The College of St. Catherine, an all-women's Catholic school in St. Paul, Minnesota, offers its serious-minded pre-professional student body a wide range of options. "The academic standards at St. Kate's are quite high, preparing students to enter the real world," explained one student who identified developing business, sales, occupational therapy, and nursing among her school's strongest areas. Another student added that despite "old lab equipment," "I feel very well prepared for a career as a biologist, which is my goal." Some students here attribute a sense of belonging in "the sciences, math, and other male-dominated fields" to the all-female environment; one student writes, "It's really empowering to walk into my organic chemistry class and see all women." Students love the school's approach to teaching, telling us that "St. Kate's is a college where the individual student is really respected. My professors are incredibly intelligent in their respective fields and teach the information in a way that is very easy to learn. They are also very accessible for outside help and also to answer questions during lecture." Small class sizes and tutoring groups also help St. Kate's undergrads negotiate the difficult curriculum. Complaints about the administration focus on their inaccessibility: one student suggests that administrators "get out of their ivory towers and pick up their phones and listen to what students have to say about the classes and teachers here." Another insists that they do actually "try to work for the students," but admits that there is a problematic "gap in communication between the majority of students and the administration." Many point out that campus buildings are in need of renovation, but the school is planning to build "a new student union and library, as well as new residence halls with the $20 million gift they received."

> **SURVEY SAYS . . .**
> *Students love Saint Paul*
> *Student publications are popular*
> *No one plays intramural sports*
> *Students don't get along with local community*
> *Students are religious*
> *Very little hard liquor*
> *Very little beer drinking*
> *Intercollegiate sports are popular*

Life

During class hours, St. Kate's campus is abuzz with activity, but once studying is done, things quiet down pretty quickly. "There is not much of a campus spirit or community life, generally because we're busy with classes, homework, and work," explains one student. Adds another, "Many people here live off campus, which makes the time they spend here their homework time." Students occasionally attend parties on campus, either in the dorms or student apartments. A few also join the sole social service sorority, and members claim participation is "the best way to party at the University of Minnesota." Overall, "campus life is pretty quiet, but . . . restaurants, clubs, shopping, etc.," keep students occupied. One student adds, "St. Paul is a great city with tons to do: dancing, movies, theatre, concerts. Minneapolis is five minutes away as well, so we have too many options to list." Respondents concur, "St. Kate's has a beautiful campus." Wrote one proud undergrad, "The College of St. Catherine was built around 1905 on 110 acres of land in St. Paul. It has lovely gates on the perimeter of the campus, big brick buildings, and lots of open grassy areas. The scenery is beautiful: slight hills, green grass, a little pond, and many trees."

Student Body

"The amount of diversity at St. Kate's is enormous," students tell us, pointing out that "The students at St. Kate's are a wide mixture of all ages and ethnicities. This is a private women's college, so there are women from just out of high school to 60-year-olds who are coming back for a degree or simply classes." Adds one undergrad, "Some women here are very mature; others still think they are in high school and play in-group/out-group games like they are running for prom queen . . . but most of us here are serious students who work hard." One woman notes that "all people are accepted here, regardless of sexual orientation, race, or other factors. We are encouraged to learn and challenge ourselves in classes and in life." A few conservatives complain that the atmosphere is "too left-wing liberal. . . . I feel that many students at CSC are very narrow-minded at times."

ADMISSIONS

Very important factors considered by the admissions committee include: secondary school record. *Important factors considered include:* class rank, essays, extracurricular activities, recommendations, and standardized test scores. *Other factors considered include:* character/personal qualities, interview, minority status, talent/ability, volunteer work, and work experience. SAT I or ACT required. TOEFL required of all international applicants. High school diploma is required and GED is accepted. *High school units required/recommended:* 19 total are recommended; 4 English recommended, 3 math recommended, 2 science recommended, 4 foreign language recommended, 2 social studies recommended, 1 history recommended, 3 elective recommended.

The Inside Word

CSC has a created a fertile setting to hatch professionals in business and science degrees. As an incoming student, however, don't become distracted by the looming bitterness many in the student body feel over their unsuccessful attempts to work with the administration to improve infrastructure.

FINANCIAL AID

Students should submit: FAFSA and institution's own financial aid form. The Princeton Review suggests that all financial aid forms be submitted as soon as possible after January 1. *Need-based scholarships/grants offered:* Pell, SEOG, state scholarships/grants, private scholarships, and the school's own gift aid. *Loan aid offered:* FFEL Subsidized Stafford, FFEL Unsubsidized Stafford, FFEL PLUS, Federal Perkins, Federal Nursing, and state loans. Federal Work-Study Program available. Institutional employment available. Applicants will be notified of awards on a rolling basis beginning on or about March 15. Off-campus job opportunities are excellent.

For even more information on this school, turn to page 340 of the "Stats" section.

COLLEGE OF SAINT SCHOLASTICA

1200 KENWOOD AVENUE, DULUTH, MN 55811-4199 • ADMISSIONS: 218-723-6046 • FAX: 218-723-5991
E-MAIL: ADMISSIONS@CSS.EDU • WEBSITE: WWW.CSS.EDU

Ratings
Quality of Life: 80   **Academic:** 75   **Admissions:** 69   **Financial Aid:** 79

Academics

Can anybody say "nursing"? Though the College of Saint Scholastica students can choose majors in 36 departments, the one that gets the most praise from students is nursing. It's also the program that graduates the most the students. "The professors in nurs-

> **SURVEY SAYS . . .**
> *School is well run, Instructors are good teachers*
> *Diversity lacking on campus, Classes are small*
> *Great food on campus, Popular college radio*
> *Student publications are popular*
> *Intercollegiate sports are popular*

ing are very caring," writes one in-the-know student. Another cites the nursing program's "excellent reputation" as her reason for choosing Saint Scholastica. But quality professors are by no means exclusive to any one department. A senior declares that across the board professors are "very helpful and willing to work with students." Because "the class sizes are small" at CSS, professors are able to offer "a lot of personal attention" to each student. Despite this small class size, writes one student, "I didn't have any trouble getting the ones I wanted, even though I was in one of the last groups to register." Another student says, "The professors really know what they are talking about and they seem genuinely glad to be there." Some undergrads find that "the administration is really friendly"; others claim "the administration does not interact enough with the students." The overriding sentiment though, is that students are "very proud to be a part of this institution."

Life

On the edge of Lake Superior, Duluth plays host to everything from the Minnesota Ballet to a thriving commercial harbor to heated rivalries in hockey and curling. Life in Duluth, according to CSS undergrads, is what you make of it. With a city population pushing six figures, "surely there are things to do in Duluth." When students go looking for the typical college nightlife, "clubs, parties, and drinking" are never out of reach. Outdoorsy types can also find their fix. With Lake Superior a stone's throw away and the Boundary Waters Canoe Area Wilderness a little more than an hour from town, water sports are popular. Close by, there are also ski resorts, hiking trails, outdoor ice skating rinks, and beaches (well, lake beaches at least). And if you'd ever want them, there are plenty of "peaceful places where you can go and be by yourself." While there may be options around here, it's often up to the individual student—or small groups of students—to take advantage of them, especially on weekends. Some students go home for the weekend, respondents tell us, and it can "get a little boring. Most of the time if you are bored, it is your own fault. There is always something to do." Students find entertainment in the 50-plus and organizations on campus, in town, or at nearby U Minnesota—Duluth. And students report that the college is getting better at "providing student social functions."

Student Body

Started by Benedictine sisters about 90 years ago, the College of Saint Scholastica continues with its Catholic emphasis, though only about half of the students here call themselves Catholic. And though 13 percent of CSS's student body hails from out of state, CSS is "not a diverse campus" by any stretch of the imagination. Still, Saint Scholastica managed to double its international contingent this year and nearly double its number of minority students. Many students choose Saint Scholastica because it's "close to home," and as a result have held onto the "cliques" that they formed in high school. Other students form their "cliques" after arriving on campus. Regardless of how it's done, social groups are pretty well formed by the end of first semester freshman year—a reality that leaves one student warning, "If you transfer in after freshman year, it's hard to meet students!" But don't be intimidated. At its core, CSS is "like a community" in which "almost everyone knows everyone" and "a lot of close friendships are developed."

ADMISSIONS

Very important factors considered by the admissions committee include: class rank, secondary school record, and standardized test scores. *Important factors considered include:* essays, interview, and recommendations. *Other factors considered include:* character/personal qualities, extracurricular activities, geographical residence, and talent/ability. SAT I or ACT required, ACT preferred. TOEFL required of all international applicants. High school diploma or GED is required. *High school units required/recommended:* 4 English recommended, 3 math recommended, 3 science recommended, 3 foreign language recommended, 3 social studies recommended.

The Inside Word

Saint Scholastica draws mostly local students who are well aware of its academic reputation. Those who can't get in don't bother to apply; hence, the high admittance rate. CSS appears to be improving its student profile despite recent increases in enrollment.

FINANCIAL AID

Students should submit: FAFSA, institution's own financial aid form, and state aid form. No deadline for regular filing. The Princeton Review suggests that all financial aid forms be submitted as soon as possible after January 1. *Need-based scholarships/grants offered:* Pell, SEOG, state scholarships/grants, private scholarships, the school's own gift aid, and Federal Nursing. *Loan aid offered:* FFEL Subsidized Stafford, FFEL Unsubsidized Stafford, FFEL PLUS, Federal Perkins, Federal Nursing, state loans, and alternative loans. Federal Work-Study Program available. Institutional employment available. Applicants will be notified of awards on a rolling basis beginning on or about March 1. Off-campus job opportunities are good.

FROM THE ADMISSIONS OFFICE

"The College of St. Scholastica is enjoying its largest-ever enrollment, as well as a vote of confidence from the federal government. St. Scholastica began its 2002–2003 academic year with a record enrollment of 2,518 students. That's a 13 percent increase over last year. Leading the growth is a largest-ever entering freshman class. 'Our incoming student body is stronger than any in recent years in terms of high school rankings, GPAs, and the ACT,' said Brian Dalton, Vice President for Enrollment Management. 'Ten percent of our freshmen are [high school] valedictorians and salutatorians. We are also glad to see our efforts at increasing the diversity of our student body showing progress. While we need to go even further, we have nearly doubled the number of students of color on campus, and more than doubled the number of international students.'

"St. Scholastica's progress also includes an award of $1.8 million by the U.S. Department of Education to use computers in an innovative way that will make the College a national model for health-care educators. The grant funds a five-year project that integrates sophisticated clinical software computer systems throughout St. Scholastica's five health science programs—nursing, physical therapy, occupational therapy, exercise physiology and health information management. St. Scholastica's computer information systems department is also involved, helping prepare IT professionals who will work in the health-care industry. St. Scholastica is ranked as a Top-Tier institution of the Midwest in *U.S. News & World Report*'s annual 'Best Colleges' rankings for 2003."

For even more information on this school, turn to page 341 of the "Stats" section.

COLLEGE OF THE OZARKS

Office of Admissions, Point Lookout, MO 65726 • Admissions: 417-334-6411 • Fax: 417-335-2618
Financial Aid: 417-334-6411 ext. 4290 • E-mail: admiss4@cofo.edu • Website: www.cofo.edu

Ratings

Quality of Life: 79   Academic: 84   Admissions: 85   Financial Aid: 93

Academics

Many students at the College of the Ozarks feel that their school is "the best place to get an affordable education in a Christian setting." The school, one of six in the country that widely offer educational opportunities to needy students in exchange for work in on-campus jobs, "provides a unique experience that cannot be found at

> **SURVEY SAYS . . .**
> *Very little drug use*
> *Lots of conservatives on campus*
> *Classes are small*
> *Students love Point Lookout, MO*
> *Beautiful campus, Very little beer drinking*
> *Very little hard liquor, (Almost) no one smokes*
> *Political activism is (almost) nonexistent*

other colleges," according to undergrads. "The college seeks to fulfill a student's needs in academic, vocational, spiritual, cultural, and patriotic areas." Students caution that "it is easier to attend because of the financial support you receive, but it is not 'free' by any means"; many students work a second, off-campus job in addition to their on-campus work in order to cover expenses. In return for their labors, students here enjoy professors who "take you in under their wing and follow you throughout college and into career placement" and an administration that "actually wants to listen if you have a concern. They don't just lock themselves in their offices; they get out and get familiar with the student body." Academic offerings at this small school cover most of the liberal arts, as well as agriculturally oriented programs, aviation, and hotel and restaurant management. Some here complain that "the academics are slightly watered down"; others, conversely, refer to their school as "Hard Work U."

Life

The academic workload, along with an average 15-hour-per-week work commitment to the school, means that C of O students "don't have a lot of free time. For the most part, however, students here find time to hang out with their friends." Many students take a second job in nearby Branson: "People work to pay for what school doesn't cover," explains one student. Students point out that "since we live in a tourist town, it's easy for everyone to be employed off-campus earning $7 an hour." As an added benefit, "being a C of O student means we get discounts on a lot of things in Branson, including movies and shows." There's a downside to living near a tourism mecca, though: "Life in Branson [occurs] among hundreds of tourists you can never escape. As students we have to learn all of the back roads." On campus, "the rules keep the school clean-cut and enjoyable for everyone." What are the rules, you ask? Reports one undergrad, "Campus gates close at 1:00 every night; opposite sexes are allowed in campus dorms for only three hours on four nights a semester; smoking is allowed only in designated areas; if you are caught drunk by a school official outside of school (even if you are over 21) you will be put on probation . . . and many [administrators] are very discriminative against the students who dress alternative or portray themselves in their own ways." Not surprisingly, "there are people who choose to take more liberties with the rules, just like everywhere. They go off campus to have fun, mostly to drink." Most, however, happily toe the line, enjoying more wholesome pursuits. Notes one, "I love the clean atmosphere: socially, environmentally, and spiritually."

Student Body

The "mostly conservative" students of College of the Ozarks pride themselves on their "outstanding moral values" (which lead at least a few to observe that "some here are really 'holier than thou.' "). Students agree that their classmates are both affable and genuinely accommodating; writes one, "People who visit here comment on how friendly and helpful we are. Maybe it's because we are in the South, but we are really, really friendly." Adds another, "I'll just put it this way: if my car broke down on campus, at least 10 people would show up to help." Students report that "This is a pretty diverse campus . . . [and] I'm glad to say that we all pretty much get along." Though they hail from far and wide, most have roots in rural America.

ADMISSIONS

Very important factors considered by the admissions committee include: character/personal qualities, class rank, essays, extracurricular activities, interview, secondary school record. *Important factors considered include:* alumni/ae relation, recommendations, standardized test scores, talent/ability, volunteer work, work experience. *Other factors considered include:* geographical residence, minority status, religious affiliation/commitment, state residency. ACT required. TOEFL required of all international applicants. High school diploma or GED is required. *High school units required/recommended:* 24 total recommended; 4 English recommended, 3 math recommended, 2 science recommended, 1 science lab recommended, 2 foreign language recommended, 3 social studies recommended.

The Inside Word

The highly unusual nature of the College of the Ozarks translates directly into its admissions process. Because of the school's very purpose, providing educational opportunities to those with great financial need, one of the main qualifiers for admission is exactly that—demonstrated financial need. Despite not being a household word, Ozarks attracts enough interest to keep its admit rate consistently low from year to year. To be sure, the admissions process is competitive, but it's more important to be a good fit for the college philosophically and financially than it is to be an academic wizard. If you're a hard worker all around, you're just what they're looking for.

FINANCIAL AID

Students should submit: FAFSA. The Princeton Review suggests that all financial aid forms be submitted as soon as possible after January 1. *Need-based scholarships/grants offered:* Pell, SEOG, state scholarships/grants, private scholarships, the school's own gift aid. Federal Work-Study Program available. Applicants will be notified of awards on or about July 1. Off-campus job opportunities are excellent.

FROM THE ADMISSIONS OFFICE

"College of the Ozarks is unique because of its no-tuition, work-study program, but also because it strives to educate the head, the heart, and the hands. At C of O, there are high expectations of students—the College stresses character development as well as study and work. An education from 'Hard Work U.' offers many opportunities, not the least of which is the chance to graduate debt-free. Life at C of O isn't all hard work and no play, however. There are many opportunities for fun. The nearby resort town of Branson, Missouri, offers ample opportunities for recreation and summer employment, and Table Rock Lake, only a few miles away, is a terrific spot to swim, sun, and relax. Numerous on-campus activities such as Mudfest, Luau Night, dances, and holiday parties give students lots of chances for fun without leaving the college. At 'Hard Work U.,' we work hard, but we know how to have fun, too."

For even more information on this school, turn to page 341 of the "Stats" section.

COLLEGE OF WOOSTER

1189 BEALL AVENUE, WOOSTER, OH 44691 • ADMISSIONS: 800-877-9905 • FAX: 330-263-2621
FINANCIAL AID: 800-877-3688 • E-MAIL: ADMISSIONS@WOOSTER.EDU • WEBSITE: WWW.WOOSTER.EDU

Ratings
Quality of Life: 88   Academic: 88   Admissions: 80   Financial Aid: 92

Academics

Like the hallmark of its curriculum—the independent study program—the College of Wooster seems intent on nurturing students into self-reliance. From the initial freshman seminar designed to foster critical thinking and writing skills, the Wooster curriculum is geared toward preparing students for their senior-year independent project. Fully integrated major requirements force students

> **SURVEY SAYS . . .**
> *Great computer facilities*
> *Great library*
> *Lots of beer drinking*
> *Low cost of living*
> *Students don't get along with local community*
> *Registration is a pain*
> *Student government is unpopular*
> *Theater is unpopular*
> *Lousy food on campus*

to master both content and methodology in their chosen fields of study before confronting the difficult but rewarding Independent Study (referred to by all on campus simply as "I.S."). Students approve, adding that Wooster's faculty is uniquely suited to the task of teaching the curriculum. "Since the school requires a two-semester independent study project of all of its seniors, the professors who choose to teach here have to (and seem to like to) put their students' research interests before their own," explains one student. Undergrads advise that "grades at Wooster are definitely earned, as classes are very challenging and involve a great deal of work." Fortunately, professors are inspiring; notes one student, "The best thing about the professors at Wooster is that you can always tell that they love what they do. When they are discussing a project of theirs, you can just see in their eyes the level of commitment [to it] that they have." Administrators are "open to suggestions and criticisms from students" although they sometimes "act too much like parents, rather than allowing us to make the mistakes that all 20-somethings need to make."

Life

Students at Wooster appreciate the wide array of activities available to them. Writes one, "There is always something going on during the week (like concerts and comedians), and there are plenty of parties on the weekends. The parties at Wooster—even the big frat parties—are open to anyone. This allows everyone to get together and have a fun time." Adds another, "People at Wooster definitely know how to have a good time. Something is always happening. We have a bar on campus, and 50-cent drafts at happy hour make Friday nights fun." Chem-free offerings? "There are always movies (either free or $1) on the weekends; we have a bowling alley (with pool and ping pong tables), and there are always plays, concerts, or dances to attend. There is never a lack of entertainment at Wooster." The campus is also host to "a million clubs and organizations, depending upon one's preferences as far as hobbies or religion." Off-campus is a different story, as "there really isn't that much to do [in town]. Until you come to Wooster you never realize how truly exciting a 24-hour Super WalMart can be!" Agrees another undergrad, "We are kind of out in the middle of a pasture, and while we don't spend our time cow tipping, we don't have as much access to museums, clubs, and good restaurants as we might were we in the middle of a big city. On the other hand, Cleveland is only an hour away, and it does have all those things."

Student Body

"Thanks to the great financial aid packages that are awarded," Wooster students "come from all different backgrounds." A large international contingent arrives primarily from Pakistan and India; international students "live mostly in one dorm, and black students live in their own sections. Wooster says it is incredibly diverse, but it is rare to see black and white students sitting together" in, say, a dining hall. Undergrads "are very active in all sorts of volunteer groups, and they actually care about the community." Observes one student, "This seems to me like a very liberal school.

ADMISSIONS

Very important factors considered by the admissions committee include: class rank, secondary school record. *Important factors considered include:* character/personal qualities, essays, recommendations, standardized test scores, talent/ability. *Other factors considered include:* alumni/ae relation, extracurricular activities, geographical residence, interview, minority status, state residency, volunteer work, work experience. SAT I or ACT required. TOEFL required of all international applicants. High school diploma or GED is required. *High school units required/recommended:* 4 English required, 3 math required, 4 math recommended, 3 science required, 4 science recommended, 2 foreign language required, 3 foreign language recommended, 3 social studies required, 4 social studies recommended, 2 elective required.

The Inside Word

Wooster has a solid academic reputation and holds its own against formidable competition for students with many national-caliber liberal arts colleges. Applicants should not take the admissions process lightly because candidate evaluations are very thorough and personal.

FINANCIAL AID

Students should submit: FAFSA, institution's own financial aid form, CSS/Financial Aid PROFILE. No deadline for regular filing. The Princeton Review suggests that all financial aid forms be submitted as soon as possible after January 1. *Need-based scholarships/grants offered:* Pell, SEOG, state scholarships/grants, private scholarships, the school's own gift aid. *Loan aid offered:* Direct Subsidized Stafford, Direct Unsubsidized Stafford, Direct PLUS, Federal Perkins, college/university loans from institutional funds. Federal Work-Study Program available. Institutional employment available. Applicants will be notified of awards on or about April 1. Off-campus job opportunities are good.

FROM THE ADMISSIONS OFFICE

"At The College of Wooster, our mission is to graduate educated, not merely trained, people; to produce responsible, independent thinkers, rather than specialists in any given field. Our commitment to independence is especially evident in I.S., the college's distinctive program in which every senior works one-to-one with a faculty mentor to complete a project in the major. I.S. comes from 'independent study,' but, in reality, it is an intellectual collaboration of the highest order and permits every student the freedom to pursue something in which he or she is passionately interested. I.S. is the centerpiece of an innovative curriculum. More than just the project itself, the culture that sustains I.S.—and, in turn, is sustained by I.S.—is an extraordinary college culture. The same attitudes of student initiative, openness, flexibility, and individual support enrich every aspect of Wooster's vital residential college life."

For even more information on this school, turn to page 342 of the "Stats" section.

CORNELL COLLEGE

600 FIRST STREET WEST, MOUNT VERNON, IA 52314-1098 • ADMISSIONS: 319-895-4477
FAX: 319-895-4451 • FINANCIAL AID: 319-895-4216 • E-MAIL: ADMISSIONS@CORNELLCOLLEGE.EDU
WEBSITE: WWW.CORNELLCOLLEGE.EDU

Ratings

Quality of Life: 77   Academic: 80   Admissions: 80   Financial Aid: 85

Academics

Most students at Cornell College chose to attend because its unique academic calendar, called "One-Course-At-A-Time" (students refer to it by its acronym, OCAAT), made intuitive sense to them. Under the system, students immerse themselves in a single course for three and a half weeks, complete a final exam, take a few days' breather, then start the whole process over again. Nearly

> **SURVEY SAYS . . .**
> *Classes are small*
> *Student publications are ignored*
> *Registration is a breeze*
> *Students aren't religious*
> *Campus easy to get around*
> *Intercollegiate sports are unpopular or nonexistent*
> *Theater is unpopular, Lousy off-campus food*
> *Class discussions encouraged*

all students find OCAAT to their liking; "The Block Plan makes learning easy, class sizes small, and one-on-one time with a professor easy. I love it here," writes a typical student. With "average class size at 14 students and classes capped off at 25," students get a "very personal teaching environment" that is heavy on discussion. More than a few professors are "'rent-a-profs,' which are faculty who visit for one or more blocks in a year." Students appreciate the expertise these outsiders bring to campus but warn that "it is difficult for these professors to adjust to the quick pace of class."

Life

"Mount Vernon is very small," explains one student. "There is a grocery store, a Subway, a Hardee's, and a couple of gas stations, all on the same corner. There are also four bars downtown that are hopping every weekend. I am from the suburbs of Chicago, so this atmosphere is really different." Many see an upside, concluding that the lack of action in town "helps our campus to become the center of activities." Students get into sports, community service, clubs, student government, and "social clubs," which are like fraternities and sororities. The school "brings in so many speakers and musical groups that I never have to leave to get some entertainment. The arts are very popular here; there is always a concert or a play." Cornell undergrads often travel to Cedar Rapids (for "a midnight run to Perkins, a movie, or a shopping trip") or Iowa City, both within relatively short driving distance. Students caution prospectives to bring plenty of warm clothing to Mount Vernon, telling us that "the Cornell campus is beautiful in the snow. And it usually snows a lot!"

Student Body

Students consider their peers extremely friendly; writes one, "I love that most people will smile and say hi to you regardless of if you know them or not. It is general Iowa hospitality!" They see another benefit of their small size; explains one student, "I think the small student body makes people much more accountable for their actions." Although "not very racially and ethnically diverse," Cornell has "our jocks, our preps, our punks, our Goths, our girlie-girls, our tom-boys, our hippies . . . whatever 'type' is out there, we have it. And no one cares what you wear or what 'group' you're in—people just love you for you." Students note that "Cornell has a strong exchange program with Korea and Japan, so a very high percentage of our exchange students are Asian."

ADMISSIONS

Very important factors considered by the admissions committee include: class rank, essays, recommendations, secondary school record, standardized test scores, talent/ability. *Important factors considered include:* character/personal qualities, extracurricular activities, interview, minority status, volunteer work, work experience. SAT I or ACT required. TOEFL required of all international applicants. High school diploma or GED is required. *High school units required/recommended:* 16 total recommended; 4 English recommended, 3–4 math recommended, 3–4 science recommended, 2–4 foreign language recommended, 3–4 social studies recommended.

The Inside Word

Given Cornell's relatively unique approach to study, it's no surprise that the admissions committee here focuses attention on both academic and personal strengths. Cornell's small, highly self-selected applicant pool is chock-full of students with solid self-awareness, motivation, and discipline. Pay particular attention to offering evidence of challenging academic course work and solid achievement on your high school record. Strong writers can do much for themselves under admissions circumstances such as these.

FINANCIAL AID

Students should submit: FAFSA, institution's own financial aid form, noncustodial (divorced/separated) parent's statement. The Princeton Review suggests that all financial aid forms be submitted as soon as possible after January 1. *Need-based scholarships/grants offered:* Pell, SEOG, state scholarships/grants, private scholarships, the school's own gift aid. *Loan aid offered:* FFEL Subsidized Stafford, FFEL Unsubsidized Stafford, FFEL PLUS, Federal Perkins, college/university loans from institutional funds, McElroy Loan, Sherman Loan, United Methodist Loan. Federal Work-Study Program available. Institutional employment available. Applicants will be notified of awards on a rolling basis beginning on or about October 1. Off-campus job opportunities are fair.

FROM THE ADMISSIONS OFFICE

"Very few colleges are truly distinctive like Cornell College. Founded in 1853, Cornell is recognized as one of the nation's finest colleges of the liberal arts and sciences. It is Cornell's combination of special features, however, that distinguishes it. An attractively diverse, caring residential college, Cornell places special emphasis on service and leadership. Foremost, it is a place where theory and practice are brought together in exciting ways through the College's One-Course-At-A-Time academic Calendar. Here, students enjoy learning as they immerse themselves in a single subject for a three-and-a-half-week term. They and their professor devote all of their efforts to that course in an engagingly interactive learning environment. This academic system also offers wonderful enrichment experiences through field-based-study, travel abroad, student research, and meaningful internship opportunities. Nine terms are offered each year; 32 course credits are required for graduation with each course equal to four credit hours. Since all classes are on a standard schedule, students are able to pursue their extracurricular interests, whether in the performing arts, athletics, or interest groups, with the same passion with which they pursue their course work. Typically, each year applicants from all 50 states and more than 40 countries apply for admission. Cornell graduates are in demand, with more than two-thirds eventually earning advanced degrees. The College's beautiful hilltop campus is one of only two campuses nationwide listed on the National register of Historic Places. Located in the charming town of Mount Vernon, Cornell is also within commuting distance of Iowa City (home of the University of Iowa) and Cedar Rapids (the second largest city in the state)."

For even more information on this school, turn to page 342 of the "Stats" section.

CREIGHTON UNIVERSITY

2500 CALIFORNIA PLAZA, OMAHA, NE 68178 • ADMISSIONS: 402-280-2703 • FAX: 402-280-2685
FINANCIAL AID: 402-280-2731 • E-MAIL: ADMISSIONS@CREIGHTON.EDU
WEBSITE: WWW.ADMISSION.CREIGHTON.EDU

Ratings
Quality of Life: 87   **Academic:** 82   **Admissions:** 79   **Financial Aid:** 81

Academics

Students can pick from more than 50 majors in three schools—the College of the Arts and Sciences, the College of Business and Administration, and the School of Nursing—at Creighton. Despite the university feel here, Creighton maintains a devotion to liberal arts education that's often found at smaller schools. "Some students don't like the liberal arts core curriculum," especially the "18 hours of theology/philosophy" they have to take "in order to graduate." But they do appreciate the attention they receive from their "absolutely phenomenal" profs. "The first thing I noticed about Creighton's professors," writes an undergrad, "[was] their availability." While the nursing and health sciences programs remain some of the most popular at Creighton, some students wish that the university would put "less emphasis on the medical fields." With a new science building, it's clear that science and technology will remain a strong part of this campus's academic life. Whether their sights are set on becoming scientists or literary critics, most students view Creighton as their ticket to the future. Declares one, "The students at Creighton are highly motivated intellectuals that always get into the top law, medical, and graduate schools."

> **SURVEY SAYS . . .**
> *Theater is hot*
> *Frats and sororities dominate social scene*
> *Very little drug use, Popular college radio*
> *Musical organizations aren't popular*
> *Students are very religious*
> *Students get along with local community*
> *Diverse students interact*
> *Lousy food on campus*

Life

Creighton's home turf is Omaha, Nebraska's largest city, with about 700,000 residents. Students regularly venture into the city for entertainment—especially to the city's "Old Market area," which has a "cool bar scene," "a lot of unique specialty shops, and excellent eats." While there's definitely some students who say that "if it were possible to change" the university's "location, say out of Omaha, then it would be perfect," others will tell you that Omaha "has a lot to offer for a midwestern city if you just get out there and look." Many students try to "balance" their social lives between on-campus and off-campus social activities. Students also divvy up some of their spare hours among campus organizations, like the Speech and Debate Club or the Gay-Straight Alliance. And "the Creighton population does everything in terms of volunteerism that you could name. The Jesuit tradition promotes the idea of going out into the community and helping others." There's another thing that the Jesuit tradition promotes that students aren't so keen on: rules. "Because this is a Catholic university, the housing regulations are rather strict." In other words, during those first two years when students live in the campus dorms, they're subject to "rules about [not] having someone of a different sex in your room past 2 A.M."

Student Body

Not many students will dispute the notion that their classmates are "extremely friendly," but some will tell you that, all in all, Creighton's 3,700 undergrads are too similar. "The majority of the students here could be poster children for Abercrombie and Fitch," whines one student. "A very conservative bunch," according to another. While many students are religious at this Jesuit institution, "actually less than 50 percent of the population is Catholic. . . . There is no religious pressure here whatsoever." Some Creighton students find "a division between students who only see each other during the day and those who live in the dorms during freshman and sophomore years." (First- and second-year students are required to live on campus.) Regardless of where they live, many Creighton students spend a fair amount of time with their noses in the books, as they tend to stress "out way too much about tests and grades and papers."

ADMISSIONS

Very important factors considered by the admissions committee include: secondary school record. *Important factors considered include:* recommendations, standardized test scores. *Other factors considered include:* character/personal qualities, class rank, essays, extracurricular activities, minority status, talent/ability, volunteer work. SAT I or ACT required. TOEFL required of all international applicants. High school diploma or GED is required. *High school units required/recommended:* 16 total recommended; 4 English recommended, 3 math recommended, 2 science recommended, 2 foreign language recommended, 1 social studies recommended, 1 history recommended, 3 elective recommended.

The Inside Word

In this world of literal translation, even colleges and universities with admit rates that are higher than Creighton's refer to themselves as selective. While it should not be particularly difficult to get in, some applicants don't.

FINANCIAL AID

Students should submit: FAFSA, institution's own financial aid form. No deadline for regular filing. The Princeton Review suggests that all financial aid forms be submitted as soon as possible after January 1. *Need-based scholarships/grants offered:* Pell, SEOG, state scholarships/grants, private scholarships, the school's own gift aid. *Loan aid offered:* FFEL Subsidized Stafford, FFEL Unsubsidized Stafford, FFEL PLUS, Federal Perkins, Federal Nursing, college/university loans from institutional funds. Federal Work-Study Program available. Institutional employment available. Applicants will be notified of awards on a rolling basis beginning on or about March 15. Off-campus job opportunities are excellent.

FROM THE ADMISSIONS OFFICE

"Students come to Creighton to become experts in their chosen fields . . . even if they haven't already chosen a field of study! About 40 percent of the graduating seniors from Creighton go immediately into medical, dentistry, pharmacy, law, and physical and occupational therapy professional graduate programs—this is the highest rate of any midwestern university. We also produce exceptional teachers, business professionals, scientists, journalists and writers, and community service advocates. Our size is ideal. With 3,700 undergraduates and, including professional school enrollment, a total of 6,300 attendees, our students feel they have the best of both worlds—first-rate academic programs and facilities but also a more intimate relationship with our faculty that often leads to involvement in research projects and internships. Creighton students tend to have a deeper focus on their careers and lifestyle choices. As students at a leading, national, Jesuit, liberal arts university our students are encouraged to examine the moral as well as factual dimension of issues. Most students also get involved in our leadership training programs and community service and/or campus ministry organizations. The campus has its own comfortable and safe sense of space, and the downtown corporate headquarters, restaurants, and music spots are just a five-minute walk away."

For even more information on this school, turn to page 343 of the "Stats" section.

DENISON UNIVERSITY

BOX H, GRANVILLE, OH 43023 • ADMISSIONS: 740-587-6276 • FAX: 740-587-6306
FINANCIAL AID: 740-587-6279 • E-MAIL: ADMISSIONS@DENISON.EDU • WEBSITE: WWW.DENISON.EDU

Ratings

Quality of Life: 77   Academic: 81   Admissions: 82   Financial Aid: 84

Academics

No, this is not your father's Denison, as students frequently made us aware. "It's more challenging and more fulfilling than I would have ever dreamed," writes one student. "It's a love/hate relationship because I know I could have gone somewhere easier and got all A's and made it to med school coasting,

SURVEY SAYS . . .
Frats and sororities dominate social scene
Diversity lacking on campus
Athletic facilities are great, Students are cliquish
Classes are small, Theater is unpopular
Lousy off-campus food
Class discussions encouraged
Low cost of living

but then I would have missed out on the great academic experience Denison offers." Agrees another, "Academically, it has become more challenging each year due to the school's increasing population of strongly academic students. The rise in standards for Denison students has motivated and made my friends and me proud." Students appreciate the attentiveness and dedication of the DU faculty; writes one undergrad, "Although I have had my doubts about attending Denison, I cannot discount the superior education I have received. The faculty is engaging, interesting, and concerned about their students. Feedback flows, and help is almost always obtainable. The professors expect a lot of you, and you work hard trying not to disappoint them." Another praises the teaching methods here, explaining that "through classes based more on discussion than lecture, I have witnessed students growing not just objectively, but becoming better thinkers, and therefore better people." The administration is similarly "top notch. Not only are they accessible, but they have given me the impression that they are very interested in the well-being of students at this institution." Popular majors at Denison include English, economics, psychology, and biology. For those studying the latter, Denison offers The Polly Anderson Field Station at the Biological Reserve, and has its own planetarium for stargazers in Olin Science Hall.

Life

Life at Denison "is pretty relaxed. Most people seem to get their work done before having fun." Writes one student, "Movies are the staple entertainment. But backing that up is the occasional spur-of-the-moment shopping trip. In general my free time is spent sitting in a friend's room laughing the day away." Students also enjoy a wide assortment of campus organizations and "activities, concerts, comedians, etc." Hometown Granville "is very small, not conducive to college students, and does not have much activity. It is a nice town though, with a few good places to eat. You have to make your own fun at Denison." Adds another student, "There is little to do off campus. Granville is not very welcoming to university students, and there is no off-campus housing allowed. The occasional house party is a big deal." Despite efforts to curb partying, "drinking is one of the most popular activities." On weekends "a lot of students make the short 30-minute commute to Columbus to enjoy the city's night-life."

Student Body

As in previous surveys, Denison undergrads note an incremental improvement in the school's demographic makeup this year. "Although our student body is predominantly white, our minority population is growing each and every year, heightening Denison's diversity. I notice on campus that most people interact with each other regardless of gender or other minority status. I feel that the campus is gradually—but surely—becoming more diverse and open-minded." Students regard classmates as "generally very friendly" and appreciate the fact that "although Denison is a small school with approximately 2,100 undergrad[s], there seems to be a group for everyone." They also note that "there is a strong separation between people who like to party and people who don't party at all, and due to [more demanding] admission standards, the latter is becoming dominant."

ADMISSIONS

Very important factors considered by the admissions committee include: essays, recommendations, secondary school record, standardized test scores. *Important factors considered include:* alumni/ae relation, character/personal qualities, extracurricular activities, interview, talent/ability. *Other factors considered include:* geographical residence, religious affiliation/commitment, state residency, volunteer work, work experience. SAT I or ACT required. TOEFL required of all international applicants. High school diploma or GED is required. *High school units required/recommended:* 16 total recommended; 4 English recommended, 3 math recommended, 3 science recommended, 3 foreign language recommended, 2 social studies recommended, 1 history recommended.

The Inside Word

Applicants who are statistically below Denison's freshman profile should proceed with caution. One of the simplest ways for a university to promote a reputation as an increasingly selective institution is to begin to cut off the bottom of the applicant pool. Only lack of success against heavy competition for students prevents Denison from being more aggressive in this regard.

FINANCIAL AID

Students should submit: FAFSA. No deadline for regular filing. The Princeton Review suggests that all financial aid forms be submitted as soon as possible after January 1. *Need-based scholarships/grants offered:* Pell, SEOG, state scholarships/grants, private scholarships, the school's own gift aid. *Loan aid offered:* Direct Subsidized Stafford, Direct Unsubsidized Stafford, Direct PLUS, Federal Perkins, college/university loans from institutional funds. Federal Work-Study Program available. Institutional employment available. Applicants will be notified of awards on a rolling basis beginning on or about April 1. Off-campus job opportunities are fair.

FROM THE ADMISSIONS OFFICE

"Denison is a college that can point with pride to its success in enrolling and retaining intellectually motivated, diverse, and well-balanced students who are being taught to become effective leaders in the 21st century. This year, nearly 50 percent of our first-year students were in the top 10 percent of their high school graduating class, their average SAT scores have risen above 1200—an increase of some 40 points over the last five years—18 percent of the class is multicultural, and 95 percent of our student body is receiving some type of financial assistance. Our First-Year Program focuses on helping students make a successful transition from high school to college, and the small classes and accessibility of faculty assure students the opportunity to interact closely with their professors and fellow students. We care about our students, and the loyalty of our 27,000 alumni proves that the Denison experience is one that lasts for a lifetime."

For even more information on this school, turn to page 344 of the "Stats" section.

DePaul University

1 East Jackson Boulevard, Chicago, IL 60604-2287 • Admissions: 312-362-8300 • Fax: 312-362-5749
Financial Aid: 312-362-8091 • E-mail: admitdpu@wppost.depaul.edu • Website: www.depaul.edu

Ratings

Quality of Life: 80   Academic: 73   Admissions: 78   Financial Aid: 86

Academics

A Catholic university with strengths in business, computer science, and pre-professional programs, DePaul University is the choice of many who crave the prestige and one-on-one interaction of a top private school but don't want to pay for a super-elite institution. DePaul is divided into three campuses. The downtown

> **SURVEY SAYS . . .**
> *Students love Chicago, IL*
> *Dorms are like palaces, Great food on campus*
> *Campus feels safe, Great off-campus food*
> *Ethnic diversity on campus*
> *Students get along with local community*
> *Diverse students interact*
> *Very little beer drinking, Very little hard liquor*

Loop campus caters to business and computer science students, while uptown Lincoln Park is home to the liberal arts, music, education, and DePaul's world-renowned drama department. Students get plenty of bang for their buck at any campus, which explains why most are so sanguine about their school. According to our respondents, "Professors are overflowing with knowledge and always extremely accessible. I would have no qualms about placing my academic experience at DePaul in the same league as our nation's most prestigious universities." Adds another, "Professors are great. They even know you outside of class on a first-name basis. There are 25 or less students in each class." Similarly, the administration "is near flawless, establishing DePaul as a well-oiled machine," according to one political science major.

Life

With its large commuter population, DePaul lacks the community base on which most schools build their extracurricular life. Add the lure of Chicago, one of the nation's top urban centers, and you begin to understand why there's not a whole lot happening on the DePaul campus once classes end. Students don't seem to mind, explaining that "the best part of DePaul is not the school itself, but rather the area surrounding the school. Anything you want to do is a block or two away." Adds another student, "Life in Chicago is great. The city has so much to offer: museums, theaters, and restaurants. In the summertime, going to the lake is the best." DePaul's few residents are housed on the Lincoln Park campus in a young, fun Chicago neighborhood. They supplement their off-campus activities with clubs, internships, and Greek life. Notes one student, "There is a club here for everyone," including ethnic, race-, and gender-based support groups, sports and games clubs, community service organizations, campus government, and hobby groups.

Student Body

Like many Catholic schools, DePaul does a good job of keeping tuition and fees down, and as a result attracts a wider variety of low- and middle-income students, among them many minorities. Students "get along" but don't see much of each other, since "most are commuter students who care little about social interaction within the student body." Among residents, "you have the jocks, the theater majors, and the Greeks," explains one undergraduate. Politically the DePaul campus is sedate: "Life at this school is far detached from important worldly issues," explains one undergrad. "Students are generally more concerned about their clothes or the party they are going to than political or social issues."

ADMISSIONS

Very important factors considered by the admissions committee include: character/personal qualities, secondary school record, volunteer work. *Important factors considered include:* class rank, extracurricular activities, minority status, recommendations, standardized test scores, work experience. *Other factors considered include:* alumni/ae relation, essays, geographical residence, interview, religious affiliation/commitment, state residency, talent/ability. SAT I or ACT required. TOEFL required of all international applicants. High school diploma or GED is required. *High school units required/recommended:* 16 total required; 4 English required, 2 math required, 2 science required, 2 science lab required, 2 social studies required, 4 elective required.

The Inside Word

Applicants to DePaul will find the admissions staff is genuinely committed to helping students. Candidates whose academic qualifications fall below normally acceptable levels are reviewed for other evidence of potential for success. The Latino student presence on campus has begun to increase significantly, due in large part to the university's major commitment to active involvement in the National Hispanic Institute, an organization that works with top Hispanic students from junior high through college.

FINANCIAL AID

Students should submit: FAFSA. Regular filing deadline is May 1. The Princeton Review suggests that all financial aid forms be submitted as soon as possible after January 1. *Need-based scholarships/grants offered:* Pell, SEOG, state scholarships/grants, private scholarships, the school's own gift aid. *Loan aid offered:* Direct Subsidized Stafford, Direct Unsubsidized Stafford, Direct PLUS, Federal Perkins. Federal Work-Study Program available. Institutional employment available. Applicants will be notified of awards on a rolling basis beginning on or about February 15. Off-campus job opportunities are excellent.

FROM THE ADMISSIONS OFFICE

"The nation's largest Catholic university, DePaul University is nationally recognized for its innovative academic programs that embrace a comprehensive 'learn by doing' approach. DePaul has three residential campuses and four commuter campuses in the suburbs. The Lincoln Park campus is located in one of Chicago's most exciting neighborhoods, filled with theaters, cafés, clubs, and shops. It is home to DePaul's College of Liberal Arts & Sciences, the School of Education, The Theater School, and the School of Music. New buildings on the 36-acre campus include residence halls, a science building, a student recreational facility, and the student center, which features a cyber café where students can surf the Web or gather with friends. The Loop campus, located in Chicago's downtown—a world-class center for business, government, law and culture—is home to DePaul's College of Commerce; College of Law; School of Computer Science, Telecommunications, and Information Systems; School for New Learning; and School of Accountancy and Management Information Systems. The Barat campus is located on 30 wooded acres in Lake Forest, Illinois, 35 miles north of downtown Chicago. Home to the interdisciplinary Barat College, it offers the feel of an intimate liberal arts college backed by the reputation and resources of a major urban teaching university."

For even more information on this school, turn to page 344 of the "Stats" section.

DePauw University

101 E. Seminary, Greencastle, IN 46135 • Admissions: 765-658-4006 • Fax: 765-658-4007
Financial Aid: 765-658-4030 • E-mail: admissions@depauw.edu • Website: www.depauw.edu

Ratings

Quality of Life: 82   Academic: 89   Admissions: 86   Financial Aid: 92

Academics

Students come to DePauw seeking a creative yet conservative approach to undergraduate education, presented by a capable and supportive faculty. By and large, most find what they come looking for, especially in the "great school of music," social sciences, media studies, and literature. Chief among DePauw's innovations is the Winter Term, a month-long session during which students can pursue "many outstanding opportu-

> **SURVEY SAYS . . .**
> *Campus easy to get around*
> *Beautiful campus*
> *No one cheats*
> *Great computer facilities*
> *Great library*
> *Student government is unpopular*
> *Very little beer drinking*
> *(Almost) no one listens to college radio*
> *Diversity lacking on campus*

nities to do things you can't do in the classroom." Winter Term allows students to undertake "internships and undergraduate research opportunities that are unparalleled." Dedicated instructors greatly enhance the Winter Term experience. Recounts one undergrad, "Professors are awesome, so accessible. I went on a trip for Winter Term with my Latin professor and had a blast. Professors here are your friends as well as teachers." Students also appreciate the fact that "class sizes are very small, yielding great personal relationships with the professors." The administration, however, is not well regarded, with many students complaining that "administrators just seem concerned with the image DePauw projects to the outside world."

Life

How students feel about social life at DePauw depends primarily on how they feel about the Greek system, which "definitely dominates the social scene." Warns one student, "If you're not into Greek life, don't come here! That's where everything is at here!" For some, "It's fine because it's free beer and a nice place to party. The majority of students stay on campus and hit the four local bars on weekends." Others find it oppressive and divisive. Making matters worse is the lack of alternative activities in hometown Greencastle, "the armpit of the earth. There is NOTHING to do here!" Given the situation, it is unsurprising that drinking "is a major pastime, perpetuated by the exclusive, gender-discriminatory Greek system." "For fun," one independent admits, "we leave town." Not all students paint such a bleak picture, though; writes one, "As an independent, I have no problem staying entertained. DePauw offers a lot of opportunities. Since it is a small school, it is very easy to become involved in all the different activities." Many participate in community service, either "through their church or through the campus ministries center." According to students, "The level of volunteer involvement with the community is amazing."

Student Body

DePauw undergrads describe a Balkanized student body, one "divided ethnically, socially, and financially." Some blame the situation on the Greeks; writes one student, "The Greek system categorizes students into a fixed mold. Often, the Greek students only converse with and befriend students in their house." Others see it as a class issue, noting that "most students here are very upper-crust. They have very definite opinions and stereotypes about our classes, and therefore tend not to mix well with others." To others still, it's racial: "The African Americans hang out with the African Americans, Hispanics with Hispanics, international students with other international students, and everyone else in whatever fraternity or sorority they joined." Politically and socially conservative, students draw such vitriolic epithets as "uncreative" and "pompous" from classmates. Is there an upside? Notes one student, "A lot of people have a 'face' they put on, but once you get to know them, they shed it."

ADMISSIONS

Very important factors considered by the admissions committee include: class rank, essays, secondary school record, standardized test scores. *Important factors considered include:* alumni/ae relation, character/personal qualities, extracurricular activities, interview, minority status, recommendations, talent/ability, volunteer work. *Other factors considered include:* geographical residence, work experience. SAT I or ACT required; SAT I preferred. TOEFL required of all international applicants. High school diploma or GED is required. *High school units required/recommended:* 4 English recommended, 4 math recommended, 4 science recommended, 2 science lab recommended, 4 foreign language recommended, 4 social studies recommended, 3 history recommended, 10 elective recommended.

The Inside Word

Students considering DePauw should not be deceived by the university's high acceptance rate. The impressive freshman profile indicates a high level of self-selection in the applicant pool.

FINANCIAL AID

Students should submit: FAFSA, institution's own financial aid form. Regular filing deadline is February 15. The Princeton Review suggests that all financial aid forms be submitted as soon as possible after January 1. *Need-based scholarships/grants offered:* Pell, SEOG, state scholarships/grants, private scholarships, the school's own gift aid. *Loan aid offered:* FFEL Subsidized Stafford, FFEL Unsubsidized Stafford, FFEL PLUS, Federal Perkins, college/university loans from institutional funds, alternative loans. Federal Work-Study Program available. Institutional employment available. Applicants will be notified of awards on or about March 31. Off-campus job opportunities are fair.

FROM THE ADMISSIONS OFFICE

"DePauw University is nationally recognized for intellectual and experiential challenge that links liberal arts education with life's work, preparing graduates for uncommon professional success, service to others, and personal fulfillment. DePauw graduates count among their ranks a Nobel laureate, a vice president and U.S. Congressman, Pulitzer Prize and Newberry Award authors, and a number of CEOs and humanitarian leaders. Our students demonstrate a love for learning, a willingness to serve others, the reason and judgement to lead, an interest in engaging worlds and cultures unknown to them, the courage to question their assumptions, and a strong commitment to community. Pre-professional and career exploration are encouraged through Winter Term, when more than 700 students pursue their own off-campus internships. This represents more students in experiential learning opportunities than at any other liberal arts college in the nation. Other innovative programs include Honor Scholars, Information Technology Associates Program, Management Fellows, Media Fellows, and Science Research Fellows, affording selected students additional seminar and internship opportunities."

For even more information on this school, turn to page 345 of the "Stats" section.

DORDT COLLEGE

498 Fourth Avenue, Northeast, Sioux Center, IA 51250 • Admissions: 712-722-6080
Fax: 712-722-1967 • E-mail: admissions@dordt.edu • Website: www.dordt.edu

Ratings
Quality of Life: 72   Academic: 76   Admissions: 74   Financial Aid: 85

Academics

Students who choose Dordt College do so most often because they appreciate "the school's emphasis on developing your spiritual life as well as other aspects of your personality. The school really focuses on developing your worldview and on mak-

> **SURVEY SAYS . . .**
> *Classes are small*
> *Students are religious*
> *Diversity lacking on campus*
> *Great off-campus food*
> *Very little beer drinking*

ing faith a part of every facet of life." As one happy undergrad put it, "I love learning at my school. While being able to learn about things from the perspective of Christian profs, they do not force feed. They teach us to think for ourselves and try to discover the truth." The Dordt approach emphasizes the Christian perspective throughout the curriculum; as school literature states, students here are "required to study history, philosophy, and contemporary problems in order to gain insight into how mankind has responded to God's call to service within his creation. Through this requirement, students are challenged to discern the spirits of the age and to work for genuine reformation in culture and society." Students describe a nurturing atmosphere at Dordt; reports one, "The greatest strengths of Dordt are the social atmosphere and overall care for the well-being of the student body by the staff." They also brag that their school "has a great off-campus program in many different countries that is available to a majority of the students."

Life

Sioux Center, hometown to Dordt College, is not exactly a bustling metropolis, students concede. "Life is mostly boring, since the town is tiny," writes one student. Many undergraduates here, however, find plenty of ways to fill their time. "Besides classes and studying," explains one, "the intramural sports are popular, as well as many other opportunities for community service and other interaction with the community." Elaborates another, "My life at school is very social and very involved. I have had a chance to participate in Student Forum, photography club, peer tutoring, as well as psychology club and a job working for security. Fun often involves a group of friends and a great movie, or a trip to Sioux City for a good-sized town." Undergrads tell us that "The school's activity committee does a great job of putting on events and such to give students things to do, such as coffeehouses with live original student music, or a dance, or a movie showing followed by a discussion about the film." Facility expansion means that soon Dordt students will have more extracurricular options; reports one, "The school is already working hard on making this school a better place to be with current work being done on a completely new student center as well as a possible pool and ice rink complex."

Student Body

Dordt undergraduates appreciate their supportive and amiable community. Writes one, "The student body here is the biggest reason that I chose this school. There is a general attitude of friendship and kindness all across campus that one cannot miss even if only here for a one-day visit. Since the school has only about 1,400 students, it is very easy to get to know a great number of people." Students note that "the only area that the school lacks in is racial diversity. It is something that they are working on and showing some improvement in, but they still have a ways to go." Some caution that "students are a bit cliquish, although they seem to be nice on the outside. Getting along is usually not a problem on the classroom/assignments level."

ADMISSIONS

Very important factors considered by the admissions committee include: religious affiliation/commitment, secondary school record, and standardized test scores. *Important factors considered include:* character/personal qualities, class rank, extracurricular activities, talent/ability, and work experience. *Other factors considered include:* alumni/ae relation, geographical residence, and recommendations. SAT I or ACT required, SAT I preferred. TOEFL required of all international applicants. High school diploma or GED is required. *High school units required/recommended:* 17 total required; 21 total recommended; 3 English required, 4 English recommended, 2 math required, 3 math recommended, 2 science required, 2 foreign language required, 2 social studies required, 2 social studies recommended, 2 history recommended, 6 elective required, 6 elective recommended.

The Inside Word

Most Dordt undergrads belong to the Christian Reformed Church, and most find their way to the school through the recommendation of their local churches. Don't let the high admit rate here fool you; Dordt's admission standards are pretty high. Borderline candidates should visit the campus and interview with an admissions officer to plead their case.

FINANCIAL AID

Students should submit: FAFSA and institution's own financial aid form. No deadline for regular filing. The Princeton Review suggests that all financial aid forms be submitted as soon as possible after January 1. *Need-based scholarships/grants offered:* Pell, SEOG, state scholarships/grants, private scholarships, and the school's own gift aid. *Loan aid offered:* FFEL Subsidized Stafford, FFEL Unsubsidized Stafford, FFEL PLUS, Federal Perkins, and college/university loans from institutional funds. Federal Work-Study Program available. Institutional employment available. Applicants will be notified of awards on a rolling basis beginning on or about March 15. Off-campus job opportunities are good.

For even more information on this school, turn to page 346 of the "Stats" section.

DRAKE UNIVERSITY

2507 UNIVERSITY, DES MOINES, IA 50311-4505 • ADMISSIONS: 515-271-3181 • FAX: 515-271-2831
E-MAIL: ADMISSION@DRAKE.EDU • WEBSITE: WWW.CHOOSE.DRAKE.EDU

Ratings

Quality of Life: 79   **Academic:** 82   **Admissions:** 77   **Financial Aid:** 78

Academics

Drake University has an "excellent academic reputation," especially in its pharmacy, business, law, and magazine journalism programs. Pharmacy students brag, "We have excellent pharmacy professors who are truly dedicated to us as students and as future pharmacists. They care about us as people." Pre-profes-

> **SURVEY SAYS . . .**
> *Student publications are popular*
> *Classes are small*
> *Class discussions encouraged*
> *Students are happy*
> *School is well run*
> *(Almost) everyone plays intramural sports*
> *Intercollegiate sports are popular*

sional programs are big here, as are the arts and sciences, particularly music performance. Students also praise the quality of instruction: "The faculty is outstanding. [The professors] are extremely knoweldgeable but also very accessible. All classes are taught by professors (no TAs) and the best professors often teach the introductory courses." Another agrees, "Accessibility to professors and administration is a strong point. It's not unusual for the school president to respond to student e-mails personally." Some students complain that "Some of the facilities are a little outdated. The lecture halls in certain buildings are old and many classrooms have old desks."

Life

At Drake, according to one undergrad, "I've found that there's a group for everyone, and if there isn't, it's possible to start one. . . . Lots of people are involved" in the more than 160 campus organizations. Another student believes that "there really isn't much to do on campus." Drake is constructing a new student union, though, which will include the coffeehouse "Cool Beans" and other amenities. "For social life,"notes one current student, "you go to the frats on Greek Street or there are functions like crush or date parties put on by the Greek houses." But the winter months can be difficult: "There is not a whole lot of things to partake in during the winter because the blistering cold prevents any outside activities. However, some sports are really our savior. Women's basketball is absolutely awesome, and there is a lot of collective excitement involved with the sports" in general. Especially, students agree, for Drake Relays, "which draws some of the top track and field athletes in the country. Although to students, Relays is less about the track events and more about getting smashed." Students describe Drake Relays as "almost an entire week of bad beer, track events, drunk alumni, and crazy streakers. What could be better?" Students give hometown Des Moines middling marks, reporting that it "is not very conducive to the social life of a young adult." Some, however, defend the city: "Des Moines has more than we give it credit for. They have a lot of stuff that I haven't seen that I would like to see before I graduate, like the local comedy club, the museums, the state capitol, etc." Students also "will get together to take a road trip to Chicago, St. Louis, Kansas City, or Minneapolis."

Student Body

At Drake, most students "come from a Caucasian, upper-middle-class, Midwest family. We all pretty much dress the same too. You know, Abercrombie, J.Crew, the Gap." Students point out that the school's "location in Des Moines, Iowa, makes it difficult to attract diverse students. Drake admissions actively recruits minority students, but the northern Midwest (where most Drake students are from) is less diverse than the coasts or the South." What diversity there is here arrives with the "nice representation of international students from all parts of the world." Sixty-five percent of the student body hails from out of state, but many of Drake's homegrown students "are from very small towns in Iowa and grew up on farms and have a totally different perspective on things. For example, they think that Des Moines is a dangerous city."

ADMISSIONS

Very important factors considered by the admissions committee include: secondary school record. *Important factors considered include:* class rank, essays, extracurricular activities, recommendations, and standardized test scores. *Other factors considered include:* character/personal qualities, interview, talent/ability, volunteer work, and work experience. SAT I or ACT required. TOEFL required of all international applicants. High school diploma or GED is required. *High school units required/recommended:* 16 total recommended; 4 English recommended, 3 math recommended, 2 science recommended, 2 foreign language recommended, 4 social studies recommended.

The Inside Word

The admissions process at Drake is competitive but compassionate; admissions officers will scour your entire application in search of justification to admit you. A solid essay, a strong record of extracurricular activities and community service, and a good, enthusiastic on-campus interview all could help offset a less-than-stellar academic record and test scores that don't demonstrate true potential.

FINANCIAL AID

Students should submit: FAFSA. The Princeton Review suggests that all financial aid forms be submitted as soon as possible after January 1. *Need-based scholarships/grants offered:* Pell, SEOG, state scholarships/grants, private scholarships, and the school's own gift aid. *Loan aid offered:* FFEL Subsidized Stafford, FFEL Unsubsidized Stafford, FFEL PLUS, Federal Perkins, college/university loans from institutional funds, and Federal Health Professional Loans. Federal Work-Study Program available. Institutional employment available. Applicants will be notified of awards on a rolling basis beginning on or about March 2. Off-campus job opportunities are excellent.

FROM THE ADMISSIONS OFFICE

"Drake University is a private, coeducational, liberal arts university in Des Moines, Iowa, the state's center for business, publishing, government, and culture. Drake offers its 5,100 students more than 70 undergraduate majors in six colleges and schools—Arts and Sciences, Business and Public Administration, Education, Fine Arts, Journalism and Mass Communication, and Pharmacy and Health Sciences. More than 96 percent of Drake graduates find professional employment or enter graduate schools within six months of earning their degrees. This fall, Drake University is offering a new foreign language initiative and a new Arts and Sciences and Law combined degree program. A new major in ethics will begin fall 2003. The largest residence hall is being renovated into three- and four-person suites, which will be completed by fall 2003. Other projects on campus include Helmick Commons, an outdoor gathering place with a reflecting pond; Cool Beans, a student-developed, -designed, and -run coffeehouse; and a conversion of the campus center into a 'real' student center."

For even more information on this school, turn to page 346 of the "Stats" section.

EARLHAM COLLEGE

801 NATIONAL ROAD WEST, RICHMOND, IN 47374 • ADMISSIONS: 765-983-1600 • FAX: 765-983-1560
FINANCIAL AID: 765-983-1217 • E-MAIL: ADMISSION@EARLHAM.EDU • WEBSITE: WWW.EARLHAM.EDU

Ratings
Quality of Life: 81   **Academic:** 91   **Admissions:** 80   **Financial Aid:** 89

Academics

The undergraduates of Earlham College agree that "the underlying Quaker values are what make this school so great . . . . It has nothing to do with religion and everything to do with community." Indeed, the "community, [and] noncompetitive atmosphere" at Earlham are what students appreciate most. Nurturing this unique environment is "Earlham's principle of according equal respect to all people."

> **SURVEY SAYS . . .**
> *Campus easy to get around*
> *Athletic facilities are great*
> *Political activism is hot*
> *Great library*
> *No one cheats*
> *Diverse students interact*
> *Students don't get along with local community*
> *Students don't like Richmond, IN*
> *Low cost of living*

This code means that "everyone, up to and including the school president, operates on a first-name basis, which really underscores the personal level of interaction." The result is a free flow of ideas and opinions; explains one undergraduate, "We are encouraged to discuss difficult issues, such as issues of diversity of religion, political views, cultural identities, etc., and people don't have to be afraid to disagree." Professors excel in the classroom. The profs here "have a lot of knowledge about and a huge passion for what they are teaching." Some students warn, "Professors in smaller majors here leave occasionally because they are not getting the support they need. It is hard to attract some newer professors because we don't pay our professors here like many competing schools." Also, because "classes are often only offered every other semester or once every two or four years, class conflicts often occur between two classes you deem necessary," cautioned one student, who proceeds to point out the benefits of attending a tiny school: "The small classes and closeness to professors allow for individual planning and independent study opportunities."

Life

Students agree that Earlham is "a place where you make your own fun," primarily because hometown Richmond "offers nothing [socially]. It is a tomb, a void of nothingness." For many, "The fun here comes from those late-night talks that last until the next morning and cost you an entire pack of cigarettes. The intellectual part of this school never stops and is so cool that the fun in daily life is many times derived from being enlightened by one of your peers." Undergrads also report, "The events (speakers, poets, musicians) that are brought to campus are usually pretty good. The movies shown on campus are often worth checking out, too." Clubs and organizations claim a good portion of students' leisure time; writes one undergrad, "The thing that I like about extracurriculars here is that they aren't really 'extra' at all. Most students are involved in activities outside of class that are also somehow related to their academic interests." The party scene here is subdued; "You won't find big frat-like parties here (no frats). Every so often there's a rowdy party, but parties usually suck or are pretty mellow (the farm party and the Hash Run are usually pretty good). Just hanging out with a group of friends is usually your best bet for a 'party.'" Those seeking more excitement suggest road-tripping, noting that "Oxford [Ohio] (Miami University), Indianapolis, and Dayton are not far, so we can go hang out there."

Student Body

The typical Earlham student is "somewhat crunchy (but post-modern intellectual, too), politically left, could be barefoot, could be smoking a cigarette, and is likely to [have] a piercing that is not in the ear." All the while any of them could be members or patrons of the college's "Hugging Club." Reports one student, "The best way to describe an Earlham student might be the absence of showering. It is probably that almighty funk that in its sticky, smelly way binds us together." Students are "politically and environmentally conscious," and "everyone seems to have practically the same views. Just about all of us are left-wing pacifists." Warns one undergrad, "We are not accepting of right-wing views." Adds one of the school's few social and political conservatives, "The school accepts everything that society apparently does not (homosexuals, alternative religions, drug use, alternative medicine, vegans . . .)". Another adds that, "Overall, Earlham is a very tolerant place where students never have to be afraid to disagree." Several students noted that Earlham could benefit from a healthy dose of "non-liberals" to offer some balance.

ADMISSIONS

Very important factors considered by the admissions committee include: character/personal qualities, essays, minority status, recommendations, secondary school record. *Important factors considered include:* extracurricular activities, interview, standardized test scores, talent/ability, volunteer work. *Other factors considered include:* alumni/ae relation, class rank, geographical residence, religious affiliation/commitment, state residency, work experience. SAT I or ACT required; SAT I preferred. TOEFL required of all international applicants. High school diploma or GED is required. *High school units required/recommended:* 15 total required; 4 English required, 3 math required, 4 math recommended, 2 science required, 3 science recommended, 2 foreign language required, 3 foreign language recommended, 1 social studies required, 1 history required, 2 elective required, 8 elective recommended.

The Inside Word

Like most colleges with a Friends affiliation, Earlham has a sincere interest in the person it admits. Essays and interviews carry virtually as much weight as the numbers. Quakers, minorities, legacies, and state residents receive special consideration in the admissions process, but special consideration is what this place is really all about. Earlham deserves a much higher national public awareness level than it has. Hopefully, this entry will help.

FINANCIAL AID

Students should submit: FAFSA, institution's own financial aid form. The Princeton Review suggests that all financial aid forms be submitted as soon as possible after January 1. *Need-based scholarships/grants offered:* Pell, SEOG, state scholarships/grants, private scholarships, the school's own gift aid. *Loan aid offered:* Direct Subsidized Stafford, Direct Unsubsidized Stafford, Direct PLUS, Federal Perkins, college/university loans from institutional funds. Federal Work-Study Program available. Institutional employment available. Applicants will be notified of awards on a rolling basis beginning on or about March 30. Off-campus job opportunities are good.

FROM THE ADMISSIONS OFFICE

"The world is full of people with good intentions. What it needs is people with the intellect, the vision, the skills, and the energy to back up their good intentions. It needs people who are able to make a difference. Although only a few students identify themselves as Quakers, Earlham retains those humanistic values of its tradition that have relevance to students of all backgrounds."

For even more information on this school, turn to page 347 of the "Stats" section.

Eastern Illinois University

600 Lincoln Avenue, Charleston, IL 61920 • Admissions: 217-581-2223 • Fax: 217-581-7060
E-mail: admissns@www.eiu.edu • Website: www.eiu.edu

Ratings
Quality of Life: 74   Academic: 74   Admissions: 70   Financial Aid: 73

Academics

When students at Eastern Illinois University say, "Price is one of the biggest factors at EIU," what they mean is that the university "is very affordable." Especially if you're coming from somewhere in Illinois. In addition to low tuition, the university has set up a

> **SURVEY SAYS . . .**
> *Student publications are popular*
> *Classes are small*
> *School is well run*
> *Students get along with local community*
> *No one cheats*

"textbook rental service," which "helps lower the cost for a semester's worth of books." But students here are quick to point out that low costs do not signify a mediocre education. One recent grad writes, "I can honestly say that I feel it was an honor to be taught by the extraordinary professors" at EIU. In fact, it's the faculty that garners the most glowing commendations from these students. "It is unbelievable how much the faculty and staff care about students," gushes an undergrad, while another nods, "They are teachers first and researchers second." Particularly dedicated students can apply to the honors program, a competitive academic track that offers priority housing, advising, registration, and increased access to grants and scholarships. Eastern Illinois has, however, as many particularly undedicated students as it does dedicated, and this causes some students to recommend that their classmates "work on not being so apathetic." One student suggests that "establishing an honor code and enforcing it at all levels" could force students to get more interested in their studies. As one undergrad put it, "Teachers provide great opportunities, but it is up to the students to take advantage of them."

Life

When you ask them about the social scene at school, EIU students take on a sarcastic tone. Life at EIU "will help you cultivate a more 'laid-back' attitude" writes one euphemistically. Another apparently sadistic schoolmate elaborates, "Fun is something that happens by sheer luck, usually when you see someone fall on ice." Another undergrad is just plain blunt: "There is virtually nil to do in this little hick town [of Charleston]." Well, not exactly nil. The typical college amusements are present, like bars, a bowling alley, a movie theatre, and, um, people falling on ice. And don't forget: this is the Midwest, which means there's plenty of open space for running around. "We have lovely fields across from the recreation center to play golf, Frisbee, and football in." Others spend time Rollerblading, biking, and hiking at nearby Fox Ridge, or lazing around the lake outside of town. For the most part, though, students turn to campus for distractions. "Every day there is something going on on campus," writes a student, offering the examples of "Campus Life Nite, What's Up Week, Greek Week, and Homecoming." Students are also proud to remind us that the university's "student government is one of the most powerful in the nation," with "veto power over tuition and fee increases." When night falls, many sets of student eyes—particularly the ones too young to legally see the inside of a bar—turn their sights to fraternity parties. Under-21ers also make the road trip to Urbana-Champaign, home of the University of Illinois, where "you only need to be 19 to get into bars."

Student Body

Though it's not hard to find students who are "serious about education" in Charleston, many EIU students "seem to simply be here to get out of the house for six years and drink lots of beer." Whether they're bookworms or book-a-phobes, the students at EIU share a friendly midwestern disposition that breeds a congenial campus environment. "Strangers will smile at you as you walk around campus," promises an undergrad. And part of the reason that these students are so good at shooting midwestern smiles is that they've grown up in the heartland. In fact, "most are from the suburbs of Chicago or small towns throughout Illinois." In one student's opinion, "The only really distinct separation [in the student body] may be between the Greeks and the non-Greeks." There's a homogeneity problem at EIU, too; writes one student, "My fellow students are mostly cut from the same mold. We have very little diversity on campus."

ADMISSIONS

Very important factors considered by the admissions committee include: class rank and standardized test scores. *Other factors considered include:* essays and recommendations. SAT I or ACT required. TOEFL required of all international applicants. High school diploma is required and GED is accepted. *High school units required/recommended:* 15 total are required; 4 English required, 3 math required, 3 science required, 3 science lab required, 3 social studies required, 2 elective required.

The Inside Word

Students who don't meet the school's GPA or standardized test score standards can apply to the Review Committee, which takes special talents, personal attributes, and other factors into consideration. Those falling well below standards may be admitted through Gateway, a provisional acceptance program that requires remedial work prior to full admission to the university.

FINANCIAL AID

Students should submit: FAFSA, parent and student federal tax returns, and institutional verification form. No deadline for regular filing. The Princeton Review suggests that all financial aid forms be submitted as soon as possible after January 1. *Need-based scholarships/grants offered:* Pell, SEOG, state scholarships/grants, and the school's own gift aid. *Loan aid offered:* Direct Subsidized Stafford, Direct Unsubsidized Stafford, Direct PLUS, and Federal Perkins. Federal Work-Study Program available. Institutional employment available. Applicants will be notified of awards on a rolling basis beginning on or about May 1. Off-campus job opportunities are fair.

FROM THE ADMISSIONS OFFICE

"Eastern Illinois University consistently shows resilience over the years as academic times change. As the smallest of the public, four-year, residential schools in the state of Illinois, it continues to provide the type of education sought out by students who wish for a personalized education with the wider scope of a public institution. Slightly more than 9,000 undergraduate students attend this multipurpose school located only 180 miles south of Chicago. The smaller size of the school and the accessible campus with professors teaching freshman-level classes are trademarks of this institution. The university prides itself on graduation rates and retention and safely listings that have been documented nationally by *U.S. News & World Report.* Eastern Illinois University (www.eiu.edu) continues to be discovered by students most interested in attending college, remaining in college, and obtaining their goals upon graduation."

For even more information on this school, turn to page 348 of the "Stats" section.

EASTERN MICHIGAN UNIVERSITY

EASTERN MICHIGAN UNIVERSITY, 400 PIERCE HALL, YPSILANTI, MI 48197 • ADMISSIONS: 734-487-3060
FAX: 734-487-1484 • E-MAIL: ADMISSIONS@EMICH.EDU • WEBSITE: WWW.EMICH.EDU

Ratings

Quality of Life: 77   **Academic:** 75   **Admissions:** 71   **Financial Aid:** 65

Academics

Students at Eastern Michigan University appreciate "the close-knit community and a faculty that cares" and cite the "location, affordability, [and] laid-back attitude," as reasons they chose EMU. The most popular majors here are

> **SURVEY SAYS . . .**
> *Frats and sororities dominate social scene*
> *Classes are small*
> *No one cheats*
> *Lots of beer drinking*

psychology, marketing, and management, but EMU is also known as a "teacher school," churning out education majors from an "excellent" program. Very few classes are taught by teaching assistants, and "professors overall are qualified [and] put the liberal in liberal arts." Some students complain that academics "should be more challenging." Putting it another way, and with a little more perspective, a recent alum believes that classes "weren't too hard," but "they weren't too easy," either. Maybe it's EMU's commitment to making sure that all students, even those not as academically gifted as others, enjoy some success. The administration gets mixed reviews; many undergrads feel that the people in charge don't "listen to the needs of the students and the faculty," while others report that the "school's administration means well and performs well despite a lack of strong reputation." Professors have gone on strike for better pay and more benefits, and students sympathize with their cause. "With a new president in place for just over 12 months, things are running reasonably well," notes one undergrad; not so, say others who worry he's spending too much money on the non-essentials, like his new home, and not on things that directly affect them, like student parking.

Life

About two-thirds of EMU students are commuters. It doesn't make for the development of a very strong sense of a campus community when, according to one student, "you go to class and get in your car and go home." Add to this the fact that EMU is a "suitcase school," in that of the students who do live on campus—about one quarter of undergraduates—most "go home on weekends or visit friends at other campuses." This can make for a dull weekend, but, nevertheless, one student claims, "We are definitely a party school. On any given Thursday to Sunday, you can walk around the neighborhoods and find at least 6 to 10 jumping house parties, not including the countless smaller parties going on in the numerous apartment complexes." Aside from partying, a favorite activity is day-tripping (or night-tripping) to nearby Ann Arbor (home to the University of Michigan) or Detroit. One enthusiastic student claims that "everything is close to the campus." That is, of course, "as long as you have a car." Those lacking vehicles stay in and watch movies when they get free time. When it comes to on-campus accommodations, we're not talking Hyatt. The dorms, students say, could use a face-lift.

Student Body

Students at EMU get along well and appreciate each other's differences; one undergraduate enthuses, "We are diverse, interesting, smart, creative, fun people living in the shadow of Ann Arbor." Another agrees, "We really don't have one set type of person on campus . . . . It is a cool experience to walk down the sidewalk and hear four different languages being spoken." Glass-half-empty types note, however, that the student body is "almost all Caucasian and African American." Also, "there is a big problem with de facto segregation in the residence halls, programming, and other campus facilities." Nontraditional students feel comfortable on campus; they don't think that their age marginalizes them at all.

ADMISSIONS

Very important factors considered by the admissions committee include: secondary school record and standardized test scores. *Other factors considered include:* character/personal qualities, essays, extracurricular activities, interview, and recommendations. SAT I or ACT required, ACT preferred. TOEFL required of all international applicants. High school diploma or GED is required. *High school units required/recommended:* 16 total recommended; 4 English recommended, 3 math recommended, 3 science recommended, 1 science lab recommended, 1 foreign language recommended, 2 social studies recommended, 1 history recommended.

The Inside Word

Nothing fancy about applying to this big school; just send them your test scores and your high school transcript and wait for the admissions office to crunch the numbers. Recent tuition increases have scared some applicants off, making EMU an easier admit than it has been in recent years.

FINANCIAL AID

Students should submit: FAFSA. No deadline for regular filing. The Princeton Review suggests that all financial aid forms be submitted as soon as possible after January 1. *Need-based scholarships/grants offered:* Pell, SEOG, state scholarships/grants, private scholarships, the school's own gift aid, and Nursing Disadvantaged Student Grant. *Loan aid offered:* FFEL Subsidized Stafford, FFEL Unsubsidized Stafford, FFEL PLUS, Federal Perkins, state loans, and college/university loans from institutional funds. Federal Work-Study Program available. Institutional employment available. Applicants will be notified of awards on a rolling basis beginning on or about March 1. Off-campus job opportunities are excellent.

For even more information on this school, turn to page 348 of the "Stats" section.

EDGEWOOD COLLEGE

1000 EDGEWOOD COLLEGE DRIVE, MADISON, WI 53711-1997 • ADMISSIONS: 608-663-2294
FAX: 608-663-3291 • E-MAIL: ADMISSIONS@EDGEWOOD.EDU • WEBSITE: WWW.EDGEWOOD.EDU

Ratings
Quality of Life: 85   Academic: 72   Admissions: 71   Financial Aid: 79

Academics

Less than one mile south of the University of Wisconsin's behemoth flagship campus in the city of Madison sits Edgewood College, a school that in most areas is the antithesis of its better-known neigh-

SURVEY SAYS . . .
*School is well run, Classes are small
Diverse students interact, Students are religious
Students love Madison*

bor. When compared to UWM, Edgewood, a Dominican Catholic school, may come up short when it comes to facilities, world-famous faculty, athletic programs, and wild parties, but it just as certainly outshines the state university in the personal touches it can offer. As one student explains, "Edgewood is a small school dedicated to giving students an excellent, well-rounded education. I think that it's most attractive characteristic is how personable this school is." Students here tell us that they "like being known around campus and knowing almost everyone else who is here. It is easier to learn in a smaller class size setting." Edgewood's faculty, undergrads agree, "are very easy to get a hold of. They are always very willing to go the extra mile to encourage and simplify learning." Administrators "are really good, too. They are easy to talk to and are very understanding." Like many small schools, Edgewood offers only "a limited number of classes to choose from each semester, [which] can be very frustrating." A "good education program" is the highlight of the largely pre-professional offerings here; nursing and business administration are also popular among undergrads.

Life

Students tell us that "Edgewood is laid back," especially on weekends when much of the school's small student body packs up and heads for home. Complains one undergrad, "I try not to spend any time that I don't have to on campus because it's so boring. We don't have a lot of interesting things going on and our school is definitely classified as a 'weekend school,' which means everyone goes home on the weekends so there is no campus life. Our turnouts at sports suck, too." Fortunately, students need not depend on Edgewood for social and entertainment opportunities because "Living in Madison gives students a great range of things to do from going to the bars, listening to bands, sporting events, and going to great restaurants." Students appreciate that the Edgewood campus is "a beautiful, quiet area in a large city" that is "close to parks and trails. Being right on a lake makes the students appreciate the beauty of nature." Students also note that "there's University of Wisconsin—Madison practically across the street, so we have lots of things to do, but I don't know if students in UW welcome us."

Student Body

Edgewood undergrads report that "since Edgewood is a fairly small campus, everyone here feels connected to each other in some way. It's like a small family." Like many small schools, the Edgewood community is "cliquey. . . . The basketball players hang out with the basketball players and so on." In the classroom, "students were very friendly and open-minded. People here are always telling each other 'good job,' being polite, and are always willing to help another student out." A sizeable portion of the student body is "from small towns in Wisconsin, and [they] don't know well about minorities, so they are a little scared to talk with people outside their races." The predominantly female student body is active in community service organizations such as Habitat for Humanity and Circle K.

ADMISSIONS

Very important factors considered by the admissions committee include: class rank, secondary school record, and standardized test scores. *Important factors considered include:* interview and talent/ability. *Other factors considered include:* alumni/ae relation, character/personal qualities, essays, extracurricular activities, geographical residence, recommendations, and volunteer work. SAT I or ACT required, ACT preferred. TOEFL required of all international applicants. High school diploma or GED is required. *High school units required/recommended:* 16 total required; 4 English recommended, 3 math recommended, 3 science recommended, 2 science lab recommended, 2 foreign language recommended, 2 social studies recommended, 2 history recommended.

The Inside Word

Edgewood makes most admissions decisions based on high school curriculum, GPA, and standardized test scores. The school requests letters of recommendation, a personal essay, and an on-campus interview only from borderline candidates. If you're asked for one or all of these, know that they will be the deciding factor in your case and proceed accordingly.

FINANCIAL AID

Students should submit: FAFSA and institution's own financial aid form. No deadline for regular filing. The Princeton Review suggests that all financial aid forms be submitted as soon as possible after January 1. *Need-based scholarships/grants offered:* SEOG, state scholarships/grants, private scholarships, and the school's own gift aid. *Loan aid offered:* FFEL Subsidized Stafford, FFEL Unsubsidized Stafford, FFEL PLUS, Federal Perkins, and college/university loans from institutional funds. Federal Work-Study Program available. Institutional employment available. Applicants will be notified of awards on or about March 15. Off-campus job opportunities are good.

FROM THE ADMISSIONS OFFICE

"As Madison's only independent liberal arts college, Edgewood College welcomes students who seek a charming campus and a great place to live. Edgewood College is only minutes away from Madison's downtown area, located on the shores of beautiful Lake Wingra.

"Edgewood is a Catholic college founded on the 900-year-old Dominican tradition of educating through study, contemplation, and action. The curriculum is based on the belief that each student is a unique individual who as a member of the global community shares a responsibility for that community. Edgewood's tradition fosters a values-based education needed for lifelong personal and professional development. A liberal arts education provides students with a background in applicable skills—communication, critical thinking, problem solving, and appreciation for culture and the arts—as well as a better understanding of the world around us. In classes and in individual conversations with professors, students will participate in the teaching and learning process that characterizes education at Edgewood.

"At the heart of campus is the Sonderegger Science Center, the only place in the United States that holds kindergarten through undergraduate education in the same building. Other campus highlights include a theatre, a chapel, the Oscar Rennebohm Library, a biological research station, several resident halls and apartments, and the Edgedome athletic facility. The Henry Predolin Humanities Center includes a full-service student center and a 265-seat amphitheater.

"Faculty members are devoted teachers and advisors who welcome questions and help students sort through academic and professional choices. They serve as an important link themselves while building a resume of experience."

For even more information on this school, turn to page 349 of the "Stats" section.

FRIENDS UNIVERSITY

2100 UNIVERSITY STREET, WICHITA, KS 67213 • ADMISSIONS: 316-295-5100 • FAX: 316-295-5101
E-MAIL: LEARN@FRIENDS.EDU • WEBSITE: WWW.FRIENDS.EDU

Ratings
Quality of Life: 75   **Academic:** 79   **Admissions:** 78   **Financial Aid:** 69

Academics

Small classes and a focus on Christian-based liberal arts education (the school is affiliated with the Quakers) are staples of the Friends University experience. Apropos to the school's affiliation, the word "friend" and many of its derivations also seem to be staples in students' descriptions of their experience here. Writes one student, "At Friends we truly have a

SURVEY SAYS . . .
Students are religious
Very little beer drinking
No one plays intramural sports
Students don't get along with local community
No one watches intercollegiate sports
Very little hard liquor
Theater is unpopular
Students love Wichita

'friendly' atmosphere. Everyone really shows that they care about you and whether or not you succeed. Professors often will check on us if we have not made it to class. They want to see us in class, and succeeding." Agrees another, "I like my school because of the small classes and very personal environment it creates between you and your teachers. I know my teachers and they know me as well." Similarly, administrators "are really friendly. The president and his cabinet are good people and seem to be out for the good of the university." Students don't hold it against the administration that things don't always run smoothly here; as one undergrad told us, "The 'business' part of the school has room to improve. The people in those positions are nice, but financial aid has messed up my files every year, for four years." Student advising, apparently, is very well regarded, as "your advisor will help you with anything, from scholarships to grad school to helping you cope with family problems." The other Friends campuses—in Topeka and Mission, Kansas, and Independence, Missouri—primarily serve the school's large continuing education population.

Life

"Community life standards are strict" at Friends University, "so it is not by any means a party school." Some students party; according to those who completed our survey, "most of the partying is done by athletes or their friends. Anyone can come. . . . Most people are very friendly, whether you want to party or not. If you don't, there's no prejudice against it. People think it's cool if you don't drink." Writes one teetotaler, "I personally have never drunk or smoked. I still go to parties; there's usually one or more somewhere each weekend. Everyone's pretty cool. They respect those who are strong in their beliefs and who choose not to drink. Overall, it's a great bunch of people to hang out with and just have fun, no matter what the activity or occasion!" Among the school's many religious students, "student ministries are big," as are the student clubs and organizations that fuel much of extracurricular life here. Students wish the dorms and physical plant were in better shape; as one told us, "Living on campus is fun, but the administrative side that's in charge has problems. In the four years I've been here, they have yet to fix the plumbing in the dorms, update the disgusting laundry facilities, etc. Though student government has been trying to push lowering the speed bumps in the business school parking lot for two years, nothing has been done. It's a great school, with great aspects. . . . It's just not well run."

Student Body

The students of Friends University are "a pretty diverse group, culture-wise. We have jocks (albeit most of our teams aren't exactly winning at this point in time!), the musicians, the singers, the psych people, the foreign language people, the computer-techno gurus, the scientists, and the zoo science people." Ethnic and geographic diversity is harder to come by here: as one student told us, "My fellow students are mostly from the Midwest. They go through life with a much different mind set than I do, being from the Northeast." Several of our survey respondents agreed that "some students are really wonderful and some are okay and others really stink, metaphorically speaking. A lot of the guys are a bunch of jerks, though not all of them. some of the girls are real gossipers, though not all. I think this is normal. Sometimes Friends resembles a high school a bit too much, with all of its cliques."

ADMISSIONS

Very important factors considered by the admissions committee include: secondary school record and standardized test scores. *Important factors considered include:* interview and recommendations. *Other factors considered include:* alumni/ae relation, extracurricular activities, minority status, religious affiliation/commitment, and talent/ability. SAT I or ACT required, ACT preferred. TOEFL required of all international applicants. High school diploma is required and GED is accepted. *High school units required/recommended:* 3 math recommended, 3 science recommended.

The Inside Word

Admissions officers will be looking to see whether you are a "good fit" with the Friends community. Students who deeply value spiritual life and who spurn alcohol, drugs, and tobacco are the best fit. Academically, you're in if the product of your composite ACT and your GPA exceeds 44.

FINANCIAL AID

Students should submit: FAFSA and institution's own financial aid form. The Princeton Review suggests that all financial aid forms be submitted as soon as possible after January 1. *Need-based scholarships/grants offered:* Pell, SEOG, and private scholarships. *Loan aid offered:* Direct Subsidized Stafford, Direct Unsubsidized Stafford, Direct PLUS, and Federal Perkins. Federal Work-Study Program available. Institutional employment available. Off-campus job opportunities are excellent.

For even more information on this school, turn to page 349 of the "Stats" section.

GOSHEN COLLEGE

1700 SOUTH MAIN STREET, GOSHEN, IN 46526-4794 • ADMISSIONS: 574-535-7535 • FAX: 574-535-7609
E-MAIL: ADMISSIONS@GOSHEN.EDU • WEBSITE: WWW.GOSHEN.EDU.

Ratings
Quality of Life: 80   Academic: 78   Admissions: 74   Financial Aid: 78

Academics

Students at tiny Goshen College dub their school "the place where you can get [someone with] a PhD [as] a personal tutor." Indeed, this Mennonite college boasts many of the resources, opportunities, and quality faculty available at much

SURVEY SAYS . . .
School is well run, Classes are small
Students are religious, Lousy food on campus
Instructors are good teachers
Students get along with local community

larger schools to a little more than 1,000 students. Undergrads report that "an ambitious student can experience as much as he or she wants. You can conduct the college orchestra, be the editor-in-chief of the newspaper, or edit a professor's manuscript." Considering its religious affiliations, its not surprising that the "Bible/Religion/Philosophy Department is strong." Students report, however, that Goshen stands out in its commitment to "student involvement in issues they learn about in class," including a required "international education program known as Study Service Term (SST)," as well as the availability of majors such as "Peace, Justice, and Conflict Studies." Students warn that "Goshen has a lot of general education requirements," which "most students don't want to take and most professors don't want to teach." In addition, many complain that "the administration has to . . . enact policies that are in line with the Mennonite Church, which makes [it] and its policies really conservative and oppressive." For example, Goshen claims "the third largest population for gays and lesbians in the state of Indiana," yet "the administration will not recognize the LGBT club on campus."

Life

"Life at Goshen College centers around campus," where students "hang out in each other's rooms and talk," "spend a lot of time discussing current political and social issues," "play sports," or head out to "theatre productions, music concerts, all-campus movies, sit-ins, open discussions, ultimate Frisbee games, [and] hymn sings." Though you won't catch many Goshen undergrads chasing dawn at urban nightclubs, most say that "life at Goshen can be great, depending on what kind of person you are." The pervasive feeling among Goshen students is that they are participating in "a big slumber party that never ends." Nestled within the Indiana cornfields, undergrads are the first to admit that "there isn't much to do in Goshen," as even the closest movie theatre is "about 45 minutes away." Students make the most of their small town, however, telling us that "many people go into town and eat at one of the few restaurants that is open late," or kick it with a book at "Electric Brew, a great local coffee shop."

Student Body

Running the gamut from "tree-hugging activists to conservative jocks," many students argue that "the greatest thing about Goshen College is the people." Students confide that divergent opinions are the roots of many "good conversations," but also cause "a lot of tension on our campus" between "those who classify themselves as liberal and those who call themselves conservative," "Mennonites and non-Mennonites," as well as "sports players and nonsports players." This may make for a slightly volatile, us-versus-them atmosphere, but neither side is by any means exclusive. One student reassures, "If a new person shows up at a party or a dorm room, they are warmly accepted," while another reveals, "Cliques are a factor, but they are usually at least somewhat permeable." Though students admit that Goshen "could use more ethnic diversity," they "are honestly concerned about gender and ethnic/racial discrimination." On that note, many Goshen students "are politically active and get involved in a number of causes," including a group of students "working to make the campus grounds chemical free."

ADMISSIONS

Very important factors considered by the admissions committee include: recommendations, secondary school record, and standardized test scores. *Important factors considered include:* character/personal qualities, class rank, and interview. *Other factors considered include:* alumni/ae relation, extracurricular activities, talent/ability, volunteer work, and work experience. SAT I or ACT required, SAT I preferred. TOEFL required of all international applicants. High school diploma or GED is required. *High school units required/recommended:* 12 total required; 16 total recommended; 4 English required, 2 math required, 3 math recommended, 2 science required, 3 science recommended, 2 foreign language required, 2 social studies required, 2 social studies recommended, 2 history required.

The Inside Word

Goshen admissions officers consider the entire application package, including extracurricular commitments, recommendations, and other indicators of personal promise. The school draws an academically solid applicant pool, though, and admissions are fairly competitive. Homeschooled candidates should provide GED scores, as well as a portfolio of academic papers representing work from grades 9 through 12.

FINANCIAL AID

Students should submit: FAFSA, institution's own financial aid form, state aid form, noncustodial (divorced/separated) parent's statement, and business/farm supplement. No deadline for regular filing. The Princeton Review suggests that all financial aid forms be submitted as soon as possible after January 1. *Need-based scholarships/grants offered:* Pell, SEOG, state scholarships/grants, private scholarships, and the school's own gift aid. *Loan aid offered:* Direct Subsidized Stafford, Direct Unsubsidized Stafford, Direct PLUS, Federal Perkins, Federal Nursing, and college/university loans from institutional funds. Federal Work-Study Program available. Institutional employment available. Applicants will be notified of awards on a rolling basis beginning on or about March 15. Off-campus job opportunities are excellent.

FROM THE ADMISSIONS OFFICE

"Goshen College is nationally recognized for integrating excellence in scholarship and active Christian faith and peacemaking on campus and throughout the world. We follow the example of Christ, serving others with passion, sensitivity, skill, integrity, and compassion. Our knowledgeable, caring faculty help you merge your mission in life with God's mission on Earth, investing your energy in meeting the needs of a changing world. Goshen College offers 70 programs of study and one of the country's most innovative study abroad programs, Study-Service Term, a semester-long program that is part of the college's emphasis on the education of global citizens. As you might expect for a school this size, the campus truly feels like a community; what you might not expect is the diversity of backgrounds, experiences, and cultures and the level of dialogue that takes place. The college's facilities include a new $24 million music facility with a concert hall designed as one of the finest acoustic settings in the Midwest. The Recreation-Fitness Center features basketball and volleyball courts, an indoor track, swimming pool, weight room, hot tub, racquetball courts and more. With an outdoor track and field facility, Goshen College's athletic complex is among the best in its conference. Goshen College's costs are lower than other schools of our type and size, and 90 percent of full-time students receive some form of financial assistance. Apply for admission to Goshen Collegeby February 15 to receive priority consideration for financial aid and scholarships."

For even more information on this school, turn to page 350 of the "Stats" section.

GRACE COLLEGE AND SEMINARY

200 Seminary Drive, Winona Lake, IN 46590 • Admissions: 800-544-7223 • Fax: 219-372-5120
E-mail: enroll@grace.edu • Website: www.grace.edu

Ratings
Quality of Life: 78   **Academic:** 80   **Admissions:** 73   **Financial Aid:** 77

Academics

Grace College offers a curriculum that incorporates "biblical values" with the aim of "strengthening character, sharpening compe-tence, and preparing [students] for service." Ask a Grace student what the greatest aspect of her school is and chances are she'll

> **SURVEY SAYS . . .**
> *Students are religious*
> *Diversity lacking on campus*
> *Classes are small*
> *Profs teach upper levels*
> *Student publications are popular*

mention straightaway the "way underpaid" professors, "men and women of God, want to see us as students become more like Him in our chosen fields." Within "small classes" that "make learning much easier," professors who "know so much I sometimes feel like bowing" form close, personal relationships with their students. This connection begins with the faculty's infectious enthusiasm; according to most it's "enjoyable to learn from professors [who] love what they're teaching." About the worst thing students have to say about their professors is that "though they want to come off as strict, they are softies underneath!" The "nasty" gener-al education classes "aren't so good," but courses in the lauded "education department, on the other hand," are "excellent." The biblical studies department also receives particular praise. If students ever feel overwhelmed by academic requirements, they can visit the Student Academic Counseling Center, which offers free tutoring for all of its students in all subjects. Unlike at many large universities, students here "feel taken care of" by the "well-organized" administration, though they also believe Grace could stand some of the effects of modernization, like an update to the campus phone system and online class registration. By and large, though, most undergraduates "wouldn't trade [their] academic experience or Grace's staff for Harvard or Yale!"

Life

According to some undergraduates, "Grace is surrounded by [the town of] Winona Lake, which has absolutely nothing to do or anywhere to go." So things do get to be "very boring at times." Fortunately there's always Fort Wayne, Indiana, which is only a half hour away by car. And, of course, there is always the Wal-Mart, an increasingly popular late-night destina-tion of college students studying in the American hinterlands—where, as one student noted, "you can always go and find someone you know." Fun for Grace students means getting off campus: in addition to water recreation at "Winona Lake, roller skating, bowling, Chicago, Indie, and Notre Dame are less then an three hours away." Strict administrative "rules (cur-few, dress code, etc.)" governing student life (though, according to students, they recently "took away the no-dancing rule") means that students rely heavily on the simple joys of inter-acting with their peers: "hanging out at friends' houses or going out to movies or bowling for fun." Athletic facilities are a big source of complaint here because the school has yet to build its own gym, forcing students to rely on the local YMCA for their bodysculpting needs. Also, as Grace expands its enrollment, students are beginning to complain of some growing pains, including a dearth of parking space.

Student Body

One student sums up how most feel about the agape vibe that permeates the student body: "I love the love that is shown on this campus." Comments another, "The other students here are like my family away from home." "We are open and honest with each other." Faith and religion at Grace are not just ideas, but something that students share and struggle with together. As one student put it, "It's typical to find a bunch of us hanging out discussing deep theological stuff and trying to apply our beliefs to our everyday lives." About 80 percent of the student body is white, but few students comment one way or the other about any diversity issues at Grace.

ADMISSIONS

Very important factors considered by the admissions committee include: character/personal qualities, class rank, recommendations, religious affiliation/commitment, and secondary school record. *Important factors considered include:* extracurricular activities, minority status, standardized test scores, and talent/ability. *Other factors considered include:* essays, interview, and volunteer work. SAT I or ACT required. TOEFL required of all international applicants. High school diploma or GED is required. *High school units required/recommended:* 14 total recommended; 4 English recommended, 2 math recommended, 2 science recommended, 1 science lab recommended, 2 foreign language recommended, 2 social studies recommended, 1 history recommended.

The Inside Word

Several annual increases in the number of freshman slots—the size of the student body has increased by nearly 10 percent in the last two years—should improve candidates' chances of getting into Grace College. Admissions officers will pay very close attention to indicators of faith and good character (such as community service and church involvement).

FINANCIAL AID

Students should submit: FAFSA. No deadline for regular filing. The Princeton Review suggests that all financial aid forms be submitted as soon as possible after January 1. *Need-based scholarships/grants offered:* Pell, SEOG, state scholarships/grants, private scholarships, and the school's own gift aid. *Loan aid offered:* FFEL Subsidized Stafford, FFEL Unsubsidized Stafford, FFEL PLUS, and Federal Perkins. Federal Work-Study Program available. Institutional employment available. Off-campus job opportunities are excellent.

For even more information on this school, turn to page 350 of the "Stats" section.

GRAND VALLEY STATE UNIVERSITY

1 CAMPUS DRIVE, ALLENDALE, MI 49401 • ADMISSIONS: 800-748-0246 • FAX: 616-895-2000
E-MAIL: GO2GVSU@GVSU.EDU • WEBSITE: WWW.GVSU.EDU

Ratings
Quality of Life: 71   Academic: 76   Admissions: 68   Financial Aid: 72

Academics

Twenty minutes west of Grand Rapids, Michigan, you'll find the "beautiful campus" of Allendale, one of Grand Valley State University's award-winning three campuses and three regional canters. "The quality of education at GVSU is skyrocketing," boasts a senior. The classroom pedagogy is

> **SURVEY SAYS . . .**
> *School is well run, Classes are small*
> *(Almost) everyone plays intramural sports*
> *Students get along with local community*
> *Lots of beer drinking*
> *Student publications are popular*
> *Intercollegiate sports are popular*

evolving from "memorizing" to "discussion and thinking," and there's also a "strong focus on writing throughout the curriculum regardless of major." Students are pleased to report that no classes are taught by TAs and "professors are truly concerned with the degree to which students are learning," especially in the Honors College, which provides "a much more thought-provoking experience than just the basic classes." But it's not all cheers at GVSU. Students say that many professors and administrators seem to live in what one student dubs "the West Michigan Bubble. . . . Many of them are unaware that there is life outside of GVSU socially, politically, professionally, and academically." More to the point, a student describes a recent hot topic within GVSU's community: "We fought for Domestic Partnership Benefits"—or benefits to include same-sex couples—but were not granted them by the board of trustees. As this suggests, western Michigan's conservatism often invades the classroom and university policies. "The school is nonchurch affiliated, but runs like it's x'ian [or Christian] affiliated," says a student.

Life

Allendale is a typical suburban Michigan community. "It is very small and quiet, and has little to no activities of interest to college students," one student reports. So what do people do here? One student reports, frankly, "If students stay in Allendale, they drink and have parties." If students don't stay in Allendale, they often head east, to Grand Rapids. One GR enthusiast raves, "Grand Rapids has so much to offer, like fine dining, tons of clubs, [and] karaoke places" while others mention the "great local music scene" and the Van Andel Arena, which frequently hosts "sporting events, concerts, and plays." And thanks to the new GVSU campus in Grand Rapids, there's a free bus service available to students that shuttles regularly from Allendale to the "downtown campus and to the mall on the weekend." Students almost unanimously favor Grand Rapids over Allendale, but let's not discard campus life altogether, as an upperclassman notes an "increase in the amount of students involved in organizations . . . [compared to] when I arrived five years ago." One student enjoys passing the time at Grand Haven on Lake Michigan: after "a bit to eat at Pronto Pups [and] some ice cream at the Peddler," watching the sunset is "a great way to relieve your college stress and to unwind after a long day."

Student Body

Only four percent of Grand Valley's undergrads come from out of state, so it shouldn't be surprising that GVSU's student body reflects the local demographic make-up. Along these lines, students tend to be "very religious"—a fact that accounts for the strong campus ministry that many in "the Laker family" (the GVSU community) applaud. Sometimes the traditional (and, perhaps, limited) views of the students translate to very evident "divisions based on class, race, and gender." But there are 16,000-plus undergrads here, so look around and you'll find "completely different views" popping up. "Friendly" is a word that many students use to describe their classmates.

ADMISSIONS

Very important factors considered by the admissions committee include: class rank, secondary school record, and standardized test scores. *Other factors considered include:* essays, extracurricular activities, interview, minority status, recommendations, state residency, talent/ability, volunteer work, and work experience. SAT I or ACT required, ACT preferred. TOEFL required of all international applicants. High school diploma is required and GED is accepted. *High school units required/recommended:* 20 total are required; 4 English required, 3 math required, 4 math recommended, 3 science required, 2 foreign language recommended, 3 social studies required, 7 elective required.

The Inside Word

Like most large state universities, GVSU looks solely at high school curriculum, GPA, and standardized test scores. The school reviews applications on a rolling basis. Apply early, before space in the incoming class grows tight.

FINANCIAL AID

Students should submit: FAFSA. Regular filing deadline is February 15. The Princeton Review suggests that all financial aid forms be submitted as soon as possible after January 1. *Need-based scholarships/grants offered:* Pell, SEOG, state scholarships/grants, private scholarships, the school's own gift aid, and Federal Nursing. *Loan aid offered:* Direct Subsidized Stafford, Direct Unsubsidized Stafford, Direct PLUS, Federal Perkins, Federal Nursing, state, and college/university loans from institutional funds. Federal Work-Study Program available. Institutional employment available. Applicants will be notified of awards on a rolling basis. Off-campus job opportunities are good.

FROM THE ADMISSIONS OFFICE

"Grand Valley State University's main campus, located in Allendale, Michigan, features modern housing and a serene suburban setting just 15 minutes from the second largest city in Michigan. Grand Valley has campuses in Allendale, Grand Rapids, and Holland and centers established in cooperation with community colleges in Muskegon, Petoskey, and Traverse City. Our downtown campus in Grand Rapids offers a distinctive urban environment with unique social, employment, internship, and community outreach opportunities.

"From international corporations and small businesses to elite graduate schools, Grand Valley has established a reputation for preparing students to excel in every field. Our focus on individual student achievement is at the heart of everything we do, creating unique learning opportunities that attract students from across the country and around the world.

"Grand Valley offers more than 200 areas of study and many diverse program options. With our challenging academic programs and liberal arts philosophy, we emphasize critical thinking, effective communications, and creative problem solving. Our students are prepared to meet new challenges with confidence and skill. Faculty choose to come to Grand Valley from some of the country's leading institutions because we encourage them to do what they do best—teach. Professors collaborate with students on innovative research projects, creating opportunities more commonly associated with master's degree programs.

"Graduates benefit from Grand Valley's reputation for preparing students to excel in leadership positions. Employers throughout the region and the country recognize the value of a Grand Valley education.

"We invite you to visit the campus for a first-hand look at Grand Valley State University."

For even more information on this school, turn to page 351 of the "Stats" section.

GRINNELL COLLEGE

GRINNELL, IA 50112-1690 • ADMISSIONS: 800-247-0113 • FAX: 641-269-4800
FINANCIAL AID: 515-269-3250 • E-MAIL: ASKGRIN@GRINNELL.EDU • WEBSITE: WWW.GRINNELL.EDU

Ratings
Quality of Life: 82   **Academic:** 94   **Admissions:** 92   **Financial Aid:** 94

Academics

Rural Iowa's Grinnell College, true to its long-held reputation, remains "a rigorous liberal arts institution in a somewhat remote location, offering a total immersion in campus life and academia." Students here praise faculty, reporting that profs are "top-notch; the number of incredible teachers is staggering, and they are all readily available and in fact eager to assist students outside of class. They are all extremely intelligent and take an active interest in their students' lives." Students also caution that the workload is "intense." Recently, however, a mood of uneasiness has descended on students, caused by the direction in which they perceive Grinnell is headed. Explains one student, "The goal seems to be to [become] 'more competitive' with our 'peer institutions,' which translates to charging students a little more every year for a little less, and putting the difference into long-term projects, such as construction." Students dislike the accompanying hassles (e.g., the attendant noise of building).

> **SURVEY SAYS . . .**
> *Campus easy to get around*
> *Campus feels safe*
> *Lab facilities are great*
> *Lots of beer drinking*
> *Political activism is hot*
> *Great library*
> *Students are happy*
> *No one cheats*
> *Campus is beautiful*
> *Great computer facilities*

Life

Grinnell, students agree, is "in the middle of nowhere in Iowa. Which is good because everyone really wants to be at the school because they like it, not because they spent their entire time in high school daydreaming about the utopian lifestyle of a college in a small farm town in Iowa." The location naturally means that "we're sometimes short on things to go out and do" and that students must "make our own fun." Fortunately, the Grinnell campus is a fairly active one. "Throughout the week, the campus attempts to keep us entertained with music/theatre events, movies, multicultural events, and colloquia," students report. When the weekend rolls around, there are "parties ranging from about four or five people in a dorm room to hundreds of people in a lounge or the Harris Center." There is no Greek system here, so "parties are almost always open to anyone who happens to walk by, and at such a small school that really helps build a sense of community." Students have mixed feelings about their hometown of Grinnell; some describe it as "small and cozy and a great place to 'escape to' within a ten-minute walk. There's a fabulous coffee shop downtown, Saint's Rest, as well as a one-screen movie theater and a bowling alley." Life here "is more enjoyable if you have a car," since "Iowa City and Des Moines are only 45 minutes to an hour away."

Student Body

"In one of the publications on campus, both prospective students and seniors were asked how popular they thought the average Grinnell student was in high school, on a scale of one to ten," reports one Grinnell undergrad. "Both agreed on the number 4." Conclusion: "Most of the students at Grinnell are the people who did not fit into a single social group in high school." Nearly all feel they have found a comfortable home at Grinnell although more than a few admit to being somewhat cowed by their peers. Writes one, "One thing I will say about the students here is that almost everyone is brilliant. I was at the top of my class in high school and was quickly humbled when I arrived as a first-year." Most students lean well to the left politically; notes one, "Part of the appeal about Grinnell is its legendary social consciousness and socio-political activism." Grinnell students are not immune to self-segregation, however: "On the north side of [campus], students are sportily clad with some kind of personal touch. On the south side: hippie styling, dreads, and barefoot."

ADMISSIONS

Very important factors considered by the admissions committee include: character/personal qualities, class rank, essays, extracurricular activities, recommendations, secondary school record, standardized test scores, talent/ability. *Important factors considered include:* interview. *Other factors considered include:* alumni/ae relation, ethnicity, volunteer work, work experience. SAT I or ACT required. TOEFL required of all international applicants. High school diploma or GED is required. *High school units required/recommended:* 17 total recommended; 4 English recommended, 4 math recommended, 3 science recommended, 3 science lab recommended, 3 foreign language recommended, 3 social studies/history recommended.

The Inside Word

Grinnell has plenty of academically talented applicants. This enables the admissions committee to put a lot of energy into matchmaking, and gives candidates who have devoted time and energy to thought about themselves, their future, and Grinnell the opportunity to rise to the top. All applicants should consider interviewing; you're likely to leave with a positive impression.

FINANCIAL AID

Students should submit: FAFSA, institution's own financial aid form, noncustodial (divorced/separated) parent's statement. Regular filing deadline is February 1. The Princeton Review suggests that all financial aid forms be submitted as soon as possible after January 1. Need-based grants offered: Pell, SEOG, state scholarships/grants, private scholarships, the school's own gift aid. *Loan aid offered:* FFEL Subsidized Stafford, FFEL Unsubsidized Stafford, FFEL PLUS, Federal Perkins, college/university loans from institutional funds. Federal Work-Study Program available. Institutional employment available. Applicants will be notified of awards by April 1. Off-campus job opportunities are fair.

FROM THE ADMISSIONS OFFICE

"Grinnell students learn initiative and leadership by taking responsibility for shaping their academic schedule and for participating in the direction of campus life. Coursework is challenging, discussion is customary, and collaborative relationships are common. The College encourages students to be critical, creative, and independent thinkers.

"Grinnell's philosophy of self-governance and the historic absence of fraternities and sororities form the residence life environment into an engaging and energetic community. An array of student groups and an abundant schedule of speakers, events, and extra-curricular programs enrich the curriculum.

"Need-blind admission guarantees access to Grinnell's educational opportunities for all qualified students."

For even more information on this school, turn to page 352 of the "Stats" section.

GUSTAVUS ADOLPHUS COLLEGE

800 WEST COLLEGE AVENUE, SAINT PETER, MN 56082 • ADMISSIONS: 507-933-7676 • FAX: 507-933-7474
FINANCIAL AID: 507-933-7527 • E-MAIL: ADMISSION@GUSTAVUS.EDU • WEBSITE: WWW.GUSTAVUS.EDU

Ratings
Quality of Life: 81   **Academic:** 82   **Admissions:** 84   **Financial Aid:** 90

Academics

At Gustavus Adophus College, a small Lutheran school in rural Minnesota, students enjoy "many opportunities to make the most out of [their] education through research, independent study, or simply the awesome, enthusiastic professors who care about what they teach." Reports one busy student, "As a sophomore, I am already involved with two

SURVEY SAYS . . .
Campus easy to get around
Musical organizations are hot
Great computer facilities
Students are happy
Athletic facilities are great
Campus feels safe
Campus is beautiful
Lots of beer drinking

research projects on campus and have come to know all three of the professors I am working with very well. The professors are really approachable and are passionate about what they teach." Business, biology, and music are among Gustavus' top departments; of the last, students crow that "the music program at Gustavus is phenomenal. Band, orchestra, or choir—the groups are just amazing, and the students are really talented. The top choir just returned from a tour of Italy, singing in places like the Duomo in Florence and the Basilica of St. Francis in Assisi." While "classes are challenging" and "professors often grade super-hard," students do not feel overburdened by their academic chores because "the school has a number of resources to help you out if you get overwhelmed," and profs "will bend over backward to help us learn." Despite the rigors of the curriculum, students find time to enjoy themselves. "The school stresses a balance between academics and extracurriculars," writes one student. Gustavus offers a short January term, during which "students try an entirely new subject for a month. It also provides a study-abroad opportunity for those that can't go abroad for an entire semester."

Life

Most students indicate a subdued but agreeable pace of life at Gustavus Adolphus: "As with all colleges, drinking is a social activity in which many students partake." Freshmen and sophomores often visit The Dive, "the on-campus dance club that has something going on every Friday and Saturday," while upperclassmen sometimes head for nearby bars. Those who abjure alcohol report that "the school does have a nice selection of on-campus, substance-free events, most of which are fun. These would include currently running movies, concerts, comedians, speakers, dancing, and other mingling events." Students also tell us that "community service organizations seem to involve a large majority of the students" and that "athletic events, both intercollegiate and intramural, are a favorite." Hometown Saint Peter is "friendly" and Mankato, home to Minnesota State University, is only 15 miles to the south. While many at this Lutheran school are religious, "religion here is what you make of it; those who want to be highly involved will find numerous opportunities to do so, but those who don't want to be involved are not hit over the head with it."

Student Body

The students of Gustavus are typically "Scandinavian, tall, blonde, attractive, intelligent, and especially nice," with "about half coming from large cities and the other half from farm areas." Most are midwestern and Lutheran, which helps explain their similarities in appearance. Despite their outward similitude, however, "there is a variety of different personality types at Gustavus," so "it is not too difficult for people to find a niche." The school also has "lots of international students that fit in with everyone." Music and athletics are the two most popular extracurricular activities. Athletes tend to live on the North Side of campus, near the athletic facilities. Reports one student, "The school has a North Side/South Side division, where the students on the North Side drink more and tend to be involved in sports, [and those] living on the South Side are more likely to be involved in the fine arts and are more serious about academics."

ADMISSIONS

Very important factors considered by the admissions committee include: essays, secondary school record, standardized test scores. *Important factors considered include:* character/personal qualities, class rank, extracurricular activities, interview, recommendations, religious affiliation/commitment, talent/ability. *Other factors considered include:* alumni/ae relation, geographical residence, minority status, volunteer work, work experience. SAT I or ACT required. TOEFL required of all international applicants. High school diploma or GED is required. *High school units required/recommended:* 17 total required; 22 total recommended; 4 English required, 3 math required, 4 math recommended, 2 science required, 3 science recommended, 2 science lab required, 3 science lab recommended, 2 foreign language required, 3 foreign language recommended, 2 social studies required, 2 history required, 2 elective recommended.

The Inside Word

While the college refers to itself as a national liberal arts college, the applicant pool is decidedly regional and mostly from Minnesota. The pool is also small and highly self-selected, which explains the high acceptance rate and solid freshman profile. Minorities and those who hail from far afield will find their applications met with enthusiasm by the admissions committee.

FINANCIAL AID

Students should submit: FAFSA, institution's own financial aid form. Students who want to receive an award by March 1 must file the CSS/Financial Aid PROFILE. Regular filing deadline is June 15. The Princeton Review suggests that all financial aid forms be submitted as soon as possible after January 1. *Need-based scholarships/grants offered:* Pell, SEOG, state scholarships/grants, private scholarships, the school's own gift aid. *Loan aid offered:* Direct Subsidized Stafford, Direct Unsubsidized Stafford, Direct PLUS, Federal Perkins, state loans, college/university loans from institutional funds, alternative loans from private lenders. Federal Work-Study Program available. Institutional employment available. Applicants will be notified of awards on a rolling basis beginning on or about March 1. Off-campus job opportunities are good.

FROM THE ADMISSIONS OFFICE

"Gustavus Adolphus, a national liberal arts college with a strong tradition of quality teaching, is committed to the liberal arts and sciences; to its Lutheran history; to innovation as evidenced by the 4-1-4 calendar, Curriculum I and II, and the writing program; and to affordable costs with its unique Guaranteed Cost Plan and Partners in Scholarship Program. The most recent additions to its excellent facilities are Olin Hall for physics and mathematics; Confer Hall for the humanities; Lund Center for physical education, athletics, and health; International Center for residential living and international education; and Jackson Campus Center."

For even more information on this school, turn to page 352 of the "Stats" section.

Hanover College

PO Box 108, Hanover, IN 47243-0108 • Admissions: 812-866-7021 • Fax: 812-866-7098
Financial Aid: 812-866-7030 • E-mail: ADMISSIONS@HANOVER.EDU • Website: WWW.HANOVER.EDU

Ratings

Quality of Life: 80   **Academic:** 87   **Admissions:** 79   **Financial Aid:** 88

Academics

Among small liberal arts schools, Hanover College scores high on the "quality-to-price ratio" scale. Hanover is a very affordable private school made even more so by a large endowment, which finances the school's generous aid packages. A Hanover education comes with a few caveats, however. Those attending must be comfortable in an extremely homogenous population, as the vast majority of students are white, midwestern, and Christian.

> **SURVEY SAYS . . .**
> Frats and sororities dominate social scene
> Theater is hot, Very little drug use
> Athletic facilities are great
> Diversity lacking on campus
> Library needs improving
> Students don't like Hanover, IN
> Political activism is (almost) nonexistent
> Lousy off-campus food, Lab facilities are great

Students must also be willing to live under an extremely—many say excessively—paternalistic administration. Complains one typical student, "The administration does not treat us like the adults we are. They are unreasonably strict. I feel like I'm back in kindergarten." Within those parameters, however, lies an excellent, well-rounded liberal arts education. Students here must complete a wide range of distribution requirements, including courses in philosophy, theology, literature, science, and nonwestern society. Approves one student, "This liberal arts school truly captures all that liberal arts means as far as linking completely different courses to one another." Professors, by all accounts, are top-notch. Writes one undergrad, "The professors really care that you learn and understand the concepts being taught. There is a strong emphasis on open-minded learning, in which, by discussion and research, the student draws the conclusion. The professor is more like a coach." Another reports that "the professors are very knowledgeable and . . . always open to one-on-one conversation."

Life

Two factors strongly influence the quality of life at Hanover. The first is the administration, which strictly enforces drinking and visitation rules. Explains one student, "Our administration's social policies are up-to-date with the 90s . . . the 1890s! The campuswide prohibition on alcohol and restrictions on times males are allowed in female rooms and vice versa are oppressive and out of date." The other is the town of Hanover and the area immediately surrounding it. Says one student, "There is not much in the way of cultural attractions in southern Indiana." Students quickly resign themselves to the fact that "since we are in the sticks, there is nothing much to do except grab a movie and/or drink." Many gravitate toward the Greeks, who "run the campus socially." Reports one senior, "If you aren't in a fraternity you're kind of screwed as far as a partying social life goes. Many upperclassmen go to the local bars to get away from campus. The social life revolves around fraternities/sororities and maybe venturing to Louisville, Indy, or Cincy." Otherwise, "for fun we have fire pits, late night Wal-Mart trips, dinner at 3 a.m., Nerf wars, and . . . the occasional band." The Hanover football program has recently made a name for itself nationally, but not all students are pleased. Writes one dissident, "Our school used to be excellent academically. Then, our football team got really good, so the school seemed to think we need[ed] more football players. It's like half the freshman class is the football team."

Student Body

The "very conservative, religious, not very open-minded, Republican majority" that makes up Hanover's student body recognize that they are "all from the same socioeconomic status. There's no diversity, and they are somewhat snobby." Writes one student, "Unless you are totally at ease living with kids from small-town Indiana, you will get an uncomfortable feeling from the total lack of diversity here." Adds another, "The administration is making extreme attempts to make the campus diverse. Hanover, Indiana, though, isn't the most appealing place for a minority because of its size and location." Students note that there are divisions among the student body and that "our differences arise from Greek affiliation rather than other factors."

ADMISSIONS

Very important factors considered by the admissions committee include: class rank, secondary school record. *Important factors considered include:* character/personal qualities, essays, standardized test scores, talent/ability. *Other factors considered include:* alumni/ae relation, extracurricular activities, geographical residence, interview, minority status, recommendations, state residency, volunteer work, work experience. SAT I or ACT required. TOEFL required of all international applicants. High school diploma is required and GED is not accepted. *High school units required/recommended:* 4 English required, 3 math required, 4 math recommended, 3 science required, 2 science lab required, 2 foreign language required, 4 foreign language recommended, 2 social studies required, 2 history required.

The Inside Word

Despite significant national publicity in recent years, Hanover still has a relatively small applicant pool. There is no doubt that these candidates are capable academically—few schools have as impressive a graduation rate or percentage of its alums going on to grad school. It pays to put some energy into the completion of the application process, especially given the sizable percentage of students awarded academic scholarships.

FINANCIAL AID

Students should submit: FAFSA. The Princeton Review suggests that all financial aid forms be submitted as soon as possible after January 1. *Need-based scholarships/grants offered:* Pell, state scholarships/grants, private scholarships, the school's own gift aid. *Loan aid offered:* FFEL Subsidized Stafford, FFEL Unsubsidized Stafford, FFEL PLUS, college/university loans from institutional funds. Institutional employment available. Applicants will be notified of awards on a rolling basis beginning on or about March 10. Off-campus job opportunities are fair.

FROM THE ADMISSIONS OFFICE

"Hanover College offers a unique community to all who live here. With 95 percent of our students and over 50 percent of our faculty and staff residing on campus, the pursuit of academic excellence extends well beyond the confines of the classroom. This is enhanced by a caring faculty, 90 percent of whom hold earned doctoral degrees. The desire to meet academic challenges and the strong sense of community may be the two greatest contributors to the 86 percent retention rate of which Hanover is quite proud. These contributions are also apparent in that over the past five years more than 65 percent of our graduates have advanced their educational degrees. Hanover's total cost qualifies the college as one of the best values in the nation, and its sizable endowment, on a dollar-per-student ratio, places it in the top 10 percent nationally."

For even more information on this school, turn to page 353 of the "Stats" section.

HASTINGS COLLEGE

HASTINGS COLLEGE, 800 N. TURNER AVENUE, HASTINGS, NE 68901 • ADMISSIONS: 402-461-7315
FAX: 402-461-7490 • E-MAIL: ADMISSIONS@HASTINGS.EDU • WEBSITE: WWW.HASTINGS.EDU

Ratings

Quality of Life: 72   **Academic:** 81   **Admissions:** 78   **Financial Aid:** 70

Academics

Yesterday's scandal is today's blessing in disguise at Hastings College, a small Presbyterian liberal arts school in south central Nebraska. In February 2000, Hastings' president was pressured into retiring after it was revealed that a recently delivered speech had been partially lifted

> **SURVEY SAYS . . .**
> *Classes are small, Student publications are ignored*
> *No one plays intramural sports*
> *Very little hard liquor*
> *Students don't get along with local community*
> *Students are religious, Very little beer drinking*
> *No one watches intercollegiate sports*

from an anonymous e-mail circulating on the Web. Explains one student, "Well, we had a little trouble last year when our president plagiarized a speech and resigned because it made us all mad." The windfall came in the person of Dr. Phillip Dudley, longtime Hastings vice president and current prez. Gushes one undergrad, "The administration at Hastings is incredible. The college president eats lunch and some dinners in the cafeteria, and he talks to students. When you see him around campus, he is always friendly, and he has tons of events at his house, which is like two blocks from campus." Agrees one student, "Last year, we got a new president; the students love him, and I feel like he really cares about us too." The cuddly vibe extends down through the faculty; reports one undergrad, "The professors are great, they have us over for cookies and paper-sharing, or movie nights for my Lit class." Students report an academic environment that is enriching but relaxed; "The classes are challenging, but I study about two to three hours a day max," notes one student. Some feel that sports programs are strongly supported "while the arts and academics are neglected. The art building is falling apart; equipment is out-of-date, broken, or in limited supply. Because of the overemphasis of sports, the students' agenda for attending college is not for an education, but to play sports or to party. Very few students want to learn or take the initiative."

Life

"Life is pretty easygoing" at Hastings College, students tell us. Explains one, "There are a couple parties every weekend, mainly off-campus because campus rules are super strict about alcohol. Students go to PJs, a local dance club, every Thursday night. You can drive to Grand Island—there are more restaurants and a better mall there, and it's about a 20-minute drive. Otherwise, there is very little to do in this town. Many students leave campus on the weekends." Drinking is popular despite the campuswide proscription, but students tell us that binge drinking isn't a problem here. "Most people I know drink at least a little, but groups such as BACCHUS [a national college association focused on preventing alcohol abuse] are pretty well known on campus too," writes one undergrad. Hastings has a fledgling Greek system; explains one frat member, "The reason that fraternities are not that popular is because the administration won't let us go national. This way we can't have huge frat houses." Hastings' 18 intercollegiate sports teams compete in the NAIA: the popular men's football team finished 18th in 2001, while the women's basketball team won the 2002 championship with an astounding overall record of 34 wins and 3 losses. Go Broncos!

Student Body

The undergrads of Hastings are "generally a bunch of preppy Midwest kids that come from upper-middle-class homes and were smart and involved in high school. They are fairly nice, although the campus can be cliquey." Some tell us that "if you like to party, you can find people to do that with; if you like to read the Bible night and day, you can find people to do that with too; and if you are somewhere in between, you'll find people like yourself here too. All of these groups seem to get along pretty well." Others have a less sanguine view of their classmates: "Many students are shallow, only interested in where's the latest party, blah, blah," moans one senior. A few secularists warn that "the damn churchy people act like they are too good for the rest of us sometimes." And nearly everyone concedes that "most of the students come from the same kind of background Our school definitely needs to try to become more open to diversity."

ADMISSIONS

Very important factors considered by the admissions committee include: character/personal qualities and secondary school record. *Important factors considered include:* class rank, interview, recommendations, standardized test scores, and talent/ability. *Other factors considered include:* alumni/ae relation, essays, extracurricular activities, geographical residence, minority status, religious affiliation/commitment, state residency, and volunteer work. SAT I or ACT required. TOEFL required of all international applicants. High school diploma is required and GED is accepted. *High school units required/recommended:* 4 English required, 4 math required, 4 science required, 1 science lab required, 1 foreign language required, 4 social studies required, 4 history required.

The Inside Word

Hastings is looking to diversify its student body. Non-Nebraskans, non-Presbyterians, and students of color willing to trek to southern Nebraska will discover a golden opportunity to attend a school better than any they may have thought would admit them.

FINANCIAL AID

Students should submit: FAFSA and institution's own financial aid form. Regular filing deadline is May 1. The Princeton Review suggests that all financial aid forms be submitted as soon as possible after January 1. *Need-based scholarships/grants offered:* Pell, SEOG, state scholarships/grants, private scholarships, and the school's own gift aid. *Loan aid offered:* FFEL Subsidized Stafford, FFEL Unsubsidized Stafford, FFEL PLUS, and Federal Perkins. Federal Work-Study Program available. Institutional employment available. Applicants will be notified of awards on a rolling basis beginning on or about February 15. Off-campus job opportunities are good.

For even more information on this school, turn to page 354 of the "Stats" section.

HILLSDALE COLLEGE

33 EAST COLLEGE STREET, HILLSDALE, MI 49242 • ADMISSIONS: 517-437-7341 • FAX: 517-437-7241
E-MAIL: ADMISSIONS@AC.HILLSDALE.EDU • WEBSITE: WWW.HILLSDALE.EDU

Ratings
Quality of Life: 73   **Academic:** 86   **Admissions:** 82   **Financial Aid:** 71

Academics

Social, political, and religious conservatism are the hallmarks of an education at Hillsdale College, a small liberal arts school in south central Michigan. Writes one student, "Hillsdale's focus on classical conservatism and Judeo-Christian/Greco-Roman heritage

> **SURVEY SAYS . . .**
> *Intercollegiate sports are popular*
> *Classes are small*
> *Popular college radio*
> *No one cheats*
> *Lots of beer drinking*

is one of its great strengths." Academics, students here agree, are rigorous; writes one, "The courses are challenging and require students to think rather than simply toss surface knowledge back at the teachers. Students are expected to both know and understand what they study." While the work is hard, the payoffs are big, "especially with regard to the humanities. The English, history, and classics departments are first-rate." Undergrads brag that Hillsdale provides "a lot of opportunities to meet high-profile people. I got to have breakfast with Clarence Thomas last semester and chatted for two hours with [author] Wendy Shalit. Larger schools may bring in high-profile people, too, but since Hillsdale is so small, we actually have a chance to meet them and talk to them." One student claims that "if three students want to take a class that the school doesn't offer, the school will find a professor willing to teach the class, hiring new faculty if necessary." Undergrads appreciate the fact that "the students and faculty all have very diverse interests. If any school is truly a liberal arts school, it is Hillsdale. One of the physics professors accompanied me on the piano for my senior recital. My journalism advisor got his MA in classics at Oxford." Summing up the Hillsdale experience, one student writes: "The program is hard. I am not going to lie—it kicked my ass—but I am learning so much and I am glad."

Life

Leisure time is hard to come by for many Hillsdale students; writes one, "Because of the challenging academic load at Hillsdale, a lot of time is spent studying. Much of a student's free time is spent at a campus job, doing volunteer work, hanging out in the student union or in the local coffeehouse, playing Frisbee in the quad, or just sitting and talking to friends." Students also "do a lot of things that may have nothing to do with our majors. There are only two music majors graduating this year, but 10 percent of the student body is in the choir and probably 20 to 30 percent take some sort of music course." They participate in clubs, too: "Students here are highly politically and religiously active. The largest organizations on campus are College Republicans and Intervarsity Christian Fellowship, followed closely by Praxis (an economics club) and Fairfield Society (a Christian organization)." Hillsdale's Greek system is "huge. About 50 percent [of nonfreshmen] go Greek, and we have some of the strongest and most award-winning chapters in the nation." Students flock to Greek events because "the town of Hillsdale has little to offer" and rules governing dorm behavior are so strict. While parties are accessible, students tend to "take their studies more seriously."

Student Body

Hillsdale's politically engaged students "are conscientious, hardworking, and serious. Most are regular churchgoers. They mostly possess fairly conservative values, and there's even a good deal of libertarians." Adds one student, "They can be a bit dogmatic sometimes, but that doesn't seem to be different from what I've seen at other schools. Overall, they're very friendly and enjoy serious discussions." Undergrads report that "we don't have many 'minority students,' but those who are here seem to have no trouble fitting in." Explains one, "Though not a widely diverse campus, Hillsdale was founded on the belief that all people should be treated equally. The application does not even ask for race or gender descriptions. Everything is merit-based. The student body works in much the same way. Taking away any inequality on the entry/application level seems to prove to the student body that everyone is on the same playing field, thus the students interact regularly." Students tell us that "while there is some tension between certain fraternities, as a whole, the student population is very congenial."

ADMISSIONS

Very important factors considered by the admissions committee include: character/personal qualities, secondary school record, and standardized test scores. *Important factors considered include:* class rank, essays, extracurricular activities, interview, recommendations, volunteer work, and work experience. *Other factors considered include:* alumni/ae relation and talent/ability. SAT I or ACT required; SAT II recommended. TOEFL required of all international applicants. High school diploma is required and GED is accepted. *High school units required/recommended:* 16 total are recommended; 4 English recommended, 3 math recommended, 3 science recommended, 1 science lab recommended, 2 foreign language recommended, 1 social studies recommended, 2 history recommended.

The Inside Word

Don't let Hillsdale's high acceptance rate fool you: at this point, the only folks who apply to this school are serious, solid candidates. As the school's national reputation grows, expect the number of applications to tick upward. While you don't have to be a political conservative to get in, a passionate and well-reasoned personal essay defending conservative values certainly can't hurt you.

FINANCIAL AID

Students should submit: FAFSA and institution's own financial aid form. No deadline for regular filing. The Princeton Review suggests that all financial aid forms be submitted as soon as possible after January 1. *Need-based scholarships/grants offered:* State scholarships/grants, private scholarships, and the school's own gift aid. *Loan aid offered:* College/university loans from institutional funds. Institutional employment available. Applicants will be notified of awards on a rolling basis beginning on or about February 15. Off-campus job opportunities are good.

For even more information on this school, turn to page 354 of the "Stats" section.

HIRAM COLLEGE

PO Box 67, Hiram, OH 44234 • Admissions: 800-362-5280 • Fax: 330-569-5944
Financial Aid: 330-569-5107 • E-mail: admission@hiram.edu • Website: www.hiram.edu

Ratings
Quality of Life: 85   **Academic:** 86   **Admissions:** 80   **Financial Aid:** 86

Academics

One satisfied undergraduate tells us, "I believe that the education that most people get at Hiram is strong and often surpasses educations from larger institutions." Students at the college "want to suck the marrow out of their educational experience" and describe the course load as "challenging enough that it isn't a walk in the park, but it's not overwhelming by

> **SURVEY SAYS . . .**
> *Lots of beer drinking*
> *Campus easy to get around*
> *(Almost) everyone smokes*
> *Hard liquor is popular*
> *Campus is beautiful*
> *Campus feels safe*
> *Lab facilities are great*
> *Students are happy*

any means." Students feel legit calling most professors by their first names: "They want to get to know me as a person and not just another student in the classroom." Professors merit gold stars because "they are very willing to devote their time to help students, or just to talk. This goes even for professors whose classes you might not be currently attending." Most instructors are "very understanding, down-to-earth people who encourage individual thought" and even grab lunch with students and send timely e-mail help over the weekends. The administration comes in a distant second in the popularity contest among the "grownups." Students cite "a lot of miscommunication" between departments. In all fairness, one student writes, "I know of very few other places where deans know many students' names." Other respondents call the staff "helpful," "attentive," and "available to explain their decisions."

Life

On certain desperate nights at Hiram, when "we'll be so bored that we'll just go and walk at night because that's the only thing to do," students have an eerie moment, and "the sudden realization that you are living in a cornfield begins to set in." Students quickly learn to accept the situation and make the best of it." Common weekend activities include "going from dorm to dorm drinking" and "driving to Taco Bell or Wal-Mart." Student organizations attempt to fill the activity void with events such as "toga parties, Springfest, Halloween, the Hiram version of Greek pledging, Homecoming, and athletic-related events." Students can hop the shuttle to Cleveland on Saturday nights, since "most programming is over by nine or so, and there's nothing else to do besides get into trouble." However, not everyone complains of tedium; in fact, there are "a lot of students who enjoy the peacefulness of Hiram," a place that manages to "teach you about the real world in a safe, almost surreal setting."

Student Body

Hiram is a school that "prides itself on being culturally diverse." Students report, "We have a very diverse group of students from all ethnic and economic groups" as well as people with "all sorts of backgrounds and belief structures." Even in this Hiram salad bowl, a few people notice that the population seems "almost segregated down racial lines sometimes." One student observes "tension between minority students or international students and white students." Nonetheless, respondents express a heartening enthusiasm regarding diversity: "It has been a great pleasure learning about so many cultures!" Reportedly, aside from being humanoid, "no two people are even remotely similar," but at the same time, "there is a group of people for everyone." These posses "tend to be a little on the exclusive side," limited to people with the same "interests, major, or residence hall," according to one respondent. Other common bonds include a past as "freaks in high school" and an interest in "discussing issues on a deeper level." One student summarizes the crew as "a friendly community who cares about what goes on around them and is accepting to new thoughts and ideas."

ADMISSIONS

Very important factors considered by the admissions committee include: secondary school record. *Important factors considered include:* character/personal qualities, class rank, essays, interview, recommendations, standardized test scores. *Other factors considered include:* alumni/ae relation, extracurricular activities, geographical residence, minority status, talent/ability, volunteer work, work experience. SAT I or ACT required. TOEFL required of all international applicants. High school diploma or GED is required. *High school units required/recommended:* 18 total required; 21 total recommended; 4 English required, 3 math required, 4 math recommended, 3 science required, 2 science lab required, 2 foreign language recommended, 3 social studies required, 1 history required, 2 elective required.

The Inside Word

Students with consistent academic records will find little difficulty in gaining admission. The applicant pool is decidedly local; out-of-state candidates benefit from their scarcity.

FINANCIAL AID

Students should submit: FAFSA. The Princeton Review suggests that all financial aid forms be submitted as soon as possible after January 1. *Need-based scholarships/grants offered:* Pell, SEOG, state scholarships/grants, private scholarships, the school's own gift aid. *Loan aid offered:* FFEL Subsidized Stafford, FFEL Unsubsidized Stafford, FFEL PLUS, Federal Perkins, college/university loans from institutional funds. Federal Work-Study Program available. Institutional employment available. Applicants will be notified of awards on a rolling basis beginning on or about February 15. Off-campus job opportunities are good.

FROM THE ADMISSIONS OFFICE

"Hiram College offers several distinctive programs that set us apart from other small, private liberal arts colleges. Over half of Hiram's students participate in our nationally recognized study abroad program at some point during their four years here. In 2001–2002, Hiram faculty will lead trips to England, France, Costa Rica, Pakistan, Greece, and Turkey; in 2002–2003, we will visit Australia, Germany, Denmark, Zimbabwe, Israel, Guatemala, and Mexico. Because Hiram students receive credits for the courses taught by faculty on these trips, studying abroad will not impede progress in their majors or delay graduation. Another unique aspect of a Hiram education is our academic calendar, known as the Hiram Plan. Our semesters are divided into 12-week and 3-week periods. Students usually enroll in three courses during each 12-week period, and one intensive course during the 3-week periods. Many students spend the 3-week periods on study abroad trips or taking unusual courses not typically offered during the 12-week periods. In addition to numerous study abroad options and the Hiram Plan, our small classes (the average class size is 15) encourage interaction between students and their professors, both in and out of the classroom. Students can work with professors on original research projects, and often participate in musical groups and intramural sports teams alongside faculty members."

For even more information on this school, turn to page 355 of the "Stats" section.

HOPE COLLEGE

69 East 10th, PO Box 9000, Holland, MI 49422-9000 • Admissions: 616-395-7850
Fax: 616-395-7130 • E-mail: admissions@hope.edu • Website: www.hope.edu

Ratings
Quality of Life: 76   Academic: 79   Admissions: 72   Financial Aid: 76

Academics

Students at Hope College, a small school affiliated with the Reformed Church, feel that their school does a good job of offering a wide range of academic options. "Hope has everything," reports one student. "We have great the-

> **SURVEY SAYS . . .**
> *No one plays intramural sports*
> *Students are religious*
> *Classes are small*
> *Diversity lacking on campus*

atre and dance programs, but also one of the best science departments in the state. And everyone (regardless of their major) can benefit from the diversity of subjects offered. I am a biology major, but I love my dance classes!" Strengths here include a strong pre-med program, a solid psychology department, and offerings in music, dance, and theatre. Students love the faculty; writes one undergrad, "The teachers here go above and beyond their duty helping students. They really want us to do well. I don't get the feeling (even in the hardest classes) that the teachers are on a mission to fail us. This is a very academically challenging school, but everyone here is committed to helping students succeed." Students have mixed feelings about the administration; as one told us, "The administration is devoted to the students, but their devotion is colored by their wish to please the more conservative financial backers of the school." This struggle between the school's religious and academic missions manifested itself last year in the administration's decision not to recognize the Gay-Straight Alliance as an official student group and to deny the group meeting space on campus. One student voiced frustration: "It's as though we live inside this sheltered safe-haven and anyone who dares to step outside the line will be shut up and ignored."

Life

Students tell us that social life at Hope is slow. "Currently there is a $2 movie each weekend and occasional entertainment in coffeehouse format or in larger shows, but other than that you have to create your own fun. It doesn't help that the town community is not targeted toward our ages but rather is a family community, so there's not a lot to do off campus, either, at least not nearby." A few students counter, "There is always something going on around campus to join in on, whether it's an official club or activity like theatre productions, dance productions, Model United Nations, and yearbook, or just spontaneous fun." Students also enjoy Frisbee golf, intercollegiate basketball games, and, when the weather is nice, hanging out on the beach at Lake Michigan. Even so, the consensus is that Hope could stand to have a little more action. Rules figure largely into student life; advises one undergrad, "We have rules known as parietals, which are that members of the opposite sex cannot be on your dorm floor or in your room after midnight on school days and after 2 A.M. on weekends. Also, Hope is a dry campus, meaning there is to be no liquor on campus, not even in apartments of people over 21." Hometown Holland "is a smallish town (60,000), but it has large minority populations (like 30 percent Hispanic) and has a wide array of ethnic eating establishments." Grand Rapids is only a half-hour away by car; longer road trips to Ann Arbor or Chicago take about two and a half hours.

Student Body

Unsurprisingly, "the majority of the campus [population] is white and Dutch Reformed." Students tell us that "many students here are religious, but there's also students who are not." Among those who are religious exists a sizeable group that their critics describe as "hyper-enthusiastic Christian, but very hypocritical about it. Close-minded, ungrateful for what they've been given in life, and a bit self-righteous." Hope undergrads "tend to be conservative and preppy, but as with religion, not everyone is the same." Some students find the homogeneity here limiting; complains one student, "Hope . . . lacks diversity within its student body. I would have enjoyed being forced into situations that challenged me in . . . understanding and tolerance." Others caution that "it seems like high school sometimes here with the extremely exclusive sororities and frats, but other than that, the students are really friendly."

ADMISSIONS

Very important factors considered by the admissions committee include: secondary school record and standardized test scores. *Important factors considered include:* class rank. *Other factors considered include:* alumni/ae relation, character/personal qualities, essays, extracurricular activities, interview, recommendations, talent/ability, volunteer work, and work experience. SAT I or ACT required, ACT preferred. TOEFL required of all international applicants. High school diploma or GED is required. *High school units required/recommended:* 20 total recommended; 4 English required, 2 math required, 3 math recommended, 1 science required, 3 science recommended, 1 science lab required, 2 science lab recommended, 2 foreign language required, 2 social studies required, 2 social studies recommended, 1 history required, 5 elective required, 5 elective recommended.

The Inside Word

Hope attracts an elite applicant pool; candidates may get away with middling test scores or less-than-optimal high school grades, but not both. The school is a natural fit for top students who are comfortable participating in the Reformed community.

FINANCIAL AID

Students should submit: FAFSA and institution's own financial aid form. No deadline for regular filing. The Princeton Review suggests that all financial aid forms be submitted as soon as possible after January 1. *Need-based scholarships/grants offered:* Pell, SEOG, state scholarships/grants, private scholarships, and the school's own gift aid. *Loan aid offered:* Direct Subsidized Stafford, Direct Unsubsidized Stafford, Direct PLUS, Federal Perkins, and state loans. Federal Work-Study Program available. Institutional employment available. Applicants will be notified of awards on a rolling basis beginning on or about March 1. Off-campus job opportunities are excellent.

For even more information on this school, turn to page 355 of the "Stats" section.

ILLINOIS INSTITUTE OF TECHNOLOGY

10 West 33rd Street, Chicago, IL 60616 • Admissions: 312-567-3025 • Fax: 312-567-6939
Financial Aid: 312-567-3025 • E-mail: admission@iit.edu • Website: www.iit.edu

Ratings

Quality of Life: 69   Academic: 77   Admissions: 84   Financial Aid: 82

Academics

Like most engineering institutions, Illinois Institute of Technology "is an intense school." Undergrads appreciate the fact that studies "are very good and career-oriented" and that "even though we are small and [aren't] that well known, we have a very challenging and strong engineering curriculum." Hoping to give its student body a leg up in the working world, IIT requires undergraduates to complete two

> **SURVEY SAYS . . .**
> *Ethnic diversity on campus*
> *Different students interact*
> *Everyone loves Chicago, IL*
> *Low cost of living*
> *Great off-campus food*
> *Unattractive campus*
> *Very little drug use*
> *Musical organizations aren't popular*
> *Students are not very happy*
> *No one plays intramural sports*

Interprofessional Projects before graduation. IPROs, as they're known at IIT, bring together undergraduate and graduate students from different academic disciplines to complete a task as a team. Recent IPROs have ranged from designing a new football stadium for the Chicago Bears to improving automated patient monitoring and diagnosis systems. In its efforts to create well-rounded students, IIT requires a wide array of courses in the humanities, writing, and social and behavioral sciences. Do students appreciate these efforts on their behalf? Well, some of the students we spoke to didn't think so. Although they appreciate the value of their academic programs, students find fault with several aspects of the school. They complain that "most professors don't utilize the small class sizes for discussions—they seem to enjoy lecturing too much," and that the administration could do more to involve students and their opinions. Most of all, they gripe about the advising system: "There is no proper guidance to choose the right courses pertaining to the interest of each student," writes a typical student.

Life

Academic demands encroach a lot on social life at IIT, to the dissatisfaction of many. Writes one typically disgruntled student: "Homework dominates our lives. We do homework all the time, including weekends." Adds another, "You really have to work in order to get involved. Classes require a lot of time and leave little left to do fun stuff." Of the campus itself, most of which was designed by legendary architect Ludwig Mies Van der Rohe, making it one of the 100 top travel destinations of the new millenium by Travel & Leisure Magazine. As one student explains life on campus, "Being involved in a fraternity has been pretty fun for me. There are also a lot of opportunities to participate in a variety of student organizations. IIT has attracted some big-name entertainment for its size . . . which is cool." Adds another, "Life in the dorms is quite fun. On weekends we [usually] have movies in the lounge." Most students try to get off campus as often as possible. The El, Chicago's version of a subway system, "runs through campus, so we have access to everything that Chicago has to offer."

Student Body

The "very diverse and intelligent" students of IIT inhabit "a very international campus," prompting one student to exclaim that "I've made friends with people from all over the world!" Some students report, however, that "to some degree cultures split off into their own groups," making interaction somewhat more difficult. Exacerbating the situation is the fact that "this school doesn't have enough facilities to get together. It makes it hard to get to know other students." Men and women alike agree that "more women are needed at this school!"

ADMISSIONS

Very important factors considered by the admissions committee include: secondary school record, standardized test scores. *Important factors considered include:* character/personal qualities, class rank, essays, recommendations. *Other factors considered include:* alumni/ae relation, extracurricular activities, interview, talent/ability, volunteer work, work experience. SAT I or ACT required. TOEFL required of all international applicants. High school diploma is required and GED is not accepted. *High school units required/recommended:* 4 English required, 4 math required, 3 science required, 2 science lab required, 2 social studies required.

The Inside Word

IIT's applicant pool is small and includes a strong element of self-selection. This means the majority get in, but not without solid academic preparation. While the committee evaluates other criteria, the bottom line is that candidates need fairly solid grades and better than average test scores in order to get admitted.

FINANCIAL AID

Students should submit: FAFSA. The Princeton Review suggests that all financial aid forms be submitted as soon as possible after January 1. *Need-based scholarships/grants offered:* Pell, SEOG, state scholarships/grants, private scholarships, the school's own gift aid. *Loan aid offered:* FFEL Subsidized Stafford, FFEL Unsubsidized Stafford, FFEL PLUS, Federal Perkins, college/university loans from institutional funds. Federal Work-Study Program available. Institutional employment available. Applicants will be notified of awards on a rolling basis beginning on or about March 1. Off-campus job opportunities are excellent.

FROM THE ADMISSIONS OFFICE

"IIT is committed to providing students with the highest caliber education through dedicated teachers, small class sizes, and undergraduate research opportunities. Classes are taught by senior faculty—not teaching assistants—who bring first-hand research experience into daily class discussion. The university's diverse student population mirrors the global work environment faced by all graduates. IIT promotes a unique interdisciplinary approach to learning. Students experience team-based, creative problem solving through two required Interprofessional Projects (IPROs). Our entrepreneurship program challenges students to develop start-up technology companies. The Leadership Academy teaches leadership skills that advance students in their personal and professional development. IIT's location in one of the nation's great cities affords many opportunities for internships and employment. A new campus center and student residence hall opening in 2003 will provide exciting new living and campus life opportunities."

For even more information on this school, turn to page 356 of the "Stats" section.

ILLINOIS STATE UNIVERSITY

Admissions Office, Campus Box 2200, Normal, IL 61790-2200 • Admissions: 309-438-2181
Fax: 309-438-3932 • E-mail: ugradadm@ilstu.edu • Website: www.ilstu.edu

Ratings

Quality of Life: 82   Academic: 72   Admissions: 69   Financial Aid: 77

Academics

Want to teach? Consider Illinois State University; according to students, "Illinois State has one of the best education programs in the country, and it shows." Students also tout the English and music program offered here. And most

> **SURVEY SAYS . . .**
> *Classes are small*
> *Frats and sororities dominate social scene*
> *No one cheats*
> *Intercollegiate sports are popular*

students feel sanguine about their instructors; one undergrad declares, "ISU is at the top of the heap when it comes to professor-undergrad friendships." While some go as far as to say that "the professors are incredible," almost everyone would at least admit of professors that "the majority of them know what they're talking about and will always make office time for you." Most students are pleasantly surprised by the accessibility of the administration. "You wouldn't think so because it's a huge university," writes one student, "but you can always spot the president talking to students on the quad." Another adds, "The new president is totally accessible and will stop and ask students questions about ISU and what they think about the school." Though some find that "the computer facilities are terrible," the majority of students at ISU are very happy with their academic surroundings. One student comments, "Everyone here is involved. . . . You can find students and professors having coffee. It actually is the stuff you see in the brochure. It's kind of cool."

Life

This is the middle of Illinois; "There is not really a whole hell of a lot to do here in town, so most students drink their minds out and have lots of sex." Located in the community of Normal, ISU does offer students accessibility to "movies, dancing, plays, and music concerts" (although one tye-dyer sadly states that, for some unknown reason, "Phish is no longer welcome at Redbird arena"). Another adds "come Wednesday, our campus is full of chalkings and signs advertising at least 30 or so events going on for the night." Others, however, "wish [they] had more options for the weekends." Indeed, the majority of students agree "school weekends pretty much consist of the same thing. People go out to some party and either end up at a friend's apartment or a fraternity house." To escape from Normal—"the town . . . is not that excited to have students there"—many choose to "hang out on [the Illinois Wesleyan University] campus" located in nearby Bloomington. But if you do stick around, be advised that "most students start to party on Thursday and do not end until Sunday." While this is fine for some, others argue, "If there were more for the sober minded to do on a weekend, it'd be nice." While some feel that the housing is less than tolerable ("sucks" was the actual word used), one student offers, "Waterson Towers has very nice rooms. Quite large and comfortable."

Student Body

Opinions vary widely regarding the students of ISU. While one student finds "the feeling of campus unity [to be] very strong, especially recently," others point to some serious divides running through the student body, not least of which is the one between Greeks and GDIs. "Those who aren't Greek don't like those who are, and even among the different houses on campus there is hostility," writes one sorority sister. An independent student corroborates that estimation succinctly: "Frats suck." So even though "the school is very good at stressing diversity," many feel that most students aren't "that welcoming to people unlike themselves." Of course, the behavior of a "small number of knuckleheads [can] ruin it for the rest of" the student body. Despite the petty disputes, "most of the people on campus are very friendly, they all want to be your friend and get to know you."

ADMISSIONS

Important factors considered by the admissions committee include: class rank, secondary school record, and standardized test scores. *Other factors considered include:* essays, extracurricular activities, and talent/ability. SAT I or ACT required, ACT preferred. TOEFL required of all international applicants. High school diploma or GED is required. *High school units required/recommended:* 15 total required; 4 English required, 3 math required, 2 science required, 2 science lab required, 2 foreign language required, 2 social studies required, 2 elective required.

The Inside Word

The quality of the applicant pool at Illinois State has improved markedly over the past few years. Those who grew up assuming that ISU was an automatic safety school may find that that this is no longer the case.

FINANCIAL AID

Students should submit: FAFSA. The Princeton Review suggests that all financial aid forms be submitted as soon as possible after January 1. *Need-based scholarships/grants offered:* Pell, SEOG, state scholarships/grants, private scholarships, and the school's own gift aid. *Loan aid offered:* Direct Subsidized Stafford, Direct Unsubsidized Stafford, Direct PLUS, Federal Perkins, and college/university loans from institutional funds. Federal Work-Study Program available. Institutional employment available. Applicants will be notified of awards on a rolling basis beginning on or about April 1. Off-campus job opportunities are excellent.

FROM THE ADMISSIONS OFFICE

"Illinois State University was founded in 1857 to educate the state's teachers. ISU is now a comprehensive institution whose early emphasis on education continues to shape the university, in particular the values-based commitment to creating an optimal learning environment for all Illinois State University students. These values include the provision of an environment emphasizing individualized attention, public opportunity, active pursuit of learning, diversity, and creative response to change. Illinois State University's vision is to create a learning environment for students seeking a small-college experience combined with the resources of a large university.

"Illinois State University freshmen can get involved in a learning communities program, CONNECTIONS, designed to assist students with their transition to college by facilitating extensive positive interactions with faculty, staff, and other students. CONNECTIONS builds bridges between ideas presented in course work, and develops ties between classroom and extracurricular activities.

"All freshmen take the Foundations of Inquiry course. The primary goal of the course is to learn about argumentation, including how to build a strong argument and how to evaluate arguments. It examines the problem-solving process of analysis and argumentation that is used in all academic disciplines (the natural sciences, social sciences, humanities, and fine arts). Students are expected to be actively involved in their own educational experience, emphasizing open communication, intellectual activities, use of technology, and use of information resources. Critical thinking is the ultimate goal of a student's education at Illinois State University."

For even more information on this school, turn to page 357 of the "Stats" section.

Illinois Wesleyan University

PO Box 2900, Bloomington, IL 61720 • Admissions: 309-556-3031 • Fax: 309-556-3411
Financial Aid: 309-556-3096 • E-mail: iwuadmit@titan.iwu.edu • Website: www.iwu.edu

Ratings

Quality of Life: 74   Academic: 84   Admissions: 91   Financial Aid: 87

Academics

Through aggressive expansion of its facilities, the "constantly building and improving" Illinois Wesleyan has transformed itself in the last decade from a well-respected regional school to a nationally renowned university; the newest additions include a library and campus center. At the same time, IWU has remained com-

> **SURVEY SAYS . . .**
> *Athletic facilities are great*
> *Frats and sororities dominate social scene*
> *Very little drug use, Everyone loves the Titans*
> *Theater is hot, Library needs improving*
> *Musical organizations are hot*
> *(Almost) no one listens to college radio*
> *Students get along with local community*

mitted to maintaining a moderate-size student body, and as a result, students here feel they get the best of both worlds. "It's just the right size: enough people but small enough that the personal attention and benefits are huge," explains one undergrad. Says another, "The reason I decided to go to this school is because I knew that I could participate in a variety of activities, and that I could work first-hand with professors." Facilities "are incredible. For a school of its size, Illinois Wesleyan has one of the best science/academic facilities in the nation." Professors "are generally really cool: interesting, knowledgeable, and real. They remember their students, even from 25 years ago. I get teased by one professor because he had my dad and recognized the name." Reports one student, "Profs have stayed past midnight in study groups when we needed help. One even came back after a tuxedo dinner and was helping us in full attire!" Students gripe that "grading is way too tough. It is extremely hard at this school to get an A," but concede that "academically, Illinois Wesleyan challenges you to be the best and does it in a way that isn't discouraging. Smaller class sizes and more attention from the professors help students become more excited about their work." Among the school's innovative offerings is May Term, which one student describes as "the best part of our academic program. It provides amazing experiential learning opportunities. Through May Term, I have traveled to eastern Europe, the Democratic National Convention, and backpacked in the Appalachians."

Life

IWU students describe a low-key but enjoyable social scene, reporting that "people at this school are hard workers and put a lot into their studies. Naturally, however, the weekends are filled with parties and dances, mostly involving fraternities and sororities. There are a lot of really good co-curricular programs, too." Agrees one undergrad, "During the week, studying is the social life, in between trips to Denny's. It's not bad, though; everyone here wants to learn, but is laid-back enough that we can still do crazy stuff like steal someone's mattress and put it outside." Intercollegiate sports "are big here: our basketball games are always packed (we won the Division III championship a few years ago)." So too are student clubs and organizations and guest lectures. Writes one student, "There is always something going on, from speakers to workshops to athletics to parties. We know how to have fun." Because "the town of Bloomington-Normal is very boring," students soon discover that "most people stay on campus for activities and entertainment." When they leave, they "either go to Chicago or to Illinois State University, which is right down the street."

Student Body

IWU students enjoy a "highly friendly atmosphere on campus," although students are also "very cliquey between Greek houses and theater, music, and other groups." The small minority populations here benefit from a support network that includes the Black Student Union, the Council of Latin American Student Enrichment, and an on-campus Multicultural Center. Still, minority students report that "being a minority student here is like you're always under someone's microscope." Agrees a white student, "Most of the students, myself included, are spoiled white middle-class suburbia. The real downfall is their narrow-minded prejudices due to a lack of exposure to diversity." Students' similarity in background fosters the "Wesleyan bubble," a sense that life begins and ends at the campus gates.

ADMISSIONS

Very important factors considered by the admissions committee include: secondary school record. *Important factors considered include:* character/personal qualities, class rank, essays, recommendations, standardized test scores, talent/ability. *Other factors considered include:* alumni/ae relation, extracurricular activities, geographical residence, interview, minority status, volunteer work, work experience. SAT I or ACT required. TOEFL required of all international applicants. High school diploma or GED is required. *High school units required/recommended:* 4 English recommended, 3 math recommended, 3 science recommended, 2 science lab recommended, 3 foreign language recommended, 2 social studies recommended.

The Inside Word

Illinois Wesleyan is selective enough that serious candidates should exceed the suggested curriculum requirements in order to improve their chances for admission.

FINANCIAL AID

Students should submit: FAFSA, institution's own financial aid form, CSS/Financial Aid PROFILE, business/farm supplement. Regular filing deadline is March 1. The Princeton Review suggests that all financial aid forms be submitted as soon as possible after January 1. *Need-based scholarships/grants offered:* Pell, SEOG, state scholarships/grants, private scholarships, the school's own gift aid. *Loan aid offered:* FFEL Subsidized Stafford, FFEL Unsubsidized Stafford, FFEL PLUS, Federal Perkins, Federal Nursing, college/university loans from institutional funds. Federal Work-Study Program available. Institutional employment available. Applicants will be notified of awards on a rolling basis beginning on or about January 1. Off-campus job opportunities are good.

FROM THE ADMISSIONS OFFICE

"Illinois Wesleyan University attracts a wide array of multitalented students—students interested in pursuing diverse fields like vocal performance and biology, psychology and German, or physics and business administration. At IWU, students are not forced into 'either/or' choices. Rather, they are encouraged to pursue multiple interests simultaneously—a philosophy in keeping with the spirit and value of a liberal arts education. The distinctive 4-4-1 calendar allows students to follow their interests each school year in two semesters followed by an optional month-long class in May. May Term opportunities include classes on campus; research collaboration with faculty; travel and study in such places as Australia, China, South Africa, and Europe; as well as local, national, and international internships.

"At Illinois Wesleyan, we assume the mind is the key to an educated person; thus, we hope to foster during the college years the knowledge, values, and skills that will sustain a lifetime of learning. We prepare our students for responsible citizenship and leadership in a democratic society and global community. Above all, whatever their course of studies, we wish to enable Illinois Wesleyan University graduates to lead useful, creative, fully realized lives."

For even more information on this school, turn to page 357 of the "Stats" section.

INDIANA UNIVERSITY—BLOOMINGTON

300 NORTH JORDAN AVENUE, BLOOMINGTON, IN 47405-1106 • ADMISSIONS: 812-855-0661
FAX: 812-855-5102 • FINANCIAL AID: 812-855-0321 • E-MAIL: IUADMIT@INDIANA.EDU
WEBSITE: WWW.ADMIT.INDIANA.EDU

Ratings

Quality of Life: 85   Academic: 72   Admissions: 75   Financial Aid: 80

Academics

Students appreciate the near-limit-less choices available at Indiana University. As one student puts it, "There's a major for everything." As at most large universities, "you really have to get into student activities or organizations and establish your community here. Otherwise, you'll get lost and become just a number." Some note encouragingly that "although IU is a very big school with some large classes, discussion classes are made

> **SURVEY SAYS . . .**
> *Campus is beautiful*
> *Lots of beer drinking*
> *Athletic facilities are great*
> *(Almost) everyone smokes*
> *Everyone loves the Hoosiers*
> *Great library*
> *Great computer facilities*
> *Frats and sororities dominate social scene*
> *Hard liquor is popular*
> *Students are happy*

to give students the opportunity to get questions answered and discuss subject matter one-on-one." Students also report that class sizes get smaller once one clears his or her intro courses. Interesting note: IU is famed for having the smallest number of large lecture halls, only two classrooms that can fit 400 max. Professors here "don't really seek you out individually, but once you go to them, they are extremely open, friendly, and helpful." Students are more critical of the administration. While they acknowledge that "IU is a giant bureaucracy with over 30,000 students—there has to be some law and order," they also complain that "it's very hard when you have a problem with something that you can't fix yourself, like parking, personal computers problems, etc. The administration will transfer you here and there and put you on hold or tell you there is nothing that can be done."

Life

At a school as large as IU, students agree that "life can be whatever you want it to be. And that's the bottom line. You can be a . . . partier, at the bars every night dancing and whoopin' it up . . . . You can go to massive house parties. . . . You can stay at home [and] watch movies with a group of friends. You can go to the mall and go out to eat. You can go to a coffee shop, smoke, and listen to music. You can study in any one of the libraries. You can join all sorts of clubs and organizations (including the Greek system). You can do whatever you want, really. And you should be able to find people to do it with." Sports are very popular here; writes one student, "One of the most exciting things to do is attend the basketball games." Student complaints center on the town of Bloomington and the school's alcohol policy ("ridiculous, and completely unreasonable for a college campus—we are dry, or at least are supposed to be. There is less tolerance for alcohol than for abusive coaches!").

Student Body

"I love the students at IU because they are so diverse! IU has something like 35,000 [sic] students and they are all different! It has really made me aware of different cultures and life choices," crows one student. Others disagree, however, like one who believes that while "the majority of people here are very friendly," the population "is very divided [by] race,

Greeks/non-Greeks, and majors. There is not a lot of intermixing unless you are in a leadership position, when you get to meet others and work with others." As for students of different races, "there is some sort of divide made by the students. Though I notice it, it isn't a big deal. Everyone does their own thing."

ADMISSIONS

The typical freshman at Indiana successfully completed 18 to 19 year-long academic courses in high school. Students are strongly encouraged to apply for admission if they have been taking four to five academic classes each year in a balanced program and earned above-average grades in those classes. Other factors considered include class rank, grade trends, and SAT or ACT results. The TOEFL is required of all international School of Music applicants and non-native speakers of English who wish to be considered for limited merit scholarships and/or an invitation to the Honors College. The admissions office says: "Students should establish a solid foundation at the high school level in English (4 years required), laboratory sciences (minimum 1 year), social sciences (minimum 2 years), and mathematics, including algebra II and trigonometry (minimum 3 years total required) to be prepared for any academic program at Indiana University. Foreign language is strongly recommended but not required for admission."

The Inside Word

A high volume of applicants makes Indiana's individual admissions review process relatively selective for a university of its size. Candidates to the School of Music face a highly selective audition process.

FINANCIAL AID

Students should submit: FAFSA. The Princeton Review suggests that all financial aid forms be submitted as soon as possible after January 1. *Need-based scholarships/grants offered:* Pell, SEOG, state scholarships/grants, private scholarships, the school's own gift aid. *Loan aid offered:* Subsidized Stafford, Unsubsidized Stafford, PLUS, Federal Perkins. Federal Work-Study Program available. Institutional employment available. Applicants will be notified of awards on a rolling basis beginning on or about April 1. Off-campus job opportunities are excellent.

FROM THE ADMISSIONS OFFICE

"Indiana University—Bloomington, one of America's great teaching and research universities, extends learning and teaching beyond the walls of the traditional classroom. When visiting campus, students and parents typically describe IU as 'what a college should look and feel like.' Students bring their diverse experiences, beliefs, and backgrounds from all 50 states and 136 countries, which adds a richness and diversity to life at IU—a campus often cited as one of the most beautiful in the nation. Indiana University—Bloomington truly offers a quintessential college town, campus, and overall experience. Students enjoy all of the advantages, opportunities, and resources that a larger school can offer, while still receiving personal attention and support. Time magazine named IU its 'College of the Year' among research universities based on the outstanding programs offered to help freshmen succeed. Because of the variety of outstanding academic and cultural resources, students at IU have the best of both worlds.

"Indiana offers more than 5,000 courses and more than 100 undergraduate programs, with many known nationally and internationally. IU—Bloomington is known worldwide for outstanding programs in the arts, sciences, humanities, and social sciences as well as for highly rated schools of business, music, education, journalism, optometry, public and environmental affairs, and health, physical education, and recreation. Students can customize academic programs with double and individualized majors, internships, and research opportunities, while utilizing state-of-the-art technology at one of Yahoo! Internet Life magazine's top five 'most wired colleges.' Representatives from more than 1,000 businesses, government agencies, and not-for-profit organizations come to campus each year to recruit IU students."

For even more information on this school, turn to page 358 of the "Stats" section.

IOWA STATE UNIVERSITY

100 ALUMNI HALL, AMES, IA 50011-2011 • ADMISSIONS: 515-294-5836 • FAX: 515-294-2592
FINANCIAL AID: 515-294-2223 • E-MAIL: ADMISSIONS@IASTATE.EDU • WEBSITE: WWW.IASTATE.EDU

Ratings
Quality of Life: 78.   Academic: 69   Admissions: 76   Financial Aid: 83

Academics

Undergraduates are drawn to Iowa State by a number of standout programs (engineering, design, agriculture, and journalism, to name a few) and its low tuition, especially for native Iowans. Like many state schools, ISU is "trying to get by with huge budget cuts"; the school's efforts to address budget shortfalls have included substantial tuition increases. Despite the still-reasonable price of an ISU education, undergrads here are not happy about the situation. Gripes one, "Tuition has been spiraling out of control." Compounding students' financial frustration are large classes ("I have six classes this semester and four of them have over 200 students in them, plus I have only one class that is under 50. That's just too big") and registration woes. Those who seek a hand-holding atmosphere, be forewarned: "Research is the purpose of Iowa State. There are a lot of excellent extension publications and extension specialists for your reference on most any subject. However, this also means that a lot of the professors don't seem to care about teaching. They are more interested in their research." While students grouse, they also understand that the university is doing the best it can in a bad financial situation; furthermore, they are not blind to the school's many assets. "Technical majors are very heavily recruited here, which makes it easier to get a job," writes one engineer. Another student points out that the Honors Program offers "smaller sections of most classes. . . . The [Honors] professors are accessible, helpful, and seem genuinely interested in teaching."

> **SURVEY SAYS . . .**
> *Campus is beautiful*
> *Everyone loves the Wildcats*
> *Lots of beer drinking*
> *Athletic facilities are great*
> *Great library*
> *Campus easy to get around*
> *(Almost) everyone plays intramural sports*
> *Great computer facilities*
> *Student newspaper is popular*
> *Frats and sororities dominate social scene*

Life

The distinguishing trait of ISU campus life, students tell us, is "the strong sense of community. I've always been amazed at how close-knit the school manages to be with [23,000] undergraduates; it's the best of both worlds because we have the feel of a small college but the resources of a large university." Those resources mean that "there is something for everyone here. There are over 500 clubs and organizations." Undergrads love their "nationally recognized football, wrestling, hockey, and men's and women's basketball" teams, as well as "plentiful intramural opportunities [and] the largest broomball participation in the country." Campus bustles most noticeably "in the spring and fall, [when] most people hang around central campus or the yards by the dorms. In the winter, there are hockey and basketball games and stuff to do on campus sometimes. Winter is more boring than the warmer months." But when a Cyclone team isn't playing, "the big thing here is drinking." Students say, "There are plenty of bars . . . with plenty of specials during the week." Alternatives for the under-21 set include "a dollar theatre at the mall for those students that don't mind seeing old movies," "ample places to eat, a nice mall, lots of places to run and road races to participate in, and many bike paths. Also, Des Moines is only 20 minutes away." Finally, "the Greek system is really popular at ISU."

Student Body

How diverse is the Iowa State student body? It depends on which yardstick you use. "Iowa State does have a diverse student population by Iowa standards, but to someone outside of Iowa it might not seem so very diverse," explains one student, who continued: "There is a very large and active lesbian, gay, bisexual, transgender group. [There are also] many students who tend to be somewhat close-minded about gays and tend to be more religious than students at other schools." Most here are "pretty small town–oriented, and Ames is a big town for them." They are "generally warm and friendly, appreciate the fact that they are at a great university, and respect other students." They also "don't spend a whole lot of time thinking about academics." ISU has "a large international student population who fit in well with the rest of the student body"; among these students is "a large population of East Asian students and, in the computer science department particularly, many people from India as well."

ADMISSIONS

Very important factors considered by the admissions committee include: class rank, secondary school record, standardized test scores. *Other factors considered include:* character/personal qualities, essays, extracurricular activities, geographical residence, interview, recommendations, state residency, talent/ability, volunteer work, work experience. SAT I or ACT required. TOEFL required of all international applicants. High school diploma or GED is required. *High school units required/recommended:* 4 English required, 3 math required, 3 science required, 2 science lab required, 2 foreign language recommended, 2 social studies required, 3 social studies recommended.

The Inside Word

With a decided lack of mystery in the admissions process and a super-high acceptance rate, Iowa State still attracts a solid student body. What we have here is living proof of the value of a good reputation and a little national press.

FINANCIAL AID

Students should submit: FAFSA. No deadline for regular filing. The Princeton Review suggests that all financial aid forms be submitted as soon as possible after January 1. *Need-based scholarships/grants offered:* Pell, SEOG, state scholarships/grants, private scholarships, the school's own gift aid. *Loan aid offered:* Direct Subsidized Stafford, Direct Unsubsidized Stafford, Direct PLUS, Federal Perkins, state loans, college/university loans from institutional funds, private alternative loans. Federal Work-Study Program available. Institutional employment available. Applicants will be notified of awards on a rolling basis beginning on or about April 1. Off-campus job opportunities are excellent.

FROM THE ADMISSIONS OFFICE

"Iowa State University offers all the advantages of a major university along with the friendliness and warmth of a residential campus. There are more than 100 undergraduate programs of study in the Colleges of Agriculture, Business, Design, Education, Engineering, Family and Consumer Sciences, Liberal Arts and Sciences, and Veterinary Medicine. Our 1,700 faculty members include Rhodes Scholars, Fulbright Scholars, and National Academy of Sciences and National Academy of Engineering members. Recognized for its high quality of life, Iowa State has taken practical steps to make the university a place where students feel like they belong. Iowa State has been recognized for the high quality of campus life and the exemplary out-of-class experiences offered to its students. Along with a strong academic experience, students also have opportunities for further developing their leadership skills and interpersonal relationships through any of the more than 500 student organizations, 60 intramural sports, and a multitude of arts and recreational activities. All residence hall rooms are wired for Internet connections and all students have the opportunity to create their own World Wide Web pages."

For even more information on this school, turn to page 359 of the "Stats" section.

JAMESTOWN COLLEGE

6081 College Lane, Jamestown, ND 58405-0001 • Admissions: 701-252-3467 • Fax: 701-253-4318
E-mail: admissions@jc.edu • Website: www.jc.edu

Ratings

Quality of Life: 78   **Academic:** 70   **Admissions:** 67   **Financial Aid:** 86

Academics

With just over a thousand students, Jamestown College offers its undergrads an intimate learning environment on its "beautiful campus" in the heart of North Dakota. One student remarks, "Classes are small enough that you can always ask questions without feeling like you're causing a

> **SURVEY SAYS . . .**
> *School is well run, Students are religious*
> *Diversity lacking on campus, Classes are small*
> *Popular college radio*
> *Student publications are popular*
> *Intercollegiate sports are unpopular or non-existent*

disturbance to the other students' learning calendar," and professors are "easily accessible" outside of class. "The professors in general are great," raves a student, "and seem to really care about how much you're learning and want to help in any way they can to ensure success in a particular course of study." But interested professors aren't necessarily interesting. One student explains, "Some of my professors, not to name names, are the walking cure for insomnia." Others complain that the collective intellect at JC is sometimes stymied by the "conservative" mentality that pervades the classrooms. "We need to be able to freely disagree on issues and feel comfortable expressing the more liberal ideas publicly, as well as the more conservative, traditional beliefs," opines a student. As far as the curriculum goes, "one major problem" at JC "is a lack of options, which is normal for a school this size." A budding scientist tells us that another issue is the lack of resources: "The science labs leave a lot to be desired, but good teachers make up for the lack of lab equipment." In fact, the sciences are among the most praised disciplines here, along with business and nursing. So while students acknowledge that "there are a few problems" here, they're quick to declare that Jamestown College "is among the top schools" in the nation.

Life

If you're in North Dakota, take Interstate 94 a hundred miles east from Bismarck (the state capitol) or a hundred miles west from Fargo (the state's largest city), and you'll find Jamestown, a hub of about 16,000 people. One student refers to Jamestown as "home of the world's largest buffalo," (a more reserved detractor simply says, "There's not much to do in Jamestown"), but the staples are available: "bars," "restaurants," "a bowling alley," "Blockbuster," and "Wal-Mart." When local social options are in shortage, students hang out in their dorm rooms, which are equipped with "computers and color printers," or venture outdoors, as "there are always activities going on" on campus, such as "sports, theatre productions, speakers, dances, or church activities," as well as events hosted by any of JC's 40 or so groups on campus. Despite the quiet, conservative exterior of the campus, "drinking is very common," according to one undergrad. That money could be better spent on a weekend in Fargo, or on about a hundred visits to Jamestown's National Buffalo Museum, home to a seven-year-old albino buffalo named White Cloud. The dedicated students at JC "study hard during the week so that when the weekend comes we can have as much fun as possible." And although "some people want more to do, more 'big city' stuff . . . most of the time we are too busy to miss what we don't have here."

Student Body

At Jamestown College, that "midwestern hospitality that you always hear about" is in no short supply. Students here describe their classmates as "really friendly" and "easygoing." Despite the pleasant demeanor of the student body as a whole, you'll also find a fair amount of exclusive "cliques" and pockets of "rude, stuck-up snobs." This cliquey-ness—and the small size of the student population—means that gossip is often prevalent at JC. "There is no need for that on a college campus," complains one student. "If I wanted to be in high school, I would go there." "Most of the students here come from small North Dakotan, Montanan, or Minnesotan towns," and, in general, tend to be "rural," "conservative," and "religious," as Jamestown College is affiliated with the Presbyterian Church.

ADMISSIONS

Very important factors considered by the admissions committee include: secondary school record. *Important factors considered include:* class rank and standardized test scores. *Other factors considered include:* alumni/ae relation, character/personal qualities, extracurricular activities, interview, recommendations, talent/ability, volunteer work, and work experience. TOEFL required of all international applicants. High school diploma or GED is required. *High school units required/recommended:* 15 total recommended; 4 English recommended, 3 math recommended, 3 science recommended, 2 foreign language recommended, 2 social studies recommended, 1 history recommended.

The Inside Word

With a 99 percent admit rate, Jamestown is truly a nonselective school. This is great news for those who feel they would perform better in a nurturing academic environment but who can't gain entrance to the more competitive small liberal arts schools.

FINANCIAL AID

Students should submit: FAFSA. No deadline for regular filing. The Princeton Review suggests that all financial aid forms be submitted as soon as possible after January 1. *Need-based scholarships/grants offered:* Pell, SEOG, state scholarships/grants, private scholarships, and the school's own gift aid. *Loan aid offered:* FFEL Subsidized Stafford, FFEL Unsubsidized Stafford, FFEL PLUS, Federal Perkins, Federal Nursing, state loans, and college/university loans from institutional funds. Federal Work-Study Program available. Institutional employment available. Applicants will be notified of awards on a rolling basis. Off-campus job opportunities are good.

FROM THE ADMISSIONS OFFICE

"Jamestown College is one of America's best private schools with average tuition about half the national average of other private, four-year colleges. After financial aid and scholarships are applied, the average net cost of attending Jamestown College is competitive with state institutions. Jamestown College is one of only a few colleges in the nation to provide a networked computer and color printer in every student room at no additional charge to the student. Jamestown College has a reputation for academic excellence and offers three degree options: Bachelor of Arts, Bachelor of Science, and Bachelor of Science in Nursing. Students can choose from 21 majors and 27 minors. The college also offers pre-professional and certification programs. Jamestown College has a strong placement rate; the college has a terrific reputation among employers and graduate programs. Jamestown College offers numerous opportunities for campus involvement. Students participate in clubs that are associated with their major and that offer leadership development. One of Jamestown College's greatest assets is the size of the school; with a student body of around 1,100, each student can enjoy personal attention from the faculty and staff. The students are recognized as individuals."

For even more information on this school, turn to page 359 of the "Stats" section.

JOHN CARROLL UNIVERSITY

20700 North Park Boulevard, University Heights, OH 44118-4581 • Admissions: 216-397-4294
Fax: 216-397-3098 • E-mail: admission@jcu.edu • Website: www.jcu.edu

Ratings
Quality of Life: 76   **Academic:** 82   **Admissions:** 79   **Financial Aid:** 75

Academics

Students agree that there are easier ways to get an undergraduate degree than to attend John Carroll University, a small Catholic school in the suburbs of Cleveland. "The professors here are more demanding and difficult than those professors of public and state colleges and universi-

> **SURVEY SAYS . . .**
> *Classes are small*
> *Students are happy*
> *Students are religious*
> *Popular college radio*
> *School is well run*
> *Theater is hot*

ties," reports one student, "thus making the overall academic experience for me more challenging, but beneficial for the future." Adds another, "Let's just say the classes that are supposed to be easy are impossible. The impossible classes are even more impossible." Why put yourself through the JCU grind? Students say it's because the quality of the education they receive is high. As one undergrad puts it, "I would have to say that the academics of this school are its greatest strength. The Jesuits attempt to educate the whole person, so there is an intense liberal arts core, which is almost half of the total number of credits that you need to graduate. This university also makes attempts to diversify the students through guest lectures, performances, or events." Students appreciate the fact that "the professors at this university are very helpful and very informative. They are easy to reach; they will e-mail or call you back." The school boasts especially strong departments in biology, psychology, and business administration.

Life

There's something for everyone at John Carroll, students say, provided you know where to look. As one student put it, "It's a nice environment. If you like to party, there is a dorm for you, and if you like quiet and volunteering, there is a dorm for you. People are very involved in community service, and religion is important to almost everyone, though not everyone is practicing." Many feel that the school's small size is a great asset, explaining that "it's nice because you can try things that you may not necessarily be able to try in a really big school, like theatre, if you are an accounting major." Indeed, "lots of kids are involved with sports, and community service is big (Habitat for Humanity, campus ministry, etc)." Some students wish campus were a bit more hopping; writes one, "Almost everything social happens off campus so it can be difficult to find things to do at times." Students tell us that there is "not a lot of partying on campus itself, but there is plenty off in frat or sport houses, etc. People like to get drunk. That's the main source of entertainment around here; either being drunk or watching all the drunks. It sucks that most parties are far from campus, so you either have to get a cab or bribe a friend into being the designated driver." Students also warn that "John Carroll has literally no surrounding campus. There are no pizza shops within walking distance or shopping centers. There is nothing to do unless you want to drive 10 minutes down the street. But since freshman and sophomores are not allowed to have cars it is hard for them to experience the surrounding culture."

Student Body

The majority of John Carroll undergraduates agree that "most of the John Carroll student body is easy to get along with, but getting along . . . really depends on the individual. The thing with JCU is that almost everyone resembles and acts like everyone else in some sense or another. We are primarily white, upper-middle-class Catholics. Is there anything wrong with that? Not unless you have something against a frighteningly robot-like appearance." Students are typically "quite conservative," as one student explains, "and there exists little intellectual diversity among them. Many students are homophobic, and consequently I feel that homosexuals are not accepted here." Undergrads caution that "John Carroll is a very clique-oriented school. Most of the students who come here went to high school together. But they are friendly." For many, "the greatest strength of the student body is its religious aspect. Almost everyone here goes to church or demonstrates some kind of faith."

ADMISSIONS

Very important factors considered by the admissions committee include: secondary school record and standardized test scores. *Important factors considered include:* character/personal qualities, essays, extracurricular activities, interview, and recommendations. *Other factors considered include:* alumni/ae relation, class rank, geographical residence, minority status, talent/ability, volunteer work, and work experience. SAT I or ACT required. TOEFL required of all international applicants. High school diploma or GED is required. *High school units required/recommended:* 16 total required; 21 total recommended; 4 English required, 3 math required, 4 math recommended, 2 science required, 3 science recommended, 2 science lab required, 3 science lab recommended, 2 foreign language required, 3 foreign language recommended, 1 social studies required, 1 social studies recommended, 1 history required, 3 history recommended, 3 elective required.

The Inside Word

A high acceptance rate masks the serious standards of the JCU admissions office because few apply here who don't already know they have a solid chance of admittance. The class of 2006, however, did include 14 percent from the bottom half of their high school graduating class, so it's not impossible for an underachiever to get in.

FINANCIAL AID

Students should submit: FAFSA. The Princeton Review suggests that all financial aid forms be submitted as soon as possible after January 1. *Need-based scholarships/grants offered:* Pell, SEOG, state scholarships/grants, private scholarships, and the school's own gift aid. *Loan aid offered:* FFEL Subsidized Stafford, FFEL Unsubsidized Stafford, FFEL PLUS, Federal Perkins, and college/university loans from institutional funds. Federal Work-Study Program available. Institutional employment available. Applicants will be notified of awards on a rolling basis beginning on or about March 1. Off-campus job opportunities are good.

For even more information on this school, turn to page 360 of the "Stats" section.

KALAMAZOO COLLEGE

1200 ACADEMY STREET, KALAMAZOO, MI 49006 • ADMISSIONS: 616-337-7166 • FAX: 616-337-7390
FINANCIAL AID: 616-337-7192 • E-MAIL: ADMISSION@KZOO.EDU • WEBSITE: WWW.KZOO.EDU

Ratings

Quality of Life: 75   **Academic:** 84   **Admissions:** 82   **Financial Aid:** 83

Academics

Kalamazoo College's unique K Plan provides students a well-rounded education through a combination of classroom instruction, study abroad, a senior thesis project, and internships. This "diverse, yet rigorous" plan "is geared toward preparing you for your future endeavors." The approach, one human development major explains, is that "here, education is a process." An enthu-

> **SURVEY SAYS . . .**
> *Classes are small*
> *Lab facilities need improving*
> *Students aren't religious*
> *Diversity lacking on campus*
> *Campus easy to get around*
> *Athletic facilities need improving*
> *No one plays intramural sports*
> *Lousy food on campus*
> *Registration is a pain*

siastic sophomore gushes, "Last quarter, I had an internship at the Philadelphia District Attorney's office. . . . Next year, I'll be studying in Thailand for five months." Though the quality of professors varies from "great" to "terrible," students believe that their professors are always accessible and incredibly dedicated. "I wholeheartedly believe that some of them never leave their offices," an English major writes. Professors expect a similar level of dedication from their students. "The work can be overwhelming," warns one sophomore, and others complain about the "ridiculous amount" of "busy work assigned." Students rave about the small class sizes, even in lower-level courses. "I expected large lectures in college and found only seven other students in my class," one first-year English major explains. "I was shocked and impressed to find that such classes are the rule, not the exception." The administration is open, friendly, and "interested in helping each and every one of their students succeed." Offers a senior biology major, "I have shown up at the president's home unannounced and [was] welcomed in with open arms." Despite its small size, Kalamazoo offers students "an amazing amount of options." Writes a sophomore, "The academics are rigorous, but extremely rewarding." Students believe that the heavy academic workload prepares them well for graduate school.

Life

Ask a student about his or her choice to attend Kalamazoo College, and a standard response might be, "I can't imagine having a more intellectually and socially stimulating environment." Students "spend way too much time studying" but still have time to participate in many extracurricular activities. Bowling and the three formal dances held every year are among students' favorite amusements. The campus improvisational group, Monkapult, is another popular diversion. Students say that the food needs to be improved. First-year students are not allowed to have cars on campus, which seriously curtails their off-campus activities. There are no fraternities on campus, and students often go to small house parties or fiestas thrown at Western Michigan University. The onerous workload means that most students restrict their partying to Friday and Saturday nights. "Study is the key word around here," a senior Spanish major advises. "Academics are by far the most important [priority]." Of course, this means that students will use words like "dull" and "boring" to describe on-campus life.

Student Body

Kalamazoo College attracts a "disparate and not entirely meshing group of students." Which is cool. The dearth of fraternities adds to the "family atmosphere" and eliminates some of the associated cliques, but "it's easy to feel inadequate with so many overachievers." Students like their peers and believe that they are genuinely friendly, "compassionate," and always willing to help. Students agree, however, that they "do not have enough ethnic diversity." Most students come from upper-middle-class backgrounds. Still, "there are lots of different people here who are respectful and tolerant," according to one sophomore biology major. Social activism could use a jump-start, too.

ADMISSIONS

Very important factors considered by the admissions committee include: extracurricular activities, secondary school record, standardized test scores, talent/ability. *Important factors considered include:* character/personal qualities, class rank, essays, recommendations, volunteer work, work experience. *Other factors considered include:* alumni/ae relation, geographical residence, interview, minority status, state residency. SAT I or ACT required. TOEFL required of all international applicants. High school diploma or GED is required. *High school units required/recommended:* 17 total required; 4 English recommended, 3 math recommended, 3 science recommended, 3 foreign language recommended, 2 social studies recommended, 2 history recommended.

The Inside Word

K-Zoo's applicant pool is small and self-selected academically, which leads to the unusual combination of a very high acceptance rate and an impressive freshman profile. The admissions committee expects candidates to show evidence of serious academic intent, suitability for the college, and a willingness to contribute to the life of the college. Those who underestimate the evaluation process risk denial.

FINANCIAL AID

Students should submit: FAFSA, institution's own financial aid form. No deadline for regular filing. The Princeton Review suggests that all financial aid forms be submitted as soon as possible after January 1. *Need-based scholarships/grants offered:* Pell, SEOG, state scholarships/grants, private scholarships, the school's own gift aid. *Loan aid offered:* Direct Subsidized Stafford, Direct Unsubsidized Stafford, Direct PLUS, Federal Perkins, state loans. Federal Work-Study Program available. Institutional employment available. Applicants will be notified of awards on or about March 21. Off-campus job opportunities are good.

FROM THE ADMISSIONS OFFICE

"The educational program offered by Kalamazoo College combines traditional classroom instruction with experiential education. During their four years, students move freely from working and learning in groups to pursuing individual academic and artistic projects. The Kalamazoo Plan, or K Plan, enables every student to participate in four different educational experiences: on-campus learning, a career development internship, overseas study, and a senior project. The Career Development internship is typically done during the sophomore year summer allowing students to 'try on' a career. Eighty percent of all Kalamazoo College students choose to participate in this valuable experience. The Senior Individualized Project provides students with the opportunity to make use of all their experiences at the college. They may choose to do research, a thesis, creative or artistic work, or other work related to their major. All students complete a Senior Individualized Project prior to graduation."

For even more information on this school, turn to page 360 of the "Stats" section.

KANSAS STATE UNIVERSITY

119 ANDERSON HALL, MANHATTAN, KS 66506 • ADMISSIONS: 800-432-8270 • FAX: 785-532-6393
FINANCIAL AID: 785-532-6420 • E-MAIL: KSTATE@KSU.EDU • WEBSITE: WWW.CONSIDER.K-STATE.EDU

Ratings
Quality of Life: 78   **Academic:** 80   **Admissions:** 82   **Financial Aid:** 84

Academics

There's no doubt about it: K-State is a big school. This means that some students end up sticking around for five or six years trying to finish their degrees. It also means lectures are common, and class sizes regularly swell into the few-hundred range. But this is all to be expected. Less expected, perhaps, are the personal bonds that many students foster with their teachers. Of her professors,

> **SURVEY SAYS . . .**
> *Frats and sororities dominate social scene*
> *Everyone loves the Wildcats*
> *Athletic facilities are great*
> *(Almost) everyone plays intramural sports*
> *Students love Manhattan, KS, Large classes*
> *Students get along with local community*
> *Student publications are popular*
> *Students are very religious*
> *Library needs improving*

one junior writes, "They want students to succeed, and this is apparent through their extra effort." A marketing/international business major concurs: "Most of my lecture professors take time to not only teach (obviously), but to tell us that they care and want us to do well." For the most part, when talk of the classroom comes up, students tell you they are "impressed with K-State and happy to be here." Undergraduates have an unusual appreciation for the People in Charge. Students report that "K-State's administration is continually being improved and constantly focused on how to provide the highest quality of education possible for the students." Regarding the academic experience, perhaps the greatest praise came in the shortest phrase. One junior wrote plainly, "I am getting my money's worth."

Life

Kansas State shares a trait with many midwestern schools: "Everyone thinks about football—if we lose, that's everyone's low for the week." K-State is a school of more than 18,000, and it's a member of the Big 12, so the importance of sports isn't surprising. Although Manhattan is a small town in a big, sparsely populated state, students will tell you that the city is "very entertaining for its size." Oddly, one of its biggest draws is a nearby superstore. "Wal-Mart is everyone's second home," explains a student. In regards to life on campus, students boast that they "have an excellent union that is fun to spend time in." And Greek life is vibrant on campus. On the weekends, it sometimes seems "there's nothing to do if you don't drink or smoke." Reflecting on his time at K-State, a senior says, yes, "drinking is very popular here." "Most guys think about getting laid, drinking beer, smoking, not going to class," notes a freshman, "and most girls don't think about these things, but still do them." So it's fair to say that this is a school with a festive mindset. But don't fret if the beer bong isn't your instrument of choice. "It's a very laid back and comfortable campus" all around. And when campus isn't comfortable, students can always get away by taking an hour-long drive to Topeka or a two-hour trip to Wichita.

Student Body

Steal a glance at the K-State student body, and you're likely to see a group of students that looks fairly uniform. Nine out of 10 students at this school are white, and as a whole the student body tends to be "very racially divided." One black student complains that the college needs to improve in its "treatment and acknowledgement of minority programs, accomplishments, and students." A white junior adds that "attending a university located in a rural 'college town' does not offer the diversity among students that I would have liked to [have been] immersed in, but K-State students' overwhelming hospitality makes up for that." Overall, friendliness is one thing you can come to count on in Manhattan, Kansas. "Smiles and nods are common," remarks one undergrad. Some are turned off by "the ultra-religious nature of this school," while still feeling comfortable in a place that's populated by many students from the Midwest—especially Kansas. "Very nice farm boys," comments a freshman. So, "if you can get past" the homogeneity of the student population, "you will meet a lot of great people."

ADMISSIONS

Very important factors considered by the admissions committee include: class rank, secondary school record, standardized test scores. *Other factors considered include:* recommendations. SAT I or ACT required. TOEFL required of all international applicants. High school diploma or GED is required. *High school units required/recommended:* 14 total required; 4 English required, 3 math required, 3 science required, 3 social studies required.

The Inside Word

As at most public universities, the admissions process is about as straightforward as it can get. Kansas high school grads are admitted with little trouble; out-of-state students are expected to be in the top half of their graduating class and to show evidence of academic potential via ACT scores. (SAT scores are acceptable, but if you haven't taken the ACT you'll have to do so once you enroll. Ouch!) Don't be deceived by the seeming lack of rigor in admissions standards—K-State is chock full of strong students. Heightened national visibility for its athletic teams over the past few years will no doubt attract more applicants.

FINANCIAL AID

Students should submit: FAFSA. No deadline for regular filing. The Princeton Review suggests that all financial aid forms be submitted as soon as possible after January 1. *Need-based scholarships/grants offered:* Pell, SEOG, state scholarships/grants. *Loan aid offered:* Direct Subsidized Stafford, Direct Unsubsidized Stafford, Direct PLUS, Federal Perkins, college/university loans from institutional funds. Federal Work-Study Program available. Institutional employment available. Applicants will be notified of awards on a rolling basis beginning on or about April 15. Off-campus job opportunities are good.

FROM THE ADMISSIONS OFFICE

"Kansas State University offers strong academic programs, a lively intellectual atmosphere, a friendly campus community, and an environment where students achieve: K-State's total of Rhodes, Marshall, Truman, Goldwater, and Udall scholars since 1986 ranks first in the nation among state universities. In the Goldwater competition, only Princeton and Harvard have produced more winners. K-State's student government was named best in the nation in 1997 and 1995. The forensics squad finished ninth in the 2003 national tournement, and K-State was the only school in the nation with two champions in individual events. A K-State team finished in the top eight at the national debate tournament in 2003. Research facilities include the Konza Prairie, the world's largest tall grass prairie preserve, and the Macdonald Lab, the only university accelerator devoted primarily to atomic physics. Open House, held each spring, is a great way to explore K-State's more than 200 majors and options and 370 student organizations."

For even more information on this school, turn to page 361 of the "Stats" section.

KENT STATE UNIVERSITY

PO Box 5190, KENT, OH 44242-0001 • ADMISSIONS: 330-672-2444 • FAX: 330-672-2499
E-MAIL: KENTADM@ADMISSIONS.KENT.EDU • WEBSITE: WWW.KENT.EDU

Ratings
Quality of Life: 83   **Academic:** 67   **Admissions:** 62   **Financial Aid:** 76

Academics

Undergrads at Kent State University truly love the "liberal attitude" of their profs, writing that the school's greatest strength "is the student-to-professor relationship." Students say the faculty encourages students "to be open-

> **SURVEY SAYS . . .**
> *Student publications are ignored*
> *Classes are small*
> *Instructors are good teachers*
> *No one plays intramural sports*

minded and to look at things for what they are" while maintaining "their sense of humor." While students are pleased that professors recognize them "outside of the classroom" and are "more than willing to help me in any way when I approached them," some feel that "the professors don't really push us students as hard as we should be pushed." This mustn't be true of all disciplines, as an architecture major tells us, "We are locked up in the towers of Taylor Hall and forced to work night and day on projects. . . . If you survive Kent State's Architecture five-year-plus program, you can survive anything." Others offer less dramatic tales but give high marks to both the College of Education and the College of Nursing. Though some call the administration "horribly inefficient," there are many who praise them "for catering to the needs of the students." Meanwhile, President Carol Cartwright is "very personable and keeps very much in the public eye" and seems to "take criticism well." One great feature of KSU is the "variety of classes you are able to take"; an extremely well-rounded student raves, "One can take a wine-tasting class or learn about pornography! How fun is that?!"

Life

Although "Kent State University offers organizations for involvement for ALL types of people," many students scream "Party, party, party!" when class is dismissed. "This school is totally party central," one undergrad writes. "If you want a school that knows how to have fun, come here." The local bars are described as "awesome" as are the "frat houses, dance clubs, or house parties." KSU's "Halloween bash is known [throughout] Ohio for being the best. You know this place rules when the city shuts down Main Street just so we can party!!" For those trying to keep their liver in check, "Kent can still provide you with stuff to do . . . free concerts, sporting events," and the new "huge" recreation center, "a really great place to meet people while working out, swimming, climbing the wall, dance classes, sitting in the hot tub, or whatever!" The campus could stand for some improvement, though, in the residence halls: "They are out of date and have trouble accommodating the college student of today," although plans "for remodeling" are "in the works." And in line with KSU's historical reputation, "there is always some controversy . . . to keep your interest. Right now there 's a controversy over whether it should be okay for a particular student to hang the American flag upside down in his window." Though Kent State students see their school as "a city within a city," fun can be found in nearby Akron or Cleveland as well.

Student Body

Although the majority of KSU's student body is Caucasian, students insist that "if you want diversity, this is the place." One student explains, "I have learned A LOT about interacting with and understanding people who have very different views from myself on things inclusive of, but not limited to, friendships, relationships, religion, and sexual orientation." Another calls Kent "a melting pot. We have every type of person and everyone respects each other." Some believe that "instead of [the student body] being divided by color or sexual preference, it is more divided by whether you're Greek or not." Kent's large student population (18,000-plus) has its pros and cons; while one student claims that "reinvention is easy and you can always find someone to fit in with," another warns, "It's hard to get to know people. My advice would be to join as many clubs and activities as possible." The typical Kent State undergrad is described by one as being "outgoing, artsy, liberal," but it's important to note that "Kent State is adaptable to unconventional students—older returning students and students with families" as well.

ADMISSIONS

Very important factors considered by the admissions committee include: secondary school record. *Important factors considered include:* standardized test scores. *Other factors considered include:* class rank. TOEFL required of all international applicants. High school diploma or GED is required. *High school units required/recommended:* 16 total recommended; 4 English recommended, 3 math recommended, 3 science recommended, 2 science lab recommended, 2 foreign language recommended, 3 social studies recommended.

The Inside Word

General admission to KSU is not so selective; however, some programs—including architecture, education, fashion design, and interior design—set the bar considerably higher. Students admitted to the university at large are not necessary guaranteed places in their program of choice. Check with the admissions office to learn more about the specific requirements of each program.

FINANCIAL AID

Students should submit: FAFSA, and University Scholarship Application Form. The Princeton Review suggests that all financial aid forms be submitted as soon as possible after January 1. *Need-based scholarships/grants offered:* Pell, SEOG, state scholarships/grants, private scholarships, and the school's own gift aid. *Loan aid offered:* Direct Subsidized Stafford, Direct Unsubsidized Stafford, Direct PLUS, Federal Perkins, Federal Nursing, state loans, college/university loans from institutional funds, and alternative loans. Federal Work-Study Program available. Institutional employment available. Applicants will be notified of awards on or about March 15. Off-campus job opportunities are good.

For even more information on this school, turn to page 361 of the "Stats" section.

KENYON COLLEGE

ADMISSIONS OFFICE, RANSOM HALL, GAMBIER, OH 43022-9623 • ADMISSIONS: 800-848-2468
FAX: 740-427-5770 • FINANCIAL AID: 740-427-5430 • E-MAIL: ADMISSIONS@KENYON.EDU
WEBSITE: WWW.KENYON.EDU

Ratings

Quality of Life: 89   **Academic:** 95   **Admissions:** 92   **Financial Aid:** 81

Academics

With its small classes, dedicated teachers, and sharp student body, Kenyon College is a classic example of a small liberal arts college. Perhaps most paradigmatic is the close relationship students enjoy with the faculty; writes one undergrad, "Professors are amazing. They are a huge part of the family known as Kenyon. We have dinner at their houses,

> **SURVEY SAYS . . .**
> *Diversity lacking on campus*
> *Beautiful campus, Classes are small*
> *Students aren't religious*
> *(Almost) everyone smokes*
> *Lousy off-campus food*
> *(Almost) no one listens to college radio*
> *Athletic facilities need improving*
> *Musical organizations are hot*

babysit their kids, and look to many of them as mentors." Adds another, "Professors here are completely approachable. We often know their spouses, their children, their dogs, and their houses. As a result, it's extremely easy to find them and to ask them questions, etc." The community atmosphere helps students deal with the considerable rigors of a Kenyon education. Explains one student, "It's not easy here, but it's satisfying in every way when you do well. I feel quite lucky to be surrounded by such a select group of intelligent students and faculty." Says another, "Kenyon is very academic in atmosphere, but it doesn't have a competitive slant to it. We have lots of interesting, specialized classes and very much focus on knowing things in depth rather than simply what you need to know to get by." Students enjoy a surprisingly wide variety of courses considering the size of the school. Says one, "Often students are heard saying there are so many courses they want to take they don't know if they'll have time to take all the ones they want in the four years they have." The administration, though it is "too politically correct," receives praise as well for its willingness "to listen and discuss anything" at practically any time.

Life

The Greek system, student organizations, and a full slate of school-sponsored events attempt to offset the relative lack of activity in Gambier, Kenyon's small hometown. Students report that "there are a TON of student organizations and activities to get involved in on campus and opportunities to create new ones each year." Writes one student, "Life at Kenyon is busy. . . . With over 90 student organizations from fencing to Zen meditation there is simply not enough time." Still, "Kenyon can be a bit boring at times. It's just such a small place that if you're not into the frat party scene, you don't have many other party environment options. But the school does try to provide other opportunities for students to have fun. There is almost always a movie showing, a musical performance, or a comedian somewhere on campus! And the college also provides shuttles to go into the little town that is near us in case we need anything. Once or twice a month there is even a shuttle that goes into Columbus." Kenyon students will soon enjoy the benefits of a much-needed new state-of-the-art fitness, recreation, and athletic facility, due to open in the fall of 2005.

Student Body

As at many private colleges, diversity at Kenyon is primarily geographic. Writes one student, "Students come here from all over the U.S. They are some of the brightest and friendliest scholars in the country. As a freshman, I was humbled by my peers. In high school, I was the valedictorian, but at Kenyon I discovered that there are so many people that are more talented and intelligent." Students acknowledge that "Kenyon has a problem with the fact that so many of its students come from well-off, two-parent households that sent them to private school. Many people led sheltered lives and continue to do that here. But not everyone is that way, and there is diversity, just not as much as there ideally would be." Students enjoy the fact that "people generally get along," which makes the "strong" community here "more close-knit than most." Undergrads are usually so absorbed in their studies that they "tend to be somewhat apathetic politically."

ADMISSIONS

Very important factors considered by the admissions committee include: character/personal qualities, class rank, recommendations, secondary school record. *Important factors considered include:* essays, extracurricular activities, interview, standardized test scores, talent/ability. *Other factors considered include:* alumni/ae relation, geographical residence, minority status, state residency, volunteer work, work experience. SAT I or ACT required. TOEFL required of all international applicants. High school diploma or GED is required. *High school units required/recommended:* 18 total required; 23 total recommended; 4 English required, 3 math required, 4 math recommended, 3 science required, 4 science recommended, 2 science lab required, 3 science lab recommended, 3 foreign language required, 4 foreign language recommended, 2 social studies required, 3 social studies recommended, 3 elective required, 4 elective recommended.

The Inside Word

Kenyon pays close attention to matchmaking in the course of candidate selection, and personal accomplishments are just as significant as academic ones. Applicants who rank the college high among their choices should definitely interview.

FINANCIAL AID

Students should submit: FAFSA, CSS/Financial Aid PROFILE, noncustodial (divorced/separated) parent's statement, completed tax returns. Regular filing deadline is February 15. The Princeton Review suggests that all financial aid forms be submitted as soon as possible after January 1. *Need-based scholarships/grants offered:* Pell, SEOG, state scholarships/grants, private scholarships, the school's own gift aid. *Loan aid offered:* FFEL Subsidized Stafford, FFEL Unsubsidized Stafford, FFEL PLUS, Federal Perkins, college/university loans from institutional funds. Federal Work-Study Program available. Institutional employment available. Applicants will be notified of awards on or about April 1. Off-campus job opportunities are fair.

FROM THE ADMISSIONS OFFICE

"Students and alumni alike think of Kenyon as a place that fosters 'learning in the company of friends.' While faculty expectations are rigorous and the work challenging, the academic atmosphere is cooperative, not competitive. Indications of intellectual curiosity and passion for learning, more than just high grades and test scores, are what we look for in applications. Important as well are demonstrated interests in nonacademic pursuits, whether in athletics, the arts, writing, or another passion. Life in this small college community is fueled by the talents and enthusiasm of our students, so the admission staff seeks students who have a range of talents and interests."

For even more information on this school, turn to page 362 of the "Stats" section.

KETTERING UNIVERSITY

1700 WEST THIRD AVENUE, FLINT, MI 48504 • ADMISSIONS: 810-762-7865 • FAX: 810-762-9837
E-MAIL: ADMISSIONS@KETTERING.EDU • WEBSITE: WWW.KETTERING.EDU

Ratings
Quality of Life: 79   Academic: 83   Admissions: 85   Financial Aid: 75

Academics

Students feel that "the professional and career experience you gain at Kettering University is unparalleled," thanks largely to a mandatory co-operative education program that requires students to work three out of every six months (the other three months are spent in

SURVEY SAYS . . .
Hard liquor is popular, Classes are small
School is well run, No one cheats
Class discussions encouraged
Popular college radio, Theater is hot
Student publications are popular

class). Explains one undergrad, "The co-op program gives you a break every three months of the year. The school is broken up into two sections: when A section is at school, B section is off in the work force and vice versa." Each academic year begins in July and is comprised of four terms. "The co-op experience is what makes this school what it is," notes one student. "As much is learned and applied at work as in the classroom." As an added bonus, "You can make up to $60,000, or more, before graduation" through co-op. Students warn that the shortened academic schedule makes for "an average course load of 19 or 20 units to get the necessary classes out of the way. . . . The classes are fairly difficult, but there are a variety of opportunities for help everywhere you look." Adds one undergrad, "Academics are very hard. . . . However, if you graduate, you'll never need to worry about finding a job, and employers will pay more, mostly because of the difficult curriculum and the co-op." Students here tell us that "the engineering program is great; the business program is quite a bit more intense than most other undergraduate business programs." They appreciate the fact that "the class size is small and the teachers are easy to get along with and help to facilitate learning. There is a very personal atmosphere between the students and the faculty."

Life

An intense academic schedule, a paucity of women students, and a co-op program that shuttles students on and off campus every three months makes for "a very, very limited social life" at Kettering. Students enjoy athletics in their spare time; writes one, "Since we have no intercollegiate sports (because of the three-month revolving academic/work terms) the intramural program is highly competitive. There are two options: 'A tourney' for the highly competitive sort, or 'R tourney' for the more relaxed, get-out-there-and-do-something sort of people. I would say the majority of people take part in these programs." Students also tell us that "About 60 percent of all students take part in some sort of fraternity or sorority. The motto of 'study hard, play hard' is put into practice with intense study during the week to fight 19 to 20 units in 11 weeks, followed by intense parties on the weekends." Hometown Flint, Michigan, is conveniently located for visits to three other large campuses: University of Michigan at Ann Arbor, Michigan State, and Central Michigan University.

Student Body

The "nice, hardworking, and original people" who attend Kettering are "fairly diverse, although the majority of the students come from Michigan or bordering states. The school pulls students from all over the nation and the world." Undergrads report that "the student

150 ■ THE MIDWESTERN COLLEGES

body here is rather small so everyone pretty much knows each other" and note that "because of the high percentage of Greek life, brotherhood and sisterhood is very prevalent in our college community." Some feel that "there are so many middle-class white males at this school that it is kind of depressing. And not just that they're all white males, but that they're engineering types as well (think comic book guy on The Simpsons)."

ADMISSIONS

Very important factors considered by the admissions committee include: class rank, secondary school record, and standardized test scores. *Important factors considered include:* character/personal qualities, extracurricular activities, talent/ability, and work experience. *Other factors considered include:* interview, minority status, recommendations, and volunteer work. SAT I or ACT required. TOEFL required of all international applicants. High school diploma is required and GED is not accepted. *High school units required/recommended:* 18 total required; 22 total recommended; 3 English required, 4 English recommended, 4 math required, 2 science required, 4 science recommended, 2 science lab required, 4 science lab recommended, 2 foreign language recommended, 4 social studies recommended, 4 elective recommended.

The Inside Word

Kettering is a competitive school with rolling admissions. Apply early—as the entering class fills, admissions standards grow tougher.

FINANCIAL AID

Students should submit: FAFSA. No deadline for regular filing. The Princeton Review suggests that all financial aid forms be submitted as soon as possible after January 1. *Need-based scholarships/grants offered:* Pell, SEOG, state scholarships/grants, private scholarships, the school's own gift aid, and Co-op Resource. While income from required professional co-op experience is not financial aid, it is a substantial resource earned by all Kettering students. *Loan aid offered:* Direct Subsidized Stafford, Direct Unsubsidized Stafford, Direct PLUS, state loans, and alternative loans. Federal Work-Study Program available. Institutional employment available. Applicants will be notified of awards on a rolling basis beginning on or about February 15. Off-campus job opportunities are excellent.

FROM THE ADMISSIONS OFFICE

"With its rich heritage, Kettering University, founded in 1919 and formerly known as General Motors Institute, is a university on the move for 2003 and beyond. Hands-on laboratories like the new Systems Design Studio, the Combustion Simulation Studio, and the Environmental Scanning Electron Microscopy Lab give students real lab experience, and that's just part of Kettering's "growth spurt." New student apartments and a $42 million mechanical engineering and chemistry center are set to open in 2003. There are outdoor soccer and baseball fields, a new outdoor track, and outdoor lighting for a recreational schedule that benefits the students and makes Kettering Park one of the finest student recreation spaces in Michigan.

"The growth, expansion, and improvements underway at Kettering are all directed toward delivering the best, real private education for future leaders. Kettering's connection to business and industry through professional co-op is one of a kind. Students may begin working as early as freshman year, receive a paycheck and work side by side with professionals, and earn up to two and a half years of real world experience by graduation. And nearly 100 percent of students have full-time employment or are accepted into grad school before they even receive their Kettering diploma.

"Its alumni validate the success of Kettering's 'Education for the REAL World.' Over the years, Kettering has produced countless innovative leaders who have revolutionized the world. And nearly one out of every six Kettering graduates becomes a company CEO, president, or business owner."

For even more information on this school, turn to page 363 of the "Stats" section.

KNOX COLLEGE

Box K-148, Galesburg, IL 61401 • Admissions: 800-678-KNOX • Fax: 309-341-7070
Financial Aid: 309-341-7149 • E-mail: admission@knox.edu • Website: www.knox.edu

Ratings

Quality of Life: 87   Academic: 92   Admissions: 81   Financial Aid: 96

Academics

"Freedom. Lots of freedom. Freedom to express, print, say, or do what you want." That's what tiny Knox College is all about, its students say, and that's why students praise this "extremely demanding" school. "If you're passionate and ambitious enough about something, you can make it happen at Knox," explains one undergrad. "New clubs are always starting, people get school money to fund trips to D.C. for protests, students direct their own plays, etc. The administration is supportive of just about anything." The student/faculty relationships here are "truly special, very relaxed, and very personal. Professors are more than educators. They dedicate their time to the students to ensure that everyone is getting out of the education what they put into it." The same holds true for student/administration relations; writes one student, "When I first visited Knox, I was greeted by Roger, who introduced himself as an alumnus. It wasn't until they introduced him in a speech that I knew he was the president of the college. But that's how it is at Knox: a very tight-knit community that works together." Knox is the kind of place that inspires long-term loyalty, which explains why "the amount of alumni that come back to speak to students is quite impressive." As one student summed up, "Rather than a school where one spends four years, Knox is a school that permeates your entire life."

> **SURVEY SAYS . . .**
> *Campus easy to get around*
> *Great library*
> *Great computer facilities*
> *Lots of beer drinking*
> *Campus is beautiful*
> *Registration is a breeze*
> *Lab facilities are great*
> *Students are happy*
> *Hard liquor is popular*

Life

If you've never heard of Knox's hometown of Galesburg, you aren't alone. Students here concede that "Galesburg is . . . well, Galesburg." Reported one undergrad, it "isn't exactly the center of the universe. Luckily for us, Knox is usually very conscious of this. They are very good about bringing in outside entertainment." Events include "student theatre, the choir, or sports, and while none of these events are sold out, they are fairly well attended. Outside speakers are sometimes scheduled and their talks are often crammed full." Other options include "movie night in the Round Room, Jazz Night at Cherry Street, or a band playing in The Gizmo." Despite the availability of such varied activity, many here tell us that Knox "definitely has a culture where all that 'happens' on the weekends is drinking at frat parties." As one student put it, "The weekends are weak, unless your friends consist of Keystone and Busch Light. Alcohol is a major factor at Knox. The Greek system is really strong." Despite the Greek presence, students tell us that the suite-style dorms, and not the Greek system, are the key to the school's social universe. "The suite system here is unique," explains one student. "Students usually live in a hall where all rooms open onto a common living area. This allows for interaction between everyone, not just the people that you live next to. In addition, you take a lot of classes together, so you can have a discussion on current issues or on an assignment for a class. It is very conducive to forming long-lasting friendships."

Student Body

Students are adamant that Knox College "has a pretty broad range of students" among its small population. "This campus is so diverse ethnically, and no one comes from the same background," writes one student. "Everyone has different interests, likes, and dislikes. We're here for a common purpose—to learn—but other than that, we're all different." Although the "majority of students here are white liberals," there is also "a crowd of more conservative and religious (mostly white American) population," and students report that relations among the various groups are remarkably stress-free. Knox's "high school jock frat boys who haven't really grown up yet, rich kids that want to be hippies, kids that actually are hippies, and geeks that are happy to be left alone and play computer games" share one more common trait: they were "probably all the kind of smart, kind of strange, but not-too-weird students in high school. We all kind of fit in but were never really popular."

ADMISSIONS

Very important factors considered by the admissions committee include: secondary school record. Important factors considered include: class rank, essays, recommendations. *Other factors considered include:* alumni/ae relation, character/personal qualities, extracurricular activities, interview, minority status, standardized test scores, talent/ability, volunteer work. SAT I or ACT required. TOEFL required of all international applicants. High school diploma or GED is required. *High school units required/recommended:* 15 total required; 18 total recommended; 4 English recommended, 4 math recommended, 3 science recommended, 2 science lab recommended, 3 foreign language recommended, 2 social studies recommended, 2 history recommended.

The Inside Word

A small applicant pool necessitates Knox's high acceptance rate. The student body is nonetheless well qualified, and candidates should show solid academic accomplishment.

FINANCIAL AID

Students should submit: FAFSA, institution's own financial aid form. No deadline for regular filing. The Princeton Review suggests that all financial aid forms be submitted as soon as possible after January 1. *Need-based scholarships/grants offered:* Pell, SEOG, state scholarships/grants, private scholarships, the school's own gift aid. *Loan aid offered:* Direct Subsidized Stafford, Direct Unsubsidized Stafford, Direct PLUS, Federal Perkins, college/university loans from institutional funds. Federal Work-Study Program available. Institutional employment available. Applicants will be notified of awards on a rolling basis beginning on or about March 15. Off-campus job opportunities are fair.

FROM THE ADMISSIONS OFFICE

"Freedom to Flourish: The idea is simple. College should be a place where you discover yourself—where your talents are nourished and your aspirations become clear. A place that prepares you to turn your dreams into reality. But this is not the only reason college is important. By helping you learn to think clearly and independently, getting you ready to face the future with confidence, college should make you free. At Knox you are challenged to think for yourself and to explain your ideas. You learn how to analyze and to write clearly. Your mind and talents are stretched by exploring new areas of knowledge. You grow, too, in unexpected ways, through the rich opportunities and challenges of life in this creative, vital community. By graduation, you have received a sound, comprehensive education and are ready for the future. You will have the skills, background, and confidence to make the future your own."

For even more information on this school, turn to page 363 of the "Stats" section.

LAKE ERIE COLLEGE

391 WEST WASHINGTON STREET, PAINESVILLE, OH 44077-3389 • ADMISSIONS: 800-639-7879
FAX: 440-352-3533 • E-MAIL: LECADMIT@LAKEERIE.EDU • WEBSITE: WWW.LAKEERIE.EDU

Ratings
Quality of Life: 80   **Academic:** 68   **Admissions:** 66   **Financial Aid:** 75

Academics

Ever hear of a Bachelor of Science in equine studies? If not, get ready. Lake Erie College is the proud owner of more than 65 horses, and among its more popular majors are equine business and facility management, and equestrian teacher/trainer—each leading to a

SURVEY SAYS . . .
School is well run
Great food on campus
Diversity lacking on campus
Classes are small
(Almost) everyone plays intramural sports

BS in equine studies. Whether learning the ins and outs of horses or honing in on one of LEC's 20 other undergrad majors, students here appreciate the small classes and liberal arts emphasis that permeates the academic halls. "The classes are so small that teachers get to know you and you get to know them," coos a student. For the most part, students have pleasant things to say about their professors: "Well-educated, enthusiastic, and professional about their subject matter and classes," is how one student describes them, and another says, "They are always willing to help when you need it." A more wary student warns that if you're not careful you'll run into profs "who do not know a thing about what they are teaching, or they can not speak the language well enough to teach for students to understand." Student ratings of the administration run the gamut, from "awesome . . . enthusiastic about helping the student body in every way they can" to "average" to "I think that the administration is real shady here at LEC." On those sunny midwestern days, though, shady might not be the worst thing in the world.

Life

There are plenty of nice things you can say about Painesville, Ohio: it's quiet, it's safe, it's cozy, and it's home to a number of great restaurants. This said, some students still claim that Painesville is an appropriate name for this town. "There is little to do," laments a student. "Therefore, we do a lot of drinking and playing cards." Nonetheless, in close proximity to campus "there are movie theatres, bowling alleys, bars, and places to eat." If these options are not your cup of tea, then you may be out of luck—unless you have a car, that is. An international student says, "Because I don't have a car, it's kind of . . . inconvenient for me to go out on weekends." If he were able to cruise around, he'd find plenty of options half an hour away, in downtown Cleveland. From pro sports to the Rock and Roll Hall of Fame, and from museums to concert halls, Cleveland is sure to provide relief from the ennui. The Cleveland Flats—"a big club district"—is a particularly hot student destination. Students here warn incomers not to depend on campus life for social outlets. "There are not enough activities on campus," says a student. Driving the point home, a resident advisor tells us, "We had a beach party in my dorm and that had about 20 to 25 people come out. For our school that is an awesome turn out." A student encapsulates the LEC experience by saying, "Life at Lake Erie College is only fun if you make it and are willing to bend some rules to do it."

Student Body

Set in quaint Painesville, in northeast Ohio, Lake Erie College is an institution that caters to students who enjoy the benefits of a small, personal school. While the smallness of Lake Erie mandates a certain sense of friendliness and camaraderie, it also perpetuates a brand of cliquey-ness. "It's like a big high school with many cliques or groups," admits a student. But if your eyes are able to focus beyond the cliques, you should have no trouble discovering that "the students here are really friendly and easy to get along with." An undergrad puts it this way: "We're like our own family"—albeit a family with a slightly lopsided gender ratio. "I heard the ratio of women to men is like 7:1," says a male student (it's actually closer to 3:1). As you may guess, not too many of the guys complain.

ADMISSIONS

Very important factors considered by the admissions committee include: secondary school record. *Important factors considered include:* interview and standardized test scores. *Other factors considered include:* alumni/ae relation, character/personal qualities, class rank, essays, extracurricular activities, geographical residence, minority status, recommendations, religious affiliation/commitment, state residency, talent/ability, volunteer work, and work experience. TOEFL required of all international applicants. High school diploma or GED is required. *High school units required/recommended:* 4 English required, 3 math required, 3 science required, 2 science lab required, 2 foreign language required, 3 social studies required, 3 social studies recommended.

The Inside Word

Lake Erie is not highly selective. Borderline candidates should visit the campus and interview with an admissions officer; a demonstration of interest could very well make the difference in such cases.

FINANCIAL AID

Students should submit: FAFSA. No deadline for regular filing. The Princeton Review suggests that all financial aid forms be submitted as soon as possible after January 1. *Need-based scholarships/grants offered:* Pell, SEOG, state scholarships/grants, private scholarships, and the school's own gift aid. *Loan aid offered:* FFEL Subsidized Stafford, FFEL Unsubsidized Stafford, FFEL PLUS, Federal Perkins, and payment plans. Federal Work-Study Program available. Institutional employment available. Applicants will be notified of awards on a rolling basis beginning on or about January 20. Off-campus job opportunities are excellent.

For even more information on this school, turn to page 364 of the "Stats" section.

LAKE FOREST COLLEGE

555 NORTH SHERIDAN ROAD, LAKE FOREST, IL 60045 • ADMISSIONS: 847-735-5000 • FAX: 847-735-6291
FINANCIAL AID: 847-735-5103 • E-MAIL: ADMISSIONS@LFC.EDU • WEBSITE: WWW.LAKEFOREST.EDU

Ratings
Quality of Life: 84   **Academic:** 92   **Admissions:** 79   **Financial Aid:** 93

Academics

The 1,300 students that rub elbows at Lake Forest College believe they receive a quality education in the context of a supportive, liberal arts environment. Boasts one, "The fact that I have seen many of my professors in the cafeteria, at sporting events, and at music concerts on campus

> **SURVEY SAYS . . .**
> *Great food on campus*
> *Student publications are ignored*
> *Classes are small, Campus feels safe*
> *Computer facilities need improving*
> *Lousy off-campus food*
> *Class discussions encouraged*

shows how concerned they are with everyone's total college experience." Not only do professors "go out of their way to make themselves accessible" both inside and outside the classroom, but the school offers free tutoring in every entry-level subject and many advanced classes. A senior sums it up, "I was challenged, but [also] given every resource I needed to succeed." Students tout not just the accessibility, but also the quality of the faculty, reporting that "Lake Forest boasts a wonderful mix of old and new professors who are second to none." Many agree that their professors "could be teaching at universities like Northwestern or University of Chicago for higher salaries," but choose LFC "because they love to teach and they believe in the liberal arts system of study." And while some call professors "nurturing," others think "overbearing" is the more appropriate word to describe them. Similarly, what some call a "supportive" environment, others describe as "a bit on the easy side."

Life

Located 30 miles north of Chicago, in the affluent, "mansion-filled" suburb of Lake Forest, it's no surprise that students "often gripe about the town shutting down too early" and declare that the surrounding area is "not a college town at all." Most see benefit to the setup, however, explaining that "being at such a small school in a small town creates a true cohesive community." Though Chicago is "an easy train ride away," many LFC students choose to hang out on campus, where they can participate in the school's "really strong drama organization" or kill some time playing and watching sports. Enthuses one undergrad, "Everyone enjoys going to support every sport, not just the big ones like basketball and football." Agrees another, "For fun we either play sports (basketball, powder puff football), support our awesome sports teams . . . go to bars, or hang out at the quad." On the weekends, "the Campus Activities department does a lot to try and help by bringing lots of stuff to the campus." The consensus is that the plentiful "all-campus parties" are the preferred venues for blowing off steam. Students describe Lake Forest as a "wet campus" and says that a large portion of the "social life revolves around drinking beer."

Student Body

Though some claim "Lake Forest is a very economically diverse school," others are skeptical of this description. However, it is undeniable that the school gives out a ton of need-based financial aid—to 70 percent of its students, to be exact. Indeed, it is reported that Lake Forest's undergraduate population primarily consists of "smart kids from the public and private high schools across the country" mixed with some "New England boarding school types." However, "there is a growing group of ethnic minorities on campus," and "faculty and staff

[are] extremely supportive of gay students." Nonetheless, Lake Forest students say that the majority of their classmates "respect the difference of others, even if they don't agree with them," and that "for the most part, people seem to get along."

ADMISSIONS

Very important factors considered by the admissions committee include: secondary school record. *Important factors considered include:* essays, extracurricular activities. *Other factors considered include:* alumni/ae relation, character/personal qualities, class rank, geographical residence, interview, recommendations, standardized test scores, talent/ability, volunteer work, work experience. SAT I or ACT required. TOEFL required of all international applicants. High school diploma or GED is required. *High school units required/recommended:* 16 total required; 19 total recommended; 4 English required, 3 math required, 4 math recommended, 2 science required, 3 science recommended, 2 science lab required, 3 science lab recommended, 2 foreign language required, 4 foreign language recommended, 1 social studies required, 2 social studies recommended, 1 history required, 2 history recommended, 3 elective required.

The Inside Word

Candidates with a solid academic record will meet with little resistance on the road to acceptance. But remember that Lake Forest definitely has a prep-school-at-the-college-level feel. It pays to keep the admissions committee's eagerness to assess the whole person in mind when completing the application.

FINANCIAL AID

Students should submit: FAFSA, CSS/Financial Aid PROFILE, federal income tax return. The Princeton Review suggests that all financial aid forms be submitted as soon as possible after January 1. *Need-based scholarships/grants offered:* Pell, SEOG, state scholarships/grants, private scholarships, the school's own gift aid. *Loan aid offered:* Direct Subsidized Stafford, Direct Unsubsidized Stafford, Direct PLUS, Federal Perkins, college/university loans from institutional funds. Federal Work-Study Program available. Institutional employment available. Applicants will be notified of awards on a rolling basis beginning on or about March 15. Off-campus job opportunities are good.

FROM THE ADMISSIONS OFFICE

"Where you go to college can have everything to do with what you get out of college. As you think about the academic challenges and resources you seek—and the overall experience you desire—consider what Lake Forest College has to offer you.

"Lake Forest College is Chicago's national liberal arts college. Located 30 miles north of downtown Chicago, the College's proximity to the city provides Lake Forest students and faculty with unique academic, cultural, and employment resources. Through partnerships with a variety of cultural, educational, financial, research, and scientific institutions in Chicago and its environs, students are engaged in an active learning process that takes them beyond the traditional boundaries of the classroom, integrating the theoretical and the practical.

"The 1,300 students represent 43 countries and 45 states. Lake Forest College fosters interaction among a diverse community of students and faculty with a significant international and minority population. The faculty are dedicated teachers and accomplished scholars, with 98 percent holding a PhD or equivalent. The faculty do all the teaching; you will not find teaching assistants at Lake Forest. The College's Career Advancement Center (CAC) begins working with students during their first year on campus, and later provides mentoring opportunities with alumni from around the globe as well as internship assistance and job placement.

"College should be demanding, but not a relentless grind. With more than 80 student-run organizations and clubs, 17 varsity NCAA Division III teams, and a variety of intramural and club sports, students find many opportunities outside the classroom."

For even more information on this school, turn to page 365 of the "Stats" section.

LAWRENCE UNIVERSITY

PO Box 599, Appleton, WI 54912-0599 • Admissions: 920-832-6500 • Fax: 920-832-6782
Financial Aid: 920-832-6583 • E-mail: excel@lawrence.edu • Website: www.lawrence.edu

Ratings

Quality of Life: 81   **Academic:** 92   **Admissions:** 85   **Financial Aid:** 91

Academics

Students at Lawrence University, a small midwestern school, brag about their "very strong" and "nationally known" biology, psychology, and music programs. Other departments are solid, too, although some students worry that the school sometimes ignores its less renowned programs in order to tout its star attractions. Across the board, "the academics at Lawrence are challenging and the class work is rigorous but fulfill-

> **SURVEY SAYS . . .**
> *No one cheats*
> *Student publications are ignored*
> *Classes are small*
> *Campus feels safe*
> *Students aren't religious*
> *Musical organizations are hot*
> *Low cost of living*
> *Diverse students interact*
> *No one plays intramural sports*

ing." Writes one student, "Lawrence is tough, but you do get a top-notch education for how hard you work. Because of the school's size, Lawrence's faculty expects each student to do their absolute best rather than fulfilling a general class requirement." Many departments place a strong emphasis on writing skills; students note approvingly that the school provides "facilities that assist students with their work, such as the writing lab, where students can go to check their paper before handing it in to the professors." Professors, students agree, "are amazing. They are great teachers and wonderful people. They are always available for student questions and concerns, or just to chat." Administrators are "very friendly and accessible. The president of the college can often be seen walking through the campus," and "the facilities are great."

Life

Lawrence is home to a pretty placid social scene, according to most students. "If partying is your scene, Lawrence probably isn't the answer. Occasionally there are frat parties, and alcohol is sometimes available if you hunt it down." Usually, though, "weekends on campus are dull," reports one typical student. Hometown Appleton "is not the most exciting place to be. The movie theatres are about two miles away, as are the grocery stores and the mall. It's crucial to know someone with a car." Students appreciate the fact that "the small community makes for a safe and cozy environment" but still wish the town had more to offer in the way of diversion. Lawrence does have a very active arts scene featuring "a lot of student and faculty (and guest) concerts to go to because of the conservatory presence." There are also "several film societies that show art films or theme-related films on a regular basis," art openings, and "guest performers at the underground coffeehouse." Students enjoy "sledding down Union Hill on cafeteria trays" during the long winter months and note that "the residence halls put on activities for us, like Capture the Flag between two halls. In the fall the frat quad will have barbeques for the campus, and everybody will go have a hot dog and play Frisbee or pass around a football." Still, many students find that "for fun, we end up watching movies or hanging out to play cards or darts."

Student Body

Lawrence's "very open-minded," "friendly" undergrads "seems to be from a specific income bracket and social background. Diversity would be nice, but it's hard to come by at a school that costs so much to attend," explains one undergrad. Students observe that "the admissions committee does a great deal to offset this homogenous group by attracting a large number of international students, which benefits the student body as a whole," although many also say that internationals tend to keep to themselves. Students also report that "conservatory students do not interact much with the other students." Despite the divisions, undergrads admire each other's "overall spunk and good humor in the face of frigid weather and snowballing homework." There is "a large homosexual population, and everyone accepts them. I've seen gay couples dancing at frat parties."

ADMISSIONS

Very important factors considered by the admissions committee include: secondary school record. *Important factors considered include:* class rank, essays, minority status, recommendations, standardized test scores, talent/ability. *Other factors considered include:* character/personal qualities, extracurricular activities, interview, volunteer work, alumni/ae relation, work experience. SAT I or ACT required. TOEFL required of all international applicants. High school diploma is required and GED is not accepted. *High school units required/recommended:* 4 English recommended, 3 math recommended, 3 science recommended, 3 foreign language recommended, 2 social studies recommended, 2 history recommended.

The Inside Word

Although the admit rate is fairly high, getting into Lawrence demands an above-average academic record. Students who are serious about the university should stick with a very challenging high school courseload straight through senior year, put significant energy into their application essays, and definitely interview.

FINANCIAL AID

Students should submit: FAFSA, institution's own financial aid form. Regular filing deadline is March 15. The Princeton Review suggests that all financial aid forms be submitted as soon as possible after January 1. *Need-based scholarships/grants offered:* Pell, SEOG, state scholarships/grants, private scholarships, the school's own gift aid. *Loan aid offered:* Direct Subsidized Stafford, Direct Unsubsidized Stafford, Direct PLUS, Federal Perkins. Federal Work-Study Program available. Institutional employment available. Applicants will be notified of awards on or about April 15. Off-campus job opportunities are excellent.

FROM THE ADMISSIONS OFFICE

"Lawrence students are characterized by their energy, commitment to community service, respect for each other, and desire to achieve their full potential. Campus activities are abundant, off-campus study programs are popular (more than half of the students take advantage of them), small classes are the norm (65 percent of the classes have 10 or fewer students in them), and, yes, winters are for the hardy! But the diversity of interests and experiences, the drive to excel, the wealth of cultural opportunities presented by the art, theater, and music departments, the quality of research students undertake alongside PhD faculty, and the general friendly attitude of everyone at the university contribute to an excitement that more than outweighs the challenge of winter."

For even more information on this school, turn to page 365 of the "Stats" section.

LOYOLA UNIVERSITY CHICAGO

820 NORTH MICHIGAN AVENUE, CHICAGO, IL 60611 • ADMISSIONS: 800-262-2373 • FAX: 312-915-6449
FINANCIAL AID: 312-915-6639 • E-MAIL: ADMISSION@LUC.EDU • WEBSITE: WWW.LUC.EDU

Ratings

Quality of Life: 73   Academic: 75   Admissions: 73   Financial Aid: 86

Academics

Top four reasons to attend this mid-sized Roman Catholic institution perched at the edge of "beautiful" Lake Michigan on Chicago's North Shore: "academic reputation, diverse student body, small class size, and great location." Many students, religious and nonreligious, still consider the school's "Jesuit character" one of its biggest draws. "Loyola's greatest strength is its commitment to providing students" with a "whole-person education," the

> **SURVEY SAYS . . .**
> *Musical organizations aren't popular*
> *Classes are small*
> *Class discussions are rare*
> *Students don't get along with local community*
> *Unattractive campus*
> *Students are not very happy*
> *Ethnic diversity on campus*
> *Intercollegiate sports are unpopular or nonexistent*
> *Lots of long lines and red tape*

mark of the Jesuits. Most students agree that "Loyola's professors are dedicated to their research, to their students (by being approachable), and to the Loyola mission—which is to provide a good education and guide to [becoming] a balanced, independent thinker." The historical Jesuit commitment to providing education for all has another benefit: true cultural, economic, and ethnic diversity amongst its faculty, staff, and student body. This diversity is enhanced by the school's division into several different campuses—one in downtown Chicago, another on the north side, and the medical center (Loyola has a popular pre-med program) in the western suburbs. Notes a sophomore, "The diverse atmosphere at the different campuses is great. Where else can you be a frat boy on Monday, Wednesday, Friday, and a corporate guru on Tuesday and Thursday?" And while some point out that Loyola has had some rough times in recent years with lack of funds, long-tenured professors, substandard facilities, and an out-of-touch administration ("Trying to talk to the administration is like trying to contact Elvis," writes a junior), a sophomore points out that "Loyola is in a transition period" and that the mood is very hopeful about the school's new president.

Life

A senior sums up the scene: "Loyola isn't your 'typical' college campus. If you are looking for big frat parties or keggers this isn't the place to be. However, if you are into smaller parties, cultural events, and the fun of Chicago, this place ROCKS!" Whether it's going down to Clarke & Belmont (a nexus for the Alternation); taking in an improv show right down the street from the uptown campus; or "heading downtown to grab some famous Chicago-style pizza," the city is "just a short El ride away," as a junior puts it, "and there's never a shortage of fun things to do." Indeed, as one first-year writes, "Life at Loyola is living in Chicago with a side of school." An international student from Ireland gives the down-low: "So far the social activities organized have been as exciting as knitting with my mum." What's needed? More sports events, a better newspaper, more funding for student events, and the renovation of key facilities are high on students' wish lists. Still, proximity to the city has its upside—"social justice and volunteer opportunities" abound, and, as a senior points out, "despite the high percentage of commuters [students], attendance at on-campus events is on the rise."

Student Body

"Choose Loyola if you're comfortable enough with yourself to handle serious diversity," writes a frank first-year, though most rave about Loyola's unique mix of people from all around the nation and the world. "I enjoy my fellow students," remarks a senior. "I have learned a lot about other cultures and religions because of them." Adds another, "If you have an open mind, you can make friends from almost every ethnic group." With such a heterogeneous community, there's bound to be cliques and divisions, which some Loyola undergrads complain can be "closed off and unapproachable."

ADMISSIONS

Very important factors considered by the admissions committee include: secondary school record, standardized test scores. *Important factors considered include:* character/personal qualities, essays, recommendations. *Other factors considered include:* extracurricular activities, geographical residence, interview, talent/ability, volunteer work, work experience. SAT I or ACT required. TOEFL required of all international applicants. High school diploma or GED is required. *High school units required/recommended:* 15 total required; 18 total recommended; 4 English required, 2 math required, 4 math recommended, 2 science required, 3 science recommended, 2 foreign language required, 3 foreign language recommended, 1 social studies required, 3 social studies recommended.

The Inside Word

The admissions process is fairly formulaic, and the standards are attainable for most competitive candidates.

FINANCIAL AID

Students should submit: FAFSA. Recommended filing by February 1. *Need-based scholarships/grants offered:* Pell, SEOG, state scholarships/grants, private scholarships, the school's own gift aid. *Loan aid offered:* FFEL Subsidized Stafford, FFEL Unsubsidized Stafford, FFEL PLUS, Federal Perkins, Federal Nursing. Federal Work-Study Program available. Institutional employment available. Applicants will be notified of awards on a rolling basis beginning on or about February 15. Off-campus job opportunities are excellent.

FROM THE ADMISSIONS OFFICE

"As a national research university, Loyola University of Chicago provides a superb academic program that is distinctive because of its personal approach. Nationally and internationally renowned scholars teach introductory freshman-level courses in classes that average 21 students. A special emphasis in our curriculum is placed on the examination of ethics and values as well as a commitment to instill intensive writing skills that will benefit the student throughout his/her life. Loyola is committed to the individual student, and its programs and policies reflect the importance of community. Students from throughout the nation are attracted to Loyola for the opportunities offered by the university, our Jesuit tradition, as well as the benefits of studying in Chicago, a world-class city."

For even more information on this school, turn to page 366 of the "Stats" section.

LUTHER COLLEGE

700 College Drive, Decorah, IA 52101-1042 • Admissions: 563-387-1287 • Fax: 563-387-2159
E-mail: admissions@luther.edu • Website: www.luther.edu

Ratings

Quality of Life: 85   **Academic:** 82   **Admissions:** 79   **Financial Aid:** 70

Academics

Nestled in the "bluffs of Northeast Iowa," Lutheran-affiliated Luther College attracts students for its "great reputation for its music programs," "friendly atmosphere," and "gorgeous" campus. Though

> **SURVEY SAYS . . .**
> *School is well run, Students are religious*
> *Classes are small*
> *Student publications are popular*

"Luther is a music-oriented school," students say that "people from all different directions can feel at home" and benefit from the school's "well-rounded" liberal arts education. What really shines at Luther is the faculty's dedication to its students and their academic success. One recounts, "If you ever need help with classes the professors are always available, and there are tutors for everything as well." Another contributes, "My professors go the extra mile to take us on field trips, advise student-led groups, and to help me think about my future. I have so many good mentors at Luther, and I know many students who have such relationships with professors, coaches, pastors, and other members of the Luther community." Despite general praises, students admit that there are some teachers who are "not friendly and not interested" in students, but in the wise words of one, "You learn to register accordingly." Many students are supportive of the administration. Writes one, "I think that the administration, although it has its fair share of problems, is really concerned about the students' welfare." "They're usually there to help you, and/or explains things to you when you're confused," offers another.

Life

Despite Luther's rural location in Decorah, Iowa, "very few people leave campus or town for the weekend, and if they do, they usually feel that they missed out on something." Though remote, students say the fun comes to them, as the "Student Activities Council is great and brings in lots of stuff to do on the weekends," from "Chinese National Acrobats and the Nutcracker on Ice" to "Dave Matthews Band." Partying is also a favored pastime, as are "trips to the local bar." But for those not inclined to imbibe (and "a lot of students choose not to drink"), students say they also enjoy "traying in the wintertime, movies, bowling, climbing trees, walks to nearby scenic outlooks," "going to movies, taking road trips," or playing "snow football." Those with cars can hightail out of town to nearby La Crosse, Wisconsin; Rochester, Minnesota; or Dubuque, Iowa. Although Luther has put to rest its tradition of "naked soccer," alternative forms of entertainment await the active student. "In fact," writes one student, "sometimes there is so much [going on] that it's hard to decide what to do."

Student Body

Students claim "the friendliest people" go to Luther, many of whom "smile and say 'hi' to whomever they pass," "have strong friendships," and "respect everyone." One undergrad bemoans, "Most students are upper class and white. . . . I have found that it is possible to find a more diverse range of people, but you have to make a conscious effort to find them." There may be "little to no racial diversity" on campus, but Luther is working to change that. Others remind us that Luther is also home to "foreign students from all over the world, a big GLBTA population, and many cultures and religions," including "a large Christian community." You'll find a "huge variety of personalities, races, cultures, and anything else here," assures an undergrad. Luther students come from religious backgrounds that include Methodist, Baptist, Presbyterian, Congregational, Hindu, Buddhist, and Muslim, but 49 percent are of Lutheran faith. Though most say the student body is accepting of all lifestyles and opinions, some report that, "It is awkward sometimes to not be Christian."

ADMISSIONS

Very important factors considered by the admissions committee include: class rank, recommendations, secondary school record, and standardized test scores. *Important factors considered include:* character/personal qualities, essays, extracurricular activities, minority status, talent/ability, and volunteer work. *Other factors considered include:* alumni/ae relation, geographical residence, and interview. SAT I or ACT required. TOEFL required of all international applicants. High school diploma or GED is required. *High school units required/recommended:* 14 total recommended; 4 English recommended, 3 math recommended, 2 science recommended, 1 science lab recommended, 2 foreign language recommended, 3 social studies recommended.

The Inside Word

Admission to Luther is competitive; the school's local reputation draws a strong applicant pool. This Evangelical Lutheran school welcomes students of all faiths, but secularists and non-Christians should visit campus to determine whether they could spend four years here.

FINANCIAL AID

Students should submit: FAFSA and institution's own financial aid form. No deadline for regular filing. The Princeton Review suggests that all financial aid forms be submitted as soon as possible after January 1. *Need-based scholarships/grants offered:* Pell, SEOG, state scholarships/grants, private scholarships, and the school's own gift aid. *Loan aid offered:* Direct Subsidized Stafford, Direct Unsubsidized Stafford, Direct PLUS, Federal Perkins, and college/university loans from institutional funds. Federal Work-Study Program available. Institutional employment available. Applicants will be notified of awards on a rolling basis beginning on or about March 15. Off-campus job opportunities are good.

FROM THE ADMISSIONS OFFICE

"In keeping with its liberal arts tradition, Luther College requires students to develop a depth of knowledge in their chosen discipline (the major) and a breadth of knowledge through exposure to a wide range of subjects and intellectual approaches (the general requirements). Learning at Luther is all about engagement—faculty who are passionate in their teaching and scholarship, students who are active and involved, and a college community characterized by personal attention, hand-on experiences, academic challenge, and community support. At Luther, all students become immersed in the liberal arts through the college's common yearlong course for first-year students called Paideia. The course, which is actually quite uncommon in its approach, helps train students' minds and develops their research and writing skills as they explore human cultures and history. A second Paideia component engages upperclassmen in values seminars.

"Luther boasts a Phi Beta Kappa chapter and several departmental honor societies, evidence of the quality of teaching and learning on campus. Luther students have recently won Rhodes, Fulbright, Goldwater, Gates Cambridge, McElroy, and Carver scholarships. A wide range of study abroad, internship, and independent research opportunities enhance the academic experience.

"At Luther, students are also encouraged to make connections between their lives in the classroom and their lives outside the classroom. The college sponsors 19 intercollegiate sports for men and women; 16 major musical ensembles; extensive theatre, dance, and visual arts experiences; numerous college ministry groups and opportunities; dozens of recreational sports; and more than 100 student organizations."

For even more information on this school, turn to page 367 of the "Stats" section.

MACALESTER COLLEGE

1600 Grand Avenue, St. Paul, MN 55105 • Admissions: 651-696-6357 • Fax: 651-696-6724
Financial Aid: 651-696-6214 • E-mail: admissions@macalester.edu • Website: www.macalester.edu

Ratings

Quality of Life: 93   **Academic:** 93   **Admissions:** 96   **Financial Aid:** 91

Academics

True to its liberal arts ideals, Macalester offers an academic environment with small classes and "close student-professor relationships." And while the courses are "challenging," the overall atmosphere is comfortable, not cutthroat. "Macalester is the kind of place where you can show up for class every day in your pajamas

> **SURVEY SAYS . . .**
> *Students aren't religious*
> *Ethnic diversity on campus, Classes are small*
> *Political activism is hot*
> *Students love St. Paul, MN*
> *Campus easy to get around*
> *Beautiful campus, Theater is unpopular*
> *Athletic facilities need improving*

and still be taken seriously and get the respect you deserve from your profs." And these accepting and accessible professors "know their [expletive]." "Even the bad profs are better than average, and the good ones are really good—innovative, attentive, and challenging," writes an enthusiastic freshman. Mac's 1,700-plus student body is spread throughout 39 majors and 31 minors. And because Macalester, like many liberal arts schools, is ripe with distribution requirements, students often mingle under the umbrella of varied topics. Over 60 percent of the students take advantage of Macalester's renowned study-abroad opportunities. You'll be hard pressed to find a Mac student talk down the academics here, while uber-accessibility is clearly the strength of administrators and staff. This place might just be undergraduate Canaan!

Life

It's hard to talk about student life at Macalester without talking about the area around campus. Located in St. Paul, Macalester offers its students easy access to Minnesota's Twin Cities. Nearby, students find things like the Mall of America, "dance clubs," "a local movie theater called 'Grandview,'" "lots of shops and cultural events," and "so many beautiful natural areas within the cities." Getting outdoors is important to Mac students. "I explore the Twin Cities on my bike," writes one student, while others cite "canoeing" and "Ultimate Frisbee" as other possible diversions. On the other side of the coin, students report some less-than-attractive features of the college's location, particularly when it comes to partying. "The parties are nonexistent because of the St. Paul police," complains a junior. But if partying is your thing, don't think you're entirely out of luck because "you can be a party animal" here if you want to. There's "lots of drinking" in the dorm rooms, as well as the use of "assorted substances." (Perhaps this is why "streaking is not a strange sight.") Though the campus brings in its fair share of speakers and performances, some students complain that if you don't drink "there's no place to have fun." However, every night Mac students feel that they've just put an active day behind them, with another active day ahead. "My friends and I are busy people," chirps a sophomore. "We try to schedule each other in for breakfasts, events in the cities, politics, or sleeping together."

Student Body

"Some schools say they're diverse, and when you get there they're all white, upper-middle-class yuppies . . . NOT Mac." In fact, diversity is one of the college's big selling points. However, says one student, "Most of the ethnic diversity is because of international students." According to the college, about one in every six students on campus comes from one of 88 foreign countries. The opinions Mac students propound are "liberal and very left-wing,"a fact that prompts one freshman to note that one will "get along fine here unless you're a Republican." And politics are on students' minds. "Very proactive, very socially aware, and justice conscious," a student writes about her classmates. Another concurs, "I like the creativity, humor, and openness of the students." Unfortunately, students don't always make an effort to widen their circles. "Minnesota cold weather sometimes makes it a little harder to be social," explains a sophomore. "It's hard to meet people when you dread going outside."

ADMISSIONS

Very important factors considered by the admissions committee include: secondary school record. *Important factors considered include:* character/personal qualities, essays, extracurricular activities, recommendations, standardized test scores. *Other factors considered include:* alumni/ae relation, class rank, interview, minority status, talent/ability, volunteer work, work experience. SAT I or ACT required. TOEFL required of all international applicants. *High school units required/recommended:* 4 English recommended, 3 math recommended, 3 science recommended, 3 science lab recommended, 3 foreign language recommended, 3 social studies recommended.

The Inside Word

Macalester is just a breath away from moving into the highest echelon of American colleges; a gift of Reader's Digest stock several years ago has recently translated into over $500 million in endowment. As the college has reaped the benefits of this generous gift, the applicant pool has grown dramatically. Macalester is already among the 25 or so most selective colleges in the country. An interview is a good idea: even though they are offered across the country, we also encourage you to visit the campus.

FINANCIAL AID

Students should submit: FAFSA, CSS/Financial Aid PROFILE, noncustodial (divorced/separated) parent's statement, business/farm supplement. Regular filing deadline is April 15. The Princeton Review suggests that all financial aid forms be submitted as soon as possible after January 1. *Need-based scholarships/grants offered:* Pell, SEOG, state scholarships/grants, private scholarships, the school's own gift aid. *Loan aid offered:* FFEL Subsidized Stafford, FFEL Unsubsidized Stafford, FFEL PLUS, Federal Perkins, state loans. Federal Work-Study Program available. Institutional employment available. Applicants will be notified of awards on or about April 1. Off-campus job opportunities are excellent.

FROM THE ADMISSIONS OFFICE

"Recent news about Macalester (Spring 2002): Macalester students come from all 50 states and 88 other countries. Before graduating, half of them will study abroad, going to more than 50 countries in any given year. For over 30 years, Macalester's debate program has been ranked among the top 10 in the nation. A Macalester team has qualified for the International Collegiate Programming Contest in four of the past seven years, and recently the team tied with Stanford, Columbia, Carnegie-Mellon, and Harvard. The women's soccer team won the 1998 NCAA Division III national championship. A new campus center opened in 2001. Each year Macalester students win an impressive number of post-graduate awards, including Fulbright Scholarships, National Science Foundation Graduate Fellowships, Truman Scholarships, Watson Fellowships, and more. Recent graduates fare well in the job market and graduate programs. One reports that she was 'accepted into top med school choices: Mayo, Stanford, UCLA and Minnesota' and another that he had a 'striking advantage over many other candidates' and is now enrolled in a PhD program in economics at Princeton University."

For even more information on this school, turn to page 367 of the "Stats" section.

MANCHESTER COLLEGE

604 COLLEGE AVENUE, NORTH MANCHESTER, IN 46962 • ADMISSIONS: 800-852-3648 • FAX: 260-982-5239
E-MAIL: ADMITINFO@MANCHESTER.EDU • WEBSITE: WWW.MANCHESTER.EDU

Ratings
Quality of Life: 76   Academic: 76   Admissions: 71   Financial Aid: 80

Academics

Whether describing the school's reputable business and accounting departments or its rare peace studies major, students say the academic programs at Manchester College are "current, dynamic, and challenging" and, "can pro-

SURVEY SAYS . . .
Student publications are popular
Instructors are good teachers, Classes are small
Students are religious, School is well run
Theater is hot

vide anyone who is serious about their education with a strong educational background." Most say it is the school's "brilliant" faculty that is at the heart of their positive experiences. "Professors here challenge students by encouraging us to think critically, figure things out on our own, and apply these skills and lessons to the 'real world,'" raves one undergrad. Testifies another, "Our professors just rock. They teach brilliantly without being stuffy and keep office doors wide open." On that note, because "the student to teacher ratio is really low," students say they receive "lots of personal attention." Some students report that the school's "friendly" administration is nonetheless "stuck in the stone age." One student suggests, "We need more technology to speed things up, instead of the handwritten paper trail."

Life

Set in a small town, students say, "Life at Manchester is peaceful but very busy if you get involved." For example, one student offers "a sampling of events that took place last week: a presentation and discussion on Ecofeminism, a teach-in about the FTAA, Love Feast (a religious ritual), Anything Goes (wrestling in puddles, swimming in ramen noodles, etc.), a concert performed by the student band Mutual Kumquat, a discussion about [how] Hispanics are being welcomed into northern Indiana, and tons more." As this list suggests, political and social issues (as well as fun) are important to most Manchester students. Many say they "spend a lot of time learning about situations in our world and trying to come up with solutions," and that "volunteerism is incredible here and the students really do a great job making this a better place for everyone." On a local level, students say, "you can always find people studying outdoors, playing ultimate Frisbee, or picking out a song on their guitar," or possibly heading out to "the nearest big city or the coffee shop down the road." Parties are also a plentiful source of entertainment. Although "MC is a dry campus," one student confides, "There does tend to be quite a bit of drinking on campus—especially on weekends."

Student Body

Undergrads say that "although most students get along, there is a diverse array of opinion on liberal and conservative issues" at Manchester. Most appreciate the stimulating environment; however, they also confide that "sometimes the level of political diversity can cause antagonism." In particular, students mention the occurrence of "conflicts between some of the religious groups and the sexual diversity group." Differences of opinion generally don't play out in the form of major conflict, though; rather, they contribute considerably to the formation of social cliques. Students tell us, "In the Union, for example, it is a fact that the 'peace studies' sit on one side and the 'athletes' sit on the other." Though politically varied, students report that the school is fairly homogenous. Says one, "They preach diversity a lot around here, but when you look around the classroom you see mostly white, middle-class students." However, many also mention that "the college has attracted a sizable population of foreign students."

ADMISSIONS

Very important factors considered by the admissions committee include: secondary school record. *Important factors considered include:* recommendations and standardized test scores. *Other factors considered include:* alumni/ae relation, character/personal qualities, class rank, interview, religious affiliation/commitment, and talent/ability. SAT I or ACT required. TOEFL required of all international applicants. High school diploma or GED is required. *High school units required/recommended:* 14 total required; 17 total recommended; 4 English required, 2 math required, 3 math recommended, 2 science required, 3 science recommended, 2 science lab required, 3 science lab recommended, 2 foreign language required, 2 social studies required, 2 social studies recommended, 1 history required, 2 history recommended, 1 elective required, 2 elective recommended.

The Inside Word

Manchester plans to soon add a brand-new, state-of-the-art science center and a new recital hall. In the near future, look for a big bump in applications to the science and performing arts programs, and a commensurate bump up in admissions standards.

FINANCIAL AID

Students should submit: FAFSA. No deadline for regular filing. The Princeton Review suggests that all financial aid forms be submitted as soon as possible after January 1. *Need-based scholarships/grants offered:* Pell, SEOG, state scholarships/grants, private scholarships, and the school's own gift aid. *Loan aid offered:* FFEL Subsidized Stafford, FFEL Unsubsidized Stafford, FFEL PLUS, Federal Perkins, and college/university loans from institutional funds. Federal Work-Study Program available. Institutional employment available. Applicants will be notified of awards on a rolling basis beginning on or about February 15. Off-campus job opportunities are fair.

FROM THE ADMISSIONS OFFICE

"What are you passionate about? At Manchester College, students are passionate about leading lives of consequence. Contributing to the communities in which they live. Making full use of their talents. Choosing jobs that make a positive contribution to society and the environment.

"Students develop skills and professional competence for career success. Fully 98 percent are employed or in graduate school within six months of graduation. And they sharpen the values that shape the contributions they make with their lives.

"Manchester offers a learning community where students and faculty are passionate about being involved. Our students get a great education in the classroom and in real-world settings. They volunteer, work as interns, tackle tough questions, connect with future employers, and work closely with faculty in small classes and one on one.

"Over 1,100 students study in 45 academic areas. The best-known programs are in accounting, pre-medicine, education, and peace studies. Faculty are well qualified, with 94 percent holding the highest degree in their field. They are also exceptional teachers. Art professor Jim Adams, who was named the 2002 US Professor of the Year, is just one example of what Manchester has to offer.

"One of our students described us well, saying we provide a collegiate environment 'in which even the most career-focused major is placed in a larger context of how it affects the community and world.'

"Our passion is graduating students with both abilities and convictions. What are you passionate about?"

For even more information on this school, turn to page 368 of the "Stats" section.

MARIETTA COLLEGE

215 FIFTH STREET, MARIETTA, OH 45750 • ADMISSIONS: 740-376-4643 • FAX: 740-376-8888
E-MAIL: ADMIT@MARIETTA.EDU • WEBSITE: WWW.MARIETTA.EDU

Ratings
Quality of Life: 78   Academic: 78   Admissions: 73   Financial Aid: 78

Academics

"The great strengths in my school," reports one Marietta College undergraduate, "are the petroleum engineering major, the sports medicine major, and the leadership program. This school is best known for those three programs, and the students seem to come out of them with lots of knowl-

> **SURVEY SAYS . . .**
> *Classes are small*
> *Student publications are popular*
> *Profs teach upper levels*
> *Class discussions encouraged*
> *Students get along with local community*

edge and background [in these fields]." The unique leadership program, available as a 20-hour minor or a 15-hour certificate, puts students through their paces with a program of seminars, team projects, internships, and community service. All undergrads must complete the Senior Capstone, "which can be a special project, show, recital, thesis, or independent research project." Students report that small classes and an engaged faculty define the Marietta experience. As one student told us, "You are only with 20 to 30 other people in your classes, and the instructors know you by name and are willing to give you extra help." Students also appreciate the fact that "the career center is so helpful in finding you an internship or a job." They are anxious, however, about changes currently being undertaken by the administration; reports one, "There's a lot of tension on campus over the proposed elimination of a few of the majors we have." Adds another, "Costs are simply skyrocketing. With the addition of new buildings and the restructuring of administrative levels, I sometimes feel like the college doesn't have it all together." Some, however, are optimistic about Marietta's future prospects; as one student wrote, "There is a lot of construction going on right now. But once completed, this place will be spectacular. They are building a new science center and a new recreation center, and they just completed the new dorms."

Life

Students report that Marietta's social options are "limited, both on campus and in town, which explains why many students choose to drink on the weekends." Agrees one student, "There's not a whole lot to do. Most of the upperclassmen go to bars like the Town House or the Dockside. Underclassmen go hang out at the suites (upperclassmen housing) or just stay at the freshman dorms." Dorm parties benefit from unofficial benign neglect, as "many RAs ignore the parties as long as they don't get out of hand. Partying usually starts at least Thursday night, which is 'college night' at the bars, and then it continues through the weekend." Students also note that "the possibility for students to get involved in any activity is here. Students who have never acted before try out for plays, and people who have never rowed before can join the crew team. People who you would have never thought would be going out if they were in high school together are able to hang out together or go on a date." They also feel that "the College Union Board (the group that sponsors on-campus events) is very active and brings a variety of entertainment types to campus." In short, there is life beyond the party scene, although many students fail to take advantage of it. Hometown

Marietta, Ohio, offers "one mall and two movie theatres within a 20-mile radius" and not much else.

Student Body

Marietta undergrads "come from different regions of the United States and the world, and it is great to learn about the different cultures." Marietta isn't exactly a perfect melting pot, however; reports one student, "The vast majority of students are white and upper-middle-class." Students tell us that "for the most part, everyone gets along, yet there are plenty of rivalries, especially within Greek life, I think." "Everyone here is really friendly," writes one upbeat undergrad. "The people are cool to hang out with on the weekends, and it is very easy to meet new people with such a small school. Everyone you walk by says 'hi!'"

ADMISSIONS

Very important factors considered by the admissions committee include: secondary school record. *Important factors considered include:* character/personal qualities, class rank, essays, extracurricular activities, interview, recommendations, and standardized test scores. *Other factors considered include:* alumni/ae relation, minority status, talent/ability, volunteer work, and work experience. SAT I or ACT required. TOEFL required of all international applicants. High school diploma or GED is required. *High school units required/recommended:* 16 total required; 4 English required, 3 math required, 3 science required, 2 science lab required, 2 foreign language required, 1 social studies required, 1 history required, 3 history recommended.

The Inside Word

Marietta admits more than nine out of ten applicants, but don't be too confident; the vast majority of candidates present solid credentials. A candidate with deficiencies in GPA and/or standardized test scores should look to pick up ground with the essay (required), recommendations, campus visit, and interview (optional, but highly recommended, especially for borderline candidates).

FINANCIAL AID

Students should submit: FAFSA and institution's own financial aid form. The Princeton Review suggests that all financial aid forms be submitted as soon as possible after January 1. *Need-based scholarships/grants offered:* Pell, SEOG, state scholarships/grants, private scholarships, and the school's own gift aid. *Loan aid offered:* Direct Subsidized Stafford, Direct Unsubsidized Stafford, Direct PLUS, FFEL Subsidized Stafford, FFEL Unsubsidized Stafford, FFEL PLUS, and Federal Perkins. Federal Work-Study Program available. Institutional employment available. Applicants will be notified of awards on a rolling basis beginning on or about March 15. Off-campus job opportunities are good.

For even more information on this school, turn to page 368 of the "Stats" section.

Marquette University

PO Box 1881, Milwaukee, WI 53201-1881 • Admissions: 414-288-7302 • Fax: 414-288-3764
Financial Aid: 414-288-7390 • E-mail: admissions@marquette.edu • Website: www.marquette.edu

Ratings

Quality of Life: 80   **Academic:** 77   **Admissions:** 78   **Financial Aid:** 82

Academics

"There is really a lot more to Marquette than just the 'community service' opportunities and excellent basketball program that they advertise so much," notes one student at this solid, demanding Catholic school in Milwaukee. Undergrads here warn that "sometimes professors forget that we are

> **SURVEY SAYS . . .**
> *Lots of beer drinking, Campus easy to get around*
> *Athletic facilities are great, Hard liquor is popular*
> *(Almost) everyone smokes*
> *Students are happy, Great off-campus food*
> *Great library, Great computer facilities*
> *Everyone loves the Golden Eagles*

college students and some of us work. The workloads can sometimes get out of hand." When students feel overwhelmed, however, they can take advantage of the "many opportunities to get help and ask questions." Marquette's faculty are "engaging, funny, and knowledgeable" and "encourage meeting outside of class and accessing them at all times, even at home. They have flexible office hours and truly try to get to know their students." Students single out for praise the "great chemistry department," the "extremely well-informed professors in the College of Engineering," and the b-school teachers "who have actual work experience." The core curriculum, required of all undergrads, earns students' approval. "While sometimes tedious, these classes provide a breadth of knowledge regardless of your major," notes one. Upperclassmen warn that "upper-division classes tend to have few sections and fill up quickly" and that "registration is done by a lottery, which prevents many upperclassmen from getting classes they need."

Life

Because academics are rigorous at Marquette, students' weekdays here are largely filled with classes, study sessions, and homework. Writes one student, "It is very typical to take heavy class loads, like at least 16 or 17 credits. I've had three 19-credit semesters, and because of that, many of us graduate on time or early. It is expected that you juggle lots of things. Otherwise it seems like you're 'lazy.'" Students know where to draw the line, however, and when the weekend comes, "the general population knows how to cut loose and have fun." How do they do that? "Marquette is a bar school. There are few house parties, and as a result of the lack of Greek life here, frat parties are also rarities. Bars are the most common form of weekend entertainment." Students also love the "major league baseball, shopping, theater, concerts, excellent nightlife downtown, Lake Michigan, etc." that Milwaukee offers and report that "the safety program here at Marquette is excellent. . . . I feel safe living in the downtown area of Milwaukee, where the school is located." On campus, Marquette offers "a lot of activities every week," and of course "Division I intercollegiate sports. The men's B-ball team, in particular, rocks our world. We are the best fans and will do anything to support the Golden Eagles." As at many Jesuit schools, "most students are involved in community service. We live in an urban area, so it is quite easy to find volunteer work. A rescue mission is just one block from campus; many of us serve meals to the homeless."

Student Body

The "studious, religious, friendly, clean-cut" students of Marquette "are typically Catholic and from Wisconsin or Illinois." As one student relates, "You will not see many ethnic differences or hippie types around the campus." Economic backgrounds vary. Wrote one undergrad, "Looking at a student, you never know their story. Some have everything paid for. Others (like me) are working their tails off to pay their own way through college." Because Catholic prep schools feed Marquette heavily, the student body does have a large preppy contingent. Students "tend to be a bit on the conservative side" and are generally very polite. As one undergrad reported, "That's the one thing that impressed me most about Marquette: the way people hold the door for each other, the way eye contact is made with strangers, and the overall inviting atmosphere of campus."

ADMISSIONS

Very important factors considered by the admissions committee include: secondary school record, standardized test scores. *Important factors considered include:* class rank. *Other factors considered include:* alumni/ae relation, character/personal qualities, essays, extracurricular activities, geographical residence, interview, minority status, recommendations, religious affiliation/commitment, state residency, talent/ability, volunteer work, work experience. SAT I or ACT required; SAT I recommended. TOEFL required of all international applicants. High school diploma or GED is required. *High school units required/recommended:* 16 total recommended; 4 English recommended, 3 math recommended, 3 science recommended, 2 science lab recommended, 2 foreign language recommended, 2 social studies recommended, 2 history recommended, 3 elective recommended.

The Inside Word

Class rank may be important to the admissions office as a required criterion, but not to worry—in practice, a little less than a tenth of Marquette's freshmen ranked in the bottom half of their graduating class. The university's low level of selectivity makes it a no-sweat proposition for most candidates.

FINANCIAL AID

Students should submit: FAFSA. Admission application required for Marquette University Ignatius Scholarship. Regular filing deadline is March 1. The Princeton Review suggests that all financial aid forms be submitted as soon as possible after January 1. *Need-based scholarships/grants offered:* Pell, SEOG, state scholarships/grants, private scholarships, the school's own gift aid, Federal Nursing. *Loan aid offered:* Direct Subsidized Stafford, Direct Unsubsidized Stafford, Direct PLUS, Federal Perkins, Federal Nursing, state loans, college/university loans from institutional funds, alternative educational loans. Federal Work-Study Program available. Institutional employment available. Applicants will be notified of awards on a rolling basis beginning on or about March 21. Off-campus job opportunities are excellent.

FROM THE ADMISSIONS OFFICE

"Since 1881, Marquette has been noted for its commitment to educational excellence in the 450-year-old Jesuit, Catholic tradition. Marquette embraces the philosophy that true education should be more than an acquisition of knowledge. Marquette seeks to develop your intellect as well as your moral and spiritual character. This all-encompassing education will challenge you to develop the goals and values that will shape the rest of your life. Each of Marquette's 7,500 undergraduates are admitted as freshman to one of six colleges: Arts and Sciences, Business Administration, Communication, Engineering, Health Sciences, or Nursing. Many co-enroll in the School of Education. The faculty within these colleges are prolific writers and researchers, but more important, they all teach and advise students. Marquette is nestled in the financial center of Milwaukee, the nation's eighteenth largest city, allowing you to take full advantage of the city's cultural, professional, and governmental opportunities. Marquette's urban experience is unique; an 80-acre campus (with real grass and trees), an outdoor athletic complex, and an internationally diverse student body (90 percent of which live on campus) all make Marquette a close-knit community in which you can learn and live."

For even more information on this school, turn to page 369 of the "Stats" section.

MAYVILLE STATE UNIVERSITY

330 THIRD STREET NORTHEAST, MAYVILLE, ND 58257-1299 • ADMISSIONS: 701-786-4842
FAX: 701-786-4748 • E-MAIL: ADMIT@MAIL.MASU.NODAK.EDU • WEBSITE: WWW.MAYVILLESTATE.EDU

Ratings
Quality of Life: 73   **Academic:** 69   **Admissions:** 62   **Financial Aid:** 77

Academics

At Mayville State University, reputedly one of America's "most wired" campuses, "each student has a laptop issued to them. Virtually the entire campus is

> **SURVEY SAYS . . .**
> *Students are happy, Diversity lacking on campus*
> *Popular college radio, Classes are small*

wired for network/Internet." The laptops are a blessing for those with chicken scratch-style penmanship, as they allow students to "type along rather than try to hand-write notes" in class. One student observes that the ever-presence of high-tech gear "makes some of the classes more interesting. Professors will design slide shows to go along with the lectures and things like that." Students at Mayville agree that "the one-on-one attention with the professors is incredible," although, they quip, "too much emphasis is placed on attendance." Mayville's education and business departments "are both excellent," but some students would like to see "more teachers in specific areas." One education major taking early childhood courses writes, "I pretty much have the same teacher for all of the classes I am taking this semester . . . which is also the same teacher I had for all my classes last semester. This gets a little old." Computerized enrollment ensures that "students have a good chance of getting into classes they want," and most consider the administrators "very professional and always ready to help." One international student, however, warns that Mayville has "an extremely weak administration when it comes to the needs of minorities and international students." The majority of undergrads at Mayville agree, though, "the programs of study are great, and for the size of the school and how little you pay, you can't get much better."

Life

"Fun? What fun? It's MAYVILLE!" While many share this despondent student's cry to the heavens, others argue that "there is a lot to do in Mayville"; students have at their disposal "a bowling alley, a movie theatre, a new ice arena/community center, parks, and numerous other places that one can go to relax off campus." Located in the Red River Valley area of North Dakota, many folks also take advantage of neighboring cities Grand Forks or Fargo "to go out to eat, shop, movies, etc." Some feel that Mayville needs to work on keeping students occupied at the home base, especially on the weekends: "Recreational student activities are generally nonexistent, "says one. "This year," one student informs us, "the college has started a new program to get students more involved on campus," so changes are abreast. Others list "sports events and intramural sports," "fine arts events," and "some of the typical 'college parties,'" as well as "four to five bars in town . . . they aren't huge bars, but they are CHEAP. Which is nice." Students complain that the dorms and buildings need upgrading, and they also gripe about the "outrageous curfews," and "quiet hours," which give some the feeling of being "babysat." If you can get past these minor issues, though, you'll find "all sorts of stuff to do at Mayville."

Student Body

If you're looking for a "small, homey atmosphere" in a college, read on. "The people who chose Mayville State University all seem to be people who know and like small towns." The school's size enables students "to know everyone on the campus," and the majority report positive findings; students tell us that "you are always meeting new people, and everyone is so friendly," and that "the students have a general respect for each other." "I am the ONLY gay student on campus," says one undergrad, "and I have received nothing but kind words and friendship. It's a great place to be." While a substantial number of "older than average students" makes for a "huge diversity in ages here," some gripe that the school is "not very ethnically diverse" and that fellow students are "rather ignorant." Differences aside, students report that in general, "Everyone at Mayville State University supports each other, and we all get along very well."

ADMISSIONS

Very important factors considered by the admissions committee include: secondary school record. *Important factors considered include:* standardized test scores. *Other factors considered include:* character/personal qualities and interview. SAT I or ACT required, ACT preferred. TOEFL required of all international applicants. High school diploma or GED is required. *High school units required/recommended:* 17 total required; 4 English required, 3 math required, 3 science required, 2 science lab required, 2 foreign language recommended, 3 social studies required.

The Inside Word

Students with average grades and standardized test scores should gain admission to Mayville State with little trouble. Shaky candidates should visit the campus and meet with an admissions officer, who can advise them on how to compile a successful application.

FINANCIAL AID

Students should submit: FAFSA. The Princeton Review suggests that all financial aid forms be submitted as soon as possible after January 1. *Need-based scholarships/grants offered:* Pell, SEOG, state scholarships/grants, private scholarships, and the school's own gift aid. *Loan aid offered:* FFEL Subsidized Stafford, FFEL Unsubsidized Stafford, FFEL PLUS, Federal Perkins, and college/university loans from institutional funds. Federal Work-Study Program available. Institutional employment available. Applicants will be notified of awards on a rolling basis beginning on or about May 1. Off-campus job opportunities are good.

FROM THE ADMISSIONS OFFICE

"As you enter Mayville State University, three early-twentieth-century buildings greet you. If you equate the red brick exterior to quaint rustic charm and the quiet serenity of a century ago, you'll be pleasantly shocked to find one of the most progressive campuses in the country. Small classes, caring faculty and staff, and a computer technology-literate campus are Mayville State hallmarks. Located in the heart of the Red River Valley, MSU's size of 750 students means an average class size of 18, no classes over 45 students, and a 14:1 student/faculty ratio.

"Nationally known for teacher education, 40 percent of MSU students plan to teach. Business administration and computer information systems are growing rapidly. Among its 67 programs of study, MSU offers the only Bachelor of Applied Science degree in North Dakota. MSU features a 100 percent job placement rate. All Mayville State students receive laptop computers. Multimedia classrooms dot the campus and faculty incorporate technology into their classes. Residence hall rooms and classrooms are wired and 24/7 Internet access is available. MSU graduates earn an information technology certificate with their degree.

"Involvement is important in campus life, as students participate in student government, drama, intramural sports, choir, speech, academic clubs, and more. Comet athletics provide excitement. Men's sports include baseball, basketball, and football. Women compete in fast-pitch softball, basketball, and volleyball.

"Mayville State offers private college advantages at a public university price. With world-class technology and graduate placement rates and outstanding faculty, you'll be thrilled by what you find at Mayville State!"

For even more information on this school, turn to page 370 of the "Stats" section.

MIAMI UNIVERSITY

301 SOUTH CAMPUS AVENUE BUILDING, OXFORD, OH 45056 • ADMISSIONS: 513-529-2531
FAX: 513-529-1550 • FINANCIAL AID: 513-529-8734 • E-MAIL: ADMISSION@MUOHIO.EDU
WEBSITE: WWW.MUOHIO.EDU

Ratings
Quality of Life: 85   **Academic:** 82   **Admissions:** 86   **Financial Aid:** 86

Academics

Students at Miami University, a highly regarded public institution, brag that their school is "very devoted to its undergraduate program." "I have to admit that in my four years at the school, I only had one or two classes with 90 students," writes one undergrad. "Most of my classes were small

> **SURVEY SAYS . . .**
> *Popular college radio*
> *Students are religious*
> *Political activism is hot*
> *No one cheats*
> *Students are happy*
> *Athletic facilities need improving*

(approx. 20 students) and were based around discussion." But this is no small liberal arts college; Miami is a full-scale university, with a wide variety of course offerings and myriad opportunities for students to distinguish themselves. "The best part of Miami is the opportunities," reports one student. "There are internships, clubs, classes, majors, minors, or traveling abroad." Adds another, "Through Miami, I've interned at the Democratic National Convention, studied a semester at our campus in Luxembourg, and attended our Washington, D.C., Media Experience Program and got to talk with people like Sam Donaldson, Bob Dole, and Tim Russert." Be forewarned that Miami's curriculum is "challenging; you need to put serious time into your work." Fortunately, profs are "very approachable and always have convenient office hours. They love teaching and love their students." Students also tell us that "the alumni network is also amazing."

Life

Miami offers "a pretty good balance as a party/academic school. Most people stay in Sunday through Wednesday nights and study. However, the weekend definitely starts on Thursday, and partying can be pretty intense." Oxford's remote location contributes to the spirited party scene. Students explain that "being surrounded by cornfields means there's not a whole lot to do other than party on the weekends. So, yeah, there is a lot of drinking. But it's fun! There are a ton of bars uptown. There are plenty of house parties to go to." The Greek houses are also abuzz with activity, as "Greek life is definitely huge." "If partying isn't your thing, you will probably find college life to be pretty boring here," many warn. That's because "the town of Oxford has nothing to offer. There is a Wal-Mart and a grocery store. It is miniscule and at times very claustrophobic." Students praise the Miami campus, calling it a "beautiful, easy-leaning environment. Lots of trees, pretty buildings, and red brick roads." They also tell us the school has a "great intramural program" that includes "broomball, a combination of hockey and soccer that is played on the ice. It is incredibly popular. It was the most fun I have ever had in a sport, and one of my most fond memories of my freshman year."

Student Body

Whether they agree or disagree with the stereotype, almost all students at Miami University concede that their school has a widespread reputation as "'J.Crew U." Writes one student, "If you were to take away the rich, white, Jetta/Audi-driving frat/sorority members, and the students who are more worried about their image than anything else, you would have a student body that could fill a small auditorium." Counters another, "Students joke about the Miami image more than they strive to conform to it. I have found most of the students to be friendly and open, and I have made many friends." Those who feel the stereotype is apt call their classmates "cliquish," "superficial," and "very unfriendly. The cement in front of them is more appealing than the person walking by. Saying 'Hi' to someone on the sidewalk seems to be a chore." Nearly everyone agrees that Miami students are "very driven," "socially conservative," and "white bread." The school is trying to recruit more minority students, but many here see it as an uphill battle. "It is somewhat difficult to attract minority students to a predominantly white, rural campus, regardless of how well the university markets itself," explains one student.

ADMISSIONS

Very important factors considered by the admissions committee include: strength of curriculum, class rank, secondary school record, standardized test scores. *Important factors considered include:* essays, recommendations. *Other factors considered include:* alumni/ae relation, character/personal qualities, extracurricular activities, minority status, talent/ability, volunteer work, work experience. SAT I or ACT required. TOEFL required of all international applicants. High school diploma or GED is required. *High school units required/recommended:* 16 total recommended; 4 English recommended, 3 math recommended, 3 science recommended, 2 foreign language recommended, 3 social studies recommended. Most students admitted to Miami exceed these minimum requirements.

The Inside Word

Miami is one of the few selective public universities with an admissions process similar to those at highly selective private colleges. The university takes into account a variety of institutional needs as well as the qualifications of individual candidates when making admissions decisions. Don't be deceived by a high acceptance rate; the academic requirements for admission are quite high.

FINANCIAL AID

Students should submit: FAFSA. No deadline for regular filing. The Princeton Review suggests that all financial aid forms be submitted as soon as possible after January 1. *Need-based scholarships/grants offered:* Pell, SEOG, state scholarships/grants, private scholarships, the school's own gift aid. *Loan aid offered:* Direct Subsidized Stafford, Direct Unsubsidized Stafford, Direct PLUS, Federal Perkins, Federal Nursing, college/university loans from institutional funds, bank alternative loans. Federal Work-Study Program available. Institutional employment available. Applicants will be notified of awards on a rolling basis beginning on or about March 31. Off-campus job opportunities are good.

FROM THE ADMISSIONS OFFICE

"Miami's primary concern is its students. This concern is reflected in a broad array of efforts to develop the potential of each student. The university endeavors to individualize the educational experience. It provides personal and professional guidance, and it offers opportunities for its students to achieve understanding and appreciation not only of their own culture but of the cultures of others as well. Selected undergraduate, graduate, and professional programs of quality are offered with the expectation of students achieving a high level of competence and understanding and developing a personal value system. Miami University is one of only eight universities in the country to produce a Rhodes, Truman, and Goldwater scholar in 2002 and one of only two public universities with this same distinction. This recognition is directly attributed to the wonderful research opportunities that exist for our undergraduate students."

For even more information on this school, turn to page 370 of the "Stats" section.

MICHIGAN STATE UNIVERSITY

250 ADMINISTRATION BUILDING, EAST LANSING, MI 48824-1046 • ADMISSIONS: 517-355-8332
FAX: 517-353-1647 • FINANCIAL AID: 517-353-5940 • E-MAIL: ADMIS@MSU.EDU • WEBSITE: WWW.MSU.EDU

Ratings
Quality of Life: 78   **Academic:** 68   **Admissions:** 74   **Financial Aid:** 81

Academics

The fact that Michigan State is such a "mega institution" has its ups and its downs. On the downside, "you do not get the advantage of having the professor's individual attention." In many cases, you don't get the advantage of having the professor, as some lower-level classes are enormous lectures taught by TAs. Another common complaint is that "many of the classes are taught by . . .

> **SURVEY SAYS . . .**
> *Everyone loves the Spartans*
> *Popular college radio*
> *No one cheats*
> *Students get along with local community*
> *Great on-campus food*
> *Musical organizations are hot*
> *Theater is hot*
> *Students are cliquish*

teachers that don't know a lick of English." An upside to MSU's size is the "plethora of academic resources" and the wide variety of "classes and majors available." And if you're really seeking a challenge, look into MSU's highly esteemed Honors College. To top students it offers "a small, personalized feel to a large campus," not to mention a streamlined registration process, access to certain graduate classes, and plenty of opportunities for independent studies, thesis work, and research projects. "James Madison College, the residential liberal arts school at Michigan State University," also draws praise. According to one JMC student, "It should be ranked in a different category from Michigan State University. It has great professors, none of the classes are taught by TAs, the faculty is always available, the classes are no more than 35 people, it's a competitive environment, and is very challenging." Engineering, business, marketing, and various social sciences are among the most popular paths of study here, and we've also heard rave reviews for the writing, nursing, and veterinary programs.

Life

School spirit is alive and well in East Lansing, Michigan, which students describe as "the happiest place on earth." Students follow Big Ten sports religiously and tell us that Spartan games are "amazing and crazily fun to watch." During football season, thousands of students "get up at the butt-crack of dawn in order to get a good spot to tailgate" outside of Spartan Stadium. Greek life provides plenty of party opportunities for the underage revelers, while upperclassmen tend to make their way to off-campus parties or the "very popular" bar scene in East Lansing. Though few students will deny that MSU's "party school" reputation is deserved, they're quick to assert that drinking has been put under control of late. If MSU sounds appealing but drinking does not, "choosing a dorm with an alcohol-free option, a quiet floor, or an honors floor will make a HUGE difference in the types of people you meet." The university offers a multitude of "volunteering" opportunities and "school activities/groups" for students who want to exercise their hobbies and talents. MSU also plays host to "many famous speakers, entertainers, and scholars." Astoundingly, nearly half of the student population is involved in intramural sports. The city of East Lansing itself is a lively town, with "bars," "a good indie band scene," and "a multitude of diverse festivities . . . such as the Native American Pow Wow of Love and the International Folk Festival and the East Lansing Arts Festival." One straight-shooting students says, "If you can't find something fun to do, you have some major social skills to work on."

Student Body

One thing's certain at Michigan State University: You're bound to run into a lot of students from Michigan. "It seems like 90 percent of our school is from Michigan," a student comments. Four-fifths of the student population is white, but there's still a mix of races and backgrounds here. "However, the different racial groups do not really socialize with each other," notes an undergrad. "Whites stick with whites, blacks stick with blacks, etc." But don't misunderstand. Most MSU students are "friendly and welcoming." One student even goes so far as to say, "I am sure that nowhere else on the planet are there 40,000+ young people [that's undergrads and grads combined] that get along as well as those attending Michigan State University."

ADMISSIONS

Very important factors considered by the admissions committee include: secondary school record. *Important factors considered include:* standardized test scores. *Other factors considered include:* alumni/ae relation, class rank, essays, extracurricular activities, geographical residence, minority status, recommendations, talent/ability, volunteer work, work experience. SAT I or ACT required. TOEFL required of all international applicants. High school diploma or GED is required. *High school units required/recommended:* 14 total required; 4 English required, 3 math required, 2 science required, 2 foreign language required, 3 social studies required.

The Inside Word

Gaining admission to MSU is a matter of following the formulas. Grades, tests, and rank—numbers, numbers, numbers. Solid extracurricular involvement and recommendations may help borderline candidates.

FINANCIAL AID

Students should submit: FAFSA, institution's own financial aid form. Regular filing deadline is June 30. The Princeton Review suggests that all financial aid forms be submitted as soon as possible after January 1. *Need-based scholarships/grants offered:* Pell, SEOG, state scholarships/grants, private scholarships, the school's own gift aid. *Loan aid offered:* Direct Subsidized Stafford, Direct Unsubsidized Stafford, Direct PLUS, Federal Perkins, state loans, college/university loans from institutional funds. Federal Work-Study Program available. Institutional employment available. Applicants will be notified of awards on a rolling basis beginning on or about March 15. Off-campus job opportunities are excellent.

FROM THE ADMISSIONS OFFICE

"Although Michigan State University is a graduate and research institution of international stature and acclaim, your undergraduate education is a high priority. More than 2,600 instructional faculty members (89 percent of whom hold a terminal degree) are dedicated to providing academic instruction, guidance, and assistance to our undergraduate students. Our 35,000 undergraduate students are a select group of academically motivated men and women. The diversity of ethnic, racial, religious, and socioeconomic heritage makes the student body a microcosm of the state, national, and international community."

For even more information on this school, turn to page 371 of the "Stats" section.

MICHIGAN TECHNOLOGICAL UNIVERSITY

1400 Townsend Drive, Houghton, MI 49931 • Admissions: 906-487-2335 • Fax: 906-487-2125
Financial Aid: 906-487-2622 • E-mail: mtu4u@mtu.edu • Website: www.mtu.edu

Ratings

Quality of Life: 77   **Academic:** 74   **Admissions:** 82   **Financial Aid:** 87

Academics

More than half of MTU's 6,000 undergrads are enrolled in its College of Engineering. The four other colleges that comprise the university are the College of Sciences and Arts, the School of Technology, the School of Business and Economics, and the School of Forestry and Wood Products. A good many students take pride in the technological bent of the institution, and frown on recent administrative investments,

> **SURVEY SAYS . . .**
> *Frats and sororities dominate social scene*
> *Popular college radio*
> *Hard liquor is popular*
> *Class discussions are rare*
> *(Almost) everyone plays intramural sports*
> *Registration is a pain*
> *Library needs improving*
> *Theater is unpopular*
> *Political activism is (almost) nonexistent*

such as "the money pit that is the Rozsa Center for Performing Arts," that threaten "to turn MTU into a more generic university rather than a technical one." Some science students tell us that they'd rather see the university spend money on improving the laboratories. "My labs are very lacking," one student gripes. "I pay extra money in my tuition for my labs and only one of them even has disk drives in the computers." In class, students often end up "trying to decipher the chopped English of some of the professors and TAs," but students at MTU still report that they're having "an excellent academic experience." Small class sizes and professor accessibility are among the aspects of the university that students love. "Tech isn't a really big school, so if you need help all you have to do is schedule a time with your professors and they will meet with you."

Life

"If you're into winter sports, this is definitely the place to be," students tell us MTU is located on Michigan's Upper Peninsula, "right on the Portage," (a large waterway) and "only a half-hour away from Lake Superior," not to mention the nearby Ottawa National Forest and the university's own Mont Ripley ski mountain. With all of these natural resources at their fingertips, MTU students regularly go "hiking and biking," "canoeing and swimming," "cross-country skiing and downhill skiing," as well as rock climbing, fishing, and snowshoeing. Competitively, hockey and broomball rule the scene. Broomball is a sport involving protective masks, brooms, a ball, and goals—not terribly unlike hockey. MTU has a Web page, www.broomball.mtu.edu, that explains the rules. They don't, however, have a Web page for "the number-one pastime at this university": drinking, especially at frat parties. One student told us that there's a rational explanation for all of the drinking that goes on here: "It is so cold and snowy, and there is an ungodly small percentage of girls that go here. So if people didn't drink, they would go insane and EXPLODE." When students get tired of life "in the boonies" and need a spark of urban energy, they'd better pull on their driving gloves. "The nearest big city is Minneapolis," an international student told us. And that's about seven hours away.

Student Body

The Tech student body is predominantly male, white, and both socially and politically conservative. Did we forget anything? Oh, yes . . . as one student succinctly puts it, "this is a very nerdy school. If you aren't a nerd and you come here, this school will turn you into one." Writes another, "Students seem too caught up in their technical selves. Students here who avoid eye contact are plentiful. I think this is mainly because they have too much technical attachment to attach their minds to anything but school." Agrees one engineer, "Students are either really gregarious, or lock themselves in their rooms. Very little in between." The relatively scarce female population get to "date frequently," but as for the men . . . well, as one student reports, "since MTU is all guys, all we think about is women. For fun, we talk about women, drink a lot and fantasize about women, and try to hit on women. It's tough being a guy in the UP!"

ADMISSIONS

Very important factors considered by the admissions committee include: class rank, secondary school record, standardized test scores. *Other factors considered include:* alumni/ae relation, character/personal qualities, essays, extracurricular activities, interview, recommendations, talent/ability, volunteer work, work experience. SAT I or ACT required. TOEFL required of all international applicants. High school diploma or GED is required. *High school units required/recommended:* 15 total required; 3 English required, 4 English recommended, 3 math required, 4 math recommended, 2 science required, 3 science recommended, 1 foreign language recommended, 1 social studies recommended, 1 history recommended, 1 elective recommended.

The Inside Word

Michigan Tech has a pretty good reputation and a highly self-selected applicant pool. In light of this, students who are interested should not be deceived by the high admit rate and should spend a little time on self-assessment of their ability to handle an engineering curriculum. There's nothing gained by getting yourself into a program that you can't get out of successfully.

FINANCIAL AID

Students should submit: FAFSA. No deadline for regular filing. The Princeton Review suggests that all financial aid forms be submitted as soon as possible after January 1. *Need-based scholarships/grants offered:* Pell, SEOG, state scholarships/grants, private scholarships, the school's own gift aid. *Loan aid offered:* Direct Subsidized Stafford, Direct Unsubsidized Stafford, Direct PLUS, Federal Perkins, state loans, college/university loans from institutional funds, external private loans. Federal Work-Study Program available. Institutional employment available. Applicants will be notified of awards on a rolling basis beginning on or about February 28. Off-campus job opportunities are good.

FROM THE ADMISSIONS OFFICE

"Michigan Tech is recognized as one of the nation's leading univesities for undergraduate and graduate education in science and engineering. Its state-of-the-art campus is located near Lake Superior in Michigan's beautiful Upper Peninsula. The university owns and operates a downhill ski area and 18-hole golf course. . . . MTU is one of Michigan's four nationally recognized research universities."

For even more information on this school, turn to page 371 of the "Stats" section.

MILLIKIN UNIVERSITY

1184 WEST MAIN STREET, DECATUR, IL 62522-2084 • ADMISSIONS: 217-424-6210 • FAX: 217-425-4669
E-MAIL: ADMIS@MAIL.MILLIKIN.EDU • WEBSITE: WWW.MILLIKIN.EDU

Ratings

Quality of Life: 79   **Academic:** 69   **Admissions:** 66   **Financial Aid:** 80

Academics

"The greatest strength of Millikin is that it is a small private school but has achieved many qualities of a large university." It's also achieved a lot of the "bureaucratic nonsense" associated with bigger institutions. Located in Decatur,

> **SURVEY SAYS . . .**
> *Students get along with local community*
> *Students are religious, Instructors are good teachers*
> *Student publications are popular*
> *Popular college radio, School is well run*

Illinois, Millikin students boast that their professors challenge "students to think critically at a level that they never have before." And according to an undergraduate, "it is extremely easy to contact and get information from professors outside of class." Consider this availability along with Millikin's small class size that makes "for interesting class discussion," and it's no surprise that students forge "strong bonds with [their] professors." Administrators, as at larger schools, don't receive such high marks. Though "the administration means well . . . they sometimes fail to realize that just because they think it is in the students' best interest doesn't mean [that] the students necessarily agree." Elementary education, marketing, biology, and nursing are among the most highly enrolled majors, but many students single out the "strong music program" as well as the fine arts program for particular praise.

Life

If the town of Decatur "is not at all a college town," the amount of activity that happens on campus completely makes up for it. The school's programming board is hailed for bringing in "nationally recognized bands, comedians (from Comedy Central and BET), local bands, [and] outdoor festivals." One content student claims that "there is always something to do on campus, and if you are not interested in participating in those activities there are opportunities for you to plan your own event and engage others." Some do just that, and "everyone is trying to balance school and extracurricular activities." If you're still intent on traveling off campus in search of fun, take heed of warnings by students that "Decatur is not a very safe town," and "east of campus the neighborhood gets rough very quickly." For those in need of an urban experience every so often, Decauter is "directly between Chicago, St. Louis, and Indianapolis"—though all are between two and three hours away by car—and "it is also very common to drive to Champaign, Illinois [home of the University of Illinois], where a more common 'college life' exists." There is also the presence of five fraternities and three sororities, which "on a small campus make for a pretty decent social environment." For those less inclined to party, "sports and theatre are both popular on this campus," and there are also "lectures, art shows, opera, dance . . . just about every evening."

Student Body

"Millikin is the home of the best college students." Such is the sentiment that many undergrads have about their fellow students here. "I like everyone at Millikin. . . . Friendships are made across racial, gender, ethnic, religious, economic, and age lines." Diversity, however, remains a "major issue on campus and is something that is constantly talked about." One student finds that "the large gay and lesbian population makes for very open-minded people." Some students have noted, however, that "there has been problems with students bashing other students because of sexual orientation, but the faculty and administration does not stand for it." While "some people [here] are ignorant to the real world," the majority like to point out the "family atmosphere" that pervades the Millikin student body. Though one student claims that "students are separated by one thing, theatre/music majors and the rest of campus," another chimes, "I like to see that vastly different backgrounds and majors can gather together and find that we all have something in common."

ADMISSIONS

Very important factors considered by the admissions committee include: secondary school record. *Important factors considered include:* class rank, interview, recommendations, and standardized test scores. *Other factors considered include:* alumni/ae relation, character/personal qualities, extracurricular activities, minority status, talent/ability, volunteer work, and work experience. SAT I or ACT required. TOEFL required of all international applicants. High school diploma or GED is required. *High school units required/recommended:* 16 total recommended; 4 English recommended, 3 math recommended, 3 science recommended, 2 foreign language recommended, 2 social studies recommended, 2 history recommended.

The Inside Word

Millikin is not highly selective, so candidates with average high school grades, a moderately challenging high school curriculum, and standardized test scores at or above the national average should be admitted. Borderline candidates should visit the campus and interview to indicate the seriousness of their intentions.

FINANCIAL AID

Students should submit: FAFSA and institution's own financial aid form. Regular filing deadline is June 1. The Princeton Review suggests that all financial aid forms be submitted as soon as possible after January 1. *Need-based scholarships/grants offered:* Pell, SEOG, state scholarships/grants, private scholarships, and the school's own gift aid. *Loan aid offered:* FFEL Subsidized Stafford, FFEL Unsubsidized Stafford, FFEL PLUS, and Federal Perkins. Federal Work-Study Program available. Institutional employment available. Applicants will be notified of awards on a rolling basis beginning on or about March 1. Off-campus job opportunities are good.

FROM THE ADMISSIONS OFFICE

"For more than 100 years, Millikin University has prepared students for professional success, democratic citizenship in a diverse and dynamic global environment, and a personal life of meaning and value. A private, primarily undergraduate institution of 75 acres and about 2,400 students, this selective, comprehensive university has four colleges or schools: Arts and Sciences, Business, Nursing, and Fine Arts. Faculty members excel at student-centered teaching and contribute scholarship appropriate to both their discipline and an institution that values and expects excellent teaching. Ninety-seven percent of Millikin students receive financial aid totaling $24 million annually. Ninety-seven percent of Millikin grads get jobs or go on to grad school within six months of graduation—87 percent in their chosen career field! Millikin has been recognized as one of the nation's Best Colleges and Universities in the Midwest for 10 straight years in the annual *U.S. News & World Report* rankings. With more than 50 majors, minors, and special programs, Millikin has something for everyone. Also, our students love to study internationally in Austria, the Dominican Republic, England, France, Germany, Italy, and beyond. Into athletics? Check out Millikin's Division III sports. For men there's baseball, basketball, cross-country, football, golf, indoor track, soccer, swimming, track & field, and wrestling. Women can choose from basketball, cross-country, golf, indoor track, soccer, softball, swimming, tennis, and volleyball. Campus Preview Days for 2003–2004 are September 13, October 18, November 10, and January 19."

For even more information on this school, turn to page 372 of the "Stats" section.

MILWAUKEE SCHOOL OF ENGINEERING

1025 NORTH BROADWAY, MILWAUKEE, WI 53202-3109 • ADMISSIONS: 414-277-6763 • FAX: 414-277-7475
E-MAIL: EXPLORE@MSOE.EDU • WEBSITE: WWW.MSOE.EDU

Ratings
Quality of Life: 77   **Academic:** 78   **Admissions:** 73   **Financial Aid:** 76

Academics

With just 16 undergraduate majors to choose from (nearly all related to engineering and business, nursing excepted), MSOE's undergrads don't simply learn engineering; they live it. Some students report that this focused curriculum can feel "limiting" at times.

> **SURVEY SAYS . . .**
> *Classes are small, Lots of beer drinking*
> *Intercollegiate sports are popular*
> *(Almost) everyone plays intramural sports*
> *Theater is hot, Students love Milwaukee*
> *Registration is a breeze, Great computer facilities*

Others believe that this focus has made MSOE's some "of the best engineering programs in the country." In the interest of educational well-roundedness, students are required to take almost one-fifth of their classes in the humanities and communications. At the same time that they fulfill these general education requirements, students "start taking engineering classes" and getting a feel for their majors. Students here find tons of work and high expectations: "I've heard a lot of underclassmen refer it as a 'boot camp mentality,'" writes one student. "What they don't realize is that this is exactly what makes MSOE such a good school—the tough, rigorous schedule is preparing you for the REAL WORLD, for going out there and being an engineer. You will WORK for you degree here. But you will also enter the workforce as one of the best damn engineers out there, ready to handle anything." Because "there are absolutely no TAs teaching," students have the chance to work closely and frequently with their professors.

Life

One student summarizes, the student body is comprised of a whole lot of "engineering majors, and many of them do act like typical engineers—not exactly the most social people." However, most undergrads assure us they have no problem finding ways to occupy their time. "There's tons of . . . stuff to do in Milwaukee, especially since MSOE is right downtown." Lake Michigan "is only a few blocks away, as is the theatre district, and both the art and science museums are within walking distance. There's even a free ice-skating rink a few blocks away." And don't forget the seemingly endless rotation of "concerts, theatre shows, movies, and festivals going on in Milwaukee." Plenty of watering holes are also nearby. "MSOE is located one block off Water Street, where many of Milwaukee's best bars can be found." It is the beer capital of the United States, after all. On campus, students will find "dances, band contests, speakers," as well as "parties."

Student Body

Imagine a world where people "sit in front of their computers all day" and deem "instant messenger an acceptable form of social interaction." This is the world of many students at the Milwaukee School of Engineering. "Most of them need to hone their social skills," opines one student. Another describes MSOE's student body as a host of 2,200 "typical nerds." Students here largely define themselves by their major—or, more accurately, by the branch of engineering they study. "Mild feudal rivalries as to which major is best" often ensue, explains a student. "After a while you voluntarily develop a sense of pride in your chosen field and will defend it to the bitter end. For example, the big debate [right now] is whether the MEs or the

EEs are better (MEs, of course) because CEs and SEs never leave their rooms . . . and what the heck is an IE!!" But don't be frightened off by abbreviations and instant messenger. Students here are also incredibly and admirably dedicated to their academics ("study freaks," offers one student). And they're a friendly, if sometimes quiet, bunch. "Almost everyone here is an overall 'good person.'"

ADMISSIONS

Very important factors considered by the admissions committee include: secondary school record and standardized test scores. *Other factors considered include:* extracurricular activities, interview, and talent/ability. SAT I or ACT required. TOEFL required of all international applicants. High school diploma is required and GED is accepted. *High school units required/recommended:* 13 total are required; 15 total are recommended; 4 English required, 4 English recommended, 4 math required, 4 math recommended, 2 science required, 4 science recommended, 1 social studies required, 1 social studies recommended, 1 history required, 1 history recommended, 1 elective required, 1 elective recommended.

The Inside Word

MSOE is a fine institution that lacks only national recognition to push it into the upper tier of engineering schools. Now is a good time to apply here; you'll get a solid education from a relatively unknown school, and you'll reap future windfalls as its reputation grows.

FINANCIAL AID

Students should submit: FAFSA. No deadline for regular filing. The Princeton Review suggests that all financial aid forms be submitted as soon as possible after January 1. *Need-based scholarships/grants offered:* Pell, SEOG, state scholarships/grants, private scholarships, and the university's own gift aid. *Loan aid offered:* Direct Subsidized Stafford, Direct Unsubsidized Stafford, FFEL PLUS, Federal Perkins, college/university loans from institutional funds, and alternative loans. Federal Work-Study Program available. Institutional employment available. Applicants will be notified of awards on a rolling basis beginning on or about March 15. Off-campus job opportunities are excellent.

FROM THE ADMISSIONS OFFICE

"MSOE reached its 100th anniversary in 2003. Although most organizations and businesses are lucky to survive five years, MSOE is thriving. This Centennial celebration is a time to reflect on how MSOE has grown in breadth to include such things the Rader School of Business and a School of Nursing, and to look forward as we continue to anticipate business and industry needs to ensure graduate preparedness well into the twenty-first century. MSOE offers 16 applications-oriented undergraduate degrees in areas such as engineering, business, technical communication, construction management, and nursing. Graduate degrees also are offered. The 2,600-person student body comes from throughout the United States and numerous countries. Approximately half the full-time students live in three modern high-rise residence halls. Ninety-eight percent of full-time students receive financial aid. MSOE's 15-acre campus is located in a historic district downtown. There are dozens of student activities, organizations, sororities and fraternities, and intramural sports. MSOE students can participate in 20 NCAA Division III intercollegiate sports, several of which will be played at MSOE's soon-to-be-built Kern Center, an athletic, health, and wellness facility.

"MSOE offers a personalized education with an 11:1 student/faculty ratio. The university has a four-year graduation guarantee for on-track students and a post-graduation placement rate of 98 percent over the past five years. Students gain invaluable experience through more than 600 laboratory hours, professional internships, and international study programs and gain research experience in the Applied Technology Center. MSOE's Technology Package provides all new students with a notebook (laptop) computer."

For even more information on this school, turn to page 373 of the "Stats" section.

MONMOUTH COLLEGE

700 EAST BROADWAY, MONMOUTH, IL 61462 • ADMISSIONS: 309-457-2131 • FAX: 309-457-2141
E-MAIL: ADMIT@MONM.EDU • WEBSITE: WWW.MONM.EDU

Ratings
Quality of Life: 78   Academic: 76   Admissions: 74   Financial Aid: 85

Academics

With the motto "What college was meant to be," Monmouth College offers "class sizes and resources for students that are ideal." One student tells us, "The science and business departments in particular have excellent faculty and very

> **SURVEY SAYS . . .**
> *Student publications are popular*
> *Classes are small, No one cheats*
> *Students are religious, School is well run*
> *(Almost) everyone plays intramural sports*

good resources," and the education program also draws praise. In all disciplines, "we are encouraged to think freely and explain our thoughts rationally and logically, and teachers don't grade just by tests but mostly by improvement and the quality of our work." Professors make themselves available to undergraduates, with one student commenting, "If you want to get to know them, they'll want to get to know you." Another respondent echoes this sentiment with his opinion: "I couldn't ask for more support and concern from the administration and faculty." The administration remains accessible, to the extent that "everyone from the president on down is very committed to talking to the students." The deans are characterized as "willing to meet with students and appear to be genuinely concerned with student troubles." The few complaints center on the unreliable Internet connections and the firewall imposed on the network, which one student calls "an impediment to my research." Course availability could also be improved, considering one student's claim that "some of the important courses needed for my major were closed by the time I got to register." However, most Monmouth attendees laud the school's "great financial plan," saying, "I would not be going here without it."

Life

At Monmouth, where life "largely revolves around partying," students agree that "bars provide a good chunk of our entertainment" and that the "strong Greek life" plays a large role in the social scene. Some students complain that "there's no alternative to attending the fraternities" and that it "gets old after a while," but others mention activities including "karaoke, mixers, and battle of the radio DJs." Students note "great opportunities to get involved," whether it be in "religious, Greek, academic, service, or athletic groups." Monmouth undergrads make regular trips to Western Illinois University in nearby Macomb, as trying to "make your own fun" is a popular pastime. Possibly due to the fact that "a movie theatre within 15 miles would be nice," undergraduates often head off campus or to nearby schools for weekend entertainment. Certain students gripe that the school "forces you to live on campus," but at least it's "extremely safe and a beautiful environment." From sporting events to alumni support, students note that "school pride really shows."

Student Body

With just over 1,000 undergraduates, Monmouth's student body demonstrates "a great acceptance among different sexual orientations, genders, and races," according to some people. Corroborating this view, others say it's "wonderful to see such a wide variety of people." Others point out that the population is "largely white due to its location," and that while some diversity is evident, "everyone tends to socialize with their own groups." Several students wish for "a more diverse group of students in leadership roles," and claim that the Monmouth crew "doesn't realize how low the number of minority students on campus actually is." On this front, the admissions committee is "trying to increase and promote diversity." In the meantime, even among the "conservative leaning" group, "there are few tensions" with the school's gay population. And though students are at times described as "apathetic," most attendees agree that "the general aura here is great."

ADMISSIONS

Very important factors considered by the admissions committee include: class rank, secondary school record, and standardized test scores. *Important factors considered include:* recommendations. *Other factors considered include:* character/personal qualities, essays, extracurricular activities, interview, talent/ability, volunteer work, and work experience. SAT I or ACT required, ACT preferred. TOEFL required of all international applicants. High school diploma or GED is required. *High school units required/recommended:* 14 total required; 20 total recommended; 4 English required, 3 math required, 4 math recommended, 2 science required, 4 science recommended, 1 science lab required, 2 science lab recommended, 3 foreign language recommended, 1 social studies required, 3 social studies recommended, 2 history required.

The Inside Word

Lack of name recognition outside the western Illinois region keeps admission at Monmouth College less competitive than it might otherwise be. The school could be a real "sleeper pick" for candidates shut out of small liberal arts colleges of similar academic quality.

FINANCIAL AID

Students should submit: FAFSA. No deadline for regular filing. The Princeton Review suggests that all financial aid forms be submitted as soon as possible after January 1. *Need-based scholarships/grants offered:* Pell, SEOG, state scholarships/grants, private scholarships, and the school's own gift aid. *Loan aid offered:* FFEL Subsidized Stafford, FFEL Unsubsidized Stafford, FFEL PLUS, and Federal Perkins. Federal Work-Study Program available. Institutional employment available. Applicants will be notified of awards on a rolling basis beginning on or about March 1. Off-campus job opportunities are good.

FROM THE ADMISSIONS OFFICE

"As the college celebrates its sesquicentennial throughout 2002–2003 academic year, the school is thriving, enjoying the best fortune in its history. Enrollment has grown by 500 students in the past decade to nearly 1,100, facilities have been renovated and constructed and the overwhelming feeling on campus and in the community is that the process will continue.

"The biggest news on campus is several ongoing facility projects, highlighted by the construction of the Huff Athletic Center, which comes on the heels of the 2001 completion of Bowers Hall, a $6 million suite-style residence facility. Other projects include renovations at the century-old auditorium and the installation of a chiller plant.

"The newly renovated Hewes Library was dedicated in 2002, giving the college community a library second to none among its peers. The $7 million project added, among other things, a 48-seat electronic classroom and wireless Internet connections.

"Unveiled in 1999, the Mellinger Teaching & Learning Center houses a 24-hour computer lab in the lower level and various tutoring resources and is another example of the changes being made on campus with an eye on technology. The college is nearly finished with an extensive curriculum review, and MC's innovative Wackerle Center gives students the resources to match their course of study to internships and future careers.

"'All of these campus improvements are designed to create a "high-performance" environment for students at Monmouth, both now and into the future,' said President Richard F. Griese."

For even more information on this school, turn to page 373 of the "Stats" section.

MORNINGSIDE COLLEGE

1501 MORNINGSIDE AVENUE, SIOUX CITY, IA 51106-1751 • ADMISSIONS: 712-274-5111
FAX: 712-274-5101 • E-MAIL: MSCADM@MORNINGSIDE.EDU • WEBSITE: WWW.MORNINGSIDE.EDU

Ratings
Quality of Life: 73   Academic: 75   Admissions: 69   Financial Aid: 90

Academics

Things come state-of-the-art at Morningside—a Methodist-affiliated, liberal arts college in Sioux City, Iowa—even the instructors: "I feel the college has done wonderful job with providing us with technology and up-to-date professors." Of professors, another stu-

> **SURVEY SAYS . . .**
> *School is well run, Classes are small*
> *Intercollegiate sports are popular*
> *(Almost) everyone plays intramural sports*
> *Hard liquor is popular, Popular college radio*
> *Lots of beer drinking, Students are religious*

dent writes, "They are the backbone of this school." Professors teach all of the classes here, intro and upper-level courses within the 55 majors and 4 pre-professional programs offered. If you're looking for the strongest academic regions at Morningside, check out "music, business, and education." Despite student gripes about the administration, there are also some bright spots. For instance, the administration is responsible for the policy that gives every student a personal computer upon arrival at Morningside. And specific departments within the administration are outstanding, such as "the people in Student Services" who "are out of this world." While students may not always agree with the college's administrators and professors, they never feel that they're a number. "The greatest strength of Morningside," offers an undergrad, "would definitely be its small, caring, community atmosphere."

Life

"If you choose to spend your weekends sitting in your dorm room, you're not going to enjoy your Morningside experience." But if you're a person who—on weekends or weekdays—has an urge to explore and get involved, you'll find plenty of satisfaction in the Morningside life. Morningside is in "Siouxland," an unofficial geographical boundary that lassos Sioux City, Iowa, Sergeant Bluff, Iowa; South Sioux City, Nebraska; and North Sioux City, South Dakota. While students will concede that Siouxland is "not the best" area in the world, they describe a large number of regional activities, such as lazing in "parks," "biking, hiking, or Rollerblading along the [Missouri] river," "a number of bars and stores and even minimalls," as well as "two ice-skating rinks and three bowling alleys." But students at Morningside don't need to rely on the off-campus action for fun. For one thing, the "very popular" fraternities and sororities net nearly a quarter of the student body. Undergrads also devote their time to "Christian groups, musical groups . . . student government, and television and radio programs." And in case you're wondering: yes, "most people party on the weekends," despite the fact that Morningside "is a dry campus." The people who stick around to party, that is. The college is often dubbed a "suitcase college, meaning that too many students leave for the weekend." But leaving for the weekend, opines one student, is a shot in the foot. "If you're like me, you will thank yourself every day for choosing this college over the others."

Student Body

Siouxland is the wellspring for Morningside College; a resounding majority of the college's students comes from the region where Iowa, Nebraska, and South Dakota meet. As one student explains, this means that "many people already know" other "prospective students" before they enroll. "Two of my aunts went to Morningside and had great experiences, which is one of the reasons that I am here today," a student offers, elucidating the personal and regional affections that students harbor for Morningside. The downside of the college's regional composition is that "Morningside can be very cliquey" because many students arrive on campus with pre-established groups of friends. Once on campus, students quickly find themselves fitting into one of two categories: athlete and nonathlete. To get a good portrait of this aspect of Morningside's social shape, an undergrad suggests peering into the cafeteria. "The athletes all sit on one side and the nonathletes sit on the other side, and if someone gets mixed up and sits in the wrong area someone will be quick to put you in your place." But boundaries are rarely insurmountable, and if students are willing to mingle with people from another "clique," they'll probably discover that "it's hard to find someone around here that you absolutely can't get along with."

ADMISSIONS

Very important factors considered by the admissions committee include: class rank, recommendations, secondary school record, and standardized test scores. *Important factors considered include:* extracurricular activities, interview, and talent/ability. *Other factors considered include:* essays. SAT I or ACT required. TOEFL required of all international applicants. High school diploma is required and GED is accepted. *High school units required/recommended:* 10 total are recommended; 3 English recommended, 2 science recommended, 3 social studies recommended, 2 math recommended.

The Inside Word

Morningside's admissions policy states, "To receive unconditional acceptance, the high school senior must have earned a composite ACT of 20 or a composite SAT of 930 and rank either in the top half of the class or have achieved a 2.5 GPA or better." The admissions office also considers the special talents and/or extenuating circumstances of candidates who do not meet these requirements.

FINANCIAL AID

Students should submit: FAFSA. No deadline for regular filing. The Princeton Review suggests that all financial aid forms be submitted as soon as possible after January 1. *Need-based scholarships/grants offered:* Pell, SEOG, state scholarships/grants, private scholarships, and the school's own gift aid. *Loan aid offered:* FFEL Subsidized Stafford, FFEL Unsubsidized Stafford, FFEL PLUS, Federal Perkins, state loans, and college/university loans from institutional funds. Federal Work-Study Program available. Institutional employment available. Applicants will be notified of awards on a rolling basis beginning on or about March 31. Off-campus job opportunities are excellent.

FROM THE ADMISSIONS OFFICE

"The Morningside College experience cultivates a passion for life-long learning and a dedication to ethical leadership and civic responsibility. Founded in 1894, Morningside College is a private, coeducational college affiliated with the United Methodist Church. Located in Sioux City, Iowa (population 120,000), Morningside offers a low student to faculty ratio of 12:1, allowing its student population to be part of a challenging but supportive community. Students learn to think creatively, work with others as a team, and gain a clear sense of where they're headed in life. They put their ideas to work writing business plans, doing research and internships, practice-teaching, and serving the community. There are more than 50 student-led organizations, including student government, honor societies, service groups, religious organizations, musical ensembles, student publications, and national fraternities and sororities. New apartment-style residence halls are currently under construction. Ninety-six percent of Morningside students receive financial aid based on merit as well as need. Talent grants are awarded in art, athletics, music, and theatre. Within six months of graduation, more than 95 percent of our students are employed or admitted to graduate school."

For even more information on this school, turn to page 374 of the "Stats" section.

MOUNT VERNON NAZARENE UNIVERSITY

800 MARTINSBURG ROAD, MOUNT VERNON, OH 43050 • ADMISSIONS: 740-397-9000 • FAX: 740-393-0511
E-MAIL: ADMISSIONS@MVNC.EDU • WEBSITE: WWW.MVNC.EDU

Ratings
Quality of Life: 77   **Academic:** 70   **Admissions:** 64   **Financial Aid:** 76

Academics

Studies both sacred and profane merge at Mount Vernon Nazarene College, a small liberal arts school northeast of Columbus, Ohio. The school excels in business administration, psychology, biology, religion, and all manner of education. (Christian and early childhood

> **SURVEY SAYS . . .**
> *Student publications are popular*
> *Students are religious, Classes are small*
> *Profs teach upper levels, Popular college radio*
> *Class discussions encouraged*
> *Theater is hot, School is well run*

physical education are among its specialties.) Students here brag that "our class sizes are so small. The biggest class I've ever been in only had 45 to 50 people in it, and it was a Bible class required of every student." Small class sizes allow for access to professors, who "are always available, even when they are at home . . . . I feel very lucky to have professors like these." Agrees one student, "God has a way of putting excellent professors on this campus." Administrators, students tell us, "give each student the feeling that they are important as individuals and not just in numbers. If MVNU is not the place for a prospective student, MVNU will suggest a good school for their area of interest." Sums up one student, "To me, MVNU is one of the best Christian colleges around. It is small, and on the outskirts of a small town, but it is the best place to go. Being here has opened my eyes to so many things: missions around the world, hunger and poverty, and so on. This school is getting us ready for when we are out in the world as missionaries, teachers, preachers, accountants, etc."

Life

As at most religiously affiliated schools, "drinking and other related activities are not allowed" at Nazarene. Students tell us that "some of the rules are a bit hard to live with . . . . Supervision is relatively tight: no members of the opposite sex in your apartment without a special 'guest pass,' for example." They also report, however, that "campus life is strict if you are on the outside looking in. We do have fun though. A lot of people see MVNU as a boring campus, but we find ways to have fun without breaking the rules." Adds one student, "We talk, hang out, watch movies, go to Columbus . . . everything normal college students do, except the majority here do not drink, smoke, or use drugs." The quality of life at MVNU is good; notes one student, "All upperclassmen live in on-campus apartments, which are spacious and generally very nice. Freshman dorms are larger than most I've seen." Hometown Mount Vernon "is so small that there is very little to do here. We have one bowling alley and one movie theatre. There are a multitude of restaurants, but not much else." Undergrads tell us that "the student government (SGA) is really good about coming up with different things to do throughout the month to keep people busy and socializing. In The Den (that's the campus hangout) we have had karaoke night, TV rerun marathons, 50s theme nights, pizza parties, ice cream socials, luaus, and much more." Intramural sports are also popular here.

Student Body

"There is a sense of mutual respect among all the students" at MVNU. "I grew up in a Christian home, and in high school I was in the minority," explains one student. "Now it is nice to be in the majority." Unfortunately, "there isn't much diversity at MVNU. I don't think anybody would be against diversity . . . but it just hasn't happened yet." Nazarenes make up the vast majority here, with Baptists (who constitute about 7 percent of the population) representing the largest minority. Students do exhibit a diversity of personalities; as one student told us, "There are many different groups: preps, jocks, art majors, science freaks, etc., but we all talk to one another and hang out . . . . There are small cliques, of course, but when it comes down to it, everyone is friends with everyone else." Undergrads here warn that "non-Christian students sometimes have a problem fitting into the strict rules and requirements (mandatory chapel three times a week!), but generally do well."

ADMISSIONS

Very important factors considered by the admissions committee include: essays, recommendations, secondary school record, standardized test scores, and state residency. *Important factors considered include:* class rank. *Other factors considered include:* character/personal qualities, extracurricular activities, geographical residence, interview, religious affiliation/commitment, and talent/ability. SAT I or ACT required. TOEFL required of all international applicants. High school diploma or GED is required. *High school units required/recommended:* 4 English required, 3 math required, 2 science required, 3 science recommended, 1 science lab required, 3 science lab recommended, 3 foreign language recommended, 3 social studies required, 3 social studies recommended, 8 elective required, 8 elective recommended.

The Inside Word

Mount Vernon Nazarene is looking for students determined to empower themselves for their calling as both academicians and Christians. Whether you are devout or not is not as important as your commitment to live up to MVNC's austere, viceless lifetstyle.

FINANCIAL AID

Students should submit: FAFSA and institution's own financial aid form. March 1 preferred deadline. The Princeton Review suggests that all financial aid forms be submitted as soon as possible after January 1. *Need-based scholarships/grants offered:* Pell, SEOG, state scholarships/grants, private scholarships, and the school's own gift aid. *Loan aid offered:* FFEL Subsidized Stafford, FFEL Unsubsidized Stafford, FFEL PLUS, Federal Perkins, alternative loans. Federal Work-Study Program available. Institutional employment available. Merit-based scholarships offered. Applicants will be notified of awards on a rolling basis beginning on or about March 1. Off-campus job opportunities are good.

FROM THE ADMISSIONS OFFICE

"At Mount Vernon Nazarene University, you'll get a great education from a distinctly Christian perspective—one that will prepare you to go wherever your heart leads you, to become the person you were created to be. Those are big ideas. We'll help you get there. Imagine a place where students are what it's all about. Where people smile and greet you wherever you go. Where you are encouraged, even inspired to explore who you are and who you want to become. Best of all, you'll make friendships for life! Our 400-acre, tree-filled campus is a busy, exciting place offering comfortable, well-equipped residence halls, great food, and a variety of things to do. Attractive townhouse-style, upperclass apartments house six students each and are complete with kitchenettes and comfortable living rooms. All feature high-speed Web connections. Your journey will begin with relevant, challenging academics. From our outstanding education, psychology, and computer science departments to our renowned ministry, pre-med, and business programs, you'll build hands-on skills and knowledge that graduate schools and employers want. Our quality education is based around small classes and lots of one-on-one face time with faculty experts, so that you have time to ask questions, share ideas, go deeper. MVNU graduates live all over the world and lead amazing lives. They've translated their knowledge, faith, and values into their careers, lives, and communities."

For even more information on this school, turn to page 374 of the "Stats" section.

NORTH DAKOTA STATE UNIVERSITY

Box 5454, Fargo, ND 58105 • Admissions: 701-231-8643 • Fax: 701-231-8802
E-mail: NDSU.Admission@ndsu.nodak.edu • Website: www.ndsu.edu

Ratings
Quality of Life: 74   Academic: 77   Admissions: 73   Financial Aid: 85

Academics

The good news at North Dakota State University in Fargo is money. The bad news, however, is also money. "The tuition is great . . . compared to other colleges," comments an undergrad, explaining the first variable of the money

> **SURVEY SAYS . . .**
> *Classes are small, Students love Fargo*
> *Diversity lacking on campus*
> *Very little beer drinking, Lousy food on campus*
> *No one watches intercollegiate sports*

equation. NDSU charges North Dakotans the least and nonresidents the most, with Minnesotans and people from all the other neighboring states receiving a generous discount that lands them somewhere in the middle of the cost scale. And while some students complain that "the profs are underpaid," there's no shortage of qualified professors. "The profs like what they are doing, and this makes the learning process more enjoyable," explains an undergrad. Others use adjectives like "intelligent," "personable," and "concerned," to describe their teachers. Despite the "cozy" atmosphere and dedicated professors at NDSU, it is a big university with both a wealth of opportunities and it's share of bureaucratic headaches. On the other hand, NDSU offers an extensive selection of majors—more than 80 in all—including some less-than-usual fields like crop and weed sciences, equine studies, food science, interior design, polymers and coatings, and recreation management. But it's departments like engineering and business that claim the hearts and minds of most students. The sciences have been gaining attention as well, thanks largely to the NDSU's president's goal to heighten NDSU's reputation as a leading research institution. "NDSU has goals in mind," asserts a student proudly, and they all amount to "full steam ahead."

Life

"If the word 'Fargo' makes you think of something other than the movie, then you must be from North Dakota," jokes one student at North Dakota State University. While it's true that Fargo, the university's hometown, is the largest city in the state, and while it's true that Fargo has a decent selection of restaurants, bars, cultural events, and odd attractions, it doesn't exactly have a "big-city" feel. "If you like tight Wranglers, cowboy boots, and cows, it's the school for you," cracks one student. Another explains, "It's a good school for people who enjoy a quiet, cozy, campus in an average-size midwestern city." Among the 17 Greek organizations at NDSU are FarmHouse, an international fraternity, and the Ceres Women's Fraternity, also international and composed of women with an interest in agriculture. The Greek system is the source of many social events, and students say "the bars are always a popular place to go." Of course, there are also over 200 student organizations on campus, and nondrinkers report that NDSU "sponsors many alcohol-free events." For instance, there's "a party event every Friday night at the Memorial Union, which is the main place [for] activities [on campus], and they have music and food and free bowling and billiards." And let's not forget Bison football at the FargoDome. "Football games are probably the most popular campus activities."

Student Body

"People in Fargo are very friendly, you betcha!" After all, "North Dakota is known for being friendly," and most of NDSU's students "come from small, rural towns" in the state or one of its neighbors. "It's hard to go through a day without a stranger smiling at you and saying 'hi' while walking to class," remarks one undergrad. The congeniality of the students here makes NDSU "a very 'comfortable' school." Some feel that because the student body is fairly uniform in race (around 95 percent white) and geography, students aren't exposed to many different backgrounds and lifestyles during their college years. Other students cite the campus' "size and diversity" as its strongest points, noting that students from nearly 60 countries attend NDSU.

ADMISSIONS

Very important factors considered by the admissions committee include: secondary school record and standardized test scores. *Other factors considered include:* class rank. SAT I or ACT required, ACT preferred. TOEFL required of all international applicants. High school diploma is required and GED is accepted. *High school units required/recommended:* 13 total are required; 4 English required, 3 math required, 3 science required, 3 science lab required, 3 social studies required.

The Inside Word

Take your ambition to get a great education in the agri-biz-engineering fields and measure it against your distance from Fargo. If your academic dreams still tower over the disproportionate out-of-state tuition, NDSU could be a compelling choice for you.

FINANCIAL AID

Students should submit: FAFSA. Regular filing deadline is April 15. The Princeton Review suggests that all financial aid forms be submitted as soon as possible after January 1. *Need-based scholarships/grants offered:* Pell, SEOG, state scholarships/grants, private scholarships, and the school's own gift aid. *Loan aid offered:* FFEL Subsidized Stafford, FFEL Unsubsidized Stafford, FFEL PLUS, Federal Perkins, Federal Nursing, state, and loans from various lending institutions. Federal Work-Study Program available. Institutional employment available. Applicants will be notified of awards on a rolling basis beginning on or about March 15. Off-campus job opportunities are excellent.

FROM THE ADMISSIONS OFFICE

"North Dakota State University is a dynamic institution dedicated to its land-grant mission of teaching, research, and service. Currently enjoying a remarkable period of growth, NDSU is an innovative, growing university that is emerging on the national scene as a leader among its peers.

"NDSU's enrollment of graduate and undergraduate students grew to a record 11,146 students during fall 2002, a 14 percent increase since 1999. At the same time, the NDSU campus is changing to meet the needs of its students. About $16 million in construction and maintenance projects have just been completed or are underway, and other projects totaling about $30 million are planned for the near future. Just completed are a $2.3 million apartment building and a $3 million Concept Pharmacy for the professional pharmacy program. Work is underway on the $7 million Living/Learning Center and the Center for Nanoscale Science and Engineering in the NDSU Research and Technology Park. Planning also moves forward on the NDSU downtown Fargo campus location, the equine studies center, and a College of Business Administration building.

"NDSU's athletic teams have been synonymous with success. Student athletes compete in first-class facilities such as the Fargodome, Newman Outdoor Field, Ellig Sports Complex, and the Bison Sports Arena. After a year of study, Bison Athletics began a transition to NCAA Division I.

"Students get individual attention and experience working directly with faculty. Ninety-five percent of graduates who sought employment in 2000–2001 found work four to six months after graduation."

For even more information on this school, turn to page 375 of the "Stats" section.

North Park University

3225 West Foster Avenue, Chicago, IL 60625-4895 • Admissions: 773-244-5500 • Fax: 773-244-4953
E-mail: admission@northpark.edu • Website: www.northpark.edu

Ratings

Quality of Life: 79   Academic: 76   Admissions: 74   Financial Aid: 80

Academics

Located six miles north of Chicago's central Loop, North Park University "is a small Christian liberal arts university." As the university puts it, NPU is rooted in "broad evangelical Christian tradition," but it differentiates itself from many other religiously affiliated institutions by describing itself as an "interactive rather than insular" Christian institution interested in drawing students from many walks of life and exposing them to the world beyond NPU's walls. The university is also interested in nurturing its 1,600 students by offering close attention and personal guidance. "The professors here are involved in what you do inside and outside of class," comments one student. Those willing to work hard soon discover that the faculty also offer "connections to many institutions and programs outside of North Park," which can be quite an asset in the Chicago area. "The professors . . . are reason enough to attend school at NPU," according to students. Many students do find the facilities inadequate, though: "We pay frickin' 20 grand a year for a couple of buildings and a dorm in the shape of a pie," groans an undergrad. In addition to getting some more space to stretch their academic legs, students also mention a desire for air-conditioning in the dorms and a student union where they can congregate rather than spending many nights "stuck in their rooms with no place on campus to go and unwind." While the small size of the university may have its limitations, it also has its virtues. "The small size meant I had some great opportunities for leadership," a recent grad recalls. Another student comments on the double-edged quality of the NPU experience, "Small school, big city . . . talk about a little bit of each world."

> **SURVEY SAYS . . .**
> *Very little hard liquor*
> *Students don't get along with local community*
> *No one watches intercollegiate sports*
> *No one plays intramural sports*
> *Very little beer drinking*
> *Students love Chicago*
> *Students are religious*

Life

As you might expect at a Christian university, many people at North Park are "very focused on growing closer to or learning more about God." And through a combination of classes, ministries, clubs, church activities, and conversations, students report that they've found "many opportunities" to do just that. But there's also a strain of NPU students "who like to party and drink." One student exclaims, "Finally, North Park has discovered the existence of beer and fun on the weekends!" Because the campus is supposedly "dry," "partying has to be done a little more secretly" than on other campuses, or on those other campuses altogether ("You can find some [parties] at surrounding colleges"). Students also take advantage of Chicago's nightlife, which is just a quick shot down the road. "This city has so much to offer that it is almost overwhelming," enthuses a biology major. Aside from going out to clubs and bars, NPU students take full advantage of the museums, shopping, dining, theatres, and sporting events that they find in the Chicago metro area. "They plan a lot of trips downtown together," observes a student of her classmates. When students want to hang around closer to campus, they'll play "Ultimate Frisbee on the Hump," cruise the area on bikes or Rollerblades, or devote some time to one of the 40 student organizations at NPU.

Student Body

"There is a huge division between the Christian and the non-Christian students on campus," explains one undergraduate. As a "religiously-based school," NPU attracts a strong contingent of students who "tend to be religious," and these students tell us that "it often disappoints" them that some of their classmates prefer to tread more secular paths. This division comes to a head when the issue of partying is mentioned. "Most people either like to party or they despise it," explains a student who happens to like it. As you might expect, "many cliques" form at the school, based on how students prefer to spend their free time. But outright disputes are rare at NPU. Instead, students are able to put their differences aside and "generally get along with one another."

ADMISSIONS

Very important factors considered by the admissions committee include: secondary school record and standardized test scores. *Important factors considered include:* class rank, essays, and recommendations. *Other factors considered include:* alumni/ae relation, extracurricular activities, interview, minority status, and talent/ability. SAT I or ACT required. TOEFL required of all international applicants. High school diploma is required and GED is accepted. *High school units required/recommended:* 4 English recommended, 3 math recommended, 3 science recommended, 2 foreign language recommended, 1 social studies recommended, 1 history recommended.

The Inside Word

This small school with a Christian attitude affords vast leadership opportunities and other ways to get involved on campus to each year's matriculating class. Applicants' views on religious and secular lifestyles are the chief factor in how well they harmonize with the rest of the community.

FINANCIAL AID

Students should submit: FAFSA. Regular filing deadline is August 1. The Princeton Review suggests that all financial aid forms be submitted as soon as possible after January 1. *Need-based scholarships/grants offered:* Pell, SEOG, state scholarships/grants, private scholarships, the school's own gift aid, and Federal Nursing. *Loan aid offered:* FFEL Subsidized Stafford, FFEL Unsubsidized Stafford, and FFEL PLUS. Federal Work-Study Program available. Institutional employment available. Applicants will be notified of awards on a rolling basis beginning on or about March 10. Off-campus job opportunities are excellent.

For even more information on this school, turn to page 376 of the "Stats" section.

NORTHERN MICHIGAN UNIVERSITY

1401 PRESQUE ISLE AVENUE, 304 COHODAS, MARQUETTE, MI 49855 • ADMISSIONS: 906-227-2650
FAX: 906-227-1747 • E-MAIL: ADMISS@NMU.EDU • WEBSITE: WWW.NMU.EDU

Ratings

Quality of Life: 76   **Academic:** 68   **Admissions:** 63   **Financial Aid:** 79

Academics

Anyone willing to brave "lots and lots of snow" will find a warm and intimate college atmosphere in Northern Michigan University. Students choose NMU for "small class sizes," an "excellent educa-

> **SURVEY SAYS . . .**
> *Classes are small*
> *Diversity lacking on campus*
> *Student publications are ignored*

tion and nursing program," and a price tag that is "reasonable for in-state tuition." They do say, however, that the most rewarding aspect of undergraduate life is the support and personal attention they receive from the faculty. One student affirms, "You'll really get to know your professors here. They'll write you letters of recommendation and be great resources if you take the time to meet them." Agrees another, "The class sizes are small (even the "big" lectures aren't that big), so it's a good environment to ask questions if you don't understand something." On that note, "there are also tutors available in almost every subject and for almost every course offered." Many warn, however, that though "the faculty is normally supportive, the administration isn't." A student elaborates: "They seem to forget that the students should have a voice concerning student issues here . . . . I've seen too many times when the administration has just ignored us and stuck with their own rulings."

Life

As NMU is located on "the snow-bound Upper Peninsula of Michigan where we have limited contact with the outside world from November to April," and Marquette is "not a typical college town," students insist that theirs is the "small-scale type of lifestyle." Given the frigid environment, it's not surprising that "winter sports are very big" at NMU. In fact, students find a million ways to entertain themselves in the snow, from "skiing (downhill and cross country)" to "ice-skating, going to the ice arena," to "snowshoeing, sledding," "snowmobiling, snowboarding," and "playing in the snow." When the ice melts, "there's a lot of nature around," and "in the spring or fall, there are plenty of places to go hiking or running, swimming, or playing outdoor sports." Though not as notorious as its weather, NMU has something of a reputation as a party school, and students admit that, "people drink a lot at Northern." Many, however, resent this characterization of student life: "It just depends on the crowd you hang out with, just like in any school."

Student Body

"Last year we had almost 300 inches of snow. . . . You wouldn't believe how people stick together through a winter like that," explains one student, describing the close-knit atmosphere on the Northern campus. Whatever the source, everyone agrees, "There is a definite sense of unity at NMU." With little exception, students characterize their classmates as "friendly and down-to-earth" and "easy to get along with." Some, however, complain that because "a vast majority of us come from small towns in Michigan and Wisconsin," the student body is "not exactly the most diverse group." Diversity, therefore, is not always embraced. Students reassure us, however, that "even though we are all the same [in some ways], there is something that characterizes each one [of us]." Confers another, "Nerds, jocks, earthy types, strongly religious . . . everyone's cool with each other."

ADMISSIONS

Very important factors considered by the admissions committee include: secondary school record and standardized test scores. *Other factors considered include:* character/personal qualities, class rank, essays, extracurricular activities, interview, recommendations, talent/ability, volunteer work, and work experience. SAT I or ACT required. TOEFL required of all international applicants. High school diploma or GED is required. *High school units required/recommended:* 12 total required; 16 total recommended; 4 English recommended, 3 math recommended, 2 science recommended, 3 foreign language recommended, 2 social studies recommended, 2 history recommended.

The Inside Word

Spending many months a year in a winter wonderland may be jarring for applicants from beyond Michigan's and Wisconsin's borders, and people of color may feel a bit socially frozen by the school's lack of ethnic diversity, but the first public university in Michigan to initiate a program providing every student a laptop can be the land of promise for committed students.

FINANCIAL AID

Students should submit: FAFSA. No deadline for regular filing. The Princeton Review suggests that all financial aid forms be submitted as soon as possible after January 1. *Need-based scholarships/grants offered:* Pell, SEOG, state scholarships/grants, private scholarships, and the school's own gift aid. *Loan aid offered:* Direct Subsidized Stafford, Direct Unsubsidized Stafford, Direct PLUS, Federal Perkins, state loans, and college/university loans from institutional funds. Federal Work-Study Program available. Institutional employment available. Applicants will be notified of awards on a rolling basis beginning on or about April 2. Off-campus job opportunities are good.

FROM THE ADMISSIONS OFFICE

"NMU is a four-year, public university offering learning opportunities in more than 180 academic programs to approximately 8,800 students. Each student is issued an IBM Thinkpad or Apple iBook as part of tuition and fees. NMU is located in an environment unrivaled by any other, on the south shore of Lake Superior in Marquette, a town with breathtaking scenery and 20,000 lucky residents. Our campus is wired and 'wireless' with state-of-the-art technology and the Internet. We're large enough to offer scenic spaces and 50 quality facilities, but we're small enough to keep everything within walking distance (which is especially nice in the winter).

"NMU has talented faulty members and a low student/faculty ratio of 20:1. They'll talk with you, not at you. They'll take time to find out who you are and how you learn best. Of the entry-level classes, 93 percent are taught by career faculty.

"NMU residence halls are organized into living areas—called houses—which actively shape their own living environments. Along with all our natural wonders, you'll also discover 200 clubs and organizations on campus, including academic, service, social, professional, religious, and special interest groups. We have a full program of intercollegiate, club, and intramural athletics.

"NMU is a tremendous tuition value, and in addition to generous financial aid offers qualified students are eligible for merit/talent scholarships, including the National Academic Award of $3,000 per year for out-of-state students.

"For more information visit www.nmu.edu or contact the Admissions Office at 800-682-9797. Better yet, come visit us!"

For even more information on this school, turn to page 376 of the "Stats" section.

NORTHWESTERN UNIVERSITY

PO Box 3060, 1801 Hinman Avenue, Evanston, IL 60208-3060 • Admissions: 847-491-7271
Financial Aid: 847-491-7400 • E-mail: ug-admission@northwestern.edu
Website: www.northwestern.edu

Ratings
Quality of Life: 89   **Academic:** 98   **Admissions:** 99   **Financial Aid:** 85

Academics

Considered by many an Ivy of the Midwest, Northwestern University is unarguably "an academically rigorous school" with an "awesome reputation" that "expects hard work from its students." Students warn that "academics here are very challenging, especially with the quarter system," which "makes the pace extremely hectic." Engineering, journalism, pre-medical studies, and the liberal arts departments are all well regarded, as is the "great theater program"—which, according to many, is "essentially a pre-professional program" that is uncommonly rigorous. Students caution that most of the professors here are among the "most important researchers in their fields" and that, while many are "genuinely interested in their students' performance" and "very generous with their time," others are "very research-oriented and lack teaching skills." During a given quarter, "it's likely that you'll take a class with the most enthusiastic and interesting person you've ever met and also one with a professor far inferior to your worst high school teacher." Fortunately, "the teacher evaluation information is excellent. There are so many classes to take here. Like anywhere, there are good and bad professors, but the evaluation system makes it easy to differentiate between them, and it's all online."

> **SURVEY SAYS . . .**
> *Frats and sororities dominate social scene*
> *Athletic facilities are great*
> *Class discussions are rare, Great library*
> *Everyone loves the Wildcats, Large classes*
> *Student publications are popular*
> *(Almost) no one listens to college radio*
> *Campus difficult to get around*

Life

There are two schools of thought about the Northwestern social scene. The first, subscribed to by those who rarely venture off campus or outside Evanston, say that life at Northwestern is pleasant but unexceptional. They report that the Greeks occupy a central position on campus. The Greek system caters to every kind of student—even the ones who would never even consider joining a fraternity or sorority." These students also enjoy the school's "great theater program. . . . There are shows going up all the time. People here are amazingly talented, and I've seen a really diverse range of shows—from mainstage musical productions to small, no-budget plays, all for pretty cheap." Finally, they commend NU's "gorgeous" campus. The second school of thought, championed by those who simply cannot wait to get off campus and into Chicago, holds that Northwestern offers the best of all possible worlds. Not only does the school boast all the above-mentioned benefits, explains one student, but "going into Chicago is a popular weekend activity. Public transportation (the 'EL') is only a block from campus and takes you directly to some of the best shopping in the world," as well as to excellent museums, restaurants, and night life. Adds another, "In Evanston," there are "great restaurants within walking distance but not much in the way of entertainment, which is why you need Chicago!" Both groups agree that "studying is a large part of student life" and also that "people here are very busy. Everyone I know has a TON on their plate, i.e. work, very difficult classes, one to five clubs/organizations, executive board positions, volunteering, sports (varsity, club, or intramural) . . ."

Student Body

Northwestern students admit that they are probably not America's coolest college kids. "It's a dork school—be forewarned," writes one student. "But it's not cutthroat or pretentious like our neighbors on the East." Even so, "there is so much pressure to succeed at everything and be involved in everything, and everyone here is so good at everything already. Because we were all overachievers and at the top of our classes in high school, we're bound to be disappointed when we realize that there are so many smarter people around us here at college." Many here are "pretty upper-, middle-class conservative," "Greek-loving, country-club types, generally talented, and lots of princess and book-smart dummies, with a few intellectual giants and truly outstanding human beings thrown in the bunch." Despite their sometimes hypercritical reviews of their peers, most students ultimately concede that their classmates are "great. They are all interesting, smart, and fun to talk to."

ADMISSIONS

Very important factors considered by the admissions committee include: class rank, essays, secondary school record, standardized test scores. *Important factors considered include:* character/personal qualities, extracurricular activities, recommendations, talent/ability. *Other factors considered include:* alumni/ae relation, interview, minority status, volunteer work, work experience. SAT I or ACT required. TOEFL required of all international applicants. *High school units required/recommended:* 16 total recommended; 4 English recommended, 4 math recommended, 2 science recommended, 2 science lab recommended, 2 foreign language recommended, 4 social studies recommended, 3 elective recommended.

The Inside Word

Northwestern's applicant pool is easily among the best in the country. Candidates face both a rigorous evaluation by the admissions committee and serious competition from within the pool. The best approach (besides top grades and a strong personal background) is to take the committee up on their recommendations to visit the campus or interview with an alumnus/a and submit SAT II scores. The effort it takes to get in is well worth it.

FINANCIAL AID

Students should submit: FAFSA, CSS/Financial Aid PROFILE, noncustodial (divorced/separated) parent's statement, business/farm supplement, parent and student federal tax returns. The Princeton Review suggests that all financial aid forms be submitted as soon as possible after January 1. *Need-based scholarships/grants offered:* Pell, SEOG, state scholarships/grants, private scholarships, the school's own gift aid. *Loan aid offered:* FFEL Subsidized Stafford, FFEL Unsubsidized Stafford, FFEL PLUS, Federal Perkins, college/university loans from institutional funds. Federal Work-Study Program available. Institutional employment available. Applicants will be notified of awards on or about April 15. Off-campus job opportunities are excellent.

FROM THE ADMISSIONS OFFICE

"Consistent with its dedication to excellence, Northwestern provides both an educational and an extracurricular environment that enable its undergraduate students to become accomplished individuals and informed and responsible citizens. To the students in all its undergraduate schools, Northwestern offers liberal learning and professional education to help them gain the depth of knowledge that will empower them to become leaders in their professions and communities. Furthermore, Northwestern fosters in its students a broad understanding of the world in which we live as well as excellence in the competencies that transcend any particular field of study: writing and oral communication, analytical and creative thinking and expression, quantitative and qualitative methods of thinking."

For even more information on this school, turn to page 377 of the "Stats" section.

NORTHWOOD UNIVERSITY

4000 Whiting Drive, Midland, MI 48640 • Admissions: 800-457-7878 • Fax: 989-837-4490
E-mail: admissions@northwood.edu • Website: www.northwood.edu

Ratings
Quality of Life: 75   Academic: 73   Admissions: 75   Financial Aid: 75

Academics

"Everyone is here" at Northwood University "for the same reason: to make better business leaders of tomorrow." That's no exaggeration; every major offered at this mid-sized private school in the middle of Lower Michigan is busi-

> **SURVEY SAYS . . .**
> *Students are happy*
> *Lousy food on campus*
> *Classes are small*

ness-related. With such a sharp focus on the subject, institutional understanding of the ever-evolving business world is of primary importance, and students agree that their professors' "real-world experience" is not in short supply. Professors are also easy to get to know one-on-one. Avers one student, "I have professors continually going out of their way to assist in my growing," and a classmate attests that the resultant "networking opportunities are great!" Some, however, partly attribute these warm student-teacher relationships to the "high school" vibe that colors the total student experience at Northwood (see Student Body, below). "Mandatory [class] attendance," for example, doesn't sit well with most undergrads. And if the administration is anything, it's business-minded. According to one student, the People in Charge "run this campus with an Iron Fist, and that is a good thing." Any suggested institutional change is approached "with the bottom-line in mind." The prospect of increasing enrollments apparently has found favor, though "the small atmosphere is being lost in their pressure to expand." Perhaps not a haven for free-spirited artsy types, but most current students "would recommend Northwood University to anyone seeking a business-related career."

Life

In Midland, Michigan, "life is dull unless you look for fun," but "seek and you shall find." Midland itself is "big enough to not be too boring and still small enough to be comfortable." Some students spend much of their time watching videos and hanging out, but for students with an outgoing disposition, there's "ice-skating, clubbing, [going] to the movies, partying, shopping, biking, Rollerblading, and other miscellaneous activities." There also happens to be "a local bike path that runs through campus. It's very easy to get on that and take a nice ride, too." Students agree that "fraternities and sororities are a very important factor for a large portion of students for their social lives." Some students feel that "if you aren't in the Greek system, sometimes you feel left out and not good enough for people who are." The biggest social event of the season? Rev your engines because "Northwood hosts the world's largest outdoor auto show every year." Even better, "the show is put on completely by the students," which gives students both some fun and hands-on event-planning managerial experience.

Student Body

Most of Northwood's student body hails from Michigan and the surrounding states, and everyone is a business major. There is, however, apparently a noticeable, if not large, contingent of international students, especially from the Netherlands ("The Dutchies rule! Without them, Northwood wouldn't be Northwood"). There are tensions of difference, though; comments one student, "I sometimes feel that I am alone because of the color of my skin and my gender." But by far the largest complaint is that "Northwood is exactly like high school. So, if you want to get away from the cliques, don't come here." Another chimes in, "Most of them [the students] are immature and need to go back to high school."

ADMISSIONS

Very important factors considered by the admissions committee include: secondary school record and standardized test scores. *Important factors considered include:* class rank and essays. *Other factors considered include:* alumni/ae relation, character/personal qualities, extracurricular activities, interview, and recommendations. TOEFL required of all international applicants. High school diploma or GED is required. *High school units required/recommended:* 4 English recommended, 3 math recommended, 2 science recommended, 1 science lab recommended, 1 foreign language recommended, 3 social studies recommended.

The Inside Word

Those who get in and excel at Northwood will respond to its exclusive business focus and what the school calls "an entrepreneurial passion for success." Though a regionally diverse group attends classes at the remote campus on the banks of the Tittabawassee River, a B-School mentality is accompanied by a sense of social immaturity.

FINANCIAL AID

Students should submit: FAFSA and state aid form. No deadline for regular filing. The Princeton Review suggests that all financial aid forms be submitted as soon as possible after January 1. *Need-based scholarships/grants offered:* Pell, SEOG, state scholarships/grants, private scholarships, and the school's own gift aid. *Loan aid offered:* Direct Subsidized Stafford, Direct Unsubsidized Stafford, and Direct PLUS. Federal Work-Study Program available. Institutional employment available. Applicants will be notified of awards on or about April 1. Off-campus job opportunities are good.

For even more information on this school, turn to page 377 of the "Stats" section.

OAKLAND UNIVERSITY

OFFICE OF ADMISSIONS, 101 NORTH FOUNDATION HALL, ROCHESTER, MI 48309-4475
ADMISSIONS: 248-370-3360 • FAX: 248-370-4462 • E-MAIL: OUINFO@OAKLAND.EDU
WEBSITE: WWW3.OAKLAND.EDU

Ratings

Quality of Life: 75   **Academic:** 77   **Admissions:** 72   **Financial Aid:** 76

Academics

Students at Oakland University, a state school located in the Detroit suburbs, proudly report that "the school's reputation is growing rapidly, especially its engineering and computer science programs, which

> **SURVEY SAYS . . .**
> *Students don't get along with local community*
> *Very little hard liquor, Classes are small*
> *Student publications are ignored*

are recognized by a lot of companies in Michigan." Undergrads here enjoy "small classes where students can get individual attention" and "excellent and well-trained" professors who "are more than professors—they are the students' problem solvers, both in academic and personal dilemma." Reports one student, "I've always been impressed with the professional attention to all subjects, no matter how rudimentary. There are no such things as TAs at Oakland; well, they do exist, but they are never 'in charge' of teaching the class. They perform other functions (e.g., proctoring) and may give occasional lectures. Having gone to the University of Michigan for a year and a half, this was easily the most appealing aspect of Oakland's education system." Students also benefit from that fact that "people from all walks of life find their way to Oakland, in part because of its easy accessibility to commuters. Many of the students are far older than your average crowd on most campuses. This gives you the opportunity to experience someone else's perspective from age and minority status. One just has to be open to such experiences." The few complaints we heard from students here involve the administration, which many feel "has very disproportionate priorities. They are only worried about the bottom line, not the students."

Life

Because Oakland University is home to "a high number of commuters, most students spend their spare time at home. On-campus life is usually pretty quiet. Those that do live on campus generally go home for the weekends." Notes one student, "On weekends the place is literally a ghost town. However, there are a number of extremely popular extra activities; chief among them is Meadowbrook Theatre, which is well-known statewide." Students benefit from the fact that "Oakland University is located at the middle of everything"; writes one undergrad; "The surrounding towns, Auburn Hills and Rochester, are two of the fastest growing new cities in Michigan. Therefore, community activity is extremely high as are job opportunities, recreation, etc." Adds another student, "It's small and in a good community with very low levels of crime. Rochester is a very small town that has good food, and nearby Pontiac has some entertainment." OU has a "small but close-knit" Greek system. Many students here complain that "it can be rough finding parking during peak hours. . . . That should be addressed."

Student Body

Oakland undergrads point out that "many of the students at this university commute to school. This does not allow for much time to get to know many of the other students." They report that "students are very nice to each other, especially for those students who study within the same program; they often study together and share their experience." They also point out that "although Oakland is a commuter school, the majority of the campus organizations are close-knit groups, and you get to know everyone fairly well" if you make the effort to get involved. OU's student body "is generally white, early 20s, well educated, and females out-number males almost two to one." A large nontraditional population is made up of "students of all ages, educational experiences, and professions, which is good."

ADMISSIONS

Very important factors considered by the admissions committee include: secondary school record. *Important factors considered include:* character/personal qualities, extracurricular activities, recommendations, talent/ability, and volunteer work. *Other factors considered include:* alumni/ae relation, essays, interview, and work experience. ACT required. TOEFL required of all international applicants. High school diploma or GED is required. *High school units required/recommended:* 4 English required, 3 math required, 3 science required, 2 foreign language recommended, 3 social studies required.

The Inside Word

Admissions officers at Oakland University review applicants' curriculum, GPA, standardized test scores, and trend (Have your grades improved as you've gotten older? Are you taking more or less challenging courses?). They then classify candidates as "admit," "deny," or "delay." Delayed candidates should immediately contact the admissions office to determine how best to improve their chances.

FINANCIAL AID

Students should submit: FAFSA. No deadline for regular filing. The Princeton Review suggests that all financial aid forms be submitted as soon as possible after January 1. *Need-based scholarships/grants offered:* Pell, SEOG, state scholarships/grants, private scholarships, and the school's own gift aid. *Loan aid offered:* Direct Subsidized Stafford, Direct Unsubsidized Stafford, Direct PLUS, and Federal Perkins. Federal Work-Study Program available. Institutional employment available. Applicants will be notified of awards on a rolling basis beginning on or about March 15. Off-campus job opportunities are excellent.

FROM THE ADMISSIONS OFFICE

"**Location:** Oakland University is located in suburban Rochester, Michigan, in Oakland County. The university boasts one of the most picturesque campuses in the country, with 1,441 acres of rolling hills, woodlands, and meadows. OU's campus is near many entertainment and recreational opportunities, including the Palace of Auburn Hills, DTE Energy Music Theatre and Great Lakes Crossing shopping mall. In recent years, this area has become one of the fastest growing suburban areas in the United States.

"**Student Centered Approach:** OU offers a small-campus setting that includes extensive support services and remarkable personal attention to help you succeed. You'll also benefit from a wide range of course offerings and rich learning experiences.

"**Personal Attention:** OU's classes average fewer than 35 students, and our 19:1 student/faculty ratio means your professors will get to know you by name. Unlike larger state universities, OU does not use graduate assistants to teach most undergraduate classes. Only 1 percent of OU's classes are taught by graduate assistants.

"**Technology-Enriched Learning:** As part of Oakland's commitment to preparing students for a rapidly changing workplace, the university has invested in the resources to prepare you for the twenty-first century. You'll use multimedia applications and interactive learning in a variety of programs to reach your potential.

"**Remarkable Job Placement Rate:** Recent statistics show more than 95 percent of OU graduates are employed within the first seven months following graduation. Oakland University Alumni work in nearly every major corporation, government agency, hospital, and school district in the region!

"Check us out!"

For even more information on this school, turn to page 378 of the "Stats" section.

OBERLIN COLLEGE

101 NORTH PROFESSOR STREET, OBERLIN, OH 44074 • ADMISSIONS: 440-775-8411 • FAX: 440-775-6905
FINANCIAL AID: 440-775-8142 • E-MAIL: COLLEGE.ADMISSIONS@OBERLIN.EDU • WEBSITE: WWW.OBERLIN.EDU

Ratings
Quality of Life: 73   **Academic:** 86   **Admissions:** 91   **Financial Aid:** 83

Academics

With a "culture unlike any other" and a "commitment to developing well- rounded, free-thinking individuals," Oberlin College consistently ranks high among college students looking for a small, politically progressive, and academically challenging liberal arts school. Its highly respected music conservatory is a major draw, as

> **SURVEY SAYS . . .**
> *Political activism is hot, Great library*
> *Students don't get along with local community*
> *Students aren't religious*
> *Musical organizations are hot*
> *Intercollegiate sports are unpopular or nonexistent*
> *Theater is popular*

are its "great double degree program," EXCO (Experimental College, where students teach courses for credit), and strong curriculum in both the arts and sciences. In a place where "students are smart and interesting, work is challenging," and there's "no red tape," it's no wonder Oberlin undergrads are so positive about their choice of college. Notes a senior, "The learning community is great, teachers are accessible, and there are great resources." The "fantastic" and "totally available" professors who "love teaching" play a big part in creating Oberlin's reputation of academic excellence. As for administration, though some claim that "the administration hates us," a senior takes the long view: "There is a lot of administration-student interaction. Students are very much involved in the politics on campus and way into creating the environment in which we learn. The administration tries to be responsive."

Life

At a place where "most learning takes place at formal and informal discussions outside of class," it's not surprising that Oberlin undergrads have a lot to say on the subject of life at this tiny college. Writes a junior, "People think about everything, and basically, that's what we do for fun." Students are, for the most part, "aware and involved" so, as a senior points out, there's "lots of activism and challenges to the status quo." A first-year sees the typical "Obie" philosophizing a little differently, however, noting that "people spend a lot of time dwelling in the saturation of their white liberalism and patting themselves on the back for their guilt." All that and a BA too? As for social pursuits, Cleveland's only 45 minutes away, but most students' social lives revolve around campus with its myriad free or inexpensive "films, lectures, speakers, recitals, performances, art openings, and theme parties" (The Drag Ball headlines the year). There aren't any frats at Oberlin, but the OSCA co-ops "are a great alternative for food and living." As for letting off all that steam built up discussing identity politics and "overdramatic interpersonal dramas," there is a "substantial party and drug scene but no pressure to do either."

Student Body

The "eclectic" and "diverse" as well as "friendly" people make Oberlin what it is, say students. Notes a junior, They're amazing, aggravating, intimidating, and intimate all at the same time. They help me to grow . . . ." And while these "open-minded" and "liberal-thinking" kids are well known for their left-of-center politics, just how left is left? A first-year explains, "The political affiliation bubble on your survey is not comprehensive enough. To the left of the 'left wing' option, there should be a bubble that says either 'radically leftist' or just 'Oberlin.'" On the other hand, one student tells us, "This is a very liberal school on the outside but I think an overwhelming amount of students are more moderate. There are conservatives [too], but they aren't as vocal." Of course, all that intense political discussion can lead to a few "closed-minded people unwilling to listen to others' points of view," but still, most like it that way.

ADMISSIONS

Very important factors considered by the admissions committee include: class rank, secondary school record, standardized test scores. *Important factors considered include:* character/personal qualities, essays, extracurricular activities, recommendations, talent/ability. *Other factors considered include:* alumni/ae relation, geographical residence, interview, minority status, state residency, volunteer work, work experience. SAT I or ACT required. TOEFL required of all international applicants. High school diploma or GED is required. *High school units required/recommended:* 4 English recommended, 4 math recommended, 3 science recommended, 3 science lab recommended, 3 foreign language recommended, 3 social studies recommended.

The Inside Word

The admissions process at Oberlin is especially demanding for candidates to the Conservatory of Music, which seeks only the best-prepared musicians for its excellent program. All applicants to the college face a thorough and rigorous review of their credentials by the admissions committee regardless of their choice of major. Take our advice—visit the campus to interview, and put extra effort into admissions essays.

FINANCIAL AID

Students should submit: FAFSA, CSS/Financial Aid PROFILE, noncustodial (divorced/separated) parent's statement, business/farm supplement. Regular filing deadline is February 15. The Princeton Review suggests that all financial aid forms be submitted as soon as possible after January 1. *Need-based scholarships/grants offered:* Pell, SEOG, state scholarships/grants, private scholarships, the school's own gift aid. *Loan aid offered:* Direct Subsidized Stafford, Direct Unsubsidized Stafford, Direct PLUS, Federal Perkins, college/university loans from institutional funds. Federal Work-Study Program available. Institutional employment available. Applicants will be notified of awards on or about April 15. Off-campus job opportunities are good.

FROM THE ADMISSIONS OFFICE

"Oberlin College is an independent, coeducational, liberal arts college. It comprises two divisions, the College of Arts and Sciences, with roughly 2,300 students enrolled, and the Conservatory of Music, with about 500 students. Students in both divisions share one campus; they also share residence and dining halls as part of one academic community. Many students take courses in both divisions. Oberlin awards the Bachelor of Arts and the Bachelor of Music degrees; a five-year program leads to both degrees. Selected master's degrees are offered in the Conservatory. Oberlin is located 35 miles southwest of Cleveland. Founded in 1833, Oberlin College is highly selective and dedicated to recruiting students from diverse backgrounds. Oberlin was the first coeducational college in the United States, as well as a historic leader in educating black students. Oberlin's 440-acre campus provides outstanding facilities, modern scientific laboratories, a large computing center, a library unexcelled by other college libraries for the depth and range of its resources, and the Allen Memorial Art Museum."

For even more information on this school, turn to page 378 of the "Stats" section.

OHIO NORTHERN UNIVERSITY

525 SOUTH MAIN STREET, ADA, OH 45810 • ADMISSIONS: 419-772-2260 • FAX: 419-772-2313
FINANCIAL AID: 419-772-2272 • E-MAIL: ADMISSIONS-UG@ONU.EDU • WEBSITE: WWW.ONU.EDU

Ratings
Quality of Life: 80   **Academic:** 80   **Admissions:** 78   **Financial Aid:** 89

Academics

"'Large enough to challenge, small enough to care' applies 100 percent at ONU!" With an average class size of under 25, students benefit from "small classes" in which professors "make [an] effort to get to know each student." Because professors take such an interest, one junior says, they "make me want to do well!" Despite being a small university, ONU offers over 60 majors and "lots of variety in classes." And the curriculum is challenging. "I didn't have to work hard in high school," a freshman reports, "but I do here!" This combination of rigor, attention, and academic variety means that "Ohio Northern has a lot to offer" the dedicated student. And after the student days are over, ONU invites its students into a web of professional and alumni networks. This prompts one senior to write that a student who decides to attend ONU "can have the opportunities to become a leader in today's world."

> **SURVEY SAYS . . .**
> *Frats and sororities dominate social scene*
> *Athletic facilities are great*
> *Classes are small*
> *Great computer facilities*
> *Student publications are ignored*
> *Lousy off-campus food*
> *Students don't like Ada, OH*
> *Students are very religious*
> *Low cost of living*
> *Lousy food on campus*

Life

Before you sign on at ONU, you should be aware that "Ada is not a booming metropolis." With just more than 5,000 residents in town, the undergrad and law-school population (which totals almost 3,300) bears the burden of finding its own fun. And "there is fun to be had," one sophomore says, "it just depends on how creative you are." Many Polar Bears find their entertainment through activities sponsored by the "SPC (Student Planning Committee), sororities, fraternities, or service organizations." Other times, students will venture into the town for "bowling, movies," or, when they're feeling especially adventurous, to the Lima Mall, in nearby Lima, a town of over 40,000. Parties are also part of the university portrait here—particularly "on Tuesday nights and weekends." But don't count on having a few too many drinks and inviting a member of the opposite sex back to your room for a little late-night, um, bonding. "Visitation hours are ridiculous and outdated," gripes a freshman student, referring to the university policy that says that guys can only go into girls' rooms, and vice versa, from 10 a.m. to 11 p.m., Sunday through Thursday, and 10 a.m. to 1 a.m. on Friday and Saturday. If this bothers you, here's some good news: the university is now reconsidering this policy. At the moment, there's even one "experimental" residential hall with 24-hour access for all.

Student Body

Ohio Northern University is a private institution with liberal arts and professional programs that's affiliated with the United Methodist Church. Not everyone who goes here is Methodist, though, and some students notice that the so-called " 'religious' students and 'nonreligious' students don't mix very much." But when you look at the big picture, "all students are friendly and seem to get along well with one another." ONU has a "pretty conservative, uniform" student body, though you're still bound to run into "diverse personalities" all over campus. Personalities, many students admit, are perhaps the only signs of diversity on campus. "I wish we had more diversity," one student complains. "Everyone is upper-middle class, white, and a science or engineering major!" says another. But they're also a "friendly" group, which is important when you're at a "small school" in a small Ohio town. In an undergraduate pool of about 3,000, "the majority of students know each other," and, with the dual spirits of competition and cooperation at work, there's a vibrant "atmosphere created by its students." One freshman admits, "I was so worried coming here because I didn't know anyone, but it's been great!"

ADMISSIONS

Very important factors considered by the admissions committee include: secondary school record, standardized test scores. *Important factors considered include:* class rank, extracurricular activities, interview. *Other factors considered include:* alumni/ae relation, character/personal qualities, essays, minority status, recommendations, talent/ability, volunteer work, work experience. SAT I or ACT required. TOEFL required of all international applicants. High school diploma or GED is required. *High school units required/recommended:* 16 total required; 22 total recommended; 4 English required, 2 math required, 4 math recommended, 2 science required, 3 science recommended, 2 science lab required, 2 foreign language recommended, 2 social studies required, 3 social studies recommended, 2 history required, 4 elective required.

The Inside Word

Solid grades from high school are a pretty sure ticket for admission to Ohio Northern. Students who are above average academically are in good positions to take advantage of a very large number of no-need scholarships.

FINANCIAL AID

Students should submit: FAFSA, institution's own financial aid form. Regular filing deadline is June 1. The Princeton Review suggests that all financial aid forms be submitted as soon as possible after January 1. *Need-based scholarships/grants offered:* Pell, SEOG, state scholarships/grants, private scholarships, the school's own gift aid. *Loan aid offered:* FFEL Subsidized Stafford, FFEL Unsubsidized Stafford, FFEL PLUS, Federal Perkins, college/university loans from institutional funds, alternative loans, Federal Health Professions Loan. Federal Work-Study Program available. Institutional employment available. Applicants will be notified of awards on a rolling basis beginning on or about February 15. Off-campus job opportunities are good.

FROM THE ADMISSIONS OFFICE

"Ohio Northern's purpose is to help students develop into self-reliant, mature men and women capable of clear and logical thinking and sensitive to the higher values of truth, beauty, and goodness. ONU selects its student body from among those students possessing characteristics congruent with the institution's objectives. Generally, a student must be prepared to use the resources of the institution to achieve personal and educational goals."

For even more information on this school, turn to page 379 of the "Stats" section.

OHIO STATE UNIVERSITY—COLUMBUS

ENARSON HALL, 154 W. 12TH AVENUE, COLUMBUS, OH 43210 • ADMISSIONS: 614-292-3980
FAX: 614-292-4818 • FINANCIAL AID: 614-292-0300 • E-MAIL: ASKABUCKEYE@OSU.EDU
WEBSITE: WWW.OSU.EDU

Ratings

Quality of Life: 78 **Academic:** 67 **Admissions:** 73 **Financial Aid:** 84

Academics

At a school "probably best known for football," many students agree that Ohio State "is growing in academic strength." Courses "emphasize critical thinking," and "the school offers every imaginable class." It can, however, be "difficult to get into the classes that you want and need. I'm even an honors student with priority scheduling, and I have problems." Another student writes, "More classes should be available so the freshman class is not shut out." Some undergraduates describe professors as "devoted to teaching" and "very intelligent and helpful," while others point out that "it is difficult to be in contact with some professors due to the amount of research that goes on here." But when professors are unavailable, "TAs are very easy to get in touch with." Advising seems to be a case-by-case matter at OSU. One student reports, "My advisor has assisted me in deciding on my major, and she set me up with a mentor." But others comment, "Students are forced to find out much more for themselves," prompting the widespread sentiment, "No wonder everyone takes five years to graduate." Widely considered the "best value for your dollar," Ohio State all in all offers "a real-world experience and worldwide access to the best of the best."

> ### SURVEY SAYS . . .
> *Students are cliquish*
> *Lots of beer drinking*
> *Everyone loves the Buckeyes*
> *(Almost) everyone smokes*
> *Lots of classroom discussion*
> *(Almost) everyone plays intramural sports*
> *Ethnic diversity on campus*
> *Student publications are popular*
> *Lab facilities are great*

Life

Ohio State social life flourishes in an atmosphere where "there are parties all the time, everywhere." The Greek community can be exclusive, with several students noting that at fraternity parties "people risk being rejected at the door because they are not cool enough or not female." Luckily, the campus offers an abundance of alternatives: "There's so much to do on any given night, it's hard to remember you're not on vacation." The size of the school provides for options galore, meaning, "If you can't find it through Ohio State, it may not exist." During warm weather, students hang out in The Oval, "the best place on Earth to socialize and relax." And of course in the fall, Buckeye football is a campuswide obsession. One student proudly points out, "There aren't too many schools that can fill a 110,000-person stadium for football games." If on-campus events ever fail to entertain, the surrounding capital city of Columbus "caters to both partiers and those who enjoy the arts." Overall, life at OSU "will surely give you the total college experience you're looking for."

Student Body

"With more than 48,000 students [undergraduate and graduate], you have just about every type of person: Rastafarians, hippies, ROTC participants, party goers, Greeks, athletes. You cannot label OSU students because there are just so many with so much diversity." Despite this variety, "the sense of community and oneness is very strong," and a common opinion is that "Ohio State is probably one of the biggest schools with such a sense of camaraderie." Racial and ethnic diversity prevails at the university, with one student commenting, "People who decide to come to Ohio State do so knowing they will be immersed in ethnicity. The community is really comfortable because of this." Other students remark, however, that it is "difficult to interact with other ethnicities." The school's residence life department "works really hard to incorporate diversity and insure that students are getting a well-rounded education." Regarding geographical variety, one student states, "As an out-of-state freshman, it can be a little difficult to make connections with people because everyone seems to be from the same small towns in Ohio." But reportedly the strongly conservative population is "friendly and accepting of anyone who is a Buckeye."

ADMISSIONS

Very important factors considered by the admissions committee include: class rank, secondary school record, standardized test scores. *Important factors considered include:* extracurricular activities, minority status, talent/ability, volunteer work, work experience. *Other factors considered include:* essays, geographical residence, recommendations, state residency. SAT I or ACT required. TOEFL required of all international applicants. High school diploma or GED is required. *High school units required/recommended:* 4 English required, 3 math required, 4 math recommended, 2 science required, 3 science recommended, 2 science lab required, 2 foreign language required, 3 foreign language recommended, 2 social studies required, 3 social studies recommended, 1 elective required.

The Inside Word

Although admissions officers consider extracurriculars and other personal characteristics of candidates, there is a heavy emphasis on numbers—grades, rank, and test scores. Although admissions standards have become increasingly competitive in recent years, OSU is still worth a shot for the average student. The university's great reputation and affordable cost make it a good choice for anyone looking at large schools.

FINANCIAL AID

Students should submit: FAFSA. The Princeton Review suggests that all financial aid forms be submitted as soon as possible after January 1. *Need-based scholarships/grants offered:* Pell, SEOG, state scholarships/grants, private scholarships, the school's own gift aid. *Loan aid offered:* Direct Subsidized Stafford, Direct Unsubsidized Stafford, Direct PLUS, Federal Perkins, Federal Nursing, college/university loans from institutional funds. Federal Work-Study Program available. Institutional employment available. Applicants will be notified of awards on or about April 1. Off-campus job opportunities are good.

FROM THE ADMISSIONS OFFICE

"The Ohio State University is Ohio's leading center for teaching, research, and public service. Our exceptional faculty, innovative programs, supportive services, and extremely competitive tuition costs make Ohio State one of higher education's best values. Our central campus is in Columbus, Ohio, the state's largest city. About 48,000 students from every county in Ohio, every state in the nation, and over 87 foreign nations are enrolled at Ohio state. Our faculty include Nobel Prize winners, Rhodes Scholars, members of the National Academy of Sciences, widely published writers, and noted artists and musicians. Our campus boasts world-class facilities like the Wexner Center for the Arts, the nation's largest medical teaching facility, and the new, multibuilding Fisher College of Business. From classes and residence halls to concerts and seminars to clubs and sports and honoraries to Frisbee games on the Oval, Ohio State offers opportunities to develop talents and skills while meeting a variety of people. At Ohio State, you're sure to find a place to call your own."

For even more information on this school, turn to page 380 of the "Stats" section.

OHIO UNIVERSITY—ATHENS

120 CHUBB HALL, ATHENS, OH 45701 • ADMISSIONS: 740-593-4100 • FAX: 740-593-0560
FINANCIAL AID: 740-593-4141 • E-MAIL: ADMISSIONS@OHIOU.EDU • WEBSITE: WWW.OHIOU.EDU

Ratings

Quality of Life: 82   **Academic:** 72   **Admissions:** 79   **Financial Aid:** 82

Academics

Students believe that the academic level at Ohio University is underrated ("Classes are definitely not as easy as some believe") and uniformly praise their education. "It's a wonderful school with great professors who are genuinely interested in the concepts they are teaching us." The journalism program earns especially high praise, though some journalism

> ### SURVEY SAYS . . .
> *Beautiful campus*
> *Athletic facilities are great*
> *Campus easy to get around*
> *Great library*
> *Great computer facilities*
> *Lousy food on campus*
> *Registration is a pain*
> *Student publications are popular*

students complain that they have a difficult time getting into classes within the major. Most professors are held in high regard and "are very nice and accessible outside of class." Ohio operates on a quarterly calendar, and many students laud the system. Though there are few teaching assistants, some students complain that in certain subjects the TAs are difficult to understand because their command of the English language is weak. First-year students speak of an excellent academic support system: "I was scared that I would get lost in classes, but the teachers were right there to help me find my way." The administration is also appreciated. The advisors are "great," and the dean of students is "personable." The university has attempted to improve the class registration system by implementing online registration which students see as "a step in the right direction."

Life

Ohio University students describe themselves as "low maintenance" when it comes to having fun. Those who are of age go to the downtown bars for dancing and partying. The annual Halloween celebration is legendary; students "party for an entire weekend," with mounted police overseeing the festivities. Students appreciate the "beautiful" campus and because "there really are not a lot of things to do in Athens," students take advantage of the 300-plus on-campus clubs and organizations. Many are associated with the Greek system, and they believe that fraternities and sororities improve campus life. Students support the athletic programs and laud the "new and huge" rec center. Movies are also a popular diversion. Many say that they spend most of their weeknights studying because it is easy to fall behind in a quarterly system if one is not diligent. The campus food needs improvement. "I gave up meat at the first glimpse of what they served me," mutters one journalism major. Students also want the parking situation upgraded.

Student Body

Nearly 91 percent of Ohio's "laid-back" students are Caucasian, and a majority of the students are "middle class, so . . . everyone seems to be on an even financial level and out to actually get an education, while at the same time enjoying the freedom and experience of college."

Students say that their peers are friendly, and only a few are bothered by the lack of on-campus diversity. "There aren't enough minorities," although the University is seeking to improve diversity through recruitment. Students feel safe on campus.

ADMISSIONS

Very important factors considered by the admissions committee include: class rank, secondary school record, standardized test scores. *Other factors considered include:* alumni/ae relation, essays, extracurricular activities, geographical residence, minority status, recommendations, state residency, talent/ability, work experience. SAT I or ACT required; ACT preferred. High school diploma or GED is required. *High school units required/recommended:* 16 total recommended; 4 English recommended, 3 math recommended, 3 science recommended, 2 foreign language recommended, 3 social studies recommended, 1 visual or performing arts recommended.

The Inside Word

There's little mystery in applying to Ohio U. The admissions process follows the formula approach very closely, and those whose numbers plug in well will get good news.

FINANCIAL AID

Students should submit: FAFSA. The Princeton Review suggests that all financial aid forms be submitted as soon as possible after January 1. *Need-based scholarships/grants offered:* Pell, SEOG, state scholarships/grants, private scholarships, the school's own gift aid. *Loan aid offered:* Direct Subsidized Stafford, Direct Unsubsidized Stafford, Direct PLUS, Federal Perkins, college/university loans from institutional funds. Federal Work-Study Program available. Institutional employment available. Applicants will be notified of awards on or about April 1. Off-campus job opportunities are good.

FROM THE ADMISSIONS OFFICE

"Chartered in 1804, Ohio University symbolizes America's early commitment to higher education. Its historic campus provides a setting matched by only a handful of other universities in the country. Students choose Ohio University mainly because of its academic strength, but the beautiful setting and college-town atmosphere are also factors in their decision. Ohio University is the central focus of Athens, Ohio, located approximately 75 miles southeast of Columbus. We encourage prospective students to come for a visit and experience the beauty and academic excellence of Ohio University."

For even more information on this school, turn to page 380 of the "Stats" section.

OHIO WESLEYAN UNIVERSITY

61 SOUTH SANDUSKY STREET, DELAWARE, OH 43015 • ADMISSIONS: 740-368-3020 • FAX: 740-368-3314
FINANCIAL AID: 740-368-3050 • E-MAIL: OWUADMIT@OWU.EDU • WEBSITE: WWW.OWU.EDU

Ratings

Quality of Life: 83   **Academic:** 88   **Admissions:** 80   **Financial Aid:** 86

Academics

Students love the academic approach at Ohio Wesleyan University, where their curriculum leads them to discover "how various disciplines can be integrated to form a greater whole, how to question what we know, and how to critically analyze the world around us." As one student put it, "The overall experience at OWU is one of practicum," a constant focus on practical application of advanced theory. Students

> **SURVEY SAYS . . .**
> *Lots of beer drinking*
> *Frats and sororities dominate social scene*
> *Hard liquor is popular*
> *(Almost) everyone smokes*
> *Registration is a breeze*
> *Students are happy*
> *Ethnic diversity on campus*
> *No one cheats*
> *Students don't get along with local community*
> *Students don't like Delaware, OH*

also brag of the "countless opportunities and experiences in a variety of fields waiting for students" at OWU. "If there's something you want," explained one student, "all you have to do is ask and someone will help you get it." Undergrads warn that "while classes can be tough, professors really want you to succeed and truly learn the material." Instructors are truly mentors. "Their real reason for being here is to teach," students agree. "They may also do research, but that is secondary and they always use us (undergrad students) to assist with any research (which looks great on our resumes)." Noted one student, "It's incredible to walk around campus and have both faculty and administrators call you by your first name. I've been able to develop great relationships with professors, which has allowed me to learn so much more on a personal level." Students also praise the "great new science center" and note that "by next semester, we are supposed to be optically connected, which should [make] our Internet run much [more smoothly]."

Life

OWU students "want to have a good time, but are very studious when it comes to class work. Students have their priorities straight at OWU." Once they've fulfilled their academic obligations, though, undergrads feel free to cut loose. Most agree that "Ohio Wesleyan always has a variety of things going on. If you really like the party scene, you can find that, but if you are not looking for that, there are many things that you can do instead." While "Greek life is popular, the Student Activities Board provides an enormous amount of fun options" away from Frat Row, as the board is "very in tune with students' wishes. They provide free movies once a month at the local movie theater and get bands to play at our Springfest concert." Undergrads also have "tons of clubs to choose from." Reports one, "There are clubs that are religious in nature: Tauheed (Islamic), Hillel (Jewish), Methodist Student Movement . . . and many others. I think these groups enrich life on campus far beyond any other aspect." Students here are "very community service–oriented. There are many opportunities for students to be engaged in serving the community in Delaware, Columbus, and pretty much anywhere in the world (every Spring Break Mission Week allows that)." Hometown Delaware gets poor marks, but OWU's proximity to OSU and Columbus eases the pain.

Student Body

OWU is home to a "diverse group of students, especially for a school with" less than 2,000 undergraduates. "The student body prides itself on its diversity. Because of this, we enjoy a gamut of ethnic clubs and social events. It creates an atmosphere in which you can learn, not only about the richness of other cultures, but more about yourself as well." The student body includes "a large international student population, which fits in wonderfully on our campus: a lot of brilliantly smart Pakistani and Indian kids," as well as "Ohio kids and a surprisingly large population from Connecticut." One thing students here share in common: they are "involved, involved, involved in many student clubs, community service organizations, and other groups."

ADMISSIONS

Very important factors considered by the admissions committee include: character/personal qualities, interview, recommendations, secondary school record. *Important factors considered include:* alumni/ae relation, class rank, essays, extracurricular activities, geographical residence, minority status, standardized test scores, talent/ability, volunteer work. *Other factors considered include:* work experience. SAT I or ACT required; SAT II recommended. TOEFL required of all international applicants. High school diploma or GED is required. *High school units required/recommended:* 16 total recommended; 4 English recommended, 3 math recommended, 3 science recommended, 3 foreign language recommended, 3 social studies recommended.

The Inside Word

OWU's high admit rate garners it both a competetive admit pool, as well as a high yield of those students. Students won't encounter super-selective academic standards for admission, but they will have to put some thought into the completion of their applications. The university's thorough admissions process definitely emphasizes the personal side of candidate evaluation.

FINANCIAL AID

Students should submit: FAFSA, institution's own financial aid form. Regular filing deadline is March 15. The Princeton Review suggests that all financial aid forms be submitted as soon as possible after January 1. *Need-based scholarships/grants offered:* Pell, SEOG, state scholarships/grants, private scholarships, the school's own gift aid. *Loan aid offered:* FFEL Subsidized Stafford, FFEL Unsubsidized Stafford, FFEL PLUS, Federal Perkins, state loans, college/university loans from institutional funds. Federal Work-Study Program available. Institutional employment available. Applicants will be notified of awards on a rolling basis beginning on or about January 15. Off-campus job opportunities are excellent.

FROM THE ADMISSIONS OFFICE

"Balance is the key word that describes Ohio Wesleyan. For example: 46 percent male, 54 percent female; 40 percent members of Greek life, 60 percent not; National Colloquium Program; Top Division III sports program; small-town setting of 25,000, near the 16th largest city in U.S. (Columbus, Ohio); excellent faculty/student ratio; outstanding fine and performing arts programs."

For even more information on this school, turn to page 381 of the "Stats" section.

PITTSBURG STATE UNIVERSITY

1701 SOUTH BROADWAY, PITTSBURG, KS 66762-5880 • ADMISSIONS: 620-235-4251 • FAX: 620-235-6003
E-MAIL: PSUADMIT@PITTSTATE.EDU • WEBSITE: WWW.PITTSTATE.EDU

Ratings
Quality of Life: 77   Academic: 68   Admissions: 64   Financial Aid: 69

Academics

Affordability and a well-regarded degree draw over 6,700 area students to Pittsburg State University, a small state institution in southeastern Kansas that "is one of the best tech schools in the region"; the business, teaching, and nurs-

> **SURVEY SAYS . . .**
> *Students are happy*
> *Campus feels safe*
> *Students love Pittsburg*
> *Great off-campus food*

ing programs here also have students crowing. Drawing largely from its home and surrounding counties, "Pitt State is a very 'home-town' school. This small, friendly atmosphere is definitely a plus" appreciated by PSU students. Faculty here "get involved with the students and organizations. It helps that we're not a 'publish or perish' school," explains one undergrad. Agrees another, "I really have enjoyed my teachers because they take time out of their schedules to find out who we are. We are not just a number on this campus." Students warn, however, that instruction in some of the required general education courses is spotty; as one told us, "As for my academic experience, most of my general education classes were either a waste of time or taught so students would pass them. As for my major classes, they were much more interesting and greatly enabled me to understand the subject material from the book and the real world." The PSU administration, according to our respondents, "is top-notch; they really care about students and PSU as a whole. Our president, Dr. Tom Bryant, is one of our greatest assets!" To some, PSU's greatest asset is that "it is also a fairly cost-effective campus. Many scholarships and forms of financial aid are offered, allowing students less stress over finances."

Life

Athletics play a central role in extracurricular life at PSU. The school's Division II teams, nicknamed the Gorillas, field competitive squads in many men's and women's sports. Students are ardent Gorilla boosters, telling us that "people at our school especially love football." And according to many, "The surrounding community is a major supporter of the athletic program" as well. The Greek system is also popular with a segment of the population because it offers a social outlet in a small town that has few of its own. As one student put it, "It's a college town so there is not much to it besides our university. There are not many activities to do here besides party. We have a movie theatre and Wal-Mart and a bowling alley." But not just any bowling alley, according to many respondents; as one told us, "For a crappy little town, we have a kick-ass bowling alley." For some, "life here is great because it is a small enough town where a person can get around easily but large enough one can have something to do." For others, though, especially those from larger cities, things here can be a tad on the dull side. Students appreciate the fact that "the appearance of this campus is quite attractive. Much renovation has been done to improve the look of campus."

Student Body

The PSU student body has a definite provincial flavor; writes one undergrad, "A lot of students have never been out of Kansas." PSU does have a large international contingent, though; writes one outgoing student, "I meet people from all over the world, and all over the states. I meet locals, older and younger. . . . It is so easy to get into the community and feel like you are a part of it." Students at PSU are generally considered "easygoing" and "very friendly"; notes one undergrad, "When I was choosing a college, that is one of the things that struck me about Pitt State—the people smiled when you looked them in the eye." One student adds, "As an out, gay college student, I come across quite a few stereotypes and ignorant people. I love the times I reach someone new, though, and almost everyone has been responsive to me. The students on campus realize we're all here to grow and learn, and we show each other that every day."

ADMISSIONS

Very important factors considered by the admissions committee include: standardized test scores. *Other factors considered include:* class rank and secondary school record. ACT required. TOEFL required of all international applicants. High school diploma or GED is required. *High school units required/recommended:* 4 English required, 3 math required, 3 science required, 1 science lab required, 3 social studies required.

The Inside Word

Admission to Pittsburg State is not highly competitive; most candidates who rank in the top third of their class or score at least a composite 21 on the ACT or earn at least a 2.0 academic GPA in high school will get in. Standards are slightly tougher for out-of-state applicants.

FINANCIAL AID

Students should submit: FAFSA. The Princeton Review suggests that all financial aid forms be submitted as soon as possible after January 1. *Need-based scholarships/grants offered:* Pell, SEOG, state scholarships/grants, private scholarships, and the school's own gift aid. *Loan aid offered:* FFEL Subsidized Stafford, FFEL Unsubsidized Stafford, FFEL PLUS, Federal Perkins, Federal Nursing, and college/university loans from institutional funds. Federal Work-Study Program available. Institutional employment available. Applicants will be notified of awards on a rolling basis beginning on or about April 1. Off-campus job opportunities are good.

FROM THE ADMISSIONS OFFICE

"Affordability, location, and class size combined with strong academic programs are the primary reasons students choose to attend Pittsburg State University in southeast Kansas. Enrollment continues to climb at this regional state university, especially undergraduate enrollment on campus. PSU also offers graduate-level programs in select academic areas.

"Pittsburg State University offers the very traditional college experience that many high school students want. Although PSU draws many of its students from within a 120-mile radius of the campus, it also has a significant international student population for a campus its size (6,751 total enrollment) and students from across the country who want access to the highly specialized baccalaureate programs in technology. Some of the academic programs earning the most accolades in recent years include teacher education, accounting, pre-med, automotive technology, and engineering technology. The university offers strong programs in the academic Colleges of Education, Business, the Arts and Sciences, and Technology.

"Well-developed student services, more than 140 student organizations and a winning tradition in intercollegiate athletics create an outstanding traditional college experience for Pittsburg State students. The university is known nationally for its strong winning tradition in NCAA Division II football. All the university's intercollegiate sports are very competitive. Students, their families, and alumni often comment on the attractiveness of the PSU campus. In recent years, the renovation of several older buildings, the construction of a new technology building, a progressive landscaping program, and other campus improvements have made this traditional college campus more attractive than ever."

For even more information on this school, turn to page 382 of the "Stats" section.

PURDUE UNIVERSITY—WEST LAFAYETTE

1080 SCHLEMAN HALL, WEST LAFAYETTE, IN 47907 • ADMISSIONS: 765-494-1776 • FAX: 765-494-0544
FINANCIAL AID: 765-494-5050 • E-MAIL: ADMISSIONS@ADMS.PURDUE.EDU • WEBSITE: WWW.PURDUE.EDU

Ratings
Quality of Life: 79   **Academic:** 68   **Admissions:** 76   **Financial Aid:** 83

Academics

Purdue is a big school, and while it can boast a stock of "great professors," it still has the expected pitfalls of most institutions of its girth. "Classes should be easier to get into," grumbles one freshman. Class sizes range from the intimate to the gargantuan, and students who get stuck in the latter wish they had "more time to associate with students one on one." Many students report that the majority of their intro classes are taught by teaching assistants, and TAs even run several upper-level courses. This can be a particular problem when "teaching assistants suck," as one sophomore puts it. The less-than-attractive aspects of Purdue's academics cause some students to think that Purdue "is not what they make it out to be." But on the flipside, some students say that you can get a terrific education if you simply go after it, like this junior, who wrote, "Even though it is a large size school, I get the help I need." And a seldom-mentioned perk of Purdue's academic plan as structured on its physical plant is that "all your classes are within walking distance of each other."

> **SURVEY SAYS . . .**
> *Everyone loves the Boilermakers*
> *Lots of beer drinking*
> *Hard liquor is popular*
> *Students are cliquish*
> *Frats and sororities dominate social scene*
> *Musical organizations are hot*
> *Campus difficult to get around*
> *Great computer facilities*
> *Lab facilities are great*
> *Lousy food on campus*

Life

It shouldn't be a shock to hear that "football games are a big thing that everyone attends" at Purdue. And it shouldn't be surprising to be told that Purdue students "like to party!" In fact, you probably won't be caught off guard by anything that you learn about Purdue's social life—except, maybe, that some students like to spend their free hours on the campus's "mud volleyball courts." Otherwise, many students adhere to a routine that goes something like this: "Go to class, eat some food, play some video games, drink some beer, & sleep." With a good number of hungry livers on campus, Purdue's social scene offers plenty of opportunities to go to "fraternities and apartment parties" and drink the night away. But it's not all fun from a keg; "there are many things to get involved with, like intramural sports, clubs, and exercising." In regard to life away from campus, students seem to think West Lafayette is an "average" town, with individual opinions ranging from calling it "excellent" to whining that "the town smells." The campus itself is "beautiful," and the students who live on it manage to find a "good mixture of school and social life." There are some, however, who would rather spend their days in bedrooms instead of classrooms. Explains a freshman, "Quite a few people are nymphos!"

Student Body

There are about 30,000 undergraduates at the main West Lafayette campus of Purdue. With a number like this, it's not surprising that people seem to "just keep to themselves." But don't let big numbers scare you—"there are so many students that it's easy to make friends and find people with common interests." Students will admit that their population is not "as diverse as we let on to be." One black student from Indianapolis writes that she "never felt what it is like to be a minority until I came to Purdue." But the Purdue stock assures that it's a "friendly" one. As one new member of campus says, "the students at Purdue are very helpful, and I know if I ever need anything, they will be there."

ADMISSIONS

Very important factors considered by the admissions committee include: class rank, secondary school record, standardized test scores. *Other factors considered include:* alumni/ae relation, recommendations, state residency. SAT I or ACT required. TOEFL required of all international applicants. High school diploma or GED is required. *High school units required/recommended:* 4 English required, 3 math required, 2 science required, 3 science recommended, 2 science lab required, 3 science lab recommended, 2 foreign language recommended.

The Inside Word

The fact that Purdue holds class rank as one of its most important considerations in the admission of candidates is troublesome. There are far too many inconsistencies in ranking policies and class size among the 25,000-plus high schools in the U.S. to place so much weight on an essentially incomparable number. The university's high admit rate thankfully renders the issue relatively moot, even though applications have increased.

FINANCIAL AID

Students should submit: FAFSA. The Princeton Review suggests that all financial aid forms be submitted as soon as possible after January 1. *Need-based scholarships/grants offered:* Pell, SEOG, state scholarships/grants, private scholarships, the school's own gift aid. *Loan aid offered:* FFEL Subsidized Stafford, FFEL Unsubsidized Stafford, FFEL PLUS, Federal Perkins, college/university loans from institutional funds. Federal Work-Study Program available. Institutional employment available. Applicants will be notified of awards on or about April 15. Off-campus job opportunities are good.

FROM THE ADMISSIONS OFFICE

"Although it is one of America's largest universities, Purdue does not 'feel' big to its students. The main campus in West Lafayette was built around a master plan that keeps walking time between classes to a maximum of 12 minutes. Purdue is a comprehensive university with an international reputation in a wide range of academic fields. A strong work ethic prevails at Purdue. As a member of the Big 10, Purdue has a strong and diverse athletic program. Purdue offers nearly 600 clubs and organizations. The residence halls and Greek community offer many participatory activities for students. Numerous convocations and lectures are presented each year. Purdue is all about people, and allowing students to grow academically as well as socially, preparing them for the real world."

For even more information on this school, turn to page 382 of the "Stats" section.

RIPON COLLEGE

300 SEWARD STREET, PO BOX 248, RIPON, WI 54971 • ADMISSIONS: 800-947-4766 • FAX: 920-748-8335
FINANCIAL AID: 920-748-8101 • E-MAIL: ADMINFO@RIPON.EDU • WEBSITE: WWW.RIPON.EDU

Ratings
Quality of Life: 79   **Academic:** 83   **Admissions:** 80   **Financial Aid:** 89

Academics

Most students here are glad they chose Ripon. As one undergrad told us, "I'm glad I went to a small school where I gets lots of personalized help and everyone—professors, administrators, town people—is so friendly because it's so small." Student satisfaction with their experiences here is especially impressive since some complained of recent staff reductions,

> **SURVEY SAYS . . .**
> *Lots of beer drinking*
> *Registration is a breeze*
> *(Almost) everyone plays intramural sports*
> *Hard liquor is popular*
> *Campus is beautiful*
> *Students are happy*
> *Very little drug use*
> *Ethnic diversity lacking on campus*

shortened library hours, and delayed improvements and additions to the school. The profs, undergrads agree, "love to teach" and offer an educational experience that is "very personalized. The faculty and staff do their best at providing a wealth of knowledge through individual interaction. Classes tend to have many discussions, and the student's opinion is the basis for learning." Agrees another student, "From the president to professors, everyone goes out of their way to cater to the students' needs. It's an open-door policy at all levels." Several students singled out the mathematics and economics departments, deeming them "superb." If you're seeking "a nice, little hometown college in the middle of Farmland, Wisconsin, with a friendly laid-back atmosphere that doesn't require too much from its students," Ripon College might just be the place for you.

Life

Because the town of Ripon "doesn't have a lot more to offer socially than bars, and the larger towns are all a half-hour to [an] hour away," life at Ripon College revolves around "the big social scene in the dorms (nearly all students live on-campus)" as well as the school's robust Greek community. Students describe an active campus, complete with an arts scene ("Virtually every play is sold out each season . . . and there are several art and photo shows"), sporting events ("We try to support our sports teams as much as possible, especially football and basketball. It's easy because you are friends with the people playing. A lot of people are involved in intercollegiate and intramural sports. We are a sports-oriented campus"), student organizations ("There are about 30 clubs on campus, and the student senate and campus political groups are very active"), and, of course, partying ("For about half of the weekends, there is usually a lounge party sponsored by a fraternity. When these occur, independents, Greeks, and freshmen all seem to come together for a night of fun"). Comedians and speakers visit this remote campus with surprising frequency; reported one student, "Groups like College Republicans bring in high-profile speakers like Ben Stein and Alan Keyes during weeknights." And while the town of Ripon itself is dead, larger towns are not too far afield. Oshkosh and Fond du Lac are about a half-hour's drive off; Milwaukee and Madison offer a wider variety of options for those up for a 90-minute trek.

Student Body

"I think there are two types of typical students" at Ripon, reported one student. "One is friendly, outgoing, majoring in at least two subjects, and involved in lots of activities. The other does nothing except varsity sports and is majoring in exercise science, but is moderately good-looking." Diversity is minimal here, since "we are a small campus in the middle of nowhere Wisconsin. The typical student is white and middle-class, usually from the Midwest." However, "there is quite a sizable minority from other places," especially from overseas. Notes one freshman, "I am from Nevada, and there are two Russians and three natives of Hong Kong on my floor alone." The majority fit the Abercrombie & Fitch mold, while "atypical students look like the remnants of a bad Nickelodeon show, all trying their hardest to be the most different."

ADMISSIONS

Very important factors considered by the admissions committee include: interview, secondary school record. *Important factors considered include:* character/personal qualities, class rank, extracurricular activities, recommendations, standardized test scores. *Other factors considered include:* alumni/ae relation, essays, talent/ability, volunteer work. SAT I or ACT required. TOEFL required of all international applicants. High school diploma or GED is required. *High school units required/recommended:* 17 total required; 4 English required, 2 math required, 4 math recommended, 2 science required, 4 science recommended, 2 foreign language recommended, 2 social studies required, 4 social studies recommended.

The Inside Word

Candidates for admission to Ripon should prepare their applications with the knowledge that they will be subjected to a very thorough and demanding review. Even though the college faces formidable competition from other top midwestern liberal arts colleges and highly selective universities, the admissions staff succeeds at enrolling a very impressive freshman class each year. That doesn't happen without careful matchmaking and a lot of personal attention.

FINANCIAL AID

Students should submit: FAFSA. No deadline for regular filing. The Princeton Review suggests that all financial aid forms be submitted as soon as possible after January 1. *Need-based scholarships/grants offered:* Pell, SEOG, state scholarships/grants, private scholarships, the school's own gift aid. *Loan aid offered:* FFEL Subsidized Stafford, FFEL Unsubsidized Stafford, FFEL PLUS, Federal Perkins. Federal Work-Study Program available. Institutional employment available. Applicants will be notified of awards on a rolling basis beginning on or about March 1. Off-campus job opportunities are good.

FROM THE ADMISSIONS OFFICE

"Since its founding in 1851, Ripon College has adhered to the philosophy that the liberal arts offer the richest foundation for intellectual, cultural, social, and spiritual growth. Academic strength is a 150-year tradition at Ripon. We attract excellent professors who are dedicated to their disciplines; they in turn attract bright, committed students from 36 states and 19 countries. Ripon has a national reputation for academic excellence—evidenced by a 2002 Rhodes Scholar, the College's third, and a 2003 Fulbright Scholar—as well as a friendly, relaxed atmosphere, small class size, and the availability of outstanding facilities. Ripon is also a community. Not only do you see your professor in the classroom, but you can relate to them in a variety of other social situations. Ripon offers a rigorous curriculum in 30 major areas, including unique preprofessional programs. There is also ample opportunity for co-curricular involvement."

For even more information on this school, turn to page 383 of the "Stats" section.

ROSE-HULMAN INSTITUTE OF TECHNOLOGY

5500 WABASH AVENUE, CM 1, TERRE HAUTE, IN 47803-3999 • ADMISSIONS: 812-877-8213
FAX: 812-877-8941 • FINANCIAL AID: 812-877-8259 • E-MAIL: ADMIS.OFC@ROSE-HULMAN.EDU
WEBSITE: WWW.ROSE-HULMAN.EDU

Ratings
Quality of Life: 79   Academic: 89   Admissions: 92   Financial Aid: 84

Academics

The engineering school with a heart: that could be the slogan for the Rose-Hulman Institute of Technology, according to students here. "Everyone here is very personable and accessible," writes one undergrad. "There aren't too many schools where the president will routinely sit down and eat lunch with the students." Agrees another,

> **SURVEY SAYS . . .**
> *High cost of living*
> *Political activism is hot*
> *(Almost) everyone smokes*
> *Popular college radio*
> *School is well run*
> *Great on-campus food*
> *Students are cliquish*

"The relationships are very personal. I've had teachers invite us to their house and even come in late at night to hold a study session. When I see a professor around town, it's so cool to talk to them. They know who you are." The "small class size and individual attention to students' needs" at Rose "ensure that a rigorous engineering curriculum is understood by all students." Rigorous indeed—as one engineer put it, "Rose is a great school if you have no problem with devoting your life to studying for four years." The workload requires "110 percent effort" and the material can be downright soporific; explains one student, "The Rose-Hulman professors' ability to send their students into a zombie-like state from the amount of homework and studying is matched only by the excitement they show during classes while teaching stuff they love." As you might expect, profs here "all have quirks ranging from being an anglophile to being a hippie to climbing Mt. Kilimanjaro." In this way, they match the students; explains one, "The professors are all really unique; you know you have the right major when they remind you of you." One such idiosyncratic student thinks—and writes—like a pirate. Quoth the scholar-brigand of his instructors: "Argh, the profs, they be good, matey. I be gettin' a good book-learnin'."

Life

As at most engineering schools, "Life at Rose is spent mostly studying and always worrying if we haven't. Everyone is excited about the good salaries they will earn after college, or the stuff they'll be equipped to do." Reports one student, "Everything revolves around homework. Last year after two guys in the sophomore engineering curriculum disagreed about an equation, one hog-tied the other and scribbled his version all over his body. This is our idea of a joke." When books are closed and computers shut down, Rose is a "very Greek-oriented" school; "For the most part, if you're an upperclassman and aren't Greek, you've got nothing to do," complains one sophomore engineer. Some here make their own entertainment ("We have hall sports. This includes shooting frozen oranges at cardboard boxes with slingshots. And lubricating the floor and sliding in your socks," reports one resourceful undergrad), while many others simply "spend a lot of time in their rooms on their computers. We like to tool it up . . . play LAN games on our kick-ass network. Yeah!" Intramural sports are also popular. Terre Haute, unfortunately, doesn't offer much in the way of off-campus diversion. Now, you are no doubt wondering: "What do the pirates at Rose-Hulman do for fun?" Answer: "Thar she blows! We enjoy math and cars and sports and women."

Student Body

Rose's "religious, conservative" students "have glasses [and] pasty white skin," and are mostly "hard working, small-town kids that learn well hands-on. There are a lot of incredibly technically gifted students here. It is a techie's paradise!" The majority "are male and have problems communicating with members of the opposite sex (welcome to an engineering school!)." These self-described "tools" like to "play video games constantly or computer games," although a sizable subpopulation is into athletics. "We're very diverse socially," notes one wry student. "We have everyone from computer nerds to computer jocks." The few women here note, kind of optimistically, that "the odds are good, but the goods are odd." Pirates here are apparently homophobes; wrote one, "Shiver me timbers, they hate gay people and love naked wenches."

ADMISSIONS

Very important factors considered by the admissions committee include: class rank, secondary school record, standardized test scores. *Important factors considered include:* character/personal qualities, minority status, recommendations. *Other factors considered include:* alumni/ae relation, extracurricular activities, interview, talent/ability, volunteer work, work experience. SAT I or ACT required. TOEFL required of all international applicants. High school diploma is required and GED is not accepted. *High school units required/recommended:* 16 total required; 4 English required, 4 math required, 5 math recommended, 2 science required, 3 science recommended, 2 science lab required, 2 social studies required, 4 elective required.

The Inside Word

Seven years ago, after 100 years as an all-male institution, Rose-Hulman opened its doors to women. The results have been largely successful—each of the last two freshman classes were 20 percent women. The Institute expects to continue at this pace as it builds up the female presence on its campus; thus, for adventurous, ambitious, and technologically-minded women, Rose-Hulman will be a relatively easy admit for the foreseeable future. "Relatively" is the key word here; academic standards are high and so are the expectations of the admissions committee.

FINANCIAL AID

Students should submit: FAFSA. No deadline for regular filing. The Princeton Review suggests that all financial aid forms be submitted as soon as possible after January 1. *Need-based scholarships/grants offered:* Pell, SEOG, state scholarships/grants, the school's own gift aid. *Loan aid offered:* Direct Subsidized Stafford, Direct Unsubsidized Stafford, Direct PLUS, Federal Perkins. Federal Work-Study Program available. Institutional employment available. Applicants will be notified of awards on or about March 10. Off-campus job opportunities are good.

FROM THE ADMISSIONS OFFICE

"Rose-Hulman is generally considered one of the premier undergraduate colleges of engineering and science. We are nationally known as an institution that puts teaching above research and graduate programs. At Rose-Hulman, professors (not graduate students) teach the courses and conduct their own labs. Department chairmen teach freshmen. To enhance the teaching at Rose-Hulman, computers have become a prominent addition to not only our labs but also in our classrooms and residence halls. Additionally, all students are now required to purchase laptop computers. Ninety million dollars in new facilities have been added in the last six years."

For even more information on this school, turn to page 383 of the "Stats" section.

SAINT LOUIS UNIVERSITY

221 NORTH GRAND BOULEVARD, SAINT LOUIS, MO 63103 • ADMISSIONS: 314-977-2500 • FAX: 314-977-3079
FINANCIAL AID: 314-977-2350 • E-MAIL: ADMITME@SLU.EDU • WEBSITE: WWW.SLU.EDU

Ratings
Quality of Life: 80   **Academic:** 79   **Admissions:** 77   **Financial Aid:** 92

Academics

Students praise Saint Louis University, a big-city Jesuit school, as "a small, private institution that really cares for its students. Due to its small size, you aren't just a 'face in the crowd' here." A renowned physical therapy/occupational therapy program, the "nationally ranked aviation school," the pre-med program, and the "recently expanded Cook

> **SURVEY SAYS . . .**
> *Student publications are popular, Lots of liberals*
> *Student government is popular*
> *Everyone loves the Billiken*
> *Musical organizations are hot*
> *Lousy off-campus food*
> *Campus difficult to get around*
> *Athletic facilities need improving*
> *Library needs improving*

School of Business" receive the highest praise here, but students report that, in all areas, "the classes are really small and teachers are really accessible, once you get past your introductory classes." Students in the most prestigious programs report that "there is a heavy workload, and everybody is pretty serious about studying during the week and even on the weekends." Others tell us that "academics are what you want them to be here. If you want a challenge, you can find those classes easily. If you want the easy way out, ask around for names of those professors" that offer them. Profs at SLU "really make an effort to reach out to the students and make us think. Also, they are available outside class and genuinely help out anyone in need." Undergrads also appreciate the way that "SLU tries to give every student the opportunity to grow and learn by offering many ways to get involved. The academic [curriculum] works together with the residence hall system, and all support the experience gained from participating in student organizations and extracurricular activities."

Life

Like most students in big cities, undergrads at Saint Louis University report that their extracurricular fun usually takes place beyond the campus gates. "The great thing about SLU is that it is located in a very urban environment with tons of cultural and entertaining things to do," explains one student. "There's never a dull moment. We have easy access . . . to museums, zoos, the Fox Theatre, and downtown sporting events." Adds another, "There's Forest Park to visit on nice days, the Arch, the Science Center, a fabulous zoo, ice skating, movie theaters, and lots of great malls." The campus is connected to most city hot spots by MetroLink, St. Louis' light rail system; some here wish the school would offer shuttle bus service, but most seem to handle the public transportation experience without much trouble. Those who choose not to venture out can enjoy "a beautiful campus, with tons of fountains, statues, and flowers." The Greeks exert a major influence on campus social life, and "there is a strong separation between Greeks and non-Greeks. Since there aren't houses—just a Greek dorm—there aren't any open parties. Greek functions tend to be exclusive."

Student Body

Drawing heavily from private Catholic schools in the Midwest, Saint Louis University is home to "many students who are preppy, snobby, rich kids." However, "since SLU gives out good scholarships, the economic classes here vary a little bit." Diversity is enhanced by the fact that "there [are] a great deal of international students, since we have our own campus in Madrid." Minority representation is considerable, too, although most here agree that "all the different races and ethnic groups are segregated." Some feel the school could do better in this area; as one put it, "I also wish there was more diversity; not only ethnically, but different kinds of personalities. It seems that while most people here are down-to-earth, everyone is preppy. I wish we had more hippie types, and musicians, and the like: something different." Many here consider themselves "smart, caring, and into volunteering/helping out the community."

ADMISSIONS

Important factors considered include: secondary school record, standardized test scores. *Other factors considered include:* character/personal qualities, essays, extracurricular activities, recommendations, volunteer work. SAT I or ACT required. TOEFL required of all international applicants. High school diploma or GED is required. *High school units required/recommended:* 20 total recommended; 4 English recommended, 4 math recommended, 3 science recommended, 3 foreign language recommended, 3 social studies recommended, 3 elective recommended.

The Inside Word

Students who are ranked in the top half of their graduating class will have a fairly easy path to admission at Saint Louis. Those who are not can find success in the admissions process by being a minority, having a top Catholic school diploma, or possessing a major talent in soccer.

FINANCIAL AID

Students should submit: FAFSA. Regular filing deadline is March 1. The Princeton Review suggests that all financial aid forms be submitted as soon as possible after January 1. *Need-based scholarships/grants offered:* Pell, SEOG, state scholarships/grants, private scholarships, the school's own gift aid. *Loan aid offered:* FFEL Subsidized Stafford, FFEL Unsubsidized Stafford, FFEL PLUS, Federal Perkins, Federal Nursing, short-term loans. Federal Work-Study Program available. Applicants will be notified of merit awards on a rolling basis beginning on or about October 15. Need-based awards notification begins February 1. Off-campus job opportunities are excellent.

FROM THE ADMISSIONS OFFICE

"A hot midwestern university with a growing national and international reputation, Saint Louis University gives students the knowledge, skills, and values to build a successful career and make a difference in the lives of those around them.

"Students live and learn in a safe and attractive campus environment. The beautiful urban, residential campus offers loads of internship, outreach, and recreational opportunities. Ranked as one of the best educational values in the country, the University welcomes students from all 50 states and 80 foreign countries who pursue rigorous majors that invite individualization. Accessible faculty, study abroad opportunities, and many small, interactive classes make SLU a great place to learn.

"A leading Jesuit, Catholic university, SLU's goal is to graduate men and women of competence and conscience—individuals who are not only capable of making wise decisions, but who also understand why they made them. Since 1818, Saint Louis University has been dedicated to academic excellence, service to others, and preparing students to be leaders in society. Saint Louis University truly is the place . . . where knowledge touches lives."

For even more information on this school, turn to page 384 of the "Stats" section.

Saint Mary's College

Admission office, Notre Dame, IN 46556 • Admissions: 219-284-4587 • Fax: 219-284-4841
E-mail: admission@saintmarys.edu • Website: www.saintmarys.edu

Ratings

Quality of Life: 77   Academic: 79   Admissions: 76   Financial Aid: 73

Academics

"Sometimes you want to go where everybody knows your name—my school is close to this," writes a student at Saint Mary's College. The college provides its undergrads with a learning environment

> **SURVEY SAYS . . .**
> *Intercollegiate sports are popular*
> *Students are religious, Diversity lacking on campus*
> *Very little hard liquor, Classes are small*

in which small classes are integral and close student-professor relationships are the norm. "The teachers truly care and are always available for consultation," raves one student. Another mentions that "Saint Mary's does not have teaching assistants teach any class." The mandatory attendance policy doesn't receive the same sort of praise: "It is not even an option to miss class unless you make an effort to pay a visit to Health and Wellness and have them call your professor." The college's administration gets mixed reviews from the student body. While some students gripe that the "administration moves like snails when it comes to change," others boast that "the administration is excellent at giving students a chance to speak out on whatever subject they wish." Ultimately, nearly all of respondents say they are pleased with their experiences at Saint Mary's. One student, justifying her satisfaction, explains that the professors and the administrators all seem to "realize that preparation for the real world is best achieved through guidance." And guidance is not in short supply at Saint Mary's.

Life

Saint Mary's students definitely have school pride. Oddly, though, the pride they hold is for the school across the street, Notre Dame University. "Notre Dame obsessed," is how one student describes her classmates. Part of the reason that Saint Mary's women make such frequent mention of their neighbor is that the Saint Mary's campus—while the center of their academic lives—provides little to fill their social lives. "Let's just put it this way," a student offers, "going to mass is a social event here." And, of course, Notre Dame has boys. Many women here say that having a coeducational institution a stone's throw away gives them the best of both worlds. "We have men right next door, down the street, actually all over," explains one undergrad. "Who needs them in class with us? We can go to class with no makeup on, pajamas on, no bras, whatever we feel like, and we don't have to worry about Jimmy sitting next to us." The administration has sunk some energy and funds into coming up with a greater amount of social events and sites. One example is the "brand new coffee house on campus." When students aren't hitting the Notre Dame parties, they'll head into South Bend, a small town that's nevertheless equipped with "very good restaurants," plenty of shopping, movie theatres, bowling alleys, and—for the "legal" students—a handful of "dance clubs and bars."

Student Body

If there's one word that accurately describes every student at Saint Mary's, it's this one: "female." At this Catholic, all-women college in South Bend, Indiana, there's an "amazingly friendly" breeze in the air. One student explains, "Students are friendly. Competition is present but not in an extreme way. Students get along with each other regardless of opposing views." Most Saint Mary's students share a common background—described by one among them as "female, white, Catholic, and well-off (although 59 percent of students receive need-based financial aid)"—and the consequent limited exposure to different lifestyles. A classmate adds, "The students here are underexposed to diverse people." But underexposure is not the same as prejudice, and students assure that no matter what your background, you won't be able to "walk to and from class without receiving and giving several 'hellos' and smiles." In class itself "the environment is competitive," an undergrad assures. "However, everyone is willing to help out one another and work together to attain academic success."

ADMISSIONS

Very important factors considered by the admissions committee include: essays, secondary school record, and standardized test scores. *Important factors considered include:* class rank, extracurricular activities, recommendations, and talent/ability. *Other factors considered include:* interview and minority status. SAT I or ACT required. TOEFL required of all international applicants. High school diploma is required and GED is not accepted. *High school units required/recommended:* 16 total required; 4 English required, 3 math required, 4 math recommended, 1 science required, 4 science recommended, 2 foreign language required, 4 foreign language recommended, 2 social studies required, 4 elective required.

The Inside Word

Slackers need not apply to "Little Notre Dame for Ladies." You may enjoy frequent trips to the Golden Dome and other events in the South Bend area, but your chances for success will go south at Saint Mary's unless you're prepared for mandatory class attendance and meager social outlets on campus.

FINANCIAL AID

Students should submit: FAFSA and CSS/Financial Aid PROFILE. The Princeton Review suggests that all financial aid forms be submitted as soon as possible after January 1. *Need-based scholarships/grants offered:* Pell, SEOG, state scholarships/grants, private scholarships, and the school's own gift aid. *Loan aid offered:* Direct Subsidized Stafford, Direct Unsubsidized Stafford, Direct PLUS, FFEL Subsidized Stafford, FFEL Unsubsidized Stafford, FFEL PLUS, and Federal Perkins. Federal Work-Study Program available. Institutional employment available. Applicants will be notified of awards on a rolling basis beginning on or about December 15. Off-campus job opportunities are excellent.

FROM THE ADMISSIONS OFFICE

"This is a time of historic growth and change at Saint Mary's College. Its multi-year Master Plan, an extensive renovation and construction effort designed to better serve students with a new dining hall, student center, and on-campus apartment-style housing, is scheduled for completion within the next couple of years. In addition, the college has begun implementation of its Strategic Plan, an initiative intended to advance the college in several areas, including curriculum and technology.

"Many of the country's top professional employers recognize the value of a Saint Mary's College education. A recruiter for Crowe, Chizek, and Company, LLP, says, 'Over the years we have developed a great respect for Saint Mary's College graduates. These graduates, many of whom are successful members of our staff today, are well prepared and well rounded. The education at Saint Mary's seems to develop individuals that are very well suited for a professional services environment.'

"Saint Mary's students come from a variety of social, economic, and ethnic backgrounds, and over 80 percent receive more than $21 million in financial aid. Saint Mary's also weaves diversity into the collegiate experience through community outreach. U.S. Secretary of Labor Elaine Chao commended Saint Mary's students for their volunteerism, saying 'Your record as students is extremely strong, with over 50 percent of you participating in community service . . . .'"

For even more information on this school, turn to page 385 of the "Stats" section.

SAINT MARY'S UNIVERSITY OF MINNESOTA

700 TERRACE HEIGHTS #2, WINONA, MN 55987-1399 • ADMISSIONS: 507-457-1700 • FAX: 507-457-1722
E-MAIL: ADMISSIONS@SMUMN.EDU • WEBSITE: WWW.SMUMN.EDU

Ratings
Quality of Life: 73   Academic: 75   Admissions: 70   Financial Aid: 74

Academics

"I would have to say the class size and the professors always knowing your name and you as a person, not just a number: those are the strengths of St. Mary's University of Minnesota," says one

> **SURVEY SAYS . . .**
> *Instructors are good teachers, Classes are small*
> *Great food on campus, Campus is beautiful*
> *Students are happy*

student at this Catholic school located about an hour southeast of the Twin Cities. Business management and biology are the two top drawing cards at this "great liberal arts school for individuals who wish to develop the overall self," including, of course, the spiritual side, through the auspices of the governing Christian Brothers. Students here enjoy access to all school officials from top to bottom: writes one undergrad, "Teachers are always available for extra help. The president of the university meets with student leaders on campus to discuss student concerns, which I think is great." Agrees another, "A major strength is how willing most of the professors are with helping students. Many are willing to say on campus till 8 or 9 o'clock to help people." As a result, students find SMU a comfortable environment in which to mature and blossom. As one student put it, "This is a good spot to come and grow for your first four years being away from home. It is also a good place to have time to develop your future career decisions and post-graduate opportunities." An added bonus of an SMU degree is that "alumni are very strong within Minnesota, Wisconsin, and Illinois."

Life

SMU undergrads warn that "life here is somewhat boring. There really isn't a whole lot of excitement on campus after about 7 P.M. If you want any sort of fun during the week, you have to find a party in town or go to a bigger city." One student agrees that "one of the few options" is participation in the "tons of drinking and partying on campus. . . . It's that or the movies." Others temper that assessment, noting that "there are the drinking and the pot-smoking crowds, but there are also the religious groups who go on weekend excursions to missions." The lack of Greek life drives the party scene into campus apartments and the dorms, much to the chagrin of the religious undergrads: "I think the punishments for drinking in the dormitories needs to be harsher," complained one such student. Opportunities for outdoor activity abound here, provided the weather isn't brutally cold, because "the school is situated on top of a bluff in Minnesota. The school also has a creek and river that runs through it. It's a beautiful campus. We go hiking in the bluffs whenever we can." Students also report that "there are plenty of opportunities to get involved in the community through school functions." Even so, most here concede that "this school needs more to do on campus." Even the intercollegiate athletic programs fail to kindle enthusiasm; "It is sad that there is so little support for sports teams here besides the softball team," says one student.

Student Body

"There is an interesting mix of urban and suburban Chicago and Twin Cities, as well as rural Iowa, Wisconsin, South Dakota, and Minnesota" at SMU, students say. Many feel that "the great thing about Saint Mary's is that because it is so small you are able to get to know a lot of people. Even if you don't have class with someone, you still will see them around campus."

Adds one student, "I love the community atmosphere surrounding the school, where book bags are openly left on campus, and students do not worry about them being stolen." Some tell us that "most students here come from a private education background. The crowd is sort of like the Abercrombie and Fitch-type looking. Everyone, however, seems to be kind to each other since there is a strong influence by the Christian Brothers to be welcoming and kind to others."

ADMISSIONS

Very important academic, and nonacademic factors considered by the admissions committee include: secondary school record and standardized test scores. *Important factors considered include:* character/personal qualities, class rank, interview, and talent/ability. *Other factors considered include:* alumni/ae relation, essays, extracurricular activities, recommendations, and volunteer work. SAT I or ACT required, ACT preferred. TOEFL required of all international applicants. High school diploma is required and GED is accepted. *High school units required/recommended:* 18 total are required; 4 English required, 3 math required, 3 science required, 2 science lab required, 3 social studies required, 3 elective required.

The Inside Word

A geographically popular choice for the Minnesota and Wisconsin crowd, Saint Mary's is ideal for those throughout the Northern Plains and Midwest in search of a Roman Catholic institution with fewer than 2,000 students. Despite its good mix of in- and out-of-staters, however, ethnic diversity is minimal.

FINANCIAL AID

Students should submit: FAFSA and institution's own financial aid form. No deadline for regular filing. The Princeton Review suggests that all financial aid forms be submitted as soon as possible after January 1. *Need-based scholarships/grants offered:* Pell, SEOG, state scholarships/grants, the school's own gift aid, and Federal Nursing. *Loan aid offered:* FFEL Subsidized Stafford, FFEL Unsubsidized Stafford, FFEL PLUS, Federal Perkins, and state loans. Federal Work-Study Program available. Institutional employment available. Applicants will be notified of awards on a rolling basis beginning on or about March 1. Off-campus job opportunities are good.

FROM THE ADMISSIONS OFFICE

"**Costs:** Undergraduate Bachelor of Arts tuition for the 2002–2003 school year is $15,280 for students carrying 24 to 34 credits a year. The average room rate is $2,750 and the average board plan is $2,170. Extra fees include a $120 activity fee, a $20 laundry fee, and a $275 technology fee.

"**Financial Aid:** Federal, state, and institutional aid programs are available for students who demonstrate need. About 80 percent of all undergraduates receive nearly $14.5 million in some form of financial aid; approximately $4.8 million is provided by Saint Mary's as need-based or merit scholarships.

"**Admission Requirements:** The pattern of high school college-preparatory courses and performance, while not the sole criterion for acceptance, is of primary importance. Rank in class, a personal essay, standardized test scores, activities, and school recommendations all provide additional data used in the evaluation of a student's academic potential for university success. The university processes admission applications throughout the year for fall or winter semester entrance.

"**Application and Information:** A completed application, a $25 nonrefundable application fee, a personal statement or essay, an official high school transcript, and standardized test scores are required. Students may apply online. Rolling admission is offered for the application process; however, Saint Mary's University applies a priority deadline of May 1 for financial aid and housing."

For even more information on this school, turn to page 385 of the "Stats" section.

ST. NORBERT COLLEGE

100 GRANT STREET, DE PERE, WI 54115 • ADMISSIONS: 920-403-3005 • FAX: 920-403-4072
E-MAIL: ADMIT@SNC.EDU • WEBSITE: WWW.SNC.EDU

Ratings

Quality of Life: 79   Academic: 84   Admissions: 82   Financial Aid: 74

Academics

St. Norbert College prides itself on its commitment to a solid liberal arts curriculum. With small classes led by "dedicated and "enthusiastic teachers," St. Norbert offers its students an intimate learning environment. "Classes are rigorous and challenging but not impos-

> **SURVEY SAYS . . .**
> *Student publications are popular*
> *Students are religious*
> *Diversity lacking on campus, Great off-campus food*
> *Classes are small, School is well run*
> *Theater is hot, Popular college radio*

sible, and call students to work to their full potential. The liberal arts curriculum makes for a well-rounded, enjoyable, and interesting education and class selection," explains one satisfied undergraduate. In addition to offering its students honors courses and freshman seminars, St. Norbert also has a host of other resources, including the Center for Adaptive Education and Assistive Technology, which trains students in the adaptation of classroom content to meet the needs of students with disabilities. The general quality of the library is a sore spot among some students, though: "A lot of their resources are out of date," grouses one undergrad. "You can still get good resources, but you have to be prepared enough to start a couple of weeks ahead of time." Luckily, St. Norbert has put together a library advisory planning committee (including students), obtained a planning grant, and begun fundraising to build a new library. And while Norbert might be home to a wide array of majors, students here definitely have some complaints about the slimness of the course catalog. Grumbles one student, "The course selection per semester doesn't always work" for people pursuing particular majors.

Life

Students here don't venture too far off campus for a good time. The favorite weekend past time is drinking, and not exactly in moderation. As one student warns, "This is a huge party school, and you have to have self control." For some students, St. Norbert's drinking and party atmosphere is exactly what they were looking for, while for others the excessive partying is a big enough turnoff to drive them to actually request "more restrictive alcohol policies." But even in a town as small as De Pere, a suburb of Green Bay, the students at St. Norbert find alternative ways of entertaining themselves and staying active. The college offers over 60 campus clubs and organizations, including 27 that are service oriented, and sponsors Your Entertainment Service (YES) to bring in outside entertainment acts. Where the administration leaves off, the students pick up with a large number of active organizations and a thriving intramural sports scene. While some students enjoy living on campus for the first three years of college. Many wish it weren't a requirement. St. Norbert does provide a variety of housing options (theme houses, single or co-ed halls), but students are calling for "more dorms" and other general improvements in dorm life.

Student Body

With just over 2,000 students, St. Norbert has the type of small, intimate, family-like feel you would expect from a liberal arts college. "After all," notes one student "having only 2,000 students can bring people together." As far as diversity, though, "St. Norbert is very homogenous." Students advise prospects to expect "white, middle- to upper-class Catholics, with some exceptions" as classmates. What they lack in variety, however, St. Norbert undergrads make up for in warmth; they are exceptionally "friendly" and "supportive," and oftentimes they have the opportunity to develop close and meaningful relationships with a lot of their peers. "You get to know a lot of people because you are in the same classes with them, and you live with them, and you pass by them every day between classes."

ADMISSIONS

Very important factors considered by the admissions committee include: secondary school record. *Important factors considered include:* recommendations and standardized test scores. *Other factors considered include:* alumni/ae relation, character/personal qualities, class rank, essays, extracurricular activities, interview, talent/ability, volunteer work, and work experience. SAT I or ACT required. TOEFL required of all international applicants. High school diploma or GED is required. *High school units required/recommended:* 18 total recommended; 4 English recommended, 3 math recommended, 3 science recommended, 2 science lab recommended, 2 foreign language recommended, 2 social studies recommended, 2 history recommended.

The Inside Word

Forcing students through precarious navigation of class schedules and limited resources is out of step with school's high academic and admission standards. Norby's lack of ergonomics and academic variety is the background, however, for a student body that bonds well together.

FINANCIAL AID

Students should submit: FAFSA, institution's own financial aid form, parent's tax return, and student tax return. The Princeton Review suggests that all financial aid forms be submitted as soon as possible after January 1. *Need-based scholarships/grants offered:* Pell, SEOG, state scholarships/grants, private scholarships, and the school's own gift aid. *Loan aid offered:* Direct Subsidized Stafford, Direct Unsubsidized Stafford, Direct PLUS, Federal Perkins, and college/university loans from institutional funds. Federal Work-Study Program available. Institutional employment available. Applicants will be notified of awards on a rolling basis beginning on or about March 15. Off-campus job opportunities are good.

FROM THE ADMISSIONS OFFICE

"Personal attention. A place students call home. Community. Service. Faculty-student collaboration. Academic challenge. Graduating in four years. These are just a few of the many things you'll experience at St. Norbert College.

"How you feel about where you live when you're learning matters. And at St. Norbert, students love where they live and the choices they have. Located on the banks of the Fox River just outside Green Bay, Wisconsin, St. Norbert provides a residential community that encourages students to grow into leaders who make a difference.

"At the heart of the college experience are faculty members committed to providing students personal attention and mentoring. Dedicated to the success of each student, professors provide real-life learning experiences. For example, students might develop marketing plans for corporations, travel on natural science field study trips, or help a community in Zambia, Africa. This practical experience leads to 95 percent of students finding employment or gaining admission to graduate school within six months of graduation.

"Living and learning are linked at St. Norbert through programs in the residence halls that provide choices from traditional to contemporary, from single and two-person rooms to four-person apartments and multi-bedroom suites or townhouses. The new Student Campus Center, initiated through student leadership, hosts entertainers, work-out rooms, a gymnasium, Phil's Pub, and docks on the Fox River.

"St. Norbert students receive more than a liberal arts and sciences degree—they are prepared for the future and to make a difference in the lives of others."

For even more information on this school, turn to page 386 of the "Stats" section.

ST. OLAF COLLEGE

1520 St. Olaf Avenue, Northfield, MN 55057-1098 • Admissions: 507-646-3025 • Fax: 507-646-3832
Financial Aid: 507-646-3019 • E-mail: admissions@stolaf.edu • Website: www.stolaf.edu

Ratings

Quality of Life: 88   **Academic:** 92   **Admissions:** 86   **Financial Aid:** 89

Academics

St. Olaf, a small Lutheran college in Minnesota, utilizes a 4-1-4 academic calendar, allowing students a winter term to travel or pursue individual projects. Study abroad is encouraged, and an adventurous group of students take advantage of the around-the-world program, which hits five countries in as many months. The school prides itself on its music department, especially its renowned choir. Students appreciate that "even nonmusic majors have the opportunity to participate in bands and choirs." Professors are caring, as is shown in their willingness to "approach you if you're struggling and express concern." Luckily, the "professors really want to be here. They want to be teaching college kids." Equally personable, the new president is "regularly spotted chatting with students outside of the commons." Students are upset, however, that certain "important programs," including the communications department, "were cut without faculty and student input." They also express a get-a-clue attitude towards the administration, claiming they are "in denial" about topics such as drinking on this dry campus. One student admonishes the Board of Regents to "open your eyes; it's the twenty-first century."

> **SURVEY SAYS . . .**
> *Great library*
> *No one cheats*
> *Campus feels safe*
> *Campus is beautiful*
> *Dorms are like palaces*
> *Very little drug use*
> *Lousy food on campus*
> *Students are cliquish*
> *Student publications are ignored*

Life

Various opinions crop up regarding St. Olaf's dry-campus policy. One student writes, "I think it [helps us] avoid a lot of potential hazards in college and generally leads to a healthier lifestyle among the student body." On the other hand, a peer counters, "Just about everyone seems to agree this is a ridiculous policy since we are all adults." Virtually everyone lives on campus for all four years, attending "student government-sponsored activities such as DJs, speakers, dances, bands, comedians." Considering the strong music department, performances draw big crowds. "A male a cappella ensemble that sings mostly Gregorian chant is actually more popular here than the football games." To get away from campus (a.k.a. "Little Suburbia"), students can take free buses to Carleton College, Timberwolves games, or other Twin Cities' happenings, all under an hour away. Those looking for politics will probably be happy here at "one of the most activist campuses in Minnesota" and one "fairly liberal in the Christian religious sphere." The environment allows for "serious contemplation of one's religious beliefs without forcing Christianity or Lutheranism on anyone."

Student Body

One student aptly explains the "cookie-cutter" quotient at St. Olaf: "Even though I'm white and upper-middle class, I sometimes feel out of place because I'm not a blond, Lutheran, Norwegian-American." A senior adds, however, that "diversity on campus and appreciation of this diversity has increased significantly since I was a freshman." St. Olaf has an active GLOW (Gay, Lesbian, Or Whatever) club, and even amid the religious environment, sexuality issues are openly discussed. A straight, Christian student who thinks homosexuality is a sin says of a friend, "He is homosexual, and yet we have loved each other and found ways to communicate through the hard issues rather than just avoiding them or each other." Full of future Peace Corps participants, St. Olaf is home to 3,000 "good citizens" who "volunteer time both on and off campus." The resilience of the campus community was recently demonstrated when three students were tragically killed by a drunk driver. One student writes, "I know it sounds morbid, but our campus was at its best when these kids died because you could really see what a family we are here at Olaf."

ADMISSIONS

Very important factors considered by the admissions committee include: secondary school record. *Important factors considered include:* essays, recommendations, standardized test scores. *Other factors considered include:* alumni/ae relation, character/personal qualities, class rank, extracurricular activities, geographical residence, interview, minority status, religious affiliation/commitment, state residency, talent/ability, volunteer work, work experience. SAT I or ACT required. TOEFL required of all international applicants. High school diploma or GED is required. *High school units required/recommended:* 15 total recommended; 3 English recommended, 3 math recommended, 2 science recommended, 1 science lab recommended, 2 foreign language recommended, 2 history or social science recommended.

The Inside Word

St. Olaf truly deserves a more national reputation; the place is a bastion of excellence and has always crossed applications with the best schools in the Midwest. Despite its lack of widespread recognition, it is a great choice. Candidates benefit from the relative anonymity of the college through an admissions process, which, while demanding, isn't as tough as other colleges of St. Olaf's caliber.

FINANCIAL AID

Students should submit: FAFSA, CSS/Financial Aid PROFILE, noncustodial (divorced/separated) parent's statement. No deadline for regular filing. The Princeton Review suggests that all financial aid forms be submitted as soon as possible after January 1. *Need-based scholarships/grants offered:* Pell, SEOG, state scholarships/grants, private scholarships, the school's own gift aid. *Loan aid offered:* FFEL Subsidized Stafford, FFEL Unsubsidized Stafford, FFEL PLUS, Federal Perkins, Federal Nursing, state loans, college/university loans from institutional funds. Federal Work-Study Program available. Institutional employment available. Applicants will be notified of awards on a rolling basis beginning on or about March 1. Off-campus job opportunities are fair.

FROM THE ADMISSIONS OFFICE

"St. Olaf College provides an education in the liberal arts that is rooted in the Christian gospel and offered with a global perspective. Sixty-seven percent of each graduating class will have studied overseas during the four years at St. Olaf. The Center for Integrative Studies and Great Conversation programs offer alternatives to the traditional curriculum."

For even more information on this school, turn to page 386 of the "Stats" section.

SOUTHERN ILLINOIS UNIVERSITY—CARBONDALE

UNDERGRAD ADMISSIONS, CARBONDALE, IL 62901 • ADMISSIONS: 618-536-4405 • FAX: 618-453-3250
E-MAIL: JOINSIUC@EDU • WEBSITE: WWW.SIU.EDU/OAR/

Ratings
Quality of Life: 76   **Academic:** 72   **Admissions:** 68   **Financial Aid:** 74

Academics

The nearly 18,000 undergrads of Southern Illinois University—Carbondale are united in their quest for a reputable degree gained at a reasonable price. In a few select departments—aviation management and flight, radio/television, and engineering among

> **SURVEY SAYS . . .**
> *No one cheats*
> *Lots of TAs teach upper-level courses*
> *Diverse students interact*
> *Class discussions encouraged, Classes are small*
> *Student publications are ignored*

them—they receive a good deal more: a hard-earned degree from a nationally renowned program. According to one student, "The quality of education is very good, especially in aviation management and flight and also in business." Adds another student, "Some professors are good—I even had Senator Paul Simon as one of my professors—and the school has a lot of dope study abroad programs." Students here appreciate the fact that "most of the classes, even the core classes, are pretty interesting, and there is definitely a wide variety of courses to take to suit your own interests." While some report that "professors have seemed pretty nice and helpful; they are usually around whenever I have questions," others observe that they "very rarely have had an actual professor teaching class; it's usually a TA." One first-year student is pleased that "everyone seems very willing to help in making the transition from high school to college as smooth as possible."

Life

Southern "is known as a party school," but does it live up to its rep? According to most students here, the answer is an emphatic "yes." "People here straight out love to party," explains one student; agrees another, "Most people at SIU-C tend to go out and party as much as they can." Some students temper their assessment, reminding us that "a lot of people at school, including myself, enjoy having a good time, which often includes drinking. But at the same time, I feel that many of those people are able to maintain their academic load. Just because somebody wants/likes to have a good time doesn't mean that he/she can't keep up with work." Another student insists that "there are plenty of things to do for those students that aren't much into the party scene." For example, "outdoor sports and activities are totally taken advantage of. Everyone here is concerned about staying fit and exercising, and there's so many ways to do so outdoors. Rock climbing, repelling, hiking, kayaking, rafting, camping, mountain biking, you name it, it's all within 20 minutes each direction. Campus is surrounded by the beautiful Shawnee National Forest." In addition, "the student activities department has about two activities per week, so there is always something to do." In quieter moments, students take time to appreciate the fact that "the school is very pretty. I love walking around the campus, especially during the fall. There are many nooks and crannies outdoors to sit and read, sit and study." Although Carbondale is "in the middle of nowhere," "St. Louis is close by" to facilitate road trips.

Student Body

Southern students are "very laid back and easygoing," perhaps too much so: notes one undergrad, "I feel like my fellow students are sometimes lazy. I often hear people complaining of the teacher not teaching well enough, but I wonder if that person ever stopped to complain that perhaps he didn't read the assigned reading or study hard enough." Undergrads in prestigious programs work hard, but many others, students here admit, are happy to coast through. "Low tuition and low acceptance standards" dilute the student population, many feel; "There are many students at SIU who are not serious about education," notes one undergrad. A "white, preppy" contingent hailing from the northwest suburbs of Chicago mix with "huckleberries from the sticks and blacks from the south side of Chicago" to create a diverse population; "a large number of nontraditional students" also add to the richness of the blend.

ADMISSIONS

Very important factors considered by the admissions committee include: class rank and standardized test scores. SAT I or ACT required, ACT preferred. TOEFL required of all international applicants. High school diploma or GED is required. *High school units required/recommended:* 15 total required; 4 English required, 3 math required, 3 science required, 3 social studies required, 2 elective required.

The Inside Word

SIU is a good value for applicants from near or far, as the school offers a broad mixture of students from every academic perspective. An applicant can look ahead and choose to either seize the opportunity to get a top-notch education or descend into apathy and alcohol.

FINANCIAL AID

Students should submit: FAFSA. The Princeton Review suggests that all financial aid forms be submitted as soon as possible after January 1. *Need-based scholarships/grants offered:* Pell, SEOG, state scholarships/grants, private scholarships, and the school's own gift aid. *Loan aid offered:* Direct Subsidized Stafford, Direct Unsubsidized Stafford, Direct PLUS, Federal Perkins, and college/university loans from institutional funds. Federal Work-Study Program available. Institutional employment available. Applicants will be notified of awards on a rolling basis beginning on or about February 20. Off-campus job opportunities are good.

FROM THE ADMISSIONS OFFICE

"Southern Illinois University—Carbondale offers students a combination of academic opportunity, student involvement, and natural beauty as unique as our mascot, the Saluki. Students can choose from over 232 different undergraduate degree options, and move on to advanced study in law, medicine, or our graduate school. SIUC is rated as one of only seven Doctoral Extensive universities in Illinois, sharing the distinction with schools such as Northwestern, Loyola, and University of Illinois—Champaign-Urbana. Even though we have big-school options, students praise us for attention that rivals any small campus. Eighty-eight percent of our undergraduate classes have 40 students or less. Every professor holds office hours to meet with students outside of class, and faculty members work with students where they live in our Academic Emphasis Floors.

"Carbondale is the quintessential college town—friendly and easy to navigate, but with a full compliment of shops, restaurants, and entertainment to keep students busy outside of class. Outdoor lovers find weekends full with hiking, mountain biking, hunting, and fishing in the Shawnee National Forest, just minutes from campus. Our 'Sweet 16' Saluki men's basketball team brought the campus and the community together in the spring of 2002, with no riotous results.

"Our students could spend thousands of dollars more at other institutions, but they consider our price, along with an average freshman financial aid package of almost $7,000, a wonderful value. At the junior and senior level, students compete for paid undergraduate research positions and undergraduate assistantships, which provide in-the-lab and on-the-job experience."

For even more information on this school, turn to page 387 of the "Stats" section.

SOUTHWEST MISSOURI STATE UNIVERSITY

901 SOUTH NATIONAL, SPRINGFIELD, MO 65804 • ADMISSIONS: 417-836-5517 • FAX: 417-836-6334
E-MAIL: SMSUINFO@SMSU.EDU • WEBSITE: WWW.SMSU.EDU

Ratings
Quality of Life: 75   Academic: 72   Admissions: 67   Financial Aid: 74

Academics

Southwest Missouri State's 15,000 undergrads are spread across an academic board of 150 majors, yet the average freshman class size is just 26 students, and by senior year, an SMSU student's average

> **SURVEY SAYS . . .**
> *Classes are small, School is well run*
> *Frats and sororities dominate social scene*
> *Instructors are good teachers*

class size is 16. Numbers can be deceiving, though, and students still report that, at times, they end up feeling more like a number than an actual person. A first-year student mutters, "It can be tiresome visiting your advisor for the sixth time and he still has no idea who you are or why you are in his office." But this is just one voice. Most students who take the time to seek out their profs report that "professors are very enthused and willing to devote extra time to students if we ask for it." Student satisfaction is further boosted by up-to-date computers, the "excellent staff," "great, new library" that's in the works, and other out-of-class resources that they have at their fingertips. The most popular college at SMSU is the College of Business Administration, followed by the College of Health and Human Services. The education department is also well reputed, and students warn us not to overlook "great" programs like "music and theatre." A student tells us that no matter what you choose to study at SMSU, you'll find that "this is an awesome place to go to college."

Life

Student life in Springfield, Missouri's third largest city, takes on many different shapes. For outdoor types, "Springfield and the Ozark area offer a lot of options," such as "boating, hiking, camping, biking, ice-skating," and jogging along the trails at the Springfield Nature Center. For the sports-oriented, the university has an array of intramural sports and NCAA Division I athletic teams that students follow with fervor. And for the partygoers, Springfield offers "dance clubs, rodeos, and concerts," and the university is alive with "costume parties, barbecues," off-campus parties—basically, in one forum or another, "drinking from Thursday night until Sunday afternoon." One student assures us that drinking is not the foremost thought on the minds of all at SMSU: "People think about everything from getting drunk and partying to the philosophical issues of life and the hereafter." "Some people say that it's a party school, but I think that it has cleaned up its reputation in the last few years," writes one student; indeed, SMSU is on a mission, and according to one, "they have almost eliminated their party school image." Now students would like to see improvements in student life, especially concerning food and parking. Still, "our dorms are palaces," says one braggart about the residential halls that are commonly regarded as among the nicest in the nation. But even breathtaking dorms aren't worth sitting idle in, so when urban adventure calls, "it is easy to drive to Kansas City or St. Louis for a weekend."

Student Body

Despite the size of SMSU's undergrad population, it does not boast a "very diverse population." One student observes, "Most kids seem to come from the area surrounding my school and consequently most of them hang around their friends from high school. It's hard coming from out of state." While there's certainly a segment of campus that comes from nearby urban areas, like

St. Louis and Kansas City, there seems to be a larger segment of rural, conservative midwesterners who are often referred to as the "Bible Belt students." "We are in the Bible Belt, and it definitely shows," says a freshman. "Non-Christian students such as myself are not discriminated against, but we do feel a little bit awkward after being invited to Bible study for the thousandth time and saying, 'No, thanks,' for the thousandth time." Not to worry—there are over 250 groups on campus other than Bible studies. One student advises, "The best way to make friends is to get involved in organizations" that suit your interests and then simply "be yourself."

ADMISSIONS

Very important factors considered by the admissions committee include: class rank, secondary school record, and standardized test scores. *Other factors considered include:* alumni/ae relation, character/personal qualities, essays, extracurricular activities, interview, minority status, recommendations, talent/ability, volunteer work, and work experience. SAT I or ACT required, ACT preferred. TOEFL required of all international applicants. High school diploma or GED is required. *High school units required:* 16 total required; 4 English required, 3 math required, 2 science required, 1 science lab required, 3 social studies required, 1 visual/performing arts required, 3 elective required.

The Inside Word

SMSU's sheer size makes it tough for faculty to match a face with a name, but its facilities provide students with everything they'll need to gain knowledge in their field of choice.

FINANCIAL AID

Students should submit: FAFSA. Recommended filing deadline is March 31. The Princeton Review suggests that all financial aid forms be submitted as soon as possible after January 1. *Need-based scholarships/grants offered:* Pell, SEOG, state scholarships/grants, private scholarships, and the school's own gift aid. *Loan aid offered:* Direct Subsidized Stafford, Direct Unsubsidized Stafford, Direct PLUS, FFEL Subsidized Stafford, FFEL Unsubsidized Stafford, FFEL PLUS, Federal Perkins, state loans, and college/university loans from institutional funds. Federal Work-Study Program available. Institutional employment available. Applicants will be notified of awards on a rolling basis beginning on or about April 30. Off-campus job opportunities are excellent.

FROM THE ADMISSIONS OFFICE

"Southwest Missouri State University offers: The **advantages of Missouri's second largest university**, with a wide range of programs, services, and activities and a growing enrollment of students from throughout Missouri, 47 states, and 90 countries; **strong academic programs** (150 undergraduate and 42 graduate majors), 700 faculty, and one of the Midwest's largest cooperative education programs, all focused on preparing students for successful entry into careers or graduate schools; **a comfortable and compact campus** with an outstanding library and student union and some of the nation's finest residence halls; **affordability and value** (our combined tuition and room and board costs are below state and national averages); and the many **opportunities for recreation, entertainment, and employment** in Springfield (Missouri's third largest city), and the surrounding Ozarks region.

"About 15 percent of SMSU students are members of fraternities and sororities, which are among our 250 student organizations. Alcohol is prohibited on campus, and we have worked proactively with students and parents to address issues such as drinking that challenge universities across the country. Our focus on public affairs earned SMSU recognition in the John Templeton Foundation's Colleges That Encourage Character Development.

"In 2001, a student satisfaction survey conducted by a national consulting firm revealed that our undergraduate students are more satisfied than students at public colleges and universities nationally on 68 of the 73 items measured by the survey. We believe that SMSU is an 'awesome place to go to college.' We invite you to visit to see for yourself."

For even more information on this school, turn to page 388 of the "Stats" section.

STEPHENS COLLEGE

1200 East Broadway, Box 2121, Columbia, MO 65215 • Admissions: 573-876-7207 • Fax: 573-876-7237
Financial Aid: 573-876-7106 • E-mail: apply@sc.stephens.edu • Website: www.stephens.edu

Ratings
Quality of Life: 79   Academic: 70   Admissions: 73   Financial Aid: 91

Academics

"It's all about theater, dance, fashion design, and marketing" at Stephens College, a small all-women's school (almost, that is; the school admits a few men to its theater department) "with an emphasis in almost every class on women's history and women's issues." Stephens is "a strict school academically, which really prepares you for the real world. Small classes and teachers who really care can be a great blessing for your education." The school's very existence and success, students say, empower them. "Stephens is about providing confidence and the ability to back that confidence up, for women, in a predominantly male world," explains one undergrad. Profs receive high marks for their "amazing real-world experience in their fields. The theatre professors have actually acted and directed in the business, the dance professors are from New York, and the Broadcasting teacher spent many years on TV." Better still, they know how to share their expertise with undergrads; as one student told us, "You really have an opportunity to bond with [profs] and make them your friend once you're done with their class. They're always willing to listen to what you have to say and how you feel about what they're teaching." On the downside, students feel that the "non-arts departments need more attention" and that "the facilities here are outdated, and the library is weak and in need of updates."

> **SURVEY SAYS . . .**
> *Athletic facilities need improving*
> *No one watches intercollegiate sports*
> *No one plays intramural sports*
> *Campus easy to get around*
> *Registration is a breeze*
> *Students are happy*

Life

Stephens students love Columbia, "a three-college town where there's always something to do." The city has a lot to offer these aesthetically inclined undergrads; explains one student, "The largest majors on campus are theater, fashion, and dance, so most of our student body is very creative. Even those not in one of these majors have an appreciation for art, and there are a lot of opportunities in downtown Columbia for us to see independent film, a poetry reading, a local musician, or the work of a local artist." Because "Mizzou is two blocks away, girls have all the chances in the world to meet guys" and "go hang out at frat parties." Students here tell us that "the majority of our student body aren't hard partiers, and those who are tend to live off-campus where they can drink and party to their own satisfaction." Most here are too busy and too deeply involved in their studies to devote much time to partying. Wrote one theater major, "As far as theater is concerned, most of us are completely consumed by the department, which is a good thing. Like Annie Potts said of her experience here, you really do 'eat, breathe, live theater.' Most of us seem to love being so busy, but others don't like the idea of rehearsing or working on a crew a good deal of the afternoon and evening and then having to do homework way into the wee hours of the morning." Just about everyone here agrees that "the food is really bad and greasy."

Student Body

"There is no 'typical Stephens woman,'" many Stephens women insist. "We are all unique: short, tall, fat, thin, black, white, Asian, Hispanic, brainiac, or sorority lover . . .we all find our niche here." Others tell us that "Stephens is mostly white students, but everyone here observes diversity and at least respects it" and report that "most students are middle class and from Missouri, or from a surrounding state. Most are in the arts (theater, dance, fashion)." Students outside the most popular majors "are respected by professors, but don't always get treated the same by students." Notes one undergrad, "While there are definite social cliques—the fashion majors, dancers, theatre people, etc.—we all get along." As at many unaffiliated women's schools, "Sexual orientation isn't an issue here. There is a good mixture of heterosexual and gay/bisexual people. It may seem like there are quite a few lesbians and bisexuals, but in reality it's just that they feel more open here."

ADMISSIONS

Very important factors considered by the admissions committee include: character/personal qualities, essays, recommendations, secondary school record, standardized test scores. *Important factors considered include:* extracurricular activities, interview, talent/ability, volunteer work. *Other factors considered include:* work experience. SAT I or ACT required. TOEFL required of all international applicants. High school diploma or GED is required. *High school units required/recommended:* 12 total recommended; 4 English recommended, 2 math recommended, 2 science recommended, 2 foreign language recommended, 2 social studies recommended.

The Inside Word

Each candidate's application is read by three members of the admissions committee, and essays carry much more significance than test scores. You'll get a lot of personal attention from the admissions staff here; with the kind of competition Stephens faces for students, they have to work pretty hard here to bring in the freshman class. Their success is a testament to the quality of the college.

FINANCIAL AID

Students should submit: FAFSA. No deadline for regular filing. The Princeton Review suggests that all financial aid forms be submitted as soon as possible after January 1. *Need-based scholarships/grants offered:* Pell, SEOG, state scholarships/grants, private scholarships, the school's own gift aid. *Loan aid offered:* Direct Subsidized Stafford, Direct Unsubsidized Stafford, Direct PLUS, Federal Perkins. Federal Work-Study Program available. Institutional employment available. Applicants will be notified of awards on a rolling basis beginning on or about February 1. Off-campus job opportunities are excellent.

FROM THE ADMISSIONS OFFICE

"A national private liberal arts college for women in the Midwest, Stephens College was established in 1833 as Columbia's first institution of higher education. Students are encouraged to arrange a campus visit.

"The women's college setting offers stimulating classroom discussion and close interaction with professors and peers. Bridging theory and application, students engage in hands-on learning opportunities (education majors in our on-campus children's laboratory school and theatre in Iowa, for example) as well as internship experiences in their first year of study. The Stephens campus is within walking distance of a thriving downtown, shared by more than 26,000 students at area colleges and universities. An extensive network of Stephens alumnae are always willing to assist students with employment searches upon graduation."

For even more information on this school, turn to page 388 of the "Stats" section.

STERLING COLLEGE

PO Box 98, Sterling, KS 67579 • Admissions: 620-278-4275 • Fax: 620-278-4416
Email: admissions@sterling.edu • Website: www.sterling.edu

Ratings

Quality of Life: 78   **Academic:** 71   **Admissions:** 66   **Financial Aid:** 75

Academics

Students come to Sterling College, a tiny Presbyterian school smack dab in the middle of Kansas, seeking a "strong Christian culture," and that is indeed what they find. Students praise Sterling's "caring students and faculty, along with its Christian atmosphere that strives and meets its Christian name." "The

> **SURVEY SAYS . . .**
> *School is well run, Very little beer drinking*
> *Students get along with local community*
> *Intercollegiate sports are popular*
> *Student publications are popular*
> *(Almost) everyone plays intramural sports*
> *Diverse students interact, Students are religious*

rules are strict" at Sterling, "but if rules are broken the administration tries to understand why and reason with the student." Requirements include chapel attendance, two religious courses, and one philosophy course as well as a number of other humanities and science classes taught from a Christian perspective. Reports one undergrad, "Most of the professors that I have had are strong Christians who wanted to get to know me and what I thought about life." Although Christians of multiple denominations attend Sterling (Baptist, Presbyterian, Methodist, and Catholic being the most predominant), a few find the religious requirements off-putting. Writes one, "Sterling should not require all the religious classes for those who are not here for that type of instruction." The faculty here receives high marks; writes one student, "The professors aim to be teachers and mentors! My personal academic experience at Sterling has been very positive."

Life

The town of Sterling, located north of Hutchinson and an hour northwest of Wichita, is "a very small community. There is not a wide range of available activities here." A short drive to Lyons will bring a greater selection of restaurants, and "movies, shopping, and all that" can be found in Hutchinson, about 30 minutes away. Life in Sterling, writes one student, "is only as boring as you make it. Rather than sitting around being bored, I am running through the dorms chasing someone or just hanging in the room watching movies. I can always find something to do. The fact is, Sterling is an alright place. The people there make it that way." It is also a safe place, safe enough that "the girls on my hall leave their doors open to each other (literally and non-literally) during the day when they aren't sleeping or studying." Campus life offers some opportunities; students tell us that "theater is always a big thing on campus. Most everyone is involved or goes to the performances." Also, "Sometimes a group of us gets together to have swing dances." Drinking, drugs, and philandering are all frowned upon and, by all reports, rare.

Students

"Most students are very friendly" at Sterling, at least according to their classmates. "I know a good deal of the student body by name and they know mine. It's like Cheers, minus the alcohol (at least from what I know and see!)." As one student put it, "The student body is like a family; we fight, but if I need help, someone is always more than willing to give me a helping hand." Some feel that "we could use more diversity" but also understand that the school's religious aspect limits the range of prospective students. A few also warn that "there is a slight division among jocks and nonjocks, but the campus is aware of that and tries to keep both sides involved with breaking the barrier." It's also important to note that "there are no openly gay or lesbian students at Sterling College."

ADMISSIONS

Very important factors considered by the admissions committee include: character/personal qualities, secondary school record, and standardized test scores. *Important factors considered include:* essays, extracurricular activities, interview, religious affiliation/commitment, and volunteer work. *Other factors considered include:* alumni/ae relation, class rank, recommendations, talent/ability, and work experience. SAT I or ACT required. TOEFL required of all international applicants. High school diploma is required and GED is accepted. *High school units required/recommended:* 4 English recommended, 3 math recommended, 2 science recommended, 1 science lab recommended, 2 foreign language recommended, 2 social studies recommended, 2 history recommended, 1 elective recommended.

The Inside Word

At Sterling, a Christian school that's big into theater arts, one can assume that the show biz "don't ask, don't tell" philosophy does not apply. But if your mission to learn is on par with Sterling's Christian structure, this school is well worth consideration.

FINANCIAL AID

Students should submit: FAFSA and a copy of prior year's tax returns. Priority deadline is April 1. The Princeton Review suggests that all financial aid forms be submitted as soon as possible after January 1. *Need-based scholarships/grants offered:* Pell, SEOG, state scholarships/grants, private scholarships, and the school's own gift aid. *Loan aid offered:* FFEL subsidized Stafford, FFEL unsubsidized Stafford, FFEL PLUS, and college/univeristy loans from institutional funds. Federal Work-Study Program available. Institution employment available. Applicants will be notified of awards on a rolling basis beginning on or about March 1. Off-campus job opportunities are fair.

FROM THE ADMISSIONS OFFICE

"What's your vision? What do you want to do with your life? Don't have that figured out yet? How about being prepared to change the world around you, one person at a time, regardless of your academic interests?

"At Sterling College, you'll find dedicated faculty and staff that will help you find your calling and assist you in making it reality. You'll find a campus community that cares about you. You'll find an academic environment that prepares you for the next step in your life . . . be it graduate school, a career in corporate business, an overseas ministry, or impacting the lives of children through education.

"Sterling College stands alone as the only college in the nation to require servant-leadership training in all 17 of its academic majors. This training teaches students how to lead by serving, following the greatest example of leadership of all time: Jesus Christ.

"Sterling College is also actively involved in developing leadership programs for nonprofit ministries throughout the world. Two world-changing organizations, Habitat for Humanity International and Feed The Children, have currently partnered with Sterling College to train their next generation of leaders.

"In athletics, Sterling College fields 12 men's and women's intercollegiate sports, and is affiliated with the NAIA and the Kansas Collegiate Athletic Conference. An active intramural schedule is also available to all students.

"Sterling College is a four-year, Christ-centered, liberal arts college located in Sterling, Kansas, with a mission 'to develop creative and thoughtful leaders who understand a maturing Christian faith.'"

For even more information on this school, turn to page 389 of the "Stats" section.

TAYLOR UNIVERSITY

236 WEST READE AVENUE, UPLAND, IN 46989-1001 • ADMISSIONS: 765-998-5134 • FAX: 765-998-4925
E-MAIL: ADMISSIONS_U@TAYLORU.EDU • WEBSITE: WWW.TAYLORU.EDU

Ratings
Quality of Life: 78   **Academic:** 88   **Admissions:** 84   **Financial Aid:** 73

Academics

Taylor University, a nondenominational Christian school, is "a small, rural campus that strongly emphasizes community," much to the students' satisfaction. Undergrads here agree that professors, administrators, and their fellow classmates bond to create a nurturing

> **SURVEY SAYS . . .**
> *Hard liquor is popular*
> *Diversity lacking on campus*
> *Profs teach upper levels*
> *Student publications are popular*
> *No one plays intramural sports*

atmosphere in which to study the world from a religious perspective. The faculty, students tell us, "are incredible people. They make themselves available and accessible to their students. They are deeply concerned with their students' well-being as well as their understanding for their class. If a professor senses that you are having difficulty in class, they are more than willing to set aside time to help you." Similarly, the administration "is great. It is always possible to get in touch with any of the administrators if you need to talk to them. They are very understanding and care for their students." Most of all, students appreciate how "most courses emphasize the text and Christian faith. The integration of faith and learning creates for an exciting aspect of class. Taylor challenges students academically and spiritually." According to some, Taylor's nondenominational status "is our biggest strength and our biggest weakness. It is our strength in that we get people from every church denomination worshiping together in unity. It is our weakness in that no one single denomination supports us financially."

Life

By nearly all accounts, Taylor students enjoy the wholesome social life one would expect of undergraduates at a devout faith-based institution. Writes a typical student, "The wild parties that a lot of college students talk about don't happen here. And contrary to belief, we like the standard that we live by. We like the fact that we can go out, have a ton of fun, and actually be able to remember what we did the next day." Students note that "we are in the middle of a cornfield, so getting off campus means going 20 to 30 minutes away. To compensate, we have different activities on campus. . . . Some favorites are the three variety shows produced every year. Air Band in early October is our lip sync competition; Our Generation Night features student groups performing songs from the '80s and '90s; and Nostalgia Night covers songs from the '70s and before." "Smaller events" include "all-night movie marathons, prayer & praises, coffee houses, and a Monopoly tournament." One student reports on the side-splitting "Welcome Weekend Square Dance. We get all decked out in our western attire and square dance in our gym with an official caller and everything. It is the most hilarious, corny, and fun event. I don't think I ever stopped laughing." Adds another, "Chapel services are excellent and well-attended even though attendance is based on an honor system. The Life Together Covenant (LTC) plays a key role in the life of the students. The LTC lays out the Christian community guidelines, which are expected to be followed. It is a type of honor code." Students tell us that "dorm life is the heartbeat of the campus. Because of our isolated location, community life thrives. Hanging out in each others rooms and playing video games are common week night activities."

Students

Students at Taylor are proud of the fact that their "very ambitious and usually well-rounded" classmates "are very friendly. Everyone says 'Hi' to each other on the sidewalks and you get to recognizing people after a while." The friendliness, most agree, is a function of the school's size; writes one, "The student body is relatively small so you can't hide from others. It forces you to talk with others even if you aren't in the mood." Some feel that "there tends to be too many of the same type of student at Taylor—perfectionist, preppy, well-off financially." Notes one student, "Our school could definitely stand more diversity. We have hardly any international students and very few minority groups represented." Students happily tolerate a lack of diversity in one area; reports one, "We share a common bond in Christ, which opens us up to one another."

ADMISSIONS

Very important factors considered by the admissions committee include: character/personal qualities, class rank, essays, interview, recommendations, religious affiliation/commitment, secondary school record, and standardized test scores. *Important factors considered include:* extracurricular activities, minority status, and talent/ability. *Other factors considered include:* alumni/ae relation, geographical residence, state residency, volunteer work, and work experience. SAT I or ACT required. TOEFL required of all international applicants. High school diploma or GED is required. *High school units required/recommended:* 15 total required; 21 total recommended; 4 English required, 3 math required, 4 math recommended, 3 science required, 4 science recommended, 3 science lab required, 4 science lab recommended, 2 foreign language recommended, 2 social studies required, 3 social studies recommended.

The Inside Word

Tough admissions standards require dexterity from applicants to gain access to a Taylor-made education. Its Christian framework nurtures every denomination and academic interest, but not every social type. The Upland campus may be a downer if mind-altering substances are your idea of a good time.

FINANCIAL AID

Students should submit: FAFSA and institution's own financial aid form. Regular filing deadline is March 1. The Princeton Review suggests that all financial aid forms be submitted as soon as possible after January 1. *Need-based scholarships/grants offered:* Pell, SEOG, state scholarships/grants, private scholarships, and the school's own gift aid. *Loan aid offered:* FFEL Subsidized Stafford, FFEL Unsubsidized Stafford, FFEL PLUS, Federal Perkins, and college/university loans from institutional funds. Federal Work-Study Program available. Institutional employment available. Applicants will be notified of awards on a rolling basis beginning on or about March 1. Off-campus job opportunities are poor.

For even more information on this school, turn to page 390 of the "Stats" section.

TRUMAN STATE UNIVERSITY

MCCLAIN HALL 205, 100 EAST NORMAL, KIRKSVILLE, MO 63501 • ADMISSIONS: 660-785-4114
FAX: 660-785-7456 • FINANCIAL AID: 660-785-4130 • E-MAIL: ADMISSIONS@TRUMAN.EDU
WEBSITE: WWW.TRUMAN.EDU

Ratings
Quality of Life: 87   **Academic:** 86   **Admissions:** 82   **Financial Aid:** 86

Academics

Truman State University, a "highly selective school that strives to provide a quality education at an affordable price," offers "students willing to be pushed academically" a demanding but worthwhile undergraduate experience. "Truman is known for its rigorous classes and is not for the faint at heart," cautions one undergrad. Others temper their warnings, reporting that "the academics can be challenging, but not overwhelming. There are some tough classes, but those only serve to teach me more." Students agree that a Truman degree is worth the hard work because "the school has a great reputation. Job recruiters know that Truman graduates are high quality." Excellent professors soften the impact of the heavy workload; "the teachers are incredibly student-oriented and they are always available for assistance," explains one undergrad. Observes another, "I think people who are willing to move to Kirksville to teach are here . . . because they like what they do." The administration makes every effort to keep class sizes small, a fact students appreciate. "The size of Truman is really one of its greatest strengths. Truman provides a very 'at home' kind of feeling," notes one student. "The classes are small and you get to know the people in your major throughout your years, so there is always great networking after college," adds another.

> **SURVEY SAYS . . .**
> *Campus easy to get around*
> *Campus is beautiful*
> *Lots of beer drinking*
> *Campus feels safe*
> *Athletic facilities are great*
> *Great library*
> *Great computer facilities*
> *Frats and sororities dominate social scene*
> *Ethnic diversity lacking on campus*

Life

The workload is heavy at Truman State, so "people at this school tend to study hard during the week and leave the weekends for partying." The weekend party scene is fairly active: "Weekend nights are usually spent at house parties or the bars, which tend to be popular hangouts for local students," one student reports, even though "alcohol rules are extremely strict. There is a bit of tension between the community and campus in the area of parties and enforcement of alcohol laws." Many here remain happily outside the party scene, telling us that they remain busy by "hiking or boating at Thousand Hills State Park; seeing a play, movie, musical, or performance on campus; participating in discussion groups; watching movies with friends; and enjoying any number of other activities." Others note that "many students join organizations to meet others with like interests." The Student Activities Board "is always bringing movies, comedians, and music acts to campus for free or a small fee." The Greek community is also active here: "Greeks lead almost every major organization on campus," writes one undergrad. All of these options help make up for the fact that hometown Kirksville "is the smallest town ever. There is not a lot to do in town on a Friday or Saturday night." Some see an upside to Kirksville's size and remote location: "Even though Kirksville is small, it is very quaint and the people are very friendly. It really grows on you," writes one student.

Student Body

If you want to envision the Truman State student body, you should "think midwestern. Think conservative living. Think very smart. Truman is not a place to come if any of these things freak you out." Truman "does not have a lot of diversity." In fact, most here agree that "Truman needs to work on recruiting a more diverse student body. There's a big need to avoid just enrolling white, straight midwesterners." Students brag, "Being a highly selective university, Truman draws some of the best and brightest in the area," but also see a downside: "Unfortunately, the typical student is pretty dorky. Many of our students care so much about academics that they care so very little about their appearance." A substantial number of Truman undergrads are "religious; we have a large Catholic population from the St. Louis area." Most "have pretty conservative views; however, they are also incredibly down-to-earth and friendly." The school has a "high female-to-male ratio."

ADMISSIONS

Very important factors considered by the admissions committee include: class rank, secondary school record, standardized test scores. *Important factors considered include:* essays, extracurricular activities. *Other factors considered include:* alumni/ae relation, character/personal qualities, geographical residence, interview, minority status, recommendations, state residency, talent/ability, volunteer work, work experience. SAT I or ACT required; ACT preferred. TOEFL required of all international applicants. High school diploma or GED is required. *High school units required/recommended:* 16 total required; 17 total recommended; 4 English required, 3 math required, 4 math recommended, 3 science required, 2 foreign language required, 3 social studies required.

The Inside Word

Truman is among the next-in-line among public universities joining the ranks of the highly selective. It's tough to get admitted here, even though application totals declined somewhat last year. Serious students with conservative attitudes make the best match.

FINANCIAL AID

Students should submit: FAFSA, institution's own financial aid form. The Princeton Review suggests that all financial aid forms be submitted as soon as possible after January 1. *Need-based scholarships/grants offered:* Pell, SEOG, state scholarships/grants, private scholarships, the school's own gift aid. *Loan aid offered:* FFEL Subsidized Stafford, FFEL Unsubsidized Stafford, FFEL PLUS, Federal Perkins, Federal Nursing, state loans, college/university loans from institutional funds. Federal Work-Study Program available. Institutional employment available. Applicants will be notified of awards on a rolling basis beginning on or about April 15. Off-campus job opportunities are good.

FROM THE ADMISSIONS OFFICE

"Truman's talented student body enjoys small classes where undergraduate research and personal interaction with professors are the norm. Truman's commitment to providing an exemplary liberal arts and sciences education with nearly 200 student organizations and outstanding internship and study abroad opportunities allows students to compete in top graduate schools and the job market."

For even more information on this school, turn to page 390 of the "Stats" section.

UNIVERSITY OF AKRON

381 BUTCHEL COMMON, AKRON, OH 44325-2001 • ADMISSIONS: 330-972-7100 • FAX: 330-972-7022
EMAIL: ADMISSIONS@UAKRON.EDU • WEBSITE: WWW.UAKRON.EDU

Ratings
Quality of Life: 78   Academic: 73   Admissions: 60   Financial Aid: 73

Academics

Students at the University of Akron praise their school for its excellent psychology program, solid offerings in international business study, and "a diversity of students, a variety of majors,

> **SURVEY SAYS . . .**
> *Classes are small*
> *Very little beer drinking*
> *Lousy food on campus*

smaller class sizes, interested professors, and many opportunities for learning." Undergrads here tell us that "for a school of over 20,000 students, Akron U runs rather smoothly. You do get the typical run-around, but most people I've dealt with are very pleasant and willing to help students out." On-line registration helps students navigate what is typically one of the worst experiences at a large university; in all administrative areas, students are satisfied that "the administration is as good as can be expected from a state school." The faculty receives mixed grades, with students telling us that "I have had some really great teachers! I have also had some really bad teachers. Many professors are very intelligent and know their subject; the problem is that they cannot make that jump to teaching ability." Students in the Honors College find the administration both more accessible and more accommodating, writing that "Honors College personnel are extremely helpful in both academic and career counseling."

Life

Life on the Akron campus is quiet, most students agree, largely because so many students commute. Even so, students tell us that "there are varied activities at school. We have the E.J. Thomas Performing Arts Hall where plays are performed, entertainment is booked for the season, and the Akron Symphony performs regularly." Also, "the campus movie theatre plays good movies at reasonable rates. The campus also has a movie channel that plays current movies (ones out on video)." The party scene, according to most, is dull and slow. "It's not a party school, although there are some partiers," reports one commuter. Adds a disgruntled resident, "School life sucks. The police and the administration have killed any type of party environment at our school. We understand the need for moderation, but we also need to be able to have fun without always checking our backs." Fortunately, "there a numerous activities available in the city of Akron: private parties, movie theatres, and many restaurants." Notes one Akron booster, "Students go to any of a number of other dance clubs in the area." Others add that "With Cleveland less than half an hour away, students often travel to places like the Flats, Tower City, and sporting events." Many warn that ongoing construction is a nuisance, leaving the campus noisy, ugly, and in dire need of more parking spaces. They strongly recommend a visit to campus before making a final decision to attend.

Students

Akron students, many here agree, "are extremely friendly. It is very hard to take a course and not make a friend in the class during the semester." Undergrads "are very down to earth and unpretentious. People are generally friendly and accepting, although the atmosphere can be somewhat anonymous because of the school size." The student body is "very diverse, with lots of urban attitude. Segregation is a definite. In fact, certain floors and dorms are segregated—not legally or even stated, but all the black people lived in townhouses on one side, and white people lived on the other side." There is also a large nontraditional population, but because nontraditionals, like other commuters, rarely spend spare time on campus, they are not well integrated into the student community.

ADMISSIONS

Very important factors considered by the admissions committee include: secondary school record and standardized test scores. *Important factors considered include:* class rank. SAT I or ACT required. TOEFL required of all international applicants. High school diploma is required and GED is accepted. *High school units required/recommended:* 15 total are recommended; 4 English recommended, 3 math recommended, 3 science recommended, 2 foreign language recommended, 3 social studies recommended.

The Inside Word

Manageable admissions standards at Akron lure applicants from around the nation looking for a big-school experience. We recommend that prospective Zips visit the campus before applying.

FINANCIAL AID

Students should submit: FAFSA and institution's own financial aid form. Regular filing deadline is No deadline. The Princeton Review suggests that all financial aid forms be submitted as soon as possible after January 1. *Need-based scholarships/grants offered:* Pell, and state scholarships/grants. *Loan aid offered:* FFEL Subsidized Stafford, FFEL Unsubsidized Stafford, FFEL PLUS, Federal Perkins, Federal Nursing, and college/university loans from institutional funds. Federal Work-Study Program available. Institution employment available. Applicants will be notified of awards on a rolling basis beginning on or about April 15. Off-campus job opportunities are excellent.

For even more information on this school, turn to page 391 of the "Stats" section.

UNIVERSITY OF CHICAGO

1116 EAST 59TH STREET, CHICAGO, IL 60637 • ADMISSIONS: 773-702-8650 • FAX: 773-702-4199
FINANCIAL AID: 773-702-8666 • WEBSITE: WWW.UCHICAGO.EDU

Ratings
Quality of Life: 73   **Academic:** 94   **Admissions:** 96   **Financial Aid:** 85

Academics

Rigor, reputation, and a world-renowned faculty. The "Three Rs (and a lower case w)"—as well as a common core curriculum—are the reasons why many students choose the University of Chicago, despite Hyde Park's bone-chilling winters, strangely aggressive squirrel population, and what some might see as the school's "elitist, pretentious" attitude.

> **SURVEY SAYS . . .**
> *Great library*
> *Students love Chicago, IL*
> *Lab facilities need improving*
> *Students don't get along with local community*
> *Students aren't religious*
> *Athletic facilities need improving*
> *Student government is unpopular*
> *Campus difficult to get around*

Chances are, you've already heard that at U of C, "academic life is central and very rigorous." Rumor has it that the faculty has racked up more Nobel Prizes than any other university in the world. One junior agrees: "The professors are world-class and know how to teach. Where else can you see a nationally known physicist launch himself out of class to demonstrate non-relativistic mechanics?" Nor is it just in the sciences that U of C excels. Notes a sophomore, "We have a writing program that actually tries to teach us to write well." Of course, such brilliance requires a sacrifice. "When you come here," warns a first-year, "you become a nerd and the library is your second home." Of course, the school's quarter system and its notable lack of grade inflation can make for a rather pressurized environment at times—"like an axe is ready to drop any minute," writes one student. Still, most wouldn't have it any other way: "Most people, although they wouldn't admit it, like the work that they do." Concludes a second-year, "The University of Chicago is the greatest academic experience of my life. It has introduced me to a world of knowledge I never before knew existed. And the Chicago weather has made me strong."

Life

On the University of Chicago's reputation as being "the place where fun comes to die," many students choose to look at the bright side: "Learning happens here," quips a glass-is-half-full type. "People go to movies, to coffee, to restaurants, to Math Club." Others aren't so zen: "With all the other core requirements we have to fulfill there should be social skills in there, too. The computer science majors need remedial bathing." A more balanced look at the school is offered by the following senior: "The academic life is the be-all and end-all of U. Chicago. If you're not into your studies and don't enjoy the intellectual life, chances are that you will think U of C is boring. "Of course, the proximity to Chicago makes even the dullest Math Club meeting an opportunity to get out and explore the Windy City, which has "one of the most beautiful skylines in the world" and where "the theatre and restaurant scenes are particularly good." Although campus itself could stand a few more social options, the administration has been trying to upgrade its image in this area over the last few years, making a more concerted effort to address quality-of-life issues such extracurricular activities, student transportation, and safety. Pluses? "Housing is exceptional," according to one student. "Where else can you have a kitchen, living room, and dining room with an excellent view of Lake Michigan?" Then there's the "legendary" Scav Hunt, quintessentially U of C: "Each spring the school nearly shuts down as students rush to answer obscure trivia, party on rooftops on other campuses, and try—successfully—to cobble together nuclear reactors."

Student Body

"Prospectives be warned," writes a junior. "We are not the stereotypical, boring, academic, nonfun students we are rumored to be!" One student argues, "People here are smart, quick-witted, and aware of the world around them." Sure, "everyone is smart, which means some very interesting people and some who are annoying and egotistical," but look at what's inside, urges a sophomore. "Their sarcasm may make them seem cynical, but it merely masks idealism struggling to exist in a nonideal world. Students here are not friendly, they're honest. You may not feel as 'welcome' or as warm and fuzzy as at other schools, but here at least you know where you stand." But if you're still concerned about the nerd factor, take heart. Writes a junior, "I'm a nerd, and I like it a lot here. So I'm guessing that, if you're a nerd, you'll like it a lot here too."

ADMISSIONS

Very important factors considered by the admissions committee include: essays, recommendations, secondary school record. *Important factors considered include:* character/personal qualities, class rank, standardized test scores, talent/ability. *Other factors considered include:* alumni/ae relation, extracurricular activities, interview, minority status, volunteer work, work experience. SAT I or ACT required. TOEFL required of all international applicants. *High school units recommended:* 4 English recommended, 4 math recommended, 4 science recommended, 3 foreign language recommended, 2 social studies recommended, 2 history recommended.

The Inside Word

While excellent grades in tough courses and high test scores are the norm for applicants to the university, what really counts is what's on your mind. This is a cerebral institution, and thinkers stand out in the admissions process. Think about yourself, think about what you'd like to know more about, think about why you want to attend the university. Once you have some answers, begin writing your essays. And remember that universities that are this selective and recommend interviews should always be taken up on their recommendation.

FINANCIAL AID

The Princeton Review suggests that all financial aid forms be submitted as soon as possible after January 1. Federal Work-Study Program available. Institutional employment available. Off-campus job opportunities are excellent.

FROM THE ADMISSIONS OFFICE

"Chicago is a place where talented young intellectuals, writers, mathematicians, and scientists come to learn in a setting that rewards hard work and prizes initiative and creativity. It is also a place where collegiate life is urban, yet friendly and open, and free of empty traditionalism and snobbishness. Chicago is the right choice for students who know that they would thrive in an intimate classroom setting. Classes at Chicago are small, emphasizing discussion with faculty members whose research is always testing the limits of their chosen fields. Our students: They take chances; they delight us when they pursue a topic on their own for the fun of it; they display an articulate voice in papers and in discussion; they do not accept our word for everything but respect good argument; they are fanciful or solid at the right time. Most often they are students who choose the best courses available, who take a heavier load than necessary because they are curious and not worried about the consequences, who let curiosity and energy spill over into activities and sports, who are befriended by the best and toughest teachers, and who finish what they set out to do."

For even more information on this school, turn to page 391 of the "Stats" section.

UNIVERSITY OF DAYTON

300 COLLEGE PARK DRIVE, DAYTON, OH 45469-1300 • ADMISSIONS: 937-229-4411 • FAX: 937-229-4729
FINANCIAL AID: 937-229-4311 • E-MAIL: ADMISSION@UDAYTON.EDU • WEBSITE: WWW.UDAYTON.EDU

Ratings
Quality of Life: 87   **Academic:** 80   **Admissions:** 78   **Financial Aid:** 82

Academics

University of Dayton, a midsize university "rooted in the Marianist tradition and Catholic faith," provides its largely career-oriented students with an ethics-based liberal arts education. "My school is all about our 'Learn, Lead, Serve' motto that comes from our Marianist influence," brags one of the many undergraduates who praise a wide array of departments, including engineering, drama, education, and mar-

> **SURVEY SAYS . . .**
> *Lots of beer drinking*
> *Campus easy to get around*
> *(Almost) everyone smokes*
> *Great computer facilities*
> *Students are happy*
> *Campus is beautiful*
> *Hard liquor is popular*
> *Registration is a breeze*
> *(Almost) everyone plays intramural sports*
> *Great off-campus food*

keting. Students appreciate that their school is large enough to maintain a broad selection of courses, yet small enough to provide mentoring and one-on-one teaching. "Since the undergraduate population is only 7,000, it is easy to have access to professors," reports one student, "while also having plenty of opportunities, such as those that are found at bigger schools." Better still, "professors are some of the best around. Many do research at Wright Patterson Air Force Base, which is nearby." Students give the new administration mixed reviews. Some tell us that administrators "seem to be very upbeat about the future, and very interested in the students, what they have to offer seems very promising." Others, however, worry that "the school's administration is out to shed itself of the party school image, and they think that throwing money and technology at the school will solve their problems, instead of getting at the root problems." One of those root problems, writes one undergrad, is that "some teachers and classes are brought down by mediocre students." Even so, most here speak highly of the overall UD experience, satisfied with the sense that "the focus at Dayton is not only grades and learning, but also taking care of us as young adults in need of mentors."

Life

Some kids go to college to escape the ghetto; at UD, the opposite occurs. "The Ghetto, an infamous neighborhood composed of old houses, most of which the University owns, [is] filled with undergrad students, mostly juniors and seniors," explains one undergrad. While "drinking in the Ghetto is the main activity" of many Dayton students, "the experience of the Ghetto is about much more than wild parties . . . . You learn to live in a community built on respect for one another." Dayton has long had a reputation as a party school, and an especially democratic one at that; "there is no such thing as 'list' parties at Dayton; rather, everyone is accepted everywhere," reports one student. "I know this is hard to believe, but it's the truth, and one of the main reasons I love this place so much." However, "while UD is known as a party school, it really isn't that bad. There are plays, movies, and special activities that Student Government sets up for those who don't want to drink. For fun we go to the movies, out to eat, or to the mall. I think the University of Dayton provides plenty of interesting things to do on the weekend." UD also has "all kinds of intramural sports that students love to play; I think we had 5,000 students play softball last spring."

Student Body

The "J.Crew and Abercrombie" crowd at UD is "dominated by white Catholic kids from private schools," primarily from Ohio, Pennsylvania, and Indiana. Writes one student, "Most students are what my friends and I call the three C's: Caucasian, Catholic (nonpracticing, of course!), and conservative. I am atypical in that I am a liberal Democrat. For students like me, there are student organizations such as Students Allies (gay, lesbian, transgender, etc.), College Democrats, Amnesty International, and Pax Christi (pacifist group)." Many here noted "the university's commitment toward making UD more diverse, reflected in its scholarship and grant-giving this year." Several students told us that "diversity is improving but could still go a long way." Many undergrads are involved in "serving the community of Dayton and reaching out to those less fortunate."

ADMISSIONS

Very important factors considered by the admissions committee include: secondary school record. *Important factors considered include:* class rank, standardized test scores, talent/ability. *Other factors considered include:* alumni/ae relation, character/personal qualities, essays, extracurricular activities, interview, minority status, recommendations, volunteer work, work experience. SAT I or ACT required. TOEFL required of all international applicants. High school diploma or GED is required. *High school units required/recommended:* 16 total recommended; 4 English recommended, 3 math recommended, 2 science recommended, 3 social studies recommended, 4 elective recommended.

The Inside Word

While Dayton reviews all applicants individually in regard to their potential for success at the university, its high admit rate means that there's little for all but the weakest applicants to worry about concerning admission.

FINANCIAL AID

Students should submit: FAFSA. The Princeton Review suggests that all financial aid forms be submitted as soon as possible after January 1. *Need-based scholarships/grants offered:* Pell, SEOG, state scholarships/grants, private scholarships. *Loan aid offered:* FFEL Subsidized Stafford, FFEL Unsubsidized Stafford, FFEL PLUS, Federal Perkins, state loans, college/university loans from institutional funds, GATE Loans. Federal Work-Study Program available. Institutional employment available. Applicants will be notified of awards on a rolling basis beginning on or about February 20. Off-campus job opportunities are good.

FROM THE ADMISSIONS OFFICE

"The University of Dayton is respected as one of the nation's leading Catholic universities. We offer the resources and diversity of a comprehensive university and the attention and accessibility of a small college. All university-owned housing is fully wired for direct high-speed connection to the Internet as well as our 78-channel cable system. The technology-enhanced learning and student computer initiative ensures students use of the tools that will prepare them for a technology-dependent workplace. Our programs of study, impressive 110-acre campus, advanced research facilities, NCAA Division I intercollegiate athletics, and international alumni network are big-school advantages. Small class sizes, undergraduate emphasis, student-centered faculty and staff, residential campus life, and friendliness are all attractive small-school qualities. The University of Dayton is committed to student success. Our educational mission is to recognize the talents you bring as an individual and help you reach your potential."

For even more information on this school, turn to page 392 of the "Stats" section.

UNIVERSITY OF EVANSVILLE

1800 LINCOLN AVENUE, EVANSVILLE, IN 47722 • ADMISSIONS: 812-479-2468 • FAX: 812-474-4076
E-MAIL: ADMISSION@EVANSVILLE.EDU • WEBSITE: WWW.EVANSVILLE.EDU

Ratings
Quality of Life: 83   **Academic:** 76   **Admissions:** 70   **Financial Aid:** 78

Academics

At the University of Evansville, each student sings the praises of his or her own department as being the best, whether it's engineering, English, theatre, biology, physical therapy, chemistry, or another discipline; they are also thrilled about study abroad opportunities at Harlaxton College, the "British Campus of the University of Evansville." U of Evansville's profs,

> **SURVEY SAYS . . .**
> *Students are religious*
> *Students are happy*
> *Classes are small*
> *Profs teach upper levels*
> *Class discussions encouraged*
> *Student publications are popular*
> *School is well run*
> *Students get along with local community*

who "actually want to help you," are reportedly "extremely easy to reach." Writes one student, "The 'spiel' they give about the availability of professors and administration here is completely true. If you want to know your professors, you will; if you don't make the effort, you won't." This accessibility is due largely to UE's size; students appreciate its "somewhat above-average academics and very small college atmosphere," and assure that UE is "a very good school, if you are looking for something small in scope," although it's "not for those who seek the frills of a big university." A few feel that some of UE's professors "should have stayed in their professional field. They know their stuff; they just can't teach it." The administration, however, "is doing a good job running the school." Students would like to see an increase in "communication between students and administration," but have high hopes that the new president "with new ideas…will ultimately be our greatest strength. There are already many changes taking place."

Life

One UE student breaks it down for us: "Evansville is not a very college-friendly town, so much of the time people have to create their own fun. Oftentimes, especially for freshmen, this involves drinking on campus. The older students go out to the bars, but often the fraternity houses will have open or closed parties where you can always get beer, and usually some liquor." While some complain that "there doesn't seem to be a lot going on on campus ever!" students testify that "there really is plenty to do." "There is a free movie once a week, plenty of intramural sports going on, lectures, club activities, and Greek life activities, and the International Students' Club has a different cultural night every Wednesday," not to mention "dancing at clubs" or the fact that you can "go out for coffee, go bowling . . . and take road trips (that's the most fun)." UE students assure us that such fun does not necessitate alcohol intake on this campus: "If you want to stay in on a Friday night and rent a movie, you can. There is no pressure to do anything that you don't want to do." Some nondrinkers "come up with creative (okay, sometimes crazy) stuff to do, like making movie shorts or having snowball fights or even hitting the town to play Wal-Mart tag." Another student describes her own brand of creative fun: "I bought two inflatable pools, we put them on the floor of my friend's dorm room, turned up the heat, got into our bathing suits, turned up the music, and sang as loud as seven girls can possibly sing. Spur of the moment things like this are really what make college fun."

Students

"Overall, I'd say that our student population gets along very well," writes a content student; an undergrad from Massachusetts finds that "everyone out here is much nicer than on the East Coast." According to some, "For a small campus with mostly Caucasian students, there is a lot of diversity, both economically and socially." Others feel that "although the group of international students is great, it would be even better if it were bigger and more diverse," and that there is "a little too much uniformity among students. They all dress alike; they all say the same things; it's like living in blahville. Anyone who is too different better learn how to be their own friend." While one postulates that Greek status determines whether you will be "accepted campuswide," another reassures that "the campus has a very relaxed family-like atmosphere," creating "camaraderie among the students. Everyone holds the door open for each other."

ADMISSIONS

Very important factors considered by the admissions committee include: secondary school record and standardized test scores. *Important factors considered include:* extracurricular activities. *Other factors considered include:* character/personal qualities, class rank, essays, recommendations, talent/ability, volunteer work, and work experience. SAT I or ACT required. TOEFL required of all international applicants. High school diploma or GED is required. *High school units required/recommended:* 4 English required, 3 math required, 2 science required, 2 science lab required, 2 foreign language recommended, 2 history recommended, 2 elective recommended.

The Inside Word

Freshmen at UE are introduced to a "total college experience," where the bar gets raised higher academically than the admissions standards may have led them to expect. Students looking for an intimate atmosphere will thrive most at Evansville.

FINANCIAL AID

Students should submit: FAFSA. The Princeton Review suggests that all financial aid forms be submitted as soon as possible after January 1. *Need-based scholarships/grants offered:* Pell, SEOG, state scholarships/grants, private scholarships, and the school's own gift aid. *Loan aid offered:* FFEL Subsidized Stafford, FFEL Unsubsidized Stafford, FFEL PLUS, Federal Perkins, and Federal Nursing. Federal Work-Study Program available. Institutional employment available. Applicants will be notified of awards on a rolling basis beginning on or about March 15. Off-campus job opportunities are good.

For even more information on this school, turn to page 393 of the "Stats" section.

UNIVERSITY OF ILLINOIS—CHICAGO

Box 5220, Chicago, IL 60680 • Admissions: 312-996-4350 • Fax: 312-413-7628
E-mail: uicadmit@uic.edu • Website: www.uic.edu

Ratings

Quality of Life: 85   **Academic:** 80   **Admissions:** 76   **Financial Aid:** 79

Academics

Many UIC students share the opinion, "My professors so far have been very knowledgeable and my classes informative despite the mediocre academic reputation of my school." Faculty is considered approachable, considering that they are "not aggravated when you call at 10 in the

evening." Students experience different degrees of personal attention; while some report that "opportunities for independent research are easily accessible," others find it "difficult to meet with teachers outside of class." Overall, undergraduates speak better of liberal arts professors than those in the science departments, but a common umbrella statement contends that the school has a "surprising number of good teachers who actually care along with some really strong TAs." Advisors reportedly "do not remotely know how to advise a student," and often "you can get a heck of a runaround just to see an advisor." The administration is similarly criticized for viewing students as "pawns to be moved around and traded." However, the school is ultimately "affordable" and boasts "very strong medical departments," considering that "we have some of the best hospitals within a few blocks of the campus."

Life

The majority commuter population greatly defines UIC life. Because approximately 90 percent of undergraduates leave campus after class, several respondents report, "Many students have little in common with other students on campus." Many people call on the administration to make life "more hospitable for those who stay after hours." Though the area directly around the school is described as "really shady," students generally cherish their urban location. The campus is "extremely close to downtown" and has "great access to the El." One student notes, "We are not limited to a college town atmosphere. When people go out, we go to 'real' bars and clubs," which perhaps explains why "people love to go clubbing." Other students comment, "When you think of a college atmosphere, UIC is not what you have in mind." A large number of students hold part-time jobs, and the concrete "riot-proof school" does not conform to the idyllic-campus image. On the whole, UIC is "less of a place to socialize and more for a serious education."

Students

Though the majority of students are "from Chicago and its suburbs," the university is "one of the most diverse schools in the United States." One student writes, "I enjoy being a white minority. It has added greatly to my learning." Others agree, saying the diversity has "expanded my knowledge in ways that would not have happened in another university." Some students point out that the diversity is "only positive when people stop hanging out with their own groups and really try to get to know other" types of people, but others claim that all "students interact in different clubs and fraternities." Basically, "it's like going to school at the United Nations." Many students express the opinion that it is "very hard to hold friendships outside of the classroom due to the fact that so many students are commuters" and that there is "not much of a community." The UIC population tends to be competitive—"a lot of students want to be at the top of their class"—as well as "very outgoing and diligent."

ADMISSIONS

Very important factors considered by the admissions committee include: class rank, secondary school record, and standardized test scores. *Other factors considered include:* character/personal qualities, essays, minority status, recommendations, talent/ability, volunteer work, and work experience. SAT I or ACT required, ACT preferred. TOEFL required of all international applicants. High school diploma or GED is required. *High school units required/recommended:* 16 total required; 4 English required, 3 math required, 3 science required, 3 science lab required, 4 foreign language recommended, 2 social studies required, 1 history required, 3 elective required.

The Inside Word

UIC is a worthy choice for liberal arts or science degrees, though its students need some stamina to deal with the hassles of big-school bureaucracy. A place to embrace the full spectrum of our nation's diversity, UIC is a worldly vessel for your college years.

FINANCIAL AID

Students should submit: FAFSA. No deadline for regular filing. The Princeton Review suggests that all financial aid forms be submitted as soon as possible after January 1. *Need-based scholarships/grants offered:* Pell, SEOG, state scholarships/grants, private scholarships, the school's own gift aid, and Federal Nursing. *Loan aid offered:* Direct Subsidized Stafford, Direct Unsubsidized Stafford, Direct PLUS, Federal Perkins, Federal Nursing, and college/university loans from institutional funds. Federal Work-Study Program available. Institutional employment available. Applicants will be notified of awards on a rolling basis beginning on or about April 15. Off-campus job opportunities are excellent.

For even more information on this school, turn to page 393 of the "Stats" section.

University of Illinois—Urbana-Champaign

901 West Illinois Street, Urbana, IL 61801 • Admissions: 217-333-0302 • Fax: 217-333-9758
Financial Aid: 217-333-0100 • E-mail: admissions@oar.uiuc.edu • Website: www.uiuc.edu

Ratings

Quality of Life: 75   Academic: 82   Admissions: 85   Financial Aid: 80

Academics

Renowned research center University of Illinois—Urbana-Champaign offers students a multitude of options and opportunities, especially in its nationally acclaimed engineering and business programs. "The size is a huge benefit because of all of the resources available," students agree. Yet as at most big schools, quality of instruction varies widely. "Like everywhere, you have to take the bad with the good," explains one student. "I think that the good outweighs the bad for the most part here." Undergrads point out that "many TAs do the 'real' teaching while the professor just makes the exams," and while some feel that "most of TAs are not experienced and do not teach adequately," others feel just as strongly that "teaching assistants have a very unfair reputation. I have found that the best teachers are TAs. They are only a few years older than you and are still students, and therefore empathetic. They also understand the material very well." Many report that "the high number of TAs and even profs who don't have the best grasp of English, however brilliant they may be, can make things unnecessarily difficult." Nearly all would warn that "the school is large. If you don't have the presence of mind to get the stuff you [need to] get done taken care of, no one else will. I would never expect extra attention from the faculty here." In terms of administrative duties, expect "huge spools of red tape. I put in a petition in October, and I still haven't heard back. It's now the end of February."

> **SURVEY SAYS . . .**
> *Frats and sororities dominate social scene*
> *Everyone loves the Fighting Illini*
> *Lots of beer drinking*
> *Ethnic diversity on campus*
> *Student publications are popular*
> *Students are cliquish*
> *Students don't like Urbana, IL*
> *Students are not very happy*
> *Lousy food on campus, Very little drug use*

Life

Many Illini tell us that they "did not know it before coming here, but the U of I is a huge party school." The campus is "very Greek; it seems like everyone is in a fraternity or sorority." Students mostly like to party at the school's numerous bars, each of which allows students 19 and over to enter (although theoretically the drinking age is 21). Writes one student, "There's not much to do in the cornfields of Champaign-Urbana [sic], but the 20-plus bars on campus really take care of that problem. Most people go out on weekends, to the bars, house/apartment parties, and after-hours parties at fraternities. During the week, many people go out as well. The weekend definitely starts on Thursday, though." Agrees another undergrad, "Nightlife for most consists of attending the campus bars. Period." Nonpartiers, including many in the school's sizeable religious contingent, "often congregate in their dorm rooms with a movie, a bunch of people from their floor, and pizza from Papa John's, a traditional campus establishment. There are a million organizations to be involved in," but according to one student, "At least a third of them are religiously affiliated, though, so unless you plan on joining every church on campus, that narrows it down a bit." Sports "seem to play a bigger role of importance than even academics, unfortunately. I guess it's pretty typical of a Big 10 university."

Student Body

"It seems like every kind of group you can imagine is represented" at U of I. "There are the Greeks, there are the athletes—either club, intramural, or Division I athletes who hang out with each other 24/7—there are the conservatives, the nerds, the ethnic groups—Hispanic, Black, Indian, Asian, European, etc.—the goths, the hippies, and on and on the list goes." Many agree that "there is not much meshing of the different ethnic and social groups" on campus. Students are united on game day, though; writes one undergrad, "For a campus of over 30,000 students, it's a pretty tight bunch. Everyone is friendly. Plus, there's a lot of school spirit. During the football season everyone is wearing orange and blue. There's definitely a sense of pride in being part of the University of Illinois."

ADMISSIONS

Very important factors considered by the admissions committee include: class rank, secondary school record, standardized test scores. *Important factors considered include:* essays, minority status, talent/ability. *Other factors considered include:* character/personal qualities, extracurricular activities, geographical residence, recommendations, state residency, volunteer work, work experience. SAT I or ACT required. TOEFL required of all international applicants. High school diploma or GED is required. *High school units required/recommended:* 4 English required, 3 math required, 2 science required, 2 science lab required, 2 foreign language required, 2 social studies required, 2 elective required.

The Inside Word

Few candidates are deceived by Illinois' relatively high acceptance rate; the university has a well-deserved reputation for expecting applicants to be strong students, and those who aren't usually don't bother to apply. Despite a jumbo applicant pool, the admissions office reports that every candidate is individually reviewed, which deserves mention as rare in universities of this size.

FINANCIAL AID

Students should submit: FAFSA. Regular filing deadline is March 15. The Princeton Review suggests that all financial aid forms be submitted as soon as possible after January 1. *Need-based scholarships/grants offered:* Pell, SEOG, state scholarships/grants, private scholarships, the school's own gift aid. *Loan aid offered:* Direct Subsidized Stafford, Direct Unsubsidized Stafford, Direct PLUS, Federal Perkins, college/university loans from institutional funds. Federal Work-Study Program available. Institutional employment available. Applicants will be notified of awards on or about April 1. Off-campus job opportunities are excellent.

FROM THE ADMISSIONS OFFICE

"The campus has been aptly described as a collection of neighborhoods constituting a diverse and vibrant city. The neighborhoods are of many types: students and faculty within a department; people sharing a room or house; the members of a professional organization, a service club, or an intramural team; or simply people who, starting out as strangers sharing a class or a study lounge or a fondness for a weekly film series, have become friends. And the city of this description is the university itself—a rich cosmopolitan environment constructed by students and faculty to meet their educational and personal goals. The quality of intellectual life parallels that of other great universities, and many faculty and students who have their choice of top institutions select Illinois over its peers. While such choices are based often on the quality of individual programs of study, another crucial factor is the 'tone' of the campus life that is linked with the virtues of midwestern culture. There is an informality and a near-absence of pretension which, coupled with a tradition of commitment to excellence, creates an atmosphere that is unique among the finest institutions."

For even more information on this school, turn to page 394 of the "Stats" section.

UNIVERSITY OF INDIANAPOLIS

1400 EAST HANNA AVENUE, INDIANAPOLIS, IN 46227-3697 • ADMISSIONS: 317-788-3216
FAX: 317-788-3300 • E-MAIL: ADMISSIONS@UINDY.EDU • WEBSITE: ADMISSIONS.UINDY.EDU

Ratings
Quality of Life: 79   Academic: 75   Admissions: 67   Financial Aid: 78

Academics

"I think the best thing about my school is the small class size," writes a typical student at the University of Indianapolis. "None of my classes had over 40 students, and my smallest class was

> **SURVEY SAYS . . .**
> *Classes are small, Theater is unpopular*
> *Students get along with local community*
> *Profs teach upper levels, School is well run*

around 15. This type of learning atmosphere is good...because you have a chance to talk to the instructor about your grades or ask questions." The largely pre-professional student body here—popular majors include education, business, and physical therapy—also enjoy the benefits of "strong programs in music, theater, and athletics." And undergrads are comfortable with the work level required at their school. Writes one, "Academically, I have been healthily challenged, but not to the point of complete frustration." Agrees another, "The college has pushed me to do my best and helped me understand what I can expect of myself and what I can accomplish." Students here believe that "because it is a small school, the professors are here to teach. Most of them form relationships with the students, learning from them as much as they try to teach the students themselves." Administrators are similarly accessible; as one student explains, "The administration includes student and faculty input whenever and as much as possible through discussions, class representatives, and surveys." Notes one student, "Many students know the president personally, and most of us just call him Jerry."

Life

Campus life is quiet at the University of Indianapolis. "There is very little to do here," complains one undergrad. "I go downtown and go shopping for fun. Because there are hardly ever parties or campus-organized events, students must find other things to do, and most go home." Adds another, "There isn't a Greek society, so therefore there isn't that much partying. You can't party in the dorms because of the drug/alcohol/noise policies." Some students resent U of I's strict regulations: grouses one, "At other schools I know of they have dance clubs on campus and they have almost nonexistent drinking rules. It is sometimes like I'm in high school again when we have to sneak around to go to parties and stuff." Because of campus rules, "parties—and there are quite a few of them!—take place at people's houses not too far from campus. Many people here like to go to those parties because it is a time for them to drink and to smoke without getting in trouble here on campus." Dormitory life lends itself to more subdued and wholesome endeavors; on a typical night a dorm resident might "go to the $1 movies, do some campus bowling, enjoy a nice place for dinner, or order a discounted pizza and rent a movie." Dorms also sponsor "ski trips, laser tag, that sort of thing." Students rarely take advantage of hometown Indianapolis; explains one, "This school is in a big city but is on the wrong side of town. There is nothing exciting around this area." Another told us that "There is not much to do in Indy unless you are 21."

Students

The "respectful, considerate, and for the most part very laid back" students of U of I are "friendly and helpful. When you walk around on campus there are always people in groups talking and it makes you feel comfortable." Students report that "U of I is a very diverse school. We take pride in the fact that we have students from so many ethnic groups on campus." Diversity manifests itself here primarily in the African American population as well as a sizeable international contingent. "Despite the size of the school, international students can be seen all around. There are people here from many different backgrounds and everyone has the chance [of] bettering themselves in the face of diversity," notes one undergrad. Some students find their classmates a tad too provincial: reports one undergrad, "'Study abroad?' someone asked me when they heard my intention. 'I wouldn't ever want to leave Indiana!'"

ADMISSIONS

Very important factors considered by the admissions committee include: secondary school record. *Important factors considered include:* class rank and standardized test scores. *Other factors considered include:* extracurricular activities, interview, and recommendations. SAT I or ACT required. TOEFL required of all international applicants. High school diploma or GED is required. *High school units required/recommended:* 15 total recommended; 4 English recommended, 3 math recommended, 3 science recommended, 2 science lab recommended, 2 foreign language recommended, 3 social studies recommended.

The Inside Word

UI is a good choice for students who are looking for a school with committed student-to-professor relationships. The absence of a Greek system and the obligation for responsible social conduct, however, can breed feelings of resentment as students cloak their behavior from the administrative radar.

FINANCIAL AID

Students should submit: FAFSA and institution's own financial aid form. No deadline for regular filing. The Princeton Review suggests that all financial aid forms be submitted as soon as possible after January 1. *Need-based scholarships/grants offered:* Pell, SEOG, state scholarships/grants, private scholarships, and the school's own gift aid. *Loan aid offered:* FFEL Subsidized Stafford, FFEL Unsubsidized Stafford, FFEL PLUS, and Federal Perkins. Federal Work-Study Program available. Institutional employment available. Applicants will be notified of awards on a rolling basis beginning on or about March 1. Off-campus job opportunities are excellent.

FROM THE ADMISSIONS OFFICE

"The University of Indianapolis is a private residential institution of higher learning. Established in 1902 and now an integral part of the educational and cultural life of Indianapolis, the university maintains a moderate size and a diverse student body, and it provides a comprehensive set of general, pre-professional, and professional programs grounded in the liberal arts.

"Students indicate that they choose the university because of its challenging yet supportive atmosphere and relatively small size, combined with the advantages of its location in the southern suburbs of a thriving state capital. As a result, there is a great sense of community and pride on the campus. The university helps students to determine and achieve their individual academic goals. The University of Indianapolis has experienced much growth and has instituted many enhancements recently, having followed the redesign and landscaping of campus with a new health science building, new facilities for the communications department, a major renovation to the student center, and a fifth residence hall.

"About 2,000 Day Division students are enrolled, and the university includes students from 60 countries and 20 states. Approximately 75 percent of the students live in on-campus housing. The warmth and sensitivity of the faculty and staff members and students alike enable those who are a part of the campus to feel a strong sense of community."

For even more information on this school, turn to page 394 of the "Stats" section.

UNIVERSITY OF IOWA

107 CALVIN HALL, IOWA CITY, IA 52242 • ADMISSIONS: 319-335-3847 • FAX: 319-333-1535
FINANCIAL AID: 319-335-1450 • E-MAIL: ADMISSIONS@UIOWA.EDU • WEBSITE: WWW.UIOWA.EDU

Ratings
Quality of Life: 85   **Academic:** 77   **Admissions:** 80   **Financial Aid:** 82

Academics

Applicants to a big state school like Iowa sometimes fear "drowning in general education classes," but many current Hawkeyes point out, "You can make it personal" with some effort, since "not very many professors have a line of students waiting to hang out at office hours, even though they'd like [them] to." Professors "have a passion for the material," and most complement that with "the passion to teach the material." As

> **SURVEY SAYS . . .**
> *Lots of beer drinking*
> *Hard liquor is popular*
> *(Almost) everyone smokes*
> *Everyone loves the Hawkeyes*
> *Great computer facilities*
> *Students love Iowa City, IA*
> *Great off-campus food*
> *Student newspaper is popular*
> *Campus is beautiful*
> *Students are happy*

at most large state universities, certain undergraduates feel their instructors stay "so buried in their research that they probably wouldn't come to class if a waiting student hadn't called them on their cell." Other students point out that "professors have a presence, but the school does rely on teaching assistants." On the whole, however, "most professors . . . attempt to present lectures in an interesting forum." Respondents single out the writing department as "highly regarded," and tout the honors program as "the ticket to ride for anyone with academic concern." Administrators receive high marks from students, who say they are "readily accessible and extremely supportive—so much so that it borders on mentoring and parental advocacy." Some students, however, see the "very parental" administration as their mortal foe, claiming that they "work with the city council on anti-student policies." Complaints also pop up surrounding the ongoing tuition hikes. In general, however, the campus "seems to run very smoothly," and the people in charge appear "attuned to students' opinions." Overall, the university offers students "a diverse and liberal learning environment" where everyone can "prepare [a] future in an atmosphere of fun and opportunity."

Life

Social life revolves around three things at Iowa: the downtown bars, Hawkeye football, and Christian groups. The "beautiful town" of Iowa City "has a lot to offer," mainly in the form of bars, "packed to capacity every night of the week." The resulting scene is "quite crazy, and most everyone seems to enjoy it." The campus' location right in the thick of things allows the "weekend to start on Tuesday and end on Sunday" even though the on-campus sororities and fraternities are dry. Some people resist the pull and take advantage of the "good restaurants and coffee shops on or near campus." Other alcohol-free options include "improv theater and musical events"; it seems "there's always some sort of live performance going on here." Hawkeye pride abounds—"It's all about sports"—and students congregate for rowdy tailgating sessions on game days during football season. Aside from drinking and cheering, many in the student body keep "involved in campus Christian groups, like, 24-7." Put it all together, and you've got a school that "offers a true big-time college experience in a very unique and exciting town."

Student Body

In the large, somewhat diverse milieu of the University of Iowa, students say, "You can be whoever you want to be and still have a big group of friends." Though many call it "your average white-dominated midwestern university," numerous students claim their school is "surprisingly open-minded, considering the location." One student expands, "The school's reputation of diversity is helped tremendously by the graduate student population." Also, the diversity lies in "social backgrounds rather than racial backgrounds." People may come from the Iowa sticks or the urban spread of Chicago, but the school still "lacks a good social atmosphere for minorities." Several surveys point out the university's intent to attract more students of color. On-campus groups do provide a framework for discussing "various ethnicities, sexual orientations, religious backgrounds, etc." Even if most people are "Christian, middle-class Dave Matthews fans who love the bars," they also share the common traits of "friendliness, enthusiasm, and openness."

ADMISSIONS

Very important factors considered by the admissions committee include: class rank, secondary school record, standardized test scores. *Other factors considered include:* alumni/ae relation, minority status, state residency, talent/ability. SAT I or ACT required. TOEFL required of all international applicants. High school diploma or GED is required. *High school units required/recommended:* 15 total required; 4 English required, 3 math required, 3 science required, 2 foreign language required, 4 foreign language recommended, 3 social studies required.

The Inside Word

Iowa's admissions process is none too personal, but on the other hand, candidates know exactly what is necessary to get admitted. The majority of applicants are fairly good students, most get in, and a lot choose to attend. That helps make Iowa the solid academic community it is.

FINANCIAL AID

Students should submit: FAFSA, institution's own financial aid form. No deadline for regular filing. The Princeton Review suggests that all financial aid forms be submitted as soon as possible after January 1. *Need-based scholarships/grants offered:* Pell, SEOG, state scholarships/grants, private scholarships, the school's own gift aid, Federal Nursing. *Loan aid offered:* Direct Subsidized Stafford, Direct Unsubsidized Stafford, Direct PLUS, Federal Perkins, Federal Nursing, college/university loans from institutional funds. Federal Work-Study Program available. Institutional employment available. Applicants will be notified of awards on a rolling basis beginning on or about March 1. Off-campus job opportunities are excellent.

FROM THE ADMISSIONS OFFICE

"The University of Iowa has strong programs in the creative arts, being the home of the first Writers Workshop and now housing the world-renowned International Writing Program. It also has strong programs in communication studies, journalism, political science, English, and psychology, and was the birthplace of the discipline of speech pathology and audiology. It offers excellent programs in the basic health sciences and health care programs, led by the top-ranked College of Medicine and the closely associated University Hospitals and Clinics."

For even more information on this school, turn to page 395 of the "Stats" section.

UNIVERSITY OF KANSAS

Office of Admissions and Scholarships, 1502 Iowa Street, Lawrence, KS 66045
Admissions: 785-864-3911 • Fax: 785-864-5017 • Financial Aid: 785-864-4700 • E-mail: adm@ku.edu
Website: www.ku.edu

Ratings

Quality of Life: 83   **Academic:** 75   **Admissions:** 81   **Financial Aid:** 81

Academics

The University of Kansas produces students satisfied with their education. Professors are always accessible. According to a biology major, "All professors have office hours and most offer workshops making them accessible to KU students." Professors are "usually at the top of their field," writes one music major. The key to being successful at KU, advises a sophomore, is to "take advantage of the resources available (i.e. TAs, libraries, instructors)." The professors make an excellent impression on first-year students; as one first-year architecture student gushes, "Every teacher I have had or met I want to chill with on the weekends, but sometimes it just doesn't work out." Dangit. While students like their professors, they are less enamored of the administration. Reports are mixed concerning the undergrad academic experience, as one student will gush, "Academically, the University of Kansas exceeded my expectations," while another will declare, "The University of Kansas will always be a good school for average kids from large midwestern cities."

> **SURVEY SAYS . . .**
> *Everyone loves the Jayhawks*
> *Students love Lawrence, KS*
> *Frats and sororities dominate social scene*
> *Great off-campus food*
> *Hard liquor is popular*
> *Large classes*
> *Registration is a pain*
> *Student publications are popular*
> *Theater is unpopular*
> *Lab facilities are great*

Life

"Lawrence is a rather alternative, obscure community, typical of a college town. The college students are the number one priority here." Students note that both the campus and the town are beautiful. A senior journalism major happily comments that "the town and university [are] very liberal and open-minded. Anyone is willing to hear you speak your mind as long as you can back it up." Students appreciate the different opportunities that life in Lawrence provides. "If you're going to stay in and do work, that's cool. If you're going to go to the bars, that's cool. If you're going to stay in and party, or go to a house party, everything is cool and fun to do." A sophomore sociology major adds that it isn't difficult to find a party in certain off-campus neighborhoods, as "you can walk down the party streets and smell the alcohol." Some believe that the city can be "a little boring" if one doesn't party. The university's basketball team is a perennial national powerhouse, and students wish that the football team would be as successful.

Student Body

As would be expected of a large, state university in middle America, students at the University of Kansas are "typical Midwest: middle-class, friendly, laid-back, and white." Most students agree that the university needs more diversity, "both ethnically and from rural areas." There is little mixing between social groups. As one junior history major puts it, "Frat boys hang out with frat boys. Nader lovers hang out with earth-friendly types. Goths chill with goths. It's segregated but united by alcohol." Still, students agree that most of their class-mates are "friendly and supportive." One first-year student testifies that his life has been altered by his classmates. "The people here are incredible. I was an edgy person when I came here, but everyone's so courteous that it changes you." A sophomore sums up life at the University of Kansas: "Everyone here is friendly. You can literally just say hi to someone on campus and they will be more than delighted to respond [in a] friendly [manner]."

ADMISSIONS

Very important factors considered by the admissions committee include: class rank, secondary school record, standardized test scores. *Important factors considered include:* geographical residence, state residency. SAT I or ACT required. High school diploma or GED is required. *High school units required/recommended:* 14 total required; 17 total recommended; 4 English required, 3 math required, 4 math recommended, 3 science required (1 year of science must be chemistry or physics), 2 foreign language recommended, 3 social studies required, 1 computer technology required.

The Inside Word

A no-sweat approach to admissions. So who gets denied? Weak out-of-state candidates, who are apparently in large supply in the Kansas applicant pool. But in-state students will have to face the music with new admissions standards starting in 2001.

FINANCIAL AID

Students should submit: FAFSA. Regular filing deadline is March 1. The Princeton Review suggests that all financial aid forms be submitted as soon as possible after January 1. *Need-based scholarships/grants offered:* Pell, SEOG, state scholarships/grants, private scholarships, the school's own gift aid. *Loan aid offered:* Direct Subsidized Stafford, Direct Unsubsidized Stafford, Direct PLUS, Federal Perkins, college/university loans from institutional funds. Federal Work-Study Program available. Institutional employment available. Applicants will be notified of awards on a rolling basis beginning on or about April 1. Off-campus job opportunities are excellent.

FROM THE ADMISSIONS OFFICE

"The University of Kansas has a long and distinguished tradition for academic excellence. Outstanding students from Kansas and across the nation are attracted to KU because of its strong academic reputation, beautiful campus, affordable cost of education, and contagious school spirit. KU provides students extraordinary opportunities in honors programs, research, internships, and study abroad. The university is located in Lawrence (40 minutes from Kansas City), a community of 80,000 regarded as one of the nation's best small cities for its arts scene, live music, and historic downtown."

For even more information on this school, turn to page 396 of the "Stats" section.

UNIVERSITY OF MICHIGAN—ANN ARBOR

1220 STUDENT ACTIVITIES BUILDING, ANN ARBOR, MI 48109-1316 • ADMISSIONS: 734-764-7433
FAX: 734-936-0740 • FINANCIAL AID: 734-763-6600 • ADMISS. WEBSITE: WWW.ADMISSIONS.UMICH.EDU
FINANCIAL AID WEBSITE: WWW.FINAID.UMICH.EDU

Ratings

Quality of Life: 80	**Academic:** 89	**Admissions:** 91	**Financial Aid:** 87

Academics

For many enrolled at the University of Michigan, attending the school has been a lifelong dream: "I've always wanted to come here—since I was a kid," writes one junior. With majors ranging from violin performance and art to aerospace engineering and molecular biology (and everything in between)—in addition to one of the best faculties in the world—it's no wonder most University of Michigan undergrads are confident in their school's

> **SURVEY SAYS . . .**
> *Everyone loves the Wolverines*
> *Lots of beer drinking*
> *Great library*
> *Great computer facilities*
> *Students love Ann Arbor, MI*
> *Hard liquor is popular*
> *Student newspaper is popular*
> *Great off-campus food*
> *Lab facilities are great*
> *(Almost) everyone plays intramural sports*

solid reputation of "quality and prestige." The school's a national powerhouse in nearly every aspect: academics (both undergrad and graduate), research, athletics, and student activism, not to mention its thriving social scene and excellent location in Ann Arbor, a town that's "not too big, but has a lot going on." On top of all this, it's a relative bargain for in-state students and still cheaper than comparable private institutions for out-of-staters. Notes another senior, "The academics at U of M are second to none—including the Ivy League." But make sure you like 'em big, because Michigan is simply that. With about 25,000 undergrads packing the lecture halls, you'll probably share this senior's desire for "more personal attention and less GSIs [graduate student instructors]." While you're first starting out you might find, like this first year did, that at Michigan it's "everyone for themselves. . . . you must seek to find your own place."

Life

Diversity, student activism, and a college town with "piles to do"—one has the sense that things are all good in Ann Arbor. A junior describes the situation this way: "The amount and quality of extracurricular activities here are phenomenal. It almost makes me want to take one class per term so I can use all my time for these activities." And that's just at the university! A classic, just-big-enough "college town," Ann Arbor, too, is known for its "great downtown restaurants and bars, and very diverse culture." U of M is also a "sports heaven" and athletics can play a big part in undergraduate life if students are so inclined. "House parties on the weekends" are also an outlet, though one senior complains that "a lot of people drink and use alcohol as a means of escapism. They think it's fun." Her social outlet? "Dancing, working out, reading"—and though finding a "social atmosphere that is moral and healthy" can be tough for chem-free students, at such a big school a kindred soul's bound to turn up sooner rather than later.

Student Body

"Students here are great," writes a junior. "There's never a shortage of new people to meet." A sophomore elaborates: "As can be expected, social groups form along distinct boundaries, but friendships abound." Sure there are your "elitists" and "spoiled rich kids," but as a senior points out, academics are the ties that bind: "People are pretty friendly," he writes, "very school-oriented." U of M can be "ethnically separated," too, but for the most part, the student vibe seems to be summed up in this junior's statement: "I really like the student atmosphere here. Lots of diversity, and I've learned a lot."

ADMISSIONS

Very important factors considered by the admissions committee include: secondary school record. *Important factors considered include:* curriculum, minority status, standardized test scores, state residency, talent/ability. *Other factors considered include:* alumni/ae relation, character/personal qualities, essays, extracurricular activities, geographical residence, recommendations, volunteer work. SAT I or ACT required. TOEFL required of all non-native speakers of English. High school diploma or GED is required. *High school units required/recommended:* Advised to take 20 total units, specific subject pattern tied to school, college, or division requirements. 1–2 science lab and 3 social studies required, 2 history recommended.

The Inside Word

Michigan's admissions process combines both formulaic and personal components in its evaluation of candidates. Making the cut is tough—and is getting even tougher for out-of-state applicants, though the university definitely wants them in large numbers. There are simply loads of applicants from outside the state. If being a Wolverine is high on your list of choices, make sure you're well prepared, and since Michigan admits on a rolling basis—apply early! Michigan establishes an enormous waitlist each year. Controversies surrounding Michigan's approach to affirmative action have resulted in significant changes in the manner in which candidates are evaluated, with greater emphasis now given to aspects of candidates' backgrounds that are not quantified by grades and scores.

FINANCIAL AID

Students should submit: FAFSA plus parent's and student's 1040s by February 15. There is no separate institutional financial aid or scholarship application. Merit scholarships are awarded based on the application for admission, therefore early application for admission (prior to November 15) is strongly advised. *Need-based scholarships/grants offered:* Pell, SEOG, state scholarships/grants, private scholarships, the school's own gift aid. *Loan aid offered:* Direct Subsidized Stafford, Direct Unsubsidized Stafford, Direct PLUS, Federal Perkins, Federal Nursing, state loans, college/university loans from institutional funds, Michigan Loan Program, Health Professional Student Loans. Federal Work-Study Program available. Institutional employment available. Applicants will be notified of awards on a rolling basis beginning on or about March 15. Off-campus job opportunities are excellent.

FROM THE ADMISSIONS OFFICE

"Michigan is a place of incredible possibility. Students shape that possibility according to their diverse interests, goals, energy, and initiative. Undergraduate education is in the academic spotlight at Michigan, offering more than 200 fields of study in 11 schools and colleges; more than 150 first-year seminars with 18 or fewer students taught by senior faculty; composition classes of 20 or fewer students; more than 1,200 first- and second-year students in undergraduate research partnerships with faculty; and numerous service learning programs linking academics with volunteerism. Some introductory courses have large lectures, but these are combined with labs or small group discussions where students get plenty of individualized attention. A Michigan degree is one of distinction and promise; graduates are successful in medical, law, and graduate schools all over the nation and world and 75 percent who enter the work force after graduation secure positions within nine months."

For even more information on this school, turn to page 396 of the "Stats" section.

UNIVERSITY OF MINNESOTA—DULUTH

SOLON CAMPUS CENTER, DULUTH, MN 55812 • ADMISSIONS: 218-726-7171 • FAX: 218-726-6394
EMAIL: UMDADMIS@D.UMN.EDU • WEBSITE: WWW.D.UMN.EDU

Ratings

Quality of Life: 72   **Academic:** 74   **Admissions:** 67   **Financial Aid:** 74

Academics

Business, biology, education, and criminology are tops at University of Minnesota at Duluth, the second-largest undergraduate campus of the University of Minnesota system. Students who choose UMD are generally looking for a campus that provides an even blend of academics and extracurricular fun. By and large,

> **SURVEY SAYS . . .**
> *Very little hard liquor*
> *No one watches intercollegiate sports*
> *Students don't get along with local community*
> *No one plays intramural sports*
> *Very little beer drinking*
> *Student publications are ignored*
> *Classes are small*

those who choose UMD are satisfied with their selection. Writes one, "I believe that UMD's greatest strength is its size. I feel that it is the perfect size. It's small enough so that you feel like you are a part of its community. You meet a lot of people, and no matter where you are in the school, you are bound to find someone you know. At the same time it is large enough to make new friends at any moment." Students enjoy a faculty and administration that "are highly available and always willing to help. They tend to do extra things, such as class websites. My advisor e-mails me with anything she feels I need to know. The staff at UMD is very helpful and caring, and they have added to my great experience here." They note that "the teachers here have either been here forever, or are very new graduates" and that most "seem so enthused to be here and teaching where they are."

Life

"If you like the outdoors, you will love UMD," asserts one Duluth undergrad. "When the weather is warm there is so much to do. There are hiking and rollerblading trails everywhere. The school sets up games and outdoor activities. There is also a great ski area only about 15 minutes away, and they offer great deals for college students." Undergrads are equally enthusiastic about the urban aspects of their hometown: "There is never a lack of things to do in Duluth. There are dance clubs, bars, bowling alleys, great restaurants, movie theaters, and a mall. The Lakewalk (a three-mile long pathway along the shore of Lake Superior) is also popular." Campus clubs and organizations also have their fans; writes one undergrad, "The more involved I become in clubs and organizations, the more people I meet and the more I like UMD. . . . I have so many great friends that are open-minded and outgoing. I never would have met them if I hadn't joined a couple of clubs." Despite the many alternatives available, drinking remains popular at UMD, a fact that has caused increased attention to alcohol education and alternative programs since an alcohol-related student death in 2001 led the school to tighten drinking restrictions on and around campus. Explains one student, since the accident, "there has been a huge move to educate the student population about alcohol awareness. However, the staff has gone a bit overboard, and that has created a lot of hostility between students who drink and the staff. While it is important to teach about the negative effects of consuming alcohol, it is also important to remember that college is a time to explore that which we may know little about. . . . And for some of us, that includes attending a few parties."

262 ■ THE BEST MIDWESTERN COLLEGES

Students

Students here, by their own accounting, "can be really fun to be around." Writes one student, "The greatest strength would have to be the students. By the end of the first two weeks everyone who doesn't want to be here has already gone home. The students respect the campus and respect their peers." Adds another, "Every weekend I meet someone new and everyone seems to get along very well. There are different groups of people that tend to stick together but everyone interacts with one another." Some undergrads find their classmates "pretty cliquey, and it is proving difficult to break into their groups of friends," but even they admit that "there are some very nice people here too." A few warn that tolerance of the gay and lesbian population here is low.

ADMISSIONS

Very important factors considered by the admissions committee include: class rank and standardized test scores. *Important factors considered include:* secondary school record. *Other factors considered include:* essays, minority status, recommendations, and talent/ability. SAT I or ACT required, ACT preferred. TOEFL required of all international applicants. High school diploma is required and GED is accepted. *High school units required/recommended:* 14 total are required; 4 English required, 3 math required, 3 science required, 2 foreign language required, 2 social studies required.

The Inside Word

UM-Duluth's small-school atmosphere can distract some from the realities of a large school; successful students will resist falling through bureaucratic cracks or floating through four years without taking advantage of great educational opportunities.

FINANCIAL AID

Students should submit: FAFSA. No deadline for regular filing. The Princeton Review suggests that all financial aid forms be submitted as soon as possible after January 1. *Need-based scholarships/grants offered:* Pell, SEOG, state scholarships/grants, private scholarships, and the school's own gift aid. *Loan aid offered:* Direct Subsidized Stafford, Direct Unsubsidized Stafford, Direct PLUS, Federal Perkins, and state loans. Federal Work-Study Program available. Institutional employment available. Applicants will be notified of awards on a rolling basis. Off-campus job opportunities are good.

For even more information on this school, turn to page 397 of the "Stats" section.

University of Minnesota—Morris

600 East Fourth Street, Morris, MN 56267 • Admissions: 320-589-6035 • Fax: 320-589-1673
E-mail: admisfa@mrs.umn.edu • Website: www.mrs.umn.edu

Ratings
Quality of Life: 84   **Academic:** 87   **Admissions:** 83   **Financial Aid:** 83

Academics

"If you want to be in an amazing jazz program, come to this school." So say the students at this small state university in western Minnesota. One student mentions with pride music professor Jim "Doc" Carlson, who recently used his connections in the jazz world to

> **SURVEY SAYS . . .**
> *School is well run*
> *Classes are small*
> *Instructors are good teachers*
> *Lousy food on campus*

allow a few "trumpet and sax" players to perform with an opening act for B.B. King. This brand of personal attention is what UM—Morris boasts. A student explains, "Being a small school allows the students and professors to develop a relationship, and this helps students a lot as they are deciding what to do after college." "Morris is a tough school," and this, coupled with the limited social life, means that "academics are the main focus here. You don't come here to play sports or to party, although either may be something you choose to do on the side." Some undergrads complain that the administration's attempts "to increase the enrollment has caused the overall quality of the student body to drop" in recent years. The good news is that students can confront the administration with this criticism, or any other criticism for that matter. "The chancellor has an office hour every week where anyone can bring their concerns about the school."

Life

"It takes a good imagination to go to school here." After all, UM—Morris "is a small public school in a small city." The town of Morris itself is fairly "boring" and lacks a "rollicking nightlife," though it does offer the hungry student "some great local eateries." When students really want a night out on the town, "groups of friends will pile into someone's car at 10 P.M. and drive to 'Alec' "—that's Alexandria—"which is the nearest 'big' town. It is 50 minutes away" and features attractions like "all-night restaurants and Wal-Mart." For the most part, students here seek out their entertainment in "the fair amount of options available on campus," like "plays, jazz concerts, dances, movies," "intramural sports, and clubs such as geology or juggling club, and if nothing else, you can always get a job." Every semester, students look forward to "the Great Pancake Break," which occurs "right before finals." At this flapjack extravaganza, "the professors serve/make the juice, pancakes, etc." for study-weary students, "and the chancellor goes around pouring coffee and juice!" While events like the Great Pancake Break keep students speaking highly of UM—Morris, some think that, overall, the campus still needs "to get more school spirit." And they wouldn't mind if someone could fidget with the outdoor thermostat a little: "It gets pretty cold in the winter out here on the prairie."

Students

If you don't have 20/20 vision, you may have a tough time spotting Morris, Minnesota, on a map. Locate the Twin Cities, pan about 160 miles northwest, and you'll eventually find Morris, the home of the University of Minnesota's liberal arts campus. That's right, UM "is in a small town of about 5,000 people, including 2,000 students." Because "most of the students are from Minnesota and the surrounding states," they're used to the "rural" feel of America's midsection. Don't think that this is a school full of farm kids, though. "Some are from rural environments, some are from cities," but regardless of where they come from, "most people make an effort to interact and learn about each other." "You can pretty much strike up a conversation with anyone," attests one student. The little ethnic variety that there is gives "students who might not be exposed to much diversity a taste of what it's like outside of mostly Caucasian rural Minnesota." Overall, students embrace all walks of life. "As an example" of the students' tolerant disposition, "this year the homecoming king was a gay man . . . and so was the homecoming queen!"

ADMISSIONS

Very important factors considered by the admissions committee include: class rank, secondary school record, and standardized test scores. *Important factors considered include:* essays, extracurricular activities, minority status, recommendations, talent/ability, volunteer work, and work experience. *Other factors considered include:* alumni/ae relation and interview. SAT I or ACT required. TOEFL required of all international applicants. High school diploma or GED is required. *High school units required/recommended:* 14 total required; 4 English required, 3 math required, 3 science required, 2 foreign language required, 2 social studies required.

The Inside Word

Among the more selective schools of the state's university system, UMM is best for applicants who are distinctly excited about the opportunities the university offers, and not just in the school's music program. Overall, the school is a terrific in-state bang for your buck.

FINANCIAL AID

Students should submit: FAFSA and institution's own financial aid form. No deadline for regular filing. The Princeton Review suggests that all financial aid forms be submitted as soon as possible after January 1. *Need-based scholarships/grants offered:* Pell, SEOG, state scholarships/grants, private scholarships, and the school's own gift aid. *Loan aid offered:* Direct Subsidized Stafford, Direct Unsubsidized Stafford, Direct PLUS, Federal Perkins, state loans, college/university loans from institutional funds, and SELF Loan. Federal Work-Study Program available. Institutional employment available. Applicants will be notified of awards on a rolling basis beginning on or about March 15. Off-campus job opportunities are good.

For even more information on this school, turn to page 397 of the "Stats" section.

University of Minnesota—Twin Cities

231 Pillsbury Drive, SE, 240 Williamson Hall, Minneapolis, MN 55455-0213
Admissions: 612-625-2008 • Fax: 612-626-1693 • Financial Aid: 612-624-1665
E-mail: admissions@tc.umn.edu • Website: Admissions.tc.umn.edu

Ratings

Quality of Life: 74   **Academic:** 71   **Admissions:** 80   **Financial Aid:** 79

Academics

Students at the University of Minnesota—Twin Cities take a pragmatic approach to their academic experiences. "I think for what I am paying I am getting a very good deal," writes one. "I have great and extremely well-qualified professors . . . . Also, at a school this large the opportunities seem nearly endless." Students identify a definite hierarchy among departments, with "star"

> **SURVEY SAYS . . .**
> *Students love Minneapolis, MN*
> *Athletic facilities are great*
> *Class discussions are rare*
> *Political activism is hot*
> *Students aren't religious*
> *Campus difficult to get around, Large classes*
> *Lots of TAs teach upper-level courses*
> *Student publications are popular*
> *Unattractive campus*

programs like business and technology receiving the most attention from the administration; other areas, such as the arts, "lack funding" and often offer too few courses. At the Carlson School of Management, the U's business program, "teachers are well experienced and offer excellent information in class. The school also has several computer labs kept in fantastic condition." The prestigious Institute of Technology receives similarly high marks, although many students complain that "professors can't speak English very well and this makes it difficult to learn." Throughout the university, "professors mostly try to get involved with us. It's hard because it's such a huge university. The lecture halls are so large that unless you make the effort, the professor probably won't be able to tell you apart from someone else." The university's administration "is pretty good except for services like the bursar or financial aid/scholarships office. They do quite poorly in this area."

Life

"There is something for everyone" at the large, urban U of M campus. Explains one student, "There are hundreds of groups, from activist groups to club sports. You can go to Dinkytown, Uptown, the Mall of America, Downtown Minneapolis, St. Paul, etc." For some, the city is the chief attraction; as one undergrad told us, "Living in Minneapolis is great! It's a friendly town, yet has all the perks of a big city: theaters, major league sports, museums, concerts!" For others, it's the myriad opportunities to get involved in campus activities; writes one student, "Sports are big . . . . This community is strong in the arts as well. It's very diverse, so if you want it, we probably have it." Many agree that "going out and having fun is what goes on on the weekends. Frat and house parties are very popular weekend activities. People also enjoy clubs and bars." The weather here, undergrads warn, is not for everyone. Writes one, "For about a week after the first snow, we all career around like horny antelopes, sliding to class in half the time it takes to walk there. After that it turns into drudgery and everybody pretty much stays inside."

Student Body

Undergrads report that "the University of Minnesota attracts a wide range of people—there are traditionally aged students and some older people as well. I've had classes with a range of 17 (still in high school) to 60." More than a few arrive from the northern countryside;

reports one caustic urbanite, "I've noticed that the city is really a foreign atmosphere to some people. They are here as tourists and are merely waiting for the day when they can return to their cornfields in relief and brag about their experiences in the big city." By Minnesotan standards, the U draws an ethnically diverse population; explains one student, "Minnesota tends to be pretty Caucasian, but the U draws people of every ethnic background, which is cool." Many warn that "[because] this university is huge . . . you have to make serious effort to keep in contact with people, because you won't see them unless you have a class with them."

ADMISSIONS

Very important factors considered by the admissions committee include: class rank, secondary school record, standardized test scores, competitiveness of curriculum. *Other factors considered include:* character/personal qualities, extracurricular activities, geographical residence, state residency, talent/ability, volunteer work, work experience. SAT I or ACT required. High school diploma or GED is required. *High school units required/recommended:* 16 total required; 4 English required, 3 math required, 3 science required, 2 foreign language required, 3 social studies required, 1 visual and/or performing arts required.

The Inside Word

Despite what looks to be a fairly choosy admissions rate, it's the sheer volume of applicants that creates a selective situation at Minnesota. Admission is by formula; only those with weak course selections and inconsistent academic records need to work up a sweat over getting admitted.

FINANCIAL AID

Students should submit: FAFSA. Priority deadline for filing is February 15. The Princeton Review suggests that all financial aid forms be submitted as soon as possible after January 1. *Need-based scholarships/grants offered:* Pell, SEOG, state scholarships/grants, private scholarships, the school's own gift aid, NSS, ROTC scholarships, academic merit scholarships, athletic scholarships. *Loan aid offered:* Direct Subsidized Stafford, Direct Unsubsidized Stafford, Direct PLUS, Federal Perkins, Federal Nursing, state loans, college/university loans from institutional funds, NSL, private loans. Federal Work-Study Program available. Institutional employment available. Applicants will be notified of awards on a rolling basis. Off-campus job opportunities are excellent.

FROM THE ADMISSIONS OFFICE

"Known globally as a leader in teaching, research, and public service, the University of Minnesota ranks among the top 25 public universities in the nation. The classic Big 10 campus, located in the heart of the Minneapolis–St. Paul metropolitan area, provides a world-class setting for lifelong learning. In addition to the top-notch academic programs (and more than 145 undergraduate degrees), the university offers an Undergraduate Research Opportunities Program that is a national model; one of the largest study abroad programs in the country; 20,000 computers available for use in labs across campus; and extraordinary opportunities for internships, employment, and personal enrichment. Students can pursue interests in more than 400 official student organizations. Committed to offering its students an education that is not only outstanding but competitively priced, the university has been recognized as a 'best value' and 'best buy.' Students from other states may qualify for discounted tuition through one of the university's reciprocity agreements. Plus, the university awards a number of academic scholarships to qualified freshmen. The university community is a broad mix of ethnic backgrounds, interests, and cultures from all 50 states and 110 foreign countries, creating a welcoming feeling on campus. Beyond campus, the dynamic communities of Minneapolis and St. Paul offer something for everyone—a nationally recognized arts and theater community, a thriving entertainment industry, a host of Fortune 500 companies, four glorious seasons of outdoor recreation, exciting professional sports, shopping, and restaurants for every taste."

For even more information on this school, turn to page 398 of the "Stats" section.

UNIVERSITY OF MISSOURI—ROLLA

106 PARKER HALL, ROLLA, MO 65409 • ADMISSIONS: 573-341-4165 • FAX: 573-341-4082
FINANCIAL AID: 800-522-0938 • E-MAIL: UMROLLA@UMR.EDU • WEBSITE: WWW.UMR.EDU

Ratings
Quality of Life: 81   **Academic:** 80   **Admissions:** 83   **Financial Aid:** 85

Academics

Students looking for "serious, no-frills engineering studies" flock to Rolla, where "research programs and post-graduation job placement" are often listed among the school's strengths. The course work is "not designed for the lazy," and a senior tells us, "Most

> **SURVEY SAYS . . .**
> *Political activism is hot*
> *High cost of living*
> *No one cheats*
> *Student publications are popular*
> *Very little beer drinking*

people here are highly dedicated, reflected by our average graduating GPA." Students relish this academic community, relieved "finally to be among my mental peers." Most students find their professors "very knowledgeable and easy to talk to" as well as "interesting and experienced." Certain respondents see the faculty as "research oriented," but others say they are "very involved with undergraduates." Instructors are known to "act tough," but a junior writes that those who are "aloof in class" can be "laid-back and human in the office." Students find themselves slaving for those top grades: "Nobody cares if you spend 30 hours a week in a two-credit-hour lab." Some students wish for more discussion in classes, complain about understaffing, and lament certain outdated facilities. But the "programs offered that assist students with their academic program and overall well-being" more than compensate for any shortcomings. However, they succeed in creating an atmosphere that "teaches great leadership qualities" and produces "graduates who know what they're doing," according to a junior in the computer engineering department.

Life

Life at UMR revolves around academics, which is reflected in the buildings themselves, "built for utility, not art." One student writes, "The reason people come to school here is not to have fun," but many people appreciate that "the environment provides very few distractions from the education that I am paying for." Those looking for a respite from the "strictly business" vibe are "forced to be creative." That translates to "climbing the abandoned nine-story building or building flame throwers" with surprising frequency. Typical geek pastimes, such as Magic tournaments, computer games, and something called the "SAE formula car group," occupy students when they aren't studying, and one respondent reports, "Role playing happens around the clock." (Meaning avatars, not French maids, we assume.) Rolla "ain't no place to party," and "people who like to drink a lot are unsatisfied because there aren't many bars," aside from the campus pub, The Grotto. The Student Union Board attempts to lure people away from the monitor's glow, but "a lot of people don't support campus activities." Though the surrounding city offers "no malls or clubs," the Ozarks provide an outdoor playground, with plenty of places for caving, fishing, hunting, and hiking. In a typically practical Rolla statement, one student concludes, "We came for the engineering degree, not the city."

Student Body

At a school full of engineers and computer scientists, it's not surprising to find high representation of "somewhat introverted white males who rarely tear themselves away from the computer." Though these "antisocial weirdos" may "not get out much," certain students assure us that they can be "very nice and social when necessary." "Frat boys" add some diversity of personality to the student body, but some respondents feel that "too much of the campus population is Greek." Many of Rolla's young men complain about the paucity of women, but one Don Juan quips, "If you eliminate all the guys who are attached or just plain pathetic, the odds are pretty even." The ladies themselves mostly enjoy the advantageous ratio, but a female student writes, "Sometimes a female will run into a person who doesn't believe that girls can be engineers." Students perceive "factions of each minority," noting that "foreign students flock together and rarely interact with the rest of us." Overall, Rolla enjoys the harmony that comes from common purpose: "Despite the diverse campus, everybody seems to get along."

ADMISSIONS

Very important factors considered by the admissions committee include: class rank, secondary school record, standardized test scores. *Important factors considered include:* recommendations. *Other factors considered include:* character/personal qualities, essays, extracurricular activities, interview, talent/ability, volunteer work, work experience. SAT I or ACT required. TOEFL required of all international applicants. High school diploma or GED is required. *High school units required/recommended:* 17 total required; 4 English required, 4 math required, 3 science required, 1 science lab required, 2 foreign language required, 3 social studies required, 1 fine arts required.

The Inside Word

This public university admissions committee functions pretty much the same as most others; admission is based on numbers and course distribution requirements. The applicant pool is small, well-qualified, and self-selected; despite the extremely high admit rate, only strong students are likely to meet with success.

FINANCIAL AID

Students should submit: FAFSA. No deadline for regular filing. The Princeton Review suggests that all financial aid forms be submitted as soon as possible after January 1. *Need-based scholarships/grants offered:* Pell, SEOG, state scholarships/grants, private scholarships, the school's own gift aid, United Negro College Fund. *Loan aid offered:* Direct Subsidized Stafford, Direct Unsubsidized Stafford, Federal Perkins, state loans, college/university loans from institutional funds. Federal Work-Study Program available. Institutional employment available. Applicants will be notified of awards on a rolling basis beginning on or about April 1. Off-campus job opportunities are excellent.

FROM THE ADMISSIONS OFFICE

"Widely recognized as one of our nation's best universities for engineering, sciences, computer science, and technology, the University of Missouri—Rolla also offers programs in information science, business, and liberal arts. Personal attention, access to leadership opportunities, research projects, and co-ops and internships mean students are well prepared for the future. A 98 percent career placement rate across all majors and a 90-plus percent placement rate to medical, law, and other professional schools tells the tale; UMR offers a terrific undergraduate experience and value for your money."

For even more information on this school, turn to page 399 of the "Stats" section.

UNIVERSITY OF NEBRASKA—LINCOLN

1410 Q STREET, LINCOLN, NE 68588-0417 • ADMISSIONS: 402-472-2023 • FAX: 402-472-0670
FINANCIAL AID: 402-472-2030 • E-MAIL: NUHUSKER@UNL.EDU • WEBSITE: WWW.UNL.EDU

Ratings

Quality of Life: 88   Academic: 75   Admissions: 91   Financial Aid: 84

Academics

Students at University of Nebraska—Lincoln tell us that their school offers "the opportunities of a large school, but with a small school feel." Nebraska achieves its "small school feel" by dividing its 18,000 undergraduates into it's undergraduate colleges: Agricultural Sciences and Natural Resources, Architecture, Arts & Sciences, Business Administration, Engineering and

> **SURVEY SAYS . . .**
> *Everyone loves the Cornhuskers*
> *(Almost) everyone plays intramural sports*
> *Frats and sororities dominate social scene*
> *Students are happy*
> *Student publications are popular*
> *Great off-campus food*
> *Class discussions are rare*
> *Large classes*
> *Library needs improving*

Technology, Fine & Performing Arts, Human Resources and Family Sciences, Journalism and Mass Communication, and Teachers. Further personal touches are supplied by "a very strong and prominent Greek system as well as one of the best residence hall systems in the area." Students brag that UNL offers "great access to research opportunities combined with good access to professors and community" and that "the full professors are quite good, although the TAs and graduate assistants often leave something to be desired." Even with all the intimate touches, UNL's scope can be a little intimidating; the resultant fears, however, are relatively easy to overcome. As one student put it, "My freshman year, I was scared to death of the large lecture halls. I took my parents' advice, though, and got to know my professors. I have discovered that they are there to help you if you just make a little effort to show that you need or want it." Surprisingly (considering this is a state school), undergrads here report "very little red tape to deal with. Bills are easy to pay in person or online, class registration is a breeze, and any concerns I have had have been answered promptly by administration."

Life

Lincoln's nation of 18,000 Cornhuskers agrees that "athletics, both intramural and intercollegiate, are a big part of the culture at Nebraska. It has a unifying effect among students and impacts the social life of most. The best part of the school year is definitely the football season." There's more to life in Lincoln than game day, however. Students here enjoy an active social life that centers on the Greek houses (especially for those under 21) and O Street and its "30+ bars that are packed with college kids on weekends." Our respondents report that alcohol is popular "even though UNL is a dry campus . . . . The rule is strictly enforced." Student opinions vary on hometown Lincoln. Some brag that "Lincoln is definitely a 'college town'" because "less than two blocks away [from campus] are the historic HayMarket, movie theaters, the Lied Center for Performing Arts, and the bar and club district." Others, noting that much of the entertainment near campus is limited to the 21-and-over crowd, complain that "there's not a lot to do in this town, so it helps to have good friends to spend time with." Summing up campus life, one student writes the following: "Sports and beer—that's Nebraska nightlife. People try to change and do different things, but it always comes back to sports and beer." Adds another, "Either you drink or you go to Bible study. That's it. And some people do both!"

Student Body

While most students at UNL "are from Nebraska or surrounding areas," "there are students from every state and many, many countries" at the university. "There are more minority and international students now than when I first started college in 1999," notes one senior, although most here agree that "there is not a lot of diversity on campus." A sizable number of students are "very religious," and "many of them try and force this on others, who do not wish it." On the upside, "most students are involved with at least one organization on campus," and "because football is so big and many of our other athletic teams are excellent (volleyball, wrestling, gymnastics, bowling), there's a real emphasis among the student body on exercise and athletics."

ADMISSIONS

Very important factors considered by the admissions committee include: class rank, secondary school record, standardized test scores. *Important factors considered include:* talent/ability. *Other factors considered include:* alumni/ae relation, geographical residence, minority status, recommendations. SAT I or ACT required. TOEFL required of all international applicants. High school diploma or GED is required. *High school units required/recommended:* 16 total required; 4 English required, 4 math required, 3 science required, 1 science lab required, 2 foreign language required, 3 social studies required, 1 history recommended.

The Inside Word

Like most large-scale universities, Nebraska—Lincoln admits a huge freshman class each year. The need for numbers is reflected in an admissions process that concentrates on them—your course selection, GPA, and test scores will be all they need to see. Unless you've had troubles academically, they're likely to welcome you aboard, though some programs have higher expectations than others.

FINANCIAL AID

Students should submit: FAFSA. No deadline for regular filing. The Princeton Review suggests that all financial aid forms be submitted as soon as possible after January 1. *Need-based scholarships/grants offered:* Pell, SEOG, state scholarships/grants, private scholarships, the school's own gift aid. *Loan aid offered:* Direct Subsidized Stafford, Direct Unsubsidized Stafford, Direct PLUS, Federal Perkins, college/university loans from institutional funds. Federal Work-Study Program available. Institutional employment available. Applicants will be notified of awards on a rolling basis beginning on or about April 15. Off-campus job opportunities are excellent.

FROM THE ADMISSIONS OFFICE

"Chartered in 1869, the University of Nebraska—Lincoln has since grown to become a major international research university, offering 149 undergraduate majors and 118 graduate programs. While 90 percent of the 23,000 students come from Nebraska, students from every state and 110 countries choose the university for its comprehensive programs and reputation for quality. Nebraska is classified as a Carnegie I Research Institution, recognizing the university's commitment to research funding and quality scholarship, and has been a member of the Association of American Universities since 1909—one of only 62 universities to claim this prestigious membership. These affiliations ensure Nebraska students are taught by nationally and internationally recognized faculty who are experts in their fields, bringing the latest discoveries into their classrooms. Lincoln—Nebraska's capital with a population of more than 213,000—offers the comfort and security of a college town with the cultural and entertainment opportunities of a larger city."

For even more information on this school, turn to page 399 of the "Stats" section.

UNIVERSITY OF NORTH DAKOTA

Box 8357, Grand Forks, ND 58202 • Admissions: 701-777-4463 • Fax: 701-777-2696
Financial Aid: 701-777-3121 • E-mail: enrolser@sage.und.nodak.edu • Website: www.und.edu

Ratings
Quality of Life: 78   **Academic:** 73   **Admissions:** 77   **Financial Aid:** 80

Academics

"A history of producing hard-working professionals and a strong alumni association" are just two of the many reasons students choose to come to the University of North Dakota. Affordability and the chance to "receive a great education while still having tons of fun" are two more. Students here brag about a variety of programs, the nationally renowned aviation program ("one of the best anywhere"), the "super business and engineering schools, and a great social work program" among them. Like most large state universities, UND offers a wide range of options, making it "great for students who definitely know what their career path is, and great for those students who are still searching for their direction." Atypically for a big school, "classes are small, which makes learning easier," and "there are a large number of professors and other faculty members dedicated to making sure every student receives the best possible education. If there is a problem or a student needs assistance, people are willing to listen and help out." To many, though, UND's large and active alumni network is the school's chief asset. Explains one student, "Alumni are amazing. They really look out for one another. It establishes an immediate connection. You say to someone in Florida, 'I graduated from UND,' and they will give you a job or find you one."

> **SURVEY SAYS . . .**
> *Lots of beer drinking*
> *Hard liquor is popular*
> *(Almost) everyone smokes*
> *Everyone loves the Fighting Sioux*
> *Frats and sororities dominate social scene*
> *Great computer facilities*
> *Ethnic diversity lacking on campus*

Life

North Dakota, its students brag, is home to "the best hockey team on earth," and most here would agree that intercollegiate sports—not just hockey, but also football, women's basketball, and swimming—are central to campus life. Some think sports are a little too central; complains one, "Don't get me wrong; I love hockey and football as much as the next guy. But when some faculty on campus literally have their offices in closets, and UND is buying the hockey players engraved suitcases and matching jackets, it's a little pathetic." When there's no game to attend, students enjoy a lively party scene. "Life at UND is study during the week and party on the weekend," explains one student. "Frats have many parties and the college has events going most weekends." Undergrads also report that "the university programming is usually really good. In the dorms, there is Residence Life Cinema, which has great movies . . . . They have concerts at the new arena." Hometown Grand Forks "isn't a huge city, so there's not a whole lot of places for students under 21 to go to." However, "once a student turns 21, there are a lot of bars, and most of them are pretty fun." Students appreciate how "the campus and the town are pretty safe," but wish the school would build some underground walkways: "It's subzero most of the year and we must often walk 10 to 15 minutes around campus!" writes one student. Road trips to Canada are popular among students with access to vehicles.

Student Body

According to some students here, geography is destiny; as one put it, "In North Dakota, the land is flat and unchanging. At UND, most of the students are the same way: everyone looks and basically acts the same. This is good and bad, and stems from the fact that most of the students here are from the tri-state region. Not many kids from other parts of the country want to go to school so far north." The exceptions to the rule "are athletes and aviation students, who add diversity. Everyone else is a Caucasian with blonde hair. We live in a Scandinavian area. It's bound to happen!" Students also note that many of their classmates "are from farms or the city of Grand Forks." Most agree that a friendly midwestern vibe pervades the campus. Writes one undergrad, "Students here are extremely nice and never put anyone down."

ADMISSIONS

Very important factors considered by the admissions committee include: secondary school record, standardized test scores. *Other factors considered include:* class rank, essays, recommendations. SAT I or ACT required; ACT preferred. TOEFL required of all international applicants. High school diploma or GED is required. *High school units required/recommended:* 4 English required, 3 math required, 3 science required, 3 science lab required, 1 foreign language recommended, 3 social studies required.

The Inside Word

North Dakota shapes up as a low-stress choice with little pressure on applicants. Its sound reputation serves as a reminder that a highly selective admissions profile isn't an indicator of the quality of a university. Who graduates is much more important than who gets admitted or denied.

FINANCIAL AID

Students should submit: FAFSA. The Princeton Review suggests that all financial aid forms be submitted as soon as possible after January 1. *Need-based scholarships/grants offered:* Pell, SEOG, state scholarships/grants, private scholarships, the school's own gift aid. *Loan aid offered:* FFEL Subsidized Stafford, FFEL Unsubsidized Stafford, FFEL PLUS, Federal Perkins, Federal Nursing, college/university loans from institutional funds. Federal Work-Study Program available. Institutional employment available. Applicants will be notified of awards on or about May 15. Off-campus job opportunities are excellent.

FROM THE ADMISSIONS OFFICE

"More than 12,000 students come to the University of North Dakota each year, from every state in the nation and more than 60 countries. They're impressed by our academic excellence, about 170 major fields of study, our dedication to the liberal arts mission, and alumni success record. Nearly all of the university's new students rank in the top half of their high school classes, with about half in the top quarter. As the oldest and most diversified institution of higher education in the Dakotas, Montana, Wyoming, and western Minnesota, UND is a comprehensive teaching and research university. Yet the university provides individual attention that may be missing at very large universities. UND graduates are highly regarded among prospective employers. Representatives from more than 200 regional and national companies recruit UND students every year. Our campus is approximately 98 percent accessible."

For even more information on this school, turn to page 400 of the "Stats" section.

UNIVERSITY OF NORTHERN IOWA

1227 WEST 27TH STREET, CEDAR FALLS, IA 50614-0018 • ADMISSIONS: 319-273-2281 • FAX: 319-273-2885
E-MAIL: ADMISSIONS@UNI.EDU • WEBSITE: WWW.UNI.EDU

Ratings
Quality of Life: 82   **Academic:** 74   **Admissions:** 73   **Financial Aid:** 78

Academics

According to one satisfied student at the University of Northern Iowa, "It's a small enough school where I regularly recognize friends on campus and all my professors know me. It has really great

> **SURVEY SAYS . . .**
> *Diversity lacking on campus, Classes are small*
> *Class discussions encouraged*
> *Students get along with local community*

programs for business and education, and the administration works hard to provide things for us to do for entertainment, career searches, and volunteer opportunities." Reports another, "As with any college campus there are those professors [who] have touched my life forever . . . and there are those that I would like to just kick sometimes for their lack of creativity and excitement in the classroom." "Instructors are usually pretty understanding and accessible." One student boasts that "friends of mine went rafting with their prof in the Canadian boundary waters." Some students complain that the "administration backs the professors 100 percent of the time and never the students no matter what the situation," which gives students little recourse in academic disputes, but most tell us that their "academic experience has been very positive." One education major applauds UNI's wide course selection, "especially in the education program. We are required to spend endless hours in surrounding classrooms doing observations and teaching lessons. No education major could leave UNI without feeling totally comfortable about teaching!!"

Life

What do people do at the University of Northern Iowa for fun? Writes one typical undergrad, "A lot of people drink on the weekends and go to the bars. But some people don't. There are only four sororities and eight fraternities, so Greek life is there, but not huge. A lot of people go home on the weekends." Another explains that "for fun here people go to the 'hill,' which is a street right next to campus that has several bars and dance clubs" and "also offers several under-21 bars. That's seriously about it." "It's very fun to live here," insists one student, "although the town itself [Cedar Falls, Iowa] is pretty boring. What makes it fun is the student population. We have parties all of the time to make sure we're always having fun." While one student has "no trouble meeting people or finding something to do," another complains that "it seems difficult to break into the social scene, especially beyond beer"; those that "don't do the bar scene" may find entertainment in "bowling," playing "board games," "doing dorm house programs that are cheap," "watching movies, or just hanging out." In addition, "intramurals are a big thing here." UNI students also hang out at the "decent student union" and "excellent wellness center" and note that "campus jobs pay well for the area and are very flexible."

Students

One UNI undergrad gives an overview of the social atmosphere: "There are enough students so that you can find whatever you're looking for, but you won't get lost in the crowd." Students describe their peers as "for the most part . . . friendly and nice; we aren't a very diversified school," but hey, "it *is* in the middle of Iowa." Only 5 percent of students here are from out of state, so many "come from a very small town" and, as some suspect, may "have never seen or even interacted with a person of a different ethnicity." This results in a student body that is somewhat "apathetic and ignorant of other religions and lifestyles." Some fret that "people stick to their friends and aren't willing to speak to strangers." Others think "most people are great and willing to talk and become your friend." Summing up, one student observes, "I don't think that this campus would serve as a great display of diversity . . . but I do know that we have all kinds of races, cultures, etc., and to my knowledge everyone works together pretty well."

ADMISSIONS

Very important factors considered by the admissions committee include: class rank, secondary school record, and standardized test scores. *Other factors considered include:* interview, minority status, recommendations, state residency, and talent/ability. SAT I or ACT required, ACT preferred. TOEFL required of all international applicants. High school diploma or GED is required. *High school units required/recommended:* 15 total required; 4 English required, 3 math required, 3 science required, 1 science lab recommended, 2 foreign language recommended, 3 social studies required, 2 elective required.

The Inside Word

Average students will stand a very good chance of admission to the University of Northern Iowa. If you have an appreciation for an environment where no one group pervades, give UNI strong consideration.

FINANCIAL AID

Students should submit: FAFSA. No deadline for regular filing. The Princeton Review suggests that all financial aid forms be submitted as soon as possible after January 1. *Need-based scholarships/grants offered:* Pell, SEOG, state scholarships/grants, private scholarships, and the school's own gift aid. *Loan aid offered:* Direct Subsidized Stafford, Direct Unsubsidized Stafford, Direct PLUS, Federal Perkins, state loans, private loans, and alternative loans. Federal Work-Study Program available. Institutional employment available. Applicants will be notified of awards on a rolling basis beginning on or about March 20. Off-campus job opportunities are good.

FROM THE ADMISSIONS OFFICE

"At UNI, more than 120 majors are offered, 90 percent of classes have 50 or fewer students, and less than 3 percent of classes are taught by teaching assistants. UNI ranks among top programs in the country for percentage of accounting graduates passing the CPA exam on the first attempt. The School of Music has the largest undergraduate program in music education in the state. The university has received a grant for more than $1 million to train native speakers of languages other than English to be bilingual classroom teachers. Full-time faculty teaches freshman-level courses as well as advanced classes. Visit www.uni.edu/pos to view the wide variety of majors and minors offered at UNI. Sixty-eight percent of UNI students drink one or fewer times per week, and 74 percent relax without using alcohol, and the university offers more than 200 student organizations, including special interest clubs, sororities and fraternities, religious groups, and academic honoraries. Living in one of UNI's 10 residence halls offers the combination of convenience, low living costs, and opportunities for involvement. UNI offers campuswide commitment to student services, with summer orientation, faculty advisors, academic advising, student health services, and the counseling and career center. UNI's Overseas Teacher Recruiting Fair is the oldest and largest in the world. More than 750 students participate in Camp Adventure, which offers them the opportunity to travel and provide summer recreation at more than 100 program sites worldwide. UNI's park-like campus contains 50-plus major buildings on 850 acres, compact enough to cross in a 10-minute walk. The renovation and addition of approximately 66,000 square feet to McCollum Science Hall includes classrooms, laboratories, and offices for the biology and chemistry departments. The Wellness and Recreation Center features the highest climbing wall in the Midwest, plus two pools, a running track, and weight and fitness rooms."

For even more information on this school, turn to page 400 of the "Stats" section.

UNIVERSITY OF NOTRE DAME

220 MAIN BUILDING, NOTRE DAME, IN 46556 • ADMISSIONS: 574-631-7505 • FAX: 574-631-8865
FINANCIAL AID: 574-631-6436 • E-MAIL: ADMISSIO.1@ND.EDU • WEBSITE: WWW.ND.EDU

Ratings
Quality of Life: 80   **Academic:** 92   **Admissions:** 99   **Financial Aid:** 84

Academics

Students at Notre Dame don't mince words when it comes to boasting about the education and experiences they've received at their beloved alma mater. Call it Irish Pride. A senior provides a perfect example: "Notre Dame, besides simply BEING college football, is great academically. You are practically guaranteed a job when you leave as long as you kept your grades at decent levels through school. What's more, ND is

> **SURVEY SAYS . . .**
> *Everyone loves the Fighting Irish*
> *(Almost) everyone plays intramural sports*
> *Diversity lacking on campus, Great library*
> *Great computer facilities*
> *Very small frat/sorority scene*
> *Students are very religious*
> *Students don't like Notre Dame, IN*
> *(Almost) no one smokes*
> *Student publications are popular*

able to attract not only some of the best students, but also the best teachers." What is it about Notre Dame that engenders such love and devotion? It's the holy trinity of "tradition, faith, and academics" that sets Notre Dame apart, argue undergrads, who also find comfort in ND's "strong sense of community" and "unparalleled school spirit." These last two—and an alumni network that's been called "the biggest fraternity in the world"—are what "make all this studying bearable," notes a sophomore. For the most part, undergrads praise Notre Dame's faculty, curriculum, and resources, noting that the school's strong emphasis on classical liberal arts courses such as theology and philosophy, its top-notch science program, as well as its honor code, exemplify ND's "commitment to instilling quality and character" in its students. Being a big research school, there are the usual complaints about TA's teaching classes (though an honors student points out that she's gotten "the cream of the crop"—"three heads of departments as teachers already, and I'm a freshman!"). This is balanced, however, by the sense that "people really care about you at Notre Dame. You're not another number, but rather, you're respected as an intelligent human. You're expected to treat others in the same way, which creates a wonderful atmosphere."

Life

A sophomore provides a window onto life at ND: "It's a Catholic university and football is so big that my friends from other schools often ask what we do: pray all the time? Or does everything shut down if the football team loses . . . ." So goes life in Notre Dame-dominated South Bend, Indiana, a few hours drive from anywhere (mostly kids go to Chicago, which is 90 minutes away, for big-city fun). Still, Domers love it: "Life is wonderful!," waxes a junior. "Football games are a little slice of heaven out here—and I am not kidding. Tailgating under a golden dome—what could be better?" Of course not everyone is so smitten with Notre Dame's "tradition of tradition," especially on matters of personal autonomy, choice, and day-to-day life at this conservative religious school. A first-year—living the "painful life of a pagan liberal at Notre Dame"—charges that "it is a sexist campus where women are rarely promoted and sometimes professors are just outright crude to women." Ouch! Yet, despite some distinctly un-twenty-first-century rules and regulations (such as single sex dorms and "parietals"—essentially curfews designed to keep men out of women's rooms and vice versa), most students are okay with Notre Dame's social set up.

Student Body

A little bit more Irish Pride—this time from a senior: "Notre Dame has the best student body in the country. The students are what make the school." Coming from a Domer, it's probably a bit of an exaggeration; still, students are, for the most part, agreed upon the fact that "the sense of community and the 'Notre Dame Family' are the most valuable part of the university." And while there's a bit of a problem with homogeneity (the typical ND student is "a rich white kid that's Abercrombie and Fitched out wearing a North Face because we do face arctic temperatures out here in Indiana . . ."), a sophomore points out that "the school is trying to become more modern/activist/chic." The problem? "We're dealing with a Catholic institution," notes our wise sophomore, "and the Catholic Church changes about as fast as molasses."

ADMISSIONS

Very important factors considered by the admissions committee include: character/personal qualities, class rank, essays, extracurricular activities, recommendations, secondary school record, standardized test scores, talent/ability. *Other factors considered include:* alumni/ae relation, minority status, religious affiliation/commitment, volunteer work, work experience. SAT I or ACT required. TOEFL required of all international applicants. High school diploma is required and GED is not accepted. *High school units required/recommended:* 16 total required; 23 total recommended; 4 English required, 3 math required, 4 math recommended, 2 science required, 4 science recommended, 2 foreign language required, 4 foreign language recommended, 2 history required, 4 history recommended, 3 elective required.

The Inside Word

For most candidates, getting admitted to Notre Dame is pretty tough. Legacies, however, face some of the most favorable admissions conditions to be found at any highly selective university. Unofficially, athletic talents seem to have some influence on the committee as well: An enormous percentage of the total student body holds at least one varsity letter from high school, and many were team captains. Perhaps it's merely coincidence, but even so, candidates who tap well into the Notre Dame persona are likeliest to succeed.

FINANCIAL AID

Students should submit: FAFSA, CSS/Financial Aid PROFILE, noncustodial (divorced/separated) parent's statement, business/farm supplement. Signed federal income tax return, and W-2 forms may be requested on an individual basis. Regular filing deadline is February 15. The Princeton Review suggests that all financial aid forms be submitted as soon as possible after January 1. *Need-based scholarships/grants offered:* Pell, SEOG, state scholarships/grants, private scholarships, the school's own gift aid, Alumni Club Scholarships. *Loan aid offered:* FFEL Subsidized Stafford, FFEL Unsubsidized Stafford, FFEL PLUS, Federal Perkins, privately funded student loans. Federal Work-Study Program available. Institutional employment available. Applicants will be notified of awards on or about April 1. Off-campus job opportunities are good.

FROM THE ADMISSIONS OFFICE

"Notre Dame is a Catholic university, which means it offers unique opportunities for academic, ethical, spiritual, and social service development. The First Year of Studies program provides special assistance to our students as they make the adjustment from high school to college. The first-year curriculum includes many core requirements, while allowing students to explore several areas of possible future study. Each residence hall is home to students from all classes; most will live in the same hall for all their years on campus. An average of 93 percent of entering students will graduate within five years."

For even more information on this school, turn to page 401 of the "Stats" section.

UNIVERSITY OF SAINT THOMAS

2115 SUMMIT AVENUE, #32-F1, ST. PAUL, MN 55105-1096 • ADMISSIONS: 651-962-6150
FAX: 651-962-6160 • E-MAIL: ADMISSIONS@STTHOMAS.EDU • WEBSITE: WWW.STTHOMAS.EDU

Ratings
Quality of Life: 81   **Academic:** 76   **Admissions:** 71   **Financial Aid:** 75

Academics

The University of St. Thomas, a small Catholic school in St. Paul, Minnesota, is best known for its "excellent business program," which, according to many students, is "second to none in the Midwest." Upon graduation, students carry a degree with a "strong reputation in the sciences

> **SURVEY SAYS . . .**
> *Students are religious*
> *Diversity lacking on campus*
> *No one cheats*
> *Instructors are good teachers*
> *Classes are small*
> *Very little hard liquor*

and the business world." Because of the business focus, one student notes that "a capitalistic aura surrounds the school." Others put it this way: "There is a lack of intellectual curiosity. Students just want to make big bucks in business." Be that as it may, the professors are "interested in getting to know you" and have the opportunity to do so because of the "small class sizes." One undergraduate writes that Saint Thomas manages to be "a challenging school while maintaining an importance on the success of all students," meaning there is a solid support system, including "a top-notch tutoring program" and "excellent technological resources." Complaints are logged regarding registration, with more than one student calling it a "crap shoot," especially for freshmen. The administration gets high praise, expressed in the comment, "I have never had trouble contacting anyone from professors to the dean." Students ask only, "Stop hiking tuition like crazy" to pay for "things other than professors." Called "as personal an experience as one can imagine," St. Thomas academics offer a "well-rounded education and a great job after."

Life

Though technically a Catholic institution, St. Thomas life compels one student to write, "As a Catholic going to a Catholic school, I don't find that it is much of a Catholic school." Perhaps the main sign of religious affiliation is rigid rules regarding alcohol, which hamper efforts on the fiesta front. "There are no parties on campus because the security is strict and there are very high fines for adult providers." If it's not the administration clamping down, the "parties always get busted by the cops." One student wants the school to "loosen up," sighing, "I mean, we are in college." Because most students are from the surrounding areas, it seems "they all go home every weekend." Those that remain complain that "on-campus events and activities are lacking." "Cultural, sporting, and entertainment events" available in the Twin Cities are popular among students to the point that "student life revolves less around campus and more around the surrounding city." Many students admire the "picture perfect" campus located in "a beautiful neighborhood," along the banks of the upper Mississippi River, though there is sometimes "friction between us and the neighborhood people."

Students

The largely "homogenous" population of 5,500 at St. Thomas (more than three quarters of which hails from Minnesota) is said to have a large contingency of "preppy, silver-spoonish kids who are using Daddy's money to get a degree in general business and then hit the work-force for a prearranged job." One student perceives a class divide between "those who have financial aid packages and those who don't," when in reality, over 95 percent of students receive some type of financial aid. Perhaps the gap isn't as wide as some students see it. Attending what they describe as the "whitest school I've ever seen," several students express the sentiment, "I wouldn't say different races integrate that well." Another undergraduate writes, "Although there are clubs available to students of different cultures, the minority pop-ulation as a whole is very small." Reportedly, a degree of diversity exists, "you just have to look for it," and generally, students are "very nice and receptive."

ADMISSIONS

Very important factors considered by the admissions committee include: secondary school record. *Important factors considered include:* class rank, essays, and standardized test scores. *Other fac-tors considered include:* alumni/ae relation, character/personal qualities, extracurricular activ-ities, geographical residence, minority status, recommendations, talent/ability, and volunteer work. SAT I or ACT required, ACT preferred. TOEFL required of all international applicants. High school diploma or GED is required. *High school units required/recommended:* 4 English rec-ommended, 3 math required, 4 math recommended, 2 science recommended, 4 foreign lan-guage recommended.

The Inside Word

Degrees here in science and business are becoming as attractive to out-of-staters as they are to students within Minnesota. A school that gets the job done without pausing to over-examine the process, UST is a largely satisfying institution of learning for applicants not desiring a strictly interpreted Catholic influence.

FINANCIAL AID

Students should submit: FAFSA. No deadline for regular filing. The Princeton Review suggests that all financial aid forms be submitted as soon as possible after January 1. *Need-based schol-arships/grants offered:* Pell, SEOG, state scholarships/grants, private scholarships, and the school's own gift aid. *Loan aid offered:* FFEL Subsidized Stafford, FFEL Unsubsidized Stafford, FFEL PLUS, Federal Perkins, state loans, and private loans. Federal Work-Study Program available. Institutional employment available. Applicants will be notified of awards on a rolling basis beginning on or about March 1. Off-campus job opportunities are excellent.

For even more information on this school, turn to page 402 of the "Stats" section.

UNIVERSITY OF SOUTH DAKOTA

414 EAST CLARK, VERMILLION, SD 57069 • ADMISSIONS: 605-677-5434 • FAX: 605-677-6753
FINANCIAL AID: 605-677-5446 • E-MAIL: ADMISS@USD.EDU • WEBSITE: WWW.USD.EDU

Ratings
Quality of Life: 81   **Academic:** 71   **Admissions:** 73   **Financial Aid:** 84

Academics

USD is made up of 100 programs in eight schools, including the state's only medical school, law school, and college of fine arts. While not every program is open to them, undergraduates here are generally pleased with the academic exposure and opportunity that surrounds them. Perhaps just as enticing as the spectrum of selection at USD is the price. South Dakota's flagship university offers notably low tuition rates, as well as "nice scholarships." Students find themselves studying under a faculty that is "very kind, understanding, and determined to make us learn." For the most part, professors here "have a good sense of humor" and give the 5,000 or so undergrads "ample time to meet with them before and after class." Some students say that niceness doesn't always make a good teacher, though. The few professors here who "babble on even when half the class is asleep" get low marks. When students need a break from the lecture hall, they find relief— and stimulation—in the range of "research and internship opportunities" available here. Overall, summarizes one student, "academics are challenging, but not enough to give you a mental breakdown."

> **SURVEY SAYS . . .**
> *Student government is popular*
> *Student newspaper is popular*
> *Frats and sororities dominate social scene*
> *Students are happy*
> *Lab facilities need improving*
> *Computer facilities need improving*
> *Athletic facilities need improving*

Life

USD is located in Vermillion, a city of 10,000 that lies on bluffs overlooking the Missouri River in South Dakota's southeast corner. While students can't deny that Vermillion is a quaint, safe, comfortable town, they find little to spark their excitement here. When they need a dose of something resembling urban life, they head 25 miles southeast to Sioux City, Iowa, or, when they're feeling particularly ambitious, 65 miles north to the even larger Sioux Falls. One student tells us that many classmates "make time for extracurricular activities," which include "academic clubs (biology club, math club, etc.), intramural sports, and the school newspaper," as well as "tae kwon do, fencing, and church activities." This being the case, one student opines, "Very rarely should anyone be bored on our campus." Sports are especially good at bringing the campus to life—particularly when one of the USD Coyote teams hosts a game at their impressive arena, the DakotaDome. But athletic match-ups and after-hours speakers don't satiate everybody's social urges. "Life is pretty boring," moans one student, and there-fore "most people party." As you'll find at almost every university, drinking and drugs have a prominent role in some students' lives, but many say they don't have much time for party-ing. "Most students here work in addition to going to school full-time," explains an English major. "The younger ones only think about the parties. The older ones are finally at the point where they know this is going to affect the rest of their lives." In other words, as the years press on, students learn to drop some of the partying and "focus on their academics."

Student Body

Undergraduates at the University of South Dakota "have the midwestern courtesy and kindness thing going on." And there's good reason for this. More than 85 percent of this student body comes from South Dakota and its neighboring states. Because of the aura of friendliness at the university, one student writes, "I always feel comfortable walking up to a fellow student and asking a question or just talking." Another agrees: "I'd feel comfortable approaching anyone. They are all very laid-back and fun-loving." The biggest complaint by USD students is the noticeable absence of "diverse peoples." At times, this lack of diversity translates to a lack of student interest in the world beyond USD. One tuned-in student mutters, "Students are very apathetic towards politics and society in general." But some of the university's alums stand as proof that this stereotype doesn't always fit. Ten South Dakotan governors have attended USD, as well as many state supreme court justices. And let's not forget news anchor Tom Brokaw, sports commentator Pat O'Brien, and USA Today founder Al Neuharth—all three earned their degrees at USD.

ADMISSIONS

Very important factors considered by the admissions committee include: class rank, secondary school record, standardized test scores. *Other factors considered include:* essays, extracurricular activities, minority status, recommendations, talent/ability. SAT I or ACT required; ACT preferred. TOEFL required of all international applicants. High school diploma or GED is required. *High school units required/recommended:* 16 total required; 17 total recommended; 4 English required, 3 math required, 3 science required, 3 science lab required, 3 social studies required.

The Inside Word

Given the relatively small numbers of college-bound students coming from South Dakota's high schools each year, the university's rolling admission policy is nearly open admission. Solid college-prep students should encounter no trouble in gaining admission.

FINANCIAL AID

Students should submit: FAFSA. No deadline for regular filing. The Princeton Review suggests that all financial aid forms be submitted as soon as possible after January 1. *Need-based scholarships/grants offered:* Pell, SEOG, private scholarships, the school's own gift aid, Federal Nursing. *Loan aid offered:* FFEL Subsidized Stafford, FFEL Unsubsidized Stafford, FFEL PLUS, Federal Perkins, Federal Nursing, college/university loans from institutional funds. Federal Work-Study Program available. Institutional employment available. Applicants will be notified of awards on a rolling basis beginning on or about May 3. Off-campus job opportunities are good.

FROM THE ADMISSIONS OFFICE

"USD, a doctorate-granting university with liberal arts emphasis, has a strong academic reputation. Old Main, the campus focal point, houses the Honors Program, high-tech classrooms, and more. Among the many programs on campus are three Centers of Excellence including the center on Ambulatory Medical Student Education. Innovative, this program has a physician-patient approach, which provides learning opportunities in primary care medicine. The Disaster Mental Health Institute, internationally recognized, provides unique programs in disaster mental health response. The W.O. Farber Center for Civic Leadership, which prepares students in leadership, offers academic, enrichment, and community-outreach programs. The center sponsors internationally prominent speakers such as retired U.S. Army General Colin Powell, former President Gerald Ford, NBC News anchor Tom Brokaw, and others. USD's alumni include: NBC's Tom Brokaw, *USA Today* founder Allen Neuharth, motivational speaker Joan Brock, writers Peter Dexter, *Penny Whistle* book author Meredith Auld Brokaw, Pat O'Brien, USD President James W. Abbott, and World War II ace Joe Foss, among others."

For even more information on this school, turn to page 402 of the "Stats" section.

University of Wisconsin—Eau Claire

105 Garfield Avenue, Eau Claire, WI 54701 • Admissions: 715-836-5415 • Fax: 715-836-2409
E-mail: ask-uwec@uwec.edu • Website: www.uwec.edu

Ratings

Quality of Life: 80   **Academic:** 73   **Admissions:** 72   **Financial Aid:** 76

Academics

Students at University of Wisconsin—Eau Claire feel that their school is the perfect size, "with an enrollment of about 10,000 so that it's big enough to

> **SURVEY SAYS . . .**
> *Diversity lacking on campus, Students are happy*
> *Classes are small, Very little beer drinking*

offer a lot of opportunities but not so big that you're just a number in a computer." This "good median size" allows professors to interact more frequently and intimately with students than they might at a larger state school, leading some to report that "professors are the greatest, they have the passion and know-how to make them the best. All of them know me by name and are very helpful when help is needed." Others are slightly less sanguine about the instruction here, telling us that "I've had a range of professors, some really excellent ones, and others who seem more interested in their personal research than teaching." Undergrads report, "The true strengths of UWEC are the education, nursing, and music schools. All of the other schools are also very good, though." The less-than-sedulous should keep in mind that "it is a hard school. When you graduate (if you do), it actually means something because this is not a school [where] a slacker can [get] by. Most employers know this." Perhaps most importantly, students agree that UWEC offers "good value for the tuition we pay."

Life

"We are in a small college town, so there is not much to do except drink" writes one undergrad. "Plus, we are in Wisconsin, so it goes without saying that pretty much everyone drinks. For the thirsty, "there are parties almost any day of the week and a street devoted to only bars one block from campus." Drinking is not the only diversion here, though. "There are a lot of campus activities you can participate in, plus concerts, plays, open mic nights, a good-sized student center, good recreational facilities, [and] free aerobics classes." Others add, "The opportunity to travel and go on weekend or winter trips through school is excellent. And the Twin Cities offer a lot of entertainment in just a short drive. Lot of concert-going up there." Even so, most who don't party concede that life in Eau Claire is often pretty slow: "It's not as easy to get distracted as [it is] at larger schools," writes one student, "but that also means that it can get boring." Students describe the campus setting as "awesome; during the fall and spring everyone is outside playing sand volleyball or sun tanning." They highly recommend dorm life: "Living in the dorms is the best deal in this area," notes one undergrad, "as students tend to get ripped off by landlords." Students warn that winters are brutal and that "the bridge that goes through campus is one of the coldest places in the United States. " Many suggest that the "really big hill dividing campus could have some sort of transportation system going up it so you wouldn't have to walk up eight flights of stairs."

Students

Many Eau Claire undergraduates remark that life at UWEC is a lot like life at a very large high school. Observes one student, "A lot of students are very gossipy and cliquey. This place is actually a lot more like high school than I ever imagined." Undergrads arrive "from white middle- to upper-class households and from the suburbs or Minneapolis or Milwaukee or

Madison or small towns throughout Wisconsin." Students who come from big cities note with caution, "A lot of students are from really small towns, and they haven't been exposed to much in life outside of their home towns." White students so dominate the student population that some here jokingly refer to the school as "UW—Eau Cracker."

ADMISSIONS

Very important factors considered by the admissions committee include: secondary school record. *Important factors considered include:* class rank and standardized test scores. *Other factors considered include:* essays, extracurricular activities, interview, minority status, recommendations, talent/ability, volunteer work, and work experience. SAT I or ACT required, ACT preferred. TOEFL required of all international applicants. High school diploma or GED is required. *High school units required/recommended:* 17 total required; 4 English required, 3 math required, 3 science required, 2 foreign language required, 3 social studies required, 2 elective required.

The Inside Word

UWEC makes a convincing case for applicants in search of a highbrow academic and social atmosphere that contrasts a lowbrow sticker price. Diversity pervades the school's scholastic climate if not the makeup of the student body.

FINANCIAL AID

Students should submit: FAFSA. No deadline for regular filing. The Princeton Review suggests that all financial aid forms be submitted as soon as possible after January 1. *Need-based scholarships/grants offered:* Pell, SEOG, state scholarships/grants, private scholarships, and the school's own gift aid. *Loan aid offered:* Direct Subsidized Stafford, Direct Unsubsidized Stafford, Direct PLUS, Federal Perkins, and college/university loans from institutional funds. Federal Work-Study Program available. Institutional employment available. Applicants will be notified of awards on a rolling basis beginning on or about April 15. Off-campus job opportunities are good.

FROM THE ADMISSIONS OFFICE

"At UW-Eau Claire you will find a challenging academic environment supported by small classes with lively discussions, classes taught by talented professors, and opportunities abounding for experiential learning, including undergraduate research, internships in most majors, study abroad, a wonderful honors program, and more.

"Of the 80 majors, the more popular degree programs are accounting, athletic training, biological sciences, chemistry, communication disorders, communications, computer science, elementary education, English, foreign languages, psychology, management information systems, nursing, the pre-professional programs, and social work. Unique majors include health care administration, Latin American studies, environmental and public health, and Indian American studies.

"Looking for the ultimate residential experience, UW-Eau Claire's residence life system is tops and provides students with high levels of satisfaction in cost and convenience. The eleven residence halls on campus provide living space for more that 3,900 students. Students have the opportunity to experience a sense of community through a variety of educational, recreational, cultural, and social programs.

"If you enjoy outdoor adventure, concerts, plays, art exhibits, leadership opportunities, or forum lectures, this is the place to be. UW-Eau Claire fields 20 NCAA Division III athletic teams, 190 clubs and organizations, a large student senate and hall council, and more. There are so many things to do that students stick around campus on the weekends.

"For those interested in visiting Wisconsin's 'most beautiful campus,' campus visits occur almost every day of the year, with two tours on most days. For additional information, please call 715-836-5415 or e-mail admissions@uwec.edu."

For even more information on this school, turn to page 403 of the "Stats" section.

UNIVERSITY OF WISCONSIN—LACROSSE

1725 STATE STREET, LACROSSE, WI 54601-3742 • ADMISSIONS: 608-785-8939 • FAX: 608-785-6695
E-MAIL: ADMISSIONS@UWLAX.EDU • WEBSITE: WWW.UWLAX.EDU

Ratings

Quality of Life: 82   **Academic: 75**   **Admissions: 71**   **Financial Aid: 77**

Academics

A "student-friendly" state school, the University of Wisconsin—LaCrosse wins recognition for its "excellent programs in physical education, sports medicine, athletic training, and other fitness-related fields," as well as allied health programs, physics, archae-

> **SURVEY SAYS . . .**
> *Student publications are popular, Classes are small*
> *Diversity lacking on campus*
> *Profs teach upper levels, School is well run*
> *Students get along with local community*
> *Intercollegiate sports are popular*

ology, and business. Professors across all departments "know how to relate to their students" and are "always willing to discuss different career options and graduate school." Several students point out that research programs are "flourishing, and not just in the sciences but in the arts and humanities as well." In testament, one student writes, "I have been doing undergraduate research in the chemistry department, and I can say only good things about my experience. I feel fortunate to be able to work so closely with a professor and learn graduate-level lab techniques." The only "major weak spot" may be advising, which some consider "useless." Administration, on the other had, receives high marks: "It is easy to get an appointment with administrators, and registration generally runs very smoothly." Even the "chancellors all answer their own e-mail." Though financial aid is "not going up in proportion to tuition," most students feel they're getting good value for their money, citing the varied "opportunities for students to develop their leadership skills." Overall they agree, "I feel as though I am studying and taking classes with the best of the best."

Life

Considering that the surrounding area comprises "an outdoor enthusiast's paradise" with spots for "skiing, hiking, kayaking, biking, camping, Frisbee, you name it," it follows that "when you get here you automatically become a fitness buff." Intramural programs offer "a sport for everyone, even dodge ball," and the athletic center is called "the best in the Midwest." All of this endorphin-inducing exercise and natural beauty serve to "greatly alleviate school stress," according to several students. As far as the party scene, a common statement goes, "You'd be surprised how many people don't drink." One undergraduate reports, "They have had a strong campaign in recent years to offer alternatives to drinking and a social norming campaign to make students realize drinking is not the norm for most students." For those who do partake, there's the free "safety bus" to shuttle them to the off-campus bars. One student writes of Greek life, "We have very few fraternities and sororities, but the ones we have are very proactive in community service and social interaction." Parties aside, the most popular nighttime activity may be attending a two-dollar movie at the popular Rivoli movie theater in town.

Students

One student characterizes UW—LaCrosse as a "very conservative, white, middle-class, heterosexual school." While "the minority groups do make themselves known," part of the school's population is "not ready to make diversity part of their everyday life." Many students comment that the student body is "becoming more diverse as the years go by" and already includes students with "diverse interests and beliefs." A sense of unity prevails nonetheless;

one student believes it's the "integration of academic and nonacademic activities that breeds nothing short of a great student body" made up of "enthusiastic students who enjoy interacting socially." The "general philosophy of 'Smile, it's contagious,'" perpetuates the ultra-friendly atmosphere.

ADMISSIONS

Very important factors considered by the admissions committee include: class rank, secondary school record, and standardized test scores. *Important factors considered include:* diversity and special talent. *Other factors considered include:* character/personal qualities, extracurricular activities, geographical residence, interview, recommendations, state residency, talent/ability, volunteer work, and work experience. SAT I or ACT required, ACT preferred. TOEFL required of all international applicants. High school diploma or GED is required. *High school units required/recommended:* 17 total required; 23 total recommended; 4 English required, 3 math required, 4 math recommended, 3 science required, 4 science recommended, 2 science lab required, 3 foreign language recommended, 3 social studies required, 4 social studies recommended, 4 elective required, 2 elective recommended.

The Inside Word

Students flourish at UW-LaCrosse when they take full advantage of the school without becoming bogged down in red tape. In return for that effort, those admitted discover a vibrant environment in the heart of the Dairy Belt.

FINANCIAL AID

Students should submit: FAFSA and the institution's own financial aid form. The Princeton Review suggests that all financial aid forms be submitted as soon as possible after January 1. *Need-based scholarships/grants offered:* Pell, SEOG, state scholarships/grants, and the school's own gift aid. *Loan aid offered:* FFEL Subsidized Stafford, FFEL Unsubsidized Stafford, FFEL PLUS, Federal Perkins, and college/university loans from institutional funds. Federal Work-Study Program available. Institutional employment available. Applicants will be notified of awards on a rolling basis beginning on or about April 15. Off-campus job opportunities are excellent.

FROM THE ADMISSIONS OFFICE

"UW-La Crosse is the place to live and learn—it's academically challenging yet offers great out-of-the-classroom activities. Set between the Coulee Region's famous bluffs and the mighty Mississippi, the campus provides a superb setting to experience 'education for the whole person.' Challenge yourself with the state's top students—our freshmen are consistently second among UW campuses in class rank and ACT scores. Choose from 85 undergraduate programs in 30 disciplines, many with national accreditations and renown. Study and work with professors who care about you. Our classes are small, averaging 30 students each. Conduct research with professors, or by yourself. Exercise your mind. Join one of 150 student organizations. Do an internship and get an advantage when looking for a job; 97 percent of our recent grads found work within six months of commencement.

"Visit campus to understand why UW-La Crosse has become a campus of choice in the Midwest. Arrangements to visit can be made by calling the Admissions Office, preferably one week in advance. Prospective new freshmen are encouraged to apply early for admission, beginning September 15 for the following fall semester. The rigor of a student's senior schedule is seriously considered in addition to their class rank, grades, ACT or SAT scores, involvement, leadership, personal statement, and letters of recommendation."

For even more information on this school, turn to page 403 of the "Stats" section.

UNIVERSITY OF WISCONSIN—MADISON

161 BEACON HALL, 500 LINCOLN DRIVE, MADISON, WI 53706 • ADMISSIONS: 608-262-3961
FAX: 608-262-7708 • FINANCIAL AID: 608-262-3060 • E-MAIL: ONWISCONSIN@ADMISSIONS.WISC.EDU
WEBSITE: WWW.WISC.EDU

Ratings
Quality of Life: 84   **Academic:** 88   **Admissions:** 91   **Financial Aid:** 82

Academics

One of the most prestigious state universities in the country, the University of Wisconsin—Madison employs professors who "are all extremely talented, and most are great teachers as well." It's said that "everyone from administration to TAs challenges students to think deeply and insightfully. They want the best all the time. They enjoy teaching, and we enjoy learning." The problem with attending an undoubtedly "great research institution," however, is that the faculty sometimes "cares less about the students than their research," comments a psychology major. Another student agrees, claiming that it's "tough for students to get in touch with professors and administration." A competitive spirit reigns at Wisconsin, and one sophomore wishes courses were geared for "success rather than hoping [other] people will fail." Difficulties lie in "finishing in four years," "getting classes of choice as a freshman," and "transferring credits" from other schools. Students also complain about a lack of career placement services and remark that "advising is a bitch. I still don't know who my advisor is."

> **SURVEY SAYS . . .**
> *Lots of beer drinking*
> *Hard liquor is popular*
> *Everyone loves the Badgers*
> *Students love Madison, WI*
> *Great library*
> *Great off-campus food*
> *Campus is beautiful*
> *Great computer facilities*
> *Student newspaper is popular*
> *Students are happy*

Life

Political activism is a cornerstone of Madison life, to a degree that one junior comments, "It can get irritating. How many rallies can you have?" When students aren't protesting, there's "lots of partying, but also lots of studying," writes a freshman. Wisconsin's reputation as a party school ("Beer goes well with all activities") has diminished in the past few years, and one senior says, "The alcohol scene is over-hyped—there's other stuff to do." That "stuff" includes "plays, concerts, an overwhelming number of organizations on campus," and Badger sporting events. The city of Madison is widely considered the ultimate college town, with a senior bragging that "State Street compares to Bourbon Street on weekend nights." The city is also a big kids' playground "for biking, running, sports, and water activities." A content math major summarizes, "No better college atmosphere can be found anywhere than in Madison with so many things to do. People come just to see how much students care for and love the opportunities the campus offers."

Student Body

The University of Wisconsin—Madison is home to "nice Midwest people" who are characterized as a "fun and crazy bunch." Amid a sea of undergraduates, one student comments, "people are friendly and willing to chat in class, which makes the large college seem smaller and more welcoming." A senior questions her classmates' priorities, opining that many are "least interested in school and the community." Some students are well-versed in studying "just enough for an A or B," but others are perpetually "way too driven and stressed out," according to a senior. The politically aware student body bends over backwards to defend the Wisconsin brand of diversity, emphasizing that the campus population is "very socio-economically diverse" even if it is "very segregated" and in sore need of "minority recruitment and retention." Interaction between students and locals is limited; one Madison native states that "most students do not know the city or its people."

ADMISSIONS

Very important factors considered by the admissions committee include: class rank, secondary school record. *Important factors considered include:* recommendations, standardized test scores, state residency, talent/ability. *Other factors considered include:* alumni/ae relation, character/personal qualities, essays, extracurricular activities, interview, minority status, volunteer work, work experience. SAT I or ACT required. TOEFL required of all international applicants. High school diploma or GED is required. *High school units required/recommended:* 17 total required; 20 total recommended; 4 English required, 3 math required, 4 math recommended, 3 science required, 4 science recommended, 2 foreign language required, 3 social studies required, 4 social studies recommended.

The Inside Word

Wisconsin has high expectations of its candidates and virtually all of them relate to numbers. Though not at the top tier of selectivity, this is admissions- by-formula at its most refined state. Nonresidents will encounter a very selective process.

FINANCIAL AID

Students should submit: FAFSA, institution's own financial aid form. No deadline for regular filing. The Princeton Review suggests that all financial aid forms be submitted as soon as possible after January 1. *Need-based scholarships/grants offered:* Pell, SEOG, state scholarships/grants, private scholarships, the school's own gift aid. *Loan aid offered:* FFEL Subsidized Stafford, FFEL Unsubsidized Stafford, FFEL PLUS, Federal Perkins, Federal Nursing, state loans, college/university loans from institutional funds. Federal Work-Study Program available. Institutional employment available. Applicants will be notified of awards on a rolling basis beginning on or about April 1. Off-campus job opportunities are excellent.

FROM THE ADMISSIONS OFFICE

"Admission decisions of quality and fairness take time. We don't promise to be the fastest out of the box, but we do guarantee a complete, fair, and thorough decision. We want applicants to provide us with as much information about themselves as they think is necessary for a group of people who don't know them to reach a favorable decision."

For even more information on this school, turn to page 404 of the "Stats" section.

UNIVERSITY OF WISCONSIN—MILWAUKEE

PO Box 749, Milwaukee, WI 53201 • Admissions: 414-229-3800 • Fax: 414-229-6940
E-mail: UWMLOOK@DES.UWM.EDU • Website: WWW.UWM.EDU

Ratings

Quality of Life: 83   Academic: 70   Admissions: 69   Financial Aid: 75

Academics

Business, architecture, engineering, nursing, education, and fine arts: our respondents believe that these are the programs that make the University of Wisconsin—Milwaukee stand out. For students with the right grades and a healthy dose of initiative, "the honors program at UWM is really wonderful" and features easy course selection, attentive advisors, and "great" professors. Honors or not, students at UWM find "the professors to be very qualified" and "extremely talented." Students gripe, though, that they have some professors who "do not speak fluently in English," which makes lecture comprehension a bit difficult; some also find it "frustrating that most of the lower-level classes and discussions are taught by teaching assistants who rarely know more than you." But in the higher-level courses, class sizes are smaller and full-time professors stand behind the lecterns—and this is when students discover "a lot of opportunity for one-on-ones with professors." Because UWM is a "highly research-oriented" university, students with drive can get their hands wet through student-faculty research. And "the school is open to funding individual projects" for ambitious young scholars. Students tell us that what UWM needs most these days is a more progressive and intelligent student body. "The administration is a bit conservative" and "not very creative" when it comes to spending money and attracting prospective students. But with some strategic spending and admissions maneuvering over the next few years, students believe that UWM's academic reputation will lift itself to a higher rung on America's academic ladder.

> **SURVEY SAYS . . .**
> *School is well run*
> *Students love Milwaukee*
> *Lots of beer drinking*
> *Classes are small*

Life

Milwaukee, America's 19th largest city, is the city that gave us Harley Davidson motorcycles, and it's the birthplace of actor Gene Wilder. It's also home to the world's largest four-faced clock, a world-famous repertoire of summer festivals, the Brewers baseball club, the Bucks basketball team, and 11 colleges and universities, including the University of Wisconsin's Milwaukee campus. "Everyone" at UWM "goes out and does things in the greater Milwaukee city area." With 1.5 million people living in the metro area, Milwaukee offers students every variety of distraction, like "downtown bars, museums, a zoo," and waterfront activities on Lake Michigan's western shore. The Miller Brewing Company's HQ is in Milwaukee, arguably "the beer capital of the world," so it should be no surprise to learn that these students like to party. There are "a lot of house parties" off campus, and the "town is full of bars"—especially on Water Street, a popular avenue for nightlife. Concerts at The Rave are popular, and there are plenty of "small bookstores and coffee shops where students are frequently found congregating for poetry readings and open mic nights." The university has more than 200 active student organizations that are regularly trying "to get people involved." Otherwise, campus is a quiet place—especially on weekends, when many students go back to their hometowns. But with Milwaukee at their fingertips, most students don't seem to mind the limits of campus life.

Students

UWM is a large, urban university in the center of the downtown Milwaukee. While most students here are from Wisconsin, the student body is a "very diverse" mix of people from all different walks of life. Many students commute to class, "most work 20-30 hours/week," and the traditional, late-teenage freshmen share the classrooms with "adult students" who "like to put their two cents of wisdom in on the subjects" being discussed. While "once in a while you'll come across someone that would be better suited for a high school," you're more likely to find people who are "intelligent" and "respectful" of one another. Perhaps a phenomenon of the urban setting, UWM students tend to "keep to themselves, walking around campus with their heads down and not making any attempts to talk to the people around them." This doesn't mean they're not a pleasant bunch. "Students are very friendly here"—that is, if you manage to get to know them.

ADMISSIONS

Very important factors considered by the admissions committee include: class rank and secondary school record. *Important factors considered include:* standardized test scores. *Other factors considered include:* essays, extracurricular activities, minority status, recommendations, state residency, talent/ability, volunteer work, and work experience. SAT I or ACT required, ACT preferred. TOEFL required of all international applicants. High school diploma or GED is required. *High school units required/recommended:* 17 total required; 19 total recommended; 4 English required, 3 math required, 3 science required, 1 science lab required, 2 foreign language recommended, 3 social studies required, 3 social studies recommended, 4 elective required.

The Inside Word

Applicants devoted to expanding their academic and social spectra can discover a supportive environment at UWM. If the school's strong professional degrees and Milwaukee location fit your plans, stress to the admissions department that you are a component in the school's ascending future.

FINANCIAL AID

Students should submit: FAFSA. No deadline for regular filing. The Princeton Review suggests that all financial aid forms be submitted as soon as possible after January 1. *Need-based scholarships/grants offered:* Pell, SEOG, state scholarships/grants, and private scholarships. *Loan aid offered:* Direct Subsidized Stafford, Direct Unsubsidized Stafford, Direct PLUS, Federal Perkins, and Federal Nursing. Federal Work-Study Program available. Institutional employment available. Applicants will be notified of awards on a rolling basis beginning on or about April 15. Off-campus job opportunities are good.

For even more information on this school, turn to page 405 of the "Stats" section.

UNIVERSITY OF WISCONSIN—RIVER FALLS

410 SOUTH THIRD STREET, 112 SOUTH HALL, RIVER FALLS, WI 54022 • ADMISSIONS: 715-425-3500
FAX: 715-425-0676 • E-MAIL: ADMIT@UWRF.EDU • WEBSITE: WWW.UWRF.EDU

Ratings

Quality of Life: 78   **Academic:** 72   **Admissions:** 73   **Financial Aid:** 78

Academics

Business, education, and agricultural studies are the feature attractions at University of Wisconsin—River Falls, a state school whose low tuition and small classes offer just the right combination for many area undergrads. Reports one student, "None of our classes are taught by teacher's assistants (I'm a tour guide, so I know this!). Our student/faculty ratio is cur-

> **SURVEY SAYS . . .**
> *Profs teach upper levels*
> *Diversity lacking on campus*
> *Great food on campus*
> *Class discussions encouraged*
> *Instructors are good teachers*
> *Theater is hot*
> *School is well run*
> *Popular college radio*

rently 19:1, and students definitely see the rewards in that . . . . Our profs are generally accessible (depending on the individual), and most are here to teach." Students here give the faculty mixed reviews for teaching ability: writes one, "We have a wide range of teaching techniques here. Some are very effective, others are down right [expletive]. You just have to ask around for the scoop on the professors before you sign up for a class." Adds another, "Some profs are unbelievably awesome, some are hard to understand and a little overwhelming. Sometimes I felt uncomfortable to talk to some of my professors if I had questions, but most were great." Fortunately, "there are tutors available for those who need additional help, and sometimes even professors will arrange a time so you can meet with them to better understand some things." UWRF offers a brief January Term that allows students an opportunity to explore a wide range of interests, including internships, practical business applications, and even glassblowing.

Life

The combination of a small-town setting and a student population drawn primarily from the surrounding region means many students leave campus on the weekends. Writes one undergrad, "During the week, school is lots of fun, but the major problem with this campus is that everyone leaves on the weekend, so there is nothing to do." Another student tells us, "On this campus, you have to be able to entertain yourself on weekends. There are always house parties, but if you're looking for something else to do, there's a movie theatre, pool hall, bowling alley, a few good restaraunts, and lots of bars." Students report that Wednesday and Thursday "are the big party nights." For fun, writes an undergrad, "my friends and I hang out, play games, cook food and serve it to the public [or] go sledding" during Wisconsin's long cold winter. Students agree, "The campus itself is absolutely beautiful . . . . There's nothing like waking up in the morning, throwing open your shades and seeing sky—no buildings, no people." When they need a more urban setting, undergrads head for the Twin Cities or Hudson, Wisconsin. Many undergrads, especially those among UWRF's sizeable commuter population, complain that "the school needs to have more places to park."

Students

"River Falls definitely has small-town charm with a li'l bit of a cosmo kick! Students come here from high schools ranging from 50 to 5,000 [students], and they definitely intermingle," reports one upbeat undergraduate. "I feel the majority of students learn to leave their prejudices behind. It's too small of a campus not to." Diversity is an issue for some; many UWRF students "come from farming communities" to form a "mainly Caucasian crowd," although "the increasing Hmong community in the Twin Cities is sending many students to River Falls, definitely increasing the diversity."

ADMISSIONS

Very important factors considered by the admissions committee include: class rank, secondary school record, and standardized test scores. *Other factors considered include:* recommendations. ACT required. TOEFL required of all international applicants. High school diploma or GED is required. *High school units required/recommended:* 17 total required; 4 English required, 3 math required, 3 science required, 2 foreign language recommended, 3 social studies required, 4 elective required.

The Inside Word

If you're not planning to join the commuter ranks of this consistently popular choice for applicants from around the River Falls region, you'd be best served bringing a healthy initiative to inject some appeal into activities that can carry the school's energy into the weekend.

FINANCIAL AID

Students should submit: FAFSA and institution's own financial aid form. The Princeton Review suggests that all financial aid forms be submitted as soon as possible after January 1. *Need-based scholarships/grants offered:* Pell, SEOG, state scholarships/grants, and private scholarships. *Loan aid offered:* Direct Subsidized Stafford, Direct Unsubsidized Stafford, Direct PLUS, and Federal Perkins. Federal Work-Study Program available. Institutional employment available. Applicants will be notified of awards on a rolling basis beginning on or about April 1. Off-campus job opportunities are good.

FROM THE ADMISSIONS OFFICE

"Founded in 1874, UW-River Falls is located in west-central Wisconsin on the eastern edge of the Minneapolis-St. Paul metropolitan area. Ranked as a top midwestern university, students can choose a major from more than 40 programs of study and find involvement in more than 120 clubs and organizations (including 18 varsity sports). Popular majors include such areas as biotechnology, computer science, business administration, psychology, art, English, environmental science, journalism, food science and technology, communicative disorders, physics, equine science, and education. The College of Education and Professional Studies is nationally recognized and is housed in a new state-of-the-art facility. The attractive 225-acre campus offers excellent facilities, laboratories, and classrooms. The university ranks second in the entire UW system in its four-year graduation rate. UW-River Falls is affordable and more than two-thirds of the students receive financial assistance. Over 40 percent of the University's 5,800 students come from out of state and find strong academic programs, a great location, and excellent opportunities for internships."

For even more information on this school, turn to page 405 of the "Stats" section.

UNIVERSITY OF WISCONSIN—STEVENS POINT

STUDENT SERVICES CENTER, STEVENS POINT, WI 54481 • ADMISSIONS: 715-346-2441 • FAX: 715-346-3957
E-MAIL: ADMISS@UWSP.EDU • WEBSITE: WWW.UWSP.EDU

Ratings

Quality of Life: 80   **Academic:** 71   **Admissions:** 70   **Financial Aid:** 76

Academics

The College of Natural Resources (CNR) is the undisputed star of the show at the University of Wisconsin—Stevens Point, but students here also praise the "great education department" as well as strong programs in biology, dance, theater, business, and political sci-

> **SURVEY SAYS . . .**
> *Very little hard liquor*
> *Students are happy*
> *Classes are small*
> *Diversity lacking on campus*
> *Profs teach upper levels*

ence. Students at CNR, the largest such undergraduate program in the nation, study forestry, soil and waste management, water management, wildlife, resource management, and paper science (the school is home to a functioning paper machine). Students report that "the quality of the professors really depends on the department. In the political science department, for example, 80 percent of them are great. In the computer information systems department, on the other hand, most of the professors are not so great." Most feel that "the majority of the profs here really enjoy their work and helping students. When you need help with anything, there is always a resource." Likewise, "the administration is always available for help," according to many. Adds another student, "I think the only problem is trying to get into classes. . . . It feels like there is not enough room for everyone." Another undergrad cries for better "availability of classes!" Even so, most graduates would agree with a student who told us that "overall, I've had a great time here. It's forced me to think thoughts I likely wouldn't have had I not gone to college. I won't miss the amount of homework or finals weeks, but I'll miss the classroom experience."

Life

Weather permitting, the students of UWSP enjoy outdoor activities in their spare time. "A lot of people that go to my school spend a lot of time outdoors," explains one student. "For fun they like to swim, jog, take walks, rollerblade, ride bikes, go to the park, etc." Many "participate in the intramural sports program and attend athletic activities." The school is also home to a budding arts scene; writes one student, "I like to go to a lot of concerts, theater performances, etc., that are sponsored by the school. A lot of these events are free or cost is minimal." Another reports that "there are a lot of plays and concerts that go on here constantly; however, they aren't very well publicized so mostly the only thing to do on the weekends is party, but UWSP is pretty good at that." Indeed, once off campus, "there isn't much to do in the town of Stevens Point. Most students, myself included, spend most of their weekend hours going out to bars downtown, or if they are underage, to house parties. The town has one small movie theatre within walking distance and another across town, as well as a new video store a block from campus. "Thirsty Thursday" is the big party night here, whether students go downtown or to on-campus parties. Green Bay and Madison are both accessible within two hours by car.

Students

UWSP students concede that "this campus is most definitely a white campus; we have very very few ethnic minorities here. We all get along though and treat each other respectfully." Because of the natural resources program, "we've got a good-sized amount of 'greens,' and I like that. The students are pretty political and aware of their place in the world." Writes one student, "There are quite a few earthy people here (i.e., hippies) because this is a big natural resources school. There are also lots of education majors." Students are pleased that their classmates "don't seem to be very judgmental, but very accepting and laid-back. They don't waste time with stereotypes and popularity; everyone kind of does their own thing and that's okay."

ADMISSIONS

Very important factors considered by the admissions committee include: class rank, secondary school record, and standardized test scores. *Important factors considered include:* talent/ability. *Other factors considered include:* character/personal qualities, extracurricular activities, minority status, recommendations, and work experience. SAT I or ACT required, ACT preferred. TOEFL required of all international applicants. High school diploma or GED is required. *High school units required/recommended:* 17 total required; 4 English required, 3 math required, 3 science required, 2 foreign language recommended, 3 social studies required, 4 elective required.

The Inside Word

Students interested in environmental studies should consider this school regardless of the distance from which they would be applying to this campus, located smack-dab in the middle of the state. Many ecology-minded in-class and extracurricular activities offer students the chance to get intensely involved in their studies.

FINANCIAL AID

Students should submit: FAFSA. Regular filing deadline is July 15. The Princeton Review suggests that all financial aid forms be submitted as soon as possible after January 1. *Need-based scholarships/grants offered:* Pell, SEOG, state scholarships/grants, private scholarships, and the school's own gift aid. *Loan aid offered:* FFEL Subsidized Stafford, FFEL Unsubsidized Stafford, FFEL PLUS, and Federal Perkins. Federal Work-Study Program available. Institutional employment available. Applicants will be notified of awards on a rolling basis beginning on or about April 1. Off-campus job opportunities are excellent.

FROM THE ADMISSIONS OFFICE

"UWSP provides a life-changing experience for students. By embracing a distinctive curriculum that emphasizes workplace learning to successfully support students' personal land professional growth, the UWSP experience significantly affects students'; lives for the years to come. Over 90 percent of our current students re satisfied with UWSP, and over 90 percent of alumni would recommend UWSP to family and friends.

"The campus enjoys a warm relationship with the Stevens Point community, which totals about 60,000 residents with the surrounding area. Students find that many partnerships are in place for their benefit—for example, outstanding co-op experiences have been arranged at regional businesses; students can use their meal counts and prepaid cash values at numerous off-campus locations; and a Collaborative Degree Program offers distance learning courses by combining video conferencing and personal instruction at three separate locations in the region.

"In a recent survey, students said that the overwhelming reason they chose UWSP was the quality of its academic programs. We now have a graduation rate second only to Madison in the entire UW system. With more than 175 extracurricular clubs and organizations, UWSP students are never at a loss for opportunities to engage with their campus, their community, and their classmates. This level of involvement compliments our students' successes in the classroom—not just for the majority of our students, but also over a variety of cultural and occupational lines. For example, UWSP students of color just experienced an 83 percent freshman-sophomore retention rate, and our varsity athletes enjoy a higher average grade point than our overall population."

For even more information on this school, turn to page 406 of the "Stats" section.

UNIVERSITY OF WISCONSIN—STOUT

ADMISSIONS UW-STOUT, MENOMONIE, WI 54751 • ADMISSIONS: 715-232-1411 • FAX: 715-232-1667
EMAIL: ADMISSIONS@UWSTOUT.EDU • WEBSITE: WWW.UWSTOUT.EDU

Ratings

Quality of Life: 75   **Academic:** 72   **Admissions:** 60   **Financial Aid:** 70

Academics

"It's all about applicable knowledge, not a philosophical education" at the University of Wisconsin-Stout, which suits the school's 7,000+ undergraduates fine. Most are drawn to this northwestern state campus by its unique career-targeted offerings. "UW Stout excels in a lot of majors that most schools don't

> **SURVEY SAYS . . .**
> *School is well run*
> *Very little hard liquor*
> *No one plays intramural sports*
> *Diversity lacking on campus*
> *Very little beer drinking*
> *Students don't get along with local community*
> *Classes are small*

have," students tell us, including a popular hospitality and tourism management program as well as degrees in apparel design and manufacturing, food services, vocational rehabilitation, and industrial production technologies. UW Stout knows how to deliver the goods to its students, which is why it was the nation's first university to receive the prestigious Malcolm Baldrige Award for efficient and effective business management, presented by the president of the United States. Students here are, not surprisingly, highly satisfied with the Stout experience. "The school promotes a very hands-on atmosphere that allows students to really experience their field of study," explains one undergraduate. "The professors are very personable. They take the time to learn students' names and greet them outside of the classroom. It is not unusual for a professor to have lunch with a group of students," writes another. UW Stout's career-minded students also appreciate that Stout's "location in a small community with access to a large-city economic base for practicums and internships is very beneficial." Budget-minded students should be pleased with both the low tuition and the opportunity to rent (rather than buy) expensive textbooks.

Life

Depending on whom you ask, UW Stout is either a bustling hub of activity or a dead zone where a keg of beer offers the only solace. Some warn that "social life at Stout has a sole focus: alcohol. If you don't drink, you won't enjoy it here." Others disagree, telling us that "there are very effective student organizations here at UW Stout. With a smaller size campus there are opportunities for anyone who wants to participate, and we are big enough to offer many resources for our experiences." Sums up one fence-straddling student, "Stout is located in a smaller town. There is not a lot to do for entertainment. While many students drink, they also have fun activities that do not involve alcohol consumption." Those activities include theater, movie nights, scavenger hunts, intramural sports, and, when the weather is warm enough, "a lot of outdoor activities." Students enjoy the homey campus, which is "big enough, but also small enough to get to a class from the bottom of the hill to the top in 10 minutes."

Students

UW Stout "is a very friendly campus," undergrads here boast. "People introduce themselves, and it is very easy to make friends. Anyone can walk into a class and pretty much sit by any random person and start up a conversation." Stout has little in the way of a minority population ("This school is so white, it blinds you," cracks one student) and "most are very small town." Diversity here comes in the form of a large nontraditional contingent. Explains one older undergrad, "There is a very good mix of traditional and nontraditional students. As a nontraditional student I think and feel I am accepted and encouraged by my fellow students, despite differing opinions." The relatively large out-of-state population here is due to the school's unusual program offerings and its proximity to Minnesota. Some caution that "students on campus are very close; however, the off-campus students tend not to mesh very well with the rest of us."

ADMISSIONS

Very important factors considered by the admissions committee include: class rank (top 50%), required SAT (1030) or ACT (22), and extracurricular activities. TOEFL required of all international applicants. High school diploma is required or completion and proof of HSED or GED and a score of 50 or better. HSED or GED applicants are not allowed to apply until 2 years before their anticipated high school graduation date. *High school units required:* 4 English required, 3 math required, 3 science required, 2 social science required, 4 elective required.

The Inside Word

UWS is a strong candidate for applicants looking for a pragmatic approach to their education. The school's "news you can use" approach benefits students in both their worldviews and their wallets.

FINANCIAL AID

Students should submit: FAFSA. Regular filing deadline is No deadline. The Princeton Review suggests that all financial aid forms be submitted as soon as possible after January 1. *Need-based scholarships/grants offered:* Pell, SEOG, state scholarships/grants, private scholarships, the school's own gift aid, and BIA. *Loan aid offered:* FFEL subsidized Stafford, FFEL unsubsidized Stafford, FFEL PLUS, federal Perkins, and alternative educational loans. Federal Work-Study Program available. Institution employment available. Applicants will be notified of awards on a rolling basis beginning on or about April 1. Off-campus job opportunities are good.

FROM THE ADMISSIONS OFFICE

"The admissions staff invites you to visit our beautiful campus to explore your career opportunities with the University of Wisconsin—Stout. You may call us at 800-447-8688 to arrange for a campus visit. We will arrange for you to tour the campus with a UW-Stout Tour Guide, meet with an advisor or program director in the program you are interested in, and meet with an admissions counselor."

For even more information on this school, turn to page 407 of the "Stats" section.

VALPARAISO UNIVERSITY

OFFICE OF ADMISSION, KRETZMANN HALL, VALPARAISO, IN 46383-9978 • ADMISSIONS: 219-464-5011
FAX: 219-464-6898 • FINANCIAL AID: 219-464-5015 • E-MAIL: UNDERGRAD.ADMISSIONS@VALPO.EDU
WEBSITE: WWW.VALPO.EDU

Ratings

Quality of Life: 73   **Academic:** 76   **Admissions:** 79   **Financial Aid:** 82

Academics

The students at Valparaiso University—affectionately called "Valpo" by all affiliated with the school—consider it a successful hybrid of large university and small liberal arts college. With 60 fields of study in four colleges (arts and sciences, nursing, business, and engineering), Valpo undergrads can select from a broad academic slate of majors the likes of which are found at large universities, and many of

> **SURVEY SAYS . . .**
> *Frats and sororities dominate social scene*
> *No one cheats*
> *Musical organizations are hot*
> *Student government is popular*
> *Lots of beer drinking*
> *Library needs improving*
> *Students are cliquish*
> *Students don't like Valparaiso, IN*
> *Very little drug use*

which train them for specific careers. Most undergrads also have to complete a battery of core requirements in order to graduate. But what the students—almost every student we surveyed—seem to appreciate the most is the easy access to professors that is often an earmark of small institutions. "Every school now seems to say that the professors are very personable, but how many schools can say that their professors have dinner with students, let them borrow their cars to take into Chicago for interviews, travel to Istanbul with them, or let them house-sit while they are away for a semester?" Aside from the strong profs, Valparaiso has built some other enticing features in its offerings, like the "neat program for freshmen called Valpo Core, which combines first-year English, history, theology, and a number of other humanities classes into one five-credit class, taken each of the first two semesters." Something that they're less enthusiastic about is the library. But one student is pleased to report that "Valpo will have a much-needed new library by fall 2004." Overall, a freshman tells us, there's no doubt that the "Valpo atmosphere is conducive to learning."

Life

Just because Valpo students tend to be religious and just because "theoretically Valpo is a dry campus" doesn't mean that these students don't know how to cut loose: "It's undeniable that alcohol is big here," and "if people don't drink in the dorms they go to the frat houses." About a quarter of all students join fraternities and sororities, and these Greeks bear the collective onus of maintaining a healthy party scene on campus. Students report, though, that "people get in trouble for alcohol on a normal basis" because of the strict campus policies and the relentless local police. Beyond the keggers, students get "involved with intramurals, student government, and the many (other) organizations that are found here." And there's always a strong turnout at the Valparaiso Crusaders men's basketball games. When students take a few steps off of campus, they find themselves in the town of Valparaiso, "the greatest hick town the world has ever seen." Still, it's "close enough to Chicago to escape the small-town atmosphere" if the students need to. And the Indiana Dunes National Lakeshore on Lake Michigan is just a quick car ride away. "It's a very relaxing and laid-back atmosphere," sums up a freshman.

Student Body

Affiliated with the Lutheran Church, the most distinctive feature of the undergraduate body is its "religious" flavor. "If you don't believe in God don't come here because it can become a very cold" place if you don't, according to one student. She estimates that "80 percent of students are ultra-conservative and are adamant about evangelizing their faith." The traditional stance taken by most students sometimes leads to problems. For instance, "sexual orientation is a sore point at Valparaiso." But overall, squabbles are rare, and this student population of 3,000 prides itself on its "friendliness." "No matter where you go you see smiling faces," raves a sophomore, a phenomenon referred to as "the Valpo Smile." Crusaders are the first to admit, however, that they're not the most diverse bunch around. "We are all upper-middle-class white kids with stable homes and not too much drama in our lives," one student tells us. Students believe, however, that their commonalities are the bedrock of many friendships.

ADMISSIONS

Very important factors considered by the admissions committee include: secondary school record. *Important factors considered include:* class rank, extracurricular activities, standardized test scores, talent/ability. *Other factors considered include:* alumni/ae relation, character/personal qualities, essays, interview, minority status, recommendations, religious affiliation/commitment, volunteer work. SAT I or ACT required. TOEFL required of all international applicants. High school diploma or GED is required. *High school units required/recommended:* 4 English required, 3 math required, 4 math recommended, 2 science required, 3 science recommended, 2 science lab required, 3 science lab recommended, 2 foreign language required, 3 social studies required, 3 elective required.

The Inside Word

Valparaiso admits the vast majority of those who apply, but candidates should not be overconfident. Places like this fill a special niche in higher education and spend a good deal of time assessing the match a candidate makes with the university, even if the expected better-than-average high school record is present. Essays and extracurriculars can help you get admitted if your transcript is weak.

FINANCIAL AID

Students should submit: FAFSA. The Princeton Review suggests that all financial aid forms be submitted as soon as possible after January 1. *Need-based scholarships/grants offered:* Pell, SEOG, state scholarships/grants, private scholarships, the school's own gift aid. *Loan aid offered:* Direct Subsidized Stafford, Direct Unsubsidized Stafford, Direct PLUS, Federal Perkins, college/university loans from institutional funds. Federal Work-Study Program available. Institutional employment available. Applicants will be notified of awards on a rolling basis beginning on or about March 1. Off-campus job opportunities are good.

FROM THE ADMISSIONS OFFICE

"Valpo provides students a blend of academic excellence, social experience, and spiritual exploration. The concern demonstrated by faculty and administration for the total well-being of students reflects a long history as a Lutheran-affiliated university."

For even more information on this school, turn to page 407 of the "Stats" section.

WABASH COLLEGE

PO Box 352, 301 W. Wabash Avenue, Crawfordsville, IN 47933 • Admissions: 765-361-6225
Fax: 765-361-6437 • Financial Aid: 765-361-6370 • E-mail: admissions@wabash.edu
Website: www.wabash.edu

Ratings
Quality of Life: 82   **Academic:** 93   **Admissions:** 87   **Financial Aid:** 89

Academics

All-male Wabash College produces graduates who exemplify "the Gentleman's Rule," Wabash's brief but all-inclusive code of conduct: "Every student should behave as a gentleman and responsible citizen on and off campus." Students report that every interaction at Wabash is colored by students', faculty members', and administrators'

> **SURVEY SAYS . . .**
> *Frats dominate social scene*
> *Everyone loves the Giants*
> *(Almost) everyone plays intramural sports*
> *No one cheats, Campus feels safe*
> *Students don't like Crawfordsville, IN*
> *Class discussions encouraged*
> *Student publications are popular*

commitment to the rule. Writes one student, "I think the Gentleman's Rule, which is our only code of conduct, not only is applicable for the students, but also for the faculty and administrators as well. They really do a good job listening to the concerns of the students and work on improving the learning environment on the campus." Professors here constitute "a knowledgeable and wonderful group of people. They push us to the furthest extent possible so that we can do the most with our given ability. I've never worked so hard in my life, and I've never gotten so much out of anything, academically, socially, and personally, as I have from Wabash." Students must complete a required core of liberal arts courses, fulfill a major concentration, and pass comprehensive written and oral examinations in order to graduate. Their efforts are abetted by access to exceptional facilities; as one student reports, "In a college as small as Wabash, it is sometimes amazing to consider all the facilities we have at our fingertips. The computer labs are all over campus and available to anyone very easily. I think our library is the best I have yet to see, and I know our recreational/athletic facilities are the envy of Division III schools."

Life

You probably wouldn't expect much in the way of wild partying from an all-male campus with demanding academics, and during weekdays, you'd be right. Weekends, however, are a whole other matter at Wabash. Reports one student, "From the start of Sunday night to Friday night students are busy studying . . . . On weekends, however, the party life here is awesome. The school is known throughout the state for having the best parties anywhere and is definitely worth the drive for girls and guys." Students brag that Wabash is a "very wet campus" where drunken misconduct is restrained not by campus police but rather by the Gentleman's Rule; writes one undergrad, "Basically, if we conduct ourselves like gentlemen, both on and off campus, no one gets in trouble. This is a very risky way of disciplining a college campus, but it works. We do a lot of drinking and partying on the weekends and a little during the week, but as long as we are mature about it, no one gets in trouble and everyone has a good time." Sports are very big with students, as is the Greek system, which reportedly snags nearly three-quarters of all undergraduates. Hometown Crawfordsville has "all of the essentials but lacks the versatility of a bigger city"; fortunately, "there are two larger cities close by that can provide the extra entertainment needed." Students occasionally "venture to other schools for parties and things because they aren't that far: Purdue, Ball State, Butler, and Indiana University are all really close."

Student Body

The "studious, disciplined, naturally intelligent, and for the most part well-spoken" undergraduates of Wabash regard each other as brothers. "Unity on campus is prevalent," students agree, "mostly because of tradition. Traditions like Chapel Sing and the Monon Bell game bring all students on campus together." These brothers do squabble on occasion. "The only problem I find is being an independent on a campus that is almost three-quarters Greek," complains one student. Responds a frat brother, "There are rivalries, but when it comes time for Wabash to compete or show her collective power, everyone is there sporting the scarlet and white." Students are "ridiculously conservative,"and while "not everyone is religious, those who are are very religious." In recent years "the student body has gotten much more diverse, and that has helped the atmosphere rather than caused problems."

ADMISSIONS

Very important factors considered by the admissions committee include: class rank, secondary school record. *Important factors considered include:* recommendations, standardized test scores. *Other factors considered include:* alumni/ae relation, character/personal qualities, essays, extracurricular activities, geographical residence, interview, minority status, state residency, talent/ability, volunteer work, work experience. SAT I or ACT required. TOEFL required of all international applicants. High school diploma or GED is required. *High school units recommended:* 17 total recommended; 4 English, 4 math, 3 science, 2 science lab, 2 foreign language, 2 social studies, 2 history.

The Inside Word

Wabash is one of the few remaining all-male colleges in the country, and like the rest it has a small applicant pool. The pool is highly self-selected, and the academic standards for admission, while selective, are not particularly demanding. However, Wabash is tough to graduate from—don't consider it if you aren't prepared to work.

FINANCIAL AID

Students should submit: FAFSA, CSS/Financial Aid PROFILE, federal tax returns and W-2 statements. Regular filing deadline is March 1. The Princeton Review suggests that all financial aid forms be submitted as soon as possible after January 1. *Need-based scholarships/grants offered:* Pell, state scholarships/grants, private scholarships, the school's own gift aid. *Loan aid offered:* FFEL Subsidized Stafford, FFEL Unsubsidized Stafford, FFEL PLUS, college/university loans from institutional funds. Institutional employment available. Applicants will be notified of awards on or about April 1. Off-campus job opportunities are excellent.

FROM THE ADMISSIONS OFFICE

"Wabash College is different—and distinctive—from other liberal arts colleges. Different in that Wabash is an outstanding college for men only. Distinctive in the quality and character of the faculty, in the demanding nature of the academic program, in the farsightedness and maturity of the men who enroll, and in the richness of the traditions that have evolved throughout its 168-year history. Wabash is, preeminently, a teaching institution, and fundamental to the learning experience is the way faculty and students talk to each other: with mutual respect for the expression of informed opinion. For example, students who collaborate with faculty on research projects are considered their peers in the research—an esteem not usually extended to undergraduates. The college takes pride in the sense of community that such a learning environment fosters. But perhaps the single most striking aspect of student life at Wabash is personal freedom. The college has only one rule: 'The student is expected to conduct himself at all times, both on and off the campus, as a gentleman and a responsible citizen.' Wabash College treats students as adults, and such treatment attracts responsible freshmen and fosters their independence and maturity."

For even more information on this school, turn to page 408 of the "Stats" section.

WARTBURG COLLEGE

100 WARTBURG BOULEVARD, PO BOX 1003, WAVERLY, IA 50677-0903 • ADMISSIONS: 319-352-8264
FAX: 319-352-8579 • EMAIL: ADMISSIONS@WARTBURG.EDU • WEBSITE: WWW.WARTBURG.EDU

Ratings
Quality of Life: 74   Academic: 76   Admissions: 70   Financial Aid: 73

Academics

A solid music education/music therapy program and a commitment to Christian values distinguish Wartburg College, a small liberal arts school in northern Iowa. As one student told us, "Our biggest strength is our music department. The bands, choirs, and symphony are really

> **SURVEY SAYS . . .**
> Classes are small
> No one cheats
> No one watches intercollegiate sports
> Students are religious
> Very little beer drinking
> Lousy food on campus

awesome. There are a lot of music events, such as guest artists and student recitals." Undergrads love the "small classrooms, great faculty, and very friendly student body" at Wartburg, but warn, "The workload is much heavier than I expected; there are a lot of papers and projects! A lot of required courses are writing intensive, meaning students will write at least 20 pages during the term. All students are required to take two Inquiry Studies classes, which are writing intensive and a lot of reading/preparation, but overall pretty pointless. Even so, most classes can be fun, especially ones that are smaller and more discussion oriented." Professors here "typically have attained the highest degrees in their fields and are easily accessible." Most are inspiring instructors, although some "are experts in their subject matter but don't teach well." Undergrads recognize both the advantages and disadvantages of the small-school experience. On the plus side, "some professors will do special stuff with smaller classes, such as serving breakfast at their house or taking the class out for pizza." Among the negatives: "We need more computers and Internet that doesn't overload or shut down. This is one of the disadvantages of going to a small school with limited resources."

Life

Wartburg undergrads reside in the "safe and friendly" small town of Waverly, Iowa, "a very small town (population 9,000)," which means "there isn't much to do in town." Undergrads "have to be creative [to entertain themselves]. . . . We grill out a lot or have campfires. We also resort to crazy sports in the middle of the night, or go out to dinner and movies. Life here is whatever you make of it." Adds another student, "There are lots of extracurricular activities. I'm definitely over-involved and a lot of my friends are too." Community service is particularly popular with Wartburg's civic-minded undergraduates. The administration does a fine job of sponsoring special events; as one student explains, "One of the best activities is Midnight Breakfast, which occurs on Sunday night going into finals week. The cafeteria opens up from 11 P.M. to 1 A.M., and professors serve us breakfast for a study break. Outfly, a random day off in the fall, is also a really great time!" Undergrads also love Wartburg's "great Division III athletic programs," which boast standout teams in football, track, men's basketball, and women's volleyball. When life in Waverly grows too quiet, students head to Cedar Falls, 20 minutes away by car; it's "a larger area with a state university [University of Northern Iowa]. A lot of students go to the bars and clubs there on the weekends." Some here complain, "We need better facilities, such as the science hall and athletic facilities. However, the college is expanding, and plans for building a new student union, a new science hall, and a new football field stadium and outdoor track are already" underway.

Students

Wartburg undergrads note a "large international student presence," adding that 32 countries are represented within the small student body. Internationals happily report that "American students are very friendly and helpful to people that they do not know well, especially international students such as myself." Some feel that "international students unknowingly segregate themselves. I think it happens because it's easier to communicate with someone you can relate to more." Most here, however, describe their fellow students as extremely open and friendly. Because Wartburg is an Evangelical Lutheran school, understandably "most of us are rather conservative." Approximately half the students here are Lutheran; Catholics make up the largest religious minority, constituting roughly one-quarter of the student body.

ADMISSIONS

Very important factors considered by the admissions committee include: class rank, secondary school record, and standardized test scores. *Important factors considered include:* character/personal qualities, interview, and recommendations. *Other factors considered include:* essays, extracurricular activities, minority status, talent/ability, volunteer work, and work experience. SAT I or ACT required, ACT preferred. TOEFL required of all international applicants. High school diploma is required and GED is accepted. *High school units required/recommended:* 15 total are recommended; 4 English recommended, 3 math recommended, 3 science recommended, 2 foreign language recommended, 2 social studies recommended.

The Inside Word

Whether or not your undergraduate goals revolve around music or religion, Wartburg offers a small-school setting and impressive academic standards to attract a wide range of applicants; keep in mind, however, that its infrastructure and facilities are playing catch-up to the quality of learning.

FINANCIAL AID

Students should submit: FAFSA. The Princeton Review suggests that all financial aid forms be submitted as soon as possible after January 1. *Need-based scholarships/grants offered:* Pell, SEOG, state scholarships/grants, private scholarships, and the school's own gift aid. *Loan aid offered:* FFEL Subsidized Stafford, FFEL Unsubsidized Stafford, FFEL PLUS, Federal Perkins, and alternative loans. Federal Work-Study Program available. Institution employment available. Applicants will be notified of awards on a rolling basis beginning on or about March 22. Off-campus job opportunities are good.

For even more information on this school, turn to page 409 of the "Stats" section.

WASHINGTON UNIVERSITY IN ST. LOUIS

Campus Box 1089, One Brookings Drive, Saint Louis, MO 63130-4899 • Admissions: 800-638-0700
Fax: 314-935-4290 • Financial Aid: 314-935-5900 • E-mail: admissions@wustl.edu
Website: admissions.wustl.edu

Ratings

Quality of Life: 82   **Academic:** 92   **Admissions:** 97   **Financial Aid:** 79

Academics

Washington University is widely recognized as one of the top institutions in the country. Most students believe that this reputation is apt. One feature of Wash U is the amount of money that it has available for research and other ventures: "The resources here are endless and the university offers the support to back them." But

> **SURVEY SAYS . . .**
> *Students love Saint Louis, MO*
> *Registration is a breeze, School is well run*
> *Great on-campus food*
> *Lab facilities need improving*
> *Intercollegiate sports are unpopular or nonexistent*
> *Large classes, Ethnic diversity on campus*
> *Students get along with local community*

there's also a downfall to studying at such a "large research institution": a number of professors "are preoccupied with becoming stars in their fields" and consequently devote minimal time to students. But this isn't the norm. Of professors, students write, "They will come in on a Sunday evening before an exam to hold a help session, stay up all night correcting tests, and regularly invite students over to their houses for dinner." Because many of the professors are leaders in their fields, they hold high expectations for their students. "The school is really, really, really tough," reports an undergraduate. "You must work very hard and put a lot of time into what you are doing," writes another. While departments in the pre-medical sciences are particularly popular, students tell us that every department has its notable strengths.

Life

There's a motto religiously intoned at Wash U: "Study hard first, then play hard." "I definitely study my butt off during the week," one typical student tells us. But when weekends come around—or free time in general—students at Wash U roll up their sleeves and roll out the party carpet. This work hard/party hard mentality has given rise to the common perception that Wash U undergrads are "the dorkiest students in the world getting [expletive] all the time. Amen. Responsibly of course, Mom." Because the university lies on the outskirts of St. Louis, it's not quite urban and not quite suburban—a sort of "in-the-middle" location that makes the school feel like "a self-sufficient bubble." Wash U undergrads get particularly excited "every semester" for the "big party called WILD." WILD "starts at noon on Friday [in the Quad] . . . and they have inflatable games, free food, and music until about 5 p.m. Then bands start playing on stage and at 8 some fairly well-known band will come on." You'll also find "cafés, sports, religious/political group activities, community service, school-sponsored raves, formal dances, costume parties," and access to about 200 student organizations. When students break out of the Wash U bubble, they often head to "The Loop, which is basically a multi-block collection of restaurants, theatres, etc." Because of the campus' location, students advise that "having a car will increase your quality of life immeasurably."

Student Body

Washington University students consider themselves Ivy League students without the Ivy League tags. Accordingly, students tell us that their classmates are "all very smart." One student amends this description slightly, writing that they're all "really smart people who like to party." Because of the university's gleaming reputation, it attracts students from "all over." In fact, only about 10 percent come from Missouri, and 55 percent hail from at least 500 miles away. "You have people from all views and walks of life," summarizes one student, "NRA members from the Midwest and rich Jewish girls from Long Island and gay male activists." Most of the causes touted at Wash U are liberal ones, leading a freshman to comment that "conservatives are a distinct minority on this campus."

ADMISSIONS

Very important factors considered by the admissions committee include: character/personal qualities, class rank, essays, extracurricular activities, recommendations, religious affiliation/commitment, secondary school record, standardized test scores, talent/ability, volunteer work, work experience. *Other factors considered include:* alumni/ae relation, interview, minority status. SAT I or ACT required. TOEFL required of all international applicants. *High school units required/recommended:* 18 total recommended; 4 English recommended, 4 math recommended, 4 science recommended, 4 science lab recommended, 2 foreign language recommended, 4 social studies recommended, 4 history recommended.

The Inside Word

No other university with as impressive a record of excellence across the board has a more accommodating admissions process. Not that it's easy to get in here, but lack of instant name recognition does affect Washington's admission rate. Students with above-average academic records who are not quite Ivy material are the big winners. Marginal candidates with high financial need may find difficulty; the admissions process at Washington U. is not need-blind and may take into account candidates' ability to pay if they are not strong applicants.

FINANCIAL AID

Students should submit: FAFSA, CSS/Financial Aid PROFILE, noncustodial (divorced/separated) parent's statement, student's and parent's 1040 tax returns or signed waiver if there are no tax returns. Regular filing deadline is February 15. The Princeton Review suggests that all financial aid forms be submitted as soon as possible after January 1. *Need-based scholarships/grants offered:* Pell, SEOG, state scholarships/grants, private scholarships, the school's own gift aid, United Negro College Fund. *Loan aid offered:* FFEL Subsidized Stafford, FFEL Unsubsidized Stafford, FFEL PLUS, Federal Perkins, state loans, college/university loans from institutional funds. Federal Work-Study Program available. Institutional employment available. Applicants will be notified of awards on or about April 1. Off-campus job opportunities are excellent.

FROM THE ADMISSIONS OFFICE

"Washington University students learn in a flexible academic atmosphere that encourages them to cross disciplines, taking courses in any of our five undergraduate divisions: arts & sciences, architecture, art, business, and engineering. We also offer graduate programs in these divisions as well as law; medicine, including occupational therapy and physical therapy; and social work. This interdisciplinary environment allows students to study alongside other academically talented students from across the country and around the world in any subject that interests them. Through research projects that start as early as the freshman year, students can participate with our world-class faculty in the creation of knowledge. This academic exploration takes place in a supportive, friendly community that provides the resources to ensure success. Outside the classroom, students participate in nearly 200 activities, including community service and multicultural groups; musical, dance, and theater groups; fraternities and sororities; intramural sports; student government; and literary groups. We invite you to visit Washington University any time to experience these outstanding opportunities firsthand."

For even more information on this school, turn to page 409 of the "Stats" section.

WAYNE STATE UNIVERSITY

OFFICE OF ADMISSIONS, WAYNE STATE UNIVERSITY, DETROIT, MI 48202 • ADMISSIONS: 313-577-3577
FAX: 313-577-7536 • E-MAIL: ADMISSIONS@WAYNE.EDU • WEBSITE: WWW.WAYNE.EDU

Ratings
Quality of Life: 81   **Academic:** 69   **Admissions:** 65   **Financial Aid:** 73

Academics

Wayne State University's 18,000 undergrads are dispersed throughout 14 colleges and schools and around 130 majors. In general, Wayne State students report that "the professors are great." "They really know what they're talking about, they are always available." The most popular majors—whether due to the "very good" professors or the professional opportunities—are in the fields of health and related sciences, education, and business administration. "If I was to give advice," writes one student, "it would be to stick with the honors program whenever possible." Though students have to achieve certain standards before receiving admission into the honors program, accepted scholars will discover that "the professors, materials, and class sizes are much better." But no matter what classes snag your interest, you'll have to deal with the administration, described as a "slow, incompetent bureaucracy." One of the more rusty cogs in these administrative wheels is the registration process; "Sometimes, I spend a couple weeks trying to hammer out a class schedule," complains one student. But when the red tape threatens to drag Wayne State students down, they remind themselves that they're attending "one of the top research universities in the nation."

> **SURVEY SAYS . . .**
> *Classes are small*
> *Diverse students interact*
> *No one cheats*
> *Lots of TAs teach upper-level courses*
> *Very little hard liquor*
> *Theater is unpopular*
> *Student publications are ignored*

Life

"Wayne State University is primarily a commuter school," which means that "there's not much to do for fun on campus." "Athletics, fraternities, and sororities, while not nonexistent, are not really very popular." That said, it's not impossible to find frat parties lighting up a Friday night on campus. For alternative amusement on campus grounds, students can cheer on any of Wayne State's nine men's NCAA sports teams and eight women's teams or participate in student organizations, including The South End, Wayne State's award-winning student paper. Commonly, students who live in the university-owned apartments close to campus (there are no dorms) take their energy into Detroit. "There are plenty of activities happening in the city," ranging from outings as down home as bowling to events as electric as late-night clubs. The campus itself is within a quick stroll from the Detroit Institute of the Arts, the Detroit Science Center, the Detroit Historical Museum, the Museum of African American Studies, and the main branch of the Detroit Public Library. And on sunny days, "the lawn and fountain area in front of the UGL (Undergraduate Library) . . . are the most popular hangouts" on campus. For commuters with children, the university offers three childcare services and provides a list of several others in close vicinity to campus on its website. "Parking availability," however, is an issue, and if you do find a spot, "you have to pay a dollar to park every day."

Students

Wayne State is a "huge" university in the hub of the cultural center in Detroit, America's 10th largest city. Perhaps because urban real estate is at such a premium, Wayne State is not a residential college. "Most people commute," and as a result of this, the sense of campus community is diminished. Students tell us that their fellows "rarely initiate any type of communication," and when they do, it's usually "through e-mail and cell phones." But this isn't to say that the students at Wayne State aren't nice people. On the contrary, once communication is established, you discover that the people at the university are "very nice and helpful." The general attitude at Wayne State is one of acceptance and tolerance. "Wayne State has one of the most diverse student bodies that I have ever seen," coos an undergraduate. "There are large numbers of minority groups including African American, Arab American, and Asian American. I have friends of just about every kind of ethnic heritage. Everybody gets along just fine inside of the classroom and out." And the mean student age on campus is 28.9, meaning that age range factors into the diversity of the institution.

ADMISSIONS

Very important factors considered by the admissions committee include: secondary school record and standardized test scores. *Other factors considered include:* class rank and extracurricular activities. SAT I or ACT required, ACT preferred. TOEFL required of all international applicants. High school diploma or GED is required. *High school units required/recommended:* 18 total recommended; 4 English recommended, 4 math recommended, 3 science recommended, 2 foreign language recommended, 3 social studies recommended, 2 elective recommended.

The Inside Word

This Motor City school offers all admitted students the chance to grow in professional studies, from those who need to rise up from humble academic origins to those in the honors program. Applicants should consider the value of this ultraresourceful, deep-pocketed state school.

FINANCIAL AID

Students should submit: FAFSA, income tax forms, and W-2 forms. The Princeton Review suggests that all financial aid forms be submitted as soon as possible after January 1. *Need-based scholarships/grants offered:* Pell, SEOG, state scholarships/grants, private scholarships, and the school's own gift aid. *Loan aid offered:* Direct Subsidized Stafford, Direct Unsubsidized Stafford, FFEL Subsidized Stafford, FFEL Unsubsidized Stafford, Federal Perkins, state loans, and college/university loans from institutional funds. Federal Work-Study Program available. Institutional employment available. Applicants will be notified of awards on a rolling basis beginning on or about April 1. Off-campus job opportunities are excellent.

For even more information on this school, turn to page 410 of the "Stats" section.

WESTERN ILLINOIS UNIVERSITY

1 UNIVERSITY CIRCLE, 115 SHERMAN HALL, MACOMB, IL 61455-1390 • ADMISSIONS: 309-298-3157
FAX: 309-298-3111 • EMAIL: WIUADM@WIU.EDU • WEBSITE: WWW.WIU.EDU

Ratings

Quality of Life: 73   **Academic:** 70   **Admissions:** 69   **Financial Aid:** 73

Academics

"WIU is an affordable, midsize university in a small town surrounded by cornfields." In fact, ask any student, and you're likely to hear that size and affordability are two of the crowning attributes of WIU. In-state students can attend WIU for less than $10,000 a year—tuition, insurance, and room

> **SURVEY SAYS . . .**
> *Classes are small*
> *Very little beer drinking*
> *School is well run*
> *Intercollegiate sports are popular*
> *Students get along with local community*
> *No one cheats*

and board included. And with about 11,000 students, WIU is big enough to offer a diversified curriculum but small enough to maintain an intimate learning environment. Professors, of course, have a lot to do with the personalized feel of the WIU experience. "Professors are always available outside the classroom, either by office hours or appointment," one student reports. Students note that some of the particularly sharp profs can be found in the foreign languages, law enforcement, and music departments—though each of the 49 undergrad programs and 13 pre-professional programs can boast its merits. For an extra challenge, look into the Illinois Centennial Honors College. "The honors program here is fantastic," raves a participant. Admission is competitive, but once accepted students not only have access to a specialized slate of honors courses, but also become eligible for scholarships, research grants, specific awards, specialized living options, out-of-class activities, and an Honors College convocation.

Life

When you attend college in a town with more cornstalks than people and where some consider Wal-Mart "the highlight of the town," there's a good chance that partying will become part of the weekly repertoire. "There are bars," assures one student, "and they are full almost every night of the week." But these students are quick to point out that while they have fun, they don't lose sight of their academics. "We get done with what we need to before any partying begins." Academics aside, another priority here is supporting the WIU Leathernecks—especially the football team. But if sports don't thrill you, you'll find plenty of other extracurricular options on campus, catering to interests ranging from theater to journalism. A student tells us, "There are a lot of organizations that you can get involved in, whether it's Greek life or cultural organizations or volunteer organizations." "If there is something you are interested in, there's a good chance WIU has it somewhere on campus," adds an undergrad. Interested in hot air balloons? You're in luck! Each year, the WIU campus is the starting point for the town of Macomb's Balloon Rally. Other annual town events include Dickens on the Square, the Festival of Trees, and County Holiday.

Students

Let's try to paint a picture of the typical student at WIU. According to one undergrad, the typical student here "likes to hang around with fellow students and friends, cares about grades, shows interest, and is friendly to talk to." Another disagrees, though, stating, "There is no typical student! We are all different! There are mothers, fathers, actors, grad students, varying religions, different races and economic structures, and so on . . . . We all melt together through programs, social events, organizations, and classroom involvement!" Many students come "from the suburban Chicago area," as well as other points in Illinois and surrounding states. Students report that people "seem to form groups of friends quickly when freshman year starts." Perhaps this is because, as one student exclaims, "Everyone is friendly to EVERYONE!"

ADMISSIONS

Very important factors considered by the admissions committee include: class rank, secondary school record, and standardized test scores. SAT I or ACT required. TOEFL required of all international applicants. High school diploma is required and GED is accepted. *High school units required/recommended:* 15 total are recommended; 4 English recommended, 3 math recommended, 3 science recommended, 3 social studies recommended.

The Inside Word

This school's strong faculty and nice price make it a popular choice among Illinois natives. The campus's collective will to party is kept in check by a peace-keeping force that means business.

FINANCIAL AID

Students should submit: FAFSA. Regular filing deadline is No deadline. The Princeton Review suggests that all financial aid forms be submitted as soon as possible after January 1. *Need-based scholarships/grants offered:* Pell, SEOG, state scholarships/grants, private scholarships, and the school's own gift aid. *Loan aid offered:* FFEL Subsidized Stafford, FFEL Unsubsidized Stafford, FFEL PLUS, and Federal Perkins. Federal Work-Study Program available. Institution employment available. Applicants will be notified of awards on a rolling basis beginning on or about February 15. Off-campus job opportunities are fair.

FROM THE ADMISSIONS OFFICE

"Western Illinois University: Real Learning. Real People

"**Four-Year Tuition, Fees, and Room and Board Guarantee:** Western will ensure that your college years will be a good investment with its guaranteed four-year rate for tuition, fees, and room and board. All new undergraduate students entering the university are automatically included in the plan, which freezes the per-hour rate you pay for a four-year period, so costs will stay the same each year you attend. Western is among the few universities in the nation—and the only university in Illinois—to offer this guarantee.

"**Here's how it works:** The rate will be fixed for a four-year period and remain in effect as long as you maintain continuous enrollment. If your major requires more than four years to complete, the guaranteed rate will be extended to cover the expected time for degree completion. Each year the university's Board of Trustees sets new rates for the entering class. If a fee is added and approved by the Board, such as funding for a new student service, the fee will apply to all students when implemented. The four-year guaranteed cost plan applies to all new undergraduate students, both full- and part-time.

"**GradTrac:** Western Illinois University is the only public university in Illinois to guarantee graduation in four years when students enroll in and comply with the GradTrac program. If you fail to graduate in four years because a course was unavailable, WIU will pay the tuition for the course!"

For even more information on this school, turn to page 410 of the "Stats" section.

WESTERN MICHIGAN UNIVERSITY

1903 W. MICHIGAN AVENUE, KALAMAZOO, MI 49008 • ADMISSIONS: 616-387-2000 • FAX: 616-387-2096
E-MAIL: ASK-WMU@UMICH.EDU • WEBSITE: WWW.WMICH.EDU

Ratings

Quality of Life: 77 **Academic:** 72 **Admissions:** 70 **Financial Aid:** 72

Academics

Students at Western Michigan University proudly report, "Some of the programs offered here are very good and nationally recognized. Every year I attend, the school improves. The school is constantly expanding, and programs and services keep getting

> **SURVEY SAYS . . .**
> *Very little hard liquor*
> *Frats and sororities dominate social scene*
> *Instructors are good teachers*
> *Lousy food on campus*
> *Lots of beer drinking*

better. It's definitely going to be a really great university some day soon!" Among the academic areas receiving students' praise are health and human services, speech pathology, "the best aviation program in the state," and "many small but brilliant programs, such as Latin, medieval studies, and counseling education." The popular business college at WMU "looks good and their program is great; it's just that there aren't enough sections of particular courses to accommodate the crowd on this campus." Overall, students report that WMU offers "good academics that aren't too challenging but not a joke either." Professors, many warn, "are research-based, and some are not specifically great teachers," but all are fairly accessible due to required office hours. Students also complain that "general education requirements are a bit restrictive" but are willing to put up with the inconvenience to benefit from "the great value" WMU provides. Students in the Honors College report a "phenomenal experience" with priority registration "to ensure that I get a place in the classes I need to take"—hardly a given for students in the general population—and "extremely helpful advisors." Some even feel that "honors classes are easier than regular classes because the professors help make sure students understand the material more carefully."

Life

"Students here have a good balance of work and play" comments one student. Others concur, "People here for the most part are in various stages of getting their lives together, so the majority are fairly focused and dedicated, but not to such an extreme that they won't go out and have fun." Students list "working out at the Rec Center," as well as "going to movies, sporting events, and hanging out with friends" as typical activities. "The Greek system is pretty huge here" as well, with the frats and sororities hosting "date parties, formals, and events." Students warn that "the architecture is about as exciting as, say, a 1960s prison complex. Every building looks suspiciously the same, in that 'massive box that just dropped out of the sky' kind of way."

Students

WMU undergrads "seem to be very friendly and offer a smile or a 'hello' when you pass on campus even if you don't know each other." Socially, "Students are somewhat segregated by class. Also, the Greeks keep to themselves, the international students keep to themselves, and the rest of us kind of float around in the middle." Many "are first- or second-generation college students. I like everyone's motivation to do better than their parents [did]." The international population includes a "large percentage of Malaysians because the school has an exchange program with another college located in Malaysia." The more studious among the population complain, "Some students are just a too lax in their studies, and they are just here to party. But there are also great people here."

ADMISSIONS

Very important factors considered by the admissions committee include: secondary school record. *Important factors considered include:* standardized test scores and talent/ability. *Other factors considered include:* character/personal qualities, essays, extracurricular activities, interview, recommendations, volunteer work, and work experience. SAT I or ACT required. TOEFL required of all international applicants. High school diploma or GED is required. *High school units required/recommended:* 16 total required; 18 total recommended; 4 English required, 3 math required, 4 math recommended, 2 science required, 1 science lab required, 1 foreign language required, 2 foreign language recommended, 2 social studies required, 1 history required, 2 elective required.

The Inside Word

Offerings at WMU are numerous, and many foster degrees in niche specialties. Interaction with professors grows along with your progress as a student, making this school worth consideration for ambitions applicants from Michigan, Ohio, Indiana, Illinois, and beyond.

FINANCIAL AID

Students should submit: FAFSA. No deadline for regular filing. The Princeton Review suggests that all financial aid forms be submitted as soon as possible after January 1. *Need-based scholarships/grants offered:* Pell, SEOG, state scholarships/grants, private scholarships, and the school's own gift aid. *Loan aid offered:* Direct Subsidized Stafford, Direct Unsubsidized Stafford, Direct PLUS, Federal Perkins, and alternative loans. Federal Work-Study Program available. Institutional employment available. Applicants will be notified of awards on a rolling basis beginning on or about April 1. Off-campus job opportunities are excellent.

For even more information on this school, turn to page 411 of the "Stats" section.

WESTMINSTER COLLEGE

501 WESTMINSTER AVENUE, FULTON, MO 65251-1299 • ADMISSIONS: 573-592-5251 • FAX: 573-592-5255
EMAIL: ADMISSIONS@JAYNET.WCMO.EDU • WEBSITE: WWW.WESTMINSTER-MO.EDU

Ratings
Quality of Life: 74   **Academic:** 82   **Admissions:** 76   **Financial Aid:** 80

Academics

At Westminster College, a well-regarded liberal arts school in central Missouri, students enjoy a "familyish" atmosphere that provides "access to professors' help academically, which often also results in the cultivation of friendships outside the classroom."

> **SURVEY SAYS . . .**
> *Classes are small*
> *Student publications are popular*
> *Hard liquor is popular, Students are religious*
> *Students get along with local community*
> *Very little beer drinking, Lousy food on campus*

Students praise the faculty for their caring attitudes, telling us, "The professors here are soooo nice!! They will know your name and remember it and you! It is very personal and they want you to succeed." Profs' teaching abilities, however, receive slightly lower marks; as one student put it, "Most of the teachers are very good, while some are downright deplorable. Even these teachers are knowledgeable, but they cannot teach worth anything." Some students warn that attending such a small school has potentially serious drawbacks. Writes one undergrad, "Academics here are rather lopsided. Some departments, such as business and biology, are top of their game here, but that leaves the rest poorly neglected. Students wanting a degree in archaeology or anthropology aren't going to get very much attention." Others caution that "because Westminster is small, sometimes it is hard to get the classes you want because they aren't offered at a lot of different times."

Life

Greek life reigns supreme at Westminster College, students report. Sixty-seven percent of male undergrads at Westminster join fraternities and 60 percent of women do the same; explains one undergrad, "Everything revolves around the fraternity parties during the weekend." Students also note that "fraternities are the source of fun on the weekends, but the school offers many activities throughout the week such as bands, parties, TGIF parties, and cultural opportunities." Many are still unsatisfied, though, and feel that the campus provides "a lack of entertainment options outside the Greek scene, which is why Greek life and partying are so prominent." Notes one student, "With so little to do with spare time, it isn't surprising the trouble the frat boys are constantly getting in. You basically have two options for fun: hang out in your room or go get wasted on fraternity row." Hometown Fulton, undergrads agree, "is small and boring. During the week there are very few activities: you can hang out with your immediate friends or go to the old smelly theater in town that shows movies two weeks after they come out." On a positive note, students note that "if you get bored, Columbia is only 20 to 30 minutes away, and there are a million things to do there. But beware, MU [University of Missouri—Columbia] people don't think very highly of Westminster students. Also, St. Louis is only an hour and a half away."

Students

With fewer than 800 undergraduates, Westminster has a "small-school atmosphere [that] allows you to get to know a lot of people on campus. You can't walk anywhere on campus without seeing someone you know." Students appreciate the fact that within the small student body "different groups are forced to interact, which is positive." Some here warn that "due to the large number of frat/sorority people, it is more difficult to live as an independent." Others caution that "everyone is the same. Diversity just doesn't exist. Everyone is Christian, middle-class Caucasian. And they all dress, walk, talk, act, and think the same way." And although its size allows rumors to elevate to "gossip city," Westminster's student body is "a very close and tight-knit community. Everybody pretty much gets along with each other."

ADMISSIONS

Very important factors considered by the admissions committee include: class rank, secondary school record, and standardized test scores. *Important factors considered include:* essays, interview, and recommendations. *Other factors considered include:* alumni/ae relation, character/personal qualities, extracurricular activities, talent/ability, volunteer work, and work experience. SAT I or ACT required. TOEFL required of all international applicants. High school diploma is required and GED is accepted. *High school units required/recommended:* 16 total are required; 4 English required, 3 math required, 3 science required, 2 science lab required, 3 foreign language recommended, 2 social studies required, 2 elective recommended.

The Inside Word

Westminster College's high price tag is offset by its admirable commitment to financial aid, affording great opportunities for future MBAs and natural science professionals. If a student population in the hundreds is too small for your tastes, try the state university down the road.

FINANCIAL AID

Students should submit: FAFSA. Regular filing deadline is February 28. The Princeton Review suggests that all financial aid forms be submitted as soon as possible after January 1. *Need-based scholarships/grants offered:* Pell, SEOG, state scholarships/grants, private scholarships, and the school's own gift aid. *Loan aid offered:* FFEL subsidized Stafford, FFEL unsubsidized Stafford, FFEL PLUS, and federal Perkins. Federal Work-Study Program available. Institution employment available. Applicants will be notified of awards on a rolling basis beginning on or about February 10. Off-campus job opportunities are fair.

FROM THE ADMISSIONS OFFICE

"'Why Westminster?' is a frequently asked question by prospective students and their parents. My response returns the question, 'What are you looking for in a college?' At Westminster, we find that prospective students and their families have five general areas of questions: academics, student life, financial aid/scholarships, location and safety of the school, and their future after graduation. Current students also value our traditions (we were founded in 1851) and our core values of Integrity, Honesty, Fairness, and Responsibility. Most of our students are actively involved in community service and service learning through our Center for Leadership and Service. Our students value being a person, rather than a number, and being able to graduate in four years (not five or six). Best of all, they enjoy and respect our faculty and staff—full-time professionals whose primary goals are good teaching and advising. Most classes are collaborative and seminar oriented, with lots of group projects that stress initiative, teamwork, and communication skills. Our alumni praise the values and skills taught and modeled by our faculty and staff. Students, faculty, and staff describe Westminster as a 'way of life!' That way of life includes demanding academic programs, varied student life activities and intercollegiate athletics (NCAA Division III), competitive financial aid and scholarships, a safe and caring environment, terrific preparation, and opportunities after graduation. Best of all, Westminster is made up of quality people—a COMMUNITY of students, faculty, and staff. Come Visit!"

For even more information on this school, turn to page 411 of the "Stats" section.

WHEATON COLLEGE

501 COLLEGE AVENUE, WHEATON, IL 60187 • ADMISSIONS: 630-752-5005 • FAX: 630-752-5285
FINANCIAL AID: 630-752-5021 • E-MAIL: ADMISSIONS@WHEATON.EDU • WEBSITE: WWW.WHEATON.EDU

Ratings

Quality of Life: 78   Academic: 89   Admissions: 92   Financial Aid: 86

Academics

Book learning means nothing at Wheaton without a Christian basis, and many students comment favorably on the "integration of academic challenges and moral principles" at their school. "It's not that I'm simply studying and earning grades. I am able to grow as a person and a student," writes a first-year undergraduate. Though some professors are accused of being "wrapped up in appearing scholarly," most are described as

> **SURVEY SAYS . . .**
> *Lots of conservatives on campus*
> *Diversity lacking on campus*
> *Very little drug use*
> *Campus feels safe*
> *Students are very religious*
> *Very little hard liquor*
> *Beautiful campus*
> *Very little beer drinking*
> *Very small frat/sorority scene*
> *(Almost) no one smokes*

"personally interested in students. There are always people willing to talk, counsel, or pray with you." The faculty "firmly yet compassionately pushes students," writes a biology student, and lectures are deemed by many as "engaging and challenging." Getting into classes can be tougher than the classes themselves, however. "The registration bureaucracy is a nightmare at worst and an annoying hassle at best," comments a senior in the philosophy department, and reportedly, underclassmen don't stand a chance of landing a spot in certain popular courses.

Life

The majority of students at Wheaton seem to support the strict rules that govern campus life, concurring that they eliminate "negative peer pressure." A junior tells us, "Although you sign something saying you won't drink, smoke, take drugs, or have sex, it is still on campus. It is just very underground, which is nice. It's there if you want it, but if you don't, it's easy to think it doesn't exist." Others complain that the tight regulations demonstrate that "This school trusts neither its students nor its faculty." With the typical party options abolished, Wheaton students are forced to be "innovative in finding ways to have fun." For example, one sophomore enjoys "dressing up in all polyester and going to Krispy Kreme." Others "sit around thinking about what we could do for fun before resigning to the fact that we will once again either study or do nothing." More commonly, students "go on road trips, see shows in Chicago, play music and sports, and attend museums." Though the dating scene is D.O.A., the school organizes "talent shows, movie nights, and concerts, and dorm life is upbeat and interesting." The Christian environment encourages "open dialogue about campus and personal issues" and builds such an environment of trust that "many of us don't even lock the doors to our rooms."

Student Body

A transfer student expresses a common view: "The majority of kids on this campus are the smart ones from high school that tended not to drink or party—we're not prudes, though." A senior communications major disagrees, writing, "Students are too worried about academics to have a healthy social life. In our attempt to pursue Godly male-female relationships, we have become sexually and socially repressed." Though some Wheaton kids are undeniably "squares" and "nerds," a freshman generally finds her classmates to be "welcoming, friendly, and inspiring. They challenge me in several aspects of life in the daily examples they set." A junior notes his classmates' personal growth process, telling us, "Many come in rich, protected, and naïve, but they expand their views as they go through." In the diversity department, a black student writes, "As a minority student on campus, I have found this to be an open-minded place."

ADMISSIONS

Very important factors considered by the admissions committee include: character/personal qualities, essays, recommendations, Christian commitment, secondary school record, standardized test scores, talent/ability. *Important factors considered include:* alumni/ae relation, extracurricular activities, interview, minority status. *Other factors considered include:* class rank, volunteer work. SAT I or ACT required. TOEFL required of all international applicants. High school diploma or GED is required. *High school units required/recommended:* 15 total required; 4 English recommended, 3 math recommended, 3 science recommended, 2 foreign language recommended, 3 social studies recommended.

The Inside Word

The admissions process at Wheaton is quite rigorous. As at most small colleges, the review of candidates focuses on far more than courses, grades, and test scores. The admissions committee will also carefully consider your essays, recommendations, and other indicators of your character as they assess how well suited you are to the campus community. Wheaton limits acceptance to students who profess Christian faith.

FINANCIAL AID

Students should submit: FAFSA, institution's own financial aid form. The Princeton Review suggests that all financial aid forms be submitted as soon as possible after January 1. *Need-based scholarships/grants offered:* Pell, SEOG, state scholarships/grants, the school's own gift aid. *Loan aid offered:* FFEL Subsidized Stafford, FFEL Unsubsidized Stafford, FFEL PLUS, Federal Perkins, state loans, college/university loans from institutional funds. Federal Work-Study Program available. Institutional employment available. Applicants will be notified of awards on a rolling basis beginning on or about March 1. Off-campus job opportunities are excellent.

FROM THE ADMISSIONS OFFICE

"At Wheaton, we're commited to being a community that fearlessly pursues truth, upholds an academically rigorous curriculum, and promotes virtue. The college takes seriously its impact on society. The influence of Wheaton is seen in fields ranging from government (the speaker of the house) to sports (two NBA coaches) to business (the CEO of Wal-Mart) to music (Metropolitan Opera National Competition winners) to education (over 40 college presidents) to global ministry (Billy Graham). Wheaton seeks students who want to make a difference and are passionate about their Christian faith and rigorous academic pursuit."

For even more information on this school, turn to page 412 of the "Stats" section.

WILLIAM JEWELL COLLEGE

500 COLLEGE HILL, LIBERTY, MO 64068 • ADMISSIONS: 816-753-7009
FAX: 816-415-5027 • FINANCIAL AID: 800-753-7009 • E-MAIL: ADMISSION@WILLIAM.JEWELL.EDU
WEBSITE: WWW.JEWELL.EDU

Ratings

Quality of Life: 82   Academic: 76   Admissions: 75   Financial Aid: 88

Academics

One William Jewell student tells a personal story that goes like this: "I was conditionally accepted to William Jewell with a 2.7 GPA. I had to take a study skills class and could only carry 14 hours. I am a real success story for Jewell. In my first semester, I ended with a 3.8

> **SURVEY SAYS . . .**
> *Lots of classroom discussion*
> *Great computer facilities, Very little drug use*
> *Student publications are popular*
> *Students are very religious*
> *Registration is a pain*

GPA. I was in Emerging Leaders, Alpha Lambda Delta," a national freshman honor society, "and am a student supervisor in the admissions office." The close-knit, nurturing atmosphere at Jewell is what allows students to live up to their potential. Students tell us that the administration cares "not only about the school and admissions and PR, but about the students." And the personal attention that professors lavish on students means that professors are more than teachers; they "become friends, role models, and even 'parents away from home.' " "They are always willing to bend over backward to help their students," adds an undergrad. And they're great teachers, too, "brilliant leaders of their disciplines," according to one student. "Perhaps the most important part of the academic program," writes a student, "is the emphasis put on . . . improving your writing skills." One of the most popular academic tracks at William Jewell is the Oxbridge Honors Program, a four-year program based on one-on-one tutorials, comprehensive exams, and a year of study in England.

Life

"Jewell is only 20 minutes from downtown Kansas City and only 5 minutes from a field full of cows," explains one undergraduate. The college's proximity to lively Kansas City is a relief to students, since "Liberty is so small that there isn't much to do." When students head to KC, they're usually in search of "eating, drinking, dancing, shopping," and the various other draws of urban life. On campus, a "solid Greek system serves as almost a social backbone for the college." And the "Campus Union Activities," a student-events group, "usually has something planned for most nights." Religious activities are particularly abundant. Writes one freshman, "Thursdays we have chapel in the morning and Worship Jam at night." Dorm life is vibrant, too: "In the residence halls you have a Resident Director, Resident Assistant," and someone called a "Shepherd." These people often join in the late-night conversations or movie-and-popcorn sessions. The party scene picks up on Wednesdays and weekends. Although Jewell's campus is considered "dry," the beer flows plentifully at off-campus frat parties and private parties alike. The restrictive nature of the rules here—from no drinking on campus to limited visitation hours in the dorms—causes some division between students and administration.

Student Body

William Jewell students are "for the most part very religious and very religiously active." A senior explains that the easiest way to describe the students is to divide them into their preferences for "Christian life" and "Party life." "The Party life . . . is very involved in drinking, dancing, and occasionally drugs. Westport in Kansas City is a favorite site for this group, along with the Corner Bar, Legends, and Lucky's Pizza—all bars that have been known as college hangouts. On the other side, there are . . . students very involved religiously and live a totally different lifestyle. They enjoy just hanging out at Waffle House [or] Steak and Shake late at night, or just playing board games with the Campus Minister and going on mission trips." Despite these distinctions, "the student body is for the most part very friendly and accepting of all people." The fact that most of the students are "white Christians" who "tend to come from Missouri" leads quite a few undergrads to long for "more diversity."

ADMISSIONS

Very important factors considered by the admissions committee include: class rank, secondary school record, standardized test scores. *Important factors considered include:* essays, recommendations. *Other factors considered include:* alumni/ae relation, character/personal qualities, extracurricular activities, interview, talent/ability, volunteer work, work experience. SAT I or ACT required. TOEFL required of all international applicants. High school diploma or GED is required. *High school units required/recommended:* 20 total recommended; 4 English recommended, 3 math recommended, 3 science recommended, 1 science lab recommended, 2 foreign language recommended, 3 social studies recommended, 2 history recommended, 4 elective recommended.

The Inside Word

Admission to William Jewell requires the usual suspects: solid grades and test scores. The college is competitive, but admission is not out of reach for the average student. Once admitted, undergrads benefit from William Jewell's leading efforts in experiential learning.

FINANCIAL AID

Students should submit: FAFSA, William Jewell Scholarship application. The Princeton Review suggests that all financial aid forms be submitted as soon as possible after January 1. *Need-based scholarships/grants offered:* Pell, SEOG, state scholarships/grants, private scholarships, the school's own gift aid. *Loan aid offered:* FFEL Subsidized Stafford, FFEL Unsubsidized Stafford, FFEL PLUS, Federal Perkins, Federal Nursing, alternative loans (nonfederal). Federal Work-Study Program available. Institutional employment available. Applicants will be notified of awards on a rolling basis beginning on or about March 1. Off-campus job opportunities are good.

FROM THE ADMISSIONS OFFICE

"William Jewell College was recently selected by *Time* magazine as the College of the Year in the liberal arts category. *Time* magazine writes, 'In selecting our 2001 Colleges of the Year among candidates recommended by our advisory board, the editors sought institutions with comprehensive freshman programs that have improved retention rates and created a sense of community for students.' William Jewell has developed an outstanding reputation for providing students with access to study abroad opportunities. Although students do not have to be in the Oxbridge Honors Program to participate in a year of overseas study, this unique honors program requires a year abroad at either Oxford or Cambridge Universities, England. The Oxbridge Honors Program has garnered much national and international attention. Placement rates into graduate school are 100 percent. Oxbridge students will study in the tutorial style of learning traditional in England's finest universities. William Jewell College is the ideal place for students who are searching for an integrated leadership development program within the liberal arts curriculum. The College offers a minor in 'not for profit' leadership in addition to a leadership certificate program. In January of 1998, the Pryor Foundation endowed one of the most unique leadership development programs in the country. The leadership certificate curriculum in the Pryor Leadership Studies Program includes a variety of internships; a 15-day Outward Bound excursion in the Florida Everglades, and training on the Tucker Leadership Lab, one of the largest experiential learning courses (ropes course) on any campus in the world."

For even more information on this school, turn to page 413 of the "Stats" section.

WITTENBERG UNIVERSITY

PO Box 720, Springfield, OH 45501 • Admissions: 800-677-7558 • Fax: 937-327-6379
Financial Aid: 800-677-7558 • E-mail: admission@wittenberg.edu • Website: www.wittenberg.edu

Ratings

Quality of Life: 83   Academic: 88   Admissions: 80   Financial Aid: 91

Academics

Undergrads at Wittenberg University, a small liberal arts and sciences school in Springfield, Ohio, report that their professors "are always there to count on for help with academics, recommendation letters, or just to talk." Students praise the fact that "classes are taught by professors (no TAs) and that they are all generally small, so that each student is given a good amount of attention." One

> **SURVEY SAYS . . .**
> *Frats and sororities dominate social scene*
> *Classes are small*
> *Everyone loves the Tigers*
> *Athletic facilities are great*
> *Students don't get along with local community*
> *Students don't like Springfield, OH*
> *Theater is unpopular*
> *(Almost) no one listens to college radio*
> *Lousy off-campus food*

recounts, "I am in a Chinese language class with two other students. That's a total of three students and a professor. It doesn't get any more personal than that." Most Witt faculty members are reputed to be friendly and laid back. A student muses, "It's nice when you can go to the bar with a professor after class on a nice day." One student notes that "the greatest strength of Witt is the academic standards which are set high to inspire achivement." However, students feel that "the administrative offices are not run very effectively and produce more problems than solutions for students."

Life

Students claim "there is never a dull moment" in "Witt World." This active campus boasts endless "clubs, awareness groups, religious groups for all kinds of religions, and never-ending opportunities for growth amongst the student body." When kicking back, Witt students can be seen at the grassy campus hollow, "a great place to study, sunbathe, nap, play Frisbee golf (on our awesome Frisbee golf course), and of course . . . streak!" Come the weekend, "Union Board usually brings in some cool events, like bands or comedians" and "parties are widespread." In addition, "Greek life is really popular." Nonetheless, students report that "there is very little pressure from others," when it comes to having fun or feeling accepted. One student attests, "Greek life is big here but you can be happy without it . . . . I am living proof!" According to another, "Alcohol is not a must here. I don't drink and have fun with lots of different people."

Student Body

"Its always easy to strike up an intellectual conversation or dance party," at Wittenberg, where "people make education fun and have fun outside the classroom." Amidst praises, many note with ambivalent disapproval that, "the students at Wittenberg are very friendly but also homogenous." One confides, "We all get along, probably because we come from such similar backgrounds." For the diversity it does have, Wittenberg students are "slightly segregated in terms of race." The lack of diversity does not necessarily translate into a lack of awareness or solidarity at Wittenberg. One student tells this story: "There was a club my freshman year that everyone went to, but the owner of the club made a racist comment to the

DJ, who was a Witt student. Once everyone heard about it, the club had to close down due to lack of business."

ADMISSIONS

Very important factors considered by the admissions committee include: secondary school record. *Important factors considered include:* alumni/ae relation, character/personal qualities, class rank, essays, extracurricular activities, interview, recommendations, standardized test scores, talent/ability, volunteer work, work experience. *Other factors considered include:* geographical residence, religious affiliation/commitment, state residency, minority status. SAT I or ACT required. TOEFL required of all international applicants. High school diploma is required and GED is not accepted. *High school units required/recommended:* 16 total required; 4 English required, 3 math required, 3 science required, 3 foreign language required, 3 social studies required.

The Inside Word

Wittenberg's applicant pool is small but quite solid coming off of a couple of strong years. Students who haven't successfully reached an above-average academic level in high school will meet with little success in the admissions process. Candidate evaluation is thorough and personal; applicants should devote serious attention to all aspects of their candidacy.

FINANCIAL AID

Students should submit: FAFSA. Regular filing deadline is March 15. The Princeton Review suggests that all financial aid forms be submitted as soon as possible after January 1. *Need-based scholarships/grants offered:* Pell, SEOG, state scholarships/grants, private scholarships, the school's own gift aid. *Loan aid offered:* FFEL Subsidized Stafford, FFEL Unsubsidized Stafford, FFEL PLUS, Federal Perkins, state loans, college/university loans from institutional funds. Federal Work-Study Program available. Institutional employment available. Applicants will be notified of awards on a rolling basis beginning on or about February 15. Off-campus job opportunities are good.

FROM THE ADMISSIONS OFFICE

"At Wittenberg, we believe that helping you to achieve symmetry demands a special environment, a setting where you can refine your definition of self yet gain exposure to the varied kinds of knowledge, people, views, activities, options, and ideas that add richness to our lives. Wittenberg is neither a huge university where students are usually mass produced, nor a very small college with few options, which can provide for the intellectual and personal growth required to achieve balance. Campus life is as diverse as the interests of our students. Wittenberg attracts students from all over the United States and from many other countries. Historically, the university has been committed to geographical, educational, cultural, and religious diversity. With their diverse backgrounds and interests, Wittenberg students have helped initiate many of the more than 100 student organizations that are active on campus. The students will be the first to tell you there's never a lack of things to do on or near the campus any day of the week, if you're willing to get involved."

For even more information on this school, turn to page 413 of the "Stats" section.

WRIGHT STATE UNIVERSITY

3640 COLONEL GLENN HIGHWAY, DAYTON, OH 45435 • ADMISSIONS: 937-775-5700 • FAX: 937-775-5795
E-MAIL: ADMISSIONS@WRIGHT.EDU • WEBSITE: WWW.WRIGHT.EDU

Ratings
Quality of Life: 83   Academic: 69   Admissions: 65   Financial Aid: 70

Academics

"A great theatre department, a good medical school, and good value for your tuition dollar," as well as strong programs in education, nursing, and accountancy are the main attractions at Wright State University, a large school located in the eastern suburbs of Dayton,

> **SURVEY SAYS . . .**
> *School is well run, Classes are small*
> *Students love Dayton, Profs teach upper levels*
> *Class discussions encouraged*
> *Intercollegiate sports are popular*
> *Lots of beer drinking*

Ohio. Students here have mixed feelings about both the faculty and administration. Writes a typical undergrad, "My professors are of all types. I have had professors where I hated being in class because they would say, 'Read Chapter 20 and come in the next class with an understanding of the material.' That to me is not teaching. On the other hand I've had professors where I wish they would be my teacher the rest of my college career. They are so helpful and are so good in making me learn the concepts. I would say that my overall academic experience has had some good times and bad times (much more good than bad)." Students say the worst teaching problems occur in required general education courses; leading these courses are "profs that are either bad teachers or you can really tell they hate teaching." Adds another, "The professors for the majors are great. As you continue your education, the classes become more interesting." Even in upper-level courses, though, most students agree the emphasis is on lecturing rather than discussion. Students also warn that "administration services can be frustrating at times, and it can be hard to get questions answered both directly and correctly." Wright State has two campuses: the main, traditional four-year campus, and the Lake Campus, an open admissions facility offering placement courses, pre-college instruction, and two-year associate's degrees.

Life

There most certainly is a party scene at Wright State University. But students also hasten to add that it's not the only game in town. Recalls one, "I have been to places where the people drink, smoke, and whatever, and then there are places where people just have a good time. Although I am not around my classmates all the time, I have seen this [latter behavior prevail]." For those seeking a party, "certain apartment buildings are popular for parties, and they are well known. Campus holidays, like May Days, become drinking fests off campus (like they would be anywhere), and the parties are very popular." For others, "there are a lot of school-sanctioned activities" as well as "a lot to do around Dayton, like comedy clubs, dance clubs, cultural events, and other activities." Students also tell us, "If there isn't something to do at Wright State, then something is happening at the other colleges around the way." Unfortunately, most off-campus action requires a car: "Because Wright State is in a suburb, access to transportation is not easy," explains one student. Some complain that the Wright campus can be downright dull at times, while others counter that "people think that it is boring and that there could be more to do, but those are the people who are usually from large cities."

Students

Wright State's efforts to recruit and accommodate disabled students are nationally known. Approximately 5 percent of students here have some type of disability. This highly visible population, along with an approximately 15 percent minority population and a large number of nontraditional students, leads many here to conclude that this is a diverse campus. A typical student avers that his experience at Wright State has given him "good insight into life outside the little town I come from." Adds another, "With the high population of handicapped students, tolerance for difference is quite high. People are pretty friendly here." Students here are also "hardworking and trying to attain their goals."

ADMISSIONS

Very important factors considered by the admissions committee include: secondary school record and standardized test scores. *Other factors considered include:* recommendations and state residency. SAT I or ACT required. TOEFL required of all international applicants. High school diploma or GED is required. *High school units required/recommended:* 15 total required; 4 English required, 3 math required, 3 science required, 3 science lab required, 2 foreign language required, 3 social studies required.

The Inside Word

Seekers of excellence in both art and science disciplines can end their search with either the traditional four year stint at Wright State or one of the school's nontraditional programs. Students who consider themselves nontraditional will likely find a host of like-minded peers in a supportive environment.

FINANCIAL AID

Students should submit: FAFSA. Priority deadline is February 15. The Princeton Review suggests that all financial aid forms be submitted as soon as possible after January 1. *Need-based scholarships/grants offered:* Pell, SEOG, state scholarships/grants, private scholarships, the school's own gift aid, United Negro College Fund, and Federal Nursing. *Loan aid offered:* FFEL Subsidized Stafford, FFEL Unsubsidized Stafford, FFEL PLUS, Federal Perkins, Federal Nursing, state loans, and college/university loans from institutional funds. Federal Work-Study Program available. Institutional employment available. Applicants will be notified of awards on a rolling basis beginning on or about April 2. Off-campus job opportunities are excellent.

FROM THE ADMISSIONS OFFICE

"Wright State University continues to grow with new majors and facilities. In 2002, new majors in criminal justice and liberal studies were added to the more than 100 majors offered by the university. Recently approved changes to the General Education curriculum will enable students to have more flexibility in selecting courses to meet core requirements.

"Two new facilities, the Honors Residence Hall complex and the Union Market, opened this fall. The Honors Residence Hall complex can house more than 400 honors students in suite-style rooms. Added amenities in the complex include computer labs, an electronic classroom, a café, and a convenience store. The Union Market features the Wright Cup coffee bar, a cybercafé, and made-to-order meals.

"New students have the opportunity to enroll in a Learning Community, designed to help students succeed in college. In Learning Communities, students with common areas of interest take two to three courses as a group during the fall quarter. One of these courses is a seminar designed to help students navigate through the university and find the resources they need to be successful.

"Wright State listens to what its students want. New student clubs and organizations including the hockey club, wrestling club, NAACP, Kappa Delta sorority, and the ski club have been started as a result of student demand. Division I athletics add excitement to campus, but students can also get involved in sports clubs and intramural teams throughout the year."

For even more information on this school, turn to page 414 of the "Stats" section.

Xavier University

3800 VICTORY PARKWAY, CINCINNATI, OH 45207-5311 • ADMISSIONS: 513-745-3301 • FAX: 513-745-4319
E-MAIL: XUADMIT@XU.EDU • WEBSITE: WWW.XAVIER.EDU

Ratings

Quality of Life: 83   **Academic:** 76   **Admissions:** 72   **Financial Aid:** 72

Academics

At Xavier University, students claim that "the academic experience is so fulfilling because of the rigorous core curriculum—every student and alum has studied Plato, great art, literature, chemistry, etc." In fact, one proud stu-

> **SURVEY SAYS . . .**
> *Popular college radio, Theater is hot*
> *Classes are small, Students are religious*
> *Students love Cincinnati, School is well run*
> *Student publications are popular*

dent credits Xavier with having "the hardest core curriculum of all 28 Jesuit universities in the United States." "Professors are better than I could have ever imagined. I truly love going to my classes just to hear them speak," raves an enamored student. The university's religious affiliation is fundamental to its academics: "The Jesuits have a strong commitment to students developing morally, intellectually, and spiritually, and helping make the society around us a better place to live." Students do complain about the registration process and the fact there is "always some construction [on campus] (but the end result is worth it!)." The administration is highly accessible; as one student boasts, "I have had the opportunity to interact one-on-one with the dean of students, the VP of student affairs, the dean of social sciences, and the president of our university . . . and I am not alone in these bragging rights, by any means." And when problems arise, as they inevitably do, students can go to "'The Man,' Adrian Schiess, who is a student advocate and will fix the problem whether it is financial aid, bursar, or housing."

Life

"There's always SOMETHING to do" in Cincinnati, students say, "whether that be a concert or a baseball game or going out to dinner or going to see a movie or a play." There are also "opportunities to see live music at a local music spot called Bogart's, which attracts some good bands," and "Main Street is a lot of fun." On Xavier's campus, there's "always something going on." One student notes that there are "always nonalcoholic activities on campus." "Xavier just opened up the Cintas Center, a 10,000-seat arena that now hosts concerts, comedy fests, and ESPN sports events," reports one student; although entertaining, some feel that "we have gotten very commercialized since the building of the 'almighty Cintas Center'—our small shrine to materialism and basketball here on campus." Some other facilities are lacking, as students wish Xavier "could improve our on-campus library." For those with philanthropic sensibilities, "service is HUGE here so a lot of people join forces to go out into the community to make a difference or to travel to third-world countries to spend a semester in service learning."

Students

Students at Xavier love being here. "I know this is really cheesy, but I always joke that Xavier, and not Disney World, is the happiest place on earth," enthuses one student. "The students at Xavier are one big family," adds another. "It's almost sickening how happy all of us are." Students feel their "fellow students are much smarter than the average person," and they're "incredibly friendly"—"everyone says 'hi' to everyone!" Another student tempers this assessment and admits that "it's not that we really have cliques, but we certainly have comfort zones." On account of these comfort zones, perhaps, little intermingling occurs. Apparently, much of the student body looks "like they stepped off a page from an Abercrombie and Fitch catalog." Still, another student suggests that "while it may appear to be a largely white university, the student body is very social-justice oriented and works for equality for members of all races."

ADMISSIONS

Very important factors considered by the admissions committee include: secondary school record (rigor and performance), class rank, secondary school record, and standardized test scores. *Important factors considered include:* character/personal qualities, essays, extracurricular activities, interview, recommendations, talent/ability, volunteer work, and work experience. SAT I or ACT required. TOEFL required of all international applicants. High school diploma or GED is required. *High school units required/recommended:* 21 total recommended; 4 English recommended, 3 math recommended, 3 science recommended, 2 foreign language recommended, 3 social studies recommended, 5 elective recommended.

The Inside Word

Xavier passes the test for many students who arrive for their freshman year expecting an accommodating place that provides all the hallmarks of a big school, academically and socially. Applicants who intend to enact a finely specialized course load must be prepared for the core courses as well.

FINANCIAL AID

Students should submit: FAFSA. No deadline for regular filing. The Princeton Review suggests that all financial aid forms be submitted as soon as possible after January 1. *Need-based scholarships/grants offered:* Pell, SEOG, state scholarships/grants, private scholarships, and the school's own gift aid. *Loan aid offered:* FFEL Subsidized Stafford, FFEL Unsubsidized Stafford, FFEL PLUS, and Federal Perkins. Federal Work-Study Program available. Institutional employment available. Applicants will be notified of awards on a rolling basis beginning on or about March 1. Off-campus job opportunities are excellent.

FROM THE ADMISSIONS OFFICE

"Founded in 1831, Xavier University is the fourth oldest of the 28 Jesuit colleges and universities in the United States. The Jesuit tradition is evident in the university's core curriculum, degree programs, and opportunities for involvement. Xavier is home to 6,700 total students; 4,000 at the undergraduate level. Each year the student population represents more than 45 states and 43 foreign countries.

"The university offers 68 academic majors and 38 minors in the colleges of arts and sciences, business, and social sciences. The most popular majors include business, communication arts, education, psychology and sport management/marketing, as well as pre-professional areas of study. Other programs of note include university scholars, Honors AB, Army ROTC, study abroad, service learning, and the Xavier service fellowship.

"There are more than 100 clubs and organizations on campus. Students participate in groups such as student government, campus ministry, performing arts, and 30 club and intramural sports teams. Xavier is a member of the Division I Atlantic 10 Conference and fields teams in men's and women's basketball, cross-country, golf, rifle, soccer, swimming, and tennis as well as men's baseball and women's volleyball.

"The university is situated on more than 125 acres in a residential area of Cincinnati, Ohio. The face of Xavier has continued to change with the addition of a 10,000-seat arena and convocation center, a complex that includes banquet facilities and a student dining hall. Also new to campus are a recreation park, apartments for upperclassmen, and a new $18 million student center with a performing arts theatre."

For even more information on this school, turn to page 415 of the "Stats" section.

PART 3

THE STATS

ALBION COLLEGE

CAMPUS LIFE
Quality of Life Rating   **77**

Type of school	private
Affiliation	Methodist
Environment	rural

STUDENTS

Total undergrad enrollment	1,548
% male/female	44/56
% from out of state	9
% from public high school	72
% live on campus	92
% in (# of) fraternities	40 (5)
% in (# of) sororities	40 (6)
% African American	2
% Asian	2
% Caucasian	86
% international	1
# of countries represented	19

ACADEMICS
Academic Rating   **78**

Calendar	semester
Student/faculty ratio	12:1
Profs interesting rating	69
Profs accessible rating	68
% profs teaching UG courses	100
Avg lab size	10-19 students
Avg reg class size	10-19 students

MOST POPULAR MAJORS
Business administration/management
English language and literature
Biology/biological sciences

SELECTIVITY
Admissions Rating   **80**

# of applicants	1,297
% of applicants accepted	87
% of acceptees attending	40
# of early decision applicants	37
% accepted early decision	95

FRESHMAN PROFILE

Range SAT Verbal	510-640
Average SAT Verbal	562
Range SAT Math	520-630
Average SAT Math	582
Range ACT Composite	22-27
Average ACT Composite	25
Minimum TOEFL	550
Average HS GPA	3.5
% graduated top 10% of class	31
% graduated top 25% of class	63
% graduated top 50% of class	88

DEADLINES

Early decision	11/15
Early decision notification	12/15
Priority admission	4/1
Regular admission	5/1
Nonfall registration?	yes

FINANCIAL FACTS
Financial Aid Rating   **87**

Tuition	$19,390
Room and board	$5,604
Books and supplies	$650
Required fees	$230
% frosh receiving aid	65
% undergrads receiving aid	60
Avg frosh grant	$16,823
Avg frosh loan	$2,610

ALMA COLLEGE

CAMPUS LIFE
Quality of Life Rating   **72**

Type of school	private
Affiliation	Presbyterian
Environment	rural

STUDENTS

Total undergrad enrollment	1,317
% male/female	43/57
% from out of state	5
% from public high school	94
% live on campus	85
% in (# of) fraternities	25 (5)
% in (# of) sororities	39 (5)
% African American	1
% Asian	1
% Caucasian	94
% Hispanic	1
% international	1
# of countries represented	12

ACADEMICS
Academic Rating   **80**

Calendar	other (4-4-1)
Student/faculty ratio	13:1
Profs interesting rating	80
Profs accessible rating	79
% profs teaching UG courses	100
% classes taught by TAs	0
Avg lab size	10-19 students
Avg regular class size	10-19 students

Business administration/management
Education
Biology/biological sciences

SELECTIVITY

Admissions Rating — **76**

# of applicants	1,502
% of applicants accepted	79
% of acceptees attending	28

FRESHMAN PROFILE

Range ACT Composite	22-27
Average ACT Composite	25
Minimum TOEFL	525
Average HS GPA	3.44
% graduated top 10% of class	33
% graduated top 25% of class	64
% graduated top 50% of class	93

DEADLINES

Nonfall registration?	yes

FINANCIAL FACTS

Financial Aid Rating — **75**

Tuition	$17,412
Room and board	$6,336
Books and supplies	$700
Avg frosh grant	$9,071
Avg frosh loan	$3,863

ANDERSON UNIVERSITY

CAMPUS LIFE

Quality of Life Rating — **77**

Type of school	private
Affiliation	none
Environment	suburban

STUDENTS

Total undergrad enrollment	1,977
% male/female	40/60
% from out of state	36
% live on campus	60
% African American	4
% Caucasian	92
% Hispanic	1
% international	1
# of countries represented	12

ACADEMICS

Academic Rating — **78**

Calendar	quarter
Student/faculty ratio	14:1
Profs interesting rating	82
Profs accessible rating	77

% profs teaching UG courses	93
% classes taught by TAs	0

MOST POPULAR MAJORS
Elementary education
Nursing
Mass communication

SELECTIVITY

Admissions Rating — **76**

# of applicants	1,552
% of applicants accepted	82
% of acceptees attending	44

FRESHMAN PROFILE

Range SAT Verbal	480-590
Average SAT Verbal	533
Range SAT Math	480-590
Average SAT Math	538
Range ACT Composite	21-26
Average ACT Composite	24
Average HS GPA	3.4
% graduated top 10% of class	23
% graduated top 25% of class	53
% graduated top 50% of class	85

DEADLINES

Regular admission	8/1
Nonfall registration?	yes

FINANCIAL FACTS

Financial Aid Rating — **78**

Tuition	$13,740
Room and board	$4,540

ASHLAND UNIVERSITY

CAMPUS LIFE

Quality of Life Rating — **76**

Type of school	private
Affiliation	Church of Brethren
Environment	rural

STUDENTS

Total undergrad enrollment	2,760
% male/female	44/56
% from out of state	9
% from public high school	89
% live on campus	72
% in (# of) fraternities	14 (4)
% in (# of) sororities	22 (5)
% African American	9
% Caucasian	83
% Hispanic	1
% international	2
# of countries represented	28

ACADEMICS

Academic Rating   **73**

Calendar	semester
Student/faculty ratio	16:1
Profs interesting rating	79
Profs accessible rating	76
% classes taught by TAs	0
Avg lab size	under 10 students
Avg reg class size	10-19 students

MOST POPULAR MAJORS
Pre-professional studies
Radio/TV
Psychology

SELECTIVITY

Admissions Rating   **68**

# of applicants	2,046
% of applicants accepted	81
% of acceptees attending	33

FRESHMAN PROFILE

Range SAT Verbal	450-550
Average SAT Verbal	515
Range SAT Math	450-580
Average SAT Math	523
Range ACT Composite	18-23
Average ACT Composite	22
Minimum TOEFL	500
Average HS GPA	3.3
% graduated top 10% of class	22
% graduated top 25% of class	45
% graduated top 50% of class	73

DEADLINES

Nonfall registration?	yes

FINANCIAL FACTS

Financial Aid Rating   **74**

Tuition	$16,764
Room and board	$6,212
Books and supplies	$600
Avg frosh grant	$5,500
Avg frosh loan	$3,000

AUGSBURG COLLEGE

CAMPUS LIFE

Quality of Life Rating   **83**

Type of school	private
Affiliation	Lutheran
Environment	urban

STUDENTS

Total undergrad enrollment	2,780
% male/female	42/58
% from out of state	10
% live on campus	35
% African American	5
% Asian	3
% Caucasian	71
% Hispanic	1
% international	1

ACADEMICS

Academic Rating   **70**

Calendar	differs by program
Student/faculty ratio	15:1
Profs interesting rating	83
Profs accessible rating	81
% profs teaching UG courses	99
% classes taught by TAs	0
Avg lab size	10-19 students
Avg reg class size	10-19 students

MOST POPULAR MAJORS
Communications studies/speech communication
and rhetoric
Education
Business administration/management

SELECTIVITY

Admissions Rating   **64**

# of applicants	910
% of applicants accepted	79
% of acceptees attending	49

FRESHMAN PROFILE

Range SAT Verbal	455-610
Average SAT Verbal	541
Range SAT Math	495-590
Average SAT Math	542
Range ACT Composite	20-25
Average ACT Composite	23
Minimum TOEFL	550
Average HS GPA	3.3
% graduated top 10% of class	17
% graduated top 25% of class	43
% graduated top 50% of class	74

DEADLINES

Regular admission	8/15
Nonfall registration?	yes

FINANCIAL FACTS

Financial Aid Rating   **79**

Tuition	$17,070
Room and board	$5,540
Books and supplies	$675
Avg frosh grant	$11,445
Avg frosh loan	$6,552

Augustana College (IL)

CAMPUS LIFE
Quality of Life Rating   **72**

Type of school	private
Affiliation	Lutheran
Environment	suburban

STUDENTS

Total undergrad enrollment	2,232
% male/female	43/57
% from out of state	12
% from public high school	87
% live on campus	70
% in (# of) fraternities	21 (7)
% in (# of) sororities	28 (6)
% African American	2
% Asian	2
% Caucasian	92
% Hispanic	3
% international	1
# of countries represented	24

ACADEMICS
Academic Rating   **84**

Calendar	quarter
Student/faculty ratio	12:1
Profs interesting rating	77
Profs accessible rating	73
% profs teaching UG courses	100
% classes taught by TAs	0
Avg lab size	10-19 students
Avg reg class size	10-19 students

MOST POPULAR MAJORS
Biology/pre-med
Business administration
English

SELECTIVITY
Admissions Rating   **79**

# of applicants	2,622
% of applicants accepted	30
% of acceptees attending	27
# accepting a place on wait list	64
% admitted from wait list	40

FRESHMAN PROFILE

Range ACT Composite	23-29
Average ACT Composite	25
Minimum TOEFL	550
Average HS GPA	3.5
% graduated top 10% of class	31
% graduated top 25% of class	64
% graduated top 50% of class	94

DEADLINES

Nonfall registration?	yes

FINANCIAL FACTS
Financial Aid Rating   **69**

Books and supplies	$675
Avg frosh grant	$10,064
Avg frosh loan	$3,358

Augustana College (SD)

CAMPUS LIFE
Quality of Life Rating   **71**

Type of school	private
Affiliation	Lutheran
Environment	urban

STUDENTS

Total undergrad enrollment	1,774
% male/female	35/65
% from out of state	49
% from public high school	97
% live on campus	67
% African American	1
% Caucasian	96
% international	2

ACADEMICS
Academic Rating   **79**

Calendar	4-1-4
Student/faculty ratio	12:1
Profs interesting rating	84
Profs accessible rating	79
% profs teaching UG courses	100
% classes taught by TAs	0
Avg lab size	20-29 students
Avg regular class size	20-29 students

MOST POPULAR MAJORS
Business administration
Biology
Nursing

SELECTIVITY
Admissions Rating   **71**

# of applicants	1,389
% of applicants accepted	85
% of acceptees attending	36

FRESHMAN PROFILE

Range SAT Verbal	520-670
Average SAT Verbal	570
Range SAT Math	540-650
Average SAT Math	550
Range ACT Composite	22-27

Average ACT Composite	24
Minimum TOEFL	550
Average HS GPA	3.5
% graduated top 10% of class	28
% graduated top 25% of class	57
% graduated top 50% of class	93

DEADLINES

Regular admission	8/15
Regular notification	rolling
Nonfall registration?	yes

FINANCIAL FACTS
Financial Aid Rating   **72**

Tuition	$15,892
Room and board	$4,668
Books and supplies	$600
Avg frosh grant	$8,430
Avg frosh loan	$5,811

BAKER UNIVERSITY

CAMPUS LIFE
Quality of Life Rating   **70**

Type of school	private
Affiliation	Methodist
Environment	rural

STUDENTS

Total undergrad enrollment	1,002
% male/female	41/59
% from out of state	25
% from public high school	95
% live on campus	96
% in (# of) fraternities	45 (4)
% in (# of) sororities	50 (4)
% African American	4
% Asian	1
% Caucasian	86
% Hispanic	2
% international	1
# of countries represented	3

ACADEMICS
Academic Rating   **78**

Calendar	4-1-4
Student/faculty ratio	11:1
Profs interesting rating	90
Profs accessible rating	90
% profs teaching UG courses	100
% classes taught by TAs	0

MOST POPULAR MAJORS
Business, Pre-medicine, Education

SELECTIVITY
Admissions Rating   **74**

# of applicants	931
% of applicants accepted	88
% of acceptees attending	30

FRESHMAN PROFILE

Range SAT Verbal	450-640
Range SAT Math	480-600
Range ACT Composite	20-26
Average ACT Composite	23
Minimum TOEFL	525
Average HS GPA	3.5
% graduated top 10% of class	21
% graduated top 25% of class	42
% graduated top 50% of class	78

DEADLINES

Regular admission	rolling
Regular notification	rolling
Nonfall registration?	yes

FINANCIAL FACTS
Financial Aid Rating   **69**

Tuition	$13,670
Room and board	$5,170
Books and supplies	$900
Avg frosh grant	$7,381
Avg frosh loan	$4,125

BALDWIN-WALLACE COLLEGE

CAMPUS LIFE
Quality of Life Rating   **74**

Type of school	private
Affiliation	Methodist
Environment	suburban

STUDENTS

Total undergrad enrollment	3,993
% male/female	38/62
% from out of state	9
% from public high school	85
% live on campus	62
% in (# of) fraternities	20 (6)
% in (# of) sororities	20 (6)
% African American	4
% Asian	1
% Caucasian	85
% Hispanic	1
% international	1
# of countries represented	15

ACADEMICS
Academic Rating   **72**

Calendar	semester

Student/faculty ratio	15:1	% in (# of) fraternities	10 (19)
Profs interesting rating	80	% in (# of) sororities	10 (16)
Profs accessible rating	76	% African American	6
% profs teaching UG courses	93	% Asian	1
% classes taught by TAs	0	% Caucasian	87
Avg lab size	10-19 students	% Hispanic	1
Avg reg class size	10-19 students	# of countries represented	86

MOST POPULAR MAJORS
Sports and fitness administration/management
Elementary education and teaching
Business administration/management

SELECTIVITY
Admissions Rating **67**

# of applicants	2,090
% of applicants accepted	81
% of acceptees attending	41

FRESHMAN PROFILE
Range SAT Verbal	520-620
Average SAT Verbal	555
Range SAT Math	510-630
Average SAT Math	567
Range ACT Composite	21-26
Average ACT Composite	24
Minimum TOEFL	500
Average HS GPA	3.5
% graduated top 10% of class	30
% graduated top 25% of class	60
% graduated top 50% of class	91

DEADLINES
Nonfall registration?	yes

FINANCIAL FACTS
Financial Aid Rating **82**

Tuition	$16,330
Room and board	$5,680
Books and supplies	$650
Avg frosh grant	$9,372
Avg frosh loan	$2,064

BALL STATE UNIVERSITY

CAMPUS LIFE
Quality of Life Rating **71**

Type of school	public
Affiliation	none
Environment	suburban

STUDENTS
Total undergrad enrollment	16,535
% male/female	47/53
% from out of state	8
% from public high school	95
% live on campus	42

ACADEMICS
Academic Rating **66**

Calendar	semester
Student/faculty ratio	14:1
Profs interesting rating	83
Profs accessible rating	79
% profs teaching UG courses	96
% classes taught by TAs	4
Avg lab size	20-29 students
Avg reg class size	20-29 students

MOST POPULAR MAJORS
Elementary education
Pre-business/business administration
Physical education teaching

SELECTIVITY
Admissions Rating **63**

# of applicants	10,462
% of applicants accepted	76
% of acceptees attending	47

FRESHMAN PROFILE
Range SAT Verbal	467-573
Average SAT Verbal	518
Range SAT Math	468-579
Average SAT Math	522
Range ACT Composite	19-25
Average ACT Composite	22
Minimum TOEFL	500
% graduated top 10% of class	16
% graduated top 25% of class	43
% graduated top 50% of class	80

DEADLINES
Nonfall registration?	yes

FINANCIAL FACTS
Financial Aid Rating **77**

In-state tuition	$3,924
Out-of-state tuition	$10,800
Room and board	$5,100
Books and supplies	$830
Avg frosh grant	$1,466
Avg frosh loan	$3,439

BELOIT COLLEGE

CAMPUS LIFE
Quality of Life Rating **84**
Type of school   private
Environment   urban
STUDENTS
Total undergrad enrollment   1,281
% male/female   38/62
% from out of state   80
% from public high school   80
% live on campus   93
% in (# of) fraternities   15 (3)
% in (# of) sororities   5 (2)
% African American   4
% Asian   4
% Caucasian   86
% Hispanic   3
% international   8
# of countries represented   54

ACADEMICS
Academic Rating **87**
Calendar   semester
Student/faculty ratio   11:1
% profs teaching UG courses   100
Avg reg class size   10-19 students

MOST POPULAR MAJORS
Creative writing
Psychology
Anthropology

SELECTIVITY
Admissions Rating **80**
# of applicants   1,677
% of applicants accepted   70
% of acceptees attending   26
# accepting a place on wait list   74
% admitted from wait list   61
FRESHMAN PROFILE
Range SAT Verbal   590-690
Average SAT Verbal   640
Range SAT Math   560-650
Average SAT Math   610
Range ACT Composite   25-29
Average ACT Composite   27
Minimum TOEFL   525
Average HS GPA   3.5
% graduated top 10% of class   30
% graduated top 25% of class   68
% graduated top 50% of class   95

DEADLINES
Priority admission   2/1
Regular notification   3/15

FINANCIAL FACTS
Financial Aid Rating **95**
Tuition $23,016
Room and board $5,268
Books and supplies $400
Required fees $220
% frosh receiving aid   71
% undergrads receiving aid   70
Avg frosh grant $12,956
Avg frosh loan $2,920

BETHEL COLLEGE (KS)

CAMPUS LIFE
Quality of Life Rating **73**
Type of school   private
Affiliation   Mennonite
Environment   suburban
STUDENTS
Total undergrad enrollment   525
% male/female   50/50
% from out of state   31
% from public high school   98
% live on campus   75
% African American   7
% Asian   2
% Caucasian   79
% Hispanic   7
% international   4
# of countries represented   15

ACADEMICS
Academic Rating **73**
Calendar   4-1-4
Student/faculty ratio   11:1
Profs interesting rating   83
Profs accessible rating   81
% profs teaching UG courses   100
% classes taught by TAs   0
Avg lab size   30-39 students
Avg regular class size   10-19 students

MOST POPULAR MAJORS
Nursing registered nurse training
(RN, ASN, BSN, MSN)
Social work
Elementary education and teaching

SELECTIVITY

Admissions Rating **69**

# of applicants	432
% of applicants accepted	75
% of acceptees attending	39

FRESHMAN PROFILE

Range SAT Verbal	450-550
Range SAT Math	440-560
Range ACT Composite	20-27
Average ACT Composite	24
Minimum TOEFL	540
Average HS GPA	3.37
% graduated top 10% of class	17
% graduated top 25% of class	42
% graduated top 50% of class	73

DEADLINES

Regular admission	8/1
Nonfall registration?	yes

FINANCIAL FACTS

Financial Aid Rating **78**

Tuition	$13,000
Room and board	$5,500
Books and supplies	$800
Avg frosh grant	$4,800
Avg frosh loan	$2,625

BETHEL COLLEGE (MN)

CAMPUS LIFE

Quality of Life Rating **75**

Type of school	private
Affiliation	Baptist
Environment	suburban

STUDENTS

Total undergrad enrollment	2,700
% male/female	39/61
% from out of state	29
% live on campus	70
% African American	1
% Asian	2
% Caucasian	95
% Hispanic	1

ACADEMICS

Academic Rating **77**

Calendar	4-1-4
Student/faculty ratio	16:1
Profs interesting rating	78
Profs accessible rating	77
% profs teaching UG courses	100
% classes taught by TAs	0

MOST POPULAR MAJORS

Education
Business
Biology

SELECTIVITY

Admissions Rating **76**

# of applicants	1,580
% of applicants accepted	67
% of acceptees attending	61
# accepting a place on wait list	213
% admitted from wait list	3

FRESHMAN PROFILE

Range SAT Verbal	520-640
Average SAT Verbal	590
Range SAT Math	520-640
Average SAT Math	593
Range ACT Composite	20-26
Average ACT Composite	23
Minimum TOEFL	525
% graduated top 10% of class	27
% graduated top 25% of class	55
% graduated top 50% of class	90

DEADLINES

Regular admission	3/1
Nonfall registration?	yes

FINANCIAL FACTS

Financial Aid Rating **72**

Tuition	$17,700
Room and board	$5,410
Books and supplies	$600
Avg frosh grant	$7,405
Avg frosh loan	$3,447

BRADLEY UNIVERSITY

CAMPUS LIFE

Quality of Life Rating **77**

Type of school	private
Environment	urban

STUDENTS

Total undergrad enrollment	5,190
% male/female	45/55
% from out of state	14
% from public high school	76
% live on campus	70
% in (# of) fraternities	34 (18)
% in (# of) sororities	33 (12)
% African American	5
% Asian	2
% Caucasian	85

% Hispanic	2
% international	2
# of countries represented	26

ACADEMICS
Academic Rating — 69

Calendar	semester
Student/faculty ratio	14:1
Profs interesting rating	92
Profs accessible rating	93
% profs teaching UG courses	100
Avg reg class size	10-19 students

MOST POPULAR MAJORS
Elementary education and teaching
Psychology
Actuarial science

SELECTIVITY
Admissions Rating — 77

# of applicants	5,506
% of applicants accepted	67
% of acceptees attending	30
# accepting a place on wait list	132
% admitted from wait list	33

FRESHMAN PROFILE

Range SAT Verbal	540-650
Average SAT Verbal	597
Range SAT Math	550-670
Average SAT Math	610
Range ACT Composite	23-29
Average ACT Composite	25
Minimum TOEFL	500
% graduated top 10% of class	33
% graduated top 25% of class	68
% graduated top 50% of class	93

DEADLINES

Priority admission	3/1
Regular admission	rolling
Nonfall registration?	yes

FINANCIAL FACTS
Financial Aid Rating — 84

Tuition	$16,800
Books and supplies	$500
% undergrads receiving aid	71
Avg frosh grant	$9,279
Avg frosh loan	$3,671

BUENA VISTA UNIVERSITY

CAMPUS LIFE
Quality of Life Rating — 75

Type of school	private
Affiliation	Presbyterian
Environment	rural

STUDENTS

Total undergrad enrollment	1,267
% male/female	48/52
% from out of state	16
% from public high school	85
% live on campus	86
% African American	1
% Asian	1
% Caucasian	95
% Hispanic	1
% international	1

ACADEMICS
Academic Rating — 80

Calendar	4-1-4
Student/faculty ratio	16:1
Profs interesting rating	83
Profs accessible rating	80
% profs teaching UG courses	100
% classes taught by TAs	0
Avg reg class size	10-19 students

MOST POPULAR MAJORS
Business
Education
Biology

SELECTIVITY
Admissions Rating — 77

# of applicants	1,233
% of applicants accepted	84
% of acceptees attending	35

FRESHMAN PROFILE

Range ACT Composite	22-26
Average ACT Composite	23
Minimum TOEFL	500
Average HS GPA	3.36
% graduated top 10% of class	20
% graduated top 25% of class	43
% graduated top 50% of class	75

DEADLINES

Regular admission	4/1
Regular notification	rolling
Nonfall registration?	yes

FINANCIAL FACTS
Financial Aid Rating — 89

Tuition	$18,738
Room and board	$5,230
Books and supplies	$500
Avg frosh grant	$11,926
Avg frosh loan	$3,322

BUTLER UNIVERSITY

CAMPUS LIFE
Quality of Life Rating **83**
Type of school | private
Affiliation | none
Environment | urban

STUDENTS
Total undergrad enrollment | 3,580
% male/female | 37/63
% from out of state | 40
% from public high school | 86
% live on campus | 62
% in (# of) fraternities | 11 (8)
% in (# of) sororities | 18 (8)
% African American | 4
% Asian | 2
% Caucasian | 91
% Hispanic | 1
% international | 2

ACADEMICS
Academic Rating **73**
Calendar | semester
Student/faculty ratio | 13:1
Profs interesting rating | 78
Profs accessible rating | 74
% profs teaching UG courses | 85
% classes taught by TAs | 0
Avg lab size | 20-29 students
Avg reg class size | 21 students

MOST POPULAR MAJORS
Elementary education and teaching
Marketing/marketing management
Pharmacy (PharmD, BS/BPharm)

SELECTIVITY
Admissions Rating **68**
# of applicants | 3,817
% of applicants accepted | 80
% of acceptees attending | 30
# accepting a place on wait list | 125
% admitted from wait list | 45

FRESHMAN PROFILE
Range SAT Verbal | 520-620
Average SAT Verbal | 571
Range SAT Math | 540-640
Average SAT Math | 588
Range ACT Composite | 23-28
Average ACT Composite | 26
Minimum TOEFL | 550
Average HS GPA | 3.6

% graduated top 10% of class | 44
% graduated top 25% of class | 67
% graduated top 50% of class | 95

DEADLINES
Regular admission | 8/15
Non-binding early admission | 12/1
Nonfall registration? | yes

FINANCIAL FACTS
Financial Aid Rating **76**
Tuition | $19,990
Room and board | $6,710
Books and supplies | $750

CALVIN COLLEGE

CAMPUS LIFE
Quality of Life Rating **93**
Type of school | private
Affiliation | other
Environment | suburban

STUDENTS
Total undergrad enrollment | 4,286
% male/female | 44/56
% from out of state | 39
% from public high school | 42
% live on campus | 58
% African American | 1
% Asian | 2
% Caucasian | 92
% Hispanic | 1
% international | 8

ACADEMICS
Academic Rating **82**
Calendar | 4-1-4
Student/faculty ratio | 13:1
Profs interesting rating | 95
Profs accessible rating | 97
% profs teaching UG courses | 100
Avg lab size | 20-29 students
Avg reg class size | 20-29 students

MOST POPULAR MAJORS
Business administration/management
Elementary education and teaching
English language and literature

SELECTIVITY
Admissions Rating **78**
# of applicants | 1,862
% of applicants accepted | 98
% of acceptees attending | 57

FRESHMAN PROFILE

Range SAT Verbal	520-640
Average SAT Verbal	584
Range SAT Math	530-660
Average SAT Math	595
Range ACT Composite	22-28
Average ACT Composite	26
Minimum TOEFL	550
Average HS GPA	3.5
% graduated top 10% of class	27
% graduated top 25% of class	52
% graduated top 50% of class	81

DEADLINES

Regular admission	8/15
Nonfall registration?	yes

FINANCIAL FACTS

Financial Aid Rating **90**

Tuition	$15,750
Room and board	$5,485
Books and supplies	$655
% frosh receiving aid	63
% undergrads receiving aid	64
Avg frosh grant	$7,600
Avg frosh loan	$4,700

CARLETON COLLEGE

CAMPUS LIFE

Quality of Life Rating **89**

Type of school	private
Environment	rural

STUDENTS

Total undergrad enrollment	1,932
% male/female	48/52
% from out of state	77
% from public high school	74
% live on campus	90
% African American	4
% Asian	9
% Caucasian	82
% Hispanic	4
% international	3

ACADEMICS

Academic Rating **98**

Student/faculty ratio	9:1
Profs interesting rating	94
Profs accessible rating	99
% profs teaching UG courses	100
Avg lab size	10-19 students
Avg reg class size	10-19 students

MOST POPULAR MAJORS

Political science and government
Biology/biological sciences
English

SELECTIVITY

Admissions Rating **97**

# of applicants	4,170
% of applicants accepted	35
% of acceptees attending	35
# accepting a place on wait list	394
% admitted from wait list	3
# of early decision applicants	367
% accepted early decision	55

FRESHMAN PROFILE

Range SAT Verbal	640-740
Range SAT Math	640-720
Range ACT Composite	27-31
Minimum TOEFL	600
% graduated top 10% of class	70
% graduated top 25% of class	93
% graduated top 50% of class	99

DEADLINES

Early decision	11/15
Early decision notification	12/15
Regular admission	1/15
Regular notification	4/15

FINANCIAL FACTS

Financial Aid Rating **83**

Tuition	$26,745
Room and board	$5,535
Books and supplies	$1,200
Required fees	$165
% frosh receiving aid	55
% undergrads receiving aid	54
Avg frosh grant	$17,184
Avg frosh loan	$2,781

CARTHAGE COLLEGE

CAMPUS LIFE

Quality of Life Rating **84**

Type of school	private
Affiliation	Lutheran
Environment	suburban

STUDENTS

Total undergrad enrollment	2,101
% male/female	42/58
% from out of state	50
% live on campus	73
% in (# of) fraternities	23 (7)
% in (# of) sororities	23 (4)

% African American	5
% Asian	1
% Caucasian	91
% Hispanic	2
# of countries represented	9

ACADEMICS
Academic Rating 72
Calendar	4-1-4
Student/faculty ratio	15:1
Profs interesting rating	79
Profs accessible rating	76
% profs teaching UG courses	100
% classes taught by TAs	0

MOST POPULAR MAJORS
Physical education teaching and coaching
Business administration/management
Education

SELECTIVITY
Admissions Rating 72
# of applicants	2,075
% of applicants accepted	91
% of acceptees attending	21

FRESHMAN PROFILE
Range SAT Verbal	460-610
Average SAT Verbal	568
Range SAT Math	470-630
Average SAT Math	562
Range ACT Composite	20-28
Average ACT Composite	23
Minimum TOEFL	500
Average HS GPA	3.1
% graduated top 10% of class	18
% graduated top 25% of class	40
% graduated top 50% of class	65

DEADLINES
Regular notification	rolling
Nonfall registration?	yes

FINANCIAL FACTS
Financial Aid Rating 75
Tuition	$19,150
Room and board	$5,750
Books and supplies	$600
Avg frosh grant	$7,851
Avg frosh loan	$3,553

CASE WESTERN RESERVE UNIVERSITY

CAMPUS LIFE
Quality of Life Rating 70

Type of school	private
Environment	urban

STUDENTS
Total undergrad enrollment	3,457
% male/female	61/39
% from out of state	40
% from public high school	70
% live on campus	78
% in (# of) fraternities	36 (18)
% in (# of) sororities	15 (5)
% African American	5
% Asian	15
% Caucasian	76
% Hispanic	2
% international	4
# of countries represented	89

ACADEMICS
Academic Rating 80
Calendar	semester
Student/faculty ratio	8:1
Profs interesting rating	88
Profs accessible rating	91
% profs teaching UG courses	72
% classes taught by TAs	5
Avg lab size	10-19 students
Avg reg class size	10-19 students

MOST POPULAR MAJORS
Business administration/management
Biology/biological sciences
Psychology

SELECTIVITY
Admissions Rating 86
# of applicants	4,428
% of applicants accepted	78
% of acceptees attending	24
# accepting a place on wait list	177
% admitted from wait list	3
# of early decision applicants	108
% accepted early decision	86

FRESHMAN PROFILE
Range SAT Verbal	590-710
Range SAT Math	630-730
Range ACT Composite	26-31
Minimum TOEFL	550
% graduated top 10% of class	66
% graduated top 25% of class	92
% graduated top 50% of class	99

DEADLINES
Early decision	1/1

Regular admission	2/1
Regular notification	4/1
Nonfall registration?	yes

FINANCIAL FACTS
Financial Aid Rating **82**

Tuition	$24,100
Room and board	$7,660
Books and supplies	$800
Required fees	$242
% frosh receiving aid	63
% undergrads receiving aid	54
Avg frosh grant	$15,865
Avg frosh loan	$5,580

CEDARVILLE UNIVERSITY

CAMPUS LIFE
Quality of Life Rating **77**

Type of school	private
Affiliation	Baptist
Environment	rural

STUDENTS

Total undergrad enrollment	2,847
% male/female	46/54
% from out of state	66
% from public high school	51
% live on campus	78
% African American	1
% Asian	1
% Caucasian	97
% Hispanic	1
# of countries represented	3

ACADEMICS
Academic Rating **78**

Calendar	quarter
Student/faculty ratio	18:1
Profs interesting rating	81
Profs accessible rating	78
% profs teaching UG courses	95
% classes taught by TAs	0
Avg lab size	10-19 students
Avg reg class size	10-19 students

MOST POPULAR MAJORS
Elementary education
Nursing
Mechanical engineering

SELECTIVITY
Admissions Rating **73**

# of applicants	1,952
% of applicants accepted	74

% of acceptees attending	50
# accepting a place on wait list	12
% admitted from wait list	8

FRESHMAN PROFILE

Range SAT Verbal	540-650
Average SAT Verbal	597
Range SAT Math	540-640
Average SAT Math	588
Range ACT Composite	23-28
Average ACT Composite	26
Minimum TOEFL	550
Average HS GPA	3.6
% graduated top 10% of class	34
% graduated top 25% of class	65
% graduated top 50% of class	93

DEADLINES

Nonfall registration?	yes

FINANCIAL FACTS
Financial Aid Rating **74**

Tuition	$11,424
Room and board	$4,929
Books and supplies	$840
Avg frosh grant	$4,200
Avg frosh loan	$8,490

CENTRAL COLLEGE

CAMPUS LIFE
Quality of Life Rating **75**

Type of school	private
Affiliation	Reformed Church
Environment	suburban

STUDENTS

Total undergrad enrollment	1,659
% male/female	42/58
% from out of state	19
% from public high school	98
% live on campus	87
% in (# of) fraternities	15 (4)
% in (# of) sororities	7 (2)
% Asian	1
% Caucasian	96
% Hispanic	1
% international	1

ACADEMICS
Academic Rating **78**

Calendar	semester
Student/faculty ratio	13:1
Profs interesting rating	81
Profs accessible rating	77

% profs teaching UG courses	100
% classes taught by TAs	0

MOST POPULAR MAJORS
Exercise science
Business administration/management
Education

SELECTIVITY
Admissions Rating	**73**
# of applicants	1,598
% of applicants accepted	86
% of acceptees attending	33

FRESHMAN PROFILE
Average ACT Composite	23
Minimum TOEFL	530
Average HS GPA	3.5
% graduated top 10% of class	26
% graduated top 25% of class	56
% graduated top 50% of class	81

DEADLINES
Regular notification	rolling
Nonfall registration?	yes

FINANCIAL FACTS
Financial Aid Rating	**79**
Tuition	$16,612
Room and board	$5,796
Books and supplies	$700

CENTRAL MICHIGAN UNIVERSITY

CAMPUS LIFE
Quality of Life Rating	**77**
Type of school	public
Affiliation	none
Environment	suburban

STUDENTS
Total undergrad enrollment	19,530
% male/female	40/60
% from out of state	2
% from public high school	95
% live on campus	31
% in (# of) fraternities	7 (19)
% in (# of) sororities	7 (14)
% African American	6
% Asian	1
% Caucasian	86
% Hispanic	2
% international	1

ACADEMICS
Academic Rating	**72**

Calendar	semester
Student/faculty ratio	23:1
% profs teaching UG courses	99
Avg lab size	20-29 students
Avg reg class size	20-29 students

MOST POPULAR MAJORS
Psychology
Teacher education, multiple levels
Advertising

SELECTIVITY
Admissions Rating	**67**
# of applicants	12,135
% of applicants accepted	67
% of acceptees attending	45
# accepting a place on wait list	300
% admitted from wait list	80

FRESHMAN PROFILE
Range SAT Verbal	465-600
Range SAT Math	490-600
Range ACT Composite	20-25
Average ACT Composite	22
Minimum TOEFL	550
Average HS GPA	3.4
% graduated top 10% of class	19
% graduated top 25% of class	48
% graduated top 50% of class	83

DEADLINES
Regular notification	rolling
Nonfall registration?	yes

FINANCIAL FACTS
Financial Aid Rating	**75**
In-state tuition	$3,686
Out-of-state tuition	$9,567
Room and board	$5,220
Books and supplies	$850
Avg frosh grant	$1,200

CENTRAL MISSOURI STATE UNIVERSITY

CAMPUS LIFE
Quality of Life Rating	**77**
Type of school	public
Affiliation	none
Environment	rural

STUDENTS
Total undergrad enrollment	9,068
% male/female	47/53
% from out of state	6

% from public high school 89
% live on campus 32
% in (# of) fraternities 16 (13)
% in (# of) sororities 13 (9)
% African American 5
% Asian 1
% Caucasian 86
% Hispanic 1
% international 3
# of countries represented 65

ACADEMICS
Academic Rating **73**
Calendar semester
Student/faculty ratio 17:1
Profs interesting rating 84
Profs accessible rating 81
% profs teaching UG courses 95
% classes taught by TAs 4
Avg reg class size 20-29 students

MOST POPULAR MAJORS
Office management and supervision
Criminal justice/law enforcement administration
Education

SELECTIVITY
Admissions Rating **71**
# of applicants 3,720
% of applicants accepted 72
% of acceptees attending 56

FRESHMAN PROFILE
Range ACT Composite 19-24
Average ACT Composite 22
Minimum TOEFL 500
% graduated top 10% of class 12
% graduated top 25% of class 40
% graduated top 50% of class 74

DEADLINES
Regular admission 8/20
Nonfall registration? yes

FINANCIAL FACTS
Financial Aid Rating **71**
In-state tuition $3,450
Out-of-state tuition $6,900
Room and board $4,410
Books and supplies $450
Avg frosh grant $2,566
Avg frosh loan $2,383

CLARKE COLLEGE

CAMPUS LIFE
Quality of Life Rating **80**
Type of school private
Affiliation Roman Catholic
Environment urban

STUDENTS
Total undergrad enrollment 1,120
% male/female 34/66
% from out of state 40
% from public high school 81
% live on campus 40
% African American 1
% Caucasian 92
% Hispanic 3
% international 3
# of countries represented 13

ACADEMICS
Academic Rating **75**
Calendar semester
Student/faculty ratio 9:1
Profs interesting rating 81
Profs accessible rating 76
% profs teaching UG courses 100
% classes taught by TAs 0
Avg lab size 10-19 students
Avg reg class size under 10 students

MOST POPULAR MAJORS
Physical therapy/therapist
Nursing/registered nurse training (RN,
ASN, BSN, MSN)
Elementary education and teaching

SELECTIVITY
Admissions Rating **72**
# of applicants 763
% of applicants accepted 55
% of acceptees attending 32

FRESHMAN PROFILE
Range SAT Verbal 420-585
Average SAT Verbal 504
Range SAT Math 460-580
Average SAT Math 501
Range ACT Composite 21-25
Average ACT Composite 24
Minimum TOEFL 525
Average HS GPA 3.3
% graduated top 10% of class 14
% graduated top 25% of class 43
% graduated top 50% of class 82

DEADLINES

Regular notification	rolling
Nonfall registration?	yes

FINANCIAL FACTS

Financial Aid Rating	**82**
Tuition	$14,685
Room and board	$5,505
Books and supplies	$600
Avg frosh grant	$7,300
Avg frosh loan	$2,518

COE COLLEGE

CAMPUS LIFE

Quality of Life Rating	**74**
Type of school	private
Affiliation	Presbyterian
Environment	urban

STUDENTS

Total undergrad enrollment	1,300
% male/female	43/57
% from out of state	34
% from public high school	92
% live on campus	84
% in (# of) fraternities	27 (4)
% in (# of) sororities	21 (3)
% African American	2
% Asian	1
% Caucasian	95
% Hispanic	1
% international	3
# of countries represented	15

ACADEMICS

Academic Rating	**80**
Calendar	semester
Student/faculty ratio	12:1
Profs interesting rating	81
Profs accessible rating	82
% profs teaching UG courses	100
Avg lab size	10-19 students
Avg reg class size	10-19 students

MOST POPULAR MAJORS
Business administration/management
Psychology
Biology/biological sciences

SELECTIVITY

Admissions Rating	**83**
# of applicants	1,285
% of applicants accepted	77
% of acceptees attending	30

FRESHMAN PROFILE

Range SAT Verbal	520-640
Average SAT Verbal	577
Range SAT Math	520-640
Average SAT Math	572
Range ACT Composite	22-27
Average ACT Composite	25
Minimum TOEFL	500
Average HS GPA	3.6
% graduated top 10% of class	30
% graduated top 25% of class	65
% graduated top 50% of class	92

DEADLINES

Priority admission	12/15
Regular admission	3/1
Regular notification	3/15
Nonfall registration?	yes

FINANCIAL FACTS

Financial Aid Rating	**80**
Tuition	$20,280
Room and board	$5,610
Books and supplies	$600
Required fees	$260
% frosh receiving aid	83
% undergrads receiving aid	80
Avg frosh grant	$13,493
Avg frosh loan	$4,000

COLLEGE OF SAINT BENEDICT/SAINT JOHN'S UNIVERSITY

CAMPUS LIFE

Quality of Life Rating	**82**
Type of school	private
Affiliation	Roman Catholic
Environment	rural

STUDENTS

Total undergrad enrollment	3,988
% male/female	47/53
% from out of state	14
% from public high school	78
% live on campus	83
% Asian	2
% Caucasian	93
% Hispanic	1
% international	3
# of countries represented	31

ACADEMICS

Academic Rating	**75**
Calendar	semester

Student/faculty ratio	12:1
Profs interesting rating	81
Profs accessible rating	82
% profs teaching UG courses	100
% classes taught by TAs	0
Avg lab size	10-19 students
Avg reg class size	20-29 students

MOST POPULAR MAJORS
Biology/biological sciences
Business administration/management
Nursing/registered nurse training (RN, ASN, BSN, MSN)

SELECTIVITY
Admissions Rating **79**

# of applicants	2,546
% of applicants accepted	83
% of acceptees attending	50
# accepting a place on wait list	80
% admitted from wait list	13

FRESHMAN PROFILE
Range SAT Verbal	520-650
Average SAT Verbal	590
Range SAT Math	540-660
Average SAT Math	600
Range ACT Composite	23-28
Average ACT Composite	25
Minimum TOEFL	500
Average HS GPA	3.6
% graduated top 10% of class	34
% graduated top 25% of class	66
% graduated top 50% of class	94

DEADLINES
Early action	12/1
Priority admission	2/1
Nonfall registration?	yes

FINANCIAL FACTS
Financial Aid Rating **85**

Tuition	$18,015
Room and board	$5,606
Books and supplies	$600
Required fees	$310
% frosh receiving aid	66
% undergrads receiving aid	62
Avg frosh grant	$11,213
Avg frosh loan	$4,600

COLLEGE OF ST. CATHERINE

CAMPUS LIFE
Quality of Life Rating **78**

Type of school	private
Affiliation	Roman Catholic
Environment	urban

STUDENTS
Total undergrad enrollment	3,600
% male/female	2/98
% from out of state	10
% from public high school	82
% live on campus	37
% African American	6
% Asian	5
% Caucasian	74
% Hispanic	2
% international	2

ACADEMICS
Academic Rating **78**

Calendar	differs by program
Student/faculty ratio	9:1
Profs interesting rating	79
Profs accessible rating	80
% profs teaching UG courses	100
% classes taught by TAs	0
Avg lab size	10-19 students
Avg regular class size	under 10 students

SELECTIVITY
Admissions Rating **70**

# of applicants	720
% of applicants accepted	85
% of acceptees attending	56

FRESHMAN PROFILE
Range SAT Verbal	470-580
Average SAT Verbal	525
Range SAT Math	490-630
Average SAT Math	561
Range ACT Composite	20-25
Average ACT Composite	22
Minimum TOEFL	500
Average HS GPA	3.4
% graduated top 10% of class	21
% graduated top 25% of class	48
% graduated top 50% of class	80

DEADLINES
Regular notification	rolling
Nonfall registration?	yes

FINANCIAL FACTS
Financial Aid Rating **80**

Tuition	$17,280
Room and board	$4,922
Books and supplies	$640

Avg frosh grant $14,180
Avg frosh loan $3,024

COLLEGE OF SAINT SCHOLASTICA

CAMPUS LIFE
Quality of Life Rating **80**
Type of school | private
Affiliation | Roman Catholic
Environment | suburban

STUDENTS
Total undergrad enrollment | 1,986
% male/female | 30/70
% from out of state | 11
% live on campus | 36
% African American | 1
% Asian | 1
% Caucasian | 88
% Hispanic | 1

ACADEMICS
Academic Rating **75**
Calendar | semester
Student/faculty ratio | 13:1
Profs interesting rating | 81
Profs accessible rating | 79
% profs teaching UG courses | 100
% classes taught by TAs | 0
Avg lab size | 16
Avg reg class size | 21

MOST POPULAR MAJORS
Education
Business administration/management
Nursing/registered nurse
training (RN, ASN, BSN, MSN)

SELECTIVITY
Admissions Rating **69**
of applicants | 1,055
# of applicants accepted | 927
# of acceptees attending | 383

FRESHMAN PROFILE
Range SAT Verbal | 510-650
Average SAT Verbal | 585
Range SAT Math | 510-650
Average SAT Math | 572
Range ACT Composite | 21-26
Average ACT Composite | 24
Minimum TOEFL | 550
Average HS GPA | 3.51
% graduated top 10% of class | 29
% graduated top 25% of class | 58
% graduated top 50% of class | 81

DEADLINES
Regular notification | rolling
Nonfall registration? | yes

FINANCIAL FACTS
Financial Aid Rating **79**
Tuition | $18,106
Room and board | $5,406
Books and supplies | $750
Avg frosh grant | $6,342
Avg frosh loan | $2,278

COLLEGE OF THE OZARKS

CAMPUS LIFE
Quality of Life Rating **79**
Type of school | private
Affiliation | Presbyterian
Environment | rural

STUDENTS
Total undergrad enrollment | 1,348
% male/female | 43/57
% from out of state | 33
% live on campus | 84
% Caucasian | 89
% Hispanic | 1
% international | 2

ACADEMICS
Academic Rating **84**
Calendar | semester
Student/faculty ratio | 14:1
Profs interesting rating | 76
Profs accessible rating | 80
% profs teaching UG courses | 100
Avg lab size | 10-19 students
Avg reg class size | under 10 students

MOST POPULAR MAJORS
Agricultural business and management
English/language arts teacher
education
Criminal justice/police science

SELECTIVITY
Admissions Rating **85**
of applicants | 2,417
% of applicants accepted | 12
% of acceptees attending | 89

FRESHMAN PROFILE
Range ACT Composite | 17-26
Average ACT Composite | 22
Minimum TOEFL | 550
Average HS GPA | 3.4

% graduated top 10% of class	11
% graduated top 25% of class	39
% graduated top 50% of class	82

DEADLINES

Priority admission	2/15
Regular admission	8/20
Regular notification	rolling
Nonfall registration?	yes

FINANCIAL FACTS
Financial Aid Rating **93**

Room and board	$3,250
Books and supplies	$600
Required fees	$250
% frosh receiving aid	90
% undergrads receiving aid	90
Avg frosh grant	$12,467

COLLEGE OF WOOSTER

CAMPUS LIFE
Quality of Life Rating **88**

| Type of school | private |
| Environment | suburban |

STUDENTS

Total undergrad enrollment	1,856
% male/female	47/53
% from out of state	44
% from public high school	73
% live on campus	97
% in (# of) fraternities	7 (4)
% in (# of) sororities	8 (6)
% African American	5
% Asian	2
% Caucasian	88
% Hispanic	1
% international	7
# of countries represented	21

ACADEMICS
Academic Rating **88**

Calendar	semester
Student/faculty ratio	13:1
Profs interesting rating	94
Profs accessible rating	97
% profs teaching UG courses	100
Avg lab size	10-19 students
Avg reg class size	under 10 students

MOST POPULAR MAJORS
History
English language and literature
Communications studies/speech
communication and rhetoric

SELECTIVITY
Admissions Rating **80**

# of applicants	2,392
% of applicants accepted	72
% of acceptees attending	30
# accepting a place on wait list	31
# of early decision applicants	83
% accepted early decision	84

FRESHMAN PROFILE

Range SAT Verbal	550-650
Average SAT Verbal	595
Range SAT Math	550-650
Average SAT Math	598
Range ACT Composite	23-29
Average ACT Composite	26
Minimum TOEFL	550
Average HS GPA	3.5
% graduated top 10% of class	46
% graduated top 25% of class	71
% graduated top 50% of class	93

DEADLINES

Early decision	12/1
Early decision notification	12/15
Regular admission	2/15
Regular notification	4/1
Nonfall registration?	yes

FINANCIAL FACTS
Financial Aid Rating **92**

Tuition	$23,687
Room and board	$5,960
Books and supplies	$700
Required fees	$153
% frosh receiving aid	65
% undergrads receiving aid	63
Avg frosh grant	$13,225
Avg frosh loan	$3,291

CORNELL COLLEGE

CAMPUS LIFE
Quality of Life Rating **77**

Type of school	private
Affiliation	Methodist
Environment	rural

STUDENTS

| Total undergrad enrollment | 1,001 |

% male/female	40/60
% from out of state	68
% from public high school	93
% live on campus	92
% in (# of) fraternities	30 (7)
% in (# of) sororities	32 (7)
% African American	3
% Asian	1
% Caucasian	90
% Hispanic	2
% international	1
# of countries represented	5

ACADEMICS
Academic Rating	**80**
Calendar	other
Student/faculty ratio	11:1
Profs interesting rating	65
Profs accessible rating	80
% profs teaching UG courses	100
Avg reg class size	10-19 students

MOST POPULAR MAJORS
Education
Psychology
Economics and business

SELECTIVITY
Admissions Rating	**80**
# of applicants	1,625
% of applicants accepted	62
% of acceptees attending	31

FRESHMAN PROFILE
Range SAT Verbal	540-660
Average SAT Verbal	599
Range SAT Math	540-640
Average SAT Math	590
Range ACT Composite	23-28
Average ACT Composite	26
Minimum TOEFL	500
Average HS GPA	3.5
% graduated top 10% of class	26
% graduated top 25% of class	59
% graduated top 50% of class	91

DEADLINES
Priority admission	3/1
Nonfall registration?	yes

FINANCIAL FACTS
Financial Aid Rating	**85**
Tuition	$20,795
Room and board	$6,032
Books and supplies	$920
Required fees	$160

% frosh receiving aid	83
% undergrads receiving aid	80
Avg frosh grant	$16,750
Avg frosh loan	$3,745

CREIGHTON UNIVERSITY

CAMPUS LIFE
Quality of Life Rating	**87**
Type of school	private
Affiliation	Roman Catholic
Environment	urban

STUDENTS
Total undergrad enrollment	3,607
% male/female	40/60
% from out of state	50
% from public high school	64
% live on campus	44
% in (# of) fraternities	26 (5)
% in (# of) sororities	25 (5)
% African American	3
% Asian	8
% Caucasian	85
% Hispanic	3
% international	2

ACADEMICS
Academic Rating	**82**
Calendar	semester
Student/faculty ratio	14:1
Profs interesting rating	94
Profs accessible rating	92
% profs teaching UG courses	100
Avg lab size	10-19 students
Avg reg class size	10-19 students

MOST POPULAR MAJORS
Biomedical sciences
Business administration
Psychology

SELECTIVITY
Admissions Rating	**79**
# of applicants	3,306
% of applicants accepted	85
% of acceptees attending	33

FRESHMAN PROFILE
Range SAT Verbal	550-640
Average SAT Verbal	590
Range SAT Math	550-660
Average SAT Math	599
Range ACT Composite	23-30
Average ACT Composite	26

Minimum TOEFL	550
Average HS GPA	3.7
% graduated top 10% of class	40
% graduated top 25% of class	70
% graduated top 50% of class	93

DEADLINES

Priority admission	1/1
Regular admission	8/1
Nonfall registration?	yes

FINANCIAL FACTS
Financial Aid Rating — 81

Tuition	$19,202
Room and board	$6,826
Books and supplies	$900
Required fees	$720
Avg frosh grant	$13,052
Avg frosh loan	$4,890

DENISON UNIVERSITY

CAMPUS LIFE
Quality of Life Rating — 77

| Type of school | private |
| Environment | suburban |

STUDENTS

Total undergrad enrollment	2,081
% male/female	46/54
% from out of state	63
% from public high school	71
% live on campus	99
% in (# of) fraternities	29 (8)
% in (# of) sororities	41 (8)
% African American	6
% Asian	3
% Caucasian	84
% Hispanic	3
% international	5
# of countries represented	34

ACADEMICS
Academic Rating — 81

Calendar	semester
Student/faculty ratio	11:1
Profs interesting rating	94
Profs accessible rating	98
% profs teaching UG courses	100
Avg lab size	10-19 students
Avg reg class size	10-19 students

MOST POPULAR MAJORS
Communications
Economics
English language and literature

SELECTIVITY
Admissions Rating — 82

# of applicants	3,289
% of applicants accepted	61
% of acceptees attending	31
# accepting a place on wait list	350
% admitted from wait list	8
# of early decision applicants	150
% accepted early decision	70

FRESHMAN PROFILE

Range SAT Verbal	550-650
Average SAT Verbal	602
Range SAT Math	560-670
Average SAT Math	615
Range ACT Composite	24-29
Average ACT Composite	26
Minimum TOEFL	550
Average HS GPA	3.5
% graduated top 10% of class	48
% graduated top 25% of class	82
% graduated top 50% of class	100

DEADLINES

Early decision I	11/15
Early decision I notification	12/1
Early decision II	1/15
Early decision II notification	2/15
Priority admission	1/1
Regular admission	2/1
Regular notification	4/1

FINANCIAL FACTS
Financial Aid Rating — 84

Tuition	$25,090
Room and board	$7,290
Books and supplies	$600
Required fees	$670
% frosh receiving aid	97
% undergrads receiving aid	98
Avg frosh grant	$12,122
Avg frosh loan	$4,625

DEPAUL UNIVERSITY

CAMPUS LIFE
Quality of Life Rating — 80

Type of school	private
Affiliation	Roman Catholic
Environment	urban

STUDENTS

| Total undergrad enrollment | 14,343 |
| % male/female | 45/55 |

% from out of state	13
% from public high school	68
% African American	12
% Asian	10
% Caucasian	57
% Hispanic	13
% international	5
# of countries represented	85

ACADEMICS
Academic Rating 73
Calendar	differs by program
Student/faculty ratio	14:1
Profs interesting rating	91
Profs accessible rating	93
Avg reg class size	20-29 students

MOST POPULAR MAJORS
Business
Accounting
Computer science

SELECTIVITY
Admissions Rating 78
# of applicants	8,932
% of applicants accepted	77
% of acceptees attending	34

FRESHMAN PROFILE
Range SAT Verbal	510-610
Average SAT Verbal	556
Range SAT Math	500-610
Average SAT Math	551
Range ACT Composite	21-26
Average ACT Composite	23
Minimum TOEFL	550
Average HS GPA	3.3
% graduated top 10% of class	16
% graduated top 25% of class	41
% graduated top 50% of class	75

DEADLINES
Priority admission	2/1
Nonfall registration?	yes

FINANCIAL FACTS
Financial Aid Rating 86
Tuition	$18,750
Room and board	$8,370
Books and supplies	$750
Required fees	$100
% frosh receiving aid	77
% undergrads receiving aid	67

DePauw University

CAMPUS LIFE
Quality of Life Rating 82
Type of school	private
Affiliation	Methodist
Environment	rural

STUDENTS
Total undergrad enrollment	2,338
% male/female	44/56
% from out of state	53
% from public high school	85
% live on campus	92
% in (# of) fraternities	77 (12)
% in (# of) sororities	69 (10)
% African American	5
% Asian	2
% Caucasian	88
% Hispanic	3
% international	1
# of countries represented	16

ACADEMICS
Academic Rating 89
Calendar	4-1-4
Student/faculty ratio	10:1
% profs teaching UG courses	100
Avg reg class size	10-19 students

MOST POPULAR MAJORS
Communications
Creative writing
Economics

SELECTIVITY
Admissions Rating 86
# of applicants	3,682
% of applicants accepted	61
% of acceptees attending	30
# accepting a place on wait list	64
# of early decision applicants	33
% accepted early decision	76

FRESHMAN PROFILE
Range SAT Verbal	560-650
Average SAT Verbal	610
Range SAT Math	570-670
Average SAT Math	620
Range ACT Composite	25-29
Average ACT Composite	27
Minimum TOEFL	560
Average HS GPA	3.7
% graduated top 10% of class	56
% graduated top 25% of class	89
% graduated top 50% of class	99

DEADLINES

Early decision	11/1
Early decision notification	1/1
Priority admission	12/1
Regular admission	2/1
Regular notification	4/1
Nonfall registration?	yes

FINANCIAL FACTS

Financial Aid Rating **92**

Tuition	$24,000
Room and board	$7,050
Books and supplies	$600
Required fees	$530
% frosh receiving aid	52
% undergrads receiving aid	53
Avg frosh grant	$16,121
Avg frosh loan	$3,141

DORDT COLLEGE

CAMPUS LIFE

Quality of Life Rating **72**

Type of school	private
Affiliation	other
Environment	suburban

STUDENTS

Total undergrad enrollment	1,396
% male/female	44/56
% from out of state	53
% from public high school	40
% live on campus	90
% African American	1
% Asian	1
% Caucasian	98
% international	12
# of countries represented	12

ACADEMICS

Academic Rating **76**

Calendar	semester
Student/faculty ratio	15:1
Profs interesting rating	84
Profs accessible rating	83
% profs teaching UG courses	100
% classes taught by TAs	0
Avg lab size	10-19 students
Avg reg class size	under 10 students

MOST POPULAR MAJORS
Education
Business
Engineering

SELECTIVITY

Admissions Rating **74**

# of applicants	793
% of applicants accepted	94
% of acceptees attending	53

FRESHMAN PROFILE

Range SAT Verbal	530-630
Average SAT Verbal	580
Range SAT Math	520-640
Average SAT Math	580
Range ACT Composite	21-27
Average ACT Composite	24
Minimum TOEFL	550
Average HS GPA	3.3
% graduated top 10% of class	15
% graduated top 25% of class	42
% graduated top 50% of class	75

DEADLINES

Regular admission	8/1
Nonfall registration?	yes

FINANCIAL FACTS

Financial Aid Rating **85**

Tuition	$13,950
Room and board	$4,000
Books and supplies	$650
Avg frosh grant	$6,000
Avg frosh loan	$4,782

DRAKE UNIVERSITY

CAMPUS LIFE

Quality of Life Rating **79**

Type of school	private
Affiliation	none
Environment	urban

STUDENTS

Total undergrad enrollment	3,577
% male/female	39/61
% from out of state	59
% from public high school	85
% live on campus	53
% in (# of) fraternities	30 (8)
% in (# of) sororities	28 (5)
% African American	3
% Asian	5
% Caucasian	76
% Hispanic	2
% international	4
# of countries represented	55

ACADEMICS

Academic Rating **82**

Calendar	semester
Student/faculty ratio	12:1
Profs interesting rating	78
Profs accessible rating	75
% profs teaching UG courses	100
% classes taught by TAs	0
Avg lab size	10-19 students
Avg reg class size	10-19 students

MOST POPULAR MAJORS
Music performance
Accounting
Pharmacy (PharmD, BS/BPharm)

SELECTIVITY

Admissions Rating **77**

# of applicants	2,735
% of applicants accepted	87
% of acceptees attending	32

FRESHMAN PROFILE

Range SAT Verbal	500-630
Average SAT Verbal	569
Range SAT Math	530-650
Average SAT Math	589
Range ACT Composite	23-28
Average ACT Composite	25
Minimum TOEFL	530
Average HS GPA	3.6
% graduated top 10% of class	35
% graduated top 25% of class	64
% graduated top 50% of class	94

DEADLINES

Nonfall registration?	yes

FINANCIAL FACTS

Financial Aid Rating **78**

Tuition	$18,190
Room and board	$5,490
Books and supplies	$700
Avg frosh grant	$11,159
Avg frosh loan	$4,276

EARLHAM COLLEGE

CAMPUS LIFE

Quality of Life Rating **81**

Type of school	private
Affiliation	Quaker
Environment	suburban

STUDENTS

Total undergrad enrollment	1,080

% male/female	44/56
% from out of state	75
% from public high school	65
% live on campus	87
% African American	8
% Asian	3
% Caucasian	77
% Hispanic	2
% international	7
# of countries represented	35

ACADEMICS

Academic Rating **91**

Calendar	semester
Student/faculty ratio	11:1
% profs teaching UG courses	100
Avg lab size	20-29 students
Avg reg class size	10-19 students

MOST POPULAR MAJORS
History
Biology/biological sciences
Psychology

SELECTIVITY

Admissions Rating **80**

# of applicants	1,269
% of applicants accepted	78
% of acceptees attending	29
# accepting a place on wait list	11
% admitted from wait list	91
# of early decision applicants	45
% accepted early decision	93

FRESHMAN PROFILE

Range SAT Verbal	550-690
Average SAT Verbal	620
Range SAT Math	530-650
Average SAT Math	590
Range ACT Composite	23-29
Average ACT Composite	26
Minimum TOEFL	550
Average HS GPA	3.4
% graduated top 10% of class	28
% graduated top 25% of class	56
% graduated top 50% of class	84

DEADLINES

Early decision	12/1
Early decision notification	12/15
Regular admission	2/15
Regular notification	3/15
Nonfall registration?	yes

FINANCIAL FACTS
Financial Aid Rating **89**

Tuition	$23,920
Room and board	$5,416
Books and supplies	$550
Required fees	$640
% frosh receiving aid	65
% undergrads receiving aid	65
Avg frosh grant	$12,651
Avg frosh loan	$3,168

EASTERN ILLINOIS UNIVERSITY

CAMPUS LIFE
Quality of Life Rating **74**

Type of school	public
Affiliation	none
Environment	rural

STUDENTS

Total undergrad enrollment	9,528
% male/female	43/57
% from out of state	2
% live on campus	46
% in (# of) fraternities	17 (13)
% in (# of) sororities	15 (13)
% African American	7
% Asian	1
% Caucasian	87
% Hispanic	2
% international	1
# of countries represented	48

ACADEMICS
Academic Rating **74**

Calendar	semester
Student/faculty ratio	17:1
Profs interesting rating	79
Profs accessible rating	76
% profs teaching UG courses	99
% classes taught by TAs	10
Avg regular class size	20-29 students

MOST POPULAR MAJORS
Family and consumer sciences/human sciences
Elementary education and teaching
Business administration/management

SELECTIVITY
Admissions Rating **70**

# of applicants	7,544
% of applicants accepted	78
% of acceptees attending	27

FRESHMAN PROFILE

Range ACT Composite	20-23
Average ACT Composite	22
Minimum TOEFL	500
% graduated top 10% of class	8
% graduated top 25% of class	27
% graduated top 50% of class	65

DEADLINES

Nonfall registration?	yes

FINANCIAL FACTS
Financial Aid Rating **73**

In-state tuition	$3,254
Out-of-state tuition	$9,761
Room and board	$6,000
Books and supplies	$120
Required fees	$1,394
Avg frosh grant	$2,528
Avg frosh loan	$1,970

EASTERN MICHIGAN UNIVERSITY

CAMPUS LIFE
Quality of Life Rating **77**

Type of school	public
Affiliation	none
Environment	suburban

STUDENTS

Total undergrad enrollment	18,502
% male/female	39/61
% from out of state	10
% from public high school	90
% live on campus	23
% in (# of) fraternities	3 (17)
% in (# of) sororities	3 (12)
% African American	17
% Asian	2
% Caucasian	72
% Hispanic	2
% international	2
# of countries represented	67

ACADEMICS
Academic Rating **75**

Calendar	semester
Student/faculty ratio	19:1
Profs interesting rating	85
Profs accessible rating	82
% profs teaching UG courses	100
% classes taught by TAs	3
Avg lab size	20-29 students
Avg reg class size	20-29 students

Elementary education and teaching
Psychology
Multi/interdisciplinary studies

SELECTIVITY

Admissions Rating	71
# of applicants	9,212
% of applicants accepted	75
% of acceptees attending	41

FRESHMAN PROFILE

Range SAT Verbal	420-560
Average SAT Verbal	493
Range SAT Math	430-570
Average SAT Math	495
Range ACT Composite	18-23
Average ACT Composite	20
Minimum TOEFL	500
Average HS GPA	3.0
% graduated top 10% of class	12
% graduated top 25% of class	34
% graduated top 50% of class	68

DEADLINES

Regular admission	6/30
Regular notification	rolling
Nonfall registration?	yes

FINANCIAL FACTS

Financial Aid Rating	65
Books and supplies	$900
Avg frosh grant	$2,050
Avg frosh loan	$2,625

EDGEWOOD COLLEGE

CAMPUS LIFE

Quality of Life Rating	85
Type of school	private
Affiliation	Roman Catholic
Environment	urban

STUDENTS

Total undergrad enrollment	1,731
% male/female	29/71
% from out of state	4
% from public high school	87
% live on campus	20
% African American	3
% Asian	2
% Caucasian	87
% Hispanic	3
% international	3
# of countries represented	21

ACADEMICS

Academic Rating	72
Calendar	semester
Student/faculty ratio	13:1
Profs interesting rating	83
Profs accessible rating	78
% profs teaching UG courses	100
% classes taught by TAs	0
Avg reg class size	10-19 students

MOST POPULAR MAJORS
Business administration/management
Nursing/registered nurse
training (RN, ASN, BSN, MSN)
Education

SELECTIVITY

Admissions Rating	71
# of applicants	952
% of applicants accepted	80
% of acceptees attending	36

FRESHMAN PROFILE

Range SAT Verbal	490-550
Average SAT Verbal	516
Range SAT Math	510-600
Average SAT Math	532
Range ACT Composite	19-24
Average ACT Composite	22
Minimum TOEFL	525
Average HS GPA	3.3
% graduated top 10% of class	12
% graduated top 25% of class	36
% graduated top 50% of class	71

DEADLINES

Nonfall registration?	yes

FINANCIAL FACTS

Financial Aid Rating	79
Tuition	$14,200
Room and board	$5,004
Books and supplies	$750
Avg frosh grant	$8,245
Avg frosh loan	$2,625

FRIENDS UNIVERSITY

CAMPUS LIFE

Quality of Life Rating	75
Type of school	private
Affiliation	Quaker
Environment	urban

STUDENTS

Total undergrad enrollment	2,614

% male/female	50/50
% from out of state	13
% live on campus	22
# of countries represented	20

ACADEMICS
Academic Rating **79**

Calendar	semester
Student/faculty ratio	10:1
Profs interesting rating	79
Profs accessible rating	79
% profs teaching UG courses	95
% classes taught by TAs	0

SELECTIVITY
Admissions Rating **78**

# of applicants	668
% of applicants accepted	93

FRESHMAN PROFILE
Range ACT Composite	17-26
Minimum TOEFL	500
Average HS GPA	3.4

DEADLINES
Nonfall registration?	yes

FINANCIAL FACTS
Financial Aid Rating **69**

Tuition	$11,050
Room and board	$3,420
Books and supplies	$750

GOSHEN COLLEGE

CAMPUS LIFE
Quality of Life Rating **80**

Type of school	private
Affiliation	Mennonite
Environment	rural

STUDENTS
Total undergrad enrollment	1,041
% male/female	42/58
% from out of state	46
% from public high school	78
% live on campus	62
% African American	3
% Asian	1
% Caucasian	80
% Hispanic	4
% international	9
# of countries represented	37

ACADEMICS
Academic Rating **78**

Calendar	semester
Student/faculty ratio	10:1
Profs interesting rating	79
Profs accessible rating	74
% profs teaching UG courses	100
% classes taught by TAs	0
Avg lab size	10-19 students
Avg reg class size	10-19 students

MOST POPULAR MAJORS
Nursing/registered nurse training (RN, ASN, BSN, MSN)
Communications and media studies
Elementary education and teaching

SELECTIVITY
Admissions Rating **74**

# of applicants	561
% of applicants accepted	46
% of acceptees attending	68

FRESHMAN PROFILE
Range SAT Verbal	490-650
Average SAT Verbal	569
Range SAT Math	480-630
Average SAT Math	556
Range ACT Composite	20-30
Minimum TOEFL	550
Average HS GPA	3.4
% graduated top 10% of class	22
% graduated top 25% of class	50
% graduated top 50% of class	77

DEADLINES
Nonfall registration?	yes

FINANCIAL FACTS
Financial Aid Rating **78**

Tuition	$14,700
Room and board	$5,450
Books and supplies	$800
Avg frosh grant	$8,856
Avg frosh loan	$3,100

GRACE COLLEGE AND SEMINARY

CAMPUS LIFE
Quality of Life Rating **78**

Type of school	private
Affiliation	other
Environment	rural

STUDENTS
Total undergrad enrollment	923
% male/female	42/58
% from out of state	53

% from public high school	63
% live on campus	78
% African American	5
% Caucasian	92
% Hispanic	1
% international	1

ACADEMICS
Academic Rating · 80
Calendar	semester
Student/faculty ratio	19:1
Profs interesting rating	77
Profs accessible rating	74
% profs teaching UG courses	100
% classes taught by TAs	0
Avg reg class size	10-19 students

MOST POPULAR MAJORS
Elementary education
Psychology
Bible/biblical studies

SELECTIVITY
Admissions Rating · 73
# of applicants	597
% of applicants accepted	88
% of acceptees attending	41

FRESHMAN PROFILE
Range SAT Verbal	480-610
Average SAT Verbal	545
Range SAT Math	470-590
Average SAT Math	530
Range ACT Composite	20-27
Average ACT Composite	23
Minimum TOEFL	500
Average HS GPA	3.4
% graduated top 10% of class	28
% graduated top 25% of class	52
% graduated top 50% of class	86

DEADLINES
| Regular admission | 8/1 |
| Nonfall registration? | yes |

FINANCIAL FACTS
Financial Aid Rating · 77
Tuition	$11,440
Room and board	$5,008
Books and supplies	$500
Avg frosh grant	$4,500
Avg frosh loan	$4,600

GRAND VALLEY STATE UNIVERSITY

CAMPUS LIFE
Quality of Life Rating · 71
Type of school	public
Affiliation	none
Environment	suburban

STUDENTS
Total undergrad enrollment	16,875
% male/female	39/61
% from out of state	4
% from public high school	86
% live on campus	25
% in (# of) fraternities	3 (10)
% in (# of) sororities	2 (11)
% African American	4
% Asian	2
% Caucasian	89
% Hispanic	2
# of countries represented	52

ACADEMICS
Academic Rating · 76
Calendar	semester
Student/faculty ratio	22:1
Profs interesting rating	80
Profs accessible rating	78
% profs teaching UG courses	90
% classes taught by TAs	0
Avg lab size	20-29 students
Avg regular class size	20-29 students

MOST POPULAR MAJORS
English
Business
Health-related fields

SELECTIVITY
Admissions Rating · 68
# of applicants	10,167
% of applicants accepted	71
% of acceptees attending	41

FRESHMAN PROFILE
Range ACT Composite	21-25
Average ACT Composite	23
Minimum TOEFL	550
Average HS GPA	3.41
% graduated top 10% of class	15
% graduated top 25% of class	42
% graduated top 50% of class	81

DEADLINES
| Regular admission | 7/31 |

Regular notification rolling
Nonfall registration? yes

FINANCIAL FACTS
Financial Aid Rating **72**
In-state tuition $5,056
Out-of-state tuition $10,936
Room and board $5,380
Books and supplies $600
Avg frosh loan $3,525

GRINNELL COLLEGE

CAMPUS LIFE
Quality of Life Rating **82**
Type of school private
Environment rural

STUDENTS
Total undergrad enrollment 1,485
% male/female 45/55
% from out of state 85
% from public high school 78
% live on campus 85
% African American 4
% Asian 5
% Caucasian 76
% Hispanic 4
% international 10
# of countries represented 52

ACADEMICS
Academic Rating **94**
Calendar semester
Student/faculty ratio 10:1
% profs teaching UG courses 100
Avg lab size 10-19 students
Avg reg class size 10-19 students

MOST POPULAR MAJORS
English
Biology
Anthropology

SELECTIVITY
Admissions Rating **92**
# of applicants 3,031
% of applicants accepted 48
% of acceptees attending 28
# accepting a place on wait list 71
% admitted from wait list 39
# of early decision applicants 119
% accepted early decision 79

FRESHMAN PROFILE
Range SAT Verbal 630-730
Average SAT Verbal 682
Range SAT Math 620-710
Average SAT Math 670
Range ACT Composite 28-31
Average ACT Composite 30
Minimum TOEFL 550
% graduated top 10% of class 59
% graduated top 25% of class 91
% graduated top 50% of class 99

DEADLINES
Early decision I 11/20
Early decision I notification 12/20
Early decision II 1/1
Early decision II notification 2/1
Regular admission 1/20
Regular notification 4/1

FINANCIAL FACTS
Financial Aid Rating **94**
Tuition $22,960
Room and board $6,330
Books and supplies $400
Required fees $570
% frosh receiving aid 58
% undergrads receiving aid 58
Avg frosh grant $12,927
Avg frosh loan $4,211

GUSTAVUS ADOLPHUS COLLEGE

CAMPUS LIFE
Quality of Life Rating **81**
Type of school private
Affiliation Lutheran
Environment suburban

STUDENTS
Total undergrad enrollment 2,536
% male/female 42/58
% from out of state 18
% from public high school 92
% live on campus 85
% in (# of) fraternities 27 (7)
% in (# of) sororities 22 (5)
% African American 1
% Asian 3
% Caucasian 95
% Hispanic 1
% international 1
# of countries represented 17

ACADEMICS
Academic Rating   **82**

Calendar	4-1-4
Student/faculty ratio	13:1
% profs teaching UG courses	100
Avg lab size	10-19 students
Avg reg class size	10-19 students

MOST POPULAR MAJORS
Communications studies/speech
communication and rhetoric
Biology/biological sciences
Psychology

SELECTIVITY
Admissions Rating   **84**

# of applicants	2,203
% of applicants accepted	77
% of acceptees attending	39
# accepting a place on wait list	70
% admitted from wait list	7
# of early decision applicants	146
% accepted early decision	97

FRESHMAN PROFILE

Range SAT Verbal	550-660
Average SAT Verbal	610
Range SAT Math	540-670
Average SAT Math	620
Range ACT Composite	23-28
Average ACT Composite	26
Minimum TOEFL	550
Average HS GPA	3.6
% graduated top 10% of class	36
% graduated top 25% of class	69
% graduated top 50% of class	94

DEADLINES

Early decision	11/15
Early decision notification	12/1
Priority admission	2/15
Regular admission	4/1
Nonfall registration?	yes

FINANCIAL FACTS
Financial Aid Rating   **90**

Tuition	$21,330
Room and board	$5,460
Books and supplies	$700
Required fees	$320
% frosh receiving aid	65
% undergrads receiving aid	65
Avg frosh grant	$7,400
Avg frosh loan	$4,500

HANOVER COLLEGE

CAMPUS LIFE
Quality of Life Rating   **80**

Type of school	private
Affiliation	Presbyterian
Environment	rural

STUDENTS

Total undergrad enrollment	1,050
% male/female	46/54
% from out of state	30
% from public high school	85
% live on campus	92
% in (# of) fraternities	33 (4)
% in (# of) sororities	47 (4)
% African American	1
% Asian	3
% Caucasian	91
% Hispanic	1
% international	4
# of countries represented	18

ACADEMICS
Academic Rating   **87**

Calendar	other
Student/faculty ratio	11:1
Profs interesting rating	94
Profs accessible rating	95
% profs teaching UG courses	100
Avg reg class size	10-19 students

MOST POPULAR MAJORS
Business administration/management
Sociology
Chemistry

SELECTIVITY
Admissions Rating   **79**

# of applicants	1,227
% of applicants accepted	76
% of acceptees attending	30
# accepting a place on wait list	78
% admitted from wait list	47

FRESHMAN PROFILE

Range SAT Verbal	500-620
Average SAT Verbal	559
Range SAT Math	520-630
Average SAT Math	576
Range ACT Composite	21-27
Average ACT Composite	24
Minimum TOEFL	550
% graduated top 10% of class	38
% graduated top 25% of class	72
% graduated top 50% of class	95

DEADLINES
Priority admission	3/1
Regular admission	3/1
Nonfall registration?	yes

FINANCIAL FACTS
Financial Aid Rating **88**
Tuition	$14,300
Room and board	$5,900
Books and supplies	$800
Required fees	$400
Avg frosh grant	$12,313
Avg frosh loan	$3,113

HASTINGS COLLEGE

CAMPUS LIFE
Quality of Life Rating **72**
Type of school	private
Affiliation	Presbyterian
Environment	rural

STUDENTS
Total undergrad enrollment	1,067
% male/female	49/51
% from public high school	90
% live on campus	50
% in (# of) fraternities	20 (4)
% in (# of) sororities	30 (4)
% African American	1
% Caucasian	86
% Hispanic	2
% international	1

ACADEMICS
Academic Rating **81**
Calendar	4-1-4
Student/faculty ratio	13:1
Profs interesting rating	84
Profs accessible rating	83
% profs teaching UG courses	100
% classes taught by TAs	0
Avg regular class size	10-19 students

MOST POPULAR MAJORS
Business administration/management
Education

SELECTIVITY
Admissions Rating **78**
# of applicants	962
% of applicants accepted	86
% of acceptees attending	37

FRESHMAN PROFILE
Range SAT Verbal	450-600

Average SAT Verbal	460
Range SAT Math	470-600
Average SAT Math	490
Range ACT Composite	21-27
Average ACT Composite	24
Minimum TOEFL	520
% graduated top 10% of class	22
% graduated top 25% of class	55
% graduated top 50% of class	90

DEADLINES
Regular admission	8/1
Nonfall registration?	yes

FINANCIAL FACTS
Financial Aid Rating **70**
Books and supplies	$650
Avg frosh grant	$7,844
Avg frosh loan	$4,090

HILLSDALE COLLEGE

CAMPUS LIFE
Quality of Life Rating **73**
Type of school	private
Affiliation	none
Environment	suburban

STUDENTS
Total undergrad enrollment	1,167
% male/female	48/52
% from out of state	49
% from public high school	65
% live on campus	87
% in (# of) fraternities	35 (4)
% in (# of) sororities	45 (4)

ACADEMICS
Academic Rating **86**
Calendar	semester
Student/faculty ratio	11:1
Profs interesting rating	77
Profs accessible rating	78
% profs teaching UG courses	100
% classes taught by TAs	0
Avg regular class size	under 10 students

MOST POPULAR MAJORS
Business
Education
Biology

SELECTIVITY
Admissions Rating **82**
# of applicants	1,008
% of applicants accepted	84

% of applicants accepted	84
% of acceptees attending	40

FRESHMAN PROFILE

Range SAT Verbal	570-690
Average SAT Verbal	590
Range SAT Math	520-660
Average SAT Math	610
Range ACT Composite	23-29
Average ACT Composite	26
Minimum TOEFL	510
Average HS GPA	3.6
% graduated top 10% of class	40
% graduated top 25% of class	73
% graduated top 50% of class	99

DEADLINES

Nonfall registration?	yes

FINANCIAL FACTS
Financial Aid Rating — 71

Tuition	$13,600
Room and board	$5,700
Books and supplies	$700
Avg frosh grant	$6,500
Avg frosh loan	$2,800

HIRAM COLLEGE

CAMPUS LIFE
Quality of Life Rating — 85

Type of school	private
Affiliation	Disciples of Christ
Environment	rural

STUDENTS

Total undergrad enrollment	1,134
% male/female	41/59
% from out of state	17
% from public high school	86
% live on campus	89
% African American	10
% Asian	1
% Caucasian	86
% Hispanic	2
% international	3

ACADEMICS
Academic Rating — 86

Calendar	semester
Student/faculty ratio	11:1
% profs teaching UG courses	100
Avg lab size	under 10 students
Avg reg class size	10-19 students

MOST POPULAR MAJORS
Business/commerce
Education
Biology/biological sciences

SELECTIVITY
Admissions Rating — 80

# of applicants	1,294
% of applicants accepted	69
% of acceptees attending	26
# of early decision applicants	38
% accepted early decision	84

FRESHMAN PROFILE

Range SAT Verbal	510-630
Average SAT Verbal	573
Range SAT Math	480-620
Average SAT Math	566
Average ACT Composite	24
Minimum TOEFL	550
Average HS GPA	3.4
% graduated top 10% of class	39
% graduated top 25% of class	53
% graduated top 50% of class	85

DEADLINES

Early decision	12/1
Early decision notification	1/1
Priority admission	2/1
Regular admission	2/1
Nonfall registration?	yes

FINANCIAL FACTS
Financial Aid Rating — 86

Tuition	$19,650
Room and board	$7,100
Books and supplies	$600
Required fees	$694
% frosh receiving aid	83
% undergrads receiving aid	83
Avg frosh grant	$10,998
Avg frosh loan	$5,176

HOPE COLLEGE

CAMPUS LIFE
Quality of Life Rating — 76

Type of school	private
Affiliation	other
Environment	suburban

STUDENTS

Total undergrad enrollment	2,999
% male/female	40/60
% from out of state	23

% from public high school	91
% live on campus	81
% in (# of) fraternities	6 (6)
% in (# of) sororities	15 (7)
% African American	1
% Asian	2
% Caucasian	93
% Hispanic	2
% international	1
# of countries represented	40

ACADEMICS
Academic Rating	**79**
Calendar	semester
Student/faculty ratio	13:1
Profs interesting rating	77
Profs accessible rating	75
% profs teaching UG courses	94
% classes taught by TAs	0
Avg lab size	under 10 students
Avg reg class size	10-19 students

MOST POPULAR MAJORS
Biology/biological sciences
English language and literature
Business administration/management

SELECTIVITY
Admissions Rating	**72**
# of applicants	2,110
% of applicants accepted	89
% of acceptees attending	39
# accepting a place on wait list	41
% admitted from wait list	85

FRESHMAN PROFILE
Range SAT Verbal	530-660
Average SAT Verbal	595
Range SAT Math	540-670
Average SAT Math	603
Range ACT Composite	22-28
Average ACT Composite	25
Minimum TOEFL	550
Average HS GPA	3.7
% graduated top 10% of class	33
% graduated top 25% of class	53
% graduated top 50% of class	89

DEADLINES
Nonfall registration?	yes

FINANCIAL FACTS
Financial Aid Rating	**76**
Tuition	$18,158
Room and board	$5,688

Books and supplies	$600
Avg frosh grant	$11,628
Avg frosh loan	$3,325

ILLINOIS INSTITUTE OF TECHNOLOGY

CAMPUS LIFE
Quality of Life Rating	**69**
Type of school	private
Environment	urban

STUDENTS
Total undergrad enrollment	1,544
% male/female	76/24
% from out of state	51
% from public high school	71
% live on campus	70
% in (# of) fraternities	19 (7)
% in (# of) sororities	10 (3)
% African American	6
% Asian	16
% Caucasian	47
% Hispanic	8
% international	11

ACADEMICS
Academic Rating	**77**
Calendar	semester
Student/faculty ratio	12:1
Profs interesting rating	90
Profs accessible rating	90
% profs teaching UG courses	74
Avg lab size	10-19 students
Avg reg class size	10-19 students

MOST POPULAR MAJORS
Architecture (BArch, BA/BS, MArch, MA/MS, PhD)
Computer science
Electrical and computer engineering

SELECTIVITY
Admissions Rating	**84**
# of applicants	2,269
% of applicants accepted	67
% of acceptees attending	24

FRESHMAN PROFILE
Range SAT Verbal	550-650
Average SAT Verbal	602
Range SAT Math	630-730
Average SAT Math	681
Range ACT Composite	26-31
Average ACT Composite	28
Minimum TOEFL	550
Average HS GPA	3.6

% graduated top 10% of class	70
% graduated top 25% of class	74
% graduated top 50% of class	94

DEADLINES

| Nonfall registration? | yes |

FINANCIAL FACTS

Financial Aid Rating	**82**
Tuition	$19,775
Room and board	$6,282
Books and supplies	$1,000
Required fees	$556
% frosh receiving aid	63
% undergrads receiving aid	54
Avg frosh grant	$14,695
Avg frosh loan	$7,534

ILLINOIS STATE UNIVERSITY

CAMPUS LIFE

Quality of Life Rating	**82**
Type of school	public
Affiliation	none
Environment	suburban

STUDENTS

Total undergrad enrollment	18,472
% male/female	42/58
% from out of state	4
% from public high school	89
% live on campus	37
% in (# of) fraternities	10 (21)
% in (# of) sororities	9 (17)
% African American	6
% Asian	2
% Caucasian	88
% Hispanic	2
% international	1
# of countries represented	60

ACADEMICS

Academic Rating	**72**
Calendar	semester
Student/faculty ratio	19:1
Profs interesting rating	81
Profs accessible rating	79
% profs teaching UG courses	93
% classes taught by TAs	7
Avg lab size	20-29 students
Avg reg class size	20-29 students

MOST POPULAR MAJORS
Elementary education and teaching
Special education
Business administration/management

SELECTIVITY

Admissions Rating	**69**
# of applicants	10,211
% of applicants accepted	77
% of acceptees attending	42

FRESHMAN PROFILE

Range ACT Composite	20-25
Average ACT Composite	23
Minimum TOEFL	550
% graduated top 10% of class	10
% graduated top 25% of class	47
% graduated top 50% of class	86

DEADLINES

| Regular admission | 3/1 |
| Nonfall registration? | yes |

FINANCIAL FACTS

Financial Aid Rating	**77**
In-state tuition	$3,465
Out-of-state tuition	$7,530
Room and board	$4,932
Books and supplies	$668
Avg frosh grant	$5,102
Avg frosh loan	$4,179

ILLINOIS WESLEYAN UNIVERSITY

CAMPUS LIFE

Quality of Life Rating	**74**
Type of school	private
Affiliation	Methodist
Environment	suburban

STUDENTS

Total undergrad enrollment	2,107
% male/female	43/57
% from out of state	11
% from public high school	82
% live on campus	82
% in (# of) fraternities	30 (6)
% in (# of) sororities	41 (5)
% African American	3
% Asian	3
% Caucasian	88
% Hispanic	2
% international	2
# of countries represented	22

ACADEMICS

Academic Rating	**84**
Calendar	4-4-1
Student/faculty ratio	12:1
Profs interesting rating	94

Profs accessible rating	94
% profs teaching UG courses	100
Avg lab size	10-19 students
Avg reg class size	10-19 students

MOST POPULAR MAJORS
Business administration/management
Biology/biological sciences
Music performance

SELECTIVITY
Admissions Rating **91**

# of applicants	3,116
% of applicants accepted	48
% of acceptees attending	39
# accepting a place on wait list	156

FRESHMAN PROFILE
Range SAT Verbal	580-670
Average SAT Verbal	635
Range SAT Math	590-690
Average SAT Math	625
Range ACT Composite	26-30
Average ACT Composite	28
Minimum TOEFL	550
% graduated top 10% of class	47
% graduated top 25% of class	83
% graduated top 50% of class	100

DEADLINES
Priority admission	11/1
Regular admission	2/15
Nonfall registration?	yes

FINANCIAL FACTS
Financial Aid Rating **87**

Tuition	$24,390
Room and board	$5,840
Books and supplies	$650
Required fees	$150
% frosh receiving aid	56
% undergrads receiving aid	54
Avg frosh grant	$11,835
Avg frosh loan	$2,816

INDIANA UNIVERSITY—BLOOMINGTON

CAMPUS LIFE
Quality of Life Rating **85**

Type of school	public
Environment	suburban

STUDENTS
Total undergrad enrollment	30,752
% male/female	44/56
% from out of state	36
% live on campus	43
% in (# of) fraternities	16 (30)
% in (# of) sororities	18 (25)
% African American	4
% Asian	3
% Caucasian	90
% Hispanic	2
% international	4

ACADEMICS
Academic Rating **72**

Calendar	semester
Student/faculty ratio	20:1
Avg lab size	20-29 students
Avg reg class size	20-29 students

MOST POPULAR MAJORS
Business administration/management
Elementary education and teaching
Biological and biomedical sciences

SELECTIVITY
Admissions Rating **75**

# of applicants	21,264
% of applicants accepted	81
% of acceptees attending	41

FRESHMAN PROFILE
Range SAT Verbal	490-600
Average SAT Verbal	543
Range SAT Math	500-610
Average SAT Math	556
Range ACT Composite	22-27
Average ACT Composite	24
% graduated top 10% of class	22
% graduated top 25% of class	52
% graduated top 50% of class	90

DEADLINES
Priority admission	2/1
Nonfall registration?	yes

FINANCIAL FACTS
Financial Aid Rating **80**

In-state tuition	$4,573
Out-of-state tuition	$15,184
Room and board	$5,676
Books and supplies	$740
Required fees	$742
% frosh receiving aid	42
% undergrads receiving aid	37
Avg frosh grant	$4,530
Avg frosh loan	$5,712

Iowa State University

CAMPUS LIFE
Quality of Life Rating   **78**

Type of school	public
Environment	urban

STUDENTS

Total undergrad enrollment	22,999
% male/female	56/44
% from out of state	19
% from public high school	93
% live on campus	35
% in (# of) fraternities	13 (31)
% in (# of) sororities	12 (18)
% African American	3
% Asian	3
% Caucasian	87
% Hispanic	2
% international	4
# of countries represented	117

ACADEMICS
Academic Rating   **69**

Calendar	semester
Student/faculty ratio	16:1
% profs teaching UG courses	86
% classes taught by TAs	17
Avg lab size	20-29 students
Avg reg class size	20-29 students

MOST POPULAR MAJORS
Management information systems
Elementary education and teaching
Mechanical engineering

SELECTIVITY
Admissions Rating   **76**

# of applicants	10,370
% of applicants accepted	89
% of acceptees attending	46

FRESHMAN PROFILE

Range SAT Verbal	510-650
Average SAT Verbal	590
Range SAT Math	550-670
Average SAT Math	620
Range ACT Composite	22-27
Average ACT Composite	24
Minimum TOEFL	500
Average HS GPA	3.5
% graduated top 10% of class	25
% graduated top 25% of class	58
% graduated top 50% of class	93

DEADLINES

Regular admission	8/1
Nonfall registration?	yes

FINANCIAL FACTS
Financial Aid Rating   **83**

In-state tuition	$4,342
Out-of-state tuition	$13,684
Room and board	$5,020
Books and supplies	$754
Required fees	$686
% frosh receiving aid	57
% undergrads receiving aid	46
Avg frosh grant	$4,260
Avg frosh loan	$5,923

Jamestown College

CAMPUS LIFE
Quality of Life Rating   **78**

Type of school	private
Affiliation	Presbyterian
Environment	rural

STUDENTS

Total undergrad enrollment	1,185
% male/female	44/56
% from out of state	38
% live on campus	60
% African American	1
% Caucasian	92
% Hispanic	1
% international	3

ACADEMICS
Academic Rating   **70**

Calendar	semester
Student/faculty ratio	17:1
Profs interesting rating	85
Profs accessible rating	83
% profs teaching UG courses	100
% classes taught by TAs	0
Avg lab size	20-29 students
Avg reg class size	30-39 students

MOST POPULAR MAJORS
Elementary education and teaching
Business administration/management
Nursing (BSN)

SELECTIVITY
Admissions Rating   **67**

# of applicants	930
% of applicants accepted	99
% of acceptees attending	36

FRESHMAN PROFILE

Range ACT Composite	13-33
Average ACT Composite	22
Minimum TOEFL	525
Average HS GPA	3.3
% graduated top 10% of class	13
% graduated top 25% of class	36
% graduated top 50% of class	63

DEADLINES

Nonfall registration?	yes

FINANCIAL FACTS

Financial Aid Rating	**86**
Tuition	$8,350
Room and board	$3,550
Books and supplies	$1,000
Avg frosh grant	$5,311
Avg frosh loan	$2,273

JOHN CARROLL UNIVERSITY

CAMPUS LIFE

Quality of Life Rating	**76**
Type of school	private
Affiliation	Roman Catholic
Environment	suburban

STUDENTS

Total undergrad enrollment	3,527
% male/female	47/53
% from out of state	27
% from public high school	55
% live on campus	59
% in (# of) fraternities	22 (12)
% in (# of) sororities	27 (7)
% African American	4
% Asian	3
% Caucasian	89
% Hispanic	2

ACADEMICS

Academic Rating	**82**
Calendar	semester
Student/faculty ratio	14:1
Profs interesting rating	84
Profs accessible rating	79
% profs teaching UG courses	99
% classes taught by TAs	3
Avg reg class size	20-29 students

MOST POPULAR MAJORS
Communications
Biology
Education

SELECTIVITY

Admissions Rating	**79**
# of applicants	2,612
% of applicants accepted	88
% of acceptees attending	36

FRESHMAN PROFILE

Range SAT Verbal	510-620
Average SAT Verbal	566
Range SAT Math	510-630
Average SAT Math	574
Range ACT Composite	21-26
Average ACT Composite	23
Minimum TOEFL	550
Average HS GPA	3.3
% graduated top 10% of class	31
% graduated top 25% of class	56
% graduated top 50% of class	88

DEADLINES

Regular admission	2/1
Regular notification	rolling
Nonfall registration?	yes

FINANCIAL FACTS

Financial Aid Rating	**75**
Tuition	$16,334
Room and board	$6,128
Books and supplies	$800
Avg frosh grant	$7,400
Avg frosh loan	$3,150

KALAMAZOO COLLEGE

CAMPUS LIFE

Quality of Life Rating	**75**
Type of school	private
Environment	suburban

STUDENTS

Total undergrad enrollment	1,265
% from out of state	21
% from public high school	85
% live on campus	75
% African American	2
% Asian	5
% Caucasian	83
% Hispanic	2
# of countries represented	20

ACADEMICS

Academic Rating	**84**
Calendar	quarter
Student/faculty ratio	12:1
Profs interesting rating	96

Profs accessible rating	99
% profs teaching UG courses	100
Avg lab size	20-29 students
Avg reg class size	20-29 students

MOST POPULAR MAJORS
Business/commerce
Biology/biological sciences
Psychology

SELECTIVITY
Admissions Rating **82**

# of applicants	1,411
% of applicants accepted	73
% of acceptees attending	33
# accepting a place on wait list	64
% admitted from wait list	50
# of early decision applicants	36
% accepted early decision	81

FRESHMAN PROFILE

Range SAT Verbal	590-680
Average SAT Verbal	631
Range SAT Math	580-690
Average SAT Math	630
Range ACT Composite	26-30
Average ACT Composite	28
Minimum TOEFL	550
Average HS GPA	3.6
% graduated top 10% of class	42
% graduated top 25% of class	74
% graduated top 50% of class	95

DEADLINES

Early decision	11/15
Early decision notification	12/1
Priority admission	2/15
Regular admission	2/15
Regular notification	4/1

FINANCIAL FACTS
Financial Aid Rating **83**

Tuition	$21,603
Room and board	$6,354
Avg frosh grant	$12,510
Avg frosh loan	$4,230

KANSAS STATE UNIVERSITY

CAMPUS LIFE
Quality of Life Rating **78**

Type of school	public
Environment	suburban

STUDENTS

Total undergrad enrollment	19,048
% male/female	52/48
% from out of state	9
% from public high school	90
% live on campus	33
% in (# of) fraternities	20 (28)
% in (# of) sororities	20 (15)
% African American	3
% Asian	1
% Caucasian	90
% Hispanic	2
% international	1

ACADEMICS
Academic Rating **80**

Calendar	semester
Student/faculty ratio	20:1
Profs interesting rating	85
Profs accessible rating	70
% profs teaching UG courses	74
% classes taught by TAs	17
Avg reg class size	10-19 students

SELECTIVITY
Admissions Rating **82**

# of applicants	8,212
% of applicants accepted	58
% of acceptees attending	74

FRESHMAN PROFILE

Range ACT Composite	19-25
Average ACT Composite	24
Minimum TOEFL	550
% graduated top 25% of class	59
% graduated top 50% of class	90

DEADLINES

Nonfall registration?	yes

FINANCIAL FACTS
Financial Aid Rating **84**

In-state tuition	$2,918
Out-of-state tuition	$10,178
Room and board	$4,500
Books and supplies	$1,000
Required fees	$526
% frosh receiving aid	55
% undergrads receiving aid	56
Avg frosh grant	$2,000
Avg frosh loan	$1,098

KENT STATE UNIVERSITY

CAMPUS LIFE
Quality of Life Rating **83**

Type of school	public

Affiliation	none
Environment	suburban

STUDENTS

Total undergrad enrollment	18,382
% male/female	40/60
% from out of state	7
% live on campus	33
% in (# of) fraternities	5 (16)
% in (# of) sororities	5 (6)
% African American	8
% Asian	1
% Caucasian	87
% Hispanic	1
% international	1
# of countries represented	64

ACADEMICS

Academic Rating	**67**
Calendar	semester
Student/faculty ratio	20:1
Profs interesting rating	82
Profs accessible rating	78
Avg reg class size	20-29 students

MOST POPULAR MAJORS
Psychology
Criminal justice studies
Architecture

SELECTIVITY

Admissions Rating	**62**
# of applicants	9,694
% of applicants accepted	90
% of acceptees attending	42

FRESHMAN PROFILE

Range SAT Verbal	450-560
Average SAT Verbal	502
Range SAT Math	450-560
Average SAT Math	501
Range ACT Composite	19-24
Average ACT Composite	21
Minimum TOEFL	525
Average HS GPA	3.1
% graduated top 10% of class	11
% graduated top 25% of class	32
% graduated top 50% of class	67

DEADLINES

Regular admission	6/1
Nonfall registration?	yes

FINANCIAL FACTS

Financial Aid Rating	**76**
In-state tuition	$4,846
Out-of-state tuition	$10,333
Room and board	$5,150
Books and supplies	$930

KENYON COLLEGE

CAMPUS LIFE

Quality of Life Rating	**89**
Type of school	private
Environment	rural

STUDENTS

Total undergrad enrollment	1,576
% male/female	46/54
% from out of state	80
% from public high school	53
% live on campus	98
% in (# of) fraternities	23 (8)
% in (# of) sororities	8 (4)
% African American	4
% Asian	3
% Caucasian	85
% Hispanic	2
% international	3
# of countries represented	26

ACADEMICS

Academic Rating	**95**
Calendar	semester
Student/faculty ratio	9:1
Profs interesting rating	97
Profs accessible rating	98
% profs teaching UG courses	100
Avg reg class size	10-19 students

MOST POPULAR MAJORS
English language and literature
History
Political science and government

SELECTIVITY

Admissions Rating	**92**
# of applicants	3,356
% of applicants accepted	44
% of acceptees attending	30
# accepting a place on wait list	169
% admitted from wait list	31
# of early decision applicants	174
% accepted early decision	78

FRESHMAN PROFILE

Range SAT Verbal	620-720
Average SAT Verbal	681
Range SAT Math	610-690
Average SAT Math	661
Range ACT Composite	27-32

Average ACT Composite	30
Minimum TOEFL	570
Average HS GPA	3.8
% graduated top 10% of class	51
% graduated top 25% of class	80
% graduated top 50% of class	97

DEADLINES

Early decision	12/1
Early decision notification	12/15
Regular admission	2/1
Regular notification	4/1

FINANCIAL FACTS

Financial Aid Rating	**81**
Tuition	$27,900
Room and board	$4,690
Books and supplies	$950
Required fees	$810
% frosh receiving aid	39
% undergrads receiving aid	45
Avg frosh grant	$22,835
Avg frosh loan	$3,577

KETTERING UNIVERSITY

CAMPUS LIFE

Quality of Life Rating	**79**
Type of school	private
Affiliation	none
Environment	suburban

STUDENTS

Total undergrad enrollment	2,487
% from out of state	36
% from public high school	83
% live on campus	43
% in (# of) fraternities	45 (14)
% in (# of) sororities	47 (6)
% African American	7
% Asian	5
% Caucasian	75
% Hispanic	2
% international	3
# of countries represented	20

ACADEMICS

Academic Rating	**83**
Calendar	continuous
Student/faculty ratio	9:1
Profs interesting rating	83
Profs accessible rating	79
% profs teaching UG courses	100
% classes taught by TAs	0

Avg lab size	10-19 students
Avg reg class size	20-29 students

MOST POPULAR MAJORS
Computer engineering
Electrical, electronics, and
communications engineering
Mechanical engineering

SELECTIVITY

Admissions Rating	**85**
# of applicants	2,433
% of applicants accepted	70
% of acceptees attending	35

FRESHMAN PROFILE

Range SAT Verbal	540-640
Average SAT Verbal	583
Range SAT Math	600-690
Average SAT Math	633
Range ACT Composite	24-28
Average ACT Composite	26
Minimum TOEFL	550
Average HS GPA	3.6
% graduated top 10% of class	35
% graduated top 25% of class	68
% graduated top 50% of class	94

DEADLINES

Nonfall registration?	yes

FINANCIAL FACTS

Financial Aid Rating	**75**
Tuition	$20,170
Room and board	$4,752
Books and supplies	$750
Avg frosh grant	$8,653
Avg frosh loan	$2,589

KNOX COLLEGE

CAMPUS LIFE

Quality of Life Rating	**87**
Type of school	private
Environment	rural

STUDENTS

Total undergrad enrollment	1,121
% male/female	47/53
% from out of state	44
% from public high school	88
% live on campus	96
% in (# of) fraternities	30 (5)
% in (# of) sororities	10 (2)
% African American	5
% Asian	5

% Caucasian	78
% Hispanic	4
% international	8
# of countries represented	32

ACADEMICS
Academic Rating **92**

Calendar	other
Student/faculty ratio	12:1
% profs teaching UG courses	100
Avg lab size	10-19 students
Avg reg class size	10-19 students

MOST POPULAR MAJORS
Psychology
Economics
Biology/biological sciences

SELECTIVITY
Admissions Rating **81**

# of applicants	1,542
% of applicants accepted	72
% of acceptees attending	27

FRESHMAN PROFILE

Range SAT Verbal	550-680
Range SAT Math	550-660
Range ACT Composite	23-29
Minimum TOEFL	550
% graduated top 10% of class	33
% graduated top 25% of class	67
% graduated top 50% of class	94

DEADLINES

Regular admission	2/1
Regular notification	3/31
Nonfall registration?	yes

FINANCIAL FACTS
Financial Aid Rating **96**

Tuition	$24,105
Room and board	$5,925
Books and supplies	$600
Required fees	$264
% frosh receiving aid	71
% undergrads receiving aid	75
Avg frosh grant	$20,531
Avg frosh loan	$4,306

LAKE ERIE COLLEGE

CAMPUS LIFE
Quality of Life Rating **80**

Type of school	private
Affiliation	none
Environment	suburban

STUDENTS

Total undergrad enrollment	509
% male/female	26/74
% from out of state	11
% from public high school	80
% live on campus	35
% African American	4
% Asian	1
% Caucasian	93
% Hispanic	2
# of countries represented	6

ACADEMICS
Academic Rating **68**

Calendar	semester
Student/faculty ratio	11:1
% profs teaching UG courses	100
% classes taught by TAs	0
Avg reg class size	10-19 students

MOST POPULAR MAJORS
Business
Education
Equestrian studies

SELECTIVITY
Admissions Rating **66**

# of applicants	336
% of applicants accepted	87
% of acceptees attending	35

FRESHMAN PROFILE

Range SAT Verbal	410-540
Average SAT Verbal	500
Range SAT Math	410-530
Average SAT Math	460
Range ACT Composite	18-24
Average ACT Composite	22
Minimum TOEFL	550
Average HS GPA	3.0
% graduated top 10% of class	15
% graduated top 25% of class	36
% graduated top 50% of class	60

DEADLINES

Nonfall registration?	yes

FINANCIAL FACTS
Financial Aid Rating **75**

Tuition	$15,140
Room and board	$5,420
Books and supplies	$530
Avg frosh grant	$5,800
Avg frosh loan	$2,650

LAKE FOREST COLLEGE

CAMPUS LIFE
Quality of Life Rating **84**

Type of school	private
Affiliation	Presbyterian
Environment	suburban

STUDENTS

Total undergrad enrollment	1,319
% male/female	41/59
% from out of state	52
% from public high school	65
% live on campus	81
% in (# of) fraternities	19 (3)
% in (# of) sororities	27 (4)
% African American	6
% Asian	5
% Caucasian	85
% Hispanic	3
% international	8
# of countries represented	42

ACADEMICS
Academic Rating **92**

Calendar	semester
Student/faculty ratio	12:1
Profs interesting rating	97
Profs accessible rating	99
% profs teaching UG courses	100
Avg lab size	10-19 students
Avg reg class size	10-19 students

MOST POPULAR MAJORS
Business/commerce
Psychology
Communications

SELECTIVITY
Admissions Rating **79**

# of applicants	1,666
% of applicants accepted	66
% of acceptees attending	33
# accepting a place on wait list	21
% admitted from wait list	43
# of early decision applicants	40
% accepted early decision	63

FRESHMAN PROFILE

Range SAT Verbal	520-620
Average SAT Verbal	570
Range SAT Math	510-620
Average SAT Math	573
Range ACT Composite	23-28
Average ACT Composite	25

Minimum TOEFL	550
Average HS GPA	3.4
% graduated top 10% of class	25
% graduated top 25% of class	53
% graduated top 50% of class	80

DEADLINES

Early decision	12/1
Early decision notification	12/15
Regular admission	3/1
Regular notification	3/15
Nonfall registration?	yes

FINANCIAL FACTS
Financial Aid Rating **93**

Tuition	$24,096
Room and board	$5,764
Books and supplies	$600
Required fees	$310
% frosh receiving aid	70
% undergrads receiving aid	70
Avg frosh grant	$17,496
Avg frosh loan	$3,599

LAWRENCE UNIVERSITY

CAMPUS LIFE
Quality of Life Rating **81**

Type of school	private
Environment	suburban

STUDENTS

Total undergrad enrollment	1,392
% male/female	47/53
% from out of state	59
% from public high school	81
% live on campus	98
% in (# of) fraternities	30 (5)
% in (# of) sororities	15 (3)
% African American	2
% Asian	2
% Caucasian	78
% Hispanic	3
% international	10

ACADEMICS
Academic Rating **92**

Calendar	trimester
Student/faculty ratio	11:1
Profs interesting rating	96
Profs accessible rating	98
% profs teaching UG courses	100
Avg reg class size	10-19 students

MOST POPULAR MAJORS
Biology/biological sciences
Psychology
Music performance

SELECTIVITY

Admissions Rating	**85**
# of applicants	1,812
% of applicants accepted	68
% of acceptees attending	29
# accepting a place on wait list	53
% admitted from wait list	21
# of early decision applicants	17
% accepted early decision	94

FRESHMAN PROFILE

Range SAT Verbal	560-690
Average SAT Verbal	620
Range SAT Math	560-670
Average SAT Math	625
Range ACT Composite	24-30
Average ACT Composite	27
Minimum TOEFL	575
Average HS GPA	3.5
% graduated top 10% of class	36
% graduated top 25% of class	73
% graduated top 50% of class	94

DEADLINES

Early decision	11/15
Early decision notification	12/1
Regular admission	1/15
Regular notification	4/1

FINANCIAL FACTS

Financial Aid Rating	**91**
Tuition	$23,487
Room and board	$5,337
Books and supplies	$555
Required fees	$180
% frosh receiving aid	69
% undergrads receiving aid	70
Avg frosh grant	$15,569
Avg frosh loan	$2,780

LOYOLA UNIVERSITY CHICAGO

CAMPUS LIFE

Quality of Life Rating	**73**
Type of school	private
Affiliation	Roman Catholic
Environment	urban

STUDENTS

Total undergrad enrollment	7,533
% male/female	34/66
% from out of state	50
% from public high school	38
% live on campus	29
% in (# of) fraternities	5 (6)
% in (# of) sororities	3 (6)
% African American	9
% Asian	11
% Caucasian	56
% Hispanic	10
% international	3

ACADEMICS

Academic Rating	**75**
Calendar	semester
Student/faculty ratio	13:1
Profs interesting rating	90
Profs accessible rating	91
Avg lab size	under 10 students
Avg reg class size	20-29 students

MOST POPULAR MAJORS
Biology/biological sciences
Psychology
Business administration/management

SELECTIVITY

Admissions Rating	**73**
# of applicants	10,214
% of applicants accepted	71
% of acceptees attending	22

FRESHMAN PROFILE

Range SAT Verbal	520-630
Average SAT Verbal	574
Range SAT Math	520-640
Average SAT Math	574
Range ACT Composite	22-27
Average ACT Composite	25
Minimum TOEFL	550
% graduated top 10% of class	29
% graduated top 25% of class	63
% graduated top 50% of class	92

DEADLINES

Priority admission	2/1
Regular admission	4/1
Nonfall registration?	yes

FINANCIAL FACTS

Financial Aid Rating	**86**
Tuition	$20,540
Room and board	$7,600
Books and supplies	$1,000
Required fees	$656

% frosh receiving aid	94
% undergrads receiving aid	77
Avg frosh grant	$13,093
Avg frosh loan	$3,958

LUTHER COLLEGE

CAMPUS LIFE
Quality of Life Rating **85**

Type of school	private
Affiliation	Lutheran
Environment	rural

STUDENTS
Total undergrad enrollment	2,575
% male/female	40/60
% from out of state	63
% from public high school	90
% live on campus	82
% in (# of) fraternities	8 (4)
% in (# of) sororities	9 (4)
% African American	1
% Asian	1
% Caucasian	86
% Hispanic	1
% international	6
# of countries represented	41

ACADEMICS
Academic Rating **82**

Calendar	4-1-4
Student/faculty ratio	13:1
Profs interesting rating	79
Profs accessible rating	75
% profs teaching UG courses	100
% classes taught by TAs	0
Avg lab size	10-19 students
Avg reg class size	20-29 students

MOST POPULAR MAJORS
Psychology
Education
Biology/biological sciences

SELECTIVITY
Admissions Rating **79**

# of applicants	1,953
% of applicants accepted	78
% of acceptees attending	40

FRESHMAN PROFILE
Range SAT Verbal	560-650
Average SAT Verbal	616
Range SAT Math	540-660
Average SAT Math	603

Range ACT Composite	22-28
Average ACT Composite	25
Minimum TOEFL	550
Average HS GPA	3.6
% graduated top 10% of class	35
% graduated top 25% of class	65
% graduated top 50% of class	91

DEADLINES
| Nonfall registration? | yes |

FINANCIAL FACTS
Financial Aid Rating **70**

Tuition	$20,310
Room and board	$4,040
Books and supplies	$710
Avg frosh grant	$8,466
Avg frosh loan	$3,332

MACALESTER COLLEGE

CAMPUS LIFE

CAMPUS LIFE
Quality of Life Rating **93**

Type of school	private
Affiliation	Presbyterian
Environment	urban

STUDENTS
Total undergrad enrollment	1,840
% male/female	42/58
% from out of state	76
% from public high school	66
% live on campus	68
% African American	4
% Asian	6
% Caucasian	85
% Hispanic	3
% international	15
# of countries represented	88

ACADEMICS
Academic Rating **93**

Calendar	semester
Student/faculty ratio	10:1
Profs interesting rating	95
Profs accessible rating	96
% profs teaching UG courses	100
Avg lab size	10-19 students
Avg reg class size	10-19 students

MOST POPULAR MAJORS
Biology/biological sciences
Psychology
Economics

SELECTIVITY

Admissions Rating	**96**
# of applicants	3,713
% of applicants accepted	44
% of acceptees attending	27
# accepting a place on wait list	93
% admitted from wait list	6
# of early decision applicants	201
% accepted early decision	54

FRESHMAN PROFILE

Range SAT Verbal	630-730
Average SAT Verbal	690
Range SAT Math	620-710
Average SAT Math	670
Range ACT Composite	27-31
Average ACT Composite	29
Minimum TOEFL	570
% graduated top 10% of class	71
% graduated top 25% of class	96
% graduated top 50% of class	100

DEADLINES

Early decision	11/15
Early decision notification	12/15
Regular admission	1/15
Regular notification	4/1

FINANCIAL FACTS

Financial Aid Rating	**91**
Tuition	$24,902
Room and board	$6,874
Books and supplies	$750
Required fees	$168
% frosh receiving aid	77
% undergrads receiving aid	69
Avg frosh grant	$15,564
Avg frosh loan	$3,113

MANCHESTER COLLEGE

CAMPUS LIFE

Quality of Life Rating	**76**
Type of school	private
Affiliation	Church of Brethren
Environment	rural

STUDENTS

Total undergrad enrollment	1,135
% male/female	45/55
% from out of state	11
% from public high school	98
% live on campus	77
# of countries represented	29

ACADEMICS

Academic Rating	**76**
Calendar	4-1-4
Student/faculty ratio	14:1
Profs interesting rating	75
Profs accessible rating	72
% profs teaching UG courses	100
% classes taught by TAs	0
Avg reg class size	20-29 students

MOST POPULAR MAJORS
Psychology
Accounting
Education

SELECTIVITY

Admissions Rating	**71**
# of applicants	1,103
% of applicants accepted	81
% of acceptees attending	37

FRESHMAN PROFILE

Range SAT Verbal	450-550
Range SAT Math	450-570
Range ACT Composite	19-25
Minimum TOEFL	550
% graduated top 10% of class	24
% graduated top 25% of class	50
% graduated top 50% of class	80

DEADLINES

Nonfall registration?	yes

FINANCIAL FACTS

Financial Aid Rating	**80**
Tuition	$15,980
Room and board	$5,930
Books and supplies	$550
Avg frosh grant	$11,883

MARIETTA COLLEGE

CAMPUS LIFE

Quality of Life Rating	**78**
Type of school	private
Affiliation	none
Environment	suburban

STUDENTS

Total undergrad enrollment	1,205
% male/female	50/50
% from out of state	50
% from public high school	82
% live on campus	91
% in (# of) fraternities	17 (4)
% in (# of) sororities	27 (4)

% African American	2
% Asian	1
% Caucasian	85
% Hispanic	1
% international	5
# of countries represented	10

ACADEMICS
Academic Rating **78**

Calendar	semester
Student/faculty ratio	12:1
Profs interesting rating	84
Profs accessible rating	77
% profs teaching UG courses	100
% classes taught by TAs	0
Avg lab size	10-19 students
Avg reg class size	under 10 students

MOST POPULAR MAJORS
Sports medicine
Education
Business areas

SELECTIVITY
Admissions Rating **73**

# of applicants	1,142
% of applicants accepted	94
% of acceptees attending	43

FRESHMAN PROFILE
Average SAT Verbal	539
Average SAT Math	547
Average ACT Composite	23
Minimum TOEFL	550
Average HS GPA	3.2
% graduated top 10% of class	24
% graduated top 25% of class	50
% graduated top 50% of class	75

DEADLINES
Regular admission	rolling
Nonfall registration?	yes

FINANCIAL FACTS
Financial Aid Rating **78**

Tuition	$19,762
Room and board	$5,774
Books and supplies	$575
Avg frosh grant	$10,000
Avg frosh loan	$2,625

MARQUETTE UNIVERSITY

CAMPUS LIFE
Quality of Life Rating **80**

Type of school	private
Affiliation	Roman Catholic
Environment	urban

STUDENTS
Total undergrad enrollment	7,644
% male/female	44/56
% from out of state	53
% from public high school	55
% live on campus	54
% in (# of) fraternities	7 (10)
% in (# of) sororities	8 (9)
% African American	5
% Asian	5
% Caucasian	86
% Hispanic	4
% international	2
# of countries represented	80

ACADEMICS
Academic Rating **77**

Calendar	semester
Student/faculty ratio	15:1
Avg lab size	10-19 students
Avg reg class size	20-29 students

MOST POPULAR MAJORS
Nursing/registered nurse training (RN, ASN, BSN, MSN)
Business administration/management
Biomedical sciences

SELECTIVITY
Admissions Rating **78**

# of applicants	7,593
% of applicants accepted	82
% of acceptees attending	30

FRESHMAN PROFILE
Range SAT Verbal	520-640
Average SAT Verbal	560
Range SAT Math	530-650
Average SAT Math	590
Range ACT Composite	23-28
Average ACT Composite	25
Minimum TOEFL	525
% graduated top 10% of class	20
% graduated top 25% of class	40
% graduated top 50% of class	94

DEADLINES
Priority admission	2/1
Nonfall registration?	yes

FINANCIAL FACTS
Financial Aid Rating **82**

Tuition	$20,350
Room and board	$7,036

Books and supplies	$900
Required fees	$374
Avg frosh grant	$11,640
Avg frosh loan	$4,385

Mayville State University

CAMPUS LIFE
Quality of Life Rating 73
Type of school	public
Affiliation	none
Environment	rural

STUDENTS
Total undergrad enrollment	755
% male/female	46/54
% from out of state	27
% from public high school	94
% live on campus	30
% African American	2
% Caucasian	92
% Hispanic	1
% international	3
# of countries represented	3

ACADEMICS
Academic Rating 69
Calendar	semester
Student/faculty ratio	15:1
Profs interesting rating	79
Profs accessible rating	77
% profs teaching UG courses	100
% classes taught by TAs	0
Avg reg class size	10-19 students

MOST POPULAR MAJORS
Business administration/management
Elementary education and teaching
Computer science

SELECTIVITY
Admissions Rating 62
# of applicants	202
% of applicants accepted	100
% of acceptees attending	72

FRESHMAN PROFILE
Range ACT Composite	17-22
Average ACT Composite	20
Minimum TOEFL	525
Average HS GPA	3.0
% graduated top 25% of class	30
% graduated top 50% of class	76

DEADLINES
Nonfall registration?	yes

FINANCIAL FACTS
Financial Aid Rating 77
In-state tuition	$2,067
Out-of-state tuition	$5,519
Room and board	$3,126
Books and supplies	$600
Avg frosh grant	$2,865
Avg frosh loan	$2,766

Miami University

CAMPUS LIFE
Quality of Life Rating 85
Type of school	public
Environment	suburban

STUDENTS
Total undergrad enrollment	15,153
% male/female	45/55
% from out of state	27
% live on campus	45
% in (# of) fraternities	24 (28)
% in (# of) sororities	27 (20)
% African American	4
% Asian	2
% Caucasian	89
% Hispanic	2
% international	1
# of countries represented	76

ACADEMICS
Academic Rating 82
Calendar	semester
Student/faculty ratio	17:1
Profs interesting rating	80
Profs accessible rating	77
% profs teaching UG courses	100
% classes taught by TAs	25
Avg lab size	20-29 students
Avg reg class size	20-29 students

SELECTIVITY
Admissions Rating 86
# of applicants	12,500
% of applicants accepted	74
% of acceptees attending	37
# accepting a place on wait list	205
% admitted from wait list	36
# of early decision applicants	839
% accepted early decision	73

FRESHMAN PROFILE
Range SAT Verbal	550-640
Average SAT Verbal	590

Range SAT Math	580-660
Average SAT Math	610
Range ACT Composite	24-28
Average ACT Composite	26
Minimum TOEFL	530
Average HS GPA	3.7
% graduated top 10% of class	37
% graduated top 25% of class	77
% graduated top 50% of class	97

DEADLINES

Early decision	11/1
Early decision notification	12/15
Regular admission	1/31
Regular notification	3/15
Nonfall registration?	yes

FINANCIAL FACTS
Financial Aid Rating   **86**

In-state tuition	$6,386
Out-of-state tuition	$15,110
Room and board	$6,240
Books and supplies	$803
Required fees	$1,214
% frosh receiving aid	34
% undergrads receiving aid	31

MICHIGAN STATE UNIVERSITY

CAMPUS LIFE
Quality of Life Rating   **78**

Type of school	public
Environment	suburban

STUDENTS

Total undergrad enrollment	35,197
% male/female	47/53
% from out of state	6
% live on campus	44
% African American	9
% Asian	5
% Caucasian	82
% Hispanic	3
% international	2
# of countries represented	100

ACADEMICS
Academic Rating   **68**

Calendar	semester
Student/faculty ratio	18:1
Profs interesting rating	82
Profs accessible rating	77
Avg lab size	20-29 students
Avg reg class size	20-29 students

MOST POPULAR MAJORS
Marketing/marketing management
Communications
Social sciences

SELECTIVITY
Admissions Rating   **74**

# of applicants	25,210
% of applicants accepted	67
% of acceptees attending	41
# accepting a place on wait list	950
% admitted from wait list	29

FRESHMAN PROFILE

Range SAT Verbal	490-610
Average SAT Verbal	552
Range SAT Math	520-640
Average SAT Math	579
Range ACT Composite	22-27
Average ACT Composite	24
Minimum TOEFL	550
Average HS GPA	3.6
% graduated top 10% of class	26
% graduated top 25% of class	66
% graduated top 50% of class	95

DEADLINES

Regular admission	8/1
Regular notification	9/1
Nonfall registration?	yes

FINANCIAL FACTS
Financial Aid Rating   **81**

In-state tuition	$6,015
Out-of-state tuition	$14,970
Room and board	$4,932
Books and supplies	$790
Required fees	$708
% frosh receiving aid	54
% undergrads receiving aid	40

MICHIGAN TECHNOLOGICAL UNIVERSITY

CAMPUS LIFE
Quality of Life Rating   **77**

Type of school	public
Environment	rural

STUDENTS

Total undergrad enrollment	5,915
% male/female	76/24
% from out of state	19
% live on campus	39
% in (# of) fraternities	9 (14)

% in (# of) sororities	16 (8)
% African American	2
% Asian	1
% Caucasian	85
% Hispanic	1
% international	6
# of countries represented	80

ACADEMICS
Academic Rating   74

Calendar	semester
Student/faculty ratio	11:1
Profs interesting rating	91
Profs accessible rating	95
% profs teaching UG courses	100
% classes taught by TAs	4
Avg lab size	10-19 students
Avg reg class size	20-29 students

MOST POPULAR MAJORS
Civil engineering
Electrical, electronics, and
communications engineering
Mechanical engineering

SELECTIVITY
Admissions Rating   82

# of applicants	2,957
% of applicants accepted	92
% of acceptees attending	44

FRESHMAN PROFILE

Range SAT Verbal	510-640
Average SAT Verbal	570
Range SAT Math	570-690
Average SAT Math	624
Range ACT Composite	23-28
Average ACT Composite	25
Minimum TOEFL	500
Average HS GPA	3.5
% graduated top 10% of class	31
% graduated top 25% of class	60
% graduated top 50% of class	89

DEADLINES

Nonfall registration?	yes

FINANCIAL FACTS
Financial Aid Rating   87

In-state tuition	$5,782
Out-of-state tuition	$14,152
Room and board	$5,465
Books and supplies	$900
Required fees	$673
% frosh receiving aid	47
% undergrads receiving aid	42
Avg frosh grant	$5,303
Avg frosh loan	$4,906

MILLIKIN UNIVERSITY

CAMPUS LIFE
Quality of Life Rating   79

Type of school	private
Affiliation	Presbyterian
Environment	suburban

STUDENTS

Total undergrad enrollment	2,389
% male/female	42/58
% from out of state	15
% from public high school	91
% live on campus	60
% in (# of) fraternities	15 (5)
% in (# of) sororities	25 (3)
% African American	7
% Asian	1
% Caucasian	84
% Hispanic	2
% international	1

ACADEMICS
Academic Rating   69

Calendar	semester
Student/faculty ratio	13:1
Profs interesting rating	81
Profs accessible rating	77
% profs teaching UG courses	100
% classes taught by TAs	0

MOST POPULAR MAJORS
Elementary education
Marketing and accounting
Biology and nursing

SELECTIVITY
Admissions Rating   66

# of applicants	2,598
% of applicants accepted	76
% of acceptees attending	33

FRESHMAN PROFILE

Range SAT Verbal	490-600
Average SAT Verbal	538
Range SAT Math	440-580
Average SAT Math	516
Range ACT Composite	21-27
Average ACT Composite	24
Minimum TOEFL	550
% graduated top 10% of class	21

% graduated top 25% of class	52
% graduated top 50% of class	84

DEADLINES

Nonfall registration?	yes

FINANCIAL FACTS
Financial Aid Rating **80**

Tuition	$17,084
Room and board	$5,594
Books and supplies	$800

MILWAUKEE SCHOOL OF ENGINEERING

CAMPUS LIFE
Quality of Life Rating **77**

Type of school	private
Affiliation	none
Environment	urban

STUDENTS

Total undergrad enrollment	2,246
% male/female	84/16
% from out of state	25
% from public high school	83
% live on campus	49
% in (# of) fraternities	9 (9)
% in (# of) sororities	6 (6)
% African American	4
% Asian	3
% Caucasian	87
% Hispanic	2
% international	4

ACADEMICS
Academic Rating **78**

Calendar	quarter
Student/faculty ratio	12:1
Profs interesting rating	84
Profs accessible rating	79
% profs teaching UG courses	100
% classes taught by TAs	0
Avg lab size	10-19 students
Avg regular class size	10-19 students

MOST POPULAR MAJORS
Mechanical engineering
Electrical engineering
Computer engineering

SELECTIVITY
Admissions Rating **73**

# of applicants	2,346
% of applicants accepted	70
% of acceptees attending	29

FRESHMAN PROFILE

Range SAT Verbal	510-620
Average SAT Verbal	580
Range SAT Math	590-680
Average SAT Math	630
Range ACT Composite	24-28
Average ACT Composite	26
Minimum TOEFL	550
Average HS GPA	3.26
% graduated top 10% of class	28
% graduated top 25% of class	58
% graduated top 50% of class	92

DEADLINES

Regular notification	rolling
Nonfall registration?	yes

FINANCIAL FACTS
Financial Aid Rating **76**

Tuition	$21,855
Room and board	$5,115
Books and supplies	$2,340
Avg frosh grant	$8,000
Avg frosh loan	$4,000

MONMOUTH COLLEGE

CAMPUS LIFE
Quality of Life Rating **78**

Type of school	private
Affiliation	Presbyterian
Environment	rural

STUDENTS

Total undergrad enrollment	1,072
% male/female	46/54
% from out of state	6
% from public high school	80
% live on campus	90
% in (# of) fraternities	21 (3)
% in (# of) sororities	24 (3)
% African American	5
% Asian	1
% Caucasian	88
% Hispanic	2
% international	3
# of countries represented	22

ACADEMICS
Academic Rating **76**

Calendar	semester
Student/faculty ratio	14:1
Profs interesting rating	83
Profs accessible rating	81

% profs teaching UG courses	100
% classes taught by TAs	0
Avg lab size	10-19 students
Avg reg class size	10-19 students

MOST POPULAR MAJORS
Education
Business administration/management
History

SELECTIVITY
Admissions Rating **74**

# of applicants	1,159
% of applicants accepted	79
% of acceptees attending	29

FRESHMAN PROFILE
Range ACT Composite	20-25
Average ACT Composite	23
Minimum TOEFL	550
Average HS GPA	3.2
% graduated top 10% of class	15
% graduated top 25% of class	36
% graduated top 50% of class	73

DEADLINES
Nonfall registration?	yes

FINANCIAL FACTS
Financial Aid Rating **85**

Tuition	$17,760
Room and board	$4,730
Books and supplies	$650
Avg frosh grant	$10,261
Avg frosh loan	$3,300

MORNINGSIDE COLLEGE

CAMPUS LIFE
Quality of Life Rating **73**

Type of school	private
Affiliation	Methodist
Environment	urban

STUDENTS
Total undergrad enrollment	806
% male/female	46/54
% from out of state	32
% from public high school	95
% live on campus	68
% in (# of) fraternities	13 (2)
% in (# of) sororities	8 (2)
% African American	3
% Asian	1
% Caucasian	88
% Hispanic	4

% international	2
# of countries represented	3

ACADEMICS
Academic Rating **75**

Calendar	semester
Student/faculty ratio	12:1
Profs interesting rating	90
Profs accessible rating	90
% profs teaching UG courses	100
% classes taught by TAs	0
Avg lab size	10-19 students
Avg regular class size	10-19 students

MOST POPULAR MAJORS
Business administration
Elementary education
Biology

SELECTIVITY
Admissions Rating **69**

# of applicants	1,127
% of applicants accepted	73
% of acceptees attending	30

FRESHMAN PROFILE
Average ACT Composite	22
Minimum TOEFL	425
Average HS GPA	3.25
% graduated top 10% of class	12
% graduated top 25% of class	37
% graduated top 50% of class	69

DEADLINES
Regular notification	rolling
Nonfall registration?	yes

FINANCIAL FACTS
Financial Aid Rating **90**

Tuition	$14,570
Room and board	$5,120
Books and supplies	$800
Avg frosh grant	$11,179
Avg frosh loan	$3,426

MOUNT VERNON NAZARENE COLLEGE

CAMPUS LIFE
Quality of Life Rating **77**

Type of school	private
Affiliation	Nazarene
Environment	rural

STUDENTS
Total undergrad enrollment	2,106
% male/female	44/56
% from out of state	12

% from public high school	84
% live on campus	53
% African American	2
% Asian	1
% Caucasian	70
% Hispanic	1
# of countries represented	6

ACADEMICS
Academic Rating **70**

Calendar	differs by program
Student/faculty ratio	18:1
Profs interesting rating	78
Profs accessible rating	74
% profs teaching UG courses	100
% classes taught by TAs	0
Avg reg class size	10-19 students

MOST POPULAR MAJORS
Biology/biological sciences
Early childhood education and teaching
Business administration/management

SELECTIVITY
Admissions Rating **64**

# of applicants	813
% of applicants accepted	83
% of acceptees attending	54

FRESHMAN PROFILE

Range SAT Verbal	560-600
Range SAT Math	500-600
Range ACT Composite	19-23
Average ACT Composite	22
Minimum TOEFL	500
Average HS GPA	3.2
% graduated top 10% of class	19
% graduated top 25% of class	42
% graduated top 50% of class	74

DEADLINES

Regular admission	5/31
Nonfall registration?	yes

FINANCIAL FACTS
Financial Aid Rating **76**

Tuition	$12,810
Room and board	$4,527
Books and supplies	$750
Avg frosh grant	$621
Avg frosh loan	$1,658

NORTH DAKOTA STATE UNIVERSITY

CAMPUS LIFE
Quality of Life Rating **74**

Type of school	public
Affiliation	none
Environment	urban

STUDENTS

Total undergrad enrollment	9,874
% male/female	57/43
% from out of state	40
% from public high school	93
% live on campus	30
% in (# of) fraternities	10 (10)
% in (# of) sororities	5 (5)
% African American	1
% Asian	1
% Caucasian	95
% international	1
# of countries represented	54

ACADEMICS
Academic Rating **77**

Calendar	semester
Student/faculty ratio	18:1
Profs interesting rating	83
Profs accessible rating	81
% profs teaching UG courses	99
% classes taught by TAs	7
Avg lab size	under 10 students
Avg regular class size	20-29 students

MOST POPULAR MAJORS
Mechanical engineering
Civil engineering

SELECTIVITY
Admissions Rating **73**

# of applicants	3,547
% of applicants accepted	60
% of acceptees attending	88

FRESHMAN PROFILE

Average ACT Composite	23
Minimum TOEFL	525
Average HS GPA	3.37

DEADLINES

Regular admission	8/15
Nonfall registration?	yes

FINANCIAL FACTS
Financial Aid Rating **85**

In-state tuition	$2,904
Out-of-state tuition	$7,754
Room and board	$4,175

Books and supplies	$700
Avg frosh grant	$2,899
Avg frosh loan	$2,897

NORTH PARK UNIVERSITY

CAMPUS LIFE

Quality of Life Rating	**79**
Type of school	private
Affiliation	other
Environment	urban

STUDENTS

Total undergrad enrollment	1,573
% male/female	38/62
% from out of state	42
% live on campus	69
% African American	12
% Asian	5
% Caucasian	61
% Hispanic	10
% international	6
# of countries represented	22

ACADEMICS

Academic Rating	**76**
Calendar	semester
Student/faculty ratio	16:1
Profs interesting rating	81
Profs accessible rating	79
% profs teaching UG courses	100
% classes taught by TAs	0

MOST POPULAR MAJORS
Business administration
Education
Nursing

SELECTIVITY

Admissions Rating	**74**
# of applicants	1,020
% of applicants accepted	74
% of acceptees attending	40

FRESHMAN PROFILE

Average SAT Verbal	572
Average SAT Math	570
Average ACT Composite	22.5
Minimum TOEFL	550

DEADLINES

Nonfall registration?	yes

FINANCIAL FACTS

Financial Aid Rating	**80**
Tuition	$17,790
Room and board	$5,830

Books and supplies	$950
Avg frosh grant	$7,216
Avg frosh loan	$2,752

NORTHERN MICHIGAN UNIVERSITY

CAMPUS LIFE

Quality of Life Rating	**76**
Type of school	public
Affiliation	none
Environment	suburban

STUDENTS

Total undergrad enrollment	7,288
% male/female	54/46
% from out of state	14
% live on campus	34
% in (# of) fraternities	1 (4)
% in (# of) sororities	2 (3)
% African American	1
% Caucasian	91
% Hispanic	1
% international	1

ACADEMICS

Academic Rating	**68**
Calendar	semester
Student/faculty ratio	20:1
Profs interesting rating	80
Profs accessible rating	77
Avg reg class size	20-29 students

MOST POPULAR MAJORS
Nursing
Education
Art & design

SELECTIVITY

Admissions Rating	**63**
# of applicants	4,467
% of applicants accepted	73
% of acceptees attending	44

FRESHMAN PROFILE

Average ACT Composite	24
Minimum TOEFL	500
Average HS GPA	3.03

DEADLINES

Nonfall registration?	yes

FINANCIAL FACTS

Financial Aid Rating	**79**
In-state tuition	$4,780
Out-of-state tuition	$7,732
Room and board	$5,630
Books and supplies	$600

Avg frosh grant $5,300
Avg frosh loan $2,625

NORTHWESTERN UNIVERSITY

CAMPUS LIFE
Quality of Life Rating   89
Type of school   private
Environment   suburban
STUDENTS
Total undergrad enrollment   7,946
% male/female   47/53
% from out of state   74
% from public high school   76
% live on campus   65
% in (# of) fraternities   30 (23)
% in (# of) sororities   40 (17)
% African American   7
% Asian   14
% Caucasian   67
% Hispanic   6
% international   5
# of countries represented   46

ACADEMICS
Academic Rating   98
Calendar   quarter
Student/faculty ratio   7:1
Profs interesting rating   92
Profs accessible rating   96
% profs teaching UG courses   100
% classes taught by TAs   2

MOST POPULAR MAJORS
Engineering
Economics
Journalism

SELECTIVITY
Admissions Rating   99
of applicants   14,283
% of applicants accepted   33
% of acceptees attending   43
# accepting a place on wait list   350
# of early decision applicants   960
% accepted early decision   53
FRESHMAN PROFILE
Range SAT Verbal   640-730
Average SAT Verbal   675
Range SAT Math   660-750
Average SAT Math   703
Range ACT Composite   28-33
Average ACT Composite   30
Minimum TOEFL   600

% graduated top 10% of class   82
% graduated top 25% of class   96
% graduated top 50% of class   99
DEADLINES
Early decision   11/1
Early decision notification   12/15
Regular admission   1/1
Regular notification   4/15
Nonfall registration?   yes

FINANCIAL FACTS
Financial Aid Rating   85
Tuition $28,404
Room and board $8,967
Books and supplies $1,326
Required fees $120
% frosh receiving aid   45
% undergrads receiving aid   44
Avg frosh grant $22,515
Avg frosh loan $2,660

NORTHWOOD UNIVERSITY

CAMPUS LIFE
Quality of Life Rating   75
Type of school   private
Affiliation   none
Environment   suburban
STUDENTS
Total undergrad enrollment   1,800
% male/female   51/49
% from out of state   30
% from public high school   85
% live on campus   55
% in (# of) fraternities   35 (5)
% in (# of) sororities   40 (5)
% African American   16
% Asian   8
% Caucasian   73
% Hispanic   39
% international   18
# of countries represented   64

ACADEMICS
Academic Rating   73
Calendar   3 terms
Student/faculty ratio   26:1
Profs interesting rating   84
Profs accessible rating   81
% profs teaching UG courses   100
% classes taught by TAs   0
Avg reg class size   20-25 students

Marketing
Management
Accounting

SELECTIVITY
Admissions Rating   75
# of applicants	2,615
% of applicants accepted	79
% of acceptees attending	40

FRESHMAN PROFILE
Range SAT Verbal	400-540
Average SAT Verbal	475
Range SAT Math	430-560
Average SAT Math	480
Range ACT Composite	18-23
Average ACT Composite	21
Minimum TOEFL	500
Average HS GPA	2.9
% graduated top 10% of class	8
% graduated top 25% of class	28
% graduated top 50% of class	60

DEADLINES
Nonfall registration?	yes

FINANCIAL FACTS
Financial Aid Rating   75
Tuition	$12,966
Room and board	$6,006
Books and supplies	$1,107
Avg frosh grant	$4,800
Avg frosh loan	$2,600

OAKLAND UNIVERSITY

CAMPUS LIFE
Quality of Life Rating   75
Type of school	public
Environment	suburban

STUDENTS
Total undergrad enrollment	12,634
% male/female	37/63
% from out of state	2
% from public high school	99
% live on campus	12
% in (# of) fraternities	3 (10)
% in (# of) sororities	2 (8)
% African American	8
% Asian	3
% Caucasian	74
% Hispanic	2
% international	1

ACADEMICS
Academic Rating   77
Calendar	semester
Student/faculty ratio	21:1
Profs interesting rating	81
Profs accessible rating	78
% profs teaching UG courses	99
% classes taught by TAs	1
Avg lab size	10-19 students
Avg reg class size	10-19 students

MOST POPULAR MAJORS
Psychology
Nursing/registered nurse training (RN, ASN, BSN, MSN)
Elementary education and teaching

SELECTIVITY
Admissions Rating   72
# of applicants	5,468
% of applicants accepted	77
% of acceptees attending	45

FRESHMAN PROFILE
Range ACT Composite	19-24
Average ACT Composite	21
Minimum TOEFL	550
Average HS GPA	3.1
% graduated top 25% of class	43
% graduated top 50% of class	87

DEADLINES
Nonfall registration?	yes

FINANCIAL FACTS
Financial Aid Rating   76
In-state tuition	$4,166
Out-of-state tuition	$11,340
Room and board	$4,978
Books and supplies	$560
Avg frosh grant	$3,010

OBERLIN COLLEGE

CAMPUS LIFE
Quality of Life Rating   73
Type of school	private
Environment	rural

STUDENTS
Total undergrad enrollment	2,848
% male/female	45/55
% from out of state	89
% from public high school	66
% live on campus	72
% African American	8

% Asian	6
% Caucasian	81
% Hispanic	4
% international	6

ACADEMICS
Academic Rating	**86**
Calendar	4-1-4
Student/faculty ratio	10:1
Profs interesting rating	94
Profs accessible rating	97
% profs teaching UG courses	100
Avg lab size	10-19 students
Avg reg class size	10-19 students

MOST POPULAR MAJORS
History
English language and literature
Biology/biological sciences

SELECTIVITY
Admissions Rating	**91**
# of applicants	5,934
% of applicants accepted	33
% of acceptees attending	38
# accepting a place on wait list	585
% admitted from wait list	19
# of early decision applicants	341
% accepted early decision	75

FRESHMAN PROFILE
Range SAT Verbal	630-740
Average SAT Verbal	691
Range SAT Math	610-710
Average SAT Math	659
Range ACT Composite	26-31
Average ACT Composite	30
Minimum TOEFL	600
Average HS GPA	3.5
% graduated top 10% of class	63
% graduated top 25% of class	93
% graduated top 50% of class	99

DEADLINES
Early decision	11/15
Early decision notification	12/20
Regular admission	1/15
Regular notification	4/1

FINANCIAL FACTS
Financial Aid Rating	**83**
Tuition	$27,880
Room and board	$6,830
Books and supplies	$734
Required fees	$170
% frosh receiving aid	56

% undergrads receiving aid	56
Avg frosh grant	$23,700
Avg frosh loan	$4,000

OHIO NORTHERN UNIVERSITY

CAMPUS LIFE
Quality of Life Rating	**80**
Type of school	private
Affiliation	Methodist
Environment	rural

STUDENTS
Total undergrad enrollment	2,281
% male/female	53/47
% from out of state	12
% live on campus	60
% in (# of) fraternities	25 (8)
% in (# of) sororities	22 (4)
% African American	2
% Asian	1
% Caucasian	96
% Hispanic	1
% international	1
# of countries represented	15

ACADEMICS
Academic Rating	**80**
Calendar	quarter
Student/faculty ratio	13:1
Profs interesting rating	92
Profs accessible rating	93
% profs teaching UG courses	100
Avg reg class size	10-19 students

MOST POPULAR MAJORS
Biology/biological sciences
Pharmacy (PharmD, BS/BPharm)
Industrial production technologies/technicians

SELECTIVITY
Admissions Rating	**78**
# of applicants	2,469
% of applicants accepted	89
% of acceptees attending	34

FRESHMAN PROFILE
Range SAT Verbal	510-610
Average SAT Verbal	560
Range SAT Math	530-650
Average SAT Math	590
Range ACT Composite	23-28
Average ACT Composite	25
Minimum TOEFL	550
Average HS GPA	3.6

% graduated top 10% of class	40
% graduated top 25% of class	69
% graduated top 50% of class	90

DEADLINES

Priority admission	12/1
Regular admission	8/15
Nonfall registration?	yes

FINANCIAL FACTS
Financial Aid Rating — **89**

Tuition	$24,935
Room and board	$6,030
Books and supplies	$900
Required fees	$210
% frosh receiving aid	86
% undergrads receiving aid	83

OHIO STATE UNIVERSITY— COLUMBUS

CAMPUS LIFE
Quality of Life Rating — **78**

Type of school	public
Environment	urban

STUDENTS

Total undergrad enrollment	36,855
% male/female	52/48
% from out of state	11
% from public high school	88
% live on campus	24
% in (# of) fraternities	5 (33)
% in (# of) sororities	6 (22)
% African American	9
% Asian	6
% Caucasian	81
% Hispanic	2
% international	4
# of countries represented	89

ACADEMICS
Academic Rating — **67**

Calendar	quarter
Student/faculty ratio	13:1
Avg lab size	20-29 students
Avg reg class size	10-19 students

MOST POPULAR MAJORS
English language and literature
Biology/biological sciences
Psychology

SELECTIVITY
Admissions Rating — **73**

% of acceptees attending	41
# accepting a place on wait list	120
% admitted from wait list	27

FRESHMAN PROFILE

Range SAT Verbal	520-630
Average SAT Verbal	575
Range SAT Math	540-660
Average SAT Math	594
Range ACT Composite	23-28
Average ACT Composite	25
Minimum TOEFL	527
Average HS GPA	4.0
% graduated top 10% of class	33
% graduated top 25% of class	66
% graduated top 50% of class	91

DEADLINES

Regular admission	2/15
Nonfall registration?	yes

FINANCIAL FACTS
Financial Aid Rating — **84**

In-state tuition	$4,788
Out-of-state tuition	$13,554
Room and board	$6,031
Books and supplies	$936
% frosh receiving aid	48
% undergrads receiving aid	45
Avg frosh grant	$3,410
Avg frosh loan	$2,702

OHIO UNIVERSITY—ATHENS

CAMPUS LIFE
Quality of Life Rating — **82**

Type of school	public
Environment	rural

STUDENTS

Total undergrad enrollment	17,343
% male/female	45/55
% from out of state	9
% from public high school	82
% live on campus	44
% in (# of) fraternities	12 (21)
% in (# of) sororities	14 (12)
% African American	3
% Asian	1
% Caucasian	95
% Hispanic	1
% international	2
# of countries represented	100

ACADEMICS
Academic Rating **72**

Calendar	quarter
Student/faculty ratio	20:1
Profs interesting rating	71
Profs accessible rating	92
% profs teaching UG courses	100
% classes taught by TAs	19
Avg lab size	10-19 students
Avg reg class size	10-19 students

SELECTIVITY
Admissions Rating **79**

# of applicants	13,195
% of applicants accepted	75
% of acceptees attending	37

FRESHMAN PROFILE
Range SAT Verbal	500-600
Average SAT Verbal	540
Range SAT Math	500-610
Average SAT Math	550
Range ACT Composite	21-26
Average ACT Composite	23
Minimum TOEFL	550
Average HS GPA	3.3
% graduated top 10% of class	18
% graduated top 25% of class	50
% graduated top 50% of class	90

DEADLINES
Regular admission	2/1
Nonfall registration?	yes

FINANCIAL FACTS
Financial Aid Rating **82**

In-state tuition	$6,336
Out-of-state tuition	$13,818
Room and board	$6,777
Books and supplies	$810
% frosh receiving aid	46
% undergrads receiving aid	45
Avg frosh grant	$3,853

OHIO WESLEYAN UNIVERSITY

CAMPUS LIFE
Quality of Life Rating **83**

Type of school	private
Affiliation	Methodist
Environment	suburban

STUDENTS
Total undergrad enrollment	1,935
% male/female	46/54
% from out of state	40
% from public high school	75
% live on campus	81
% in (# of) fraternities	44 (13)
% in (# of) sororities	34 (8)
% African American	5
% Asian	2
% Caucasian	79
% Hispanic	2
% international	11
# of countries represented	52

ACADEMICS
Academic Rating **88**

Calendar	semester
Student/faculty ratio	13:1
% profs teaching UG courses	100
Avg lab size	10-19 students
Avg reg class size	10-19 students

MOST POPULAR MAJORS
Business/managerial economics
Zoology/animal biology
Psychology

SELECTIVITY
Admissions Rating **80**

# of applicants	2,212
% of applicants accepted	80
% of acceptees attending	31
# accepting a place on wait list	6
% admitted from wait list	100
# of early decision applicants	29
% accepted early decision	86

FRESHMAN PROFILE
Range SAT Verbal	540-650
Average SAT Verbal	602
Range SAT Math	540-650
Average SAT Math	608
Range ACT Composite	23-28
Average ACT Composite	27
Minimum TOEFL	550
Average HS GPA	3.3
% graduated top 10% of class	26
% graduated top 25% of class	50
% graduated top 50% of class	76

DEADLINES
Early decision	12/1
Early decision notification	12/30
Priority admission	3/1
Nonfall registration?	yes

FINANCIAL FACTS
Financial Aid Rating **86**

Tuition	$25,080
Room and board	$7,110
Books and supplies	$800
Required fees	$360
% frosh receiving aid	60
% undergrads receiving aid	55
Avg frosh grant	$12,861
Avg frosh loan	$3,586

PITTSBURG STATE UNIVERSITY

CAMPUS LIFE
Quality of Life Rating	**77**
Type of school	public
Affiliation	none
Environment	suburban

STUDENTS
Total undergrad enrollment	6,753
% male/female	51/49
% from public high school	85
% live on campus	15
% African American	2
% Caucasian	75
% Hispanic	2
% international	6

ACADEMICS
Academic Rating	**68**
Calendar	semester
Student/faculty ratio	19:1
Profs interesting rating	82
Profs accessible rating	77
% profs teaching UG courses	100
% classes taught by TAs	10

MOST POPULAR MAJORS
Biology
Engineering technology

SELECTIVITY
Admissions Rating	**64**

FRESHMAN PROFILE
Average ACT Composite	21
Minimum TOEFL	520
% graduated top 25% of class	38
% graduated top 50% of class	75

DEADLINES
Nonfall registration?	yes

FINANCIAL FACTS
Financial Aid Rating	**69**
In-state tuition	$2,338
Out-of-state tuition	$7,192

Room and board	$3,890
Books and supplies	$300
Avg frosh grant	$750

PURDUE UNIVERSITY—WEST LAFAYETTE

CAMPUS LIFE
Quality of Life Rating	**79**
Type of school	public
Environment	suburban

STUDENTS
Total undergrad enrollment	30,908
% male/female	58/42
% from out of state	24
% in (# of) fraternities	18 (46)
% in (# of) sororities	17 (25)
% African American	3
% Asian	4
% Caucasian	82
% Hispanic	2
% international	6
# of countries represented	120

ACADEMICS
Academic Rating	**68**
Calendar	semester
Student/faculty ratio	16:1
Profs interesting rating	91
Profs accessible rating	92
Avg lab size	20-29 students
Avg reg class size	20-29 students

SELECTIVITY
Admissions Rating	**76**
# of applicants	22,872
% of applicants accepted	76
% of acceptees attending	36

FRESHMAN PROFILE
Range SAT Verbal	500-610
Average SAT Verbal	555
Range SAT Math	530-660
Average SAT Math	595
Range ACT Composite	23-28
Average ACT Composite	26
Minimum TOEFL	550
% graduated top 10% of class	28
% graduated top 25% of class	62
% graduated top 50% of class	93

DEADLINES
Priority admission	3/1
Nonfall registration?	yes

FINANCIAL FACTS
Financial Aid Rating **83**
In-state tuition $5,580
Out-of-state tuition $16,260
Room and board $6,340
Books and supplies $830
% frosh receiving aid 38
% undergrads receiving aid 36

RIPON COLLEGE

CAMPUS LIFE
Quality of Life Rating **79**
Type of school **private**
Environment rural
STUDENTS
Total undergrad enrollment 987
% male/female 47/53
% from out of state 32
% from public high school 75
% live on campus 90
% in (# of) fraternities 49 (5)
% in (# of) sororities 27 (3)
% African American 2
% Asian 1
% Caucasian 89
% Hispanic 4
% international 2

ACADEMICS
Academic Rating **83**
Calendar semester
Student/faculty ratio 14:1
% profs teaching UG courses 100
Avg lab size 10-19 students
Avg reg class size 10-19 students

MOST POPULAR MAJORS
Business administration/management
Education
Biology/biological sciences

SELECTIVITY
Admissions Rating **80**
# of applicants 934
% of applicants accepted 84
% of acceptees attending 32
FRESHMAN PROFILE
Range SAT Verbal 570-640
Average SAT Verbal 599
Range SAT Math 540-670
Average SAT Math 602

Range ACT Composite 22-26
Average ACT Composite 24
Minimum TOEFL 550
Average HS GPA 3.3
% graduated top 10% of class 26
% graduated top 25% of class 53
% graduated top 50% of class 85
DEADLINES
Priority admission 3/15
Nonfall registration? yes

FINANCIAL FACTS
Financial Aid Rating **89**
Tuition $19,700
Room and board $5,055
Books and supplies $500
Required fees $240
% frosh receiving aid 77
% undergrads receiving aid 76
Avg frosh grant $11,125
Avg frosh loan $2,751

ROSE-HULMAN INSTITUTE OF TECHNOLOGY

CAMPUS LIFE
Quality of Life Rating **79**
Type of school private
Environment suburban
STUDENTS
Total undergrad enrollment 1,800
% male/female 82/18
% from out of state 51
% from public high school 87
% live on campus 54
% in (# of) fraternities 47 (8)
% in (# of) sororities 46 (2)
% African American 2
% Asian 3
% Caucasian 94
% Hispanic 1
% international 1
# of countries represented 12

ACADEMICS
Academic Rating **89**
Calendar quarter
Student/faculty ratio 13:1
Profs interesting rating 80
Profs accessible rating 74
% profs teaching UG courses 100

Avg lab size	20-29 students
Avg reg class size	20-29 students

MOST POPULAR MAJORS
Electrical, electronics, and
communications engineering
Mechanical engineering
Chemical engineering

SELECTIVITY
Admissions Rating	**92**
# of applicants	3,207
% of applicants accepted	65
% of acceptees attending	22

FRESHMAN PROFILE
Range SAT Verbal	570-670
Average SAT Verbal	620
Range SAT Math	640-720
Average SAT Math	680
Range ACT Composite	27-31
Average ACT Composite	29
Minimum TOEFL	550
% graduated top 10% of class	73
% graduated top 25% of class	96
% graduated top 50% of class	100

DEADLINES
Priority admission	12/1
Regular admission	3/1

FINANCIAL FACTS
Financial Aid Rating	**84**
Tuition	$24,255
Room and board	$6,720
Books and supplies	$900
Required fees	$435
% frosh receiving aid	77
% undergrads receiving aid	73
Avg frosh grant	$5,649
Avg frosh loan	$5,000

SAINT LOUIS UNIVERSITY

CAMPUS LIFE
Quality of Life Rating	**80**
Type of school	private
Affiliation	Roman Catholic
Environment	urban

STUDENTS
Total undergrad enrollment	7,178
% male/female	46/54
% from out of state	47
% live on campus	51
% in (# of) fraternities	16 (11)
% in (# of) sororities	17 (4)
% African American	7
% Asian	4
% Caucasian	71
% Hispanic	3
% international	3
# of countries represented	80

ACADEMICS
Academic Rating	**79**
Calendar	semester
Student/faculty ratio	12:1
Profs interesting rating	73
Profs accessible rating	72
Avg lab size	20-29 students
Avg reg class size	10-19 students

MOST POPULAR MAJORS
Business
Biology/biological sciences
Psychology

SELECTIVITY
Admissions Rating	**77**
# of applicants	5,992
% of applicants accepted	72
% of acceptees attending	33

FRESHMAN PROFILE
Range SAT Verbal	530-640
Average SAT Verbal	585
Range SAT Math	530-655
Average SAT Math	595
Range ACT Composite	23-28
Average ACT Composite	26
Minimum TOEFL	525
Average HS GPA	3.5
% graduated top 10% of class	32
% graduated top 25% of class	61
% graduated top 50% of class	88

DEADLINES
Priority admission	12/1
Regular admission	8/1
Nonfall registration?	yes

FINANCIAL FACTS
Financial Aid Rating	**92**
Tuition	$20,840
Room and board	$7,310
Books and supplies	$1,040
Required fees	$168
% frosh receiving aid	73
% undergrads receiving aid	67
Avg frosh grant	$13,575
Avg frosh loan	$6,797

SAINT MARY'S COLLEGE

CAMPUS LIFE
Quality of Life Rating   **77**

Type of school	private
Affiliation	Roman Catholic
Environment	suburban

STUDENTS

Total undergrad enrollment	1,409
% from out of state	73
% from public high school	52
% live on campus	78
% African American	1
% Asian	1
% Caucasian	91
% Hispanic	5
% international	1
# of countries represented	13

ACADEMICS
Academic Rating   **79**

Calendar	semester
Student/faculty ratio	12:1
Profs interesting rating	79
Profs accessible rating	77
% profs teaching UG courses	100
% classes taught by TAs	0
Avg lab size	10-19 students
Avg reg class size	20-29 students

MOST POPULAR MAJORS
Elementary education
Business administration
Communication

SELECTIVITY
Admissions Rating   **76**

# of applicants	1,041
% of applicants accepted	83
% of acceptees attending	49
# of early decision applicants	165
% accepted early decision	83

FRESHMAN PROFILE

Range SAT Verbal	530-620
Average SAT Verbal	571
Range SAT Math	520-610
Average SAT Math	562
Range ACT Composite	23-27
Average ACT Composite	25
Minimum TOEFL	550
Average HS GPA	3.6
% graduated top 10% of class	31
% graduated top 25% of class	68
% graduated top 50% of class	96

DEADLINES

Early decision	11/15
Regular admission	3/1
Regular notification	rolling
Nonfall registration?	yes

FINANCIAL FACTS
Financial Aid Rating   **73**

Tuition	$16,994
Room and board	$5,962
Books and supplies	$800
Avg frosh grant	$7,530
Avg frosh loan	$3,351

SAINT MARY'S UNIVERSITY OF MINNESOTA

CAMPUS LIFE
Quality of Life Rating   **73**

Type of school	private
Affiliation	Roman Catholic
Environment	rural

STUDENTS

Total undergrad enrollment	1,654
% male/female	47/53
% from out of state	31
% from public high school	60
% live on campus	66
% in (# of) fraternities	0
% in (# of) sororities	0
% African American	2
% Asian	1
% Caucasian	79
% Hispanic	2
% international	2
# of countries represented	21

ACADEMICS
Academic Rating   **75**

Calendar	semester
Student/faculty ratio	12:1
Profs interesting rating	81
Profs accessible rating	79
% profs teaching UG courses	100
% classes taught by TAs	0
Avg lab size	10-19 students
Avg regular class size	10-19 students

Marketing/marketing management
Biology/biological sciences
Early childhood education and teaching

SELECTIVITY
Admissions Rating 70
# of applicants	1,122
% of applicants accepted	79
% of acceptees attending	35

FRESHMAN PROFILE
Range ACT Composite	19-25
Average ACT Composite	23
Minimum TOEFL	520
Average HS GPA	3.1
% graduated top 10% of class	17
% graduated top 25% of class	42
% graduated top 50% of class	74

DEADLINES
Regular admission	5/1
Nonfall registration?	yes

FINANCIAL FACTS
Financial Aid Rating 74
Tuition	$15,280
Room and board	$4,920
Books and supplies	$800
Avg frosh grant	$6,095
Avg frosh loan	$5,380

ST. NORBERT COLLEGE

CAMPUS LIFE
Quality of Life Rating 79
Type of school	private
Affiliation	Roman Catholic
Environment	suburban

STUDENTS
Total undergrad enrollment	2,059
% male/female	42/58
% from out of state	28
% from public high school	80
% live on campus	75
% in (# of) fraternities	25 (6)
% in (# of) sororities	25 (5)
% African American	1
% Asian	2
% Caucasian	93
% Hispanic	1
% international	3
# of countries represented	27

ACADEMICS
Academic Rating 84
Calendar	semester
Student/faculty ratio	14:1
Profs interesting rating	76
Profs accessible rating	73
% profs teaching UG courses	100
% classes taught by TAs	0
Avg lab size	10-19 students
Avg reg class size	10-19 students

MOST POPULAR MAJORS
Elementary education
Communications studies
Business administration

SELECTIVITY
Admissions Rating 82
# of applicants	1,603
% of applicants accepted	84
% of acceptees attending	41
# of early decision applicants	58
% accepted early decision	88

FRESHMAN PROFILE
Range ACT Composite	22-26
Average ACT Composite	24
Minimum TOEFL	550
Average HS GPA	3.3
% graduated top 10% of class	31
% graduated top 25% of class	56
% graduated top 50% of class	90

DEADLINES
Early decision	12/1
Regular notification	9/15
Nonfall registration?	yes

FINANCIAL FACTS
Financial Aid Rating 74
Tuition	$19,034
Room and board	$5,472
Books and supplies	$430
Avg frosh grant	$8,847
Avg frosh loan	$3,090

ST. OLAF COLLEGE

CAMPUS LIFE
Quality of Life Rating 88
Type of school	private
Affiliation	Lutheran
Environment	rural

STUDENTS
Total undergrad enrollment	3,041

% male/female	41/59
% from out of state	46
% from public high school	85
% live on campus	96
% African American	1
% Asian	4
% Caucasian	89
% Hispanic	1
% international	1
# of countries represented	28

ACADEMICS

Academic Rating	**92**
Calendar	4-1-4
Student/faculty ratio	13:1
Profs interesting rating	97
Profs accessible rating	98
% profs teaching UG courses	100
Avg lab size	10-19 students
Avg reg class size	20-29 students

MOST POPULAR MAJORS
Economics
Biology/biological sciences
English language and literature

SELECTIVITY

Admissions Rating	**86**
# of applicants	2,624
% of applicants accepted	73
% of acceptees attending	41
# accepting a place on wait list	56
% admitted from wait list	18
# of early decision applicants	125
% accepted early decision	88

FRESHMAN PROFILE

Range SAT Verbal	590-690
Average SAT Verbal	639
Range SAT Math	580-690
Average SAT Math	635
Range ACT Composite	25-30
Average ACT Composite	27
Minimum TOEFL	550
Average HS GPA	3.6
% graduated top 10% of class	50
% graduated top 25% of class	79
% graduated top 50% of class	97

DEADLINES

Early decision	11/15
Early decision notification	12/15
Priority admission	2/1
Nonfall registration?	yes

FINANCIAL FACTS

Financial Aid Rating	**89**
Tuition	$23,650
Room and board	$4,850
Books and supplies	$850
Required fees	$0
Avg frosh grant	$12,210
Avg frosh loan	$3,680

SOUTHERN ILLINOIS UNIVERSITY—CARBONDALE

CAMPUS LIFE

Quality of Life Rating	**76**
Type of school	public
Affiliation	none
Environment	suburban

STUDENTS

Total undergrad enrollment	16,863
% male/female	56/44
% from out of state	17
% from public high school	80
% live on campus	24
% in (# of) fraternities	3 (14)
% in (# of) sororities	2 (10)
% African American	14
% Asian	2
% Caucasian	76
% Hispanic	3
% international	4
# of countries represented	103

ACADEMICS

Academic Rating	**72**
Calendar	semester
Student/faculty ratio	18:1
Profs interesting rating	84
Profs accessible rating	79
% classes taught by TAs	17
Avg lab size	20-29 students
Avg reg class size	20-29 students

MOST POPULAR MAJORS
Health professions and related sciences
Engineering
Education

SELECTIVITY

Admissions Rating	**68**
# of applicants	7,832
% of applicants accepted	76
% of acceptees attending	40

FRESHMAN PROFILE

Range ACT Composite	20-24
Average ACT Composite	22
Minimum TOEFL	520
% graduated top 10% of class	10
% graduated top 25% of class	30
% graduated top 50% of class	60

DEADLINES

Nonfall registration?	yes

FINANCIAL FACTS

Financial Aid Rating	**74**
In-state tuition	$5,521
Out-of-state tuition	$9,766
Room and board	$4,903
Books and supplies	$660
Avg frosh grant	$6,990

SOUTHWEST MISSOURI STATE UNIVERSITY

CAMPUS LIFE

Quality of Life Rating	**75**
Type of school	public
Affiliation	none
Environment	urban

STUDENTS

Total undergrad enrollment	14,699
% male/female	45/55
% from out of state	8
% from public high school	93
% live on campus	26
% in (# of) fraternities	12 (14)
% in (# of) sororities	9 (10)
% African American	3
% Asian	1
% Caucasian	87
% Hispanic	1
% international	2

ACADEMICS

Academic Rating	**72**
Calendar	semester
Student/faculty ratio	18:1
Profs interesting rating	81
Profs accessible rating	77
% profs teaching UG courses	98
% classes taught by TAs	5
Avg lab size	20-29 students
Avg reg class size	under 10 students

MOST POPULAR MAJORS

Elementary education
Psychology
Accounting

SELECTIVITY

Admissions Rating	**67**
# of applicants	5,828
% of applicants accepted	87
% of acceptees attending	51

FRESHMAN PROFILE

Range ACT Composite	21-26
Average ACT Composite	23
Minimum TOEFL	500
Average HS GPA	3.4
% graduated top 10% of class	20
% graduated top 25% of class	48
% graduated top 50% of class	81

DEADLINES

Regular admission	8/1
Nonfall registration?	yes

FINANCIAL FACTS

Financial Aid Rating	**74**
In-state tuition	$3,330
Out-of-state tuition	$6,660
Room and board	$4,032
Books and supplies	$800

STEPHENS COLLEGE

CAMPUS LIFE

Quality of Life Rating	**79**
Type of school	private
Environment	suburban

STUDENTS

Total undergrad enrollment	596
% male/female	5/95
% from out of state	57
% from public high school	75
% live on campus	70
% in (# of) sororities	8 (2)
% African American	9
% Asian	1
% Caucasian	84
% Hispanic	4
# of countries represented	5

ACADEMICS

Academic Rating	**70**
Calendar	semester
Student/faculty ratio	10:1
% profs teaching UG courses	100

Avg lab size	under 10 students
Avg reg class size	under 10 students

MOST POPULAR MAJORS
Fashion/apparel design
Drama and dramatics/theatre arts
Education

SELECTIVITY

Admissions Rating	**73**
# of applicants	335
% of applicants accepted	83
% of acceptees attending	44

FRESHMAN PROFILE

Range SAT Verbal	510-630
Average SAT Verbal	566
Range SAT Math	480-580
Average SAT Math	513
Range ACT Composite	21-26
Average ACT Composite	24
Minimum TOEFL	550
Average HS GPA	3.5
% graduated top 10% of class	43
% graduated top 25% of class	67
% graduated top 50% of class	88

DEADLINES

Regular notification	rolling
Nonfall registration?	yes

FINANCIAL FACTS

Financial Aid Rating	**91**
Tuition	$17,360
Room and board	$6,900
Books and supplies	$750
% frosh receiving aid	73
% undergrads receiving aid	65
Avg frosh grant	$10,600
Avg frosh loan	$2,000

STERLING COLLEGE

CAMPUS LIFE

Quality of Life Rating	**78**
Type of school	private
Affiliation	Presbyterian
Environment	rural

STUDENTS

Total undergrad enrollment	466
% male/female	47/53
% from out of state	39

% from public high school	80
% live on campus	78
% African American	6
% Asian	1
% Caucasian	84
% Hispanic	4
% Native American	2
% international	3

ACADEMICS

Academic Rating	**71**
Calendar	4-1-4
Student/faculty ratio	12:1
% profs teaching UG courses	100
% classes taught by TAs	0
Avg lab size	10-19 students
Avg regular class size	10-19 students

MOST POPULAR MAJORS
Elementary education
Biology
Business administration

SELECTIVITY

Admissions Rating	**66**
# of applicants	359
% of applicants accepted	57
% of acceptees attending	48

FRESHMAN PROFILE

Range SAT Verbal	480-610
Average SAT Verbal	560
Range SAT Math	400-580
Average SAT Math	530
Range ACT Composite	19-26
Average ACT Composite	23
Minimum TOEFL	520
Average HS GPA	3.34
% graduated top 10% of class	28
% graduated top 25% of class	41
% graduated top 50% of class	71

DEADLINES

Nonfall registration?	yes

FINANCIAL FACTS

Financial Aid Rating	**75**
Tuition	$12,750
Room and board	$5,090-$5,388
Books and supplies	$550
Avg frosh grant	$6,000
Avg frosh loan	$2,625

TAYLOR UNIVERSITY

CAMPUS LIFE
Quality of Life Rating **78**

Type of school	private
Affiliation	none
Environment	rural

STUDENTS
Total undergrad enrollment	1,861
% male/female	48/52
% from out of state	69
% from public high school	79
% live on campus	83
% African American	1
% Asian	2
% Caucasian	93
% Hispanic	2
% international	1
# of countries represented	17

ACADEMICS
Academic Rating **88**

Calendar	4-1-4
Student/faculty ratio	15:1
Profs interesting rating	78
Profs accessible rating	77
% profs teaching UG courses	100
% classes taught by TAs	0

MOST POPULAR MAJORS
Business/managerial operations
Bible/biblical studies
Elementary education and teaching

SELECTIVITY
Admissions Rating **84**

# of applicants	1,390
% of applicants accepted	78
% of acceptees attending	46
# accepting a place on wait list	262
% admitted from wait list	24

FRESHMAN PROFILE
Range SAT Verbal	461-678
Average SAT Verbal	594
Range SAT Math	470-677
Average SAT Math	597
Range ACT Composite	22-28
Average ACT Composite	26
Minimum TOEFL	550
Average HS GPA	3.7
% graduated top 10% of class	43
% graduated top 25% of class	70
% graduated top 50% of class	93

DEADLINES
Nonfall registration?	yes

FINANCIAL FACTS
Financial Aid Rating **73**

Tuition	$16,350
Room and board	$4,990
Books and supplies	$600
Avg frosh grant	$7,200
Avg frosh loan	$3,300

TRUMAN STATE UNIVERSITY

CAMPUS LIFE
Quality of Life Rating **87**

Type of school	public
Environment	rural

STUDENTS
Total undergrad enrollment	5,636
% male/female	41/59
% from out of state	24
% from public high school	78
% live on campus	48
% in (# of) fraternities	30 (19)
% in (# of) sororities	21 (11)
% African American	4
% Asian	2
% Caucasian	90
% Hispanic	2
% international	4
# of countries represented	49

ACADEMICS
Academic Rating **86**

Calendar	semester
Student/faculty ratio	15:1
% profs teaching UG courses	97
% classes taught by TAs	4
Avg lab size	20-29 students
Avg reg class size	20-29 students

MOST POPULAR MAJORS
Business administration/management
English language and literature
Biology/biological sciences

SELECTIVITY
Admissions Rating **82**

# of applicants	5,132
% of applicants accepted	79
% of acceptees attending	36

FRESHMAN PROFILE
Range SAT Verbal	560-680
Average SAT Verbal	614

Range SAT Math	550-660
Average SAT Math	606
Range ACT Composite	25-30
Average ACT Composite	27
Minimum TOEFL	550
Average HS GPA	3.8
% graduated top 10% of class	47
% graduated top 25% of class	82
% graduated top 50% of class	98

DEADLINES

Priority admission	11/15
Regular admission	3/1
Nonfall registration?	yes

FINANCIAL FACTS
Financial Aid Rating 86

In-state tuition	$4,600
Out-of-state tuition	$8,400
Room and board	$5,072
Books and supplies	$600
Required fees	$56
% frosh receiving aid	26
% undergrads receiving aid	36
Avg frosh grant	$4,103
Avg frosh loan	$3,462

UNIVERSITY OF AKRON

CAMPUS LIFE
Quality of Life Rating 78

Type of school	public
Affiliation	none
Environment	urban

STUDENTS

Total undergrad enrollment	20,180
% male/female	48/52
% from out of state	1
% live on campus	10
% African American	14
% Asian	1
% Caucasian	78
% Hispanic	1
% international	1

ACADEMICS
Academic Rating 73

Calendar	semester
Student/faculty ratio	15:1
Profs interesting rating	84
Profs accessible rating	80
% profs teaching UG courses	97
Avg lab size	10-19 students
Avg regular class size	20-29 students

MOST POPULAR MAJORS
Lberal arts and sciences
General studies and humanities
Business administration/management

SELECTIVITY
Admissions Rating 60

# of applicants	7,057
% of applicants accepted	85
% of acceptees attending	60

FRESHMAN PROFILE

Range SAT Verbal	430-570
Average SAT Verbal	477
Range SAT Math	430-570
Average SAT Math	471
Range ACT Composite	17-23
Average ACT Composite	20
Minimum TOEFL	500
Average HS GPA	2.88
% graduated top 10% of class	12
% graduated top 25% of class	29
% graduated top 50% of class	58

DEADLINES

Regular admission	rolling
Regular notification	rolling
Nonfall registration?	yes

FINANCIAL FACTS
Financial Aid Rating 73

In-state tuition	$4,350
Out-of-state tuition	$10,552
Room and board	$5,600
Books and supplies	$704
Avg frosh grant	$2,500

UNIVERSITY OF CHICAGO

CAMPUS LIFE
Quality of Life Rating 73

Type of school	private
Environment	urban

STUDENTS

Total undergrad enrollment	4,236
% male/female	50/50
% from out of state	78
% from public high school	70
% live on campus	66
% in (# of) fraternities	12 (9)
% in (# of) sororities	5 (2)
% African American	4
% Asian	16

% Caucasian	71
% Hispanic	8
% international	8
# of countries represented	34

ACADEMICS
Academic Rating **94**

Calendar	quarter
Student/faculty ratio	4:1
Profs interesting rating	91
Profs accessible rating	92
% profs teaching UG courses	90

SELECTIVITY
Admissions Rating **96**

# of applicants	8,139
% of applicants accepted	42
% of acceptees attending	33
# accepting a place on wait list	754
% admitted from wait list	10

FRESHMAN PROFILE
Range SAT Verbal	660-750
Range SAT Math	650-750
Range ACT Composite	28-32
Minimum TOEFL	600
% graduated top 10% of class	79
% graduated top 25% of class	94
% graduated top 50% of class	100

DEADLINES
Regular admission	1/1
Regular notification	4/1

FINANCIAL FACTS
Financial Aid Rating **85**

Tuition	$27,324
Room and board	$8,728
Books and supplies	$1,061
Required fees	$501
% frosh receiving aid	58
% undergrads receiving aid	56
Avg frosh grant	$20,616
Avg frosh loan	$4,000

UNIVERSITY OF DAYTON

CAMPUS LIFE
Quality of Life Rating **87**

Type of school	private
Affiliation	Roman Catholic
Environment	suburban

STUDENTS
Total undergrad enrollment	7,085
% male/female	50/50
% from out of state	33
% from public high school	51
% live on campus	95
% in (# of) fraternities	15 (14)
% in (# of) sororities	18 (10)
% African American	4
% Asian	1
% Caucasian	88
% Hispanic	2
% international	1
# of countries represented	46

ACADEMICS
Academic Rating **80**

Calendar	semester
Student/faculty ratio	15:1
% profs teaching UG courses	97
Avg lab size	10-19 students
Avg reg class size	20-29 students

MOST POPULAR MAJORS
Business/marketing
Engineering
Education

SELECTIVITY
Admissions Rating **78**

# of applicants	7,496
% of applicants accepted	84
% of acceptees attending	26
# accepting a place on wait list	37
% admitted from wait list	100

FRESHMAN PROFILE
Range SAT Verbal	500-610
Average SAT Verbal	557
Range SAT Math	510-630
Average SAT Math	575
Range ACT Composite	22-27
Average ACT Composite	24
Minimum TOEFL	550
% graduated top 10% of class	18
% graduated top 25% of class	41
% graduated top 50% of class	75

DEADLINES
Priority admission	1/1
Nonfall registration?	yes

FINANCIAL FACTS
Financial Aid Rating **82**

Tuition	$18,390
Room and board	$5,890
Required fees	$570
Avg frosh grant	$6,406
Avg frosh loan	$4,263

University of Evansville

CAMPUS LIFE
Quality of Life Rating	**83**
Type of school	private
Affiliation	Methodist
Environment	urban

STUDENTS
Total undergrad enrollment	2,624
% male/female	40/60
% from out of state	44
% live on campus	60
% in (# of) fraternities	24 (6)
% in (# of) sororities	23 (4)
% African American	2
% Asian	1
% Caucasian	88
% Hispanic	1
% international	8
# of countries represented	48

ACADEMICS
Academic Rating	**76**
Calendar	semester
Student/faculty ratio	13:1
Profs interesting rating	78
Profs accessible rating	75
% profs teaching UG courses	100
% classes taught by TAs	0
Avg lab size	10-19 students
Avg reg class size	10-19 students

MOST POPULAR MAJORS
Engineering
Business

SELECTIVITY
Admissions Rating	**70**
# of applicants	1,722
% of applicants accepted	91
% of acceptees attending	36

FRESHMAN PROFILE
Average SAT Verbal	573
Average SAT Math	574
Average ACT Composite	26
Minimum TOEFL	500
Average HS GPA	3.5
% graduated top 10% of class	28
% graduated top 25% of class	61
% graduated top 50% of class	90

DEADLINES
Regular admission	2/1
Regular notification	2/15
Nonfall registration?	yes

FINANCIAL FACTS
Financial Aid Rating	**78**
Tuition	$15,850
Room and board	$5,220
Books and supplies	$700
Avg frosh grant	$9,421
Avg frosh loan	$3,375

University of Illinois—Chicago

CAMPUS LIFE
Quality of Life Rating	**85**
Type of school	public
Affiliation	none
Environment	urban

STUDENTS
Total undergrad enrollment	15,887
% male/female	45/55
% from out of state	2
% from public high school	79
% live on campus	12
% in (# of) fraternities	3 (11)
% in (# of) sororities	3 (13)
% African American	10
% Asian	24
% Caucasian	44
% Hispanic	17
% international	2
# of countries represented	87

ACADEMICS
Academic Rating	**80**
Calendar	semester
Student/faculty ratio	14:1
Profs interesting rating	86
Profs accessible rating	83
% profs teaching UG courses	82
% classes taught by TAs	14
Avg lab size	20-29 students
Avg reg class size	20-29 students

MOST POPULAR MAJORS
Psychology
Biology/biological sciences
Information science/studies

SELECTIVITY
Admissions Rating	**76**
# of applicants	9,512
% of applicants accepted	64
% of acceptees attending	45

FRESHMAN PROFILE
Range ACT Composite	21-26

Average ACT Composite	23
Minimum TOEFL	520
% graduated top 10% of class	24
% graduated top 25% of class	60
% graduated top 50% of class	93

DEADLINES

Regular admission	5/1
Nonfall registration?	yes

FINANCIAL FACTS
Financial Aid Rating 79

In-state tuition	$3,330
Out-of-state tuition	$9,990
Room and board	$6,206
Books and supplies	$850
Avg frosh grant	$9,000
Avg frosh loan	$2,600

UNIVERSITY OF ILLINOIS—URBANA CHAMPAIGN

CAMPUS LIFE
Quality of Life Rating 75

Type of school	public
Environment	urban

STUDENTS

Total undergrad enrollment	28,750
% male/female	52/48
% from out of state	7
% live on campus	30
% in (# of) fraternities	17 (55)
% in (# of) sororities	22 (30)
% African American	7
% Asian	14
% Caucasian	72
% Hispanic	6
% international	2
# of countries represented	51

ACADEMICS
Academic Rating 82

Calendar	semester
Student/faculty ratio	15:1
Profs interesting rating	90
Profs accessible rating	90
% profs teaching UG courses	89
Avg lab size	20-29 students
Avg reg class size	20-29 students

MOST POPULAR MAJORS
Biology/biological sciences
Psychology

SELECTIVITY
Admissions Rating 85

# of applicants	19,930
% of applicants accepted	62
% of acceptees attending	51

FRESHMAN PROFILE

Range SAT Verbal	550-670
Average SAT Verbal	613
Range SAT Math	600-720
Average SAT Math	660
Range ACT Composite	25-30
Average ACT Composite	27
Minimum TOEFL	550
% graduated top 10% of class	55
% graduated top 25% of class	86
% graduated top 50% of class	99

DEADLINES

Regular admission	1/1
Nonfall registration?	yes

FINANCIAL FACTS
Financial Aid Rating 80

In-state tuition	$5,226
Out-of-state tuition	$13,046
Room and board	$6,090
Books and supplies	$740
Required fees	$1,304
% frosh receiving aid	40
% undergrads receiving aid	38

UNIVERSITY OF INDIANAPOLIS

CAMPUS LIFE
Quality of Life Rating 79

Type of school	private
Affiliation	Methodist
Environment	suburban

STUDENTS

Total undergrad enrollment	2,854
% male/female	34/66
% from out of state	8
% live on campus	50
% African American	8
% Asian	1
% Caucasian	78
% Hispanic	1
% international	5
# of countries represented	60

ACADEMICS
Academic Rating 75

Calendar	other
Student/faculty ratio	14:1
Profs interesting rating	81
Profs accessible rating	77
% profs teaching UG courses	100
% classes taught by TAs	0
Avg lab size	under 10 students
Avg reg class size	under 10 students

MOST POPULAR MAJORS
Nursing/registered nurse training (RN, ASN, BSN, MSN)
Education
Business administration/management

SELECTIVITY
Admissions Rating	**67**
# of applicants	2,289
% of applicants accepted	80
% of acceptees attending	31

FRESHMAN PROFILE
Range SAT Verbal	450-560
Range SAT Math	450-580
Range ACT Composite	18-25
Minimum TOEFL	500
Average HS GPA	3.0
% graduated top 10% of class	22
% graduated top 25% of class	50
% graduated top 50% of class	79

DEADLINES
Nonfall registration?	yes

FINANCIAL FACTS
Financial Aid Rating	**78**
Tuition	$15,820
Room and board	$5,660
Books and supplies	$600
Avg frosh grant	$12,112

UNIVERSITY OF IOWA

CAMPUS LIFE
Quality of Life Rating	**85**
Type of school	public
Environment	suburban

STUDENTS
Total undergrad enrollment	20,487
% male/female	45/55
% from out of state	33
% from public high school	89
% live on campus	28
% in (# of) fraternities	12 (23)
% in (# of) sororities	13 (17)

% African American	2
% Asian	3
% Caucasian	88
% Hispanic	2
% international	1
# of countries represented	122

ACADEMICS
Academic Rating	**77**
Calendar	semester
Student/faculty ratio	15:1
% profs teaching UG courses	100
Avg lab size	20-29 students
Avg reg class size	10-19 students

MOST POPULAR MAJORS
Business administration/management
Communications studies/speech communication and rhetoric
Psychology

SELECTIVITY
Admissions Rating	**80**
# of applicants	13,079
% of applicants accepted	84
% of acceptees attending	38

FRESHMAN PROFILE
Range SAT Verbal	520-650
Range SAT Math	540-670
Range ACT Composite	22-27
Minimum TOEFL	530
Average HS GPA	3.5
% graduated top 10% of class	21
% graduated top 25% of class	50
% graduated top 50% of class	89

DEADLINES
Regular admission	4/1
Nonfall registration?	yes
Priority Application	2/1

FINANCIAL FACTS
Financial Aid Rating	**82**
In-state tuition	$4,342
Out-of-state tuition	$14,634
Room and board	$5,930
Books and supplies	$840
Required fees	$651
% frosh receiving aid	38
% undergrads receiving aid	42
Avg frosh grant	$1,650
Avg frosh loan	$2,250

UNIVERSITY OF KANSAS

CAMPUS LIFE
Quality of Life Rating **83**
Type of school | public
Environment | urban

STUDENTS
Total undergrad enrollment | 20,605
% male/female | 48/52
% from out of state | 33
% live on campus | 18
% in (# of) fraternities | 15 (25)
% in (# of) sororities | 18 (18)
% African American | 3
% Asian | 4
% Caucasian | 83
% Hispanic | 3
% international | 7
# of countries represented | 118

ACADEMICS
Academic Rating **75**
Calendar | semester
Student/faculty ratio | 15:1
Profs interesting rating | 92
Profs accessible rating | 95
% profs teaching UG courses | 100
% classes taught by TAs | 24
Avg lab size | 10-19 students
Avg reg class size | 20-29 students

MOST POPULAR MAJORS
Biology/biological sciences
Psychology
Business administration/management

SELECTIVITY
Admissions Rating **81**
# of applicants | 9,573
% of applicants accepted | 67
% of acceptees attending | 63
# accepting a place on wait list | 175
% admitted from wait list | 71

FRESHMAN PROFILE
Range ACT Composite | 21-27
Average ACT Composite | 24
Average HS GPA | 3.4
% graduated top 10% of class | 28
% graduated top 25% of class | 56
% graduated top 50% of class | 87

DEADLINES
Priority admission | 1/15
Regular admission | 4/1

Regular notification | rolling
Nonfall registration? | yes

FINANCIAL FACTS
Financial Aid Rating **81**
In-state tuition | $2,921
Out-of-state tuition | $10,124
Room and board | $4,822
Books and supplies | $750
Required fees | $563
% frosh receiving aid | 44
% undergrads receiving aid | 46
Avg frosh grant | $3,777
Avg frosh loan | $2,502

UNIVERSITY OF MICHIGAN—ANN ARBOR

CAMPUS LIFE
Quality of Life Rating **80**
Type of school | public
Environment | urban

STUDENTS
Total undergrad enrollment | 24,547
% male/female | 49/51
% from out of state | 34
% from public high school | 80
% live on campus | 37
% in (# of) fraternities | 38 (16)
% in (# of) sororities | 22 (15)
% African American | 8
% Asian | 12
% Caucasian | 64
% Hispanic | 4
% international | 4
# of countries represented | 129

ACADEMICS
Academic Rating **89**
Calendar | trimester
Student/faculty ratio | 15:1
Avg lab size | 20-29 students
Avg reg class size | 10-19 students

MOST POPULAR MAJORS
Mechanical engineering
Economics
English language and literature

SELECTIVITY
Admissions Rating **91**
# of applicants | 25,081
% of applicants accepted | 49

| % of acceptees attending | 42 |
| # accepting a place on wait list | 1,150 |

FRESHMAN PROFILE

Range SAT Verbal	570-670
Average SAT Verbal	622
Range SAT Math	610-720
Average SAT Math	661
Range ACT Composite	26-30
Average ACT Composite	28
Minimum TOEFL	570
Average HS GPA	3.8

DEADLINES

Regular admission	2/1
Nonfall registration?	yes

FINANCIAL FACTS

Financial Aid Rating	**87**
In-state tuition	$7,765
Out-of-state tuition	$24,489
Room and board	$6,620
Books and supplies	$938
Required fees	$187
% frosh receiving aid	77
% undergrads receiving aid	63
Avg frosh grant	$8,309
Avg frosh loan	$5,937

UNIVERSITY OF MINNESOTA— DULUTH

CAMPUS LIFE

Quality of Life Rating	**72**
Type of school	public
Affiliation	none
Environment	suburban

STUDENTS

Total undergrad enrollment	9,144
% male/female	49/51
% from out of state	12
% from public high school	95
% live on campus	31
% in (# of) fraternities	1 (1)
% in (# of) sororities	1 (1)
% African American	1
% Asian	2
% Caucasian	89
% Hispanic	1
% international	2
# of countries represented	42

ACADEMICS

Academic Rating	**74**
Calendar	semester
Student/faculty ratio	20:1
Profs interesting rating	84
Profs accessible rating	81
% profs teaching UG courses	100

MOST POPULAR MAJORS
Biology/biological sciences
Elementary education and teaching
Business administration/management

SELECTIVITY

Admissions Rating	**67**
# of applicants	6,202
% of applicants accepted	77
% of acceptees attending	43

FRESHMAN PROFILE

Range ACT Composite	20-24
Average ACT Composite	23
Minimum TOEFL	550
Average HS GPA	3.22
% graduated top 10% of class	15
% graduated top 25% of class	41
% graduated top 50% of class	83

DEADLINES

Regular admission	8/1
Nonfall registration?	yes

FINANCIAL FACTS

Financial Aid Rating	**74**
In-state tuition	$5,580
Out-of-state tuition	$15,840
Room and board	$4,960
Books and supplies	$1,020

UNIVERSITY OF MINNESOTA— MORRIS

CAMPUS LIFE

Quality of Life Rating	**84**
Type of school	public
Affiliation	none
Environment	rural

STUDENTS

Total undergrad enrollment	1,924
% male/female	41/59
% from out of state	18
% from public high school	80
% live on campus	51
% African American	5

% Asian	3
% Caucasian	80
% Hispanic	2

ACADEMICS
Academic Rating **87**
Calendar	semester
Student/faculty ratio	16:1
Profs interesting rating	79
Profs accessible rating	77
% profs teaching UG courses	100
Avg lab size	10-19 students
Avg reg class size	10-19 students

MOST POPULAR MAJORS
Economics
Elementary education and teaching
Biology/biological sciences

SELECTIVITY
Admissions Rating **83**
# of applicants	1,268
% of applicants accepted	84

FRESHMAN PROFILE
Range SAT Verbal	550-650
Average SAT Verbal	600
Range SAT Math	560-680
Average SAT Math	620
Range ACT Composite	23-28
Average ACT Composite	25
Minimum TOEFL	600
% graduated top 10% of class	45
% graduated top 25% of class	75
% graduated top 50% of class	98

DEADLINES
Early decision	12/1
Regular admission	3/15
Regular notification	4/1
Nonfall registration?	yes

FINANCIAL FACTS
Financial Aid Rating **83**
In-state tuition	$5,549
Out-of-state tuition	$11,097
Room and board	$4,470
Books and supplies	$600

UNIVERSITY OF MINNESOTA— TWIN CITIES

CAMPUS LIFE
Quality of Life Rating **74**

Type of school	public
Environment	urban

STUDENTS
Total undergrad enrollment	28,103
% male/female	48/52
% from out of state	18
% live on campus	22
% African American	4
% Asian	8
% Caucasian	82
% Hispanic	2
% international	2

ACADEMICS
Academic Rating **71**
Calendar	semester
Student/faculty ratio	15:1
Profs interesting rating	90
Profs accessible rating	89
Avg lab size	10-19 students
Avg reg class size	10-19 students

SELECTIVITY
Admissions Rating **80**
# of applicants	14,724
% of applicants accepted	74
% of acceptees attending	47

FRESHMAN PROFILE
Range SAT Verbal	540-660
Average SAT Verbal	593
Range SAT Math	550-670
Average SAT Math	612
Range ACT Composite	22-28
Average ACT Composite	25
Minimum TOEFL	550
% graduated top 10% of class	30
% graduated top 25% of class	65
% graduated top 50% of class	92

DEADLINES
Regular admission	12/15
Nonfall registration?	yes

FINANCIAL FACTS
Financial Aid Rating **79**
In-state tuition	$5,420
Out-of-state tuition	$15,994
Room and board	$5,696
Books and supplies	$730
Required fees	$860
% frosh receiving aid	48
% undergrads receiving aid	46
Avg frosh grant	$6,346
Avg frosh loan	$3,874

UNIVERSITY OF MISSOURI—ROLLA

CAMPUS LIFE
Quality of Life Rating   **81**
Type of school   public
Environment   rural

STUDENTS
Total undergrad enrollment   3,849
% male/female   75/25
% from out of state   22
% from public high school   85
% in (# of) fraternities   27 (20)
% in (# of) sororities   24 (6)
% African American   5
% Asian   3
% Caucasian   86
% Hispanic   2
% international   3
# of countries represented   38

ACADEMICS
Academic Rating   **80**
Calendar   semester
Student/faculty ratio   14:1
Profs interesting rating   80
Profs accessible rating   74
% profs teaching UG courses   88
% classes taught by TAs   14
Avg lab size   10-19 students
Avg reg class size   20-29 students

MOST POPULAR MAJORS
Computer science
Electrical, electronics, and
communications engineering
Mechanical engineering

SELECTIVITY
Admissions Rating   **83**
# of applicants   1,976
% of applicants accepted   90

FRESHMAN PROFILE
Range ACT Composite   25-30
Average ACT Composite   27
Minimum TOEFL   550
Average HS GPA   3.5
% graduated top 10% of class   40
% graduated top 25% of class   70
% graduated top 50% of class   94

DEADLINES
Priority admission   12/1
Regular admission   7/1
Nonfall registration?   yes

FINANCIAL FACTS
Financial Aid Rating   **85**
In-state tuition $4,602
Out-of-state tuition $13,755
Room and board $5,230
Books and supplies $850
Required fees $778
% frosh receiving aid   49
% undergrads receiving aid   50
Avg frosh grant $5,900
Avg frosh loan $3,400

UNIVERSITY OF NEBRASKA—LINCOLN

CAMPUS LIFE
Quality of Life Rating   **88**
Type of school   public
Environment   urban

STUDENTS
Total undergrad enrollment   18,118
% male/female   52/48
% from out of state   14
% live on campus   25
% in (# of) fraternities   15 (26)
% in (# of) sororities   17 (16)
% African American   2
% Asian   2
% Caucasian   89
% Hispanic   2
% international   3
# of countries represented   124

ACADEMICS
Academic Rating   **75**
Calendar   semester
Student/faculty ratio   19:1
Profs interesting rating   80
Profs accessible rating   75
% classes taught by TAs   17
Avg lab size   20-29 students
Avg reg class size   20-29 students

SELECTIVITY
Admissions Rating   **91**
# of applicants   7,631
% of applicants accepted   90
% of acceptees attending   53

FRESHMAN PROFILE
Range SAT Verbal   500-640
Average SAT Verbal   570
Range SAT Math   520-660

Average SAT Math	589
Range ACT Composite	21-27
Average ACT Composite	24
Minimum TOEFL	525
% graduated top 10% of class	26
% graduated top 25% of class	53
% graduated top 50% of class	85

DEADLINES

Priority admission	1/15
Regular admission	6/30
Nonfall registration?	yes

FINANCIAL FACTS
Financial Aid Rating 84

In-state tuition	$3,345
Out-of-state tuition	$9,938
Room and board	$4,875
Books and supplies	$756
Required fees	$780
% frosh receiving aid	41
% undergrads receiving aid	40
Avg frosh grant	$3,934
Avg frosh loan	$2,588

UNIVERSITY OF NORTH DAKOTA

CAMPUS LIFE
Quality of Life Rating 78

Type of school	public
Environment	urban

STUDENTS

Total undergrad enrollment	10,277
% male/female	53/47
% from out of state	42
% from public high school	85
% live on campus	26
% in (# of) fraternities	9 (13)
% in (# of) sororities	9 (7)
% African American	1
% Asian	1
% Caucasian	95
% Hispanic	1
% international	2
# of countries represented	61

ACADEMICS
Academic Rating 73

Calendar	semester
Student/faculty ratio	18:1
% profs teaching UG courses	85
Avg lab size	20-29 students
Avg reg class size	20-29 students

MOST POPULAR MAJORS
Nursing/registered nurse training (RN, ASN, BSN, MSN)
Elementary education and teaching
Aeronautics/aviation/aerospace science and technology

SELECTIVITY
Admissions Rating 77

# of applicants	3,628
% of applicants accepted	72
% of acceptees attending	77

FRESHMAN PROFILE

Range ACT Composite	20-26
Average ACT Composite	23
Minimum TOEFL	525
Average HS GPA	3.4
% graduated top 10% of class	16
% graduated top 25% of class	40
% graduated top 50% of class	74

DEADLINES

Regular admission	7/1
Nonfall registration?	yes

FINANCIAL FACTS
Financial Aid Rating 80

Out-of-state tuition	$8,594
Room and board	$3,987
Books and supplies	$700
Required fees	$708
% frosh receiving aid	47
% undergrads receiving aid	53
Avg frosh grant	$2,512
Avg frosh loan	$5,102

UNIVERSITY OF NORTHERN IOWA

CAMPUS LIFE
Quality of Life Rating 82

Type of school	public
Affiliation	none
Environment	urban

STUDENTS

Total undergrad enrollment	13,927
% male/female	43/57
% from out of state	6
% live on campus	30
% in (# of) fraternities	2 (7)
% in (# of) sororities	2 (4)
% African American	3
% Asian	1
% Caucasian	93

% Hispanic 2
% international 2

ACADEMICS
Academic Rating **74**
Calendar semester
Student/faculty ratio 16:1
Profs interesting rating 85
Profs accessible rating 80
Avg lab size 20-29 students
Avg reg class size 20-29 students

MOST POPULAR MAJORS
Elementary education
Accounting
Biology

SELECTIVITY
Admissions Rating **73**
# of applicants 4,688
% of applicants accepted 81
% of acceptees attending 56

FRESHMAN PROFILE
Range SAT Verbal 440-610
Range SAT Math 450-600
Range ACT Composite 21-25
Average ACT Composite 23
Minimum TOEFL 550
% graduated top 10% of class 18
% graduated top 25% of class 48
% graduated top 50% of class 91

DEADLINES
Regular admission 8/15
Nonfall registration? yes

FINANCIAL FACTS
Financial Aid Rating **78**
In-state tuition $3,692
Out-of-state tuition $10,000
Room and board $4,640
Books and supplies $797
Avg frosh grant $3,076
Avg frosh loan $5,196

UNIVERSITY OF NOTRE DAME

CAMPUS LIFE
Quality of Life Rating **80**
Type of school private
Affiliation Roman Catholic
Environment suburban

STUDENTS
Total undergrad enrollment 8,261

% male/female 53/47
% from out of state 88
% from public high school 50
% live on campus 75
% African American 3
% Asian 4
% Caucasian 84
% Hispanic 8
% international 3
# of countries represented 80

ACADEMICS
Academic Rating **92**
Calendar semester
Student/faculty ratio 12:1
Profs interesting rating 92
Profs accessible rating 92
% profs teaching UG courses 94
% classes taught by TAs 7
Avg lab size 10-19 students
Avg reg class size 10-19 students

MOST POPULAR MAJORS
Pre-medicine/pre-medical studies
Business administration/management
Engineering

SELECTIVITY
Admissions Rating **99**
# of applicants 9,744
% of applicants accepted 34
% of acceptees attending 58
# accepting a place on wait list 477
% admitted from wait list 48

FRESHMAN PROFILE
Range SAT Verbal 620-720
Average SAT Verbal 665
Range SAT Math 650-730
Average SAT Math 685
Range ACT Composite 30-33
Average ACT Composite 31
Minimum TOEFL 550
% graduated top 10% of class 82
% graduated top 25% of class 95
% graduated top 50% of class 100

DEADLINES
Regular admission 1/9
Regular notification 4/1

FINANCIAL FACTS
Financial Aid Rating **84**
Tuition $25,510
Room and board $6,510

Books and supplies	$850
Required fees	$342
% frosh receiving aid	46
% undergrads receiving aid	40

University of Saint Thomas

CAMPUS LIFE
Quality of Life Rating **81**

Type of school	private
Affiliation	Roman Catholic
Environment	urban

STUDENTS
Total undergrad enrollment	5,429
% male/female	48/52
% from out of state	18
% from public high school	75
% live on campus	43
% African American	2
% Asian	5
% Caucasian	89
% Hispanic	2
% international	1
# of countries represented	33

ACADEMICS
Academic Rating **76**

Calendar	4-1-4
Student/faculty ratio	14:1
Profs interesting rating	78
Profs accessible rating	75
% classes taught by TAs	0
Avg lab size	11 students
Avg reg class size	21 students

MOST POPULAR MAJORS
Business administration
Journalism/mass communication
Sociology

SELECTIVITY
Admissions Rating **71**

# of applicants	3,094
% of applicants accepted	87
% of acceptees attending	41

FRESHMAN PROFILE
Range SAT Verbal	520-620
Average SAT Verbal	571
Range SAT Math	530-640
Average SAT Math	587
Range ACT Composite	22-27

Average ACT Composite	25
Minimum TOEFL	550
Average HS GPA	3.6
% graduated top 10% of class	26
% graduated top 25% of class	58
% graduated top 50% of class	90

DEADLINES
| Nonfall registration? | yes |

FINANCIAL FACTS
Financial Aid Rating **75**

Tuition	$19,120
Room and board	$6,858
Books and supplies	$600
Avg frosh grant	$8,143
Avg frosh loan	$3,723

University of South Dakota

CAMPUS LIFE
Quality of Life Rating **81**

| Type of school | public |
| Environment | rural |

STUDENTS
Total undergrad enrollment	5,769
% male/female	39/61
% from out of state	23
% from public high school	93
% live on campus	19
% in (# of) fraternities	20 (8)
% in (# of) sororities	12 (4)
% African American	1
% Asian	1
% Caucasian	86
% Hispanic	1
% Native American	2
% international	1
# of countries represented	38

ACADEMICS
Academic Rating **71**

Calendar	semester
Student/faculty ratio	14:1
Profs interesting rating	77
Profs accessible rating	81
% profs teaching UG courses	94
% classes taught by TAs	6
Avg reg class size	under 10 students

MOST POPULAR MAJORS
Psychology
Biology
Business administration/management

SELECTIVITY
Admissions Rating **73**
# of applicants 2,539
% of applicants accepted 86
% of acceptees attending 51

FRESHMAN PROFILE
Range ACT Composite 19-25
Average ACT Composite 22
Minimum TOEFL 560
Average HS GPA 3.1
% graduated top 10% of class 10
% graduated top 25% of class 31
% graduated top 50% of class 63

DEADLINES
Nonfall registration? yes

FINANCIAL FACTS
Financial Aid Rating **84**
In-state tuition $2,163
Out-of-state tuition $6,875
Room and board $3,505
Books and supplies $700
Required fees $2,042
% frosh receiving aid 58
% undergrads receiving aid 59
Avg frosh grant $2,127
Avg frosh loan $2,065

UNIVERSITY OF WISCONSIN— EAU CLAIRE

CAMPUS LIFE
Quality of Life Rating **80**
Type of school public
Affiliation none
Environment urban

STUDENTS
Total undergrad enrollment 10,700
% male/female 40/60
% from out of state 22
% from public high school 95
% live on campus 39
% in (# of) fraternities 1 (5)
% in (# of) sororities 1 (3)
% African American 1
% Asian 3
% Caucasian 93
% Hispanic 1
% international 1
# of countries represented 48

ACADEMICS
Academic Rating **73**
Calendar semester
Student/faculty ratio 20:1
Profs interesting rating 82
Profs accessible rating 78
% profs teaching UG courses 100
Avg lab size 10-19 students
Avg reg class size 28 students

MOST POPULAR MAJORS
Biology/biological sciences
Marketing/marketing management
Business administration

SELECTIVITY
Admissions Rating **72**
# of applicants 6,784
% of applicants accepted 68
% of acceptees attending 46
# accepting a place on wait list 361
% admitted from wait list 47

FRESHMAN PROFILE
Range SAT Verbal 490-630
Average SAT Verbal 580
Range SAT Math 520-630
Average SAT Math 599
Range ACT Composite 21-25
Average ACT Composite 24
Minimum TOEFL 525
% graduated top 10% of class 19
% graduated top 25% of class 54
% graduated top 50% of class 93

DEADLINES
Regular notification rolling
Nonfall registration? yes

FINANCIAL FACTS
Financial Aid Rating **76**
In-state tuition $3,472
Out-of-state tuition $11,984
Room and board $3,560
Books and supplies $330
Avg frosh grant $3,379
Avg frosh loan $2,949

UNIVERSITY OF WISCONSIN— LACROSSE

CAMPUS LIFE
Quality of Life Rating **82**
Type of school public

Affiliation	none
Environment	urban

STUDENTS

Total undergrad enrollment	8,148
% male/female	42/58
% from out of state	16
% live on campus	32
% in (# of) fraternities	1 (3)
% in (# of) sororities	1 (2)
% African American	1
% Asian	2
% Caucasian	93
% Hispanic	1
% international	1

ACADEMICS

Academic Rating	**75**
Calendar	semester
Student/faculty ratio	22:1
Profs interesting rating	85
Profs accessible rating	81
% profs teaching UG courses	100
% classes taught by TAs	0
Avg lab size	20-29 students
Avg reg class size	20-29 students

MOST POPULAR MAJORS
Education
Biological sciences/life sciences
Marketing

SELECTIVITY

Admissions Rating	**71**
# of applicants	5,385
% of applicants accepted	59
% of acceptees attending	47
# accepting a place on wait list	405
% admitted from wait list	11

FRESHMAN PROFILE

Range ACT Composite	22-26
Average ACT Composite	24
Minimum TOEFL	550
Average HS GPA	3.5
% graduated top 10% of class	27
% graduated top 25% of class	70
% graduated top 50% of class	98

DEADLINES

Nonfall registration?	yes

FINANCIAL FACTS

Financial Aid Rating	**77**
In-state tuition	$4,229
Out-of-state tuition	$10,122
Room and board	$3,450
Books and supplies	$200
Avg frosh grant	$400
Avg frosh loan	$1,885

UNIVERSITY OF WISCONSIN— MADISON

CAMPUS LIFE

Quality of Life Rating	**84**
Type of school	public
Environment	urban

STUDENTS

Total undergrad enrollment	29,708
% male/female	47/53
% from out of state	30
% from public high school	70
% live on campus	26
% in (# of) fraternities	9 (25)
% in (# of) sororities	8 (9)
% African American	2
% Asian	5
% Caucasian	90
% Hispanic	2
% international	3
# of countries represented	100

ACADEMICS

Academic Rating	**88**
Calendar	semester
Student/faculty ratio	13:1
% profs teaching UG courses	90
Avg lab size	20-29 students
Avg reg class size	10-19 students

MOST POPULAR MAJORS
Psychology
Communications studies/speech
communication and rhetoric
Political science and government

SELECTIVITY

Admissions Rating	**91**
# of applicants	21,211
% of applicants accepted	60
% of acceptees attending	43

FRESHMAN PROFILE

Range SAT Verbal	560-670
Average SAT Verbal	613
Range SAT Math	610-710
Average SAT Math	652
Range ACT Composite	25-30

Average ACT Composite	27
Minimum TOEFL	550
Average HS GPA	3.6
% graduated top 10% of class	55
% graduated top 25% of class	93
% graduated top 50% of class	99

DEADLINES

Priority admission	2/1
Regular admission	2/1
Nonfall registration?	yes

FINANCIAL FACTS

Financial Aid Rating	**82**
In-state tuition	$4,426
Out-of-state tuition	$18,426
Room and board	$4,005
Books and supplies	$680
% frosh receiving aid	30
% undergrads receiving aid	31

UNIVERSITY OF WISCONSIN—
MILWAUKEE

CAMPUS LIFE

Quality of Life Rating	**83**
Type of school	public
Affiliation	none
Environment	urban

STUDENTS

Total undergrad enrollment	19,959
% male/female	45/55
% from out of state	3
% live on campus	13
% African American	9
% Asian	4
% Caucasian	81
% Hispanic	4
% international	1

ACADEMICS

Academic Rating	**70**
Calendar	semester
Student/faculty ratio	19:1
Profs interesting rating	86
Profs accessible rating	79
Avg lab size	10-19 students
Avg reg class size	20-29 students

MOST POPULAR MAJORS
Business administration
Education
Nursing

Admissions Rating	**69**
# of applicants	7,340
% of applicants accepted	79
% of acceptees attending	52

FRESHMAN PROFILE

Range SAT Verbal	460-580
Range SAT Math	470-600
Range ACT Composite	20-24
Average ACT Composite	22
Minimum TOEFL	500
Average HS GPA	2.8
% graduated top 10% of class	7
% graduated top 25% of class	27
% graduated top 50% of class	69

DEADLINES

Nonfall registration?	yes

FINANCIAL FACTS

Financial Aid Rating	**75**
In-state tuition	$4,057
Out-of-state tuition	$15,028
Room and board	$4,850
Books and supplies	$700
Avg frosh grant	$3,069

UNIVERSITY OF WISCONSIN—
RIVER FALLS

CAMPUS LIFE

Quality of Life Rating	**78**
Type of school	public
Affiliation	none
Environment	suburban

STUDENTS

Total undergrad enrollment	5,399
% male/female	38/62
% from out of state	48
% from public high school	95
% live on campus	45
% in (# of) fraternities	5 (5)
% in (# of) sororities	5 (4)
% African American	1
% Asian	3
% Caucasian	94
% international	1

ACADEMICS

Academic Rating	**72**
Calendar	semester
Student/faculty ratio	19:1

Profs interesting rating	84
Profs accessible rating	80
% profs teaching UG courses	100
% classes taught by TAs	0

MOST POPULAR MAJORS
Business administration
Elementary education
Animal science

SELECTIVITY
Admissions Rating	**73**
# of applicants	3,545
% of applicants accepted	75
% of acceptees attending	54

FRESHMAN PROFILE
Range ACT Composite	21-24
Average ACT Composite	23
Minimum TOEFL	500
% graduated top 10% of class	17
% graduated top 25% of class	42
% graduated top 50% of class	83

DEADLINES
Regular admission	1/1
Nonfall registration?	yes

FINANCIAL FACTS
Financial Aid Rating	**78**
In-state tuition	$3,674
Out-of-state tuition	$13,720
Room and board	$3,774
Books and supplies	$200
Avg frosh grant	$4,080
Avg frosh loan	$2,616

UNIVERSITY OF WISCONSIN— STEVENS POINT

CAMPUS LIFE
Quality of Life Rating	**80**
Type of school	public
Affiliation	none
Environment	suburban

STUDENTS
Total undergrad enrollment	8,512
% male/female	43/57
% from out of state	8
% live on campus	36
% in (# of) fraternities	2 (4)
% in (# of) sororities	1 (3)

% African American	1
% Asian	1
% Caucasian	94
% Hispanic	1
% international	2
# of countries represented	30

ACADEMICS
Academic Rating	**71**
Calendar	semester
Student/faculty ratio	20:1
Profs interesting rating	82
Profs accessible rating	79
% profs teaching UG courses	100
% classes taught by TAs	0
Avg lab size	20-29 students
Avg reg class size	20-29 students

MOST POPULAR MAJORS
Biology
Communication
Business administration

SELECTIVITY
Admissions Rating	**70**
# of applicants	4,151
% of applicants accepted	77
% of acceptees attending	47

FRESHMAN PROFILE
Range SAT Verbal	473-588
Average SAT Verbal	531
Range SAT Math	490-580
Average SAT Math	537
Range ACT Composite	20-25
Average ACT Composite	23
Minimum TOEFL	550
Average HS GPA	3.4
% graduated top 10% of class	15
% graduated top 25% of class	45
% graduated top 50% of class	95

DEADLINES
Regular admission	rolling
Regular notification	rolling
Nonfall registration?	yes

FINANCIAL FACTS
Financial Aid Rating	**76**
In-state tuition	$3,377
Out-of-state tuition	$11,890
Room and board	$3,738
Books and supplies	$450

University of Wisconsin—Stout

CAMPUS LIFE
Quality of Life Rating   **75**

Type of school	public
Affiliation	none
Environment	rural

STUDENTS
Total undergrad enrollment	7,316
% male/female	52/48
% from out of state	29
% live on campus	37
% in (# of) fraternities	2 (5)
% in (# of) sororities	4 (3)
% African American	1
% Asian	2
% Caucasian	95
% Hispanic	1
% international	1
# of countries represented	30

ACADEMICS
Academic Rating   **72**

Calendar	4-1-4
Student/faculty ratio	19:1
Profs interesting rating	80
Profs accessible rating	79
% profs teaching UG courses	100
% classes taught by TAs	0
Avg lab size	20-29 students
Avg regular class size	20-29 students

MOST POPULAR MAJORS
Early childhood education and teaching
Design and applied arts
Business administration/management

SELECTIVITY
Admissions Rating   **60**

# of applicants	3,383
% of applicants accepted	70
% of acceptees attending	55
# accepting a place on wait list	332
% admitted from wait list	41

FRESHMAN PROFILE
Range ACT Composite	19-23
Average ACT Composite	22
Minimum TOEFL	500
Average HS GPA	3.2
% graduated top 10% of class	8
% graduated top 25% of class	33
% graduated top 50% of class	82

DEADLINES
Nonfall registration?	yes

FINANCIAL FACTS
Financial Aid Rating   **70**

In-state tuition	$3,150
Out-of-state tuition	$13,196
Room and board	$3,830
Books and supplies	$300
Avg frosh grant	$2,992
Avg frosh loan	$3,720

Valparaiso University

CAMPUS LIFE
Quality of Life Rating   **73**

Type of school	private
Affiliation	Lutheran
Environment	rural

STUDENTS
Total undergrad enrollment	2,910
% male/female	47/53
% from out of state	66
% from public high school	81
% live on campus	65
% in (# of) fraternities	24 (8)
% in (# of) sororities	20 (7)
% African American	3
% Asian	2
% Caucasian	88
% Hispanic	3
% international	3
# of countries represented	37

ACADEMICS
Academic Rating   **76**

Calendar	semester
Student/faculty ratio	13:1
Profs interesting rating	93
Profs accessible rating	91
% profs teaching UG courses	100
Avg lab size	10-19 students
Avg reg class size	10-19 students

MOST POPULAR MAJORS
Elementary education and teaching
Biology/biological sciences
Nursing/registered nurse training (RN,
ASN, BSN, MSN)

SELECTIVITY
Admissions Rating   **79**

# of applicants	3,117

% of applicants accepted	84
% of acceptees attending	27

FRESHMAN PROFILE

Range SAT Verbal	530-630
Average SAT Verbal	583
Range SAT Math	530-650
Average SAT Math	596
Range ACT Composite	23-29
Average ACT Composite	26
Minimum TOEFL	550
% graduated top 10% of class	34
% graduated top 25% of class	68
% graduated top 50% of class	93

DEADLINES

Priority admission	1/15
Regular admission	8/15
Nonfall registration?	yes

FINANCIAL FACTS
Financial Aid Rating   **82**

Tuition	$20,000
Room and board	$5,480
Books and supplies	$700
Required fees	$638
% frosh receiving aid	69
% undergrads receiving aid	64
Avg frosh grant	$12,533
Avg frosh loan	$5,661

WABASH COLLEGE

CAMPUS LIFE
Quality of Life Rating   **82**

Type of school	private
Environment	suburban

STUDENTS

Total undergrad enrollment	912
% from out of state	26
% from public high school	92
% live on campus	99
% in (# of) fraternities	65 (10)
% African American	7
% Asian	3
% Caucasian	84
% Hispanic	6
% international	3
# of countries represented	13

ACADEMICS
Academic Rating   **93**

Calendar	semester
Student/faculty ratio	11:1

Profs interesting rating	98
Profs accessible rating	99
% profs teaching UG courses	100
Avg lab size	10-19 students
Avg reg class size	10-19 students

MOST POPULAR MAJORS
History
English language and literature
Political science and government

SELECTIVITY
Admissions Rating   **87**

# of applicants	1,287
% of applicants accepted	50
% of acceptees attending	42
# accepting a place on wait list	86
% admitted from wait list	7
# of early decision applicants	58
% accepted early decision	81

FRESHMAN PROFILE

Range SAT Verbal	530-620
Average SAT Verbal	576
Range SAT Math	560-655
Average SAT Math	609
Range ACT Composite	23-28
Average ACT Composite	26
Minimum TOEFL	550
Average HS GPA	3.6
% graduated top 10% of class	32
% graduated top 25% of class	68
% graduated top 50% of class	95

DEADLINES

Early decision	11/15
Early decision notification	12/15
Priority admission	12/15
Nonfall registration?	yes

FINANCIAL FACTS
Financial Aid Rating   **89**

Tuition	$20,829
Room and board	$6,717
Books and supplies	$600
Required fees	$386
% frosh receiving aid	77
% undergrads receiving aid	68
Avg frosh grant	$18,668
Avg frosh loan	$3,301

WARTBURG COLLEGE

CAMPUS LIFE
Quality of Life Rating   **74**

Type of school	private
Affiliation	Lutheran
Environment	rural

STUDENTS

Total undergrad enrollment	1,695
% male/female	43/57
% from out of state	23
% from public high school	95
% live on campus	82
% African American	4
% Asian	1
% Caucasian	85
% Hispanic	1
% international	4
# of countries represented	32

ACADEMICS
Academic Rating   **76**

Calendar	other
Student/faculty ratio	14:1
Profs interesting rating	81
Profs accessible rating	82
% profs teaching UG courses	100
% classes taught by TAs	0
Avg lab size	20-29 students
Avg regular class size	20-29 students

MOST POPULAR MAJORS
Biology/biological sciences
Elementary education and teaching
Business, management, marketing,
and related support services

SELECTIVITY
Admissions Rating   **70**

# of applicants	1,828
% of applicants accepted	84
% of acceptees attending	37

FRESHMAN PROFILE

Range SAT Verbal	500-680
Range SAT Math	510-660
Range ACT Composite	21-27
Minimum TOEFL	480
Average HS GPA	3.55
% graduated top 10% of class	35
% graduated top 25% of class	60
% graduated top 50% of class	87

DEADLINES

Nonfall registration?	yes

FINANCIAL FACTS
Financial Aid Rating   **73**

Tuition	$17,150
Room and board	$4,800
Books and supplies	$500

WASHINGTON UNIVERSITY IN ST. LOUIS

CAMPUS LIFE
Quality of Life Rating   **82**

Type of school	private
Environment	suburban

STUDENTS

Total undergrad enrollment	7,219
% male/female	47/53
% from out of state	89
% from public high school	62
% live on campus	80
% in (# of) fraternities	27 (11)
% in (# of) sororities	21 (5)
% African American	8
% Asian	10
% Caucasian	66
% Hispanic	3
% international	4
# of countries represented	104

ACADEMICS
Academic Rating   **92**

Calendar	semester
Student/faculty ratio	7:1
Profs interesting rating	91
Profs accessible rating	92
% profs teaching UG courses	90
Avg lab size	10-19 students
Avg reg class size	10-19 students

MOST POPULAR MAJORS
Psychology
Biology/biological sciences
Finance

SELECTIVITY
Admissions Rating   **97**

# of applicants	19,514
% of applicants accepted	24
% of acceptees attending	29

FRESHMAN PROFILE

Range SAT Verbal	640-730

Range SAT Math	670-750
Range ACT Composite	28-32
Minimum TOEFL	550

DEADLINES

Early decision	11/15
Early decision notification	12/15
Regular admission	1/15
Regular notification	4/1

FINANCIAL FACTS

Financial Aid Rating	**79**
Tuition	$28,300
Room and board	$9,240
Books and supplies	$960
Required fees	$753
% frosh receiving aid	41
% undergrads receiving aid	45

WAYNE STATE UNIVERSITY

CAMPUS LIFE

Quality of Life Rating	**81**
Type of school	public
Affiliation	none
Environment	urban

STUDENTS

Total undergrad enrollment	18,489
% male/female	40/60
% from out of state	1
% live on campus	2
% in (# of) fraternities	2 (7)
% in (# of) sororities	2 (8)
% African American	32
% Asian	5
% Caucasian	48
% Hispanic	3
% international	4

ACADEMICS

Academic Rating	**69**
Calendar	semester
Student/faculty ratio	11:1
Profs interesting rating	82
Profs accessible rating	82
% profs teaching UG courses	62
% classes taught by TAs	13
Avg lab size	under 10 students
Avg reg class size	under 10 students

MOST POPULAR MAJORS
Criminal justice/safety studies
Elementary education and teaching
Fine/studio arts

SELECTIVITY

Admissions Rating	**65**
# of applicants	5,972
% of applicants accepted	72
% of acceptees attending	60

FRESHMAN PROFILE

Range ACT Composite	17-24
Average ACT Composite	21
Minimum TOEFL	550
% graduated top 25% of class	31
% graduated top 50% of class	56

DEADLINES

Regular admission	8/1
Regular notification	rolling
Nonfall registration?	yes

FINANCIAL FACTS

Financial Aid Rating	**73**
In-state tuition	$3,888
Out-of-state tuition	$8,910
Books and supplies	$654
Avg frosh grant	$3,000
Avg frosh loan	$2,600

WESTERN ILLINOIS UNIVERSITY

CAMPUS LIFE

Quality of Life Rating	**73**
Type of school	public
Affiliation	none
Environment	rural

STUDENTS

Total undergrad enrollment	10,755
% male/female	49/51
% from out of state	3
% from public high school	88
% live on campus	52
% in (# of) fraternities	11 (17)
% in (# of) sororities	8 (10)
% African American	6
% Asian	1
% Caucasian	84
% Hispanic	3
% international	2
# of countries represented	54

ACADEMICS

Academic Rating	**70**

Calendar	semester
Student/faculty ratio	17:1
Profs interesting rating	81
Profs accessible rating	78
% profs teaching UG courses	97
% classes taught by TAs	5
Avg regular class size	20-29 students

MOST POPULAR MAJORS
Law enforcement & justice administration
Elementary education

SELECTIVITY
Admissions Rating **69**

# of applicants	8,115
% of applicants accepted	61
% of acceptees attending	36

FRESHMAN PROFILE
Average ACT Composite	22
Minimum TOEFL	550
% graduated top 10% of class	8
% graduated top 25% of class	29
% graduated top 50% of class	66

DEADLINES
| Regular admission | 7/31 |
| Nonfall registration? | yes |

FINANCIAL FACTS
Financial Aid Rating **73**

In-state tuition	$3,165
Out-of-state tuition	$6,330
Room and board	$5,062
Books and supplies	$800
Avg frosh grant	$5,003
Avg frosh loan	$2,492

WESTERN MICHIGAN UNIVERSITY

CAMPUS LIFE
Quality of Life Rating **77**

Type of school	public
Affiliation	none
Environment	urban

STUDENTS
Total undergrad enrollment	23,156
% male/female	48/52
% from out of state	6
% from public high school	90
% live on campus	28
% in (# of) fraternities	8 (21)
% in (# of) sororities	8 (13)
% African American	5
% Asian	1

% Caucasian	87
% Hispanic	2
% international	4
# of countries represented	104

ACADEMICS
Academic Rating **72**

Calendar	semester
Student/faculty ratio	16:1
Profs interesting rating	84
Profs accessible rating	79
% profs teaching UG courses	100

MOST POPULAR MAJORS
Education
Health professions and related sciences
Finance

SELECTIVITY
Admissions Rating **70**

# of applicants	13,517
% of applicants accepted	84
% of acceptees attending	40

FRESHMAN PROFILE
Range ACT Composite	20-25
Average ACT Composite	22
Minimum TOEFL	550
Average HS GPA	3.3
% graduated top 10% of class	15
% graduated top 25% of class	33
% graduated top 50% of class	71

DEADLINES
| Regular notification | rolling |
| Nonfall registration? | yes |

FINANCIAL FACTS
Financial Aid Rating **72**

In-state tuition	$3,897
Out-of-state tuition	$9,653
Room and board	$5,517
Books and supplies	$804

WESTMINSTER COLLEGE

CAMPUS LIFE
Quality of Life Rating **79**

Type of school	private
Affiliation	Presbyterian
Environment	suburban

STUDENTS
Total undergrad enrollment	1,340
% male/female	34/66
% from out of state	21
% from public high school	90

% live on campus | 78
% in (# of) fraternities | 50 (5)
% in (# of) sororities | 50 (5)
% African American | 1
% Caucasian | 83
% Hispanic | 1

ACADEMICS
Academic Rating | **77**
Calendar | semester
Student/faculty ratio | 13:1
Profs interesting rating | 93
Profs accessible rating | 90
% profs teaching UG courses | 100
Avg lab size | 10-19 students
Avg reg class size | 10-19 students

SELECTIVITY
Admissions Rating | **75**
# of applicants | 1,191
% of applicants accepted | 78
% of acceptees attending | 38

FRESHMAN PROFILE
Range SAT Verbal | 480-580
Average SAT Verbal | 544
Range SAT Math | 480-590
Average SAT Math | 543
Range ACT Composite | 19-26
Average ACT Composite | 24
Minimum TOEFL | 500
Average HS GPA | 3.3
% graduated top 10% of class | 20
% graduated top 25% of class | 55
% graduated top 50% of class | 87

DEADLINES
Regular admission | 4/15

FINANCIAL FACTS
Financial Aid Rating | **88**
Tuition | $18,100
Room and board | $5,590
Books and supplies | $1,700
Required fees | $860
% frosh receiving aid | 82
% undergrads receiving aid | 78
Avg frosh grant | $7,500
Avg frosh loan | $3,100

WHEATON COLLEGE

CAMPUS LIFE
Quality of Life Rating | **78**
Type of school | private

Affiliation | other
Environment | suburban

STUDENTS
Total undergrad enrollment | 2,395
% male/female | 49/51
% from out of state | 77
% from public high school | 64
% live on campus | 86
% African American | 2
% Asian | 6
% Caucasian | 88
% Hispanic | 3
% international | 1
# of countries represented | 44

ACADEMICS
Academic Rating | **89**
Calendar | semester
Student/faculty ratio | 11:1
Profs interesting rating | 71
Profs accessible rating | 71
% profs teaching UG courses | 90
Avg lab size | 10-19 students
Avg reg class size | 10-19 students

MOST POPULAR MAJORS
English language and literature
Business/managerial economics
Music

SELECTIVITY
Admissions Rating | **92**
# of applicants | 1,968
% of applicants accepted | 54
% of acceptees attending | 53
# accepting a place on wait list | 229
% admitted from wait list | 10

FRESHMAN PROFILE
Range SAT Verbal | 620-710
Average SAT Verbal | 661
Range SAT Math | 610-700
Average SAT Math | 658
Range ACT Composite | 26-31
Average ACT Composite | 28
Minimum TOEFL | 550
Average HS GPA | 3.7
% graduated top 10% of class | 54
% graduated top 25% of class | 84
% graduated top 50% of class | 97

DEADLINES
Priority admission | 1/15

Regular admission	1/15
Regular notification	4/10

FINANCIAL FACTS
Financial Aid Rating **86**

Tuition	$18,500
Room and board	$6,100
Books and supplies	$660
% frosh receiving aid	47
% undergrads receiving aid	46
Avg frosh grant	$7,051
Avg frosh loan	$3,754

WILLIAM JEWELL COLLEGE

CAMPUS LIFE
Quality of Life Rating **82**

Type of school	private
Affiliation	Baptist
Environment	suburban

STUDENTS

Total undergrad enrollment	1,168
% male/female	42/58
% from out of state	20
% from public high school	95
% live on campus	71
% in (# of) fraternities	39 (3)
% in (# of) sororities	37 (4)
% African American	2
% Asian	1
% Caucasian	90
% Hispanic	2
% international	2
# of countries represented	12

ACADEMICS
Academic Rating **76**

Calendar	semester
Student/faculty ratio	13:1
Profs interesting rating	85
Profs accessible rating	86
% profs teaching UG courses	100
Avg lab size	under 10 students
Avg reg class size	under 10 students

ADMISSIONS
Admissions Rating **75**

# of applicants	1,102
% of applicants accepted	76
% of acceptees attending	45

FRESHMAN PROFILE

Range SAT Verbal	530-650
Average SAT Verbal	580
Range SAT Math	500-640
Average SAT Math	560
Range ACT Composite	21-27
Average ACT Composite	24
Minimum TOEFL	550
Average HS GPA	3.6
% graduated top 10% of class	31
% graduated top 25% of class	64
% graduated top 50% of class	93

DEADLINES
Nonfall registration?	yes

FINANCIAL FACTS
Financial Aid Rating **88**

Tuition	$16,500
Room and board	$4,820
Books and supplies	$650
% frosh receiving aid	69
% undergrads receiving aid	64
Avg frosh grant	$9,500
Avg frosh loan	$6,629

WITTENBERG UNIVERSITY

CAMPUS LIFE
Quality of Life Rating **83**

Type of school	private
Affiliation	Lutheran
Environment	suburban

STUDENTS

Total undergrad enrollment	2,320
% male/female	43/57
% from out of state	46
% from public high school	78
% live on campus	90
% in (# of) fraternities	22 (6)
% in (# of) sororities	35 (7)
% African American	8
% Asian	1
% Caucasian	84
% Hispanic	1
% international	2

ACADEMICS
Academic Rating **88**

Calendar	semester
Student/faculty ratio	14:1
Profs interesting rating	94
Profs accessible rating	95
% profs teaching UG courses	100
Avg reg class size	20-29 students

MOST POPULAR MAJORS
Business/commerce
Biological and physical sciences
Teacher education, multiple levels

SELECTIVITY
Admissions Rating **80**

# of applicants	3,200
% of applicants accepted	73
% of acceptees attending	30
# of early decision applicants	40
% accepted early decision	83

FRESHMAN PROFILE
Range SAT Verbal	490-680
Average SAT Verbal	576
Range SAT Math	484-684
Average SAT Math	582
Range ACT Composite	24-29
Average ACT Composite	26
Minimum TOEFL	550
Average HS GPA	3.6
% graduated top 10% of class	34
% graduated top 25% of class	65
% graduated top 50% of class	90

DEADLINES
Early decision	12/1
Early decision notification	1/1
Priority admission	12/1
Regular admission	3/15
Regular notification	rolling
Nonfall registration?	yes

FINANCIAL FACTS
Financial Aid Rating **91**

Tuition	$24,948
Room and board	$6,363
Books and supplies	$800
Required fees	$150
% frosh receiving aid	74
% undergrads receiving aid	75
Avg frosh grant	$16,000
Avg frosh loan	$4,400

WRIGHT STATE UNIVERSITY

CAMPUS LIFE
Quality of Life Rating **83**

Type of school	public
Affiliation	none
Environment	suburban

STUDENTS
Total undergrad enrollment	12,220
% male/female	44/56
% from out of state	3
% from public high school	85
% live on campus	20
% in (# of) fraternities	3 (11)
% in (# of) sororities	4 (7)
% African American	11
% Asian	2
% Caucasian	87
% Hispanic	1
% international	1
# of countries represented	60

ACADEMICS
Academic Rating **69**

Calendar	quarter
Student/faculty ratio	20:1
Profs interesting rating	84
Profs accessible rating	80
% profs teaching UG courses	95
% classes taught by TAs	5
Avg lab size	under 10 students
Avg reg class size	20-29 students

MOST POPULAR MAJORS
Psychology
Nursing
Accountancy

SELECTIVITY
Admissions Rating **65**

# of applicants	4,488
% of applicants accepted	92
% of acceptees attending	52

FRESHMAN PROFILE
Range SAT Verbal	450-570
Average SAT Verbal	502
Range SAT Math	450-570
Average SAT Math	501
Range ACT Composite	19-25
Average ACT Composite	21
Minimum TOEFL	500
Average HS GPA	3.0
% graduated top 10% of class	16
% graduated top 25% of class	34
% graduated top 50% of class	65

DEADLINES
Regular notification	rolling
Nonfall registration?	yes

FINANCIAL FACTS
Financial Aid Rating   **70**

In-state tuition	$5,360
Out-of-state tuition	$10,524
Room and board	$5,700
Books and supplies	$900

XAVIER UNIVERSITY

CAMPUS LIFE
Quality of Life Rating   **83**

Type of school	private
Affiliation	Roman Catholic
Environment	suburban

STUDENTS

Total undergrad enrollment	4,006
% male/female	42/58
% from out of state	65
% live on campus	42
% African American	10
% Asian	2
% Caucasian	84
% Hispanic	1
% international	1
# of countries represented	40

ACADEMICS
Academic Rating   **76**

Calendar	semester
Student/faculty ratio	17:1
Profs interesting rating	76
Profs accessible rating	73
% profs teaching UG courses	95
% classes taught by TAs	0
Avg lab size	10-19 students
Avg reg class size	20-29 students

MOST POPULAR MAJORS
Natural sciences
Marketing
Psychology

SELECTIVITY
Admissions Rating   **72**

# of applicants	3,534
% of applicants accepted	83
% of acceptees attending	27
# accepting a place on wait list	45

FRESHMAN PROFILE

Range SAT Verbal	540-640
Range SAT Math	520-640
Range ACT Composite	23-28
Minimum TOEFL	500
Average HS GPA	3.5
% graduated top 10% of class	31
% graduated top 25% of class	63
% graduated top 50% of class	88

DEADLINES

Regular admission	2/1
Regular notification	rolling
Nonfall registration?	yes

FINANCIAL FACTS
Financial Aid Rating   **72**

Tuition	$16,540
Room and board	$7,230
Books and supplies	$700

PART 4

INDEX

Index By State

ABOUT THE AUTHORS

Robert Franek is a graduate of Drew University and has been a member of The Princeton Review Staff for four years. Robert comes to The Princeton Review with an extensive admissions background, most recently at Wagner College in Staten Island, New York. In addition, he owns a walking tour business and leads historically driven, yet not boring, tours of his home town!

Tom Meltzer is a graduate of Columbia University. He has taught for The Princeton Review since 1986 and is the author or co-author of seven TPR titles, the most recent of which is *Illustrated Word Smart*, which Tom co-wrote with his wife, Lisa. He is also a professional musician and songwriter. A native of Baltimore, Tom now lives in Hillsborough, North Carolina.

Roy Opochinski is a graduate of Drew University and has been a member of The Princeton Review staff since 1990. He has taught courses for TPR for 11 years and has edited several other books for TPR, including *Word Smart II* and *Math Smart*. In addition, Roy is the executive editor at Groovevolt.com, a music website. He now lives in Toms River, New Jersey.

Tara Bray is a resident of New York City by way of Hawaii, New Hampshire, Oregon, and Chicago, and is a graduate of Dartmouth College as well as Columbia University's School of the Arts. When she's not writing, Tara likes to spend her time figuring out how to pay the rent. She is also the author of The Princeton Review's guide to life after college, *Why Won't the Landlord Take Visa?*

Christopher Maier is a graduate of Dickinson College. During the past five years, he's lived variously in New York City, coastal Maine, western Oregon, central Pennsylvania, and eastern England. Now he's at an oasis somewhere in the midwestern cornfields—the University of Illinois—where he's earning his MFA in fiction. Aside from writing for magazines, newspapers, and The Princeton Review, he's worked as a radio disc jockey, a helping hand in a bakery, and a laborer on a highway construction crew. He's trying to avoid highway construction these days.

Carson Brown graduated from Stanford University in 1998, and after getting paid too much for working for various Internet companies for several years, sold her BMW and moved to Mexico. She has now overstayed her welcome south of the border and is returning to San Francisco to be responsible and further her career working as a writer and editor.

Julie Doherty is a freelance writer, Web designer, and preschool teacher. She lives in Mexico City.

K. Nadine Kavanaugh is pursuing her Master of Fine Arts at Columbia University. Her fiction has appeared on NYCBigCityLit.com and SlackFaith.com.

Catherine Monaco—ACADEMICS: Graduated from Dickinson College and earned a master's degree from Fordham University. STUDENT BODY: Bigger hair, bushier eyebrows (but learned to pluck after junior year). LIFE: Works as NYC public school teacher, lives in Tribeca, and "always has fun quoting other people for The Princeton Review."

Dinaw Mengestu is a graduate of Georgetown University and is currently completing his MFA in fiction at Columbia University. He lives in Brooklyn, New York.

Countdown to the SAT:
The Week Before the Test

Studying Tips

- Make sure that you get enough sleep every night. Try going to bed earlier and waking up earlier.
- Get up early on the weekend and take a practice test. You need to train your mind to be alert in the morning and able to think for three hours. Treat the practice test as the "real thing."
- Get into a pattern of doing 30-45 minutes' worth of SAT problems each day from now until the test day. You're probably really busy, but think of it this way: you can make this tiny sacrifice now, or go through the entire process all over again.
- When you practice at home, do so under timed conditions. You need to get the feeling of what it will be like on the day of the test. As always, don't do your homework in front of the television or with the radio playing.
- Review all of the formulas and strategies that you've learned so far.

Got What You Need?

- Make sure you have your admission ticket. If you lose it or if it hasn't arrived at least one week before the test, call ETS at (609) 771-7600.
- Put new batteries in your calculator.
- Buy some No. 2 pencils, an eraser, and a sharpener.
- Confirm the location of the test center and make sure you know exactly where it is. If you haven't been there before, take a test run. How long does it take to get there? What's traffic like on Saturdays? Where should you park?
- Make sure you have a picture ID (e.g., driver's license, school ID with photo, passport). If you don't have one, see your counselor. Have him or her write a brief physical description of you on school stationery, and then both you and your counselor should sign it.

Extra Study Tip

Get a 5" x 7" index card; write math strategies on one side and verbal strategies on the other. Keep this card with you all week. Study it whenever you have free time: in study hall, in between classes, or on the ride home.

Countdown to the SAT:
The Day Before the Test

The Week Before the Test

Studying Tips

- DON'T STUDY!!! Cramming just won't help. Put your books away on a high shelf where you can't see them.
- Take it easy and let your brain relax. Catch an early movie or have dinner with friends.

At Night

- Go to bed at a reasonable hour. However, don't try to go to sleep at 7:00 p.m. It won't work.
- Set your alarm clock.

"Don't Forget" Checklist

Prepare everything that you'll need for the morning of the test:

- Admission ticket
- Photo ID
- No. 2 pencils
- Eraser
- Sharpener
- Calculator
- Watch or clock (one that doesn't beep)
- Morning warm-up problems

Countdown to the SAT: The Morning of the Test

At Home

- Eat a healthy breakfast. It will give you the energy you need to make it through three hours of testing. However, don't give your body what it's not used to. For example, don't eat steak and eggs if you normally have toast and a glass of juice.
- Wear comfortable clothes. Also, dress in layers. You never know whether the test center will be unusually hot or cold.
- Take everything from the "Don't Forget" Checklist with you.
- Leave yourself 20 minutes more than you think you'll need to get to the test center. Be sure to arrive at least 20 minutes before the scheduled test time.

At the Test Center

- Use the bathroom before the test starts. You'll also have a chance to go to the bathroom during the first break (after Section 2). However, you will not have a chance to go during the second break (after Section 4).
- Do your warm-up problems. A great time to work on these questions is before you're seated.
- Try to maintain your focus. Do not listen to what other people say about the test, including which section they think is the experimental one.

Classroom Courses From The Princeton Review

The Classic Way to Prep

Classrooms may remind you of school, but in Princeton Review classes, the feeling is different. You're in a friendly, supportive place where everyone has the same goal: to beat the test.

Teachers that really know their stuff.

Not only do our teachers know how to keep you interested and involved, they also know our methods inside out. And by the end of your course, so will you.

Small, focused classes.

We never put more than 12 students in any class. So you'll get the personal attention you need and work at a pace that's right for you.

Extra help when you need it.

Admit it: occasionally you might need a little bit of extra help. Your Princeton Review teacher is available to meet with you outside of class at no extra charge. (And no one else has to know.)

Online resources 24/7.

Our Online Student Center is just a click away. You can go there whenever you want to check on your class times and locations, email your teacher, review lessons, practice tough concepts, or make up a missed class.

Materials that work for you.

Ask anyone who's taken our course: our manuals are the best. They have it all. Plus, you'll take a series of full-length practice tests, so you can monitor your progress and get comfortable with the exam.

Guaranteed results.

We know our courses work. In fact, we guarantee it: your SAT score will improve by at least 100 points, or your ACT score by 4 points, or we'll work with you again for up to a year, FREE.

Classroom Courses Available: *

SAT
ACT
SAT II – Writing, Math IC and IIC,
   Biology, Chemistry, Physics
PSAT
Word Smart, Math Smart

* Availability of specific courses varies by month
   and by location.

1-2-1 Private Tutoring From The Princeton Review

The Ultimate in Personalized Attention

If you're too busy for a classroom course, prefer learning at your own kitchen table, or simply like being the center of the universe, *1-2-1* Private Tutoring may be for you.

The focus is on you.

Forget about what some other kid doesn't understand. With *1-2-1* Private Tutoring, it really is all about you. Just you. So you'll get the best instruction in less time than you'd spend in a class.

Your tutor is your coach.

1-2-1 tutors are our best, most experienced teachers. Your tutor will work side-by-side with you, doing whatever it takes to help you get your best score. No push-ups are required.

Pick a time, any time.

We know you're very, very (very) busy. So you and your tutor will meet when it's convenient for you.

Guaranteed results.

As with our classroom and online courses, your results with a full *1-2-1* Private Tutoring program are guaranteed: your SAT score will improve by at least 100 points, or your ACT score by at least 4 points, or we'll work with you again for free.

Tutoring programs available: *

SAT
ACT
SAT II (all subject tests)
PSAT
AP tests
Academic subjects

*Availability varies by location.

Online Courses
From The Princeton Review

The Best of Both Worlds
Take the newest and best in software design, combine it with our time-tested strategies, and voilà: dynamic test prep where, when, and how you want it!

Lively, engaging lessons.
Our online courses are totally different from others you may have seen. You'll never passively scroll through pages of text or watch boring, choppy video clips. These courses feature animation, audio, interactive lessons, and self-directed navigation. We put you in the driver's seat.

Customized, focused practice.
The course software will discover your personal strengths and weaknesses and will help you to prioritize. You'll get extra practice only in the areas where you need it. Of course, you'll have access to dozens of hours' worth of lessons and drills covering all areas of the test. So you can practice as much or as little as you choose. (Just don't give yourself carpal tunnel syndrome, okay?)

Real-time interaction.
Our *LiveOnline* course includes eight additional sessions that take place in a virtual classroom over the Internet. You'll interact with your specially certified teacher and your fellow students in real time, using live audio, a virtual whiteboard, and a chat interface.

Help at your fingertips.
Any time of the day or night, help is there for you: chat online with a live Coach, check our Frequently Asked Questions (FAQ) database, or talk to other students in our discussion groups.

Guaranteed results.
We stand behind our *Online* and *LiveOnline* courses with complete confidence. Your SAT score will improve by at least 100 points, or your ACT score by at least 4 points. Guaranteed.

Online Courses Available:*
SAT *Online*
SAT *LiveOnline*
SAT *ExpressOnline*
ACT *Online*
ACT *LiveOnline*
ACT *ExpressOnline*

*Available EVERYWHERE!

Hit Parade

abstract general; not concrete
aesthetic having to do with the appreciation of beauty
alleviate to ease a pain or a burden
ambivalent simultaneously feeling opposing feelings
apathetic feeling or showing little emotion
auspicious favorable; promising
benevolent well-meaning; generous
candor sincerity; openness
cogent convincing; reasonable
comprehensive large in scope or content
contemporary current, modern; from the same time
conviction a fixed or strong belief
diligent marked by painstaking effort; hard-working
dubious doubtful; of unlikely authenticity
eclectic made up of a variety of sources or styles
egregious conspicuously bad or offensive
exculpate to free from guilt or blame
florid describing flowery or elaborate speech
gratuitous given freely; unearned; unwarranted
hackneyed worn-out through overuse; trite
idealize to consider perfect
impartial not in favor of one side or the other; unbiased

imperious arrogantly domineering or overbearing
inherent inborn; built-in
innovative introducing something new
inveterate long established; deep-rooted; habitual
laudatory giving praise
maverick one who resists adherence to a group
mollify to calm or soothe
novel strikingly new or unusual
obdurate stubborn; inflexible
objectivity treating facts uninfluenced by emotion
obstinate stubbornly adhering to an opinion
ornate elaborately decorated
ostentatious describing a pretentious display
paramount of chief concern or importance
penitent expressing remorse for one's misdeeds
pervasive dispersed throughout
plausible seemingly valid or acceptable; credible
profound having great depth or seriousness
prosaic unimaginative; dull
quandary a state of uncertainty or perplexity
rancorous hateful; marked by deep-seated ill will
spurious not genuine; false; counterfeit
stoic indifferent to pleasure or pain; impassive
superfluous extra; unnecessary
tenuous having little substance or strength; unsure; weak
timorous timid; fearful about the future
transitory short-lived; temporary
vindicated freed from blame

SAT vs. ACT

	SAT	**ACT**
Preferred by?	Private schools, and schools on the east and west coasts.	Public schools, and schools in the middle of the country. ACT is preferred by more U.S. colleges than the SAT.
Accepted by?	Nearly all U.S. colleges and universities.	Nearly all U.S. colleges and universities.
When is it administered?	Seven times per year.	Six times per year.
Test structure	Seven-section exam: Three Verbal, three Math, and one Experimental. The Experimental section is masked to look like a regular section.	Four-section exam: English, Math, Reading, and Science Reasoning. An Experimental section is added to tests on certain dates only, and is clearly experimental.
Test content	Math: up to 9th grade basic geometry. No science section. Reading: one passage with roughly one minute to answer each question. Stresses vocabulary. A test of strategy and testmanship.	Math: up to trigonometry. Science section included. Reading: four passages with less than one minute to answer each question. Stresses grammar. A test of time management and studiousness.
Is there a penalty for wrong answers?	Yes	No
How the test is scored/highest possible score	200-800 for each subject, added together for a combined score. A 1600 is the highest possible combined score.	1-36 for each subject, averaged together for a composite score. A 36 is the highest possible composite score.
Are all scores sent to schools?	Yes. If a student requests a score report be sent to specific colleges, the report will include the scores the student received on every SAT taken.	No. There is a "score choice" option. Students can choose which schools will receive their scores AND which scores the schools will see.
Other uses for the exams	Scholarship purposes.	Scholarship purposes. Certain statewide testing programs.
When to register	At least six weeks before the test date.	At least four weeks before the test date.
For more information	Educational Testing Service (ETS) (609) 771-7600 www.ets.org The College Board www.collegeboard.com	ACT, Inc. (319) 337-1270 www.act.org

To help you decide which test is right for you, take a side-by-side glance at these important exams.

The Princeton Review Admissions Services

At The Princeton Review, we care about your ability to get accepted to the best school for you. But, we all know getting accepting involves much more than just doing well on standardized tests. That's why, in addition to our test preparation services, we also offer free admissions services to students looking to enter college or graduate school. You can find these services on our website, *www.PrincetonReview.com*, the best online resource for researching, applying to, and learning how to pay for the right school for you.

No matter what type of program you're applying to—undergraduate, graduate, law, business, or medical—**PrincetonReview.com has the free tools, services, and advice you need to navigate the admissions process.** Read on to learn more about the services we offer.

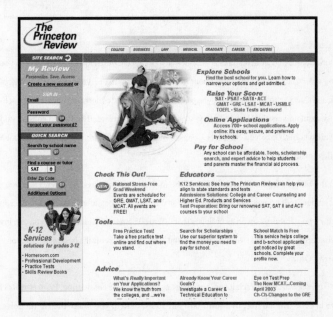

Research Schools
www.PrincetonReview.com/Research

PrincetonReview.com features an interactive tool called **Counselor-O-Matic.** When you use this tool, you enter stats and information about yourself to find a list of your best match schools, reach schools, and safety schools. From there you can read statistical and editorial information about thousands of colleges and universities. In addition, you can find out what currently enrolled college students say about their schools. Once you complete Counselor-O-Matic make sure you opt in to School Match so that colleges can come to you.

Our **College Majors Search** is one of the most popular features we offer. Here you can read profiles on hundreds of majors to find information on curriculum, salaries, careers, and the appropriate high school preparation, as well as colleges that offer it. From the Majors Search, you can investigate corresponding Careers, read **Career Profiles**, and learn what career is the best match for you by taking our **Career Quiz.**

No matter what type of school or specialized program you are considering, **PrincetonReview.com has free articles and advice, in addition to our tools, to help you make the right choice.**

Apply to School
www.PrincetonReview.com/Apply

For most students, completing the school application is the most stressful part of the admissions process. PrincetonReview.com's powerful **Online School Application Engine** makes it easy to apply.

Paper applications are mostly a thing of the past. And, our hundreds of partner schools tell us they prefer to receive your applications online.

Using our online application service is simple:

- Enter information once and the common data automatically transfers onto each application.
- Save your applications and access them at any time to edit and perfect.
- Submit electronically or print and mail in.
- Pay your application fee online, using an e-check, or mail the school a check.

Our powerful application engine is built to accommodate all your needs.

Pay for School
www.PrincetonReview.com/Finance

The financial aid process is confusing for everyone. But don't worry. Our free online tools, services, and advice can help you plan for the future and get the money you need to pay for school.

Our **Scholarship Search** engine will help you find free money, although often scholarships alone won't cover the cost of high tuitions. So, we offer other tools and resources to help you navigate the entire process.

Filling out the FAFSA and CSS Profile can be a daunting process, use our **Strategies for both forms** to make sure you answer the questions correctly the first time.

If scholarships and government aid aren't enough to swing the cost of tuition, we'll help you secure student loans. The Princeton Review has partnered with a select group of reputable financial institutions who will help **explore all your loans options**.

If you know how to work the financial aid process, you'll learn you don't have to **eliminate a school based on tuition.**

Be a Part of the PrincetonReview.com Community

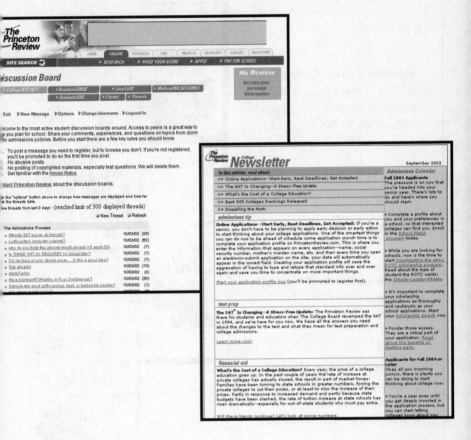

PrincetonReview.com's **Discussion Boards** and **Free Newsletters** are additional services to help you to get information about the admissions process from your peers and from The Princeton Review experts.

MORE BOOKS FOR YOUR
COLLEGE SEARCH

America's Elite Colleges
The Smart Buyer's Guide to the
Ivy League and Other Top Schools
0-375-76206-X • $15.95/C$23.95

Best 351 Colleges
The Smart Student's Guide to Colleges
2004 Edition
0-375-76337-6 • $21.95/C$32.95

Complete Book of Colleges
2004 Edition
0-375-76339-2 • $24.95/C$37.95

Guide to College Majors
Everything You Need to Know
to Choose the Right Major
0-375-76276-0 • $21.00/C$32.00

The Internship Bible
2003 Edition
0-375-76307-4 • $25.00/C$38.00

The K&W Guide to Colleges
for Students with Learning
Disabilities or Attention
Deficit Disorder
7th Edition
0-375-76357-0 • $27.00/C$41.00

Paying for College
Without Going Broke
2004 Edition
0-375-76350-3 • $20.00/C$30.00

The Scholarship Advisor
5th Edition
0-375-76210-8 • $26.00/C$40.00

Taking Time Off
2nd Edition
0-375-76303-1 • $13.00/C$20.00

Visiting College Campuses
6th Edition
0-375-76208-6 • $20.00/C$30.00

Book Store
www.PrincetonReview.com/college/Bookstore.asp

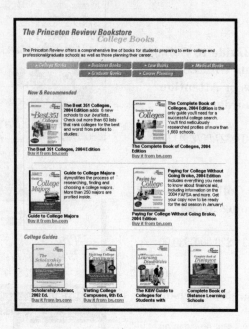

In addition to this book, we publish hundreds of other titles, including guidebooks that highlight life on campus, student opinion, and all the statistical data that you need to know about any school you are considering. Just a few of the titles that we offer are:

- Complete Book of Business Schools
- Complete Book of Law Schools
- Complete Book of Medical Schools
- The Best 351 Colleges
- The K&W Guide to Colleges for Students with Learning Disabilities or Attention Deficit Disorder
- Guide to College Majors
- Paying for College Without Going Broke

For a complete listing of all of our titles, visit our **online book store**:

www.princetonreview.com/college/bookstore.asp